BROADCAST COPYWRITING

BROADCAST COPYWRITING

THIRD EDITION

PETER B. ORLIK
Central Michigan University

ALLYN AND BACON, INC.

Boston   London   Sydney   Toronto

Managing Editor: Bill Barke
Senior Production Administrator: Jane Schulman
Editorial/Production Services: Wordsworth Associates
Cover Coordinator: Linda Dickinson

Library of Congress Cataloging-in-Publication Data

Orlik, Peter B.
    Broadcast copywriting.

    Includes index.
    1. Broadcasting—Authorship.   2. Broadcast
advertising.   I. Title.
PN1990.9.A8807   1986   808'.066791   85-22935
ISBN 0-205-08750-7

Printed in the United States of America

10 9 8 7 6 5 4 3 2 1   91 90 89 88 87 86

To
CBO, DAO, and BTO

*in gratitude for your continued
and continuous help and patience;
and to Nipper, who lacked the chance
to do paste-ups, but contributed ever
so much more.*

CONTENTS

LIST OF ILLUSTRATIONS

PREFACE

Some writers are motivated by the challenge of their craft, others by the monetary rewards it promises. Broadcast copywriting offers the exciting opportunity to have a foot in each world: to experience the divergency of constantly changing tests of your skill and to enjoy significant financial rewards for successfully meeting those tests. Whether you are already a broadcast professional seeking to hone your writing ability or a novice wordsmith striving to apply your talents to radio and television, this book is intended for you.

Broadcast Copywriting, third edition, introduces you to the special requirements and pitfalls of creating the continuity and commercials that are so central and pervasive a part of the broadcast industry. Neither a book in program-length script development nor a treatise on broadcast journalism, this volume is, instead, geared toward acquainting you with the basic building blocks of radio and television writing: the station IDs, program promos, public service announcements, and commercials that facilitate and justify broadcasting's entertainment and information offerings.

Unlike the comparatively circumscribed world of dramatic and documentary writing, broadcast copywriting is a function that every station, no matter how small, must perform for itself and its clients; it is an activity in which every advertising agency using the electronic media must engage. Developed skill in continuity and commercial creation is therefore a valuable and needed asset for writers wishing access to or advancement in the radio and television industries. Though they are very abbreviated, commercial and continuity pieces also exemplify all the requisites of media form and content demanded in broadcast journalism as well as in series script formulation. Thus, guided exposure to these short but standard parts of the copywriter's repertoire will help prepare you, simultaneously, for a possible career as a creator of much more extended news and entertainment materials.

Still, if you're like many broadcast wordsmiths, you may find the opportunity, the pay, and the challenging diversity of *copywriting* to be a hard field to abandon in favor of the more sober environment of the newsroom or the unstable world of program script creation. Do not be surprised if you decide to spend your entire career as either a copywriter, or a continuity supervisor, promotions director, agency creative director, or account executive; these and others all are satisfying and lucrative positions that can flow from a practiced facility in commercial and continuity generation.

To get you started or, in the case of those already in the industry, to accelerate your growth as a copywriter, *Broadcast Copywriting* is divided into four main sections. After an appraisal of the broadcast copywriter's world, and the communication process to which that world is subject, the Copywriter's Perspective section continues with an inventory of the tools and procedures that radio and television writing collectively share. This sets the stage for both the second section, which discusses the advantages, limitations, and copy formats of radio writing, and the parallel third section, which covers the same ground in regard to television. Finally, the fourth section delves into the interlocking process of campaign construction; first for the conventional broadcast campaign; next for the hazardous practice of political, controversial and crisis copywriting; and last, for the cross-media effort. This fourth section examines how an entire advertising or promotions strategy is constructed and the individual messages within it coordinated into a mutually reinforcing whole.

Through it all, a great many rules and precepts are presented. Though each of these rules has been tested time and time again in the intensely competitive broadcast arena, each (except for those ordained by government or industry regulators) also can be broken, given a specific and unique set of circumstances. Knowing the rules, however, ensures that when you do decide to ignore one, your decision is not inadvertent but is based on a careful, conscious, and calculated appraisal of why this proven principle cannot govern the assignment or marketing problem at hand.

You are also cautioned not to view the separate chapters of this book as independent and self-standing wholes. Do not, for example, think that you will acquire all information pertinent to writing *radio commercials* simply by reading the chapter that carries that name. The fourteen chapters in *Broadcast Copywriting* are, instead, mutually complementary. Each strives to add additional perspectives to what has been covered in previous chapters. Guidelines introduced in conjunction with television public service announcement writing, for instance, may be equally applicable to commercial creation, and vice-versa. In the constantly mutating world of broadcast copy, nothing remains totally discrete from anything else for very long. Thus, though subjects have been grouped into digestible segments under the topics to which each has greatest application, keep in mind that every chapter contains elements that are relevant to the concerns of one or several others.

Like the two previous editions, this third edition of *Broadcast Copywriting* seeks to deepen your understanding of the subject through numerous examples and illustrations. Many of these models are quite current. Others are more historic and are featured here because they have made enduring contributions to furthering effective radio/television communication. It is especially gratifying to be able to include recent work contributed by some of my former students: Paul Boscarino, Gerald Downey, Susan Montgomery, Dan Nelson, Sheila O'Donnell, Ginger Raymond, Ann Rittenhouse, and Steve Serkaian. They are true professionals who have established themselves in the communications business and who continue to excel there as they did in the classrooms we once shared.

Now, one last bit of housekeeping. In an effort to expand the number of copy examples while still keeping the size of the book within reason, please note that the format of many of the sample scripts has been condensed. This is especially true of radio copy. Readers are encouraged, therefore, to consult the sections on radio format (pp. 125–232) and on television format (pp. 233–357) when typing up their own scripts.

IN ACTUAL PRACTICE, ALL COPY THAT IS SINGLE-SPACED IN THIS BOOK NORMALLY WOULD BE DOUBLE-SPACED, AND ALL COPY HEREIN DOUBLE-SPACED WOULD BE TRIPLE-SPACED.

ACKNOWLEDGMENTS

First and foremost, the author wishes to thank his wife, Chris, for her unswerving faith in this project and its author, as well as for her patience, understanding, and encouragement in *Broadcast Copywriting*'s evolution through three editions.

Appreciation is also expressed to the many professionals in the broadcasting, advertising, and publishing industries who collectively provided the wealth of script and other illustrative material on which this third edition of *Broadcast Copywriting* was able to draw. Many of their names appear in the text in conjunction with the copy or other creative achievements they made available.

Recognition also goes to Allyn and Bacon's John DeRemigis, whose interest and attention resulted in *Broadcast Copywriting*'s first edition, and to Bill Barke, who provided the same impetus and support for the book's successors. My thanks also to Grace Sheldrick, Wordsworth Associates, for her fine editorial/production assistance on both the second and third editions. A special debt of gratitude continues to be owed to Melba Marlett, prolific novelist and premier writing teacher, whose perceptive high standards provide an unwavering beacon.

Finally, thanks go to Darcy and Blaine, our two children, who gave up use of the den and numerous outings so that all three editions of *Broadcast Copywriting* could be accomplished on schedule.

Thank you for reading this far and, it is hoped, for the chance now mutually to explore all of *Broadcast Copywriting*'s specific aspects and elements.

P.B.O.

BROADCAST COPYWRITING

PART ONE

THE COPYWRITING PERSPECTIVE

The Broadcast Copywriter's World

The Components of Communication

The Broadcast Copywriter's Tools

Rational and Emotional Appeals and Structures

The CDVP Process

Chapter One

THE BROADCAST
COPYWRITER'S WORLD

To begin to understand the pressures and prerequisites of radio and television copywriting, it makes sense to learn something about the employment contexts into which the copywriter is thrust. We are not talking about the rarefied and largely inaccessible world of the drama or documentary script-writer. These jobs (and the writing assignments that fuel them) are few and far between. Instead, our focus is that multitude of employment situations in which *copy*, the life's blood of broadcast content, is created. Copy is the short piece of written craftsmanship that propels, or promotes, or defines, or pays the bills for every carrier of radio and television programming. Unlike full-length scripts, which are the province of a few isolated specialists, pieces of copy must be produced by writers at every station and almost every cable system, no matter how large or how small. Copy must also be generated by the many agencies, corporations, and institutions who seek to make an impact on and through those telecommunications delivery vehicles.

The typical piece of copy is ten, thirty, or sixty seconds long. However, like the full-length script, it must tell a tale or reveal a truth within the time allotted. Some people seek to make creating copy their long-term profession. Other writers see it as preparation for long-form composition. Still others aspire to media management and realize that success in both media and management depends on the deft supervision of written words. Whatever the case, study of and practice in the sources and techniques of copywriting can pay significant professional dividends. Most of this book is about techniques. But for a few pages, let's first look at sources—at where (and from whom) the copy comes.

FREELANCE

This term has an unmistakably mercenary origin. It was first applied to knights too poor or unaccomplished to have their own land or liege lord. They hired themselves and their lances out to anyone who would have them in order to establish a reputation and accumulate a little wealth. The freelance copywriter is in much the same position in today's media world, where the pen, if not mightier, at least has more utility than the sword. Freelancing is a way for many young copywriters to test, even in a part-time way, their ability to create market-place material that successfully serves a commissioned need. Initially, this might be constructing anything from public service spots for the local YMCA to commercials promoting a home-town merchant. Ultimately, if such little assignments are successfully dealt with, the freelancer may expand operations to become a one-person advertising agency: "pitching" area businessfolk on the need for radio and television exposure, writing the commercials, supervising their production, even handling the actual time buys with area stations.

Unquestionably, part-time freelancing is a prudent way for the fledgling writer, like the obscure knight, to fashion a reputation and make a little money before attempting to slay the fiercer dragons of full-time campaigns. And for a few talented people who do not see themselves as "team players," permanent freelancing can be a creative and psychologically satisfying way to earn a living. Freelancers, as advertising chronicler Ed Buxton points out, have "something sweet and precious: independence. In this age of economic bondage, the right to sleep until noon, to take a two-month holiday or to tell a client to go jump are fringes that no corporation is likely to pass out to wage slaves."[1]

On the other hand, former freelancer Gojan Nikolich feels compelled to state that such conditions may be the exception. From his experience, "freelancers rarely sleep until noon, and unless they do boffo work at boffo prices, hardly ever manage to take a two-month sortie into vacationland. I've known many a freelancer who has bitten the dust because he/she figured telling a client 'to jump' was preferable to working hard and playing a delicate game of compromise. True, a freelancer's destiny IS more firm. Still, the realities of doing business outweigh the often romanticized aspects of a hired gun's 'hard' life."[2] Like any self-employed workers, freelance copywriters have only themselves to lean on when times get tough. "Freelance beats every other job in advertising," affirms freelancer Ed Butler, "except on Friday or twice a month depending on payroll."[3]

Freelancing may be full-time anxiety at part-time pay. For this reason, many copywriters do not freelance. They appreciate that in the creative warfare of today's business world, most of us are only too glad to have other auxiliaries around. That is also why slaying today's assignment dragons tends to be a group crusade.

IN-STATION

Despite the prevalence of canned (preproduced) video and audio material, all radio and television stations and most cable systems must generate some aired copy on their own. These self-created writing efforts are not limited to news material; they also include such items as station identifications (known as

---

1. Ed Buxton, "When the Going Gets Tough, the Agencies Get Freelancers," *ADWEEK/Midwest*, August 2, 1982, p. 6.
2. Gojan Nikolich, letter to the editor, *ADWEEK/Midwest*, August 30, 1982, p. 16.
3. Ed Butler, "Confessions of a Freelance Copywriter," *ADWEEK/Midwest*, September 20, 1982, p. 32.

"ID's"), program promotions, public service copy for the ubiquitous "community calendar," and, most lucratively for the station, commercial messages (called "spots") to serve the needs of local advertisers. Station employees who turn out such writing may or may not be called—or even paid as—writers, but they nonetheless draw the scripting assignments.

The paradox has been that those major-market stations with the largest staffs have needed in-station writers least. Virtually all their "spot load" (schedule of commercials) accrues from substantial national or regional advertisers whose agencies deliver the commercials prepackaged and ready for airing. Large stations, in short, had the greatest capability to hire writers but, unless their local program production effort was substantial, the least need for them.

With more stations coming on the air, however, and with new cable services entering the competitive arena, even large operations have recognized a need for writers in their expanded promotions efforts. The burgeoning options available to listeners and viewers require greater efforts by existing stations to hold the audience and aggressive marketing on the part of new services to establish a niche in the consumer's listening/viewing patterns. Thus, at both large and small media entities, promotions departments have been strengthened or newly established.

At major stations, particularly television, the old promotions unit (which used to be staffed by a secretary sending out bumper stickers) has been upgraded into a Creative Services Department that handles everything from on-air promotion to complete client and press information packets. The creative services director is a member of the management team and is often a former copywriter who now supervises other writing personnel. The escalating activity in this area has meant new prestige and new job opportunities for broadcast copywriting professionals.

Small stations also are increasingly sensitive to the fact that a continuity and commercial writer is economically vital in both station image-building and courting local clients through market-attuned commercials. Small stations have either scraped together enough money to hire one full-time person to perform the writing chores or have retained only those time salespeople and air personalities who can be counted on to generate effective copy in conjunction with their other duties. This fact demonstrates that good broadcast writing skills are important to your employability whether you are seeking to sustain a career in broadcasting as a pen-pusher or in some other job capacity.

As with the freelancer, even the full-time in-station writer may discover that the alleged "writing" duties also encompass responsibility for producing, announcing, and actually selling the end-product of these processes to clients and their representatives. In the case of station promotion materials, this selling job is initially to one's own bosses rather than to external powers; but it makes the workload no less demanding. Whether freelancing or in-station, if you are the only writer around, be prepared to shepherd your concept from the typewriter right through its placement on the station's program log and its ultimate projection over the airwaves.

ADVERTISING AGENCY

Much popular sociology, and a bad Hollywood movie or two, have spent a lot of time exposing the foibles of the typical ad person who spouts catchy clichés and snappy slogans that would sour in the mouth of a backwoods con artist. Contrary to this stereotype, agency copywriters tend to be the top professionals in their fields from the standpoint of talent as well as take-home pay. In most cases, they have had to prove themselves in one or more other jobs in the media before an advertising agency would consider hiring them. As *ADWEEK* editor Geoffrey Precourt states, "The agency business is image-intensive—a nice way of saying that it employs a lot of people who have extraordinarily high opinions of their own work. Often those opinions are not exaggerated."[4]

In the United States, the top fifty broadcast advertising agencies spent $14.4 billion in radio–television–cable during 1984.[5] This figure represents a tremendous amount of copy as well as dollars—a volume that could not be generated by an unreliable industry replete with hucksters.

Though it used to be possible for novice copywriters to enter agency work without previous experience, the tightening economy of the seventies made this impractical. Hans Carstensen, N. W. Ayer's former vice president of media, pointed out at the time that advertisers concerned with "taking the water out" of their advertising budgets were no longer willing to pay for trainee overhead at their agency.[6] This attitude still largely prevails. Clients and consequently the advertising agencies themselves have come to expect that each writer at the agency is already a seasoned professional.

"By nature," observes advertising veteran Whit Hobbs, "the ones who do well at it are very bright, ambitious, articulate, good with ideas, good with people, dissatisfied with anything less than excellence. They are also stubborn, egotistical, restless and greedy. They want success as quickly as possible, as much of it as possible."[7]

Assuming you do make it into an advertising agency creative department either directly or, more probably, via the freelance, in-station or similar apprenticeship route, you will encounter one of two main types of structures. You may be working in a creative department, where all copywriters serve the total media needs of the clients to which they are assigned. In this case, you will be creating newspaper and magazine layouts, even direct-mail pieces, point-of-purchase displays, and billboards, in addition to radio and television copy. This diversity forces the copywriter to be much more of a generalist and to be equally familiar with the divergent requirements of print and broadcast communication. A few key aspects of the print side are presented in chapter 14.

Alternatively, you may be in one of the far fewer number of agencies that segregate their *broadcast* writers from those servicing print-related media. This

4. Geoffrey Precourt, "The Big Step," *ADWEEK/Midwest*, August 29, 1983, p. 20.
5. "Broadcasting's Top 50 Agencies," *Broadcasting Magazine*, February 4, 1985, p. 40.
6. Hans Carstensen, address to Central Michigan University business and media students, April 27, 1973.
7. White Hobbs, "Roots and Wings," *ADWEEK/Midwest*, August 2, 1982, p. 14.

pattern goes back at least to the fifties, when the new medium of television caused many clients to demand advertising that reflected the talents of video specialists or, if that was impossible, writers who were striving mightily to become such specialists. Later, when the integrated, cross-media campaign became the focal point, most agencies abandoned this dual pool organization. Nonetheless, some full-service agencies continue to claim that specialists are the only way to maximize the impact of their radio and television messages. These agencies have been joined in this attitude by the small specialty or boutique shops that give heavy attention to the creative aspect of advertising, especially advertising designed for the broadcast media.

No matter what particular structure a given advertising agency adopts, no matter how few or how many functions it serves besides actual message creation, the primacy of the message developer is being reasserted. "Today's top creative minds," says author William Meyers, "are the establishment. In fact, sixteen of the top twenty agencies in America are currently managed by former copywriters or art directors. After more than a century in existence, Madison Avenue has finally gotten around to institutionalizing its most precious asset— the big idea. The surge of customer-oriented, corporate-backed creativity today stems in large part from the fact that advertising has become a serious bottom-line issue, an essential profit-booster for many companies. A single breakthrough commercial—'Where's the Beef?'—can dramatically distinguish one enterprise from the rest of the competition in the public's mind; a series of riveting half-minutes on prime-time can be the ultimate weapon that sends sales soaring."[8] The advertising agency is thus more ready to advance skilled copywriters than ever before.

CORPORATE IN-HOUSE

Certain types of firms prefer to fashion their own advertising rather than to contract it out to a separate agency. They therefore set up units within their own organization—often in conjuction with their public relations division—to plan and execute the advertising effort. Utility companies and financial institutions are especially prone to this approach. Their managements feel that corporate policy and attitude can be properly communicated only by writers who thoroughly understand it. And what better way to stimulate understanding than by making the writer a full-time part of the firm and dependent on it for that weekly paycheck?

This rationale points up the greatest weakness of the in-house system: lack of objectivity. Writers or creative directors who are a part of the institution they are publicizing are leery of criticizing its promotional plans and reluctant to question a defective campaign or outmoded corporate slogan. In-house writers come to know their company's sacred cows so well that a whole system of untouchable subjects can, by accretion, come to clog the entire creative process

---

8. William Meyers, "The Big Idea: Reborn in the USA," *ADWEEK/Midwest*, February, 1985, p. C.R. 5.

and stifle the universal need for constant creative evolution and campaign updating. Further, the in-house pattern can be stifling to the writer forced to deal exclusively with the same product or service year after year without the opportunity to grow through new and divergent assignments and clients.

Giving it its due, the in-house system does provide the writer with a generally greater chance for job stability and a heightened opportunity to analyze fully the products and services the copy will promote. Such in-depth knowledge can result in clearer and more truthful messages through the writer's increased familiarity with the subject. Inadvertent deception arising from writer misunderstanding of client data is minimized, and corporate decision makers can be kept more closely in touch with consumer opinions about both their advertising and the product or service marketed.

GOVERNMENT/INSTITUTIONAL IN-HOUSE

Much of what was said about the corporate in-house situation carries over to the government/institutional setting. Working for a nonprofit organization does not make the writer's problems significantly different from those faced by an in-house counterpart at a profit-making corporation. The lack of objectivity is still a real danger and is perhaps heightened by the fact that an allegedly beneficient public or charitable institution is doing the communicating. The controversial CBS documentary of the early seventies, *The Selling of the Pentagon,* probed what can happen when a large and entirely self-contained communications staff promotes its public institution without the healthy interplay and cross-checking that come from continuous association with the communicators from cooperating but independent media agencies.

Still, the in-house situation is the only practical organizational pattern for many small charities, institutions, and foundations that cannot afford outside talent but must rely on the work of regular employees who often perform other functions as well. The municipality, the college, the religious organization, and several like establishments need people who thoroughly understand their institution's role and philosophy and can explain them in a consistent manner whatever the specific issue involved. This is another generalist environment to which the writer trained only in broadcasting may have difficulty adapting. But if you have a strong commitment to the city, church, or charity involved, such a setting can be personally appealing and, given the breadth of jobs you may have to perform, professionally stimulating as well. Just remember to keep a place in your pencil box for well-sharpened objectivity. Mayors and bishops can be just as shortsighted as marketing vice presidents.

OTHER EMPLOYMENT OPTIONS

Even though the above five categories encompass the majority of full-time broadcast writing positions, a number of other options may present themselves. Since the two key wire services separate print and broadcast subscription lines as well as maintain their own "audio networks," broadcast writers with training in journalism may find a home at the Associated Press, United Press International, or other more regional and specialized news agencies that cater to the electronic media. Broadcast journalism is also an important function at the network and local station level. Here, too, the emphasis is on a good sense of the spoken message, which will be emphasized in this text, together with a solid familiarity with journalistic principles, which constitutes material beyond this book's province.

In alluding to networks, it also should be pointed out that they need an additional small band of non-news writers to create the promotion and other brief material used between program segments. This type of writing can be an especially challenging, high-stakes adventure. If it had to pay for the airtime it uses, the promotions department of any of the networks would be its own network's biggest client. With such multimillion dollar time investments at stake, network promotion writers must be especially facile.

In a similar manner, specialty service firms such as FirstCom, TM Productions, and Radio Arts use high-talent writers in creating jingle, promotion and station identification packages that enhance programming flow and appeal on behalf of local stations around the country. Station slogans, comedy bits, musical sell lines, and community service blurbs may all be a part of the specialty service's highly attractive output.

Finally, commercial and educational film and video production houses must be mentioned. Although much of their activity revolves around the creation of full-length scripts, they are also often involved in short industrial films for corporate training or promotion, tape/slide presentations, and the creation of audio cassettes that accompany school textbooks and study materials. As all of these functions depend on copy meant to be heard rather than read, the broadcast writer is uniquely qualified to handle such assignments.

CONTINUITY—THE COPYWRITER'S MAIN ARENA

In all of the employment contexts mentioned here, the broadcast copywriter is engaged in the business of *continuity* creation. This term, which is so central to the writer's role, has both a broad and a narrow definition. To understand our responsibility in copy creation, it is essential that we be aware of the parameters of each use of the term.

In the broad sense, continuity encompasses *all short, nonprogrammatic broadcast-related material.* Thus, within this use of the term, everything that is not an actual part of a self-contained information or entertainment program can be called continuity. Even though such a definition excludes news copy, it still includes commercials and public service announcements as well as program promotion, station identification, time/weather, and similar between-program matter. As you can see, the continuity writer's job that would be specified within this context would include the creation of actual commercials for paying clients, the construction of public service announcements (PSAs) for noncommercial entities, even the tape/slide presentations and textbook cassettes previously mentioned.

These latter tasks would be largely excluded under continuity's more narrow delineation. This much more specific approach to the term defines continuity as *the short, nonprogrammatic and nonspot broadcast material that serves to promote, interlock, and increase interest in and understanding of the aired programs and commercials.* This definition is much more station-based. In fact, it would be difficult for anyone but a writer working in-station or at a specialty firm serving stations to be in a position to accomplish such a restricted purpose.

Many stations maintain a traffic and continuity department or person with the responsibility for preparing the station program logs and the directed scheduling of all material segments to be aired. Under such an arrangement, a natural relationship exists between the scheduling function, which sets down all the programs and announcements in sequence, and the writing function, which seeks to make the flow between all those disparate parts as smooth as possible. The traffic and continuity person is thus an organizer as well as a writer. In each of these contexts, the focus is on the *segue.* Originally borrowed from the field of music, *segue* is now used in broadcasting as verb and noun—both to describe the process of one sound merging without a break into another and to denote the result of this process.

The radio and television industries place a high premium on these segues in order to give the listener or viewer as little excuse as possible to tune out mentally; as little time as possible to flip the dial or push the zap button. The writer who constructs stimulating and informative copy is just as important to segue achievement as is the technical director or disc jockey. Conversely, dead air and dead copy can be equally lethal to the maintenance of program and audience flow. The aim, of course, is to give the audience the feeling that pleasing and interesting stimuli are proceeding in an unbroken stream that deserves the continuing investment of their time as well as the more or less constant devotion of their attention.

The construction of meaningful, listener-holding transitions is a vital part of the writer's craft and a core duty whether you deal with continuity in the broad or narrow sense. Further, transitions are as essential to a full-length drama or documentary as they are to the interlocking of a news show with the dance program that is to follow. Practice and skill-honing in broadcast transitions bring carryover benefits to any full-length or self-contained manuscript that you might later be called on to write. We therefore can look on continuity writing, even in its most limited sense, as both a valuable training ground for more expansive writing efforts and a means of employment in its own right.

It is not necessary to justify continuity writing as merely a necessary proving ground for bigger things. Hundreds upon hundreds of writers are making lucrative and satisfying livings creating program promotions, station IDs, and, in the broader sense, radio and television commercials and PSAs. Indeed, it might be argued that the writer who can surmount the immense time problems inherent in a 30-second spot and still create a memorable, attention-holding, and complete vignette has to possess and exhibit a cogent writing style that few novelists or playwrights could ever hope to attain.

PORTFOLIO CREATION

Just as the novelist or playwright collects scenario ideas and character sketches for possible use in some future project, continuity writers should be gathering, preserving, and upgrading the copy assignments on which they have worked in order to advance to better accounts or stations in the months and years ahead. Plainly stated, this means that developing a professional portfolio is essential. Unlike playwrights and novelists, a copywriter's name does not adorn each spot or station ID he or she has penned. In fact, the writer of commercial and continuity copy remains anonymous to all but the supervisor. This absence of attribution is the price we pay for the relative security of a salaried job and a regular paycheck. To secure that first media job in whatever the employment context, and then to move on and up, copywriters must have a tangible record of what they have done to serve as a promise of what they will do.

ADWEEK reports "general consensus that a portfolio is essential for ascending to the creative hierarchy. Even if their entry-level jobs don't provide the opportunity, juniors can put together a professional quality spec book on their own."[9] To give yourself every advantage, it is strongly suggested that you begin your portfolio now with the exercises and assignments with which you will wrestle as you study broadcast copywriting. A piece of continuity or a half-minute spot need not have been actually aired in order to demonstrate your skill as a writer any more than a conventional author's character sketch must be actually published before it has merit. The important thing is that the spot or the sketch exposes a true writer's insight and manner of handling.

You will find that portfolio development is easier if you don't have to think up both the problem and the solution. Use and improve classroom or self-practice exercises whenever possible since they invariably set the boundaries within which you must work. Dreaming up *assignments* for portfolio examples, on the other hand, can be not only tedious but also misleading. It is far too easy to create a problem for a solution you've already conceived or to avoid instructive pitfalls by bending the task around them. As opposed to the playwright or novelist, the continuity writer can seldom choose the subject and can virtually never select the length of time expended in addressing it. Get your assignments from someone or somewhere else as your new portfolio begins to take shape. Learn to work within the unbending time and subject constraints that are an intrinsic part of the continuity writer's world and let your portfolio reflect this reality.

Above all, don't wait until you are in the job market to get your portfolio started. Under the pressure of finding employment quickly, the range of your work will be all too limited and the scope of your talent all too blurred. Certainly, the pressure of fulfilling assignments is a constant part of the writer's lot, but pressure to come up with what those assignments *should be* is not. Further, no writer, novice or veteran, can create, in a short period of time, a copy catalog sufficient to demonstrate either versatility or breadth of experience.

9. Gail Belsky, "Head-Hunting for Young Turks," *ADWEEK/Midwest,* October 31, 1983, p. 65.

Writing style and character are in a constant process of evolution; they exist, as Aaron Copland said about music, "in a continual state of becoming."[10] Not even a hint of this evolution can be frozen into a portfolio created within a single month. So start your portfolio now. Add to it gradually throughout your career. Keep thinning it out so that only the hardiest hybrids from each copy species remain. Then let that portfolio help carry you toward whatever part of the writer's world best suits your aims, goals, and self-demonstrated abilities.

Despite trends away from books and newspapers, the broadcast copywriter's world will always be well populated. Because, as copy chief Michael Plemmons notes, "No matter how many people stop reading, they'll never stop listening to speeches and broadcast spots and all the audio entertainment that will assault their ears. That noise won't just happen. It'll have to be in writing first."[11] You can be the person to accomplish this task, but only if you can surmount some of the barriers to communication that are present in the broadcast environment. These barriers are explored in the following chapter.

10. Aaron Copland, *Music and Imagination* (Cambridge, Mass.: Harvard University Press, 1952), p. 2.
11. Michael Plemmons, "Some Words to the Wise," *ADWEEK/Midwest*, November 8, 1982, p. 14.

Chapter Two

THE COMPONENTS
OF COMMUNICATION

Like anyone professionally engaged in reaching large and diverse groups of people, the broadcast copywriter must be aware of the dynamics of the communication process. The fact that your messages intrinsically involve the electronic media of radio and television does not lessen the need for you to appreciate the most basic components of human communication. If they concentrate only on the electronic implements of the delivery system, broadcast writers may find themselves constructing messages attuned primarily to media agencies rather than to the audiences those media agencies are attempting to serve. Since, in the final analysis, we are paid, not to reach the media, but to reach *people through* the media, there should be no misconception as to the primacy of individual perceivers, grouped into masses of various sizes and types, in determining what we write and how we write it. The unemployment lines continue to be fed by practitioners who write "for" radio or television rather than for people.

THE BASIC SYSTEM

All people-aimed communication, no matter how simple or sophisticated its delivery system, includes and uses the four components discussed below. (See Figure 2–1.) Any or all components can exist in multiple form and still not change the fundamental functioning of the process.

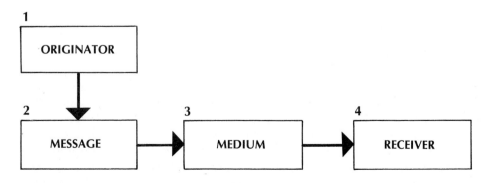

Figure 2–1. Basic Communication Process

Originator

Limiting ourselves to human communication (this is not, after all, a text on computer programming or animal husbandry), we assume the *originator* to be a human being with some desire, at times stimulated by money, to communicate with another human being or beings. The originator's task is to attempt to establish a temporary linkage with at least one other person in order that they both will focus on the same object, event, or idea. The duration of this linkage and the clarity of this focus are influenced by every component in the process but initially depend on the overt and covert behavior of the originator. We have all experienced situations in which an originator's overt action clashes so strikingly with his or her covert or secondary behavior that real doubt is cast on the originator's motives. The man who shakes your hand warmly but studiously avoids your gaze becomes as suspect as the woman whose warm "hello" is accompanied by physically backing away. A link, of course, has been established, but with a much different impact than the originators intended, or thought they intended.

In certain instances, originators might even fool themselves as to the fundamental motivation for their communications. (More than one inadvertently bad peanut butter advertisement can be traced back to some poor copywriter who could never stand the stuff.) Since the originator does have some financial, social, or professional stake in the results of every communication he or she initiates, the most successful originators are those who have learned to probe their own behavior before seeking to influence the behavior of others.

This influencing may consist of nothing more than the acquiring of attention, which, on radio and television, is itself no small task. Nevertheless, if the linkage has been thus established, the originator has met the objective as far as the simple mechanics of the communication process are concerned. Whether the outcome of the linkage is favorable or unfavorable to the originator is a more long-range and subjective judgment. It goes far beyond the functional question about whether the linkage was, in fact, achieved. As we shall see in later chapters, it is not too difficult to secure fleeting attention. Holding and parlaying such attention toward ends deemed acceptable or advantageous to the originator, however, are much more extensive and intensive tasks.

Message

A message is a commodity one must possess in order to be justifiably labelled an originator. It is a commodity one must also transmit in order to function as an originator. This should not be taken to mean that originators are always aware of the content they are transmitting or even that they are transmitting at all. Human beings, in sensory proximity to other human beings, can receive messages that are products of that proximity rather than of any conscious desire on the part of the unwitting originator to communicate. What is interpreted as a "come hither" look on the part of that handsome male across the aisle may result only from a slippage of his contact lens. Similarly, though he is certainly not conscious of the fact, the dozing student in the back of the classroom may be the originator of a distinctly unpleasant message as far as his instructor is concerned, and one that will not have its impact diminished simply because it was inadvertent.

Except in total isolation from others, it is very difficult if not impossible for human beings to avoid assuming the more or less constant role of originators, transmitting a steady stream of intended and unintended messages to people with whom they are somehow brought in contact. While most of us are self-consciously aware of the inevitability of our message divulgence when placed in unfamiliar or strained social situations, we must also remain cognizant of this factor during our calculated and premeditated attempts to communicate. Sending a message when none was intended is one thing, but sending an unintended message that obscures or negates what we are actively seeking to transmit can be much more detrimental to one's professional or social interests. If the situation was important enough to instill in us an active desire to transmit, it should be important enough to justify special efforts to avoid possible blurring or contradiction by the simultaneous sending of seemingly conflicting messages.

Medium

The vehicle through which originators transmit or project their messages can be simple or complex and can involve components completely external to the originator. Some authorities divide media into two broad categories: *communication* vehicles and *communications* vehicles. In the former group are the means of transmission not requiring implements external to the originator. Thus, oral behavior using the human vocal apparatus as well as physical gestures and other visible body movements would constitute *communication*. Writing on a blackboard, typing a letter, or marking a forest trail with piled rocks would, on the other hand, all be considered *communications*, since they rely on components external to the human body as message carriers. Communications media therefore extend one's ability to communicate in time and/or space. A note left on a bulletin board or on the dining room table will convey the originator's message even though it may have been written several hours ago and the originator be hundreds of miles distant by the time the message is discovered.

Mass communications vehicles constitute a special subgroup of communications media since their extreme efficiency extends the ability to communicate in time and space and also makes it possible to reach large and diversified audiences quickly, if not instantaneously. As the broadcast writer soon learns, however, the optimum use of mass communications requires that each individual within the mass audience comes to feel that he or she is being addressed directly and singly. In fact, the mass media of broadcasting in particular are at their most effective when they can skillfully simulate a *communication* rather than a *communications* setting. The script that assists an announcer in seeming to talk "across the table" to you (a communication setting) has a much better chance of succeeding than one that screams at "all you folks out there in radioland" and thereby focuses more on the medium than on the message it carries.

Receiver

The receiver in human communication is the *detector* of the message the originator has transmitted via some medium. We say detector, rather than target, simply because receivers spend much of their time picking up messages that are not really aimed at them. In the most alarming sense, this occurs in such cases as bugging and other forms of electronic eavesdropping, where a conscious and technologically sophisticated effort is made to intercept the messages of others. In many cases, however, detection of messages by nonintended receivers is simply a case of being mistaken for the sought-after receiver or being in sensory proximity to that receiver. We have all heard conversations of people at adjoining restaurant tables or nearby bus seats. We have all glanced over others' bulletin board notes and postings. In doing so, we became receivers even though the originator of the message sent via a communication or communications vehicle was not seeking to establish a link with us.

Straightforward originators usually do not concentrate on whether people other than those at whom they aim have, in fact, become receivers of the message. What is of concern is whether you have been able to make receivers of the people you have actively tried to reach. Ultimately, the true success of the communication process is not assured by the mere mechanical meshing of originator, message, medium, and receiver. Instead it requires:

> an originator
>   with a conscious desire to communicate
>   a message of significance
>   through an appropriate medium
>   in such a way that
>   a receiver will attach like sig-
>   nificance to that message
>   *and respond in a manner acceptable*
>   *or advantageous to the originator.*

THE COMMUNICATION PROCESS IN THE BROADCAST SETTING

As indicated, the originator, message, medium, and receiver are components basic to any and every manifestation of the communication process. As various situations, vehicles, and communication goals require greater specificity or productivity, we must consider additional subelements. In the broadcast setting, which is the prime concern of this book, we might dissect the process in the following manner. (Figure 2–2.)

Originator

In this as well as the other three components of our communication process, one can see that, with the complexities of a broadcast system, we have acquired various subcomponents; have broken down or shared the function between

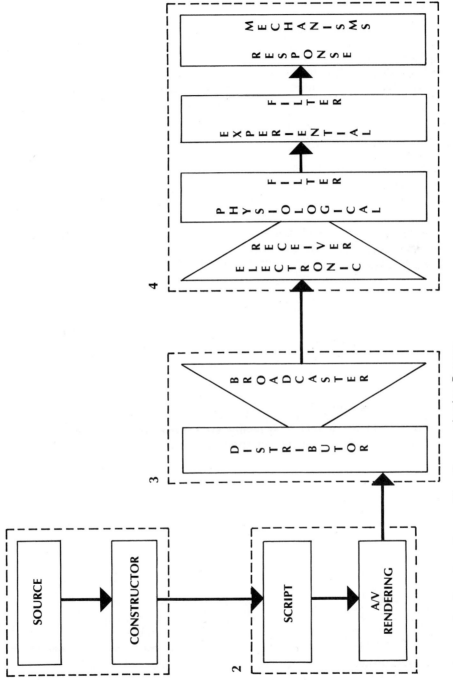

Figure 2-2. Broadcast Copywriting Communication Process

SOURCE

CONSTRUCTOR

SCRIPT

A/V RENDERING

2

DISTRIBUTOR

BROADCASTER

3

ELECTRONIC RECEIVER

PHYSIOLOGICAL FILTER

EXPERIENTIAL FILTER

MECHANISM RESPONSES

4

two or more interactive agents. Unless one owns, operates, and creates all the advertising for a firm, the origination function is shared by a source working in cooperation with a message constructor. The *source*, then, is most often referred to as the *client*. It may be a bank, cereal manufacturer, or fast-food palace. In noncommercial situations (generally called *public service* announcements), the source may be the United Way, CARE, even the local Society for the Preservation of Hibernating Chipmunks. Since broadcast journalism is outside the scope of this book, we shall not mention the wide variety of agencies and individuals outside broadcasting itself who may function as broadcast news sources to accomplish more indirectly their own communication goals. It is sometimes charged, for example, that public relations people are really news *constructors* striving to present themselves to other constructors as objective news *sources*.

Whatever its nature, it is this source whose aims are being promoted and who tries to set the agenda for what is to be communicated. The other half of the originator function, the *constructor*, then strives to achieve these aims by putting together a message that is appropriate to the broadcast media and maximally adapted to the unique capabilities of either radio or television. Presumably, you are reading this book as a means of preparing yourself to be, or work with, such a constructor. You may labor at a station, an advertising agency, or in any of the several other contexts discussed in chapter 1. Whatever the environment, it is vital to realize at the outset that a mass media message constructor seldom has the last (or even the first) word as to what will be communicated. To a general or a specific degree, it is the source who pays the bills—the constructor's salary included—and therefore who calls the shots.

Shaller Rubin Associates' Executive Vice President Paul Goldsmith illustrates this point by recalling:

> "The greatest hype a copywriter has is at the moment the 'final' version of the copy comes out of the typewriter. It's all downhill from that moment. My ideal copywriter is fully aware of the downhill realities of the advertising process—recognizing that his work will go through more sieves, more review than any other piece of work in the agency. After it's submitted to the scrutiny of his supervisor, it goes to the creative director. On to the account group for its suggestions and changes before it reaches the client who will surely incorporate his ideas and alterations. This tedious trip through a creative person's chamber of horrors unfortunately comes with the territory."[1]

Message

When we think of the broadcast message, we logically focus on the audio and/or visual form in which that message reaches us and the millions of colleague broadcast consumers who populate the landscape. Yet, that message has first had to have been set in the more traditional written form, to constitute a *script*. On rare occasions, the message is extemporized, entirely ad-libbed, or edited down from recorded actualities and real-life interviews. In these instances, the script is required only for contractual and station record-keeping purposes. In most cases, however, the script constitutes the evolved creative

1. Paul Goldsmith, writing in "Monday Memo," *Broadcasting Magazine*, September 22, 1980, p. 12.

end product which, once approved by the appropriate sources, is translated into "live," on-air readings, or audio tape, video tape, or film dubs for easy playback by the stations involved. As shall be subsequently seen, the success of this script depends almost as much on its form as on its content. The best-laid concepts can be maimed, if not destroyed, by an improperly executed script.

Assuming that the script is cast into the industry-recognized pattern, it must then be transformed into one of the audio or video formats mentioned. This transformation must be as true to the original script as possible; but we also should recognize that the printed word is but an imperfect method for describing actuality. A picture, a snatch of music, or a vocal inflection can be generally indicated in the script, but their finalized on-air rendering will have a whole new, and much more specific, dimension. This same principle applies to the broadcast message as a whole, which can include all of these elements. Thus, though the printed script is both a creative chronicle and a contractual promise, its final form in sight and/or sound is a discrete phenomenon unto itself. This is a maddening fact of life for both sources and constructors but is the price gladly paid for the potential dynamism of the radio or television message.

Medium

The transmission of the broadcast message also proceeds through two stages. Even though it may often be nothing more than a clerical processing, a non-broadcast *distributor* mechanism precedes the actual airing of the precon-structed message. If the project begins and culminates entirely within a single station, this distributor function may be nothing more than placing copies of the completed script in the appropriate continuity books for on-air reading by station announcers. The process is slightly more involved if the message is to be put on tape to be broadcast in a preproduced or canned form. In that instance, the production staffer uses the script or cue sheet in recording and editing the message into an audio/video cartridge (cart) or open-reel format suitable for airing. In many stations, the writer will also handle this function and thereby has actual control over the translation of the message into the aural/visual mode.

As larger numbers of stations and more substantial sources are involved, the distributor function becomes more comprehensive. Scripts engendered by the creative departments of advertising agencies and produced by them or by independent production houses result in the dubbing and dissemination of multiple copies of the air-ready message to scores of stations. Copies may also be sent to network continuity acceptance departments and to the offices of stations and station groups in order to insure that the message does not violate the self-policing standards imposed by these organizations. (A sample of these standards appears in Appendix C.) Whatever the case, we must realize that an intermediate step exists between creation and actual airing of the broadcast preplanned message. Depending on the scope of the project involved, this step can inject a few more or a great many more people and institutions into the broadcast communication process.

The message is then transmitted over the airwaves by each station involved as per its own broadcast schedule or simultaneously aired by a large number of stations or cable systems taking the feed from a network. This *broadcaster* function is the factor that gives the message potential access to thousands, even millions, of people. We will not get into the immense variety of electromagnetic equipment that plays a part in this dissemination process. Nor will we attempt to isolate all the technical malfunctions beyond the control of the writer that may interfere with the optimal transmission of the message. At this point, science takes over from art, and the writer must rely on the specialized expertise of the engineers and the highly improved reliability of our solid-state and satellite-facilitated technology.

Receiver

This same reliance must be granted to the first stage in the receiver function. Broadcast transmitters do not talk directly to people—they talk to people's radio and television receiving sets from which we human beings are able to perceive the message. These *electronic receivers* vary widely in cost, age, sensitivity, and ability of their owners to adjust them properly. Stressing the particular color of a product on television through the visual alone may be a risky venture on home sets that make Johnny Carson look like the Jolly Green Giant. Having your key selling point buried in an audio crowd scene may not be the wisest choice over pocket radios operating on six-month-old, discount-store batteries. Despite our transistorized and electronic sophistication, there are a lot of malfunctioning and misadjusted receiving sets in use by audience members. The less you, the writer, take for granted as to these units' performance, the more care you will come to exercise in preserving clarity of content in your message.

The final three stages of the receiver function are all internal to each human being in our audience. The first stage, the *physiological filter,* describes the varying sensory limitations inherent in each of us. People with hearing losses will obviously have greater difficulty in picking up the radio transmission or television sound track than those with unimpaired auditory mechanisms. People with sight problems will experience trouble in perceiving certain elements of the television picture but may acquire greater auditory acuity as a compensation. As in the case of the electronic receiver, the broadcast writer cannot assume too much as regards the functioning level of the physiological components of our human receptors. Even those who hear or see fairly well may have trouble discerning a brand name read over a "heavy" music backdrop or a television "where to call" line projected in small, indistinct numerals. Remember also that some individuals with well-functioning eyes and ears take longer to process this sensory information through the brain. Say it or show it too quickly and they, too, will miss the message.

Given that these sensory barriers are successfully penetrated, the message must then encounter the much more varied and sometimes downright bizarre hurdles presented by the *experiential filter.* This is the sum total of all the events, episodes, and situations through which we have acquired knowledge of our world and of ourselves. Since no two people have experienced exactly the same things, each of us sees the world through different "eyes," or, as Marshall

McLuhan put it, through different "goggles." Our preconceptions, preferences, fears, and prejudices are all part of this filter that guarantees that each of us constitutes and behaves as a unique individual.

Fortunately for the mass communicator, though all of us are one-of-a-kind items, we can be grouped into broad categories delineated by such factors as age, sex, educational level, geography, income, and national origin. Labelled *demographic characteristics*, market research experts and other social scientists use these factors to make predictions as to the programs we will watch, the products we will use, and the candidates we will vote for or, in some cases, against. As mass communications institutions, unable to monitor feedback from audiences until well after the message has been sent, radio and television use these demographic data in formulating the structure and content of everything from ten-second station identifications to multipart entertainment presentations.

In short, the broadcast/cable industry is engaged in a giant guessing game that tries to predict not only the demographic composition of a potential audience, but also the words and images that best appeal to that group. Through still more indepth *psychographic* research, media strategists even attempt to probe life-style and other psychological preference patterns that can cut across, or subdivide, individual demographic clusters. But however the population pie is sliced, its constituent parts remain relatively large, their precise physiological and experiential characteristics still obscured by the massiveness of their numbers. Standardized or common denominator message level is therefore inevitable as we try to reach those research-targeted phantoms without boring them, on the one hand, or confusing and overloading them on the other.

Two common expressions graphically illustrate these two undesirable extremes. The dulling, oversimplified message that seems to assail us with a "Ding-dong School" vocabulary is diagrammed in Figure 2–3. The message gets through our sensory system without difficulty but is so blandly basic that it seems to insult our intelligence. "They're *talking down* to me" is our reaction, and our attention either goes down or entirely ceases.

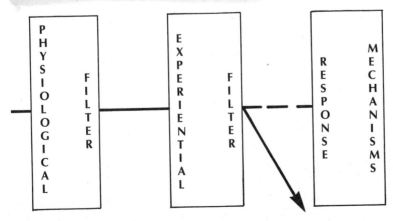

Figure 2–3. Talking Down

At the other end of the continuum is the overly esoteric message that is so cabalistic or recondite that almost no one understands it. Such a message is charted out in Figure 2–4. Here, again, the message successfully penetrated the sensory system but was acutely deflected by the individual's lack of familiarity with the terms or concepts used. "They're *talking over* my head" is the conclusion, and our further attention or response is minimal. Now, look back to the terms *esoteric, cabalistic,* and *recondite.* Did those words and the sentence that contains them turn you off? If so, you've experienced this "over my head" conundrum (or should we say, *problem*) first hand.

Hopefully, however, the radio or television set is working properly, most of our audience have functioning eyes and ears, and our writer has constructed a message that features understandable and interesting concepts for the people at whom it is aimed. Finally, the receiver's *response mechanisms* are able to be engaged. Perhaps our audience members will buy it, vote for it, donate to it, or mix it with the cat's food once a week. At least, the originator wishes that they *remember* it so that a gradual familiarity with and favorable disposition toward the product or idea will be built up in the weeks and months ahead.

The appropriateness or inappropriateness of audience responses in terms of the originator's expectations for the message are stringently evaluated after the fact by rating points, sales curves, votes cast, or other relevant measuring devices. If possible, field trials and other test marketing have been undertaken to sample results on a limited basis as a preliminary step to the costly full-scale campaign. In any event, if the responses are found deficient in character or quantity, the message must be changed. Worse, if the responses are adjudged *negative* in nature, it may be that the constructor must be changed. For unlike the dog in Pavlov's psychology experiment, it is not the subject audience that is "punished" for inappropriate responses. Instead, it is the experimenter/constructor!

If this irksome condition fails to diminish your interest in broadcast writing and writers, congratulations. You obviously possess two ingredients essential for work in the creative side of radio and television: an uncommon appetite for

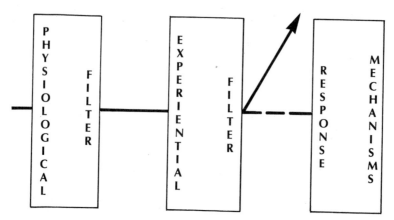

Figure 2–4. Talking Over

pain and a thirst for constant challenge. The subsequent pages will seek to analyze further your commitment to the field and probe the outer limits of your talent. As either a broadcast writer or interdependent colleague of such writers, good luck! And, as radio's Bob and Ray used to say, *write* when you get work.

Chapter Three

THE BROADCAST COPYWRITER'S TOOLS

Now that we have surveyed the various work situations in which broadcast copywriters might be placed and have seen the communications complexities to which they can be subjected, we are ready to inventory the writing implements usually required. Broadcast copywriters call on many of the same devices as other wordsmiths to accomplish their tasks. They also work in an environment in which clarity, conciseness, and speed are of paramount importance.

Excess is the radio/television scribe's greatest enemy—whether an excess of ideas that muddles a PSA, an excess of words that forces a commercial into longer (and more expensive) form, or an excess of time in completing an assignment that puts an entire campaign off schedule. The writing tools most important to us, therefore, are those replacing excess with functional frugality, helping us communicate on target, on budget, and on time.

Punctuation is vital since it provides the mechanism for grouping words into their most cogent and quickly understandable patterns. It is no overstatement to say that punctuation is a major, perhaps even the prime tool for successful broadcast copywriting.

PRINT PUNCTUATION VERSUS BROADCAST PUNCTUATION

Though both print and broadcast writers use words set to paper as the means of initially snaring their thoughts, this paper prototype plays a significantly different role in the two categories of media. In the case of print, the writer's arrangement is in fundamentally the same form in which the intended audience will ingest it. Certainly, some editor or typesetter may perform minor alterations, but we still have a message captured on the page that the audience will pick up and read from the page.

For the broadcast writer, on the other hand, the written copy is only a linguistic halfway house in the communication process. As we saw in chapter 2, the written broadcast message comes to life for the audience only after it has been translated into aural or visual form. The broadcast audience does not *read* the script but *hears* and, in the case of television, also *sees* the translation of that script into real-time actuality. They can neither go back and reread it nor scan ahead to preview it. Thus, broadcast punctuation must strive to translate the writer's message to and through the announcer or other performer so it finally reaches the audience as natural *sounding* speech. In the final analysis, broadcast punctuation consists of systematic stage directions to an intermediary, whereas print punctuation is direct and largely unaltered communication between writer and receiver.

Unfortunately for the broadcast writer, any punctuation system, no matter how modified, remains somewhat print-bound. No written symbology can ever indicate entirely all the nuances of a spoken message any more than a musical score is a true blueprint for a heard composition. Both the score and the broadcast script require the services of competent performer/interpreters. What the composer or copywriter must do is make certain that the notation or punctuation is as systematic and standardized as possible so that, at least, it does not convey something different than what the originator intended. Though no system of broadcast punctuation is universally accepted, the following guidelines serve to keep the various punctuation marks mutually discrete so each fulfills its specific function as discretely as possible.

With that aim in mind, let us now examine the various punctuation marks used in broadcast copy. As an overview, remember that for radio and television copy, your ear rather than printed-oriented grammatical rules should be the final adjudicator of what constitutes proper broadcast punctuation.

Period

As in print media, the period indicates that a whole thought, complete in itself, has been concluded. Moreover, the period in broadcast copy tells the performer to insert a pause, the duration of which depends on the overall pace of the copy, before beginning the next thought. At their option, broadcast writers may decide to put a period after a sentence that is *grammatically* incomplete, if the sense, flow, and memorability of the copy will thereby be enhanced:

<u>Visit Lou's.</u> For shoes.

Thirteen thousand sympathetic towtrucks. Your Acme Auto Club.

Radio. Red hot because it works.

<u>Your best deserves the best.</u> Butter. Real Butter.

Notice that there are nine effective *idea units* in these examples but only two grammatical *sentences* (which have been underlined).

Because the period denotes a pause, it is wise to avoid its use in abbreviations, since a performer may not know whether a pause is desired after "Dept." or not. Abbreviations are undesirable anyway since announcers, reading an extended piece of copy, have been known temporarily to draw a blank as to the full pronunciation of the term represented by such shortcuts as "Corp.," "Msgr.," "lb.," or "GA." Imagine yourself stumbling across the following sentence in the middle of a long on-air stint.

The Brockett Corp., charged Msgr. Foster, dumped its contaminants by the lb. in GA.

Even a single abbreviation can trip up an announcer on a bad day—and announcers, like copywriters, are never immune to bad days. Take every precaution to use periods only at the end of sense-complete thought units. Whether the thought unit is also *grammatically* complete is largely irrelevant.

The only exception to this singular use of the period should be in abbreviations that are virtually never written out and that, in fact, are much more commonly used than the words they might stand for. Basically, there are six of these:

Dr.   Mr.   Mrs.   Ms.   A.M.   P.M.

As four of these words are always followed by a proper noun (Ms. Hanson), and the remaining two are preceded by numerals (11 A.M.), the use of the period with them cannot, by itself, be easily mistaken for the end of a thought unit. The acceptable indication for doctor (Dr.) does, however, make it doubly important that we never write

```
Lakeside Dr. or Clive Dr.
```

when we mean

```
Lakeside Drive and Clive Drive.
```

Question Mark

A question mark comes after a direct query in broadcast copy just as it does in print copy. In addition, the broadcast writer must realize that, in our culture, most spoken questions end with an upward inflection. We thus must be especially careful to keep questions in our copy short so that the performer can easily perceive that the thought unit is indeed a question and prepare that upward inflection in a smooth and gradual manner. Otherwise, the poor announcer may realize it's a question only after most of the sentence has passed. The sudden inflection that results may be humorous to listen to but hardly contributes to meaningful communication of the message. Even if the talent detects a long question early, it is almost impossible to sustain the proper rising modulation for very many words. Try reading the following copy segment aloud in such a way that it continuously sounds like a question:

```
Doesn't there have to be a reason why Sims' Fruit Emporium has
been the best place for pears, apples, oranges, peaches and plums
since Grampa Sims put up his first striped awning back in the
quiet Clintondale summer of nineteen-ought-six?
```

For better clarity, and unstretched vocal chords, the essence of the question should be isolated like this:

```
Why is Sims' the best place in Clintondale for fruit? Well, since
1906 when, etc.
```

Keep queries short and to the point so the question mark can be easily seen and accommodated by the announcer as well as easily "heard" and felt by the audience.

Exclamation Mark

Both print and broadcast punctuation use the exclamation mark (!) after complete thought units that demand special emphasis. Comic strip characters seem to talk in nothing but exclamation marks, and this fact should not be lost on broadcast writers. Since we strive for copy that sounds natural and believable, the constant use of exclamation marks is at best an irritant to the listener and at worst an indication that Daffy Duck was the writer. In most cases, emphasis should be built naturally into the copy through your choice of words and the arrangement of the words you've chosen. A piece of continuity permeated with exclamation marks can do nothing but cast real doubt on your wordsmith's ability. Wield this punctuation symbol with extreme reluctance. If you've already developed an exclamation problem, make a pact with yourself to donate a dollar to your favorite charity each time you end up using an exclamation mark in your copy creation. In the long run, this practice will either make you a much better writer or lower your income tax. (Note the absence of an exclamation mark after that last sentence.)

Comma

Just as in print, the *broadcast* comma generally indicates a separation of words, phrases, or clauses from others that are part of the same thought unit and of a similar or like type:

```
Bertha's Breakfast Grotto for the tummy yummyist waffles,
pancakes, omelets, and sweet rolls.
```

```
Rain, snow, ice, and fog. Terrible weather well presented on
Channel 10.
```

In a like manner, commas are used to set off the name of a person addressed from the rest of the sentence:

```
But golly, Mr. Whipple, I can't help squeezing.
```

More important to broadcast performers, the comma also provides a short breathing space that can be used as necessary to keep the tone round and the head clear. We thus insert commas wherever needed to facilitate announcer breathing and to gather words more clearly into effective rhythmic groupings. In using commas to promote copy flow, the broadcast writer may find it necessary to employ them in some places not called for by conventional grammatical rules.

```
Taco Heaven, it's the place, where real sour cream, drips down,
your face.
```

In other instances, broadcast copy may omit commas where a grammar book would demand their placement.

```
At the Deli and the Baker and the Ice Cream Maker.
```

Here again, the resultant *sound* of the message rather than the strictures of print-oriented grammar must be the decisive factor.

Semicolon

The semicolon, too, is a very helpful tool in promoting copy rhythm. It is used between main clauses within a single thought unit and takes the place of such drab, time-wasting connectives as *and, for, but,* and *or.* Notice how the pace and forward motion of the following sentence,

```
Something had happened but she didn't know what.
```

is enhanced by replacing the connective with a semicolon:

```
Something had happened; she didn't know what.
```

To the announcer, the semicolon indicates a short vocal pause between two closely related thoughts. This contrasts with the proportionately longer pause that the period deserves, coming as it does at the end of a self-sufficient thought unit. The semicolon gives a pleasing sense of balance to the two sub-parts of its thought unit while still keeping them in close temporal proximity to each other. Finally, semicolon patterns like the following provide additional breathing opportunities to be used at the performer's option.

```
                        (that)
Radio 93's Midday News;          brings you the action in time for
lunch.
```

```
                                        (and)
The Norseman blanket saves you cash today;        keeps you cozy
tonight.
```

Quotation Marks

For the commercial and continuity writer, quotation marks are more to be avoided than embraced. Their main legitimate use is to set off direct quotations that must be read exactly as written. Occasionally, the testimonial spot or PSA will use such word-for-word statements, but it is in news copy that these punctuation symbols are primarily employed. In most cases then, if your writing job keeps you out of the newsroom, keep away from quotation marks. They clutter copy appearance and can therefore serve to inhibit a smooth delivery of the message by announcers who are reading the copy "cold." (Notice how those just-used quotation marks caused a brief stop in even your silent reading flow.)

Apostrophe

Since this symbol makes use of only one ' instead of two ", it has only half the potential for script clutter that the quotation marks possess and helps reserve their use solely for direct quote indication. If not underlined, a program or record title can be set apart with paired apostrophes. This symbol is especially practical when your copy must identify a specific part of a larger work as well as the larger work itself. The apostrophe can clearly indicate the subunit, while underlining identifies the work as a whole:

We now hear 'Let Me Say Just One Word' from Puccini's <u>The</u> <u>Girl</u> <u>of</u> <u>the</u> <u>Golden</u> <u>West.</u>

That was 'Big D,' a salute to the home of the Cowboys from the hit musical, <u>The</u> <u>Most</u> <u>Happy</u> <u>Fella.</u>

From Bill Cosby's hilarious album <u>To</u> <u>Russell,</u> <u>My</u> <u>Brother,</u> <u>Whom</u> <u>I</u> <u>Slept</u> <u>With,</u> here's a tribute to 'The Apple.'

Colon

This symbol, too, performs one of the tasks in broadcast copy that quotation marks would otherwise be called on to serve. It is used to set up each line of dialogue in a spot, PSA, or other continuity writing that calls for speeches by separate characters. When combined with proper spacing, the colon insures that the copy will be definitive and easy to read without the necessity for a jungle of quotation marks. Imagine the copy clutter in the following 60-second spot if quotation marks had to be used in place of each colon:

BRUCE: So that's when she starched my shorts. You'd think I drove the car into the ditch.

ED: How'd she get out?

BRUCE: Oh, she finally found a phone booth about a mile up the road.

ED: Called you from there?

BRUCE: No. Called her mother. That was my bowling night.

ED: Good grief. So then what happened?

BRUCE: They got this gas station guy to pull her out. Cost her mother thirty bucks.

ED: Why didn't your wife pay for it?

BRUCE: I borrowed her last five for beer money.

ED: You're lucky she only starched your shorts.

BRUCE: Maybe you're right. So then she gets this idea she could join that Acme Auto Club thing so we could get <u>free</u> road service.

ED: Your wife said this?

BRUCE: Yeah. But I think it came from her mother.

ED: Why don't you?

BRUCE: Join Acme Auto Club? I've already got car insurance.

ED: So what? Acme Auto Club only sells insurance as an extra service. The important thing is the membership.

BRUCE: You belong?

ED: You bet. Costs me thirty-five bucks but it's worth it. I get road aid and notary service and all the help I want in trip planning. Acme even taught my wife to drive.

```
BRUCE:  Mine could use that. Costs you thirty-five bucks for Acme
        membership?
ED:     Right. Sit down and I'll tell you about it.
BRUCE:  Can't.
ED:     Why not?
BRUCE:  My shorts.
ED:     Oh.
```

In addition to dialogue clarification, the colon also paves the way for any direct quotations called for in the message. It puts the performer on notice that a distinct and generally extensive passage is to follow.

```
TV 22 is helping you. Bob Lane of the Stoltz City United Fund
says: ''We have exceeded our pledge goal for this year's
campaign. And much of the credit goes to the folks at TV 22 in
helping to publicize how the United Fund helps us all.'' TV 22.
Serving Stoltz City; serving you.
```

In a similar vein, the colon can prepare the announcer for a long list of items that are to follow as component parts of the same thought unit.

```
Today, the Sharkville Diner and Car Wash is featuring: veal
surprise, chicken over-easy, potted pork pie, and ham hock
delight.
```

Dash

The dash serves functions similar to, but more exaggerated than, those accommodated by certain of the other punctuation symbols. Like the semicolon, it can be used to improve copy rhythm and flow by replacing drab words. It is preferred over the semicolon if more than one word is being omitted:

```
                      (when you)
Keep a garden in your kitchen---keep a cupboard full of cans.
```

```
        (it has)
Radio 97---the greatest tunes this side of Boston.
```

In both of these examples, the dash creates a longer pause than that indicated by the semicolon while still helping to convey that the phrases on either side of it are both component parts of the same thought unit.

Like paired commas, paired dashes can be called on to segregate a single word or phrase from the rest of the sentence. But whereas commas serve to underplay that isolated segment, a duo of dashes strives to heighten and emphasize it. In our previous example:

```
But golly, Mr. Whipple, I can't help squeezing.
```

we want the listener to focus, not on Mr. Whipple, but on what you can't help doing to the product. Paired commas are thus appropriate. The following specimen, on the other hand, has the product name (always our most important information) within the separated segment. Since we wish to accent that product name, paired dashes are mandated.

```
The smoothest way---the Finster way---to blend the best in tea.
```

As an experiment, let's reverse our punctuation use in these two instances. Read the two lines aloud in the manner the broadcast punctuation decrees.

```
But golly---Mr. Whipple---I can't help squeezing.
```

```
The smoothest way, the Finster way, to blend the best in tea.
```

Note the difference in effect and impact? So would your listener. Appropriate words must go hand in hand with appropriate punctuation.

In a more specialized way, a dash can be used to denote a sudden breaking off of a thought either because of hesitancy on the part of the speaker,

```
All of a sudden I wanted to---
```

or because that speaker was interrupted by another.

```
SAM:   Florida grapefruit is---
ANN:   Great fruit.
```

Underlining

An underlined word, which is placed in italics if set in type, is another way of requesting special emphasis from the performer. As in the case of the "great fruit" line above, underlining is especially helpful at directing attention to words on which we normally don't focus or that occur at a place in the sentence that prohibits the use of alternative punctuation:

```
I don't know why my wash is grayer than yours.
```

Any of the other means of directing attention via emphasis would only inject an unwanted pause or pauses into this thought unit and, consequently, inhibit copy flow. Note how the following punctuation marks either misdirect or hobble the thought.

```
I don't know why. My wash is grayer than yours.
```

```
I don't know, why my wash is grayer than yours.
```

```
I don't know why, my wash is grayer than yours.
```

```
I don't know; why my wash is grayer than yours.
```

```
I don't know why; my wash is grayer than yours.
```

```
I don't know---why---my wash is grayer than yours.
```

As discussed in conjunction with the apostrophe, underlining is also used to denote the titles of complete literary works, programs, albums, or complete musical compositions. Because we normally wish to direct attention to these titles anyway, underlining in such instances serves two mutually compatible functions.

Ellipsis

The ellipsis is a series of three dots which, when used more than once, can make your copy appear to have contracted the pox.

> Use of the ellipsis . . . should therefore . . . be avoided . . . like the plague.

Its sole recognized function in broadcast writing is to indicate clearly that words have been omitted from a direct quote and that the announcer should make that fact clear in the way the copy is read. Yet, for some reason, lazy copywriters blissfully substitute the ellipsis for commas, dashes, semicolons, and even periods. They therefore deprive their copy of the subtle but effective shadings that the discrete and specialized use of each of these punctuation marks can help bring to their writing.

Parentheses

Though often used in print media for asides and stage whispers, the parentheses have a much more circumscribed and mechanistic task in broadcast copy. Simply stated, they are used to set off stage directions and technical instructions from the words the announcer is supposed to read aloud. In the follownng example which was actually read on air, the copywriter neglected to use his parentheses:

```
It's 8 P.M. Bulova watch time. On Christmas, say Merry Christmas.
On New Year's, say Happy New Year.
```

The correct translation of the copywriter's intent should, of course, have been punctuated this way:

```
It's 8 P.M. Bulova watch time. (On Christmas, say Merry
Christmas. On New Year's, say Happy New Year.)
```

Don't omit parentheses around any private communications between you and the talent who will read your copy. Similarly, don't persist in the print-oriented approach to parentheses and put anything between them that you *do* wish the listener to hear. In the following piece of broadcast copy, parentheses have been used in a manner common to print media.

```
Ever been in a Lumber camp? (If you had, you'd remember the meals
the guys stowed away.) They needed good, hot food (and plenty of
it) for all that muscle work. And no meal was as important as
breakfast. They wanted a hot breakfast that stayed with them (a
hot meal like Mama Gruber's Corn Mush cereal). No, her Mush isn't
modern. (In fact, Mama Gruber's Corn Mush is kind of old-
fashioned). But so is hard work.
```

The announcer accustomed to the broadcast employment of parentheses would quite properly read the commerical this way:

```
Ever been in a Lumber camp? They needed good, hot food for all
that muscle work. And no meal was as important as breakfast. They
wanted a hot breakfast that stayed with them. No, her Mush isn't
modern. But then, so is hard work.
```

Does the spot still make sense? Not only are we left with at least ten seconds of dead air in a 30-second spot, but we have also lost the name of our product and sponsor. Restrict parentheses to their intended broadcast use. If your copy contains words and phrases that, in print, would constitute parenthetical expressions, use dashes or commas in your broadcast script to set these expressions off.

A final caution pertaining to all broadcast punctuation must here be reemphasized. Even when used correctly and in accord with widely accepted broadcast practices, punctuation of copy meant to be read aloud remains a comparatively tenuous and approximate tool. In his eighteenth century *A Course of Lectures on Elocution,* English authority Thomas Sheridan focused on the "unprintable components of good speech"; components that words and spaces arranged uniformly on a page were incapable of indicating. The ancients, he pointed out, had no system of punctuation whatever but used written material merely to enable a speaker to learn the words by rote so he could recite them, in his own unique manner, from memory.[1] Since broadcast announcers don't often memorize their scripts and because the broadcast industry as a whole has some more or less uniform expectations for the way copy is to be read, today's copywriters *need* punctuation, no matter how tentative. A commonly accepted system of punctuation is essential if broadcast writers are even to hope for an adequate means of communicating with the announcers and other performers who will bring their copy to life.

TOOLS TO READ/CONSULT

Punctuation is only one of the broadcast copywriter's implements. Reference books comprise another. Though the following list does not attempt to be comprehensive, it does include the types of volumes that are an essential part of the copywriter's library. Basically, these works group themselves into three categories: dictionaries, word-finders, and style aids.

Dictionaries

Any writer must be an ardent dictionary user if for no other reason than its utility as a spelling aid. Because words are our prime stock in trade, misspelling is inexcusable and makes the writer seem as incompetent as the physician unable to read a thermometer. A dictionary is also helpful to writers in separating the syllables within a word to facilitate proper hyphenating of it at the end of a line. For broadcast writers, however, this is a function that should rarely be used. Announcers' eyes do not like to have to jump lines in the middle of a word, and there is no reason why the copywriter should require them to do so.

---

1. Thomas Sheridan, *A Course of Lectures on Elocution* (London: J. Dodsley, 1787).

If the word does not fit completely on one line, it should be moved in its entirety to the one below. Whole words are more important to copy comprehension than is an unwavering right-hand margin.

For most people, a dictionary is consulted primarily to learn the meaning of words. As a mass communicator, the copywriter should seldom need to use this dictionary capability: at least in selecting words for a broadcast script. If you, a supposed wordsmith, don't already know the meaning of that term, how do you expect members of the mass audience to be able to understand it as the word goes flitting past their ears? Of course, if your spot is aimed at a highly specialized or technically oriented audience (auto engineers or dairy farmers, for example), words unfamiliar to you as well as to the general public may need to be used and their precise meanings sought out in the dictionary.

In most cases, however, a standard abridged dictionary will serve the copywriter better than some massive unabridged volume that is difficult to handle and store and that will include thousands of words, or archaic definitions for words, of which most of your audience will be totally ignorant. Since broadcast commercial and continuity copy is intended to be understandable to the audience *as it is* rather than striving to increase their vocabularies, exotic words and meanings are communication hindrances. If the word and the meaning you seek to use are in a good abridged volume, you can proceed with at least a little more confidence in considering its employment in your copy.

Besides the standard dictionaries, a number of specialty ones are on the market to serve the requirements of certain professions. Unless you find yourself consistently writing copy aimed at doctors, computer specialists, or similarly distinct groups, such volumes will not be required. The one type of specialized dictionary that is a helpful addition to any copywriter's library is the rhyming dictionary. Even in straight copy, and especially in campaign slogans or tag lines at the end of spots, a simple rhyme can greatly enhance memorability. The rhyming dictionary can be of significant assistance in this regard as long as we never distort message meaning and clarity in pursuing some forced doggerel.

Word-finders

The most commonly known book in this category is *Roget's Thesaurus,* which is a complete compilation of *synonyms* (words meaning the same) and *antonyms* (words meaning the opposite) active in American and British usage. Any writer develops a preference for, or a pattern in, the selection of certain words. The *Thesaurus* helps break these patterns by giving the writer alternate choices of words and thereby avoid interest-robbing redundancy in the copy. Further, this type of volume allows you to find and select a word possessing a more precise meaning or one with a syllabic construction or phonetic makeup that better promotes sentence rhythm and rhyme. To the broadcast writer, this latter function can be of prime importance given the preeminence of sound in effective oral communication. Consequently, you may well discover a word-finder like the *Thesaurus* to be your most often consulted reference work.

Roget's is the classic, but by no means the only, volume in the field. Since to use it, you must first look up a word category and are then referred to various subcategories, several writers find the volume to be somewhat time-wasting.

They prefer books like J. I. Rodale's *The Synonym Finder,* which lists the specific word and its specific alternatives in the same place. Though such works do not generally possess the scope of *Roget's* or provide closely associated categories of words, their ease and speed of use are important advantages in such a volatile and time-bound field as broadcast copywriting.

Style Aids

Generally referred to as grammar books, these references are of significant help to copywriters in reacquainting them with standard and accepted patterns of word arrangement. Although, as we've previously indicated, broadcast style and punctuation frequently break print-oriented practices in striving for conversational speech, the mechanics of good composition are more applicable than inapplicable to broadcast writing as a whole. As will be seen in other parts of this book, you need to know what the proven principles are before you can recognize why they won't work in the situation at hand. A good stylebook or English usage handbook such as Strunk and White's venerable *The Elements of Style* provides you with that essential broad view of our language. Periodic sessions with such a book help insure that you never become so specialized as a broadcast writer that, should the time come, you are incapable of branching out into print media, memo composition, or the myriad of other verbal tasks that call for a wordsmith's talents.

TOOLS TO POUND ON, WRITE WITH, WRITE ON

Once we have the germ of a message, know how to spell words it requires, and how to uncover alternative word choices, we need some vehicle in which to contain all this verbiage while we trim and refine it. Though everyone is aware of the implements serving this function, here are some special considerations that pertain to the copywriter's use of them.

Typewriter

In *Shopping in Oxford,* English poet laureate John Masefield described the typewriter as:

> the black-bright, smooth running,
>   clicking clean
> brushed, oiled and dainty
>   typewriting machine.[2]

This is as apt and memorable a description as any broadcast writer could ask for in regard to the "care and feeding" of this prime appliance on our creative production line. The ability to use and maintain a typewriter is essential in a copywriter's fashioning of readable ideas, quickly captured. No one's penmanship is, at the same time, both as rapid and discernible as can be the typewriter's

2. From "Shopping in Oxford" in *Gautama the Enlightened and Other Verse* by John Masefield (Copyright 1941 by John Masefield, renewed 1969 by Judith Masefield). By permission of Macmillan Publishing Company Inc., and the Society of Authors as the literary representative of the Estate of John Masefield.

recording via the fingers of even a relatively slow keyboard pounder. The machine needs neither to be electric nor even have Masefield's "black and dainty" attributes. If the rest of the poet's specifications are followed, however, it will serve you and your career well. A new ribbon, clean keys, and a standard, nonscript typeface not only make for legible copy but also signify to others your craftsperson-like approach to your profession. And even for yourself, there is something psychologically stimulating in watching those laboriously fashioned ideas given birth in crisp, clean impressions.

Word Processor

Crisp, clean impressions are also available from this solid-state typewriter surrogate. Basically, a word processor is a microcomputer primed with the proper software (program) and tied to a printer that can produce hard (paper) copy. The massive growth of and technological advancements in the microcomputer industry have put the word processor within reach of most working copywriters—should they wish to exploit its advantages and put up with some of its quirks.

The advantages are several, particularly in television, with its comparatively complex script format. The word processor largely eliminates the tedium involved in setting up a left side/video, right side/audio piece of TV copy and, provided the proper software is used, will maintain the proper spatial relationship between two columns. Word processors can also condense or expand type size to fit a variety of script formats up to and including large characters that could be read by the talent directly off a teleprompter. Since the processor can generate perfectly typed copy, it also has definite appeal in producing radio material. Moreover, the microcomputer makes spacing changes, deletion, and editing particularly easy. Rather than manually retyping an entire script, the writer can simply work with the lines or words that require modification and reinsert them; the corrected copy then will be delivered in its entirety. This facet is especially helpful when the changes involve no more than moving words and phrases around. Several rearrangements can be tried and quickly compared before the best pattern is selected and printed out.

Nonetheless, for the broadcast copywriter, the word processor also has some potential disadvantages that must be considered. First, you must be willing to train yourself to understand the processor—or more to the point, to make certain the processor understands *you*. Two separate functions must be comprehended. The first, the *editing* function, is the input portion of the operation. This is where you create, modify, and finalize your piece of copy. In the output or second function, called *formatting*, the finished draft is delivered in the proper arrangement. Some software packages perform these two functions as a single operation; in many others, they are handled separately and require discrete and systematic instruction from the user (that's *you*) to create a script that looks like a script. In some cases, such as with short, basic radio scripts, it might therefore be more efficient just to clack out the copy on a conventional typewriter.

In addition, some systems possess a slight time lag between the time you press a key and the time the character appears on the screen. Although a minor point to many writers, this aspect of the word processor has been known to unsettle creators accustomed to capturing ideas and slogans in rapid bursts of typed and immediately documented verbal energy. Finally, some diehards believe writing is an intensely *physical* activity that is totally out of character with the word processor's intellectual patter.

Pens and Pencils

Since all broadcast copy must be typed (or processed) before it can be shown to anyone important, pens and pencils are selected for their utility in a variety of preliminary and subsidiary roles. Pencils are ideal for sketching out material, whether alone or with a colleague copywriter or art director. When married to a pliable eraser, a pencil allows us to play with words, diagrams, and pictures without having to sit in front of a keyboard. Soft pencils can be used to correct or modify copy while it is still in the typewriter; the higher-numbered, harder leads, which may tear through the copy and mar the roller, should be avoided. Many writers also find that a cheap pocket pencil sharpener, available in any five-and-ten-cent store, is handy to keep on one's person to prevent disruptive trips to a wall-mounted model just as the creative juices are starting to flow.

When it comes to pens, don't be taken in by the "eight for a dollar" specials that litter our discount stores. Jotting down fleeting ideas is difficult enough without being distracted by a constantly clogging pen or one whose burred tip scratches across the paper like a cat clawing through the screen door. Shop around for pens that have a pleasing shape and weight in your hand. Note taking and copy editing are both much easier if you can grip the pen firmly without the scrawl that results from having to squeeze it. The pen point should be narrow enough to make a neat, clean, editing incision on a piece of typed copy, though not so pointed that it pierces the paper being corrected in the typewriter.

Paper

Once you go to work for a station, agency, or other institution, your stationery needs will be provided for and should not be of overt concern. You will be issued, or can ask for, pads of lined paper for note taking and brainstorming, plain typing paper for creating your first draft work, and printed letterhead or other formatted manuscript for preparing subsequent drafts that have to be seen and evaluated by a supervisor or client. If word processors are used in the office, printer paper also will be available. Your only responsibilities will be to make certain that you keep your desk stocked with a sufficient quantity of each variety and that you follow whatever format is mandated by preprinted letterhead and copy worksheets (format will be discussed further in subsequent chapters).

If you are freelancing or otherwise self-supervised, you must provide this paper supply for yourself. You will find that having three distinct varieties of stock (lined pads, plain typing paper, and letterhead) will help you to divide your tasks mentally and put you in the proper frame of mind for idea exploration, first-draft experimentation, and final-draft polishing, respectively. When

ordering your own stationery on which you will prepare the actual scripts that
go to clients and stations, these two considerations should be kept in mind:

1. Even if you are only a part-time freelancer, professional looking, preprinted letter-
    heads will help establish an initial presumption that you know your business. A
    sleek letterhead won't save a bad piece of writing, but it does help to open doors
    for a good one. Give your copy every chance for a favorable evaluation by clients
    and a positive treatment by performers. Showcase a solid copy painting within a
    suitable frame.
2. For durability, paper on which finished scripts are typed should be of at least
    medium weight and definitely *not* onion-skin or corrasible bond. The thin paper
    issued forth from some cheap word processing printers also does not pass muster in
    this regard. Performers need to be able to hold the script without its crackling or
    rustling. Such extraneous sounds will be picked up by the station or sound studio
    microphone and, at best, become distractions to the listener. At worst, they
    resemble the old radio sound effect used to signify fire, and your message might
    sound as if it's coming from hell.

TIME—THE TOOL THAT'S MASTER OF ALL

Speaking of hell, the inexorable demands of the clock on everything the
commercial and continuity writer produces can create our own occupational
torment. A 30-second spot was not, is not, and will never be a 35-second spot.
No matter what the message and regardless of the writer's talent, all elements
of broadcast communication must ultimately conform to the rigorous demands
of the station program day, the network feed schedule, the amount of money
our client has to spend, and the amount of time the station has available on
which to spend this money. Unlike a newspaper or magazine, a broadcast
station cannot add "pages" onto its broadcast day when advertising volume is
high, or contract itself when that volume is down. On the contrary, the radio or
television station or cable system is on the air for a set number of hours each
day, and all available program matter, commercial fare, and continuity segments
must fill and compete for this time.

The following time standards constitute a general yardstick of spot length as
reflected by word count. Copy requiring a relaxed and languid style should
contain fewer words than these norms, and material meant to be more rapid
and upbeat may contain slightly more. Because the majority of video spots do
not have wall-to-wall audio copy, these guidelines can be helpful in television
only to provide a rough indication of how much time individual copy segments
within the spot will expend.

"Sixties"

Though television is increasingly abandoning the one-minute message, in
radio, sixty seconds remains by far the dominant spot type. Industry figures
show that approximately four out of five commercials aired on United States
radio stations were one minute in length. A 60-second radio script will usually
contain from 130 to 145 words. As will be seen later, this number is proportionately less than the word count for two "thirties." Such a determination is based
on the presumption that we cannot expect our audience to take in quite as

much copy in one continuous minute of perceiving as they can in two separate messages of thirty seconds each. In short, once initial attention is gained, we can anticipate people's vigilance dwindling the longer the message progresses. If a nonprerecorded radio spot exceeds 150 words, the station may charge the client an additional premium. Because PSAs depend on the station for gratuity airing in the first place, public service announcements that are supposedly "sixties" but contain more than 150 words will probably not be aired at all.

"Thirties"

Since the mid-sixties, and as a result of both the increasing cost of air time and of research showing that many video messages can be as effective in half-minute as in full-minute form, the 30-second spot has vastly eclipsed the "sixty" as the most commonly used unit of television commercial time. This phenomenon has had a spin-off effect on both PSAs and in-station continuity, whose lengths must now conform to the type of schedule openings mandated by this buying pattern. Tables 3–1 and 3–2, based on data garnered by the Television

Table 3–1
Nonnetwork Television Commercial Activity
by Length of Commercial

	10's	20's	30's	P/B's	45's	60's+	Total
1965	16.1%	13.3%	0.8%	5.1%	—%	64.0%	100.0%
1966	15.6	12.7	0.8	8.8	—	61.5	100.0
1967	16.1	12.3	3.0	11.5	—	56.7	100.0
1968	14.0	10.6	16.0	11.8	—	47.2	100.0
1969	12.3	7.7	32.0	11.4	—	36.2	100.0
1970	11.8	4.5	48.1	9.0	—	26.5	100.0
1971	12.1	2.4	60.5	4.1	—	20.7	100.0
1972	11.6	1.2	67.4	1.8	—	17.8	100.0
1973	9.8	0.9	72.7	1.2	—	15.2	100.0
1974	8.9	0.6	77.0	0.8	—	12.6	100.0
1975	9.1	0.5	79.2	0.8	—	10.4	100.0
1976	8.1	0.5	82.2	0.9	—	8.3	100.0
1977	8.2	0.4	82.2	0.8	—	8.3	100.0
1978	7.8	0.2	83.8	—	—	7.4	100.0
1979	8.2	0.2	83.9	—	0.1	7.6	100.0
1980	7.8	0.2	85.1	—	0.2	6.7	100.0
1981	7.1	0.1	86.2	—	0.5	6.1	100.0
1982	6.0	0.1	87.5	—	0.8	5.6	100.0
1983	6.0	0.1	87.8	—	1.2	4.9	100.0
1984*	5.9	0.3**	88.0	—	0.7	5.1	100.0

Note: 60's+ were broken down for the first time in 1980 as follows:

	1980	1981	1982	1983	1984*
60's	3.9%	3.4%	3.3%	2.9%	2.8%
90's	0.2	0.2	0.2	0.1	0.2
120's	2.6	2.5	2.1	1.9	2.1

*January through June, 1984
**Includes 15's as well as 20's
Source: BAR, annual average as provided by Television Bureau of Advertising, courtesy of Hal Simpson

Table 3–2
Network Television Commercial Activity
by Length of Commercial

			Percent of Total		
	10's	30's	45's	P/B's	60's	Total*
1965	--%	0.0%	--%	23.3%	76.7%	100.0%
1966	--	0.0	--	31.5	68.5	100.0
1967	--	6.4	--	43.3	49.2	100.0
1968	--	7.9	--	50.4	40.1	100.0
1969	--	14.4	--	50.8	33.9	100.0
1970	--	25.1	--	47.2	27.0	100.0
1971	--	53.3	--	30.3	15.8	100.0
1972	--	67.6	--	21.9	10.3	100.0
1973	--	71.8	--	19.4	8.5	100.0
1974	--	75.4	--	17.5	6.8	100.0
1975	--	79.0	--	14.7	5.6	100.0
1976	--	80.2	--	13.3	5.8	100.0
1977	--	81.8	0.1	12.9	4.5	100.0
1978	0.5	82.6	0.7	12.6	3.3	100.0
1979	0.6	83.3	0.8	12.3	2.8	100.0
1980	0.7	85.2	0.7	11.2	2.1	100.0
1981	1.0	86.5	0.2	10.6	1.6	100.0
1982	1.0	87.2	0.2	9.9	1.6	100.0
1983	1.0	87.3	0.2	9.1	1.9	100.0
1984	1.1	85.1	0.1	10.8**	2.1	100.0

120's accounted for 0.1% in 1982 and 0.5% in 1983 and 1984
*Includes miscellaneous lengths
**Includes splits of 30/30, 45/15, 45/30, 45/45, and 15/15
Source: BAR, annual averages as provided by Television Bureau of Advertising, courtesy of Hal Simpson.

Bureau of Advertising, graphically illustrate just how pervasive is the half-minute length in both network and local buying patterns. (On the tables, the column P/B stands for *piggybacks*—longer length units that are split into two discrete spots by the advertiser. Originally limited to two 30-second messages within one minute of time, piggybacks now also occur in splits of 45/15, 45/30, 45/45, and 15/15.)

Half-minute wall-to-wall television soundtrack copy or the same-duration radio spot can each accommodate from 70 to 80 words. Some radio stations, however, will levy a penalty charge for "thirties" of more than 75 words, since such spots, if not pretimed and preproduced, may therefore spill over into the station's own air space. "Thirties" are the second most common radio commercial length but tend to be priced in such an inflated way that, given radio's need to establish a picture through more extended sound, the "sixty" is the more prudent and economical buy.

"Tens"

Having reached their high water mark in the mid-sixties, these units became comparatively rare due to industry concern about commercial clutter (too many separate spots within a single time frame). Now that this concern has receded in light of many advertisers' inabilities to afford the high cost of 30-second (particularly network) television time, it remains to be seen whether economic realities will mitigate clutter fears enough for the "ten" to stage a major comeback. As we discuss below, the growth of "fifteens" may also influence the resurgence or further decline of the 10-second spot. "Fifteens" can be paired with other "fifteens" and "forty-fives" to make tidy half-minute and one-minute packages, but "tens" can be linked only with exceedingly rare "twenties." Ten seconds remains a good length for *shared IDs* in which the station's call letter/city of license identification can be married to a brief commercial pitch for a given sponsor. "Tens" are also effectively exploited to convert bits and pieces of left-over radio and (much less frequently) television air time into program promos as well as PSAs; the latter further to bolster the station's public service record while requiring from it but a minimal donation of its airtime.

Some advertising executives, such as Romann & Tannenholz's Gad Romann, believe that television stations and advertisers, too, should be far more willing to use the "ten." Romann found that this brief unit, from a creative standpoint:

> forced us to compress a concept into a visual metaphor, to use ideas where other advertisers would have used the much more time-consuming approach of location and mood to make the same point—and not get the same impact. Brevity, we discovered, added strength. . . . Stop thinking of television as a film medium and start thinking of it as a "visual telegraph station" that contains the fewest words and communicates the most information with one, single, powerful visual.[3]

Mel Rubin, chairman of Shaller Rubin Associates, uses a three-question yardstick to determine whether a "dime length" spot makes communication sense. "In opting for the 10-second format," he says, "We ask ourselves:

> Can you 'say it all' in 10 seconds clearly and concisely and have the message stand on its own as a valid communication?
> Is there enough frequency to the target market to insure that the commercial registers with resounding impact?
> Is there a fundamental marketing strategy that is appropriately served by a 10-second spot?"[4]

An example of a "ten" that does stand on its own, clearly makes its point, and frames the new nature of an old establishment is this TV approach for Howard Johnson's. Titled "Frankenstein Mob," the spot registers its client-relevant description in both audio and video.

---

3. Gad Romann, writing in "Monday Memo," *Broadcasting Magazine*, June 30, 1980, p. 16.
4. Mel Rubin, writing in "Monday Memo," *Broadcasting Magazine*, May 11, 1981, p. 18.

Video	Audio
USING STOCK FOOTAGE WE SEE A MOB OF VILLAGERS, AT NIGHT, WITH TORCHES. ONE POINTS OFF CAMERA.	<u>VILLAGER:</u> There it is!
THEY ALL DASH OFF.	<u>ANNCR (VO):</u> When a fresh new restaurant opens in town, word gets around pretty fast.
CUT TO THE LOGO OF THE DELI BAKER ICE CREAM MAKER.	<u>SUNG:</u> THE FRESH-LOOKING FRESH-COOKING NEW HOWARD JOHNSON'S.

(Courtesy of Campbell-Ewald Advertising and Howard Johnson Company.)

When used on radio, a ten-second spot can include up to twenty-five words, which is also the usual maximum permitted by a station. The television "ten" may, of course, use far fewer words depending on the composition of the visual.

"Fifteens"

   Though scarcely encountered on American radio, where it would be allowed to consume up to 40 words, this newest length has become the most controversial unit on the television scene. It began through efforts by Alberto-Culver, Beecham, Gillette, and other package goods advertisers to sell two separate products within a 30-second spot. This created the "split thirty"—actually two 12½-second messages with a brief segue line (such as, "Here's news of another fine product from ___") between. Under intense pressure from these major advertisers, the television networks acceded to experimental acceptance of "split thirties." When station groups (companies owning several local outlets) refused to accept these same-length messages, Alberto-Culver brought a class action antitrust suit against them. The group owners backed down and the "split thirty" became a fact of life. Just as important, Alberto-Culver's agreement with the groups did not impose on the advertisers "production requirements such as opening statements identifying the message as advertising 'products from ___' or bridges between the two messages."[5] In short, the way had been paved for the entirely self-contained 15-second spot.

   The quarter-minute commercial may be new to the United States, but it has been well established in television systems elsewhere. Barry Day, vice-chairman of McCann-Erickson Worldwide, points out that "85 percent of Japanese commercials are 15 seconds."[6] That these appear successful is indicated not only by

5. "Alberto-Culver Wins Split-30 Battle, Drops Anti-Trust Suit," *Broadcasting Magazine*, March 19, 1984, p. 42.
6. "Splitsville: Agency Execs Explore 15-Second Ads," *ADWEEK/Midwest*, January 28, 1985, p. 38.

the experience in Japan but also by American research, in which "it appears that the 15-second commercial performs, on average, about two-thirds as well [as the "thirty"] on the basis of recall—not a bad buy at half the cost."[7] Doyle Dane Bernbach's Mike Drexler believes "fifteens" can be effectively exploited when:

1. The shorter commercial length can provide additional reinforcement in *combination* with 30-second commercials.
2. Additional frequency is required during the purchase cycle or, as a continuous reminder, over time, to maintain top-of-the-mind awareness.
3. The creative message can be effectively communicated in a shorter length to serve a limited budget.
4. A single point (or main point of a larger commercial) is the central focus of the advertising.
5. Television is used to further support the main point of an established and familiar print campaign.
6. Specific price or item advertising is required during a concerted period of time.[8]

The "fifteen" may even create more employment opportunities for copywriters. "Pools of 15-second spots will have to contain more executions than pools of 30-second spots—because 'wearout' seems likely to occur so much faster with 15's."[9] Larger pools, of course, mean more spot assignments that can require more copywriters.

Still, the shorter length means even less margin for error on the copywriter's part. Richard Morgan cautions that "15's can be neither stepped-up 30's nor slowed down 10's. Rather, they must be as creatively constructed as recent blockbuster 90's, as psychologically satisfying as well-paced 60's and as financially fulfilling as the earlier move to 30's."[10] The key to fashioning an appropriate quarter-minute spot, agrees Barry Day, is

> that you look at what you can do in 15 seconds rather than worry about cutting down 30's or 60's. People will begin to stop thinking of the 15 as being a short 30 after a while, but as a thing in its own right. And once you devise 15-second ideas, 30's will become viewed, ironically, as 15 seconds with room to breathe. So I think that from a creative point of view, the way into it is to start thinking about the potential of the spot: It promises a miniature effect, if you like, a simplicity that is not easy to come by in 30's, 60's or longer spots.[11]

Twenties

"Twenties," which can encompass up to 50 words, have never been a significant factor in radio and, as the Television Bureau of Advertising charts indicated, have declined to virtual oblivion on television. The interest in "split thirties" may, however, have given the "twenty" new life. Packaged goods sponsors like

7. Mike Drexler, "DDB Says Split 30's Here to Stay," *ADWEEK/Midwest*, January 28, 1985, p. 32.
8. Ibid.
9. Richard Morgan, "Agencies Stand to Gain the Most from Split 30's," *ADWEEK/Midwest*, February 4, 1985, p. 25.
10. Richard Morgan, "15's to Offer Profit, Creative Opportunities," *ADWEEK/Midwest*, January 28, 1985, p. 28.
11. "Splitsville: Agency Execs Explore 15-Second Ads," *ADWEEK/Midwest*, January 28, 1985, p. 33.

Mennen have started to use 20/10's in which the first two-thirds of the message is for one product, and the last 10 seconds for another. An "and also from ____" bridge usually connects the two. This division allows more time to be spent on describing one product with a reminder message devoted to another.

"Forty-Fives"

The recent attention paid to "three-quarter" length spots is much more apparent in piggyback than self-standing configurations. Spearheaded by Procter & Gamble, "forty-fives" are coming to be linked with a "fifteen," or paired into ninety-second combinations or, much less often, placed in tandem with a "thirty." Avon, the door-to-door cosmetics firm, has been especially successful in exploiting the 45/15 pattern. The "forty-five" sells the breadth of the company's line while the "fifteen" promotes an individual Avon product.

> "This is real retail selling, and the agency (Ogilvy & Mather), has produced 25 different 15-second tags in a year, updating each spot every two weeks. The tags are simple: as the camera examines the product against a graphic backdrop, we hear delicate music and a pleasing female voiceover. Even coming as they do—at the end of big-budget commercials—the tags are not disruptive and offer solid product information."[12]

The flexibility in such a scheme is obvious. A major production "forty-five" can be used for years as a locomotive to pull a variety of easily hitched-up product cargos. William Claggett, vice president of marketing for Ralston Purina, calls the 45/15 process the firing of "bullets and cannons." His company will use the "cannon" 45 to sell cat food, for example, and then follow up with a 15-second reminder "bullet" for dog chow.[13]

With end-to-end copy, a TV "forty-five" could consume up to 105 words. This computation would, of course, also be true for radio. But few, if any, radio stations have chosen to offer the length, and advertisers have not, to this point, found it viable in the auditory medium.

"Nineties" and "One-Twenties"

The modest growth in one-and-a-half and two-minute message units has occurred chiefly in cable television, which has the flexibility (and the comparatively lower advertising demand) to handle these extended commercials. Technically, the "one-twenty" is called an *infomercial* and, as the name implies, provides the advertiser with the time to offer in-depth information about the product and its benefit range. For this reason, the format has special appeal to sellers of such things as magazine subscriptions, book clubs, and special-purpose products aimed at specific occupational and hobby groups.

The "ninety" allows for a little less detailing but also a significantly reduced air-time charge. General Foods has used the length to communicate "client-specific, consumer information programming" and then piggybacks it with a

12. Barbara Lippert, "Avon Puts on a New Face for the '80s," *ADWEEK/Midwest*, July 9, 1984, p. 24.
13. "Purina's Claggett Reports Success," *Broadcasting Magazine*, March 5, 1984, p. 57.

conventional "thirty". In this arrangement, the "ninety" is referred to as a "Shortcut."[14]

Trade terminology labels both "nineties" and "one-twenties" *short-form programming* rather than commercials. Tim Conner, a Young & Rubicam USA senior vice president, has found that many consumers seem to prefer these units over conventional-length spots. "We've discovered," he says, "that short-form programming in general is perceived for the most part by viewers as helpful, interesting, entertaining and contemporary."[15] Other researchers concur and find that viewers actually seek out the "short-form" over increasingly more brief, more numerous, and what they believe to be more pushy TV spots.

Up to this point, our discussion of "nineties" and "one-twenties" has pertained exclusively to television. Few radio advertisers, outside of financial, insurance, and religious clients, have shown any interest in attempting to force stations to offer these lengths. When they do, a "ninety" can service approximately 190 words and a two-minute spot a maximum of 225 words.

"Time Compression"

We cannot leave the subject of time without mentioning a new technique designed to manipulate it. Dubbed a *Lexicon,* after the Massachusetts company that developed it, this time compressor-expander machine allows material to be played back at faster or slower speed without changing the pitch of the audio. The television version of this process has been christened "Squeezeplay" by one of its chief users, John Blair Marketing. Frames are electronically lifted from thirty-second commercials to compress them into twenty-five seconds. The salvaged five seconds can then be used to mention a consumer promotion campaign or other time-bound sales event such as telling consumers where to get expiration-dated coupons.

The process is not to be entered into lightly and should be undertaken with extreme care. A Blair spokesman emphasizes that "the difference between a spot shortened from 30 seconds to 25 seconds, and the same spot reduced to 24 seconds, can be remarkable. The former might seem undetectable, the latter 'hurried.' "[16] True, in both radio and television, "dramatic effects may be added by speeding up program segments," boasts Lexicon, Inc. "Slow-paced programs can be given higher energy levels. News reports can be made to sound more brisk and exciting."[17] When it comes to commercials, however, the copywriter is well advised to follow time guidelines carefully and not depend on electronic wizardry to condense bloated writing. Time compression is a valuable tool for adding seasonal information to expensive commercials without having to completely reproduce them. It should not be prostituted and used as a gimmick to repair carelessly overextended copy.

14. Joe Mandese, "General Foods Cooks up New Ad Vehicle," *ADWEEK/Midwest,* October 1, 1984, p. 3.
15. Ibid.
16. "Blair Squeezes TV Ads to Give Room for Tags," *ADWEEK/Midwest,* September 13, 1982, p. 28.
17. "Squeeze Technique," *Broadcasting Magazine,* March 9, 1981, p. 147.

TOOLING UP

Now that we've discussed the tools available to the broadcast copywriter, we can begin to apply them to the situations and problems to be encountered in the chapters and tasks ahead. But in wielding all of these tools, we must not make the mistake of thinking that our listener is breathlessly waiting for us to apply them, like some chair-encased patient alert to the dentist's next probe. For unlike that dental patient, our listener is neither captive nor in abject need of the message we sell. As copywriters, we have to use our tools to be as creative, as appealing, and as stylish as possible in coaxing our audience first to *attend to,* and then to *agree with* the message our tools have helped us construct. More than a decade ago, Bernard Owett, creative director for J. Walter Thompson/ New York, stated the matter well in the following comment, which, though focusing on television, can be applied at least as well to the radio listener:

> One of the great mistakes made by people in this business is to think of the viewer—our potential customer—as one who sits in front of a television set, eyes alert, mind honed to a keen edge, all interior and exterior antennae eagerly adjusted to receive the message. I think it's far better, far sager and far more realistic to think of the viewer as maybe lightly dozing—maybe semicomatose.
>
> If he's thinking at all, it's probably about his child's orthodontist bill, his wife's scrappiness, his latest problem on the job. . . . So what do we have to do to make this worthy, troubled citizen listen to our pitch? First, we have to get his attention. Then we have to be ingratiating, disarming and, above all, persuasive. And this we have to do through execution, through style.[18]

In gaining attention and being persuasive, copywriters use a potent arsenal of emotional and rational appeals. These appeals will be examined in the next chapter.

18. Bernard Owett, writing in "Monday Memo," *Broadcasting Magazine*, October 13, 1975, p. 11.

Chapter Four

RATIONAL AND EMOTIONAL
APPEALS AND STRUCTURES

Deriving successful broadcast messages is more than choosing words and phrases that sound appealing. The process also transcends the elements of proper punctuation and tidy typing. Though all of these aspects play a part in effective continuity writing, they cannot, by themselves, comprise a cohesive and purposeful communication. Such a communication can accrue only from combining all of these ingredients within an overall structure that reflects a thorough understanding of human motivation. Especially in broadcasting, where the absence of immediate feedback forces us to make continuous hypotheses about how the members of our audience will react, we must constantly refine our cognizance and questioning of human response patterns.

As Harvard marketing professor Theodore Levitt urges, copywriters must be able "to tap into what it is that lies deep in the hidden recesses of the human consciousness . . . to find the hot button . . . to see things with a third eye . . . to transcend the ordinary without being too cute or too clever."[1] "If you can emotionally trigger [the consumer's] fantasy," adds psychologist Carol Moog, "then it's okay if you're selling a product along with it. People aren't offended by that, and their minds are open to the message because they haven't put up any defenses. The pathway to that emotional trigger, once again, is through symbols and knowing which symbolic imagery will be important to what consumer. The next step is to link that imagery to the product."[2]

No, you don't have to be a psychologist to write broadcast copy, but it is important to understand human nature. As advertising giant William Bernbach once remarked, human nature "hasn't changed for a billion years; it won't even vary in the next billion years. Only the superficial things have changed. . . . One thing is unchangingly sure, the creative man with an insight into human nature, with the artistry to touch and move people, will succeed."[3]

There are several human-nature-based reasons that would make someone want to buy your client's product, listen to a program your station is promoting,

---

1. Richard Morgan, "A Conversation with Harvard Guru Theodore Levitt," *ADWEEK/Midwest,* August, 1983, p. M.R. 14.
2. Betsy Sharkey, "Emotional Pitch Can Take the Chaos Out of 15's," *ADWEEK/Midwest,* February 11, 1985, p. 31.
3. "The Quotable Bill Bernbach," *ADWEEK/Midwest,* October 11, 1982, p. 26.

or patronize the civic function described in your PSA. But all of these reasons relate in some way to *solving a problem*—even if the problem is simply finding something to do on Saturday night. For this reason, Levitt advocates cultivating what he calls "the marketing imagination," which, "by asserting that people don't buy things but buy solutions to problems—makes an inspired leap from the obvious to the meaningful."[4]

Whatever the problem to be solved, its solution can be expressed as attaining a fundamental human want. Many complicated systems have been devised for defining and categorizing these wants. For our purposes, and as a memory aid, however, just think "SIMPLE."

RATIONAL APPEALS

"SIMPLE" is a mneumonic (memory-building) device to help you recall the six rational appeals that motivate people to buy, use, or listen to the subject of your message. Each letter of "SIMPLE" is the first letter in the word that denotes one of these six appeals. Specifically, "SIMPLE" stands for:

Safety
Indulgence
Maintenance
Performance
Looks
Economy

Let's examine each of these rational needs in more detail. Keep in mind that every persuasive message—and that's virtually every piece of broadcast continuity—must cater to at least one of these appeals in order to trigger an appropriate solution-seeking response by each member of our target audience. As will be seen, a given message can be constructed several different ways to focus on and stress a separate need than that being emphasized by competitors. If, for example, they're all pushing the *economy* of their products, your accentuating of *safety* or *performance* will help your client to stand apart from the pack and stand out more in the minds and memories of your audience.

Safety

Though this has always been a buyer's or user's consideration, the rise of the consumer movement in the sixties gave it much greater prominence in people's hierarchy of values. Listeners and viewers want to know if the product or service being marketed will make them sick, ruin their plumbing, or injure the psyches of their children. With the prodding of the Federal Trade Commission, the Food and Drug Administration, and many other consumer and industry action groups, the question of safety, of absence from probable harm, is being addressed in more and more pieces of copy. The banning entirely of cigarette advertising from the airwaves is an extreme example of this phenomenon; other examples include car ads stressing the steel-beam construction around

4. Morgan, "Conversation with Levitt," p. M.R. 14.

the passenger compartment, the laxative commercials focusing on the gentleness of their ingredients for people of all ages, and even the program promotions emphasizing a show's suitability for viewing by the entire family.

Particularly in today's unsettled climate, the question of safety is an extremely potent factor in listener and viewer decision making. If it's a concern clearly associated with your product or service category, as in the Curad bandage photoboard in Figure 4–1, you can't afford to ignore it when constructing your message.

But even if safety is not the prime element people might think of in relation to your subject, you may be able to fashion a unique and therefore attention-holding presentation through its exploitation. Notice how safety is used in the following radio spot to provide a new twist for the old candy market:

ANNCR: So, you're satisfied with that candy bar you pop into your mouth at lunchtime, eh? The one with all the chocolate and

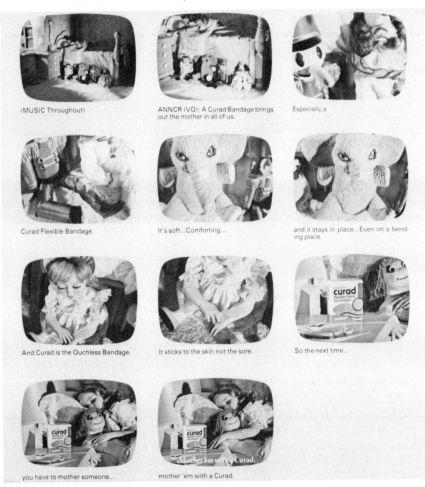

(MUSIC Throughout!)

ANNCR (VO): A Curad Bandage brings out the mother in all of us.

Especially a

Curad Flexible Bandage.

It's soft...Comforting...

and it stays in place...Even on a bending place.

And Curad is the Ouchless Bandage.

It sticks to the skin not the sore.

So the next time...

you have to mother someone...

mother 'em with a Curad.

Figure 4–1. *(Courtesy of Antoine Willaume, Foote, Cone & Belding.)*

goo. It tastes all right, but can your complexion take it?
Any chocolate may bring out those ugly facial blemishes.
And blemishes do nothing for your social life. Sure, you
need that shot of sugar at lunch. It gives you that energy
boost to keep going in the draggy afternoon.

But skip the chocolate. Rainbow Rock Candy Crystals can
give you that sugary boost without the chocolaty problems.
Open a box of Rainbow. Take out a clear, shining nugget
and let it melt away in your mouth. Enjoy Rainbow's
crystal smoothness sliding down your throat. Feel that
needed strength surging through your bod. Now you're ready
for the afternoon's challenges. Next time, when you start
to think about candy, think about your complexion. Then
get some Rainbow Rock Candy Crystals.

Indulgence

We all like to be comfortable, to be self-indulgent. And we'll frequently be willing to sacrifice one of the other rational appeals in order to accrue this quality, which is so integral to the good life. Water beds and bean bag chairs are ugly—but they feel so good. Subcompact cars are cheaper to purchase and operate—but they jar your bones and cramp your style. Frozen dinners aren't as tasty as home-cooked—but just look at the time and dirty dishes they save. Because, in the words of a famous beer campaign, we "only go around once in life," the indulgence appeal, and its comfort and convenience corollaries, are oft-used devices in a consumer-oriented society such as ours. The rosier financial conditions are, the more susceptible most of us become to the siren song of self-indulgence.

In the following spot for Saginaw Steering Gear's "Tilt-Wheel," comfort and convenience are intertwined with an economy appeal so you don't feel guilty enjoying yourself.

(MUSIC:	SHORT VAMP.)
SINGERS:	MAKE YOURSELF COMFORTABLE, TILT-WHEEL.
SONG/	
VOICE:	Tilt-Wheel.
(SFX:	CAR COMING TO A STOP.)
GUY:	This looks like a great spot for our picnic. Pass the chicken and potato salad.
GIRL:	We're not getting out of the car?
GUY:	What for? Now that we've finally got a new GM car, we've got the most comfortable with Tilt-Wheel Steering.
GIRL:	(Scoldingly) Harold!
GUY:	Just click, click, click to position four and I've got room for a feast!

GIRL:	(Still unimpressed) Amazing.
GUY:	Sure, and adjust the Tilt-Wheel just so and it's a convenient rest for—
GIRL:	(Impressed) Lemonade!
GUY:	Lemonade! Clever, eh?
GIRL:	And look, you can drape the napkins over the spokes and Tilt-Wheel lever!
GUY:	Pass another drumstick, Hon.
GIRL:	Any more chicken, Harold, and you'll have to adjust the Tilt-Wheel <u>all</u> the way up.
GUY:	Position six? Why?
GIRL:	To make room—for your tummy.
SINGERS:	<u>TILT-WHEEL HAS A SPOT THAT'S GOT A FEEL JUST RIGHT FOR YOU.</u> <u>SIX GREAT POSITIONS AND IT COSTS SO LITTLE, TOO.</u> <u>NO NEED TO CRAMP YOUR STYLE, JUST MAKE YOURSELF COMFORTABLE,</u> <u>WITH TILT-WHEEL.</u>
(MUSIC:	BUTTON.)
TAG:	Tilt-Wheel Steering from GM.

(Courtesy of Roger W. Bodo, Leo Burnett Company of Michigan, Inc.)

Maintenance

If a product maintains its usefulness for a long time, or if a service has long-term benefits, we are in a much better position to justify a comparatively high cost or overlook drawbacks in comfort/convenience. Automotive accounts such as Jeep and Volkswagen, the lonely Maytag repairman, and the entire stainless steel industry have had significant success by accenting maintenance factors over any of the other rational appeals. In what many people complain is a plastic society, the possibility that something will actually survive into downright longevity is an enticing prospect indeed. If a meaningful durability claim can be made and substantiated, it weaves aspects of performance, economy, and indulgence into a very compelling and logical stand. To function in the future, a maintenance-efficient product must certainly work now (performance). Because its life expectancy is long, it saves on replacement costs (economy) while eliminating the bother and inconvenience of having to do without while the thing is being fixed (indulgence).

Just as with all of our other rational appeals, maintenance can be most persuasive when used within a product category in which it is not generally made a salient factor. Many television set manufacturers talk about how long their receivers last without the need for major servicing. Thus, their commercials all tend to sound much the same, and no one, under such circumstances, is able to feature the maintenance appeal to its full advantage. How often, on the other hand, does a business like a restaurant dare to stand out from the crowd by stressing maintenance-related benefits? It should be recognized that this appeal, a blend of durability and longevity, is potentially available to *any* client, even a client like Spike's:

```
REPORTER:  Madame?
LADY:      Yes?
REPORTER:  Here's two hamburgers from you-know-who's. I'll trade
           both for that Spike-burger you're eating.
LADY:      No thanks.
REPORTER:  How about a box of chicken from a bearded old man?
           Swap that for your Spike-burger?
LADY:      (Emphatically) No!
REPORTER:  What if I say we've got your pet cat? And if you ever
           want to see him again you'll give me that
           Spike-burger?
LADY:      I'd say good-bye, kitty. I'm keeping this
           Spike-burger.
REPORTER:  What's so special about the Spike-burger?
LADY:      It's so big and meaty. Stops the hungries for hours.
           You should try one.
REPORTER:  But nobody will trade with me.
LADY:      Then just go to Spike's on North Elm and buy one.
REPORTER:  Only one? I've got to last all afternoon.
LADY:      One Spike-burger satisfies just about anybody. And for
           hours.
REPORTER:  All afternoon?
LADY:      Right.
REPORTER:  Wow!
LADY:      But once you get one, hang on tight. People will try
           to trade almost anything for an appetite-quenching
           Spike-burger.
```

Performance

Even though this rational appeal often overlaps with several of the others, its essence is workability. Will the product work for me? Will my donation help solve that community problem? Will staying up late to watch that movie really "round out my weekend on a happy note"? With performance, we are not primarily concerned with what it looks like, how much it costs, how long we can maintain it, even with how safe it might be. Instead, we simply want to be shown that the product, or service, or charity drive will meet the need at hand. "But does it work?" is a question being articulated and then answered in more and more of today's broadcast advertising copy, often through a stark, slice-of-life approach, such as Anacin's "Medical Student" portrayal in Figure 4–2.

Here, as in any meaningful performance spot, the product-in-use unveiling seems in perfect harmony with both (1) the situation as painted in the commercial and (2) the situation consumers themselves would encounter. Thus, though few viewers are themselves medical students, they find it easy to relate to the pain of long, pressure-filled days like those presented in this "Medical

Figure 4–2. *(Courtesy of Carol A. DiSanto, William Esty Company, David Rockwell, copywriter.)*

Student" spot and in its companions such as "Waitress," "Miner," "Teacher," and "Mother."

Looks

Often the least rational of our rational appeals, the looks element promotes a subject because it's pleasing to the eye. Housepaint, flower seeds, and racing stripes can seldom be sold without a discussion of their visual effect. But soda pop, peanut butter, and even dog food can also benefit from an appearance-oriented approach, especially in contrast to competitors who are stressing more usually linked appeals. Further, radio as well as television can use the physical likeness of an object in its promotion. In fact, the looks appeal may be even more potent on radio since we can actively involve listeners in constructing their own mind pictures. If properly stimulated, such a radio portrait will also be more memorable since the listeners have had to fashion it out of their own past experiences rather than being presented with someone else's completed picture on a television screen.

In this spot for Mr. B's, a well-crafted looks appeal not only conjures up an image for the eye but also engages the senses of smell and taste. And all this from copy that originally comes to the consumer in a sound-only mode.

ANNCR: Look deep into your subconscious. Picture full, red, ripened tomatoes. Tender, young onions. Oregano. Basil. Parsley. Ladled lavishly onto our own fresh, enriched, wheat flour dough. Crown it with mozzarella. Grated parmesan cheese. Fresh mushrooms. Pepperoni. Italian sausage. And garden fresh peppers. Slide it into the oven. The aged cheeses begin to bubble. Sizzle. And bake themselves into the completed creation. Now comes the time for the ultimate test. Your first bite. Then and only then, you'll know why people call it Best. Mr. B's Best pizza. We bring out only the best. It's what you deserve. Mr. B's.

(Courtesy of Stewart Sacklow, Wolkcas Advertising Inc.)

Economy

Few of us, and few members of our various target audiences, can totally ignore the cost of the goods and services used to make our lives safer or more self-indulgent. Even the decision to devote our time to watching that program or listening to this station must often be weighed against the other more productive responsibilities to which we might better attend. Life is a constant cost/benefit comparison, and the disbursement of our time and of the money that is a product of that time is a more or less continuous concern. Nothing comes free, and the farther from free it is, the higher will be consumer resistance to obtaining it. It is probably easier for most of us to decide on a brand of cereal than on what new car to buy; simpler to determine that we'll watch a thirty-minute show than a six-hour movie, which expends three nights' viewing.

Depending on the product category, asking *how much* is at least as important to consumers as asking *how safe* or *how long* it will maintain itself. Because of its conspicuous relationship to our own self-interest, an economy appeal can be made very concisely, as in the enduring 10-second spot for the California Milk Advisory Board in Figure 4–3.

Sometimes, the most effective economy appeal is one that presents a comparison between doing it the way our copy suggests and the alternative. In the following radio commercial, this alternative is ludicrously misunderstood by a stubborn noncustomer who thereby makes the economy point in an even more graphic manner.

CONSUMER: You know that SEMTA bus commercial of yours?

SEMTA REP: Uh, the one where we say you can save eight dollars a day by riding the—

CONS: Hold it right there, that's the one.

REP: What about it?

CONS: Well, your figures, they just don't add up.

REP: First of all, do you live in Birmingham?

CONS: Right.

REP: Do you ride the bus to and from work?

CONS: Every day.

REP: Well, by not having to pay gas and oil and parking, we conservatively figure eight dollars a day is what you'll save.

CONS: Save! Ha! It cost me $112 a day!

REP: Impossible!

CONS: Okay, you just check my math, buddy.

REP: Go ahead.

CONS: First, there's $72,000 for a used bus—

REP: You bought a bus?

CONS: Interest, gas and parking is $12,000—

REP: He bought a bus.

CONS: And there's $6,000 to raise the roof on my garage—

REP: He bought a bus.

CONS: Finally, I spent six bucks for snow chains.

REP: Hold it! You save eight dollars a day if you ride <u>our</u> bus.

CONS: <u>Your</u> bus?

REP: SEMTA.

CONS: SEMTA?

REP: Yes.

CONS: Oh, I see.

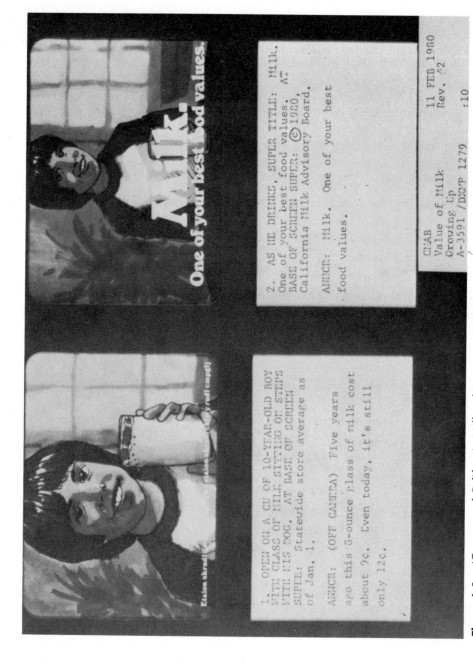

Figure 4-3. (Courtesy of California Milk Advisory Board and Cunningham & Walsh, San Francisco.)

REP: See?

CONS: You already probably got them tall garages and everything, huh?

REP: Exactly.

CONS: Okay. How'd you like to buy a good used bus real cheap?

REP: (Yelling to someone off-stage) He bought a bus!

(Courtesy of John J. Saunders, Southeastern Michigan Transportation Authority.)

EMOTIONAL APPEALS

The rational appeals are the basic justifications for why anyone chooses to buy, use, listen to, or watch something. But for any of these appeals to have their impact on the audience member's decision-making process, the attention of those jaded broadcast viewers must be engaged. The emotional appeals are our most potent weapons in grabbing this attention. Like Mary Poppins's "spoonful of sugar helping the medicine go down," the emotional appeals offer an immediate reward for stopping to listen and watch. "You do not sell a man the tea, but the magic spell that is brewed no where else but in a teapot," adman James Wallin once observed.[5] Similarly, Revlon's Charles Revson knew that: "In the factory, we make cosmetics, in the store we sell hope."[6] The emotional triggers in our copy are what provide the incentive for the members of the audience to stick around long enough to absorb that rational appeal that should then motivate them to follow the action or belief the copy is designed to instill. As we made it "SIMPLE" to remember the rational appeals, we can make it a "PLEASURE" to keep the emotional appeals in mind. "PLEASURE" is decoded this way:

People interest
Laughter
Enlightenment
Allurement
Sensation
Uniqueness
Rivalry
Eminence

Even though there are many ways to categorize and subdivide the various factors that solicit an emotional response, this "PLEASURE" approach is an uncomplicated yet reasonably comprehensive one as regards the appeals put into play in broadcast continuity and commercial writing. In its simplicity, "PLEASURE" may not please many psychologists or motivational research experts, but it does have a real use for the preoccupied copywriter (and it is the nature of the business for all of us to be preoccupied). "PLEASURE" serves constantly to remind us that human beings are emotional as well as rational creatures. As

5. Edwin Diamond, "The Day Fantasy Arrived," *ADWEEK/Midwest,* August 8, 1983, p. 46
6. Morgan, "Conversation with Levitt," p. M.R. 14.

patrons of a primarily entertainment medium, broadcast audiences especially must be catered to emotionally before one can hope to register a persuasively rational case. And, as Dr. Larry Light of BBDO Advertising correctly predicted at the top of the decade, emotional appeals have become even more important in the eighties since

> It's going to be hard to make a price claim because most of us will be raising our price, not lowering it, and it's going to be harder to find a performance claim that distinguishes our product. So value in the 1980's, value in the era of emotion, will have to be a function of performance plus emotion.
>   Telling isn't selling. This applies to every product and service we buy. In the era of emotion, every sale is a personal sale. Every sale is an emotional sale. Product claims can no longer be either performance claims or price claims. That is value in the traditional, but limited, way. The consumer of the 1980's wants to feel good about what he buys. In the era of emotion, feeling good is a right.[7]

Almost five years after Light's observation, advertising expert William Meyers came to the supporting conclusion that "almost any product can be sold on an emotional level these days, and maybe that's why Pepsi, Hallmark, Coke, McDonald's and Ronald Reagan have become such important national brand names."[8]

Let's now examine, in order, each of these powerful feeling-good PLEASURE vehicles.

People Interest

This appeal might less charitably be called "nosiness." We tend to have a well-developed and, occasionally, even malicious fixation on what others are doing and the way they are doing it. The testimonial spot seeks to exploit this characteristic by showing what the stars are drinking, wearing, or shaving with. But, as will be seen in later chapters, we have equal interest in the doings and preferences of "real people," people we ourselves can identify with and relate to.

In a more uplifting way, a concern with the lives and problems of others is a very warm and charitable phenomenon that motivates people to give of their time and treasure in the service of others. Many PSAs seek to tap this aspect of the audience's humanity. Whichever cause it aids, the people interest appeal works only if the characters it features and the way they are presented can compel the audience's curiosity.

Here is a spot that, from the beginning, heightens our heed by promoting the feeling of eavesdropping on someone else's awkward revelations. Its people interest works in conjunction with the rational appeals of performance and, in a subordinate way, of economy.

```
AD TAKER:    (Female with sing-songy nasal voice) Detroit Free
             Press Valentine's Day Ads, may I help you?
```

7. "TvB at NAB: No Need to Fear the Next 10 Years," *Broadcasting Magazine*, April 21, 1980, p. 63.
8. William Meyers, "How Do Academics Feel about Emotion?" *ADWEEK/Midwest*, December, 1984, p. F. 32.

MAN: (Stage whisper—gruff voice) Uh, ya, I'm calling from
                 work and I'm a little embarrassed to read my
                 Valentine's Day ad out loud.

AD TAKER: There's nothing to be embarrassed about, sir. We've
                 heard just about everything. Sweetie Pie. Cutie Pie.
                 Doll-face. Poopsie. Even a Popsicle Toes. As
                 professionals, it's our job to be totally objective.

MAN: Okay. Here goes. Snookums, I love you. Uh, can you
                 spell love L-U-V and make the you a letter 'U'?

AD TAKER: You got it.

MAN: And can, can you put lacey little hearts and flowers
                 around the border?

AD TAKER: Consider it done.

MAN: Sign it Hun Bun. Capital H-U-N. Capital B-U-N.

AD TAKER: How would you like that billed, Mr. Bun? Tee hee hee—
                 excuse me—snort, snort, ha, ha (Fades under)

ANNCR: Call 222-5000 before 4 P.M., February twelfth to place
                 a Free Press Valentine's Day Happy Ad. Four lines for
                 just five dollars. It doesn't cost a lot to get cute.

(Courtesy of Dan Nelson, W. B. Doner & Company, Advertising.)

This next spot uses the same emotional appeal but is noteworthy because it
successfully invests people interest in an entity that is not alive. This technique
is called *anthropomorphizing*—endowing nonhuman subjects with human
attributes. Anthropomorphizing can be a potent copywriting technique if you
remember to (1) keep the spokesthing in character throughout the spot, and
(2) re-identify that thing for late tuners-in so they are not confused as to who
(or really, *what*) is speaking. This Fensterwald commercial, for example, identifies the loquacious bank deposit at least three times.

ANNCR: Dear Fred. Remember me? Yes, Fred, I'm that little bank
                 deposit you made at Fensterwald Fidelity Bank a while ago.
                 Well, I just wanted to let you know I've been doing all
                 right. I've grown, Fred. Really grown. Even while you were
                 out on the golf course last weekend, I was sitting here
                 quietly piling up that interest. Why, with that five
                 percent interest compounded daily, little deposit me is a
                 lot bigger now. You ought to stop around and see me
                 sometime, Fred. I'm right downtown at Fensterwald Fidelity
                 Bank. They've got some mighty nice people here at
                 Fensterwald. They'll treat you right because they want to
                 keep you as a friend, Fred. They take good care of me—your
                 personal deposit—too. Yes sir, I think I'll just sit back
                 in my cozy steel vault here at Fensterwald Fidelity Bank
                 and grow, and grow, and grow (repeat to fade out).

Laughter

Human beings need to laugh, need to have the capacity to stand back and make light of the problems and conditions around them. Individuals who trudge through life taking themselves and everything else completely seriously are asking for a mental breakdown or a peptic ulcer. Laughter is a vital release mechanism for all of us—copywriters especially. That is why we seek it in our entertainment fare and try to use it to our advantage every chance we get. Comedy is disarming. It can effectively break down a reluctance to listen and at the same time build good will. Though every product, service, or program cannot be approached in a humorous vein, laughter tends to be the most coveted emotional appeal in a family-oriented, home entertainment medium such as broadcasting. If it's appropriate (something we'll discuss in depth later), comedy can scale attention barriers that, for some functionally disagreeable subjects, are all but insurmountable via any other emotional approach. In this "I Love New York" spot, the comedy team of Stiller and Meara take the negative of careless litter and entertainingly convert it into a positive corrective experience. Along the way, they rationally dramatize why *looks* are more important than *indulgence*—even high-class indulgence.

MAN: Hi.

WOMAN: Hi. This is some way to meet a neighbor—taking out the garbage.

MAN: You're the opera magazine.

WOMAN: Pardon me?

MAN: The opera magazine. There. Falling out of your garbage next to the anchovy can. I notice it every week.

WOMAN: Oh, do you like opera?

MAN: *Pagliacci's* my favorite.

WOMAN: Mine too.

MAN: I also love anchovies.

WOMAN: Oh, we have so much in common.

MAN: I feel as though I've known you forever through your garbage. Do you mind if I ask you a question?

WOMAN: Oh, ask. Ask.

MAN: Why are you always dumping on New York?

WOMAN: Huh? I love New York.

MAN: Maybe, but your garbage is always all over the street and that's the worst kind of dumping there is.

WOMAN: Gee, I never realized. *Your* trash is beautiful.

MAN: Thank you.

WOMAN: Tied up so neatly in that plastic bag.

MAN: Thank you. I always sweep my sidewalk and close my garbage can tight.

WOMAN: You're so civic-minded.

MAN: Perhaps I can show you how to bag your trash over some
         La Boheme.

WOMAN: Oh, would you? I'll open a can of anchovies and maybe some
         day---we could bag our garbage together?

(Courtesy of Barbara Klee and Manny Perez, Young & Rubicam.)

Laughter can also be deftly used to attack competitors' alleged benefits without making the listener feel that you're being unfair or surly. Humor works especially well in puncturing flawed economy arguments. It can raise otherwise threatening predictions without actually scaring consumers or losing them in a sea of numbers.

ANNCR: Southwest Airlines presents, 'How the Other Guys Getcha
         with the Gotcha's.'

CAPT: Enjoying the flight, sir?

DICK: Maybe I am, maybe I'm not.

CAPT: I'm Captain Dave—

DICK: So?

CAPT: Are you the gentleman who wrote, 'This Flight Bites It' on
         the restroom mirror?

DICK: Maybe I did, maybe I didn't.

CAPT: Are you upset about something, sir?

DICK: Why should I be upset?

CAPT: I don't know.

DICK: I got on a plane in El Paso to go to Houston—

CAPT: Uh huh.

DICK: Two weeks ago!

CAPT: Oh, you're on our special bargain flight. Well, there are
         some layovers, time limits, restrictions, you know.

DICK: It's very uncomfortable in this overhead luggage rack.

CAPT: Sir, we moved you from the beverage cart!

DICK: I know. Ice was going down my shirt!

CAPT: But sir, it's a bargain fare and that means—

BOTH: Limited seating.

ANNCR: If you don't read the fine print, some airline bargain
         fares can get you in a fine mess. Southwest Airlines
         thinks low fares should mean low fares—no restrictions, no
         limitations. And that's Southwest: every seat, every
         flight, every day. So don't let the gotcha's getcha!

DICK: Is my wife okay?

CAPT: Yes sir, she's still strapped to the wing.

```
DICK:   Oh good!
CAPT:   You can wave to her—
DICK:   Hi, Sylvia! Another three hours, hon. Hang on!
ANNCR:  Call Southwest or your travel agent for a 'no gotcha'
        reservation today.
```

(Courtesy of Dick Orkin, The DOCSI Corporation.)

Enlightenment

Though we often do not recognize it as such, the need for enlightenment, the need to know, is itself an emotional function. Human beings can feel more in control of themselves and their environment if they are aware of what is going on around them. If you've read *Man without a Country*, been in solitary confinement, even survived a week in the wilderness minus radio and newspapers, you are aware of the real emotional ramifications that flow from a lack of information about the places, people, and institutions with which you are familiar. Our increasing reliance on near-instantaneous broadcast news has deepened our information dependency. The promise that we will receive useful data on a subject or event is often enough to initiate attention that can be sustained as long as valuable and relevant data seem to keep coming.

The Exxon Office Systems photoboard in Figure 4–4 projects the viewer into an enlightenment-producing situation (both immediate and future) that seems to suggest all manner of functional product advantages.

Enlightenment is especially important to people, like ourselves, in the communication business. This trade ad, aimed at fellow communicators, makes the most of the enlightenment appeal to hit the hot buttons of the client publication's potential readers.

```
(SFX:    COCKTAIL LOUNGE SOUNDS)
PHIL:    Hi, Bob.
BOB:     Hi, Phil
PHIL:    Can I buy you a drink?
BOB:     Do squirrels eat nuts?
PHIL:    (Shout) Scotch over here, barkeep.
BOB:     So, how's the old ad game going?
PHIL:    Pretty good. We just won the Beamer Bowling Ball Bag
         account from Bowzer, Bingham, Bibber and Bub.
BOB:     I read in Adweek they pitched the Kooper Kazoo
         business.
PHIL:    Yeah, but they lost to Loofty, Libitz, Lumper and Low.
LADY:    That's not what I read in Adweek.
PHIL:    Really?
LADY:    According to Adweek, Kooper Kazoo went with Kibble,
         Kop, Kibbitz and Kabobo.
```

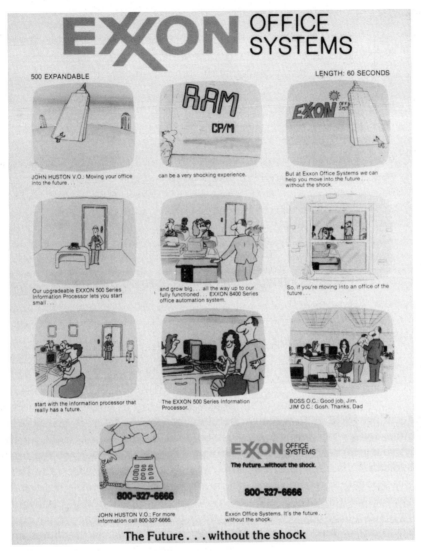

Figure 4-4. *(Courtesy of Kathryn Spiess, Marsteller Inc.)*

BOB:	I thought Kabobo left Kibble, Kop and Kibbitz.
PHIL:	He did. He joined Dooper, Dink and Diddle.
LADY:	According to <u>Adweek,</u> they just lost Doofus Drugs.
BOB:	To who?
LADY:	Morrelli, Mooseman, and Mung.
PHIL:	Mung just got the Royal Shaft.
BOB/LADY:	Oh, too bad—
PHIL:	No, no. It's an Ad Club Award. The story is in—

BOB/LADY:	<u>Adweek!</u>
PHIL:	Last year, Wiffle of Waller, Wiffle and Winky won that award.
BOB:	I read that Winky went with Kabobo over to Dooper, Dink and Diddle.
LADY:	Boy, that's gonna make Kabobo, Dooper Diddle, Winky and Dink a name to reckon with.
PHIL:	I thought Diddle got top billing?
LADY:	Over Winky and Dink's dead body!
ANNCR:	Sometimes it's hard to keep up with who's coming, who's going, who's hot and what's not. That's why so many top ad executives read <u>Adweek</u> magazine.
BOB:	I heard Pee, Picked, Peck and Olepepper joined Tairpiper, Abe, O'Pick and Smythe.
LADY:	Now they're called—
ALL:	PETER PIPER PICKED A PECK OF PICKLED PEPPERS—and Smythe.
(SFX:	OUT)

(Courtesy of Dick Orkin, The DOCSI Corporation.)

Allurement

Few red-blooded copywriters require a detailed explanation of this emotional appeal, which, in a more exploitative sense, is called "sex." Actually, allurement is something of a hybrid as it contains elements of people interest, sensation, and sometimes rivalry or eminence all rolled into one. Because the use of allurement is so widespread in several product categories, however, we tend to treat it as a distinct classification. But one definite caution must be raised in regard to this appeal, a caution that has nothing to do with taste or moral standards. Because allurement has such utility, it has been exploited in irrelevant contexts; in contexts in which it was totally unrelated to the copy approach and rational appeals of the message as a whole. In such a case, sex becomes an unjustified attention-getter that makes promises the subsequent copy never fulfills. This has caused listeners and viewers to develop a real suspicion, if not deep distrust, of any message using the allurement appeal, even those where its solicitation is pertinent.

Allurement can be an effective emotional appeal. It also can be appropriately adapted to a wide variety of adult-oriented products and services with which it is not now paired. The copywriter must, however, make certain that the use of sex is both relevant and helpful to the assignment at hand and is an effective vehicle for the rational appeal or appeals that are stressed.

The KRST promo in Figure 4–5 demonstrates how allurement can be recruited to project a young adult image to a music format (country) which is sometimes

Figure 4–5. *(Courtesy of Jerry K. Williams, American Image Productions.)*

mistaken for an oldsters' vehicle. The copy, of course, is in lyric form, but the appeals pairing of allurement and indulgence is accomplished just as well, or better, than if the spot employed wall-to-wall speech.

A lighthearted, almost satiric view of allurement is featured in the "Little Red" spot for Dr Pepper (Figure 4–6). It illustrates that the appeal need not be steamy or exploitative but can work well in tandem with laughter to characterize the fun and sugar-free performance inherent in the product.

LITTLE RED

Figure 4–6. *(Courtesy of Lee Kovel, Young & Rubicam New York.)*

Video	Audio
OPEN ON A 18-YEAR-OLD RED HEAD IN CONTEMPORARY SHORT-SHORTS & HALTER TOP ROLLER SKATING TOWARD A VERY OLD FOREST ON A PAVED PATH. SHE'S CARRYING A PICNIC BASKET AND IS OBLIVIOUS TO HER SURROUNDINGS BECAUSE SHE IS LISTENING TO HER WALKMAN	<u>SFX:</u> HOWL (Unheard by Little Red)
SHE ENTERS MYSTERIOUS WOODS LADEN W/MIST AND RAYS OF LIGHT	<u>RED:</u> (Humming to herself) <u>SFX:</u> GROWL (Close by)
CU RED AS SHE PICKS UP ONE OF HER EARPHONES	<u>RED:</u> Say wha?
CUT TO ECU OF WEREWOLF	<u>WOLF:</u> (Growls)

Video	Audio
	RED: Please—I'm on my way to grandma's.
WOLF LOOKS HER UP AND DOWN; SHE REALIZES HE MAY NOT ATTACK. OFFERS HIM APPEASEMENT IN THE FORM OF COTTAGE CHEESE	RED: Low fat cottage cheese?
WEREWOLF SLAPS IT AWAY	WOLF: (Howls)
RED RUMMAGES IN HER BASKET, OFFERS HIM A CAN OF DIET COLA	RED: Mmmaybe a diet cola?
WOLF IS INTERESTED; INSPECTS THE CAN WITH AN INSERT CLAW; SNIFFS THE CONTENTS & CRUSHES CAN	WOLF: (Menacing growl)
RED DIGS DEEPLY INTO BASKET AND PULLS OUT BOTTLE OF SUGAR-FREE DR PEPPER	RED: Well, I was saving this for myself but—
WOLF DRINKS DR PEPPER	SONG: HOLD OUT FOR SUGAR FREE DR PEPPER—
WOLF TRANSFORMS TO HUMAN BEING AS HE DRINKS	SONG: HOLD OUT FOR SUGAR FREE DR PEPPER—
TRANSFORMS INTO DAVID NAUGHTON COMPLETE W/VEST	SONG: DON'T BE SOLD OUT, IT'S THE TASTE THAT'S EXTRAORDINARY—
THEY DRINK & SKATE TOGETHER	SONG: THERE'S NO DOUBT, IT'S OUT OF THE ORDINARY
DR PEPPER GRAPHIC ROLLS IN	SONG: HOLD OUT FOR SUGAR FREE DR PEPPER.
AS THEY SKATE AWAY TOGETHER, NAUGHTON WAGS HIS TAIL. RED TURNS TO HIM W/A SMILE	RED: My mother always warned me about wolves!

Sensation

The sensation appeal requires no literacy, no social insight or ambition on the part of the audience. Instead, it uses the basic senses of sight, sound, taste, smell, and touch to achieve its emotional impact. Even a very small child can respond to the taste-whetting stimulus of that rich chocolate cake or the depicted softness of that Downy-washed blanket. Adults may bring more depth to their appreciation of the beads of condensation running down that bottle of beer, but the same fundamental emotional appeal is in operation.

Sensation requires less social or scholastic experience of its audience than do any of its colleague appeals. That is why it is recruited so often to market the low-cost, mass-consumed products and services sold to such broad sections of the listening and viewing public. When properly selected and employed, the sensation appeal enables the audience to participate most rapidly in the message-building process by plugging in their own sensory experiences almost as soon as the copywriter-stimulated image reaches them.

In this 60-second radio spot, indulgence and performance are appropriate outgrowths of the setting established through sensation's application:

```
Attention people who like to see, smell, take home and even eat
fresh food.

At the Deli and the Baker and the Ice Cream Maker
In the fresh-cooking, fresh-looking new Howard Johnson's

Try our famous ice cream flavors
Extra rich and extra creamy
We've got sprinkles, nuts and jimmies
We'll make your Sundaes dreamy.

At the Deli and the Baker and the Ice Cream Maker
In the fresh-cooking, fresh-looking new Howard Johnson's

We've got loads of tempting goodies
To take home by the pound
Blocks of savory cheeses
Coffees all fresh ground

At the Deli and the Baker and the Ice Cream Maker

Shop with your eyes wide open
Follow your nose around
There's nothing so delicious
Anywhere else in town.

At the Deli and the Baker and the Ice Cream Maker

Make your own. Made to order.
Have it here or take it out.
Luscious dishes. So delicious
That's what this is all about.
```

At the Deli and the Baker and the Ice Cream Maker
In the fresh-cooking, fresh-looking new Howard Johnson's
In Camp Hill and Carlisle

(Courtesy of Campbell-Ewald Advertising and Howard Johnson Company.)

Because it brings us the actual visual, television's use of the sensation appeal usually asks even less verbal acuity of the audience than does radio. Nevertheless, television sensation can be heightened still further by orchestrating the counterpoint of compelling copy, as is accomplished in this Canadian Dairy Foods Service Bureau script:

Video	Audio
MASTER SHOT: ECU OF A CHEESE KNIFE AS IT STARTS TO SLICE THE FRONT OF A WEDGE OF CHEDDAR IN SLOW MOTION.	MUSIC UNDER ANNOUNCER VO: This could make you very hungry for the taste of Canadian Cheddar.
CUT TO ECU OF A CHEDDAR SANDWICH. CUT TO ECU OF CHEDDAR ON PIE.	VOICE: Cheddar in a sandwich. Cheddar with some pie.
CUT BACK TO MASTER SHOT AS KNIFE CONTINUES TO SLICE.	ANNOUNCER VO: Think of the clean, honest taste of Cheddar. Think about Cheddar and something crisp and tangy with it.
CUT TO ECU OF CHEDDAR ON CRACKER.	VOICE: Cheddar on a cracker.
CUT TO ECU OF CHEDDAR AND PEAR.	Cheddar and a pear.
CUT BACK TO MASTER SHOT.	ANNOUNCER VO: Or maybe melted, golden Cheddar.
CUT TO CHEDDAR ON OPEN 'BURGER.	VOICE: Cheddar on a 'burger.
CUT TO ECU BROCCOLI DIPPED IN CHEDDAR FONDUE.	Cheddar in a pot.
CUT BACK TO MASTER SHOT AS KNIFE BREAKS OFF PIECE AND LIFTS IT TOWARDS CAMERA.	ANNOUNCER VO: Go on. Your Cheddar's waiting.

Video	Audio
	<u>MUSIC</u> <u>UP:</u> Show your Cheddar more warmth.
PIECE OF CHEDDAR DISAPPEARS.	<u>ANNOUNCER</u> <u>VO:</u> That's the way!
CU OF CHEDDAR GOING INTO SHOPPING BASKET. <u>SUPER:</u> C.D.F.S.B. LOGO.	<u>MUSIC:</u> Take it home from the store more often!

(Courtesy of Mary Jane Palmer, Vickers & Benson Ltd.)

Uniqueness

Alternately referred to as "newness" or "novelty," this emotional appeal is exploited unmercifully in the marketplace as just-developed products and services try to make their mark and old established items attempt to demonstrate how up-to-date they've become. Being "where it's at" is an important concern to many consumers—especially younger ones with higher expendable incomes. Since these are the people most advertisers most like to reach, not only commercials but also whole programs and the continuity that promotes them will often invoke this novelty aspect.

Because the Federal Trade Commission allows the term *new* to be applied to a product characteristic, in general, for only the first six months of national advertising, the novelty approach as applied to the product has a severely circumscribed lifespan. But fortunately for clients and copywriters, the uniqueness appeal can also be exploited in the way in which we write and design the message itself. Even vintage products, services, and programs can appear fresh and modern within the proper contemporary framework.

What follows is a unique way to present the benefits of radio; a way that, by implication, makes the old sound medium itself seem more novel. Clearly, the rational appeals of performance and economy are also major considerations that this spot brings forth.

CUSTOMER:	Your ad agency is highly recommended.
AD REP:	Oh, thanks. What do you sell?
CUST:	Fruits and vegetables. Here, I brought some along.
REP:	Great. We'll do some TV spots.
CUST:	Oh, I'd rather use radio.
REP:	Why?
CUST:	TV is too expensive.
REP:	Well, look—
CUST:	Anyway, people don't have to see my fruits and vegetables as long as they can hear them.

REP:	What?
CUST:	When we play music on them.
REP:	Are you kidding?
CUST:	No. See, I put an all-produce band together just for our radio commercial.
REP:	Oh, come on now.
CUST:	Hand me that squash there.

(MUSIC: LONG SAXOPHONE RIFF)

REP:	How did you do that?
CUST:	Practice. I'm also proficient on three leafy vegetables and two tropical fruits.
REP:	Really?
CUST:	It's economical to advertise on radio, and I can target the people who like to listen to fresh fruits and vegetables.
REP:	This, uh, band you—
CUST:	Seven rutabagas, five cucumbers, and a bass broccoli.
REP:	Uh-huh.
CUST:	So, we'll play our theme song, 'Yes, we have no bananas,' and then we'll eat our instruments. Okay?
REP:	(Laughs) Okay!
CUST:	You'll buy radio for us then?
REP:	Sure. Listen, could you teach me?
CUST:	Sure. Here, start with the celery.

(SFX: BLOWING SOUND)

You don't blow on celery. You strum it.

REP:	Oh, sorry.

(MUSIC: GUITAR STRUM)

CUST:	Beginners!
ANNCR:	Radio. Red hot because it works. For all the facts, call this station or the Radio Advertising Bureau.

(Courtesy of Dick Orkin, The DOCSI Corporation.)

One caution about uniqueness must be observed. Raymond Rubicam's copy chief, Roy Whittier, suggested it decades ago when he tersely stated: "In advertising, the beginning of greatness is to be different, and the beginning of failure is to be the same."[9] If the difference is not significant to our customers, if it doesn't make functional sense within their frames of reference, we have uniquely miscommunicated, or not communicated at all.

9. David Ogilvy, "Six Giants Who Invented Modern Advertising," *ADWEEK/Midwest,* August 8, 1983, p. 38.

Rivalry

Dramatists and literary experts tell us that no good story can be without this element. The rivalry or conflict between two opposing entities or points of view provides the motive force for a story and constitutes a constant pull on our attention. As ministories, many pieces of commercial and continuity writing must use similar conflict mechanisms but within a very reduced time frame. On several classic occasions ("Will Shell with Platformate Out-Perform Other Gasolines?"; "Can the Timex Take This Licking and Keep on Ticking?"), the conflict itself has become the message's prime emotional appeal, with the attainment of the advocated rational appeal constituting the specific rivalry resolution. Yes, our Timex has that maintenance reliability and can take that licking. Yes, our client's vinyl covering does have the looks, the appearance, and feel of real leather. Yes, our margarine is more economical than the high-priced spread but still tastes just as good. These and dozens of other little contests are constantly played out before listeners and viewers.

If the rivalry is too contrived, if its results and main copy point are telegraphed from the beginning, the impact and, consequently, the emotional appeal will be seriously impaired. In order to constitute the primary emotional appeal, the conflict must build and heighten as the message progresses.

Such is the case with the following spot that adds a comedic twist to what would otherwise be a very trite and predictable rivalry. The hypothetical client is Firmstrand, and the rational appeals are performance and safety:

AGNES: (Quietly triumphant) Marge, for years I've tried and I've finally done it.

MARGE: Done what?

AGNES: I've finally found a product that's better than yours.

MARGE: (Snidely) Oh yeah? Like what?

AGNES: These toothpicks. Firmstrand Round Toothpicks to be exact.

MARGE: (Still haughty) Those are just plain, old wooden toothpicks. What's so special about them?

AGNES: Firmstrand's are round. They're stronger than your flimsy flat toothpicks.

MARGE: (Defensive) Oh yeah? Well, mine come in different colors.

AGNES: What's more beautiful than Firmstrand's natural polished wood? Besides, your toothpicks left stains in all the sandwiches you made for last week's party. Not that anyone wanted to eat them anyway.

MARGE: Oh yeah? My wash is still whiter than yours.

AGNES: Maybe so. But my Firmstrand Round Toothpicks are safer than yours too. My husband got slivers from your flimsy party toothpicks. Firmstrand Round Toothpicks would never do that.

MARGE: (More subdued) My hands are softer than yours.

AGNES: (Closing in for the kill) Admit it, Marge. Firmstrand
          Round Toothpicks <u>are</u> better than yours.
MARGE: (Sulkily) <u>My</u> husband can still out-bowl <u>your</u> husband.

Rivalry is also the motivating force in the man versus nature sagas in which the product is shown to tip the balance in favor of man. In this Mortein spot from Australia, of which the last frame is reproduced as Figure 4–7, the conflict is unabashedly exaggerated but, through clever writing and visualization, seems all the more believable.

Video	Audio
OPEN ON WIDE HORIZONS SHOT OF TYPICAL OUTBACK STATION HOMESTEAD. SUPER: <u>NO FLIES ON BAKKABURK STATION.</u>	MUSIC: <u>MORTEIN THEME UNDER THROUGHOUT.</u>
DISSOLVE TO DROVER APPROACHING SCREENED FRONT VERANDAH OF HOMESTEAD TRAILED BY HIS CATTLEDOG. HE SPEAKS TO CAMERA AS HE ENTERS THROUGH SCREEN DOOR AND DROPS HIS SADDLE IN A CLOUD OF DUST ON THE FLOOR.	DROVER: You think you've got flies. Out here we've got more flies than a zipper factory.
CUT TO CU OF DROVER AS HE DELIVERS LINE WITH LACONIC GRIN.	And big---they're big enough to shear!
CUT WIDER AS HE APPROACHES HIS WIFE WHO IS SITTING IN AN OLD ROCKER AT THE END OF THE VERANDAH SHELLING PEAS IN MECHANICAL MANNER. SHE IS CHEWING AND STARING INTO SPACE AND HARDLY NOTICES AS THE DROVER APPROACHES HER AND PICKS UP A CAN OF MORTEIN FAST KNOCKDOWN FROM A TABLE BESIDE HER. HE HOLDS CAN UP CLOSE TO CAMERA.	So, the missus got this can of Mortein Fast Knockdown and those flies went down quicker than cold beer in a dust storm.
CUT TO FRONT ROOM OF HOMESTEAD AS DROVER ENTERS THROUGH FRONT	And it's a new formula—

Video	Audio
DOOR WITH CAN IN ONE HAND AND HAT IN THE OTHER. HE PLACES HAT ON PEG AND SPRAYS SOME PRODUCT INTO THE AIR. HE SNIFFS THE SPRAYED PRODUCT.	doesn't smell like sheep dip.
CUT TIGHTER ON DROVER. AS HE SPEAKS A GUST OF WIND BLOWS HIS HAIR AND HE LOOKS UP. QUICK INTERCUT OF CATTLEDOG LOOKING AROUND WARILY. THE DROVER SPRAYS UP INTO THE AIR.	Good for blowies, too. Here's one now—
CUT WIDE TO SEE DROVER REACT TO THUNDERING CRASH OFF CAMERA. GREAT CLOUDS OF DUST RISE FROM THE FLOOR, TABLES AND CHAIRS CLATTER AND BANG. QUICK INTERCUT SHOWS DOG HIGH-TAILING IT OUT OF THE WINDOW WITH A WHIMPER.	<u>SFX:</u> VARIOUS CRASHING FX, WHIMPERING OF DOG.
CUT TIGHTER ON DROVER AS HE REGATHERS HIS COMPOSURE. ONE OF THREE FLYING DUCKS ON WALL BEHIND FALLS TO GROUND IN FINAL PROTEST.	<u>DROVER:</u> and that was just a baby!
CUT TO PACK SHOT—MORTEIN FAST KNOCKDOWN CAN IN FOREGROUND ON TABLE IN HOMESTEAD FRONT ROOM. SUPER: <u>AUSTRALIA'S FASTEST FLYSPRAY.</u> ON WALL BEHIND WE SEE SHADOW OF THE DROVER HUMPING OUT THE HUGE ''BLOWFLY.''	<u>ANNCR VO:</u> Mortein. Australia's fastest flyspray. <u>DROVER OFF CAMERA:</u> Get the door, luv!

Eminence

This particular category may be more readily recognized as snob appeal; keeping up with the Joneses; becoming a beautiful person. Goods that are among the most expensive in their product category often use this approach in an attempt to turn an unfavorable economic rationale into a positive statement.

Figure 4–7.   *(Courtesy of Kilner Mason, McCann-Erickson Advertising Pty Limited.)*

Long ago, when Cadillac Motors stopped focusing on the technical aspects of its automobile and began simply to feature it within regal and ultra-stylish tableaus, the effectiveness of the eminence appeal became and remains fully entrenched in twentieth-century advertising (see Figure 4–8).

When combined with ego-building copy that compliments the audience member's taste, professional life-style, or value to the community, the eminence appeal can be a potent generator of charity pitches in PSAs as well as an effective means to cultivate consideration of commercial products. Even in program promos and station IDs, the eminence appeal can be used to get audience members to watch the program or listen to the station that "astute people like you are talking about." In short, the eminence appeal is why you display your client's toilet tissue on a golden baroque holder instead of dangling it from a bent coat-hanger.

In this next spot, eminence is intertwined with its frequent rational partner, indulgence. Notice how the ego-builders help bolster the appeal, even from the beginning of the commercial.

ANNCR: You've got a lot to do in your working day. A lot of
         people depend on you. For the right decisions. At the
         right time. So who can blame you if your personal
         decisions sometimes take a back seat? Like the decision

CADILLAC MOTOR CAR DIVISION
1985 SEVILLE
Polo
GMEK2035   30 Seconds

(SFX: ALL NATURAL AND MIX WITH CADILLAC THEME.)

(Anncr VO): All out is...

the only way you go...

(MUSIC AND SFX)

and it earns you...

the rewards of success.

Naturally, that includes the car you drive. Distinctive. Elegant.

Seville goes all out...to achieve your high goals for luxury travel.

Drive the 1985 Seville...

the car for those, who like you...

choose to go first class all the way. SINGERS: BEST OF ALL, IT'S A CADILLAC.

Figure 4–8.   *(Courtesy of John Johnson, D'Arcy MacManus Masius.)*

about where to deposit your hard-earned money. At the Bank
of Richton, we know you're busy. And our drive-in windows
get you in and out quickly. But we also know you've got
enough professional worries without keeping day by day
track of your private cash flow. That's why the Bank of
Richton's Exec-Assist provides for automatic transfers
between your savings and checking account. We cover for
you so you can concentrate on those big decisions at the
job. The Bank of Richton; easing little problems for big
decision makers.

AUDIENCES AND ATTITUDES

Now that "SIMPLE PLEASURE" is fully in mind, we can focus on the types of audiences at which these coupled rational and emotional appeals are directed. We are not dealing here with the various age, sex, geographic, and socio-economic characteristics into which audiences can be demographically segmented. Such marketplace delineations are discussed later. Instead, we are at this point concerned with the general opinion orientations, to which any demographic group might be prone.

As our "SIMPLE PLEASURE" discussion recognizes, any broadcast audience presents a unique psychological challenge to the communicator. The listeners or viewers must be approached with a balanced blend of both emotional and rational appeals because, though they constitute a mass audience, it is an audience listening and watching in very small units.

Psychologically, they share certain characteristics common to both large and small groupings. Since it is a mass, the broadcast audience needs an emotional stimulus to cut through the impersonality of the one-to-many communication setting. Like Marc Antony's "Friends, Romans, and Countrymen" speech in Shakespeare's *Julius Caesar*, broadcast copy must quickly strike emotional chords that each member of the audience can easily personalize, even though the audience is not being addressed as separate individuals.

But because the broadcast audience is also largely separated one from another, pure emotion alone normally won't compel and convince them. As solitary units of one and two, they are not prey to the sort of mob psychology that can sharpen the response and dull the inhibition of individuals who find themselves part of the crowd at a rock concert, revival, or football game. When we are addressed alone, or as part of a very small group, we expect our intellect to be solicited; we are less susceptible to purely emotional pitches.

Aiming at a quantitative mass that is physically isolated into very small, even single-person units, the broadcast copywriter must not only resort to both rational and emotional appeals, but must also be aware of the fundamental attitudinal set of that mass. Without immediate feedback and within only thirty or sixty seconds, the broadcast writer cannot construct a message that first probes the audience's attitude and then begins the process of adapting to it. Rather, using as much market and polling data and raw intuition as are available, the copywriter must astutely select from among the "SIMPLE PLEASURE" attributes and construct a systematic communication that will be in consonance with the predominant audience feeling about the product, service, station, or program to which the copy pertains.

There are four main attitudinal orientations that an audience may take. Each of these must be dealt with somewhat differently in order to achieve maximum copy effectiveness. These four varieties can be identified respectively as the "you bet," "heck no," "yes but," and "so what" audiences.

"You Bet" Audience

Unfortunately, this audience is relatively rare in the broadcast writer's world. It is the one already favorably impressed with whatever your copy is trying to promote and simply needs to be coaxed into tangible action or, at least, into maintaining a continued positive posture. This audience needs to be shown as graphically as possible why they should finally energize their belief. It's fine that they agree taking movies of the kids is a swell idea, but unless they are activated into buying the camera, you haven't sold many Kodaks. It's great that they think our candidate is tops, but unless we motivate them to the ballot box, he's not going to win no matter how far ahead the polls put him. It's gratifying to know how highly they think of our news program, but it doesn't mean much unless they develop the habit of tuning in. With the "you bet" audience, as in this Hot Springs Auto Wash spot, we don't have to persuade folks that a clean car is better than a dirty one. They accept that. Rather, we must reinforce the reasons for taking the trouble to keep the car clean and explain how our client can help.

ANNCR: This year, billions of bugs will lose their lives on the nation's highways. Chances are, a lot of them will end up on the front of your car. And if you don't get them off, they'll come back to haunt you.
(EERIE MUSIC: FEATURE AND UNDER)
You see, as bugs decompose, they give off a strong acid that actually eats away at your car's chrome and paint—making it dull. The hotter the weather, the faster the acid is made. But there is a brighter side to all of this. Come to Hot Springs Auto Wash. We've developed a way to completely remove bugs before they kill your car's finish. In fact, Hot Springs is the only car wash to make this guarantee: if you find as much as one single little mosquito on your car after we've washed and dried it, we'll give you your two dollars and ninety cents back.
(MUSIC: OUT)
Next time, we'll talk to you about the problem with birds.
(SFX: BIRDS CHIRPING)

(Courtesy of Diana L. Monroe, Siddall, Matus & Coughter Inc., Advertising.)

"Heck No" Audience

These folks have a real bone to pick either with your client's category in general or, worse, with your client in particular. There is no way you are going to sell them on anything until you first alleviate their antipathy. One way to accomplish this is to approach them with total frankness. Bring the element they don't like right up front and then show why it isn't so bad after all or why there are other factors that outweigh this disadvantage. Volkswagen pretty well neutralized the negative eminence appeal its "Beetle" had with upper-income types through a campaign called "Live Below Your Means." A & P supermarkets put "Price and Pride" together to repair the damage done in a previous approach that had stressed economy at the expense of the company's long-time reputation for quality and integrity (performance). The copy admitted

A & P had strayed and most people forgave them. Listerine turned the "Taste People Hate Twice a Day" from an anti-indulgence debit into a positive performance credit.

If frankness is too hard for the client to swallow, your copy can take a more indirect approach that starts by establishing some common ground; some principles with which both the copy and the audience can agree. That gives you some place figuratively to hang your hat before tackling the point of controversy. Nobody, for example, likes to endure the cost and potential discomfort of trips to the dentist. But if we can show people the ravages of untreated gum disease, they'll be more likely to make regular appointments. Your liquid deodorant may take longer to dry than a spray, but if we can first appeal to an audience interest in saving money, the inconvenience may be shown to be worth it. As in the following spot, the positive aspect must be both well presented and unequivocally held now by the audience. If they don't subscribe to even your alleged common ground principle, you'll be selling two concepts and they'll buy neither.

ANNCR:　We all like peace and quiet. It's nice to hear yourself think. So the noise in downtown Carrington must be driving you up the walls. Jackhammers; riveting; truck engines. When will it stop? It'll stop by the end of next year. It'll stop when our new mall is ready for your enjoyment. It'll stop when we all have a downtown mall that we can comfortably shop in; winter or summer. Your Carrington Chamber of Commerce asks that you let us continue to make some noise about the new downtown mall. Things will be peaceful again when it's done. Much more peaceful, much more relaxing than they were before we started. The New Carrington Mall. Better shopping, better business, a better city. The Carrington Mall. It'll be the quietest ever then; because we're raising the roof now.

"Yes But" Audience

An audience with this psychological set is certainly not hostile to your product or cause but neither are they preconvinced. If anything, the "yes but" audience would like to buy what you have to sell but has a nagging doubt or two that needs resolution. For them, you have to present evidence and validation that your claim is true; that more people do watch your news team than the crew down the street; that (even) "for a dollar forty-nine, it's a pretty good lighter." All the common ground in the world won't satisfy the "yes but" audience if you don't come to grips with their objection. And ignoring weaknesses in your evidence or documentation may convert them into diehard "heck noers." The "yes but" audience, unlike the other three types, is passing through a temporary stage rather than displaying a stable condition. If you ignore them, they may become a "so what" group. If you try to mislead them, they'll be interested enough to exhibit a very active "heck no" attitude. But if you can convince them with appropriate and sensible validation, they'll be "you bets" for a long time to come.

In the Goodwill Industries approach (Figure 4–9), the copywriter avoids, at first, specific mention of the qualms people have about whether a handicapped person can do the job. Instead, the proof is presented before the speaker's disability is revealed. This makes it difficult for the viewer mentally to introduce an objection that has already been neutralized.

"So What" Audience

This is by far the most numerous attitudinal set that the broadcast copywriter will encounter. Most mass consumable products and services do not create a strong enough impression on people to engender love, hate, or even the interest needed to be actively suspicious or skeptical. So many commercials, PSAs, and other continuity copy fill the airwaves that audiences can muster little more than a profound indifference to most of them. The copywriter's life is a

For years I never had a reason to get up in the morning.

No one would hire me.

But then a friend told me about Goodwill Industries

and their job training programs.

Now I go to work just like my neighbors.

I'm making a real contribution and the people here respect me and my ability.

I'm still disabled, but I'm lucky. Because of Goodwill Industries, I've not only learned to live with my disability, I've learned to work with it.

Goodwill Industries. Our business works. So people can.

Figure 4–9. *(Courtesy of Gerald Downey, Needham, Harper & Steers, Inc.)*

constant battle against this malaise, a continuous struggle to break through that "so what" attitude long enough to make an impression and stick in the memory. Since the "so what" audience commands so much of the copywriter's time, we need to devote special attention to the tiered persuasive structure of messages aimed at receivers with this orientation. We'll call this structure Progressive Motivation.

PROGRESSIVE MOTIVATION: THE DOUBLE-E, DOUBLE-D, A

Though the study of multistep persuasion is an age-old phenomenon pre-dating both broadcasting and the twentieth century, it acquired one of its most lucid forms in a book called *Principles and Types of Speech* by Alan H. Monroe. Monroe coined the term *Motivated Sequence* to refer to a persuasive process, which, for his purposes, was divided into five steps identified as attention, need, satisfaction, visualization, and action.[10] To Monroe, one needed first to attract the indifferent listener (attention), then identify the problem (need), give the solution (satisfaction), project that solution into the future (visualization), and, finally, get the solution manifestly adopted (action).

Though Monroe did apply his Motivated Sequence to several types of human communication situations, it is clear that the broadcast message normally does not provide the time to follow a formula whose precursor is the comparatively leisurely platform speech. Further, since people are not socialized to give the same initial attention to a radio or television set that they give to other people, broadcast communicators must devote a greater proportion of their already scarce time than Monroe's Motivated Sequence allows to the matter of height-ening that attention—to making certain that the "so what" audience is with us before plunging ahead into the actual selling line.

Therefore, the more that broadcast-oriented Progressive Motivation allows more focus on the attention-*building* process, the better to reach the indifferent radio-television audience not enthused enough ("you bet"), angry enough ("heck no"), or skeptical enough ("yes but") about the subject to give it heed just because an electronic box is attempting to describe it to them. To assist recall of Progressive Motivation's constituent parts, you can think of them as "The Double-E, Double-D, A," which is an acronym for:

1. Entice
2. Engage
3. Disclose
4. Demonstrate
5. Activate

In other words, we must first entice audience notice (1), which is usually the job of one of the "PLEASURE" elements. Then we must engage that notice (2) by providing stimuli that involve audience members' past experiences in a way that gets them to help us construct our selling scene. Next, we apply this

---

10. Alan H. Monroe, *Principles and Types of Speech*, 3rd ed. (Chicago: Scott, Foresman and Company, 1949), p. 310.

involvement toward the disclosure of a consequent need (a rational appeal) the listener or viewer has for our product or service (3). We then demonstrate how our product or service can fulfill this need (4), and, finally, encourage the audience to make some overt, activated response (5)—even if only to remember the name of our product or the call letters of our station.

The PSA in Figure 4–10 is a prime illustration of Progressive Motivation. In fact, the purpose of many public service announcements is not just to circumvent the audience's "who cares" attitude but instead directly to combat and dispel it. Roman numerals have been added to the photoboard to indicate where each of the five "Double-E, Double-D, A" steps begins. The "Double-E, Double-D, A" can fight an audience's "who cares" attitude in commercials and on radio, too. Here is a rivalry-charged spot delivering performance and economy. It also has numbers added in order to expose its internal persuasive structure:

(MUSIC: EERIE ORGAN MUSIC UNDER)

ANNCR: [I](Dramatic) There's a sound that strikes terror in
                 the hearts of men.

MAN: No!! Oh nooo!

ANNCR: [II]It'll send cold chills down your spine.

LADY: Help!
                 (MUSIC: UP DRAMATICALLY AND UNDER)
                 (SFX: GAS PUMP: DING—DING—DING—DING—DING)

ANNCR: [III]It's the sound of a gas pump.

MAN/LADY: Noooooo!!!

ANNCR: And now with the recent gas tax increase—

MAN/LADY: The gas tax increase!? Ahhhhhh!! Nooo!

ANNCR: —gas prices are really a horror.[IV] But a fresh set
                 of Champion Spark Plugs can help put an end to your
                 fears. They'll put an end to missing, stalling, and
                 dead starts---things that make your car burn more
                 gas than it should. Because Champion Spark Plugs can
                 help protect against the build-up of carbon and
                 grime that can cause other plugs to foul.[V] So put an
                 end to the gas tax nightmare—
                 (MUSIC: ORGAN UP DRAMATICALLY AND UNDER)
                 (SFX: GAS PUMP: DING—DING—DING—DING—DING)
                 —with a new set of Champion Spark Plugs. You'll
                 sleep easier tonight. Nothing sparks like a
                 Champion.

(Courtesy of Dan Nelson, W. B. Doner & Company, Advertising.)

Now turn back to the spots listed below that have been used in this chapter. Put your own numbers on each message to indicate where the five Progressive

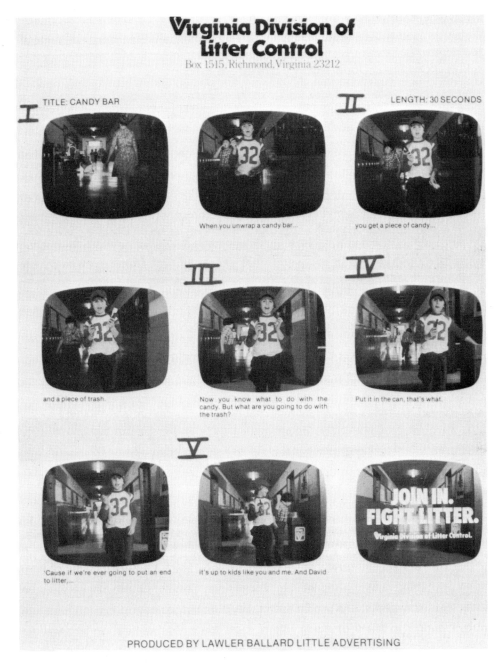

Figure 4–10. *(Courtesy of Virginia Raymond, Virginia Division of Litter Control.)*

Motivation steps begin. You should discover that, though the proportional length of each step may vary from spot to spot, their order remains the same as it strives to penetrate the "who cares" barricade. Go back and reveal for yourself the "Double-E, Double-D, A" structure as used in:

```
the Rainbow Rock Candy example of a ''safety'' appeal

the I Love New York example of a ''laughter'' appeal

the Southwest Airlines example of a ''laughter'' appeal

the Dr Pepper example of an ''allurement'' appeal

the Bank of Richton example of an ''eminence'' appeal
```

The functionally "SIMPLE" appeals, the emotional "PLEASURE" appeals, audience attitudinal analysis, and Progressive Motivation's "Double-E, Double-D, A" all are elements designed to make broadcast copy secure its intended impact and secure that impact within the very brief time frame allowed by the dynamics of radio and television. When combined with appropriate and well-fashioned words and phrases, these devices can make even the shortest pieces of communication have both relevance and salience for those semi-isolated and "semicomatose" folks the copywriter is expected to reach.

APPEALS CLUSTERING: PSYCHOGRAPHICS

In today's complex and sophisticated marketing world, some campaign designs go beyond the concept of basic appeals to look at which appeals groupings best seem to pull the emotional triggers of certain types of people. The typologies that have evolved comprise the study of *psychographics*—the analysis of lifestyles and preferences rather than the mere categorization of consumers into demographic pigeonholes. Advertising and public relations executive Henry J. Kaufman explains the difference this way:

> Years ago, everything was demographics. Age. Sex. Wealth. Education. Now there's a thing called psychographics that deals with lifestyles. Like cancer or the common cold, psychographics are not based on your social status or your wealth. You can have a taste for great books and be poor as a churchmouse, and be willing to spend your last sou on them. Or you can be poor as a churchmouse and own a Leica camera, if your interest is photography.[11]

Thus, people in the same demographic category may, through their preferences, self-concepts, and world views, be distributed among several separate psychographic categories. In like manner, people from different demographic groups may cluster together in the same psychographic category. The impoverished Leica camera owner to whom Kaufman referred, may be in the same psychographic circle as people with twice the education and ten times the income. This would depend on how salient the values associated with the practice of advanced photography are to the people in question.

11. "At Large: Henry Julian Kaufman," *Broadcasting Magazine*, June 25, 1979, p. 72.

This market or *life-style segmentation* orientation, while increasingly prominent on the media scene, is not universally accepted, nor, really, is it a single
approach. Different companies and different researchers have developed distinct methodologies for trying to segment that mysterious audience pie—and
different terminologies to describe the pie's individual pieces. The Research &
Marketing Services Department at Doyle Dane Bernbach, for example, broke
down the marketplace by identifying "what distresses us most and least, then
assigned each of us to what it deems our appropriate 'contentment climate.' "[12]
Four such climates have been isolated by DDB and are made up, respectively,
of people labelled:

1. The Easy Streeters
2. The Resigned
3. The Service Seekers
4. The Environmentally Concerned

The Easy Streeters are thought to have the greatest overall satisfaction with
life—satisfaction that comes from the dovetailing of money, education, and the
ready availability of a variety of comfort possessions and services. The Resigned,
on the other hand, are the working poor whose financial concerns are so
pressing that any other subjects (and discretionary goods/services) are largely
irrelevant. Service Seekers are like The Easy Streeters in terms of income but
have achieved this income only through the hard work of both spouses. They
labor to acquire money, not just to survive (as is the case with The Resigned)
but to purchase the comforts The Easy Streeters take for granted. Finally, The
Environmentally Concerned, though the best educated group, is also the most
tense about the condition of their surroundings and of everyday life. This
smallest group is average in income, above average in job satisfaction, and far
above the norm in terms of the stressful conditions they feel emanating from
the world around them.[13]

A more widely known and used psychographic schema is VALS—the Values
and Lifestyles research tool developed principally by Arnold Mitchell of SRI
International. As in other psychographic models, "the underlying thesis of VALS
is that people and their buying habits are driven by their values and lifestyles,
as well as their needs. It looks to the motivation behind the act. . . . Using
values enables them [companies and agencies] to give consumers shape and
texture—a face and a psychology as well as a demography."[14] In its standard
form, VALS is divided into four categories and nine segments as outlined below:

Need-Driven
   1. Survivors
   2. Sustainers

12. Richard Morgan, "Doyle Dane Bernbach Slices Up the American Pie," *ADWEEK/Midwest*,
    September 13, 1982, p. 22.
13. *Ibid.*
14. Betsy Sharkey, "The Father of VALS Looks Ahead," *ADWEEK/Midwest*, December, 1984,
    p. F. 6.

Outer-Directed
  3. Belongers
  4. Emulators
  5. Achievers
Inner-Directed
  6. I-Am-Me's
  7. Experientials
  8. Societally Conscious
Integrated
  9. Integrateds

Need-Driven people correspond roughly to the Resigned in the Doyle Dane Bernbach typology. The Survivors tend to be rooted in poverty while The Sustainers' fortunes drastically ebb and flow with the state of the economy. As a result, some advertisers, particularly those offering costly or upscale items, will avoid this group entirely, whereas "necessity" product producers (such as grocery chains and staple foods manufacturers) must put their advertising focus on price and guarantees.

Outer-Directed individuals want, above all, to fit in. Often referred to as Middle America and comprising up to two-thirds of the United States population, they perceive of products as status symbols. Belongers are the largest (and least wealthy) segment in this category and the ones for whom being accepted is of overwhelming importance. They are seldom likely to try something new, preferring instead what are often labelled "heritage" brands—even if these brands are not price competitive. Emulators want not just to be accepted but to be noticed (even envied) for how well-accepted they are. In rational appeals terms, Emulators usually sacrifice indulgence and performance for looks. They are seeking to pattern themselves after the Achievers, who may be the most driven segment in the VALS typology. Achievers already possess the success for which the Emulators are striving but continue to push themselves for more socially prized material goods. Unlike the less secure Emulators, Achievers know they have made it but don't want to be patronized by advertising that tells them that.

Representing approximately 20 percent of the United States (and assumedly, other developed Western countries') population, the *Inner-Directeds* are most concerned with self-expression. They believe more in social responsibility and meeting personal goals than in conforming to an external standard. The I-Am-Me segment is a group in transition from Outer- to Inner-Directed values. Thus, they tend to be impulsive, rather self-consciously independent, and highly unpredictable. Because of the small size of this segment and its volatility, it is extremely difficult (perhaps, even counterproductive) to attempt to aim a campaign at them.

Experientials, conversely, are secure in their inner-directedness and whole-heartedly pursue a rich, personal life regardless of how other people may perceive their possessions and activities. Since they do not necessarily subscribe to status quo values, they are most likely to try a new product or brand if it can be shown to meet their intensely personal needs. For the Societally Conscious segment, meanwhile, personal needs are defined by what they believe to be society's needs. They closely parallel The Environmentally Concerned group in the Doyle Dane Bernbach matrix and seek not status but to act in harmony with what is best for the world as they see it—even if that course of action is not seen as socially popular. Generally highly educated, they look for real value and environmental harmony in their product purchases. Thus, safety and maintenance appeals would be especially useful in reaching the Societally Conscious.

Integrateds are the smallest category and segment in the VALS universe. Making up no more than 2 percent of the population, they are so mature and self-assured that they can deftly combine both inner- and outer-directed values in their preferences without self-contradiction. Because of the small number of Integrateds and their variegated behavior, few marketers make them a prime target.

To illustrate how VALS principles translate into copywritten communication, here are five separate television scripts prepared by Ketchum Advertising/ Philadelphia for Provident National Bank. Each spot is aimed at a different VALS segment: Belongers, Emulators, Achievers, Experientials, and Societally Conscious. Each script features the financial product most likely to appeal to the needs of the VALS segment being addressed. Notice how the copywriter has zeroed in on the product and its associated need. Notice, too, that VALS is so central to the creative concept that it becomes a key part of each script's visual description. Finally, review our earlier VALS descriptions to determine why Provident National did not target in this campaign the other four VALS segments (Survivors, Sustainers, I-Am-Me's, and Integrateds).

Spot 1: Outer-Directed Belonger

Video	Audio
1. OPEN ON PROTOTYPE OF BELONGER TENDING HER PLANTS. THIS MIDDLE-AGED WOMAN WHO LIVES IN CHELTENHAM WAS WIDOWED EARLY IN LIFE (5 YEARS AGO) AND IS IN CHARGE OF HER OWN FINANCES.	1. <u>SFX:</u> NATURAL SOUNDS <u>PERSON (OC):</u> I thought I should have a money market account. I mean, everyone else was talking about high interest---why shouldn't I get it. So I went down to my bank---The Provident. And they took the time to explain things to me. Helped me turn my savings account into a Gold Edge Money Market Account. Imagine. For my money, The Provident was the right place to start. And a pretty good place to stay, too.

Video	Audio
2. FADE TO BLACK <u>SUPER:</u> THE PROVIDENT PROVIDENT NATIONAL BANK MEMBER FDIC WE'RE PREPARED TO HELP.	2. <u>SFX:</u> NATURAL SOUNDS

Spot 2: Outer-Directed Emulator

Video	Audio
1. OPEN ON PROTOTYPE OF EMULATOR HAVING LUNCH. HE'S BLACK, LATE 20's TO EARLY 30's. HAS A CLERICAL JOB, BUT STILL WEARS A 3-PIECE SUIT. HE'S MARRIED WITH ONE OR TWO YOUNG CHILDREN.	1. <u>SFX:</u> NATURAL SOUNDS <u>PERSON (OC):</u> The money wasn't the problem. In fact, I had to do something before I filed my tax return. And I'd seen all the ads, but I still didn't really understand Individual Retirement Accounts. Well, The Provident is my bank— so I decided to start there. You know what? I didn't have to worry. By the time I left The Provident, I knew all I needed to know about IRAs. (HUMOROUSLY) Tax deductions. Investment options. Ask me anything!
2. FADE TO BLACK <u>SUPER:</u> THE PROVIDENT PROVIDENT NATIONAL BANK MEMBER FDIC WE'RE PREPARED TO HELP. LEGAL SUPER: SUBSTANTIAL PENALTIES FOR EARLY WITHDRAWAL	2. <u>SFX:</u> NATURAL SOUNDS

Spot 3: Outer-Directed Achiever

Video	Audio
1. OPEN ON PROTOTYPE ACHIEVER IN THE LOCKER ROOM OF HIS COUNTRY CLUB. HE'S A BRIGHT ENGINEER WHO'S MADE A GO OF HIS OWN COMPANY. AND EVEN THOUGH HE STILL WORKS EVERYDAY HE HAS MADE A GOOD DEAL OF MONEY.	1. SFX: NATURAL SOUNDS ACHIEVER (OC): We were just college kids with a good idea. Ever since, it's been good business. But while I was getting ahead professionally, I was getting nowhere managing my own money. Professional investment management; protect my family with a Trust? Well, I called The Provident; my company bank, they're known for their trust department. Now I understand personal financial management. I'm doing this, because they're helping me do that.
2. FADE TO BLACK SUPER: THE PROVIDENT PROVIDENT NATIONAL BANK MEMBER FDIC WE'RE PREPARED TO HELP.	2. SFX: NATURAL SOUNDS

Spot 4: Inner-Directed Experiential

Video	Audio
1. OPEN ON PROTOTYPE OF EXPERIENTIAL WORKING OUT IN A GYM. THIS YOUNG LAWYER LIVES IN CENTER CITY OR THE MAIN LINE WITH HIS GIRLFRIEND. BECAUSE HE IS A SPECIALIST HE IS ALREADY MAKING A DECENT INCOME.	1. SFX: NATURAL SOUNDS PERSON (OC): I have always made my own decisions. And after all, I have been following the stock market since law school. So it made sense to switch to a discount broker. Which one? Well, I called my

Video	Audio
	bank, The Provident. After I explained my needs, they explained Trade$aver— Provident's brokerage alternative, that executes and clears through BHC Securities. Now I have access to my brokerage account where I have my bank account, at The Provident.
2. FADE TO BLACK SUPER: THE PROVIDENT PROVIDENT NATIONAL BANK MEMBER FDIC WE'RE PREPARED TO HELP. LEGAL SUPER: TRADESAVER IS AN INITIATED BROKERAGE SERVICE ACCOUNT CARRIED BY BHC SECURITIES, INC., A REGISTERED BROKER/ DEALER.	2. SFX: NATURAL SOUNDS

Spot 5: Inner-Directed Societally Conscious

Video	Audio
1. OPEN ON PROTOTYPE OF SOCIETALLY CONSCIOUS PERSON SITTING IN HER DEN, WORKING WITH A HOME COMPUTER. SHE'S A MIDDLE MANAGEMENT TECHNICIAN OR PROFESSIONAL WHO'S BEEN OUT OF COLLEGE FOR A WHILE.	1. SFX: NATURAL SOUNDS PERSON (OC): Like everyone else I started an Individual Retirement Account when they first came out. Opened one at my bank—The Provident. But I decided I could do more with the money in it—like put it into a mutual fund or money market

Video	Audio
	investment. So I went down to The Provident. Explained what I wanted to do. And guess what! They explained to me I could do everything I wanted with my IRA right there at The Provident. That's my bank.

2. FADE TO BLACK
    SUPER: THE PROVIDENT
          PROVIDENT NATIONAL
          BANK
          MEMBER FDIC
          WE'RE PREPARED TO
          HELP.
    LEGAL SUPER: SUBSTANTIAL
      PENALTIES FOR EARLY
      WITHDRAWAL
	2. SFX: NATURAL SOUNDS

(Courtesy of Lynda M. Lee, Ketchum Advertising. Philadelphia.)

VALS, as we've stated, is one example of how psychographic research is impacting the copywriter's work and resulting creations. It is a new, but by no means the only, way of thinking about who the consumer is. Bryant Robey, former editor of *American Demographics* magazine, maintains that "VALS and demographics are different ways of carving up the same marketplace. They complement each other and should not be regarded as competing approaches. The next step may be to find better ways to link the findings of attitude research with the broadly available numbers that demographers collect."[15]

As a copywriter, you must endeavor to ascertain the type of audience you are striving to reach, both in terms of its demographic make-up and its predominant attitudinal and values sets. Develop copy goals and strategy based on these sets and then execute this strategy through calculated use of compatible rational and emotional appeals.

Building on the experiences and needs of our audience requires effective broadcast copy that is neither involving imagery nor stark product data but a painstakingly tailored blend of both. As we have seen in this chapter, successful broadcast copywriting is an endeavor dependent on an appeals-cognizant

15. Bryant Robey, "From Classroom to Boardroom," *ADWEEK/Midwest*, December, 1984, p. F. 21.

content within an attitudinally attuned structure. Our scripts may be brief, but they are still required to impact those hot buttons and emotional triggers we discussed at the beginning of the chapter. As Dean Robert Smith of Temple University so succinctly put it,

> Commercials are shorthand devices for relating the potent emotions associated with parenthood, love, sex, greed, status and social acceptance to the sponsor's products. They are the Greek vases or Navajo sand paintings of our time—they give meaning to the ephemeral by relating it to the timeless.[16]

16. Robert R. Smith, *Beyond the Wasteland: The Criticism of Broadcasting*, rev. ed. (Annandale, Va.: Speech Communication Association, 1980), p. 19.

Chapter Five

THE CDVP PROCESS

Before proceeding to discuss the specifics of radio and television writing, it is necessary to lay out some additional ground rules that apply equally to copy creation for both media. In an overall fashion, we need to ascertain what we are striving for, how to describe and evaluate the results of this striving, and the nature of the functional and regulatory boundaries within which the whole game must be played. All of this can be referred to, via shorthand sloganeering, as the copywriter's "CDVP PROCESS":

Creation
Definition
Validation
Prohibition

CREATION

Creativity is probably the most often used and often abused word in our business. It is used to describe what we intend to do, how we intend to do it, and what we'll have when we're through. Creativity is used to excuse our faults and failings ("I just can't *create* whenever I want to.") and is cited as justification for the ignoring of market realities ("How do they know what's *creative*? They only make the product."). Most importantly, creativity is what we're paid to exercise (when feasible) and why we're paid more than somebody else to exercise it. So what is creativity?

This question has lots of answers, and many of them consume whole volumes on aesthetics. Since we don't have the space for that, the following definition is proposed to encompass the creative tasks the broadcast copywriter faces:

Creativity—Forging a logical link twixt two previously unattached subjects.

This is a real-world orientation that well serves the copywriter who deals in real-world products and services. For, unlike some of art's more mystic extremities, the copywriter's creative product must be openly logical; must make sense, and the *same* sense, to a very large number of people on the other side of those radio and television sets. This is the kind of creativity that everyone has the chance to bring to his or her life's work and, therefore, that everybody can appreciate.

Robert Fulton (hardly an avant-garde weirdo) brought this kind of creativity to bear when he put together a tea kettle's steam and a boat's ability to traverse water. The consequent steamboat was dubbed Fulton's Folly—until it worked, until the logical nature of the link was established. The World's Fair concessionaire who ran out of ice cream containers exercised this same sense of creativity when he bought funnel-shaped cookies from the booth next door and gave birth to—the ice cream cone. And the copywriter who had a ball-point pen write right through a thick butter smear got a no less creative result in the process of proving that pen wouldn't skip.

Here are some further classic examples, some other manifestations of our definition in action in broadcasting. The "two previously unattached subjects" are spotlighted as is the link, the central copy point, which logically ties them together:

```
                                   (proves)
The Polaroid print in the goldfish bowl    =    the camera's
self-processed photos are moisture resistant.
```

```
                                   (proves)
The Jergens Lotion and the dry, autumn leaf    =    the
softening attributes of this creme.
```

```
The ''playful'' gorilla and the piece of American Tourister
       (proves)
luggage      =    the luggage's maintenance attribute.
```

```
                                  (proves)
The monk scribe and the Xerox machine    =    quality,
fine-detailed copies are ''miraculously'' easy for the new Xerox
machine.
```

```
                                   (proves)
The flamenco dancer with the Bic pen on his boot    =    a cheap
pen can still have a tough point.
```

```
                                   (proves)
The six-foot submarine sandwich in the AMC Pacer    =    a small
car need not be uncomfortably narrow.
```

To reiterate, the copywriter's logical link will be, simultaneously: (1) the central copy point and (2) the piece of information we want the listener or viewer to discern and retain.

Though the examples above all flow from television "commercialdom," this need for our defined creativity and its *central copy point link* is just as pronounced, with results just as effective, in PSA construction. Figure 5–1 showcases a message for the National Heart, Lung and Blood Institute. The two previously unattached subjects are (1) a time bomb and (2) high blood pressure. What is the logical-link central copy point?

Another television PSA that also demonstrates our creativity in action is seen in Figure 5–2 on pp. 96–97. What are the two previously unattached subjects and the logical-link message presented there?

A Public Service Campaign of the Advertising Council

NATIONAL HEART, LUNG AND BLOOD INSTITUTE/ U.S. Dept. of Health, Education & Welfare

Volunteer Advertising Agency: DKG, Inc.

Volunteer Campaign Coordinator: Sanford Buchsbaum, Revlon, Inc.

Figure 5-1. *(Courtesy of The Advertising Council, Inc.)*

Radio as well as television seeks to capitalize on the sort of creativity we've defined to make and hold an impression on the audience. That radio's linkage must be engendered entirely through the audio increases not only the challenge but also the need for a clean, clear relationship that stands out and draws its conclusion in a memorable way. The following radio spot juxtaposes museums with feather dusters to prove that our *purchased* product is astutely superior to (and safer than) the *free* rags the listener would otherwise use.

> <u>Production Note:</u> Male announcer with refined, but not
> haughty diction.

ANNCR: Today we're talking to the original "Share the Ride with a Friend" man.

Uh, you sir, are Noah of Noah's Ark Fame.

NOAH: That's right. I had two lizards, two monkeys, two snails,

two snakes and two rhinos get together and share the ride.

ANNCR: Then actually when you did do the whole number with the...
NOAH: whole number...is that a thing you say nowadays...?

ANNCR: That's a current terminology.
NOAH: Yea, O.K. fine.

ANNCR: Well, one of the great things about Carpooling is all the money you can save.
NOAH: Absolutely!

ANNCR: Uh, huh.
NOAH: Two falcons...boy, were they hard to get aboard.

ANNCR: So today the best thing you could advise people to do would...
NOAH: Share the Ride.

It worked out for us and so when you share a ride with somebody, make an animal noise—it's kinda fun.

ANNCR: Uh, by the way, did you call it carpooling way back then?

NOAH: No, we did not have that word. We called it Kalaka.

ANNCR: Kalaka. Is that the same...
NOAH: Kalaka, yes. In Babylonian, that meant carpool.
ANNCR: Oh, yes.
NOAH: Yea.

SINGERS: DOUBLE UP EVERY MORNIN' DOUBLE UP GOIN' HOME AT NIGHT. DOUBLE UP

EVERY DAY, IT'S A BETTER WAY. YOU'RE GONNA HAVE MORE FUN TOGETHER.

BEATS DRIVIN' ALONE.

A public service campaign of the Advertising Council.

Volunteer Advertising Agency:
VanSant Dugdale & Company, Inc.

Volunteer Campaign Coordinator: John P. Kelley, The Goodyear Tire & Rubber Company

Figure 5–2. (*Courtesy of The Advertising Council, Inc.*)

```
ANNCR:   I'm the curator of this world-renown museum of art. What
         would you say is the most valuable thing in our
         collection? No, it's not a Rembrandt; nor is it a Picasso.
         (Chuckles) No, the most valuable property at our art
         museum is the Frisky Feather Duster. What could possibly
         be so valuable about a Frisky Feather Duster? Well,
         imagine a two-hundred-pound cleaning woman named Bertha.
         Now imagine Bertha pushing an unwieldy rag at an Etruscan
         vase (VAZ) worth 50,000 dollars. Or SCRAAY-PPING a coarse
         dustcloth across a million dollar oil painting. That's why
         a Frisky Feather Duster is so valuable. I can sit back in
         my curator's chair and watch Bertha safely flick dust away
         from even our most fragile pieces with the Frisky Feather
         Duster I bought her. The Frisky delicately brushes the
         nooks and crannies of our best sculptures. It gets deep
         into the corners of our most famous framed paintings
         without a scratch or a crumple. For valuable museum
         pieces, or treasured home nicknacks, the Frisky Feather
         Duster is a must. Frisky is the duster with the true
         artist's touch.
```

To find examples of other treatments that likewise exhibit our creativity characteristics, turn back to chapter 4 and examine the following spots. Once again, sharpen your ability to appreciate true copy creativity by isolating both the two subjects and the linkages that interlock them:

```
the Curad example of a ''safety'' appeal

the Tilt-Wheel example of an ''indulgence'' appeal

the ''I Love New York'' example of a ''laughter'' appeal

the Dr Pepper example of an ''allurement'' appeal

the Adweek example of a ''uniqueness'' appeal
```

Is creativity achieved in every commercial and continuity segment being broadcast? Just spend some time in front of a radio or television set with a pencil and paper. Try to detect two previously unattached subjects and the new, logical linkage between them in each spot, PSA, and extended piece of continuity to which you are exposed. You will undoubtedly find a great many messages discussing subjects that have been not only long related but that draw identical relationships to those being dwelled on by same-category competitors. Alternately, you may also find copy that strives to construct a new relationship but ends up with a linkage that is either illogical or unrelated to the message's central copy point.

Real, functional creativity is difficult to achieve within broadcasting's unyielding time limits. If it weren't, the manufacturers and humanitarians would be tempted to turn out their own spots and PSAs. No one would feel they needed the special talent and expertise of the copywriter. And that could make us very hungry indeed.

In many situations, a competent, straightforward description of the subject and what it will do for the prospect is all that is mandated—and difficult enough for even expert copywriters to supply. Forced, irrelevant creativity can be counterproductive and get in the way of the task to be done. Still, creativity, as we have defined the term, is something often to be reached for if seldom attained. Robert Browning's observation that "a man's reach should exceed his grasp, or what's a heaven for?" is an apt encouragement for the copywriter in this regard. Ken Robbins, chairman of SSC&B, reminds us that "The creative process is nothing more than a function of all your observations and knowledge, constantly resynthesized and reapplied in terms of your own personal experience. Therefore, one can never read enough books, watch enough television, understand enough political positions, etc. in the search for the germ of fresh and surprising ideas."[1]

Keep searching, whenever the assignment permits, for that logical link twixt two previously unattached subjects. Keep in mind that the link must also be your central copy point and that one of those two subjects is often, though not always, the product or service itself. But whatever you do, don't get too scientific about the process because, as Backer & Spielvogel's Ed Butler warns, "creative is not an exact science. It's not even a science. It's a curious amalgam of talent, smarts, experience, instinct and guts—qualities that can easily be mistaken for flight of fancy, ego, grass, poor judgment and instrument flying."[2]

DEFINITION

In the mass communications setting, creativity means very little if even a small minority of your target audience fails to decipher the meaning of the terms you've used to achieve it. An appropriate and logical linkage can seem both inappropriate and illogical if couched in language that is vague or obscure. It is therefore most important that copywriters clearly define the terms inherent in the subject category with which they are dealing. Writers must also beware of introducing terms of their own that are more in need of definition than those with which they started.

There are five categories of terms that, when used in your copy, may need to be defined. These categories can be identified as abstractions, analogies, generalities, technicalities, and multiplicates.

Abstractions

Words lacking tangibility are difficult for many people to deal with because nothing activates their "mind's eye." The undefined abstraction is therefore especially dangerous on radio, where a successful communication requires

1. Jeffrey Lener, "Some Friends Stopped By to Chat Recently," *ADWEEK/Midwest*, February, 1984, p. C.R. 30.
2. Ed Butler, "A Few Kind Words about Clients," *ADWEEK/Midwest*, April, 1984, p. B.W.C. 30.

active participation and concrete picture-building by the listener. General Electric must always provide a specific and tangible example of the "good things they bring to life." Banks may talk about customer *service,* but to little effect without graphic descriptions of the forms that service takes. The *love* stressed in some PSAs exists in a vacuum unless illustrated with concrete referents of love in action. And since, by their nature, public service announcements usually contend with abstractions, the copywriter should approach PSAs with a special dedication to be vivid, distinct, and explicit. This is also why PSAs must often strive for true *creativity* in order to achieve tangibility in a graphic and meaningful manner.

Analogies

Many products have been christened with highly symbolic names by their parent companies. Sometimes these symbolic or figurative terms may be wonderfully appropriate. For other clients, however, like the hypothetical "April Showers Diaper" account, the analogy can be ludicrously counterproductive. Either way, since one normally can't change the brand name, the copywriter must make certain that the relevance of the analogy is understood by the audience, and understood in a way that puts the product in the most favorable light possible. "The Little Zephyr" may be a potent characterization of the way a fan works, but unless the audience is made aware that a zephyr is a cooling, west wind, such potency never materializes. Barracuda may have been a meaningful name for a fish but, when applied to a compact car, it was hard to pronounce and dredged up a gobbling image that hinted of voraciousness at the gas pump.

Generalities

Some terms have such broad meaning that, unless we can stake out the particular aspect of the meaning we're using, our audience members will be thinking in several, mainly irrelevant directions. To some pharmaceutical companies, it is essential that broadcast consumers be aware of the characteristics of a *capsule* which differentiate it from other entities within the broader classification of *pills.* Likewise, some beauty bar manufacturers are especially concerned that you not lump their cake of "whatever" under the general category called *soap.* Generalities are seldom as graphic as good broadcast copy requires and may blur the key distinction your product needs in order to stand out from the competition. Worse, if generalities in your copy are allowed to multiply, they may give the impression of deliberate vagueness with a consequent rise in receiver mistrust.

Technicalities

Unless the message is aimed at a narrow and specially educated audience, jargon-like references can also be counted on to repel the audience either by making them feel inferior because they don't speak that language or by making them peeved that you haven't cared enough about them to select the plain talk they can understand. If milk is people's only referent for the term *homogenized,* telling them your peanut butter is homogenized will not, by itself, have a positive or meaningful impact. A skin cream designed to penetrate the *epidermis* had better be described in a message that shows and tells just what that epidermis is.

Sometimes, a technical word or phrase is deliberately enlisted early in the copy as a means of heightening the seeming importance of the subject being discussed. This is most often done in spots promoting products for your body, your dental work, or your car. *Eczema, iron deficiency anemia, plaque, halitosis, hydroplaning,* and *rotary power plant* are all used to document the seriousness of the communication to follow and thereby to increase consumer attention. But unless you then clearly articulate what type of malady eczema is, plaque's character and location, and the fact that the rotary power plant in "the Mazda goes hhmmm," the technicality alone won't hold beneficial attention long enough to accomplish your purpose.

Multiplicates

This word is itself a technicality that refers to terms having more than one use or application. If the members of the audience think the Malaga *Pipe* Company turns out products for plumbers when it in fact makes the kind you smoke, your message won't move many meerschaums. In the case of a multiplicate like *pipe,* some people might even be imaging flutes and fifes unless you define that term quickly. With the capability to illustrate from the very first frame, television can stake out the relevant ground much more quickly than radio, but it must be staked out nonetheless. The longer you allow your audience to play mentally with their own favorite referent for *pipe, plane,* or counterpart words having multiple meanings (like *conductor, organ,* and *range*), the greater the probability they will be irretrievably off on their own mental tangents. If your message inadvertently stimulates the listener or viewer to muse about a keyboard instrument (one type of *organ*), he or she will seldom be in the mood to begin worrying over a bodily organ's excess acidity.

Now that we are aware of the kinds of terms requiring definition, we can focus on the available mechanisms for accomplishing this definition. Generally speaking, a word or phrase can lend itself to clarification via any of five methods: negation, location, correlation, derivation, and exemplification.

Negation

This very old rhetorical device sets a thing apart by showing what it is *not* or by demonstrating the conditions to which it does *not* apply. Definition by negation can be a very effective device for the copywriter since it often lends itself to a highly developed copy rhythm in which both the sound and the sense push the message forward:

```
Not a roll-on, not a creme, new Mennon with Pers-stop . . .
```

Provided we don't attempt to milk it too long, negation is also an effective suspense-builder that encourages the listener or viewer to stay tuned to discover just what the thing *is:*

If you think it's butter, but it's not, it's---Chiffon.

The beer that isn't for snobs or the ignorant masses; the beer that's Guiness.

Definition by negation can also be more subtle. It can be used to encourage the audience to reevaluate a product or policy in order to see it in its proper light; to see that its attainment is easier than the audience has heretofore been led to believe. This is the brand of negation used below to explain that eliminating litter does *not* require immense self-sacrifice on the part of anyone.

ANNCR: Presenting great discoveries during Stamp Out Litter Week:
          Three years ago, little Tommy Ferguson discovered that his
          arm would not fall off if he held onto his candy wrapper
          until he reached a wastebasket. Two years ago, Miss Edwina
          Perkins discovered it would not take forever to walk
          twenty extra feet and trashcan the newspaper she'd
          finished reading. Just last year, Alvin 'Big Al' DeAngelo
          discovered that bagging his empties, instead of stomping
          them into the pavement, did not destroy his macho image.
          This Stamp Out Litter Week, you <u>too</u> can discover how easy
          it is NOT to litter. You'll also discover how suave it is
          not to have litter around. This Stamp Out Litter Week,
          start making your own sweeping discoveries.

Location

This definitional device is the most straightforward and the least time-wasting of the five methods available. Through its application, the meaning of the term is made clear by the context in which the term is placed, by the words and phrases that precede and/or follow it:

We <u>pasteurize</u> to purify.

<u>Le</u> <u>Car</u>—Renault's answer to the small car question.

The <u>Serta</u> <u>Perfect-Sleeper</u> mattress

A particularly intense application of definition by location is demonstrated in the following television (Figure 5–3) and radio spots for the Culligan Water Conditioner. In this instance, the copywriter doesn't just equate the word *water with* Culligan but facetiously suggests that the former term be *replaced* by the latter. The radio spot also is notable for its 45/15 construction (refer to our chapter 3 discussion of spot lengths). This division allows the major portion of the commercial to be paired with any of a number of seasonal 15-second bumpers.

(MUSIC: UNDER THROUGHOUT)
(SFX: WATER RUNNING IN SHOWER)
GUY: (YELLING) Come out of the shower Alice---you're gonna
             use up all the hot Culligan!

Figure 5–3. *(Courtesy of Kathy Mullins, Marsteller Inc.)*

ANNCR:	Ordinary hard or problem household water can be annoying and expensive. So more and more people are thinking 'Culligan' instead!
TEEN GIRL:	Mom, do we wash Dad's funny golf pants in hot or cold Culligan?
ANNCR:	A Culligan Water Conditioner saves you money on soaps. Helps keep your tub and sinks cleaner. Even reduces dishwater spots on glassware!
	No one can meet the growing need for high-quality water like Culligan. So maybe today, you call it 'water'---but tomorrow?

```
(SFX:       BIRDS CHIRPING, POWERFUL GOLF SWING.)
GUY:        Aw, tough luck, Jay—
(SFX:       KER-PLUNK)
GUY:        —right in the Culligan!
:10
(first
optional):  Right now your Culligan Dealer is talking turkey! Just
            buy or rent a Culligan Water Conditioner or Drinking
            Water System before December 24, and you'll get a
            coupon good for a delicious Swift's Butterball Turkey!
SING:       The future calls—
MAN:        Hey, Culligan man!
SING:       The future calls for Culligan.
:05
(final
opening):   Offer good through December 24 at your Chicago area or
            Northwest Indiana Culligan Dealer. Void where
            prohibited.
```

(Courtesy of Kathy Mullins, Marsteller Inc.)

Definition by location can be an important tool in continuity writing, too, since it preserves a sense of unbroken flow and idea unity while still identifying the term in question. In the following continuity lyric, the listener is fully apprised of just what WMAQ 'truckin' programming is without the necessity of giving the *process* of definition a distracting and pace-slowing profile:

```
Well I been pushin' this big ol' heavy rig, and I still got miles
to go;

But I'm never lonesome through the night, I got Country Music
Radio.

Push that button and set that dial on 6-7-0.

And keep on truckin' with WMAQ.

It helps me keep my wheels a-rollin',

It helps me stay right on the line;

Tells me where it's rainin' and where it's clear,

An' keeps me right on time.

Well it's a friendly voice through the lonely night while I'm
clickin' off those miles,

I keep on truckin', with WMAQ, I keep on truckin', with WMAQ
(repeats and fades)
```

(Courtesy of TM Productions.)

Correlation

Comparing the term in question to other terms that can be shown to have a somewhat similar meaning is the process of definition by correlation. Through this device, we are systematically and colorfully attempting to *connect* the less known or less vibrant term with one possessing much more image potential for our audience. Thus, definition by correlation is often intrinsically *creative:*

Like a thousand busy fingers, Lustre Creme goes to work to smooth wrinkles.

Wash 'N Dry is soap and water to go.

Peak Anti-Freeze is like chicken soup for your car.

Hathaway Car Cleaners treats your car as gently as a mother bathes her baby.

Sometimes the script doesn't articulate both parts of the correlation but rather, provides the audience with only the selected analogy. The television treatment in Figure 5–4 shows a single tree to be a living artifact of our country's history. The vague term *history* is not even mentioned but instead becomes totally correlated with, and tangibly represented by, the progressive growth of the tree itself and the sound of the epoch the tree has survived. History is effectively defined and exploited on behalf of the central copy point without the word itself ever having to be used.

Derivation

Speaking of history, the presentation of a term's derivation, of its semantic or geographic heritage, is another definitional method. The original meaning of the whole term can be illuminated, or we can break down the term into its constituent parts and show the specific significance of each:

In Europe, where our beer originated, <u>Fass</u> beer meant <u>draft</u> beer.

Penny Ante: the beauty soap inspired by the beauty queen.

Engelsen's Danish Bon-Bons---Old World candy with a New World zing.

When our country was still young, people from both sides of the Alps came to settle in California. With them came their long tradition for vintage excellence; the <u>Italian-Swiss Colony</u> tradition.

Though a dictionary quotation can sometimes be used to present the derivation, many audience members will be anything but captivated by such a boring and stilted approach. It is true that, in the case of a professional-technical market already interested in the field from which the term comes, the dictionary blurb may be the quickest way available to show the word's heritage. For less well delineated target groups, however, a less clustered and cluttered derivational definition must be used to retain attention:

<u>Production</u> <u>Note</u>: Gladys is irreconcilably cheery
throughout while Howard is surly and groggy until
consuming the product

GLADYS: Good morning, dear.

HOWARD: What's good about it?

GLADYS: Any morning you can wake up to Ginger Pops is a good
morning.

HOWARD: Ginger who?

GLADYS: Ginger <u>Pops,</u> dear. <u>Foggarty</u>'s Ginger Pops. Old-fashioned
gingerbread in a new, round shape.

HOWARD: So what, Gladys? Who needs some off-the-wall ginger
what—

ANNCR: (V.O.) In the time it
takes to grow a tree, you can
grow a country.

SFX: SOUND MONTAGE: YANKEE
DOODLE; LINCOLN'S GETTYSBURG
ADDRESS; OH SUSANNA;

OVER THERE; "WE HAVE
NOTHING TO FEAR BUT FEAR
ITSELF"...F.D.R; YOU OUGHTA
BE IN PICTURES;

JACK ARMSTRONG, THE ALL-
AMERICAN BOY- "WAVE THE
FLAG FOR HUDSON HIGH";

"BENNY WAS BORN IGNORANT
AND HAS BEEN LOSING GROUND
EVER SINCE"...LAUGHTER-- FRED
ALLEN;

THE FLAT FOOT FLOOGIE;
JOHN DALY'S RADIO REPORT OF
ATTACK ON PEARL HARBOR;
SENTIMENTAL JOURNEY;

"ASK NOT WHAT YOUR COUNTRY
CAN DO FOR YOU..." J.F.K.;
COUNTDOWN AND ROCKET
LAUNCH.

ANNCR: (V.O.) But it only takes
a minute to wipe out a century.

A flash. And nothing. And even
the birds won't come any more.

A Public Service Campaign of the Advertising Council

On behalf of the U.S. Forest Service, State Foresters, U.S. Dept. of Agriculture
Volunteer Advertising Agency: Foote, Cone & Belding, Inc. (Los Angeles)
Volunteer Campaign Coordinator: James P. Felton, AVCO Financial Services

Smokey Bear Series 52
CNFF-6260
(formerly released as
FS68-FP55-60)

Figure 5–4. *(Courtesy of The Advertising Council, Inc.)*

```
GLADYS:   Pops, dear. Foggarty's Ginger Pops. Gramdma depended on
          Foggarty's Ginger in her baking. And now they've come
          out with these new little nuggets to pop you out of bed
          and wake you up right.
HOWARD:   Okay, okay, I'll try the stuff. But I'm in a hurry. Make
          it snappy.
GLADYS:   Not snaps, dear, Pops. Fogarty's Ginger Pops. They're
          ready to eat right out of the box.
HOWARD:   Oh, swell.
GLADYS:   Or with milk and sugar. Here, Howard.
HOWARD:   (Chewing) Hey! I haven't tasted a gingerbread this good
          since Mom used to make it for me and Pops.
GLADYS:   Right, dear.
HOWARD:   Huh?
GLADYS:   Pops. Fogarty's Ginger Pops.
```

The *tradition* of the product (another name for its derivation) can be shown on television, too, and this definitional approach works even if the "product" is an institution like the National Guard (see Figure 5–5).

Exemplification

Finally, we can define a term by citing examples of situations to which it applies or, alternatively, by enumerating the essential components of what the term represents. With the first method, we help to define *Excedrin* by saying:

```
Excedrin is great for relief of mild headache pain. If pain
persists, see your doctor.
```

Thus, we have been both truthful with our audience and respectful of the Federal Trade Commission and Food and Drug Administration in citing, in exemplifying, conditions for which the product is and is not intended.

With the second method, we can illuminate the performance of the Little Zephyr Fan through an exposition, an exemplification, of its namesake's effect and behavior as a gentle, cooling breeze. We can identify the key characteristics of the original "zephyr" and thereby also identify the manner in which the product that preempted the term is promised to perform.

The Kraft Miracle Whip photoboard (Figure 5–6) skillfully blends both exemplification procedures. The spot cites uses to which the product can be put and ties it to the old term's essence (salad dressing) as well as to the new term (bread spread). The commercial thereby defines how central Miracle Whip is to any sandwich's attainment.

In our study of definition so far, we have isolated five categories of terms that require defining (abstractions, analogies, generalities, technicalities, and multiplicates) as well as five techniques for defining them (negation, location, correlation, derivation, and exemplification). It should not be surprising that there are also, as a consequence, five criteria to be applied; five questions to be asked, as to whether the term under scrutiny has been defined successfully. We

Figure 5-5.   *(Courtesy of Gerald Downey, Needham, Harper & Steers, Inc.)*

need to ascertain if the definition we've chosen has truly been able to categorize, familiarize, particularize, synonymize, and (to coin a word) "discriminatize" the term with which we've had to deal.

Categorize

The chosen definition must always make it clear into what category, into what classification, the spotlighted word or phrase fits. Does the listener or viewer know that a Celica is a car and not a carpet? That STP is an engine additive and not a toothpaste ingredient? That the public service "Double Up" campaign is promoting car pooling and not free love? That Fat Freddie is a meat snack and not an overweight cigar?

ANNCR: Chips, chips, chips. Candy, candy, candy. Day in and day out. You get tired of the same snacks all the time. It's enough to drive your tastebuds into a permanent stupor. So give your taste buds a break. Try Fat Freddie beef summer sausage. It's not hard and crunchy, or soft and gooey--- just chewy and delicious. Fat Freddie summer sausage is a

KRAFT   MIRACLE WHIP
"Diner" :30

WAITRESS: Yeah?

1ST MAN: Club sandwich. Heavy on the Miracle Whip Salad Dressing.

COOK: No Miracle Whip.

WAITRESS: No Miracle Whip today.

1ST MAN: Oh, no. Well, I'll have the soup.

WAITRESS: Yeah?

2ND MAN: Ham on rye. Miracle Whip Salad Dressing on both sides.

WAITRESS: No Miracle Whip today. 2ND MAN: Oh, no. Well, I'll have the soup.

ANNCR: A sandwich just isn't a sandwich, without the tangy zip of Miracle Whip Salad Dressing.

The Bread Spread from Kraft.

WAITRESS: We're out of Miracle Whip. 3RD MAN: Oh, then I'll...

WAITRESS: We're out of soup.

Figure 5–6. *(Courtesy of Leslie Berger, J. Walter Thompson USA.)*

```
snack-size stick of real beef, mildly seasoned. Look for
the yellow wrapper at your local Showtime Market. Treat
your taste buds to the meaty pick-me-up. Fat Freddie beef
summer sausage.
```

Familiarize

The definition selected must also use words that are more familiar to the target audience than the term we set out to define. Otherwise, we're worse off than when we started, and what was originally a small clarification problem can become a semantic quagmire in which all understanding is bogged down.

```
The Acme Heat Pump is a temperature and condensation-sensitive
thermostatic mechanism that utilizes calibrated aperture closure
activity to manage thermal emissions.
```

By this juncture, the perplexed listener can't even *remember* the term *heat pump,* let alone understand what it is or does. An explanation like the following, on the other hand, casts the term in a simpler and more graphic mold:

```
The new Columbia dynagroove process will make your stereo sound
better than ever. If you look at one of our records under a
microscope you can see the little valleys. . . .
```

Though a "dynagroove" is outside of most people's frame of reference, virtually everyone can visualize what "a little valley" looks like, and the familiarization test has therefore been successfully passed.

Particularize

The essential characteristics of the term, the aspects pertaining to it we wish our audience to remember, must all be addressed in the definition. In its most succinct form, the particularization process normally entails consumer cognizance of the product, service, or station *name,* and of just *what* that product, service, or station can do for each consumer out there. A listener or viewer without this knowledge will be in no position to select what we offer or, even, to keep us in mind. For a subject like Danish Fruitcake Pipe Tobacco, the writer must preserve the imagery of the name while still deliberately specifying the actual use to which the product is put.

```
ANNCR:  You are a self-made man. You've worked hard to get where
        you are today. That's why you'd like smoking Danish
        Fruitcake Pipe Tobacco in your pipe. The pipe tobacco that
        stands up for itself and for you. Danish Fruitcake Tobacco
        may cost more. But you'd know this mild, fruity blend is
        well worth it. That old Danish recipe is always fresh—
        because it's vacuum-packed. Watch heads turn as you light
        up your pipe, and that rich, fruitcake-like aroma teases
        the air. Like its namesake, Danish Fruitcake Tobacco is
        never harsh, never bitter, never dull. So indulge
        yourself. Danish Fruitcake is not your run-of-the-pack
        pipe tobacco. And you're not a run-of-the-pack man.
```

Synonymize

Whatever the words from which we've constructed our definition, they had better be terms other than the words or phrases to be defined. Gertrude Stein's "a rose is a rose is a rose" may have made it big in the poet business, but it's no way to peddle American Beauties. Telling the listener unfamiliar with a carburetor that "Phelps Carburetor Cleaner will improve carburetion" is an exercise in futility. And praising the "top-notch security provided by Jones Security Service" is not meaningful praise at all.

Using a term to define itself rather than employing associated synonyms is a bad broadcast practice for two reasons. First, mere repetition of the same word will never sharpen the clarity of that word. At best, the consumer may remember the word—but not its meaning or affiliated brand. And "ingredient" terms that exist in such a vacuum—terms like Penetresence and Acrisil—are themselves seldom remembered for long. Second, the redundant use of the same word, whether part of a definition or not, simply doesn't make for vivid or colorful copy. It will therefore not engage the attention or the imagination of our audience, and the term and its message will simply vanish without a trace in that sea of continuity in which every listener and viewer is awash.

Everyone, for example, knows the term *heart attack*. But not everyone knows its varied signals, and the constant repetition of the "heart attack" phrase does nothing to clarify them. So this American Heart Association PSA literally illuminates the symptomatic synonyms that signal and define the main term.

Video	Audio
SILHOUETTE OF HUMAN BODY IN LIMBO	SFX: HEART BEAT ANNOUNCER: The American Heart Association wants you to know the signals of heart attack.
MULTI COLOR LIGHT PULSE ON THAT AFFECTED PART OF THE BODY, IN SYNC WITH NARRATION.	Pressure or pain in the middle of your chest lasting approximately two minutes or longer---the pain may spread through the chest and down the left arm---Pain in your neck or jaw---or, through the shoulders and down both arms.
LIGHTS STOP PULSING—BACKGROUND BECOMES GREENISH	Sweating, nausea, or shortness of breath may also accompany these pains.
Z/N TO HEART AREA	If you experience any of these, don't take any chances; get to your doctor.
DIS AHA LOGO	The American Heart Association. We're fighting for your life.

(Courtesy of Virginia Tannebring, American Heart Association.)

"Discriminatize"

Finally, the definition we've constructed must separate the term to be defined from all other terms with which it is likely to be confused; must make sure that our audience is well prepared to "beware of imitations." Since the term to be defined is often a brand name, a product function, or an essential ingredient, the audience's ability to discriminate our product or service from competitors' with which it might accidentally or intentionally be confused is of paramount importance to the copywriter and the client. Because the term *spearmint* is not, in itself, a protected trademark, the Wrigley people who so prominently display "spearmint" as part of their brand name had to make a point of telling their audiences:

```
Many gums have the name 'Spearmint.'
But only one has the Wrigley name.
```

The Xeroxes, Jellos, and Kleenexes of the world have a special problem in this regard since, in common usage, their brand name has been appropriated as the generic referent for their entire product category. Even though this has some beneficial aspects in the area of brand recall, it also creates a constant need to remind consumers to buy Jello *brand gelatin,* rent Xerox *photocopiers,* and blow their noses in Kleenex *facial tissues.*

If such generic/brand confusion is often an inadvertent marketplace phenomenon, other misconceptions are more deliberately contrived. The company that put out the low-cost "English Sterling" cologne was not entirely unaware of the much more expensive "English Leather," "British Sterling," and the huge media budgets that were helping to promote both. The discount "Vacation" car wax that came packaged in a bottle virtually identical to that holding the full-price "Holiday" was an interesting if not wholly accidental variation on the same theme. It cannot be stressed too strongly, therefore, that every copy effort possible must be made to delineate clearly and to discriminate your client's brand or service from others for which it might accidentally or purposely be mistaken. When the term to be defined is a brand or trademark, proper definition is not just important but may be essential to the survival of the account (or at least, to your survival as a copywriter for it).

The subject of definition cannot be put to rest without a brief mention of a special advertising phenomenon that might be referred to as "antidefinition." As a means of capturing audience attention and boosting memorability, some firms have deliberately positioned a term without any initial definition and have almost baited the audience to synonymize for themselves. When the term is also part of the brand name, a coy little innuendo is set up that tickles the receiver without really inhibiting brand recognition:

```
Dad, can I have a glass of Culligan?

Midacize that car!

Can you imagine what it's like to go a whole year without
flicking your Bic?

Ever been beeped on top of a ladder? I have. By my People Beeper.
(a pocket signaling device)
```

The New York woman; when her needs are financial, her reaction is Chemical. (a slogan for Chemical Bank New York Trust Company)

VALIDATION

Let's suppose you've achieved our logical link between two previously unattached subjects. Let's even assume that the link is unbreakable. And let's further assume you've isolated the terms in need of defining, used one or more of the five definitional methods, and found the result to be categorized, familiarized, particularized, synonymized, and "discriminatized." You are now ready, not to relax, but to take a step back from your copy and attempt to evaluate it as a whole; to predict its overall effect on those listeners and viewers who are definitely *not* waiting breathlessly for your next message to reach them.

This stepping back, this process of speculating on how your piece of copy will be received, can be dubbed "validation." It's a process encompassing three separate perspectives which, when all brought to bear, are effective protections against losing the market forest in the trees of your copy. These three mechanisms are lovingly known as The Boss's Haymaker, The Fuller Brush Odyssey, and The Proletariat Promenade.

The Boss's Haymaker

This potentially knock-out punch might be delivered by an agency creative director, a station sales manager, or even the corner druggist for whom you're freelancing. The Boss's Haymaker is usually thrown right after he or she has read your proposed message and entails nothing more than one simple question: "But what does this *mean?*"

See how unstylish and clumsy it is? No seeming attention to motivational research, psychological appeals, or the tag line that's sheer inspiration. Not even the courtesy and sportsmanship to debate copy imagery or how slickly it flows off the page. Instead, The Boss's Haymaker just flails right into the *solar plexus* of the whole matter; to the fundamental purpose your message was supposed to achieve. If you can't respond with a lightning, one-sentence answer, maybe you never even took the trouble to think about the assignment before stepping into the ring. Maybe you just started writing with no thought whatever to your overall game plan.

Yet, even if you manage a counter to "But what does this mean?" you may still be disqualified. For, if you respond by saying that your treatment is intended to show the Mack-the-Knife Vegetable Cutter's durability, but your copy pays homage to a big tossed salad, The Boss's Haymaker has hit home. Somewhere in the writing process you backed out of contention and ignored your copy's main event.

Get into training by asking yourself "But what does this mean?" after you've finished writing a piece of copy. If there is time, ask that question again the following day. The message may look much different to you after a night away from it because time is a great refresher of objectivity. Either way, turning the

Boss's Haymaker on yourself *now* will avoid the need for a lot of fancy footwork in somebody's office *later.*

The Fuller Brush Odyssey

This copy validation vehicle was pioneered by radio's first great salesman, Arthur Godfrey. In forced convalescence and with nothing to do but listen to the radio, Godfrey tried to discern why some commercials were so much more effective in grabbing and convincing him than others. The answer seemed to be that many spots simply blabbed at "you folks out there in radio land." There was little or no personalization; little or no attempt at simulating and stimulating a sense of one-to-one communication before dragging the product in by the foot. The successful messages, on the other hand, took the time and trouble to establish a feeling of friendly conversation before waving the product in front of the listener's ear.

Good copy, in other words, seemed to present the same warmth yet direct-ness that a Fuller Brush salesperson must exhibit on your porch. Good copy, like a good "brush pusher," has first to sell itself. That keeps the door to the listener's or viewer's attention open long enough to get the product out of the sample case. Advertisers and their copywriters "tend to forget that they are door-to-door salespeople, invading people's privacy for less than altruistic pur-poses," chides Malcolm MacDougall, former president and creative director of SSC&B. "They seem to ignore the fact that people are just as wary of the adver-tising that knocks on their door—and just as quick to slam that door. People slam the door on almost 80 percent of the advertising we send them. When you look at some of the commercials on the air today, it's easy to see why."[3]

The Fuller Brush Odyssey, then, asks copywriters to put themselves in the place of door-to-door salespersons. Imagine yourself standing on a long street of stoops mouthing the essence of the message you've constructed for broad-cast. If that conjures up doors being slammed in your face, The Fuller Brush Odyssey should cause you to rethink your copy's style and thrust before hitting the copy development pavement once more.

The Proletariat Promenade

This third validation test requires you to reverse the role-playing that you exercised in The Fuller Brush Odyssey. In The Proletariat Promenade, pretend that you're a gas station attendant, a check-out clerk, or the person who sat next to you on the bus. Forget that you're a copywriter; forget that you've written the spot; forget everything about the whole assignment and just go blank. (If going blank is easy for you, consult another book.)

Now, as that attendant, clerk, or bus-rider—does this piece of copy make sense? Is it credible? Does it come across in terms with which you can identify? Or does the message make you want to walk away, take a coffee break, or move to another seat? Vary the roles you mentally play to represent several segments of the audience at which your copy is aimed. But remember—The

3. Malcolm MacDougall, "Getting the Foot in the Door," *ADWEEK/Midwest,* March 12, 1984, p. 32.

Proletariat Promenade does not involve talking down to people (you might want to review the pertinent section of chapter 2).

"What do I want to see in my living room?" asks Keller-Crescent Advertising's Al Samuelson. "Simply, commercials that haven't forgotten the basics. Commercials that have some regard for me as something other than a sales target, and that recognize they are guests in my home. I want to see commercials that have such a fitting balance between strategy and execution that they beguile me into paying attention to them, and after they've finished, leave me feeling rewarded for having done so."[4]

It is deadly to assume that, because you are writing for a mass or non-elite audience, there is no need to worry about receiver common sense. It may be true that educational levels vary from demographic group to demographic group, but common sense is randomly distributed among all ages, income levels, and social strata. Proportionately, there are just as many (or just as few) foolish souls in Fat Cat City as there are on Poverty Row; and the copywriter who doesn't appreciate this verity will have trouble communicating with both places. As the Fuller Brush Odyssey should have helped to point out, your copy needs listener/viewer friendship, and this does not flow from patronization. The Proletariat Promenade should help you to evaluate continually whether the words you write are enabling the types of people at which your message is aimed to put themselves in the picture; to see themselves using that product or service you are striving so hard to describe. Lois Korey, Needham, Harper & Steers' executive vice president, states the matter this way:

> A healthy respect for the audience would cause a lot of storyboards to get junked before they can junk up the air waves. Given the budget, the talent, the technical innovations, the bright, creative minds available to produce a single 30-second commercial, it is inexcusable that such a high percentage of them would insult the intelligence of a brussels sprout. Not in production or casting. But in the essence of the commercial: the story—the dialogue—the message.
>   Underestimating the public is not just foolish; it's costly (as many advertisers have discovered to their sorrow). People can no longer be charmed out of their money by a good musical arrangement, a pretty smile or the dulcet assurances of the voice-over announcer (followed by four legal-department disclaimers). Audiences have become too sophisticated for such sleight of mind. They are demanding, and are entitled to, credibility.[5]

PROHIBITION

In addition to all of our other concerns as copywriters, we must avoid certain techniques no matter how much they might seem to assist or enhance our creation, definition, and validation enterprises. Several of these prohibitions are mandated by the laws and regulations associated with the Federal Communications Commission, the Federal Trade Commission, the Food and Drug Administration, or a host of other agencies. Since this is not a legal casebook, suffice it

4. Al Samuelson, writing in "Monday Memo," *Broadcasting Magazine*, April 18, 1983, p. 18.
5. Lois Korey, writing in "Monday Memo," *Broadcasting Magazine*, September 10, 1979, p. 24.

to say that commercial broadcasting, in countries where it is even allowed, is among the most regulated of enterprises, with large and complex bodies of law and litigation to back up this regulation. If anything in your copy seems at all questionable in its (1) legal, or (2) "good taste" aspects, it should be checked out long before you even think about hitting the airwaves. Even a giant like General Foods had to reverse engines quickly when a copywriter's inspired "explore the outer reaches of your mind" line was used to promote its *Space Dust* candy. The slogan may have been creative, but the link it forged for children was euphemistically unacceptable. Likewise, when California's Jack-in-the Box drive-in restaurants decided to make their image more adult—and accomplished this with the on-camera dynamiting of their happy clown emblem—the impact was immediate and unanticipated. Viewers complained loudly about the depicted violence and brutality, and the spots met a quick and well-deserved demise. Though this example involved audience resentment rather than a governmental raised eyebrow, the negative spin-off for the advertiser was no less real.

For their own protection, the broadcasting networks, group-owners, and individual stations have devised a number of guidelines and policies governing what is and is not permissible in broadcast program, commercial, and continuity content. A general reading of these specific corporate documents should give you a reasonable feel for the concerns and constraints relative to the airing of what you write. This is important. For, if a network, group, or station "continuity acceptance" executive refuses your copy, it can play havoc with the most finely tuned media schedule, bring you and your client into disrepute, and create public relations problems that nobody needs and few can solve. Appendix C contains samples of these broadcasting policies, from networks and individual station sources.

In 1983, for example, ABC said "that fully 35 percent of the 32,500 original storyboards it will review this year will be returned for changes or additional information. NBC says it asked for more information or substantiation of claims on about 25 percent of the 55,000 storyboards it reviewed; it asked for changes in another 10 percent. About 3 percent will be rejected altogether at ABC and NBC. CBS' figures were not available."[6]

Should a complaint arise *after* station/network airing, the National Advertising Division (NAD) of the Council of Better Business Bureaus may investigate it as another part of the industry's self-regulatory structure. If no voluntary resolution is achieved at this level, the National Advertising Review Board (NARB) then may come into the picture as a final, but still nongovernmental, adjudicator. As of 1984, the NAD was reviewing an average of 15 cases per month, according to its senior vice president, Lorraine Reid, with about six months required to settle a case. Because of this time lag, a dispute between competing advertisers is likely to result, instead, in a lawsuit. NAD's Reid herself admits that "there are times when it is very appropriate for advertisers to go right to court. . . . If

6. Paul Farhi, "Agencies, Networks Battle over Censors' Role," *ADWEEK/Midwest*, November 14, 1983, p. 50.

they're aggrieved enough and want an immediate [remedy,] they can't go through us."[7] The expense of litigation, of course, is easily expressed in multiples of even the best-paid copywriter's salary—a salary that could well be terminated if the suit was the result of careless writing.

If the government gets into the act, it's hard to say where things might end. Your client may, for example, be required by the Federal Trade Commission to engage in *corrective advertising;* a process whose constitutionality was upheld in 1978 by the Supreme Court in a case involving Listerine. In this instance, the FTC order required that the advertiser, Warner-Lambert, include the following statement in the next $10 million of its advertising (an amount equal to Listerine's annual advertising budget for the years 1962–72):

Listerine will not help prevent colds or sore throats or lessen their severity.[8]

In 1984, the FTC also reaffirmed and refined its commitment to its advertising substantiation program whereby advertisers and agencies must be certain they have the proper evidence in hand before disseminating product performance claims.

Several years before, Benton & Bowles' group executive Frederick Sulcer had surveyed the regulatory landscape and lamented: "I honestly believe we often spend more hours clearing commercials than creating them. . . . There are special guidelines for children, over-the-counter drugs, automobiles, alcoholic beverages, savings stamps, guarantees, the Boy Scouts, government buildings, federal agencies, the President and the First Lady. There's always the chance some regulator will decide we have disparaged a competitor, shown an ethnic group in what they think is a disparaging setting, shown behavior they find anti-social or violated their personal standard of good taste."[9]

In the intervening years, these adversarial conditions have certainly not diminished. If anything, they have merely shifted, in the United States, at least, to a greater proportion of civil as compared to governmental actions. "Court action over advertising claims will almost certainly multiply during the next few years," predicts William Wilkie of the University of Florida Business School, "partly because of the intense market-share battles being waged in so many categories, but also because of the FTC's recent disappearing act. All companies have the right to fair advertising, and if the government doesn't help provide this, then private litigation may be the only answer. It may be one of the best ways to protect market standing against competition."[10]

Whether self-regulatory, governmental, or judicial, prohibitions against deceptive, unsubstantiated, offensive, or just plain sloppy advertising are not about to disappear. Broadcasting is too powerful and high-profile a medium to escape

7. Gail Belsky, "Playing the Short Suit Against 'False' Ad Claims," *ADWEEK/Midwest*, February 13, 1984, p. 26.
8. "FTC Power on Corrective Ads Left Untouched by Supreme Court," *Broadcasting Magazine*, April 10, 1978, p. 80.
9. Frederick Sulcer, writing in "Monday Memo," *Broadcasting Magazine*, July 23, 1979, p. 22.
10. William Meyers, "Here Comes the Judge," *ADWEEK/Midwest*, December, 1984, p. F. 17.

such regulatory notice. Yet, the prudent copywriter must also be guided by four operational prohibitions. Though not specific parts of governmental or industry policy, they are of such broad and continuing concern as to require special mention and highlighting. Because they may dovetail with so many provisions common to official edicts and statutes, these four prohibitions should perhaps be accorded the status of occupational commandments to be engraved on the top of your typewriter:

I.   Don't Be Irrelevant
II. Don't Be Nasty
III. Don't Stay Ugly
IV. Don't Make Saints

Don't Be Irrelevant

Some people will do anything to attract attention to themselves—or to their copy. As we've seen previously, a good attention-getter is vital if your message is to grab the audience's eyes and ears. But an attention-getter that has nothing to do with the copy's main point, or main point that has nothing to do with the offered product or service, is a lie and a theft. It promises the receiver something your message is never prepared to give and robs him or her of the time each expended in taking the whole message in. Loud noises, screams, and other "now that I've got your attention" rip-offs resurrect the spectre of the huckster copywriter. Spots like this may show imagination, but an imagination that is both unprincipled and undisciplined:

(SFX: WAILING SIREN UP AND UNDER)

ANNCR: (In a panic) Fire! Fire! What a tragedy! What a disaster! All those poor people and what it does to them. Makes you sick right down to your stomach. Yes, the tragedy of heartburn, of excess acidity that comes from eating all that 'fast food,' is a national calamity. But all the flaming agony can be prevented. Stop burning yourself out at those plastic food palaces and start enjoying how 'cool' a good meal can be at Barney's Beefsteak Bistro. Barney's Beefsteak Bistro, corner of Fulton and Business Route 9, takes the time and care to prepare a meal that stays with you; but stays with you the right way. A lunch or dinner at Barney's leaves you cool and collected; not hot and bothered. Plan now for a relaxing noon or evening at Barney's Beefsteak Bistro, Fulton and Business Route 9. Barney fires up his trusty charcoal; not your tender stomach.

(SFX: WAILING SIREN UP AND OUT TO TIME)

Barney's itself deserves to burn, most listeners would conclude. And so does the copywriter who wrote such irrelevant trash.

Don't Be Nasty

People do not enjoy having their egos bruised—especially by some jerk on the television or radio. So copy that tries to bludgeon the audience into accepting your point of view through sarcasm and ridicule is bound to go down in flames, just like Barney's steaks. Few writers deliberately attempt to disparage their audience, but ill-considered lines like the following do no less harm just because they are oversights:

```
Even you can operate a Sharkfin outboard on the very first try.
```

```
Well, Mom, are you about to bake another batch of those drab,
dull, everyday cookies?
```

```
It's time the Hades Oil and Gas Company showed you a few things
about home heating.
```

```
Banking is simpler than ever at Fensterwald. That's why we know
you'll enjoy it.
```

Nastiness is also a problem when directed at the competition. Until 1971, both CBS and ABC refused to accept advertising that "named names," and their stance helped keep both fair and unscrupulous product comparisons off most of the airwaves. If two of the networks wouldn't accept the copy, it was just too hard to get proper penetration for it. Then the Federal Trade Commission ruled that euphemisms such as "Brand X" and "our larger competitor" were confusing the public and depriving them of meaningful consumer information. The two networks got the message and joined NBC in permitting the specification of which "Brand X" the copy was talking about. This resulted in a significant upswing in what are officially known as "comparative" commercials and in the consequent rise in the previously mentioned advertiser versus advertiser litigation.

It must be made clear that comparison, by itself, is neither evil nor nasty. As long as the focus of the message is on the positive aspect of your product (comparison) and not on the alleged negative attributes of the competition's product (disparagement), the practice can play a beneficial role for both the advertiser and the consumer. But if a marketer "can prove that consumers are picking up a false or misleading message from a competitor's commercial, then the spot will, in all probability, be found objectionable in a court of law," cautions advertising expert William Meyers.[11] University of Wisconsin Journalism Professor Ivan Preston adds that "In the legal arena, an ad's literal statements don't matter nearly as much as its implications. The bottom line for judicial judgments is how the public perceives a sales message rather than how the copy reads."[12] So keep in mind that the thrust of any honest comparative message is to place your client's product or service in the best verifiable light.

11. Ibid.
12. Ibid.

The aim is not to place the competition under some unsubstantiated cloud, a cloud that all too likely could rain on your own parade.

The following radio spot illustrates a *positive* comparison. Ajax candles aren't disparaged—in fact, they're conceded to look the same and be less expensive. But the Re-lites advantage is described in such a manner that a key superiority shines through—a superiority that comes from concentrating on an honest Re-lites *attribute* rather than on a competitor *flaw.*

ANNCR: If you're looking for something to brighten up your next
          birthday party, then you're looking for Re-lites. Re-lites
          look just like ordinary Ajax birthday candles. And Ajax
          candles are a lot cheaper. But unlike ordinary candles,
          when you blow Re-lites out, they re-light. By themselves.
          Magically. And they'll keep on relighting as long as you
          have the breath to keep blowing them out. Don't miss out
          on the laughs that Re-lites can bring to your next
          birthday party. Re-lites. The more you blow, the more they
          glow.

Don't Stay Ugly

This copywriter's commandment addresses the issue of offensive or unpleasant words and pictures. Particularly with an entertainment medium such as radio or television, people will be patently unwilling to expose themselves voluntarily to extended periods of agony. Gone is that poor suffering mortal with the pounding hammers and the flashing lightning echoing through his skull. Gone, too, are the people bent over with the torture of constipation and assailed by the torment of skin itch. Spots that dwell on such images can appeal only to masochists—and there aren't enough of them to bolster many sales curves. If you must depict a discomforting image in your commercial, don't wait too long before introducing relief. And in order to avoid breaking our first copywriter's commandment, that relief had better be a relevant result of using our product.

Public service announcements may be tempted to ignore this commandment more than are their commercial counterparts. How many PSAs expend virtually their entire time in showing us starving orphans or ravaged wildlife? Certainly these are vital concerns. But the message that illuminates nothing but the grotesque effects of this or that calamity will cause listener/viewer tune-out before folks learn how they can help. It does the starving orphans or endangered species little good if the people who could have mitigated their plight were driven away prematurely.

Don't stay ugly. If you must use a repelling image, get through it as soon as possible to make way for the relief. And make certain such relief is a tangible and logical outgrowth of the product or service for which you have drawn the assignment. The Exxon Office Systems commercial shown in Figure 5–7 fully respects this stricture. The grating sound of loud banks of business machines is introduced early, and then quickly eliminated as the relief-giving Ink Jet Printer is brought on the scene.

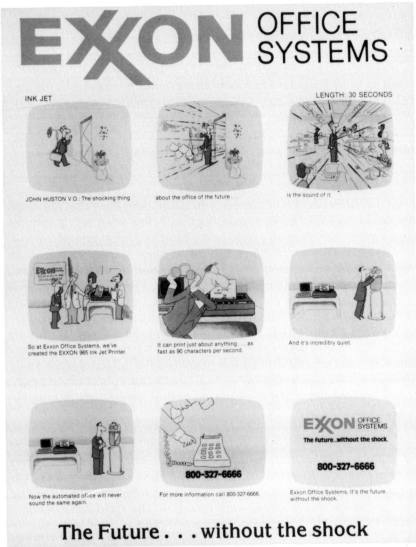

Figure 5–7. *(Courtesy of Kathryn Spiess, Marsteller Inc.)*

Don't Make Saints

Inexperienced copywriters tend to try too hard; they tend to oversell the product or service to such a degree that the listener or viewer may well conclude it is just too good to be true. If the product, service, or program sounds so unbelievably spectacular that we expect the Three Wise Men to come over the hill, the copy needs total rethinking. Superlatives (words of overpraise), will simply not be credible to an audience that is bombarded daily by hundreds of spots and promotion pieces. Our jaded receiver is well aware that heaven is not "just around the corner from where you live" or "yours by mail for only three ninety-eight." Copy that attempts to say different is begging to be scorned. Imagine how you would react to the following pitch:

ANNCR: Spectacular! Stupendous! Those are just some of the words
         used to describe Gramma Hubbard's Hominy Bread. Gramma
         Hubbard's Hominy is the best thing ever to come out of an
         American oven. Its texture is unsurpassed. Its taste is
         incredibly delicious. And Gramma Hubbard's Hominy Bread
         makes the most tremendous toast your taste buds have ever
         experienced. Try a loaf of this fantastic bread
         breakthrough. Witness the marvel of real milled hominy.
         Gramma Hubbard's Hominy Bread.

In fact, even if your product is as good as you claim, describing that goodness too enthusiastically may still be counterproductive. A few years ago, a spot for Dupont's Xerex antifreeze showed a hole being punched into a can of the stuff and the product package then resealing itself. The claim seemed so incredible that many viewers thought it was phoney. So did the Federal Trade Commission. They required Dupont to substantiate the claim that Xerex would work in a similar way to seal small holes in a car's cooling system. Dupont did substantiate it and the FTC backed off. But some viewers still could not believe a coolant could perform so amazingly. Moral: sometimes even a truly spectacular product needs more humility than it deserves.

Don't canonize your product or service. Don't make a saint out of every account to which you're assigned. Overzealous praise causes mistrust to mushroom and may prevent the audience from accepting suggestions that would otherwise have been truly beneficial for them.

If it seems as though everyone—government, industry, client, and consumer—is looking over your shoulder, you have acquired a healthfully paranoic view of copywriting today. By its very nature, broadcasting's power and potency attract the close scrutiny of a wide variety of groups with both legitimate and self-serving axes to grind. It is not easy to balance the conflicting pressures and crosspurposes of the various forces at work in and on the radio and television industry. But try to keep it all in perspective or you'll drive yourself looney.

Try to see the humor in even a pressure-cooker situation. For along with the four parts of the "CDVP Process," a sense of humor must also accompany the copywriter as part of the baggage he or she brings to each new assignment. Recognizing the incongruity if not the downright ludicrousness of some work situations will do a lot to keep your blood pressure down and your enthusiasm up.

The resilient ability to find humor in all things—especially in those most worrisome job-based harassments—is what preserves a copywriter's freshness. The "Evolution of Advertising" presentation (Figure 5–8) demonstrates this quality. Inspired by Kenyon & Eckhardt's former chairman of the board, Stanley I. Tannenbaum, it should serve to remind each of us that we needn't be sour to be serious; that we don't have to drape our afflictions in black. As Tannenbaum's "Evolution of Advertising" shows, even (and especially) under pressure, copywriting *can* be fun. There is no better observation with which to conclude

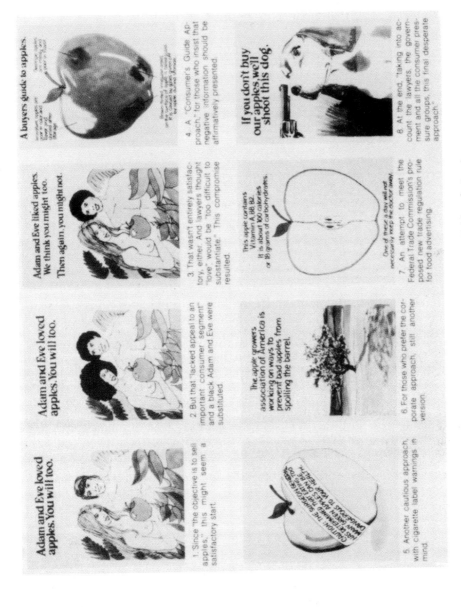

Figure 5–8. (*Courtesy of Stanley I. Tannenbaum, Kenyon & Eckhardt, Inc.*)

this chapter and, for that matter, this entire five-chapter section on The Copywriting Perspective.

Don't follow the sardonic advice of Tannenbaum's eighth panel and succumb to "shooting that dog." Forging logical links that make sense to regulators as well as to target audiences may not be an easy task, but it will insure the survival of your copy as well as that of poor Fido. Focused CREATIVITY that is properly DEFINED and VALIDATED and that respects the multitude of PROHIBITIONS outlined earlier is more than a match for generalized critical carping from whatever the source.

Radio commentator Earl Nightingale put the whole struggle in reassuring perspective when he reminded us that:

> Most products advertised and sold in this country are good products. A lot of hard work, research and brains have gone into them, and there's a market for them. So all we have to do is tell the truth about them, in a straightforward, interesting and even creative way. There's an interesting story lurking in every product or service. It is the job of the advertising people, and especially the copywriter to ferret it out and present it in an interesting and believable way to the consumer.[13]

In undertaking the ferreting of which Nightingale spoke, the copywriter's main governor is not some external regulator but a sense of professional *responsibility*. As described by advertising veteran Whit Hobbs, this means that,

> "When I sit down to write, I feel a strong sense of responsibility to a lot of people—to my client, to my associates, to my customer/reader/viewer. This is what creative people in advertising are *supposed* to feel, and I wish all of them did. . . . I keep seeing advertising that seems to be designed by creative people in agencies primarily to impress *other* creative people in other agencies— inside jokes that leave the customers out there relatively unmoved. It is very nice to win praise from one's peers, but it's far more important to win *customers.*"[14]

The *responsible* winning of customers is The Copywriting Perspective's focal point, the central and honest goal that motivates everything we write. Let's now turn our attention to how this goal can be achieved on radio.

13. Reprinted with permission of the Nightingale-Conant Corporation, Chicago, 1979 copyright, producers of the Earl Nightingale radio program OUR CHANGING WORLD.
14. Whit Hobbs, "Biting the Brands That Feed You," *ADWEEK/Midwest*, October 4, 1982, p. 20.

PART TWO

RADIO COPYWRITING

Chapter Six

KEY ELEMENTS OF RADIO
WRITING

Ad man Richard J. Mercer once fashioned the following hypothetical classified for radio copywriters:

> Attention playwrights, unfulfilled geniuses, humorists, composers: Come right
> to the theater, the greatest theater of them all, the theater of the mind. Write
> for radio, the land of the [Stan] Frebergs and the home of rave reviews.[1]

Mercer's implied list of qualifications is still an apt one because the successful
and effective radio writer has a bit of the dramatist, comedian, muse, and
mastermind all rolled into one adaptable package. Writing for radio is a unique
adventure that transcends the limitations of the shooting schedule and the
costliness of the camera lens. As CBS/Broadcast Group President Gene Jankowski recalled,

> When television became the nation's theatre, people felt radio had suffered a
> crippling blow. But what actually happened was that radio did something
> daring. . . . It walked right off the stage and into the audience. Radio learned
> how to speak to the audience 'one on one,' one person at a time. So it
> achieved an intimacy which, to this day, no other medium possesses.[2]

Radio writing manifests a respect for language like that print accords but
must dole out this respect into comparatively miniscule units that are most
often read in a minute or less. For the creative copywriter, such enforced
brevity is a constant frustration. Nevertheless, as a wordsmith-in-training and/or
a creative student of the broadcast media as a whole, you should still aspire to
answer Mercer's want ad and to strive for the raves that it promises. The next
three chapters will do what they can to assist you.

TAPPING RADIO'S ADVANTAGES:
SUCCINCT SOUND APPEAL

If, as a copywriter, you think radio is no more than video's farm team, your
appraisal differs radically from that of many successful practitioners. John V.
Chervokas, chief creative officer of Warwick Advertising, maintains that radio is

---

1. Richard Mercer, writing in "Monday Memo," *Broadcasting Magazine,* May 23, 1966, p. 24.
2. "Jankowski Foresees Shakeout in Radio," *Broadcasting Magazine,* November 5, 1984, p. 37.

"the best way to arrest the human intelligence, to visualize and to fantasize; it presents an opportunity to create outstanding advertising for unglamorous products; it doesn't require the use of the eyes and therefore the music is more penetrating and the copy more emotionally effective; radio is also 'a great presentation tool.'"[3]

But in order to tap these intrinsic radio advantages for whatever the assignment at hand, your copy must conform to the medium's dynamics. It must mirror but not flaunt all the qualities making for what we shall call *Succinct Sound Appeal.* Copy that manifests *SSA* does not acquire it by accident but rather achieves it through the interaction and combined effect of all of the following procedures:

Succinct Sound Appeal requires
1. Painting a backdrop
2. Varying length
3. Averting "printese"
4. Concluding with energy
5. Reading aloud
6. Timing as read

Painting a Backdrop

Whenever possible, radio commercials and continuity should seem to have a locale, should seem to arise from some specific setting. With the camera's opening shot, television can easily let the viewer know just what the context is for the message to follow. Radio has no such automatic establishing device, and unless special care is taken to provide the equivalent orientation via other means, the radio piece will seem to lack substance. The listener will receive it in a vacuum, tied to nothing and associated with nothing. Like a curtain that rises on a carefully dressed stage, the opening seconds of your radio presentation should frame and augment the action to follow. True, you don't want the listener to "walk out whistling the scenery" to the detriment of your central copy point, but you do want a habitat that heightens memorability. Even straight copy as in the following Porsche spot can, if well selected, quickly sketch the situation most appropriate to the communication's purpose:

```
(MUSIC:  UP AND UNDER THROUGHOUT)
ANNCR:   In the Arctic Circle, there's a place where reindeer
             struggle to make their way through the blizzards.
         It is here that a Porsche Nine Two Four began one of the
             greatest challenges that any car can face. A journey
             from the North Cape in Norway to Cape Horn in Tierra
             del Fuego---the northernmost and southernmost points
             on earth that can be reached by car.
         In this brutal trial, the Porsche Nine Two Four endured
             glacial temperatures of minus 56 degrees and tropical
             heats of 122 degrees.
```

3. "Radio, an Answer in Troubled Times," *Broadcasting Magazine*, June 14, 1982, p. 66.

The route plowed through deep mud and heavy snow. And
when the Nine Two Four reached its goal, not so much
as a fan belt needed replacing.

The Nine Two Four. The most affordable Porsche. Come see
it at your Porsche Audi dealership. Where dream cars
become a reality.

TAG: 10 SECOND LOCAL DEALER TAG HERE

(MUSIC: UP AND OUT)

(Courtesy of Doyle Dane Bernbach Inc.)

Note how the first sentence clearly circumscribed the environment to which
the message pertained and in which it seemed to take place. The second and
third sentences then helped enlarge and intensify that environment.

Sometimes the encompassing environment is less important and serves only
as a neutral canvas on which to paint the product itself. In such instances, the
product must be capable of commanding and holding attention since it becomes
both backdrop and foreground on the stage of the listener's mind:

(MUSIC:	SHORT VAMP IN)
SINGERS:	MAKE YOURSELF COMFORTABLE—TILT-WHEEL.
GIRL:	Nervous?
GUY:	Me? Why do you ask?
GIRL:	You've been sitting there pawing the steering wheel for 15 minutes.
GUY:	I'm trying to find the Tilt-Wheel control.
GIRL:	Silly, there isn't one.
GUY:	No Tilt-Wheel?! Now I'll never get comfortable.
GIRL:	But it's Daddy's favorite sports car.
GUY:	But it doesn't have Tilt-Wheel.
GIRL:	Poor boy.
GUY:	Now, a GM car you can order with Tilt-Wheel. It adjusts up, down. Six different driving positions.
GIRL:	But you look so macho sitting there.
GUY:	I don't like macho. I like Tilt-Wheel position six, all the way up like an 18-wheeler.
GIRL:	And that makes you feel comfortable?
GUY:	Yeah, that and—
GIRL:	What?
GUY:	Tilt-Wheel makes it easy in and easy out.
GIRL:	Don't tell me. You're—
GUY:	Stuck behind the wheel?
GIRL:	Yeah. What will we tell Daddy?

```
GUY:          Shoulda got Tilt-Wheel?
SINGERS:      TILT-WHEEL HAS A SPOT THAT'S GOT A FEEL JUST RIGHT
                 FOR YOU
              SIX GREAT POSITIONS AND IT COSTS SO LITTLE TOO.
              NO NEED TO CRAMP YOUR STYLE, JUST MAKE YOURSELF
              COMFORTABLE WITH TILT-WHEEL.
TAG:          Tilt-Wheel Steering from GM.
```

(Courtesy of Roger Bodo, Leo Burnett Company of Michigan, Inc.)

Despite its brevity, even station continuity can create a sense of locale. That may, in fact, be its prime mission in encouraging listener identfication with the program or station being plugged. The following two snippets illustrate how time and place can be quickly communicated and capitalized on in your continuity:

```
Don't you just love coming back to work on Monday? Well, I do.
This is The Bill Robinson Show and I'm ready to go with Big Lake
Country music on KJCK.
```

```
It's springtime where the hills meet the plains. What a great
place to be, in 1420 country and The Bill Robinson Show.
```

(Courtesy of Jon R. Potter, The Musicworks, Inc.)

Varying Length

As we've mentioned before, good copy has flow. And a feeling of flow is enhanced best by a progression of thought units that vary in length. If all of its sentences expend about the same number of metric beats, a message will develop a lock-step character that may be totally appropriate as a music lyric but monotony incarnate as unaccompanied copy. In a modified jingle like this Howard Johnson's spot, the pulsating stanzas provide a propelling flow in an ear-pleasing, foot-tapping progression that is both expected and required for psychological acceptance.

```
It looks like Howard Johnson's on the outside
but you should see what's going on inside.

At the Deli and the Baker and the Ice Cream Maker
In the fresh-cooking, fresh-looking new Howard Johnson's

Have a nibble here---a snack there
A slice or wedge to go
Stand up, wander around, or have a
meal real slow

At the Deli and the Baker and the Ice Cream Maker
In the fresh-cooking, fresh-looking new Howard Johnson's

If you're into calorie counting
We've got salads by the score
```

```
And if you're in a hurry
We can speed you
out the door.
```

```
At the Deli and the Baker and the Ice Cream Maker
```

```
Have a nosh, have a nibble,
Breakfast, dinner or lunch
Make it nice, take a slice,
have a bite or a brunch.
```

```
At the Deli and the Baker and the Ice Cream Maker
```

```
So forget your basic eatery
Hey, fast food place, you're through
Try somethin a bit familiar,
yet deliciously brand new.
```

```
At the Deli and the Baker and the Ice Cream Maker
In the fresh-cooking, fresh-looking new Howard Johnson's
In Camp Hill and Carlisle
```

(Courtesy of Campbell-Ewald Advertising and Howard Johnson Company.)

With straight copy, conversely, the task of promoting beneficial flow variety is totally dependent on the words and sentences themselves, which should proceed in contrasting short and medium units. For flow, after all, is best seen when balanced by ebb. The shorter units help hold the thought up momentarily before the medium ones propel it ahead again.

The copywriter should be enough of a craftsman that the listener will not notice the means by which flow is regulated but only experience its pleasing effect. The tedium of unaccompanied same-length sentences, on the other hand, is a dulling distraction for audience attentiveness. Often, listeners may not be able to identify consciously what caused their attention to wander. But the lack of contrast inherent in uniform-length thought units takes its toll no matter how glowing the word choices that made up those units. The sample Talbot Reinforcement spot below demonstrates the sluggish sameness undiversified length begets. Each succeeding thought unit has the same five beats, which pound relentlessly on without regard to copy meaning or aural flow. The beats are marked to identify further the lack of variety in sentence duration:

```
1       2            3       4       5       1     2
Paper's cheap but your time and effort aren't. Torn paper

        3       4   5   1      2      3          4
means valuable work lost. Take no foolish chances and stop

    5           1       2         3     4
misfortunes. Fix those tears with Talbot Gummed

        5               1       2     3       4
Reinforcements. Preserve the time and effort you put in your
```

```
5              1      2      3      4        5    1
work. Ripped binder holes demand you use Talbot now. Keep
     2      3        4          5           1
that valuable work right there in your notebook. Talbot
2          3        4       5      1     2
effectively heals that wounded paper. Talbot Gummed
   3           4        5       1     2
Reinforcements can put you at ease. Get Talbot Gummed
   3           4          5
Reinforcements before it's too late.
```

Length, then, is measured in *beats,* which combine to create copy *rhythm.* It is not the number of words but the number and arrangement of beats that comprise the framework for copy flow. Take the measure of some of your material in the way we've just measured the Talbot spot. That should help you detect monotony in the making and result in copy that seems to soar rather than metronomically plod.

Contrast the mechanical effect of the Talbot commercial with the nonrepetitive progression in this Pawprint dog food spot. Compute the beats in each thought unit. Here, the sentence lengths are varied enough to retain rhythmic interest without eclipsing the copy's meaning and sense:

```
ANNCR:  Life. It's a beautiful thing to behold. From a newborn
        baby to a newborn puppy. Remember that old cardboard box
        and all those puppies clinging to their mother? Remember
        smiling? When you finally decided which puppy was going to
        be yours? That was a big decision. You took on
        responsibility for another's life. And you handled that
        responsibility by making sure your puppy got the best.
        Pawprint dog food. Pawprint nurtured your pet from a
        clumsy pup, to a mature adult. And Pawprint's rich beef
        flavor gave your dog all he needed to live a long, healthy
        life. That beautiful dog's still part of your life. And so
        is Pawprint dog food. Because when something's this
        genuine, you want to keep it.
```

Averting "Printese"

As we've mentioned several times before, radio copy is meant to be *heard,* not *read,* by the people at whom it is aimed. A newspaper or magazine reader always has the option of rereading a certain passage to get the meaning that was originally missed. A radio message, however, exists and evaporates in real time. Unless the listener is exposed to that same communication at another time or on another station, meaning missed the first time may be meaning missed forever.

Radio copy, therefore, must be conversational, not only because that quality helps simulate an essential feeling of one-to-one communication but also because conversation is the style in which we are most conditioned to pick up aural meaning and to pick it up the first, and often the only, time the message is delivered. The sentence just completed is a good example of print communication. It is an extended thought unit that pulls several related elements together into one package whose meaning can be garnered by rereading or simply reading more slowly the first time. For radio communication, on the other hand, we have to sacrifice the unity of one extended "lead" idea for shorter thought units that will cumulatively give us the same information in a more "aurally digestible" serving. Rewriting this paragraph's lead sentence to meet radio's requirements might give us something like this:

```
Radio copy has to be conversational. A conversational quality
helps simulate the needed feelings of one-to-one communication.
Besides, we're most used to picking up aural meaning when it's
delivered in a conversational style. And we realize conversation
won't often be repeated. So we work harder to understand
conversation, the first time.
```

Sometimes, as this example shows, radio must use just as many if not more words than print to cover the same ground. That's why on radio, where real-time communication is so brief, we can seldom afford to deal with more than one main point in any commercial or piece of continuity. Yet, too many writers still try to send out the same piece of copy to both newspapers and radio stations. This results either in print copy tht does not offer enough information to hold a reader's focus or, more often, in radio copy that is just too congested for most listeners to decipher. Here is a piece of newspaper copy that was sent to radio without rewriting. Is it styled conversationally? Does it make one main point? Does that point come through clearly?

```
Honest Abe is the wood burner for big jobs. For $269 you can heat
your entire home with this amazing wood-burning stove and save
one half or more in fuel costs. Clean and safe burning, it's free
of smoke and fireplace odor. Minimum maintenance with easily
emptied ash drawer. Roomy 24 by 20 firebox allows one fire to
burn for hours. And Honest Abe is easy to install. Call Harry's
Heating at 320-8865.
```

Though the copy conforms to the word limit inherent in a 30-second spot, there is little else about it that shows adaptation to the radio medium. In reaching the *listener* as opposed to the *reader,* some of the technical data would have to be omitted so that the main copy point can be allowed to surface:

```
It's been a cold winter, with more to come. And those high
heating bills have probably given your budget a real chill, too.
Harry's Heating has the solution; the Honest Abe wood-burner
which can cut those fuel costs in half. The easily installed,
```

```
Honest Abe wood-burner is the clean, safe, economical way to
bring cheery warmth to you and your budget. Call Harry's Heating
at 320-8865. Get Honest Abe warming for you. Call 320-8865.
```

Radio copy obviously cannot depend on the typeface alterations, layout patterns, and other graphic implements through which print can present and arrange a comparatively vast quantity of information. And unless they are composed into the very essence of the copy, paragraphing and headlining are not discernible to the radio listener, who receives the message only one word at a time in the order in which the announcer's voice is unveiling it. On the other hand, radio can paint pictures in the mind—pictures that can be far more involving and multidimensional than the pen-and-ink starkness on which print must so often depend. If our radio copy can escape "printese," it can attain what Richard Mercer recognized as the "freedom from print's static vulnerability. Radio doesn't just stand there like a four-color proof begging to be nit-picked into appalling mediocrity."[4]

Concluding with Energy

Varying the length, the number of beats, in succeeding thought units will do much to support copy flow. The motivating force behind that flow, the careful revealing of sense, is equally important to the overall effectiveness of the radio message. In short, our radio sentences should conclude with strong, forward-leaning endings, just as the copy as a whole should end strongly. Announcers need something to *read up to* so that they experience the copy's natural impact and, through their voices, their listeners experience it also. Both announcer and listener need to feel that each succeeding sentence was worth their time and trouble. This helps insure and heighten further attention as the spot progresses. The anticlimactic sentence or message ending that seems to let the listener down rather than confer a reward for listening is like Aunt Eleanor's bright-tinseled Christmas packages with the perennial underwear inside. The result never lives up to how it was wrapped or the time expended opening it.

Don't be an "Aunt Eleanor Copywriter." Make sure your messages for radio are not only packaged in an ear-pleasing rhythm, but also reveal engaging discoveries as the sentence-by-sentence unwrapping proceeds. A particularly good example of such continuous "expectation fulfillment" aimed at the college crowd is this dialogue spot for Mr. Johnnie's:

```
Production Note:  Residence Hall Director is a middle-aged
   female; Delivery Boy should sound about seventeen.
RHD:  Hey, you there with the food.
BOY:  Who, me?
RHD:  Yes. I'm the Residence Hall Director. And I want to know
      what you're doing with all that food.
BOY:  I do have quite an assortment, don't I?
RHD:  You certainly do. How many restaurants did you rob?
```

4. Mercer, *Broadcasting Magazine*, May 23, 1966, p. 24.

BOY: Oh, I didn't steal this food, ma'am. I'm the delivery boy from Mr. Johnnie's.

RHD: Mr. Johnnie's?

BOY: That's right, Mr. Johnnie's. The place with more than just delicious pizza.

RHD: Hmmm. That stuff certainly smells good.

BOY: Room twelve ordered it. Let's see---five different kinds of subs, two poor boys, a roast beef sandwich, a salami sandwich, lasagna, two pizzas gargantua, and chips.

RHD: Very appealing. But can't one order beverages from Mr. Johnnie's?

BOY: Sure. Coffee and all kinds of soft drinks. And free delivery on everything.

RHD: But you aren't delivering any beverages.

BOY: The guy on the phone said they already had a keg.

RHD: A keg??!!

BOY: Uh-oh. (Fading off rapidly) Got to run. Mr. Johnnie's promises quick delivery. And it's getting quicker all the time.

Reading Aloud

The achieving of *Succinct Sound Appeal* obviously requires the generating of some sound. And this must occur not just at the completed message's moment of recording or airing but during the copy's entire evolution. So the copywriter needs to check the effectiveness of every piece of material by reading it aloud. Words and sentences that look spectacular on paper can sound terribly stilted, awkward, or even incomprehensible when launched onto the airwaves.

Great writing is not necessarily great *radio* writing, and the actual articulation of the proposed copy is the only way to test accurately the words in an environment comparable to that for which they are ultimately intended. Here is a piece of great writing from William Faulkner's *Light in August*. Can it also be used as great *radio* writing? Try reading it aloud to find out:

> All the men in the village worked in the mill or for it. It was cutting pine. It had been there seven years and in seven years more it would destroy all the timber within its reach. Then some of the machinery and most of the men who ran it and existed because and for it would be loaded onto freight cars and moved away. But some of the machinery would be left, since new pieces could always be bought on the installment plan—gaunt, staring, motionless wheels rising from mounds of brick rubble and ragged weeds with a quality profoundly astonishing, and gutted boilers lifting their rusting and unsmoking stacks with an air stubborn, baffled and bemused upon a stumppocked scene of profound and peaceful desolation, unplowed, untilled, gutting slowly into red and choked ravines beneath the long quiet rains of autumn and the galloping fury of vernal equinoxes.[5]

5. From *Light in August* by William Faulkner. Copyright 1932 and renewed 1960 by William Faulkner. Reprinted by permission of Random House, Inc. and Curtis Brown, Ltd., London.

Vocalize everything you write for radio as you write it. Your copy may not approximate classic writing but, as we've just seen, classic writing will often not succeed as acceptable aural copy. Perform the message you've created exactly the way you would want an announcer to read it. If something trips you up, change it. That same imperfection is likely to cause similar problems later for both talent and listeners.

Timing as Read

While reading aloud, you should also obtain the actual running time of the copy. Word count, as noted in Chapter 3, is only a general indication of the number of seconds a given piece of material will expend. The only exact method is to put a stopwatch to the copy as you are voicing it. And make sure you do *really* voice it. Some copywriters invariably come up with material that is overtime because they whisper the message to themselves. Since it takes longer to actually vocalize a word than it does simply to form it with the mouth, lip-read copy will always time out shorter than when fully articulated by an announcer. The result (assuming that stations accept the material at all) is a forced accelerating at the end of the copy as the talent strives to fit it into the allotted time. Nothing can be more detrimental to listener attention than this involuntary speeding up. Avoid it by careful timing of several fully articulated run-throughs performed at the tempo at which you would wish the announcer to read. In this way, your message will be as succinct in form as it should be in content, and this final ingredient in achieving *Succinct Sound Appeal* will have been successfully incorporated into your finished radio presentation.

THE RADIO COPYWRITER AS POET

The previous section indicated that great writing is not always great *radio* writing. Yet, a particularly strong bond exists between one class of great writers—the poets—and the copywriters who labor for the sound mass medium.

Webster's New Collegiate Dictionary describes a poet as "one endowed with great imaginative, emotional, or intuitive power and capable of expressing his conceptions, passions or intuitions in appropriate language." The radio copywriter's job, in fact, is to find words and other sound elements that are *so appropriate* to our message that the listener will not only comprehend but also remember them as the means of recalling the workings of our product or service. Thus, we know what will "double our pleasure, double our fun," what makes our pet cat "chow, chow, chow," whom to call "when it absolutely, positively has to be there over-night," and maybe even how to get "off the can and on the stick."

These broadcast slogans are simply the latest manifestations of an age-old tradition. For, before the age of print and, consequently, before the age of significant literacy, fables, sagas, and folklore in general were passed down orally. From the ancient Greek rhapsodes and Biblical psalmists to the medieval minstrels and beyond, poets seeking to communicate with significant numbers of "common folk" did so by casting their messages into concise yet colorful verses that could be understood easily by all and remembered, at least in part, by many.

Like these earlier poets, the radio copywriter performs in a totally oral and fundamentally nonliterary environment. Our listeners, like those of our historic predecessors, have no concrete, permanent record of the subject being communicated. Everything the radio audience carries away with them has not only to be visualized but also implanted in the mind through an unusually harmonious juxtaposition of sounds and ideas. In a process with which any past or present minstrel can identify, the radio writer is continually in search of the perfect marriage between *sound and sense;* a marriage that will enable the message to spring to life and stay alive in the listeners' memories during the days and weeks to follow. Semanticist S. I. Hayakawa long ago observed that the "copywriter, like the poet, must invest the product with significance so that it becomes something beyond itself. . . . The task of the copywriter is the poeticizing of consumer goods."[6]

Yet, in many ways the radio copywriter's task is even more difficult than that faced by most other poets. Poets in the conventional sense can usually choose their own subject, the orientation that will be taken as regards that subject, the form to be employed, and the length to which that form will extend. Radio copywriters, conversely, virtually always have the subject assigned to them together with a compulsory subject orientation which is nearly always positive (unless it is something like an *anti*-litter PSA). The form is certain to be budget- and time-bound. If there is no time or money for a dialogue spot to be produced, for example, the copywriter must proceed with a uni-voice approach regardless of personal or professional preference. And the dictated length is precisely the length decreed by the campaign managers and the media selection plan they have adopted; no longer and no shorter.

The nonradio poet can decide to write in praise of a solitary stalk of corn. The copywriter is told to pen a corn flakes spot. The conventional poet may decide this particular cornstalk represents man's constant search for independence. The radio poet is instructed to demonstrate how that one brand of corn flakes meets the whole family's breakfast requirements. The traditional poet decides to discuss the corn stalk in Italian sonnet form: fourteen lines in iambic pentameter grouped into two subsections of eight and six lines. The broadcast writer has thirty seconds of air-time to be devoted to a uni-voice housewife testimonial. The remarkable aspect of all this is that, despite the comparatively cramped boundaries within which they have to maneuver, radio copywriters must still construct a message that is just as meaningful and memorable to the mass audience as the traditional poet's message is to his or her far fewer and initially more attentive constituents.

Just for a moment, let's see how a conventional poet and a "copywriter poet" might approach and describe the identical subject. In this case, the topic is the same small-town cafe. As in the case of the Faulkner passage, the nonradio

---

6. S. I. Hayakawa. *Language in Thought and Action.* (New York: Harcourt Brace and World, 1964), p. 262.

writer's imagery may be more descriptive and extended. But would it be as clear and discernible coming over the radio as the copywriter's 30-second spot that follows it? For poets, too, good or even great writing is not necessarily great or even functional on radio:

DINER

A new day's procrastination
Lets night's veil still opaque the sun.
The silky mist floats on the highway
And the dew embosoms the grass,
While sleepy truckers and travelers,
Draped in coats, soon discarded,
Gather in bleary-eyed company,
Sipping the heaven-sent coffee.

The morn's high tide arrives.
Rays of sunshine put neon to shame;
The grey-white road crawls toward tomorrow
And the ground is a mottled pastel,
A carpet which grade school boys
Imprint with rubber-ribbed gym shoes
In their jumbled, vibrant rush
To the charm-filled gum machine.

Exhausted, a spent afternoon
Plods by in thankful surrender,
Leaving a dusked thoroughfare
Flanked by the darkening earth
Where the bachelors and creased businessmen
Stretch out their day-piled stiffness
While stepping from autos and vans
In pursuit of the house specialty.

A suit with a moon for lapel pin—
The ebony mystery of midnight—
Makes the highway a concrete river,
Gives each blade of grass a new boldness
To the starry-eyed couples,
As linked pairs of feet
Drift through the door,
For the evening's last talk.

ANNCR: A place to start the day off right; a place to stop before
         saying good-night. Tempting food, relaxing atmosphere, and
         an always-here-to-please-you attitude. That's what you'll
         find every day, twenty-four hours a day, at Bannerman's
         Diner. From that first up-and-at-em cup of coffee, to a
         late-night home-cooked snack, Bannerman's Diner serves you
         the food you like—when you like it. Bannerman's Diner on
         Route 23. Your any-time, every-time restaurant.

POETIC PACKAGING

In comparison with the poem, the copywriter's radio-tailored effort may seem banal. But despite the obvious and necessary differences in the above two treatments of Bannerman's Diner, let's not forget the broad task and goal similarities that bind nonbroadcast poets and radio copywriters into a common society. In the final analysis, both groups are required to take nonvisual media and, through inspired blends of sound and sense, energize and activate the listener's visual and other senses in order to extend both attention and memorability. Award-winning copywriter Robert C. Pritikin once noted that "When you write a radio commercial for the eye, instead of for the ear, you can expect to achieve enormous recall value. The most elementary memory course will teach you that to remember something, you must visualize it."[7] Pritikin himself created one of modern radio writing's best illustrations of this principle in a series of spots that illuminated a paint's very visual essence via the supposedly "blind" radio medium:

ANNCR: The Fuller Paint Company invites you to stare with your
         ears at---yellow. Yellow is more than just a color. Yellow
         is a way of life. Ask any taxi driver about yellow. Or a
         banana salesman. Or a coward. They'll tell you about
         yellow. (PHONE RINGS) Oh, excuse me. Yello!! Yes, I'll
         take your order. Dandelions, a dozen; a pound of melted
         butter; lemon drops and a drop of lemon, and one canary
         that sings a yellow song. Anything else? Yello? Yello?
         Yello? Oh, disconnected. Well, she'll call back. If you
         want yellow that's yellow-yellow, remember to remember the
         Fuller Paint Company, a century of leadership in the
         chemistry of color. For the Fuller color center nearest
         you, check your phone directory. The yellow pages, of
         course.[8]

This Fuller Paint spot is a perfect example of radio's using its own unique advantages to capitalize on television's disadvantages. Every member of the audience was enticed into painting, in their own minds, what was most appealing about yellow to them. There was no forced dependence on the film processor's yellow, video-tape's yellow, the kind of yellow that the television station engineer admired, or even the brand of yellow the home receiver was adjusted to reproduce. Instead, it was everyone's perfect yellow displayed in everyone's most perfect showcase—their own minds.

Like any successful radio copywriter, Pritikin engaged in a little *poetic packaging*—he isolated the element of the subject on which he wanted to focus

7. Robert C. Pritikin, writing in "Monday Memo," *Broadcasting Magazine*, March 18, 1974, p. 22.
8. Ibid.

and then derived some picture-potent symbols to bring that element to mind's-eye life. Broken down, the development of the above commercial, like the development of any image-filled piece of *poetically packaged* radio, results from a unified process that nonetheless springs from three separate though succeeding questions:

1.   What is my subject? (Yellow Fuller Paint)
2.   What is its key element or quality that I want the listener to appreciate? (the vibrancy of its yellow color)
3.   How can I *poetically package* this quality? (relate it to other prominent examples of the color yellow; taxis, bananas, dandelions, melted butter, lemon drops, a canary, even the yellow pages and cowards)

Many aspiring writers realize they must use imagery to make their message come alive, but they neglect the vital second step. They mistakenly try to describe, to *package poetically,* the product or service *as a whole* rather than first selecting its key attribute and the central copy idea that must be fashioned to display that key attribute. Since no short piece of copy can ever be expected to make more than one memorable point, the adopted *poetic package* must likewise work in service of that point instead of attempting to characterize the product or service's totality.

For practice, take the following items and try to pull out what the key element or quality of each might be:

a ball-point pen
a pizza pie
a life insurance policy
a watchband
an automobile shock absorber
an underarm deodorant

Do you and, given your subject's specific advantages, *should* you focus on the pen's shape, the pizza pie's convenience, the policy's low monthly cost, the watchband's strength, the shock absorber's gentleness, and the deodorant's aroma? Or do you stress the pizza pie's shape, the deodorant's convenience, and the policy's strength? Whatever you decide, you must then as a radio writer encase that central concept in the most vivid and meaningful wrapping you can derive. Does the pen fit your hand like an extra finger? Does the watchband's strength come from "tank-track" weave? Does the deodorant go on "gentle as a goldfish's kiss"? And what about that pizza with its shape or convenience? Keep digging until you find your subject's most appropriate element and a convincing *poetic package* to match. It's not easy, and a lot of seemingly unproductive "think time" may be expended before you ever start setting your copy to paper. But hang in there. For, once you have successfully dealt with all three of *poetic packaging's* questions as they apply to the assignment at hand, you'll have a message that is truly effective because it's intrinsically *radio*.

Isolate how poetic packaging's trio of queries might have been answered in the formulation of this PSA:

(MUSIC: BACH UP AND UNDER)

KEN NORDINE: Handel's oratorios, The symphonies of Brahms,
Mozart and Beethoven. The piano music of Chopin.
The concertos of Rachmaninoff. The music of
Tchaikovsky. The rhapsodies of Liszt. The operas of
Wagner. The ballets of Stravinsky. The great
masterpieces of man are also the great masterpieces
of our forests. Take away the wood in pianos,
organs and harpsichords, and you take away the
medium through which these geniuses communicated
their inspiration. A symphony of life abounds in
every tree, in every forest. Please allow that
music to be appreciated by our children and our
children's children. Only Bach could have written
the Toccata and Fugue in D minor. But only you can
prevent forest fires.

(MUSIC: UP AND OUT)

(Courtesy of The Advertising Council, Inc.)

GENERAL RADIO FORMAT

Also intrinsic to radio is the need for clarity in copy arrangement. The efforts toward *Succinct Sound Appeal, poetic packaging,* and all the rest do not automatically spring from the writer's head to the announcer's mouth. Rather, as discussed in the second chapter, even the most appealing and image-filled message must be translated into proper script form as a prelude to proper performance.

The body of the copy, the script's working section, is what we need to concern ourselves with here. For it is in the body that we must indicate our precise arrangement and manipulation of any or all of the parts of radio's sound element triumvirate: words, music, and sound effects. The following commercial has been constructed not as a "hall of fame" spot but to demonstrate a useful and cogent pattern for script organization. It features all of the key ingredients that might need to be scripted. Reference numbers have been added to facilitate dissection.

[1]Production Note: All talent should convey lines like
actors in an early thirties movie.

ANNCR: Motion sickness; that queasy feeling. And it's hard to
imagine a better place for it than this choppy cruise.
Doesn't seem to bother that guy out on deck though.
[2](Fading off) Let's try to find out why—
        [3](FADE IN: CREAKING TIMBERS, SPLASHING WAVES)

BILL: (Fading on) What? No, I'm no sailor. I'm Bill the Bookie
from Davenport. [4](TIMBERS/WAVES OUT) Motion sick? Not

> me. Not since that day (Fading off) back at George's
> Drug Store—

[5](STORE SOUNDS UP QUICKLY AND GRADUALLY OUT)

GEORGE: Hey, Bill. [6](MUSIC: <u>OFF-KEY</u> <u>WHISTLING</u> <u>OF</u> <u>'CAMPTOWN</u>
<u>RACES'</u> <u>FIRST</u> <u>FOUR</u> <u>BARS)</u> Know this tune?

BILL: Give it some hay, George. Oh, that bumpy flight from
Vegas. Like riding a swayback steer.

[7](<u>TWO</u> <u>MORE</u> <u>WHISTLED</u> <u>BARS</u> <u>OF</u> <u>'CAMPTOWN</u> <u>RACES')</u>

GEORGE: Then saddle up to this. It's Owen's Elixir.

BILL: Owen's what?

GEORGE: Owen's Elixir. Makes you feel like it's post time.

[8](MUSIC: <u>TRADITIONAL</u> <u>'AT</u> <u>THE</u> <u>POST'</u> <u>TRUMPET</u> <u>CALL)</u>

[9](CROSSFADE TO SHIP SOUNDS UP AND UNDER)

BILL: From then on, it was Owen's for me. You can bet your
calm stomach on it. It's Owen's Elixir to win, every
time.

As [1] shows, an indented production note may precede the actual copy and is used to give a general casting or stage direction that will pertain throughout the script. This keeps clutter within the copy to a minimum and segregates continuing elements from those relevant only to limited sections.

Specific movement and stage directions, such as the one marked by [2], exist in parentheses with the first letter capitalized. These directions are placed in the copy at exactly the point when they're to become operative.

Sound effects are likewise in parentheses and, unlike stage directions, are entirely in CAPS. They may or may not be preceded by the designator SFX. When they occur between character speeches but within the same scene, sound effect directions are indented at least three spaces more than are lines of dialogue. The [3] marks such a situation. When sound effects occur within a speech they, like stage directions, are placed at the actual point of occurrence as [4] demonstrates. Sound effects' FULL CAPS format thereby becomes the prime means by which the actor can distinguish these technician-activated devices from the stage directions for which he himself is more likely to be responsible. Lastly, when sound effects comprise the bridge between scenes or are the prime means of initial scene establishment, their cue begins at the far left margin, as [5] points out.

Music cues are also in parentheses and are also in CAPS. They are further distinguished from sound effects by being fully <u>underlined</u> but may or may not begin with the term MUSIC. As reference numbers [6], [7], and [8] illustrate, the location of music cues within speeches, between speeches, and as scene-bridging devices respectively, follows the same rules as do sound effects serving similar functions. Finally, when separate music and sound effect cues assist each other to shift the scene, both directions are normally placed at the left margin with a separate line for each, as [9] strives to designate.

The spacing of each subsequent line of copy is also important in providing both talent and sound engineers with the clearest possible blueprint of what the copywriter has in mind. Typical broadcast practice is to DOUBLE SPACE WITHIN SPEECHES and TRIPLE SPACE BETWEEN THEM (a practice we usually, in this book, reduce to single and double-spacing respectively to keep this edition's size and cost down).

This includes triple-spacing between a speech and a sound effect or music cue that completely separates that speech from another character's line to follow (see [3] and [7]). It also applies to the triple-spacing that precedes and follows music or sound-effect bridges between separate scenes (such as [5] and [8-9]).

A commercial announcement or piece of continuity will seldom be extensive enough to require the use of even half the specialized cues called for in the above Elixir script. In fact, a cluttered productional orgy like this would be a technical and brand-recall nightmare. The Owen's Elixir presentation does, however, demonstrate a standardized plan for message typography; a plan that promotes consistent script layout and ungarbled communication with the skilled individuals, the voices and technicians, who must mold your copy into sound-propelled images.

PRODUCTIONAL TERMINOLOGY

The copywriter's adaptability to the technical requirements of radio is more than a matter of proper format. It also encompasses an understanding of those basic radio terms that, for the writer, translate into sound capabilities. For our purposes, we will divide terminology into three categories: (1) talent instructions, (2) control booth instructions, and (3) other writer-used technical terms. It is not our intent here to cover all of radio production's specialized vocabulary. Instead, we call attention only to those words the copywriter is most likely to need in preparing the actual script.

Talent Instructions

This category can be thought of as traffic-directing devices, several of which were included in the above Owen's Elixir commercial. In essence, they tell the talent where he or she should be in relationship to the microphone and whether he or she should stay there. Because talent is expected to be *on mike* unless told otherwise, this instruction requires writing out only when needed to indicate the desired completion point of a long move toward the microphone. Walking toward the microphone is called *fading on,* as Bill's portrayer does in his first Elixir spot speech. The reverse effect is called, not surprisingly, *fading off.* The Elixir announcer does it to give the impression that he is walking away from the listener and out on deck to Bill. Bill does the same thing at the end of his first speech to give us the feeling of a gradual flashback in time. If we instead want the talent to stay "in the distance" for any significant portion of his or her dialogue, we simply use the term *off mike* at the beginning of the first line to be delivered in that mode.

Moving talent in and out creates a much more realistic sound picture than the mere adjusting of volume in the control room. When someone walks away from us in real life, for example, our ears do not suddenly pick up less sound from our total environment. Instead, quieter but closer sounds grow more prominent as the receding person's voice grows less distinct in the distance. That total sense of presence is what radio seeks, and we therefore move people accordingly. As a slightly more sophisticated application of this principle, we will sometimes use the terms *behind barrier* or *thru soundscreen* when we want the effect of someone talking through a wall, behind a closed door, or locked in a trunk, to name just a few possibilities. A special acoustical panel is placed between the talent and the microphone to facilitate this condition. When the fictional door is opened or the trunk is unlocked, the talent can simply move quickly around the barrier to be instantaneously *on mike*. Alternatively, if our aural scene features a long wall or pictures a door that is supposed to be some distance from the listener's central vantage point, the talent can be instructed to *fade on* (either *quickly* or *slowly*) *from behind barrier*.

Control Booth Instructions

As mentioned above, volume is the most obvious productional function to be manipulated by the control booth engineer. Sound effects and music are commanded to *FADE IN* or *FADE OUT* when respectively introduced, and removed from the scene. Sound effects and music that are *already present* in the scene may be requested to FADE UP or FADE DOWN in order to enlarge or diminish their part in the total sound picture. We can also use refinements to these general directions, such as ESTABLISH, SNEAK IN/SNEAK OUT, FEATURE/ FEATURE BRIEFLY, or use hybrids, such as FADE UP AND OUT, FADE DOWN AND UNDER, FADE UP AND UNDER, and FADE DOWN AND OUT. As the conclusion to the Elixir spot demonstrates, we can, in addition, CROSSFADE one music or sound-effect cue with another by overlapping the receding element with the sound source just taking the stage. Especially when both elements are musical in nature, the CROSSFADE is also known as a SEGUE.

You may occasionally need certain more rarefied control booth instructions, too. The FILTER MIKE effect may be accomplished by having the talent talk into a tin can but is often accommodated through a more sophisticated microphone or control room modification of the input line that carries the talent's voice. A FILTER MIKE mechanism is used to give the effect of a voice coming over a telephone, through a public address system, or to denote unspoken thoughts and musings in a character's mind. As these musings get more and more unreal or frenzied, we may also want to bring REVERB—electromechanical echo—to the sound source. Varying amounts of REVERB are also effective in denoting such specialized locations as an empty warehouse, the bottom of a well, the Grand Canyon floor, or the inside of your refrigerator. (In a precise engineering sense, "echo" is *delayed* sound whereas "reverb" is *deflected* sound that is then "bounced back" to the listener's ear.)

In distinguishing control booth instructions from talent instructions, remember that people fade *on* and *off* whereas control booth originated sounds fade *IN* and *OUT,* and *UP* and *DOWN.* In addition, as the Elixir commercial shows, stage ("people") directions are not in full caps. Control booth directions and music and sound effects cues, on the other hand, are entirely set IN CAPS even in those rare instances when the sound is created "live" in the studio rather than in the control booth.

Other Writer-used Technical Terms

The following miscellany is comprised of additional productional terms commonly understood in the broadcast industry and, more important for our purposes, will sometimes find their way into or bordering the body of a piece of radio copy:

Actuality: production that seems to be originating live from some scene external to the studio

Ad Lib: impromptu dialogue not written out in the script. We might, for example, ask a background "crowd" to *ad-lib* reactions to what is being said or portrayed by the characters *on mike.*

Ambient Sounds: sounds that are a normal and expected part of the scene/environment being presented (train station, jungle, cocktail lounge, etc.)

ANNCR: the standard abbreviation for "announcer"

Attenuate: reducing the level of an electrical signal via volume or loudness controls or by using acoustically absorbing materials

BB: abbreviation for *billboard*

BG: abbreviation for background; normally referring to sound that will not be at full volume

Billboard: a brief announcement that identifies the sponsor at beginning and/or end of program

Bridge: aural transition (normally via music or sound effects) between two separate scenes or vignettes

Chain Break: station or network identification occurring between programs

Continuity Book: loose-leaf collection of spots and promos in the order they are to be read or played over the air; also called *copy book*

Cowcatcher: a portion of time that precedes the actual start of a program and thus allows space for unrelated spots or continuity

Cut: a particular band on a disc recording from which a specific music bed or sound effect is retrieved

Dead Air: period of time when no discernible sound is being transmitted

Distant Miking: placing microphones several feet from performers to accomplish a listener feeling of physical distance from the subject

Dry: a recording made without the introduction of any echo or reverberation

ET: an electrical transcription; a recording. This abbreviation can be used to indicate that a scripted music or sound effect is already available in a prerecorded form.

Flight: a series of announcements for the same product or service that are usually done in the same style and format

Gain: the radio sound term for "volume"

Hitchhiker: a portion of time that follows a program and thus allows time for unrelated spots or continuity

Jingle: customized musical creation used throughout a spot or as the articulation of a key copy point or brand identification

Kill Date: last day on which a particular piece of copy is authorized to be aired

Live Tag: a line at the end of a recorded message that is added by a local announcer to help adapt the copy to local/seasonal programming, personalities, and conditions

Logo: the visual or auditory/musical corporate symbol used by a station or client to identify itself

Master: the "original" recording of a disc or taped message from which duplicates can be dubbed

Mix: two or more separate signals brought into a desired collective balance

Out Cue: last word of a message and the signal for the next message/program to begin

Out Take: recorded segment not used in creating the final production

Pad: material added at the end of a message to bring it to the exact time specified; also referred to as *fill*

ROS: abbreviation for "run of schedule"; the announcement may be rotated anywhere in the broadcast day rather than remaining at a particular time or near a particular program

SC or SP: abbreviations for "station continuity" or "station promotion"; designates local copy meant to further the station's image or activities

SFX: the standard abbreviation for "sound effects"

Sign On: the piece of continuity used to begin the broadcast day

Sign Off: the piece of continuity used to end the broadcast day

Sitting Mike: a microphone placed on a table rather than mounted on a floor-length stand *(stand mike)* or from an overhead boom *(boom mike)*

Sounder: short musical/copy identification of a particular programmatic element

Stab: a musical or sound exclamation used at the beginning of or within a spot

Sting: a *stab* used at the end of a spot

Synthesizer: audio signal processor that can produce conventional sounds (including music) or create entirely new sounds

TF: abbreviation for "'til forbid"; announcement may be run until originating source instructs otherwise. May also be designated *TFN*—"'til further notice"—or *TN*—"'til notified".

Timbre: the tonal make-up and quality of any sound that is the sum of its frequencies and overtones

Universe: the particular demographic group, the particular part of the total available audience, at which the message is directed

Voice Over (VO): an announcer reading over a music segment

Wet: a recording to which reverberation or echo has been added

USING SOUND EFFECTS

Unlike the days before the extensive use of ETs (review above definition), few of today's sound effects need be "custommade" during the production of the radio message. Readily available sound effects libraries like those provided by the Thomas Valentino, TM, or Sound Ideas Sound Effects companies contain virtually every effect piece a copywriter might need to specify. But whether a

SFX is "canned" or specially produced, the vital thing to keep in mind is that it should be used to further the message rather than as an end in itself. The spot or PSA that becomes "that pitch with the locomotive" instead of "that pitch *for*" whoever the client might be, is a waste of everybody's effort (unless you're really selling locomotives).

Whether used to set locale, heighten a product-use situation, or give substance to something that is silent in real life, a sound effect must (1) advance message progression, (2) enhance the main copy point (3) integrate well with the copy's style and form, and (4) accomplish its task without creating aural clutter. Sound effects should not be used in a misguided attempt to duplicate reality. The only result will be a muddled jumble of noise. Instead, the writer should select, as the human ear selects, the most prominent or most relevant sounds in a given situation, use these with discretion, and forget about the rest.

In addition, Foote, Cone & Belding's group copy head Larry Rood has long cautioned that, "If you are going to use sound effects, make sure they register. The sound of a car skidding and crashing is easily recognizable. A boulder rolling down a mountainside may not be. It helps to describe the action at the same time you use the sound effect."[9] The "slamming door" PSA featured below is a good illustration of this principle and also demonstrates how even a single, stark sound effect can be used to characterize a complex condition.

(SFX: SLAMMING DOORS, RAPID FIRE, REVERBERATING)

ANNCR: Behind millions of doors in America, people are trapped
        alone—(SLAMMING DOOR) suffering from a contagious disease;
        which has reached epidemic proportions. (SLAM) The disease
        can be passed from parents to children and from those
        children to the children of the next generation. (SLAM)
        Every year, that disease hurts an estimated one million
        children. Countless others are emotionally crippled for
        life. An estimated eighty percent of America's prison
        inmates have suffered from the disease. That disease
        (SLAM) is child abuse. (SLAM) Child abuse hurts everybody.
        But it doesn't have to happen. With enough people who
        care, we could help form crisis centers and self-help
        programs. Together, we could help prevent child abuse.
        For more information on child abuse and what you can do,
        write: Prevent Child Abuse, Box 2866, Chicago, Illinois
        60690. What will you do today that's more important?

(Courtesy of The Advertising Council, Inc.)

Alternatively, as in the following message for the National Council on the Aging, specific copy identification of the sound effect can be deliberately withheld for a few moments to build listener interest. This approach should be risked, however, only when (1) you have but a single sound effect, (2) it well

9. Larry Rood, writing in "Monday Memo," *Broadcasting Magazine*, November 11, 1974, p. 14.

represents your central copy point, and (3) you don't try to string the listener on too long before providing unequivocal verification of just what that sound *is*.

```
(SFX:    CREAKING OF ROCKING CHAIR---FEATURE)
MAN:     Do you know you're slowly becoming part of the fastest
         growing minority in the country?
WOMAN:   What?
MAN:     Would you mind standing up for a moment?
WOMAN:   Huh---(SFX: CREAKING STOPS) Hey, where are you going with
         my rocker?
MAN:     Are you willing to take old age sitting down?
WOMAN:   Sitting-?
MAN:     You are going to be old some day.
WOMAN:   All right, all right; but you didn't have to take my
         rocker to prove your point, did you?
MAN:     You have to get off your rocker to stand up. Stand up, or
         be prepared to just sit back and rock your life away.
WOMAN:   I see what you mean.
MAN:     This message has been brought to you by this station, The
         Advertising Council, and the National Council on the
         Aging.
WOMAN:   Thank you.
```

(Courtesy of The Advertising Council, Inc.)

Sometimes, sound effects are most effective when contrasted with a much quieter if not entirely silent condition. In a classic commercial, Farrell Lines, a large shipping firm, once used this principle to undercut some executives' stereotypes about Australia by dramatizing the vitality of its business climate. Against a cacophony of bustling, industrial SFX, the voice-over copy pointed out that:

```
Australia is so booming that you can't hear the sheep being
sheared. You can't hear tennis balls pinging off rackets. You
can't hear koala bears eating leaves off eucalyptus trees. Listen
to the sounds of booming Australia.[10]
```

One caution: sound effects should never be expected to accomplish identifications beyond their intrinsically recognizable aural capabilities. Examples like the following are impossible to portray adequately without the assistance of spoken copy.

```
(SFX: WATER BEING POURED INTO CAR RADIATOR)
How does listener know the receptacle is a radiator?
How does listener know it's water and not some other liquid?
```

10. Emery Dobbins, writing in "Monday Memo," *Broadcasting Magazine*, May 18, 1970, p. 18.

```
(SFX: HORSE CHOMPING ON APPLE)
```
How does listener know it's a <u>horse,</u> not a slovenly human?
How does listener know it's an <u>apple?</u>
```
(SFX: 10-YEAR-OLD GIRL GOING UP STAIRS)
```
How does listener know she's <u>10?</u>
How does listener know she's a ''she''?
How does listener know she's going <u>up</u> and not <u>down</u> stairs—or on stairs at all?

USING MUSIC

Like sound effects, music is readily available to the commercial and continuity writer in conveniently prepackaged form from a wide variety of sources such as TM Productions, Network Production Music, Thomas Valentino, and Capitol Production Music. This availability is especially helpful to the in-station writer because if the station has purchased the library or service from any of these or several other firms, all relevant copyright fees have already been paid, and the often formidable task of obtaining copyright clearances is thereby avoided. While this is not a casebook on copyright law, it must be emphasized that music virtually never comes "free." Mechanical, synchronization, performance, and grand dramatic rights may all be involved in your using even a brief musical cut and may often be held by several different firms or individuals. The fact that your station has ASCAP, BMI, and SESAC performance rights licenses does *not* give you the automatic prerogative to take popular compositions licensed to them as background music for your continuity. In fact, such unauthorized appropriation may constitute overt copyright infringement.

Especially if you're a freelancer or in-station writer directly involved in the production of your message, make certain the music you've selected has been properly cleared—and for more than just performance rights. Advertising agencies and other larger organizations will normally have specific employees who assist with these clearance concerns.

And wherever the music comes from, take special care that it is of professional quality in styling and sound reproduction. As more and more sources of production music come on the scene, there is a natural tendency on the part of some companies to underprice the competition by offering an underproduced product. If the music bed sounds like it emanated from the group shown in Figure 6-1, don't use it to accompany your copy. Bargain basement music is a cellar, not a stellar commodity. If it is cheap, it will sound cheap and so will your client.

As the third of radio's trio of potential sound elements, music has unsurpassed utility in quickly and comprehensively constructing an environment for the message it complements. William Stakelin, president of the Radio Advertising Bureau, observes that "music is the most natural way to stimulate thought and action. . . . Music sets up our expectations—brings a pastoral scene into focus, swells up feelings of love or affection, hints at troubles to come, establishes movement and, using a basic sound motif, heralds an important idea or event. Music plays to the moods and desires of customers. The right music, in the right format, on the right stations establishes an instant unspoken bond with your

Figure 6–1.   Have you ever wondered where some production music is recorded?

(Courtesy of Michael Anderson, Network Production Music, Inc.)

target audience."[11] The necessity for this appropriateness cannot be overstated. The copy style, the product or service category, the situation being conveyed in the spot, and the station(s) on which the spot will be run must all be considered in music specification. Because, for the radio copywriter,

M	U	S	I	C
e	s	e	n	o
a	i	n		n
n	n	t		t
s	g	i		e
		m		x
		e		t
		n		
		t		
		s		

Intrinsically, music *does* mean using sentiments in context. Music can tap, simulate, and stimulate a wide variety of feelings in even a very short passage. And even a very short passage will, because of its "sound power," constitute a milieu, a context, that had better not be self-standing but a complementary

11. William Stakelin, writing in "Monday Memo," *Broadcasting Magazine*, December 10, 1984, p. 26.

component of the message as a whole. If your music says one thing and your copy another, it will probably be music's point of view that predominates in both the listener's short- and long-term recollection. Never start off with a musical "bed" just because you like it and then try to construct a message around it. You may end up with a nice commercial for the tune but only at crippling expense to your central copy point.

In radio, the introduction of music will be much more attention-getting than it is on television, where audience focus is already heavily oriented toward the visual. But if the music's style or character at all clashes with the flow and approach of the copy, the melody will invariably become a disrupting rather than an enabling element. Don't be afraid *not* to use music in your copy. In fact, if surrounding messages tend to make heavy use of music, a solid piece of univoice writing will stand out very well by comparison. This is especially true when all your client's competitors have tripped down Melody Lane and you want your campaign to be distinct. Imagine how this antijingle jingle stands out in a market where each of the competition has tried to outdo all the others with slick lyrics.

WOMAN:	We'll be recording your jingle in Studio B.
DICK:	Is this singer a good—
WOMAN:	Oh, it'll be the best jingle ever for J. K. Chevrolet.
DICK:	Gee, I don't even know how it goes.
WOMAN:	Well, it goes something like, 'Nice friendly place, sing, sing, something, something—'
DICK:	Fine.
WOMAN:	'—no pressure, no hype—'
BOTH:	'Sing sing sing—'
DICK:	Yeah.
WOMAN:	Then 'something about a relaxed friendly place—'
DICK:	Good. Very good.
WOMAN:	Then 'talk talk talk, more'—
BOTH:	'Sing sing'—
WOMAN:	Then with a big finish: 'J. K. Chevrolet!'
DICK:	Fine.
WOMAN:	Is that okay?
DICK:	Let's do it.
WOMAN:	(Shouting) Alrighty, J. K. Chevrolet Jingle, take one.
SINGER: (MALE)	(Sings, kind of) 1, 2, 3, 4. <u>NICE FRIENDLY PLACE—SING SING, SOMETHIN' SOMETHIN', NO PRESSURE, NO HYPE SING SING, TALK, TALK, TALK TALK, SING, BIG FINISH: J. K. CHEVROLET!</u>
WOMAN:	Well, how do you like it?
DICK:	It's just like you said.

WOMAN: (Shouting) Okay, Mac, that's a wrap.
DICK: Man knows how to sing, no doubt about it.
WOMAN: Isn't he good—
ANNCR: J. K. Chevrolet. 3901 North Broadway at the Bypass.

(Courtesy of Fran Sax, FirstCom.)

If your script idea really calls for music, and if the music is selected *in light* of the copy and not vice versa, you can create a very relevant and focused aural portrait. Just make certain that the audience does not already have some competing referent for the music you've used. Thus, stay away from lyric tunes or movie sound tracks that have had a previous life of their own unless, as in the following, the original lyrics or context can be shown to have direct bearing on the subject of your copy.

                    Production Note: Music is Don McLean's recording of
                        Wonderful Baby.
(MUSIC:) WONDERFUL BABY
          LIVING ON LOVE
          THE SANDMAN SAYS MAYBE
          HE'LL TAKE YOU ABOVE
          UP WHERE THE GIRLS FLY
          ON RIBBONS AND BOWS
          WHERE BABIES FLOAT BY
          JUST COUNTING THEIR TOES
          (CONTINUES UNDER:)
ANNCR: While some babies float by counting their toes, this
          country endures a reported one million cases of child
          abuse every year and at least two thousand children die.
(MUSIC: UP FULL)
          —AT THE BEGINNING
          OR IS IT AT THE END?
          GOES IN AND COMES OUT
          AND STARTS OVER AGAIN.
          (CONTINUES UNDER:)
ANNCR: Volunteer groups and child abuse crisis centers can help
          prevent these needless, painful deaths. For more
          information on child abuse and how you can help, write
          Prevent Child Abuse, Box 2866, Chicago, Illinois 60690.
          What will you do today that's more important?
(MUSIC: OUT)
ANNCR: A public service message of this station, The
          Advertising Council, and the National Committee for
          Prevention of Child Abuse.

(Courtesy of The Advertising Council, Inc.)

Much of the music a copywriter might choose will be of the straight instrumental variety and, unlike the above, will have no lyric cues to be used as script referents. In such instances, there are several possible methods for specifying in your copy the way you wish music to be handled:

1. In the case of many music services and libraries, you can identify the music you want via the catalogue number and/or the musical segment title that the packaging firm has assigned to it. Thus, your music cue might look like this:

(MUSIC: <u>FADE IN</u> 'COUNTRY TWANG,' EZQ 634-R2)

2. Similarly, a particular passage within a larger work that exists independently of a sound library can be specified as follows:

(MUSIC: <u>ESTABLISH SECOND THEME FROM BEETHOVEN'S</u> 'EGMONT OVERTURE')

(MUSIC: <u>SNEAK IN FLUTE SOLO FROM RIFKIN'S</u> 'THREE JAZZ NIGHT'—SOLO IS 2:40 <u>INTO THE PIECE</u>)

3. Alternatively, for the copywriter who does not have direct access to a music library, it is sufficient to construct a phrase that specifically describes the musical effect sought. The tempo, the style, and, if possible, the arrangement of the desired passage should be indicated. If the particular musical effect is important and precise enough to be used in your copy, you as a writer should have little trouble finding the proper adjectives to describe it:

(MUSIC: <u>FADE UP LANGUID, OBOE DAYDREAM</u>)

or, for an entirely different effect:

(MUSIC: <u>FEATURE FRANTIC PERCUSSION EXPLOSION</u>)

In this Milk Advisory Board treatment, the phrase "TRAVELING ROCK. SMALL GROUP" sets down the essential requirements for the music but without locking in to any one song or recording that might be unclearable or prohibitively priced. This is generally the most feasible practice. Identify the musical specifications you desire but try not to make them so inflexible that the whole spot must be junked if a single tune or cut is unobtainable.

(MUSIC:	<u>TRAVELING ROCK. SMALL GROUP. ESTABLISH, THEN CUT FOR DIALOGUE.</u>
TOUGH GUY:	Better baste that barbequed chicken with butter!
SOCIALITE:	Otherwise it's underprivileged chicken.
(MUSIC:	<u>CONTINUE, THEN CUT FOR DIALOGUE</u>)
GOOD OL' GAL:	Fresh corn! Ah barbeque mah ears with butter.
ENGLISHMAN:	Isn't that painful?
(MUSIC:	<u>CONTINUE, THEN CUT FOR DIALOGUE</u>)
SEX SYMBOL:	Mmm, hot buttered French bread in foil.
ESTABLISHMENT TYPE:	That wraps it up!

(MUSIC:	<u>CONTINUE, THEN FADE TO END</u>)
SINGERS:	<u>BUTTER, BUTTER! BUTTER, BUTTER, BUTTER, BUTTER</u>— (Fade to end)
ANNCR(VO):	Your barbeque deserves the best. Butter. Real Butter.
LOCAL LIVE ANNCR:	Manufacturing Milk Advisory Board

(Courtesy of California Manufacturing Milk Advisory Board and Cunningham & Walsh, San Francisco.)

Succinct Sound Appeal and *Poetic Packaging,* as well as proper format, terminology, sound effects, and music use (or avoidance) are the key elements to be relied on in styling radio copy that truly engages the "theater of the mind." Whether it's a short piece of continuity, a public service announcement, or a commercial for the client's new room freshener, radio can be any copy-writer's great challenge. "After all," urges associate creative director Ed Butler, "radio is all yours. You create it. You select the talent. You may even get the chance to direct your brainchild. And, more often than not, radio is 60 seconds. Epic proportions in a world that seems to be measured in 10- and 30-second segments. It's my opinion that if you can write good radio, you can write great television."[12] Besides, radio doesn't have the hobbling blinders of TV's picture tube casing or print's column inch. Radio, when professionally written, is as expansive and unbounded a medium as you can induce yourself and your listener to make it.

12. Ed Butler, "Why Creatives Avoid Radio," *ADWEEK/Midwest,* October, 1983, p. R.R. 38.

Chapter Seven

RADIO HOUSEKEEPING COPY

Fundamentally, radio housekeeping copy can be divided into two categories: continuity (in the narrow sense of the term) and public service announcements. Even though these varieties of copy may seem far more mundane and far less lucrative than the world of radio advertising, both can present challenges and problems that, once met and solved, will make you a more competent commercial creator. For continuity demands the best marriage of clarity and brevity, and PSAs provide incomparable practice in bringing intangibles to vibrant and concrete life. This clarity, brevity, vibrancy, and tangibility are esteemed qualities to which every good commercial writer, every good *broadcast* writer, should aspire.

In this chapter, we will first examine the main types of continuity writing with which you will most likely be faced and then devote a separate discussion to the workings and requirements of public service announcement construction. Although they will not be reintroduced here, don't forget that the elements of good radio writing discussed in the previous chapter apply just as much to continuity and PSAs as they do to advertising copy.

IDs AND STATION PROMOS

These two varieties of continuity writing can occur separately or as one and the same thing. A station identification may just give the information required by governmental regulations—the call letters and city to which the station is licensed—and then apply the remainder of the ten seconds to a brief "pop-in" or billboard commercial. This, as mentioned earlier, constitutes a *shared ID*. Alternatively, the ID may be entirely devoted to station self-promotion, once the legal niceties are out of the way. In fact, most stations schedule far more IDs than required by law as a means of reasserting their identity for the listener. Since these additional announcements are not compulsory, they need not even contain the name of the station's home city but can be completely appropriated for the station's image-building tasks. They may therefore be shorter, or a good deal longer, than the traditional 10-second identification.

An example of the first type of identification, with two seconds for the government and eight seconds for the station's sales department, would typically be fashioned like this:

This is KTRE, Cedarton. Enrich your day with Nestor's Ice Cream in fifteen dairy-delicious flavors. Nestor's Ice Cream makes any meal a party.

For variety, the two parts of the ID can also be reversed:

Keep your smile, keep your teeth. Cranston's Sugarfree Gum satisfies without danger of cavities. Chew Cranston's for enjoyment and safety. This is KTRE, Cedarton.

A legal ID that is pressed into service for station promotion can be set up this way:

This is KTRE, Cedarton. The week's best music, today's news and tomorrow's weather. All for you on the Big 102. KTRE—your hits-happy radio station.

Or, it too can be juxtaposed and a mini-PSA thrown in as a public relations gesture:

Your hits-happy radio station doesn't want trees to be only a thing of the past. Be careful with campfires. This is hits-happy radio, KTRE—Cedarton.

Optional IDs, of course, cover a much wider spectrum since they are played when the station wants to play them and contain whatever information the station most desires to lodge in the listener's memory. These IDs may be only 2–3 second "cut-ins" or entire features in themselves. They are most often straight copy that ties into a particular format, show, or personality while always making certain that the station is clearly positioned for the listener:

It's good to have you with me today on <u>The Bill Robinson Show</u> on KJCK.

1340 AM, your flagship station for the Kansas City Kings. And you're with <u>(Personality's Name)</u> on KCKN.

You're spending your morning with 'Wire.'. W-I-R-E. 1430 Radio in Indy. And this is Bill Robinson.

(All of the above courtesy of Jon R. Potter, The Musicworks, Inc.)

A taste of the Big Bands, the best of the crooners, and the rest of your all-time favorite melodies. We've got the 'Music of Your Life' every day here on WMAS, Springfield.

We've got <u>all</u> the songs you grew up with. They're part of the 'Music of Your Life' right here on WMAS, Springfield.

Soft as velvet, smooth as silk. The 'Music of Your Life' flows on at WMAS, Springfield.

The words of a loved one. Tender moments. A joyful reunion. The 'Music of Your Life' brings it all back crystal clear at WMAS, Springfield.

(Courtesy of Al Ham, Research Center, Huntington, Ct.)

Optional IDs like those above, are also known as *separators* and should be regularly rewritten, updated, personalized, and localized for maximum listener impact. The station strives to rotate these throughout various parts of the day and on a week-to-week basis in order to have well-established identity without listener-boring redundancy. Thus, many such separators are usually required from the copywriter.

Transitional copy is a separator designed to segue from one program type to another. Here are two examples of transitional separators that assist flow from news and into music. In the first, the news was just read by the disc jockey. In the second, where a separate newscaster is on duty, the newsperson escorts the listener back to the record spinner.

It's (temperature) at (time). I'm (d.j. name), and I've got more of the 'Music of Your Life' on WMAS, AM-1430.

It's (temperature) at (time). I'm (newscaster name), WMAS News. Now, (d.j. name)—with more of the 'Music of Your Life' on WMAS, AM-1430.

(Courtesy of Al Ham, Research Center, Huntington, Ct.)

Optional ID material can also be in lyric form, usually obtained from a specialty production house. The collection of WFYR identifications that follow illustrate the wide divergency in running time that optional lyric IDs exhibit. These were all produced as lyric copy and set into customized musical "beds" by TM Productions of Dallas. As you will note, some of these lyric sets are written with parentheses. This is done to indicate a *musical echo* effect. Since the copy is prerecorded, there is no need to worry about any announcer confusion resulting from this unorthodox use of parenthetical punctuation.

1. :10 You are the words (you are),
   We are the music (you are the music),
   W F Y R, Chicago.

2. :14 We are the music.
   Liftin' your spirits
   when you're feelin' low,
   feelin' low
   W F Y R
   W F Y R.

3. :16 We are the music.
   We are the sweet, sweet music.
   We are your music,
   W F Y R.

4. :19 We are the music.
         A song that lasts the whole day long,
         W F Y R.

5. :26 You, You are the words,
         and we, we are the music.
         We'll make a song that lasts the whole day long.
         We'll make it last all day
         W F Y R.

6. :37 Like a guitar without a hand to play it,
         no music will it bear.
         Like a symphony with no ear to hear it,
         wasted in the air.

         Like a beautiful harmony waiting for its melody,
         where would we be without you, Chicago?
         Where would we be without you?

         You are the words—we are the music,
         we are the song, but you are a star
         on W F Y R.

7. :49 You are the words
              You are the words
                  You are the words
                      You are the words—
         You are the words.
         You give the laughter meaning,
         the tears, their feeling,
         in everything we play.

         We are the music.
         We put the rhythm and the melody into the songs
         as you sing along.
         Come on and sing along.

         You are the words, we are the music.
         Together we make the music of Chicago on
         W F Y R.

         You are the words and we are the music.
         W F Y R,
         you are the words and we are the music.

8. 3:15 Anytime or anywhere you go,
         listen in on the music show.
         For all those little things
         you might wanta know,
         turn on your radio (turn on your radio).

              You are the words, (we are the music),
              we are the music, (make it last, make it last).
              We'll make a song that lasts the whole day long,
                WFYR.

```
        You are the words, (we are the music)
        we are the music;
        together is where we belong.
    So bring your dreams along and make 'em real,
    'n get a little closer to the way you feel (the way
        you feel)
    lift your spirits when you're feelin' low,
    turn on your radio (turn on your radio).
        You are the words, (we are the music),
        we are the music, (make it last, make it last).
        We'll make a song that lasts the whole day long,
            WFYR.
        You are the words, (we are the music)
        we are the music;
        together is where we belong.
    Just to make you happy or just be where you are,
    we are the story and you are the star.
        You are the words, (we are the music),
        we are the music, (make it last, make it last).
        We'll make a song that lasts the whole day long,
            WFYR.
        You are the words, (we are the music)
        we are the music;
        together is where we belong.
```

(Courtesy of TM Productions.)

It should be obvious from these examples that IDs, when linked with music, will usually expend far fewer words in the time alloted than would straight copy. You can't pack a music bed with words and still expect that bed to play a balanced role in the total impact of the message. It must be made clear, too, that the style of the music and the swing of the copy should mesh, not only with each other, but also with the overall "sound," with the particular program format, that the station is striving to exemplify. Obviously, the format of WOLF, as epitomized in the following lyric, is a much more up-tempo sound than that of WFYR.

```
The city's got me runnin',
I ain't losin' ground.
The music's got me hummin',
movin' to the sound.
Oh, Syracuse, like a lover
    you're always in my heart.
Oh, your rhythm rocks me to and fro
and gets me where I wanna go.
Oh, move me, move me,
    rhythm of the city is WOLF.
```

(Courtesy of TM Productions.)

IDs constitute a station's most available and most important continuing public relations device. It is therefore vital that they be well written, well produced, and carefully oriented in consultation with station programming executives. More than any other type of material a copywriter creates, the ID will reflect on the character and identity of the station for which it is constructed. Consequently, it is essential that copy and program personnel be operating on exactly the same wavelength when it comes to aural definition of what the station is, and of what it is striving to say about itself. In today's radio, *format* is everything. It imbues everything the station airs and everything the station sells or fails to sell. Continuity/programming clash makes for a disjointed, schizophrenic station personality that disrupts format design and integrity. The format will *never* be changed to fit the style of your continuity so your continuity had better be a mirror image of that format from its very inception. This rule applies to all continuity but especially to the ID material, which is supposed to promote and exemplify the format's very essence. Notice how both format essence and station location are communicated in this lyric ID for Washington D.C.'s WRQX:

```
Move right on Q
Go right to the top.
On Q107 the hits never stop.
Yeah, 107—it's right on Q
Less talk—more music
comin' to you.
So slide to the right
'bout as far as you can
the hits are just waitin'
for a twist of your hand.
Hits happening right on Q
Q107
Q107
Hits happening right on Q
Riiiii-ght!
```

Courtesy of WRQX Radio.

At the same time as they are reflecting station format, IDs can acquire heightened relevance to the listener by blending in with what is in the audience's mind at the moment—by merging with the particular time of day, local event, or season of the year.

```
Look for sunny skies through tomorrow in the Sioux Empire. Anita
Mason has the complete forecast at the top of the hour on KIOV.
```

```
It's a February 19th already in KIOV Country and the town is
filling up with some beautiful ladies. This is the opening day of
the Miss South Dakota Beauty Pageant at the Jeschke (JESS-key)
Fine Arts Center.
```

(Both the above courtesy of Jon R. Potter, The Musicworks, Inc.)

There is no happier sound than the music of Christmas. For the
next 36 hours WOOD-FM presents the sounds of the season for your
holiday enjoyment. Please share with us this continuous gift of
song.

(Courtesy of Joe Borrello and Paul Boscarino, WOOD Broadcasting, Inc.)

Seasonal IDs can even be exploited to push the station's own promotions,
thereby getting the audience excited about these events and about listening to
the station to which they are linked. In this WMAQ stanza, the outlet's current
contest is given clear definition and unmistakably tied to station character and
identity.

Listen to the country, 6-7-0, WMAQ, Country Music Radio.
He was seekin' his fortune, didn't have much dough,
Just a suitcase, new boots, and an' old radio.
Found an all-night cafe and played his radio,
Had a cup of coffee, had no place to go.
The announcer spoke up, said 'Hello my friend,
    We got money and prizes for you, won't you listen
    and win on WMAQ.'
So he listened and played, he had nothin' to lose.
The DJ said, 'Son, you've won' on WMAQ.
Listen to the country, 6-7-0, WMAQ, Country Music Radio.

(Courtesy of TM Productions.)

Music cuts and copy can also be combined in generating excitement for a
station-sponsored outing, as in this high-energy promo piece for a WRQX
concert:

(MUSIC: <u>DRIVING ROCK AND ROLL INSTRUMENTAL UP AND UNDER QUICKLY</u>)
ANNCR: Q107 presents the greatest summer of rock and roll in
        Washington's history. All summer long, see your favorite
        rock and roll groups:
        (REVERB VOICE)
        The Doobie Brothers.
        Chicago.
        The Cards.
        Jackson Brown.
        The Beach Boys.
        The Blues Brothers.
        Tom Petty and the Heartbreakers.
        (END REVERB)
        and more. The Q has the best seats right down in front
        reserved for you at Merriweather Post Pavilion. The best
        summer of the eighties promises to be your greatest
        summer of fun from the Q. We'll have the Q Party Van on

the streets and at your party with thousands of Q-shirts
for you. And start planning for the Second Annual Beach
Party. It's coming up. So are many other surprises we'll
be telling you about soon. Keep it on the Q for the
greatest summer of rock and roll in Washington's
history. And your greatest summer of fun. From your Q.
Q107.

(MUSIC OUT QUICKLY)

(Courtesy of WRQX Radio.)

In a necessarily more generalized way (to extend playability), ID lyric packages
can also possess this "in tune with the time" quality. In these ID sets for KNBR,
each focuses on a distinct daypart or time-of-year, but all exhibit the same
carefully integrated styling:

1. :22 morning
    It's a Great California Mornin' from San Jose clear across
    the Golden Gate. Have a Great California Morning here on
    KNBR 68.

2. :20 weekend
    It's a Great California Weekend, there's a whole wide world
    that doesn't want to wait. So come on and just begin to do
    whatever you are into and take KNBR 68.

3. :48 Thanksgiving
    Look around you, see the wonder; look inside you, find the
    joy; touch the beauty, feel the love that's everywhere. It's
    a time for sharing blessings with your family and your
    friends. It's a time for giving thanks for being here. For
    the holidays and all the days you'll never be alone, 'cause
    KNBR 68 feels a lot like home.

4. :47 Christmas
    It's so warm and sentimental when there's Christmas in the
    air; it's so good to hear the laughter and the joy. It's a
    time when every woman is a little girl again, it's a time
    when every man becomes a boy. For the holidays and all the
    days you'll never be alone, 'cause KNBR 68 feels a lot like
    home.

5. :48 New Year's
    There's another year behind you, there's a bright new year
    ahead, and you're thinkin' 'bout the things you want to do.
    Makin' promises to keep and keepin' track of where you're
    goin', feelin' happy New Year feelin's through and through.
    For the holidays and all the days you'll never be alone,
    'cause KNBR 68 feels a lot like home.

(All of the above courtesy of TM Productions.)

Though several of these packaged musical IDs are comparatively lengthy, cut-down versions, often referred to as "lift-outs," are also available in a wide variety of timings to lend themselves to almost every conceivable segment in the station's program day or "format clock." The more than three-minutes-long composition for WFYR, for example, was the source of several shorter lift-out variations. Conversely, the KNBR "Weekend" ID was itself a 20-second lift-out from a 60-second piece. Particularly as you create longer IDs, whether lyric or straight copy, consider if and how they will be adaptable to lift-out derivation. In fact, it is often a good practice to ascertain what is the longest ID that the program executive wants, write this one first, and then strive to make it the fountainhead out of which the shorter IDs spring.

Even the shortest ID should center on the essence of your station image line—the one overriding statement that must adhere like glue to the listener's entertainment-seeking consciousness. This may be expressed in straight copy, a musical statement, or very likely, a combination of the two, as orchestrated in Figure 7–1. But whatever its form, the line must embody the station and be almost infinitely expandable from both length and seasonal standpoints.

Figure 7-1. *(Courtesy of Al Ham, Research Center, Huntington, Ct. © 1978 Mayoham Music [ASCAP])*

PROGRAM PROMOS

Many of the principles introduced into the ID discussion pertain equally to constructing promotional continuity for individual programs, station personalities, or program series. Program promos, too, must mesh with the station's overall sound or character and, even more specifically, must attempt to capture the particular offshoot of that character that the program being pushed epitomizes.

```
Gary Havens playing the country hits in KIOV Country. And by the
way, there's more great country music with your favorite stars on
Live from the Lone Star Cafe every Sunday night at 10:05 here on
KIOV.

Big Lake Country Radio and Bill Robinson here on KJCK. Listen to
Swap Shop Monday through Saturday from 9:30 to 10:00 in the
morning. If you have anything to buy, sell, or trade, call us
during Swap Shop at 238-0151.

Jerry Heart keeps you up on what's going on in Kansas City when
he joins Dave Bryan, 6 to 10 in the morning on 1340 AM. Listen
for the news and your favorite music with Dave and Jerry on
Kansas City Country—KCKN.
```

(All of the above courtesy of Jon R. Potter, The Musicworks, Inc.)

Program promos should also exploit seasonal subjects in order to tie the show more closely to what is in the listener's mind, and environment, at the time:

```
(MUSIC:  ESTABLISH AND UNDER)
TIM:     Hi! This is Tim Moore. Do you believe this weather,
         fellow early risers? Sometimes I wonder why I ever
         started doing morning shows. You really have to be a
         little different to wade through snowbanks at 5:30 in
         the morning! But—as the song says, 'We do it for you' at
         106 KHQ. When you need to get started in the morning, we
         bring all the players to the game:
            our sky-watching Sperry Radar,
            our number one news team with Gill Fox and Bob White,
            Doris Craft checks driving conditions,
            Scott Stillings analyzes the ski slopes,
            and Paul Harvey adds his comments.
         No wonder the Northern Michigan Morning Show is number
         one. When you need help starting your day, just picture
         our call letters written in the snow:
         (SFX: SNOW SCRATCH) K____H____Q!
         Who else in the morning but 106, K____H____Q!
(MUSIC:  FEATURE AND OUT)
```

(Courtesy of Tim Moore, WKHQ.)

Short or long, lyric or straight, program promotional continuity must, like all good broadcast copy, convey a sense of immediate, present-tense vibrancy. Radio is a "right-now" medium. So features, guests, or attributes of *future* programs are nonetheless still cast in *present* tense form whenever possible. This not only makes the program benefit easier for the audience to anticipate and visualize, but also cuts down on the drab, time-wasting helping verbs that can destroy continuity's essential conciseness. And in case you were a scholar who slept through seventh-grade English, here is a list of those helping verbs that your broadcast copy should avoid. They are divided into five segments to encourage familiarity if not downright memorization:

1. be, am, is, are, was, were, been
2. have, has, had
3. do, does, did
4. may, might, must
5. can, could; will, would; shall, should

Thus, it's "Jerry Heart keeps you"—not "Jerry Heart WILL keep you;" "we play it for you on 93 KHJ"—not "we WILL play if for you." Similarly, we write that "Tonight, Sportscaster Biff Bicep talks to Cougars' coach . . ." rather than "Bicep WILL talk." Keep it direct. Keep it immediate so the continuity does its job and gets out of the way.

The WKHQ promo had this sense of present-tense "nowness" and so does this spot for Earl Nightingale's *Our Changing World*. Like the WKHQ piece, Nightingale's copy recruits the program's own host as presenter to illuminate the show's essential character and pacing.

EARL: Hello. This is Earl Nightingale with a word for you. The
        word is <u>understanding.</u> It's been my impression that our
        success on the job and off---with our families and with
        the world in general---depends largely upon how well we
        understand ourselves and those by whom we're surrounded. I
        discuss this---and more---here on <u>Our Changing World.</u>

(Courtesy of Bryant W. Gillespie, Nightingale-Conant Corporation.)

Two writing tools are especially helpful in constructing copy such as program promos, which must make a purposeful sound impact in a very short time span. The first of these tools is *evocative phonetics* and the second is the *fulcrum phrase*. Let's look at the contribution each can make.

Evocative Phonetics

Because there is such a compressed time frame in which you must not only identify but also characterize the spirit of the program being promoted, the deft copywriter will choose words not only for the precision of their meanings but also for the appropriateness of their phonetic makeups.

Audiences as a whole tend to respond in different ways to different sounds. They are conditioned by certain quirks of the language to perceive some words as much for their aural composition as for their denotative meaning.

The i sound as in the word li̲ttle, for example, very often occurs in words that depict something little: bit, kid, mitten, chick, tiff, whiff, pill, kilt, thin, pin, inch, lint, snip, wisp, even witticism. Similarly, a crisp, decisive effect is auditorially suggested by words that end emphatically, such as pep, jet, swept, attack, act, clap, clout, and catapult. Or, a rapid, lightning-like impression can often be conveyed more fully by words that begin with the "fl" sound such as: flash, flurry, fling, flay, flag, flaunt, flail, flare, flee, flame, and fluorescent. And, as one more example, words featuring the syllable "-ain" can help to paint a generally listless or unpleasant image, as evidenced in pain, bane, rain, drain, stain, strain, sprain, wane, abstain, complain, inane, mundane, and profane. Thus, a sensitivity to evocative phonetics would cause you to take care that the "-ain" sound is enlisted to describe the condition your product or service is designed to alleviate and not the product or service itself.

Examine the following program promo. How are evocative phonetics used to further its pitch and portray program character?

If talk is a pain and country's a drag, flip your dial to rockin'
98 and The Andy Acne Show. Join the jump to Denver's fast track.

Contrast that characterization of Andy's show with the way evocative phonetics help to depict this one:

The mystery of moonlight on Lake Erie landscapes. Midnight in
Buffalo with the mellow melodies of Larry Languid's Sonatas 'til
Sunrise.

Lyrics, of course, are especially deft evocative tools when instrumental and copy sounds combine to further the same overall mood. The dulcet music that bedded the following "Here with You Tonight" song was complemented by euphonious long vowel sounds as in radi̲o, lo̲w, two̲, kno̲w, go̲ and yo̲u. This last word possesses special utility because, other than his or her own name, *you* is the most pleasing sound in the world to any listener.

Sitting here with you
The lights and the radio way down low
We listen to a song or two
And I know it's gonna be awhile before I go

Here with you tonight
Everything is just exactly right
Here with you tonight
Chicago 101 is our special friend
WKQX playing our song again
Here with you tonight
WKQX Chicago 101
We hear it with you tonight
Here with you tonight

(Courtesy of Jim West, FairWest.)

Fulcrum Phrase

A *fulcrum* can be described as the brace-point of a seesaw. When positioned exactly halfway between the board's two ends, it can hold the board perfectly horizontal once the weight on each end is in balance. Linguistically, the *fulcrum phrase* possesses this same capability. It is a thought unit constructed in such a way that its midpoint is obvious because there is a metrically balanced load on each end. Such a line is intrinsically pleasing to the ear and, therefore, like any pleasing rhythm, makes it easier to remember the message being carried. True, listeners may not be able to define just what a fulcrum phrase *is* but, to paraphrase Justice Stewart's comment on obscenity, they'll "know it [and appreciate it] when they hear it."

The yellow Fuller Paint commercial, which was reproduced in the previous chapter, contains an excellent example of the fulcrum phrase. Not coincidentally, that phrase is also the company's identity line:

```
a century of leadership in the chemistry of color
```

Where is the fulcrum? Between the words *leadership* and *in*. This balance point as shown in Figure 7–2, is literally *composed* into the line and gives it the appealing sense of proportion, of stability, so important in aiding and stimulating recall.

If the fulcrum phrase is a valuable asset for an identity line in a spot, it can be downright vital to the comparatively dwarf-life program promo that often has a *total* of only one or two lines in which to accomplish its objective. There, the fulcrum phrase may well be a necessity to add interest to a line that exists in virtual isolation. Notice how even these one-liner promos seem confident and complete in themselves because they are conscientiously balanced:

```
The tunes roll on with Mel St. John ∧ and they never stop 'til
ten.
```

```
Let Dialing for Dollars ∧ give your purse a silver lining.
```

Here are four more fulcrum program promos. Plot the balance point in each for yourself:

```
Take the pressure out of rush hour with The Jim Mead Show.
```

```
Lou Day has better weather 'cause he helps you understand it.
```

```
Cool, mellow sounds for a warm Akron night as Kay Lenox grooves
jazz just for you.
```

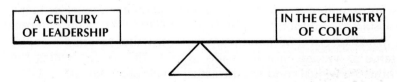

Figure 7–2.

```
Play-by-play baseball with Ken Arcane sticks the bat and ball in
your ear.
```

Fulcrum phrases can also be double-paired. Below is a radio promo in support of a television news department. In addition to making one clear and overriding promise to the listener, it ends with the double fulcrum:

```
Channel 7 ⌃ Action News. It isn't easy ⌃ being first.
```

Through this device, the writer was able to stress both client ID and key listener/ viewer promise while still keeping the spot concise and snappy. Thus, the slogan's sound mirrors the qualities we expect to find in the newscast product.

```
ANNCR:  At Channel 7, we know we're only as good as our last news
        broadcast, because we know that's the newscast you'll
        judge us by. Just because we did a great job of covering a
        story in Lansing yesterday, doesn't help you today when
        the story's in Washington. Yesterday our coverage of City
        Hall may have been brilliant, but today's story is at the
        bargaining table in Warren.
        That's why, everyday, Channel 7 commits everything it has
        to the news. Everything. And everything is a lot. More
        news trucks than any other station, more reporters, more
        writers and more equipment.
        But the important thing is we make this commitment
        everyday.
        So tune in to Channel 7 tonight---not because of what we
        did yesterday, but because of what we're doing today.
        Channel 7 Action News. It isn't easy being first.
```

(Copyright © 1983 American Broadcasting Company.)

INTERVIEWS AND SEMISCRIPTS

Today, the broadcast interview seems to be a more common part of the programming landscape. Playing no small role in this phenomenon is the need for stations to prove themselves more in tune with their localities in the face of increasing competition from other electronic media. The community conversation program type, consisting primarily of interviews, is both the simplest and often the most relevant mechanism by which a local station can show itself *to be* vibrantly local.

Nonetheless, *any* interview requires detailed preparation if it is to jell properly and make a substantive contribution. The broadcast interview is no different and generally needs special ministrations by the copywriter to bring it to full fruition. The same provisions must be made whether the person writing the copy or some other individual conducts the actual on-air proceedings.

In a manner much like that of program promo creation, the copywriter needs to construct an enticing and vibrant interview introduction. This introduction, though brief, must serve three distinct functions: (1) arouse listener interest, (2) provide a tight capsule of information that puts the guest and host in perspective, and (3) make the guest feel comfortable and at home. The same attention-getting devices discussed in previous chapters can be used to accomplish the first objective. The writer might need to structure these opening lines in such a way that they can also be used as lift-outs that serve periodically to advertise the interview for several days before its airing.

Second, the interview intro needs to trace the essential parameters of the subject without being deliberately evasive on the one hand, or giving away the discussion's main revelation on the other. To open a drug abuse show by saying, "Here is a man who was hooked on heroin but after ten months of the new chemotherapy is healthy and free," would leave the listener with little reason to stay tuned.

Finally, since many guests are not professional communicators, the interview introduction must strive to put the individual at ease. In this context, overpraise is just as dangerous as unabashed derision. Too many guests have suffered through introductions that were so overzealous they hardly dared open their mouths for fear of destroying that image. Write a deserved compliment or two for the guest but refrain from using intimidating superlatives.

The interview's closing or "outro" also has three intertwined purposes: (1) reidentify the guest and his or her topic/qualifications for late tuners-in, (2) also reidentify the host and program as well as (3) briefly promo today's next guest or the guest on the series' next show. As in the intro, it is the third function that is fraught with the greatest dangers. The audience must be sufficiently intrigued about the next guest that they will tune in or stay tuned. But at the same time, you cannot demean the contribution just made by the current guest. The outro that seems to imply, "Once we get this turkey out of here, there's a really great person we want you to meet," is an unintentional but unforgivable disservice to the guest who's just finished. The opposite extreme, which might be accidentally conveyed as, "Wish we could bring you back but we've already scheduled some city sewage guy," serves the future guest no better.

The body of the interview may also require the copywriter's attention. You may be asked to prepare a list of key questions that can be put to the guest and that are guaranteed to elicit more than a one-word response. Many program hosts do not have the time, and a few do not have the brainpower, to read up on the topic on which the guest is going to expound. Carefully worded and prechecked questions make the host look suitably knowledgeable, keep the guest comfortable and self-assured, and allow the interview to harvest the expertise or point of view for which the guest was invited in the first place.

Particularly if accompanied by commercial and continuity inserts, this list of questions, together with the fully scripted intro and outro, could be said to constitute a semiscript—a skeletal framework that allows the show to be extemporaneous while still adhering to an established announcement schedule and preordained set of objectives. The continuity writer must therefore sketch in the essential subject, pace, and tone of the show while allowing persons actually on-air to flesh out the program within those guidelines. In semiscripting, the writer succeeds when the show displays a structured spontaneity that keeps the listener unaware it was preplanned at all.

A more open derivation of the standard semiscript entirely omits the questions as well as most outros. It concentrates almost exclusively on carefully fashioned intros and tight transitions between the program and the commercial messages that punctuate it. Normally, this version of the semiscript is used when (1) both a staff announcer and an interviewer are assigned "live" to the program and (2) that interviewer is an experienced communicator/interrogator adept at drawing out guests without major reliance on a set of preplanned questions. *FOCUS*, a daily talk/discussion show aired by Detroit's WJR, possesses both these attributes. A composite semiscript that amalgamates the various pieces of continuity prepared for a single *FOCUS* program is reproduced below:

FOCUS

DIRECTOR:	Hal Youngblood	GUESTS:	
ANNOUNCER:	Hal Youngblood		Dudley L. Carlson
			Buzz Ramsey

ANNCR: From Studio D, this is J. P. McCarthy's <u>Focus.</u>

(MUSIC: <u>THEME</u> <u>UP</u> <u>UNDER</u> <u>AND</u> <u>OUT</u>)

ANNCR: WJR presents an active view of life and living in the Great Lakes area: a lively look at people, places, events and attitudes. Put into focus by---J. P. McCarthy.

J.P.:   Hal, thank you very much. In focus today, Commodore Dudley L. Carlson, newly appointed Chief of the Office for Legislative Affairs, United States Navy. He's manning a desk these days---must be awful for an old submariner. He is the man who serves as the Navy's liaison with the ever-budget-conscious Congress. So we'll get the Navy's position with regard to its role in national security versus the new mood in Congress to slash Defense's piece of the pie.

And then we'll meet the only man I've ever met that, when he tells you a fish story, you can believe most of it. He is a nationally acclaimed fishing expert, Buzz Ramsey, who can tell you anything and everything you ever wanted to know about landing the Big Ones; the Big Ones out west in his native British Columbia. You, right now, believe it or not Buzz, are in the heart of one of the great fishing spots in the country. It's hard to believe, but it's true. We'll get to that, and see how convincing the Commodore's story is, from the Navy's point of view, in just a minute.

```
POS. #1: Free Press spot (R)                    :60
POS. #2: Fisher Buick/Subaru spot (R)           :60
POS. #3: Lawson's Stores spot (R)               :30
```

J.P.:   My first guest is a veteran Navy line commander and
          submariner. He also has served at the Pentagon as a
          member of the Strategic Plans and Policy Section, served
          as executive assistant to the Commander-in-Chief, U.S.
          Atlantic Fleet, and was recently named as Chief of the
          Navy's Legislative Affairs; a liaison, I guess, between
          the Navy and the ever-more-budget-conscious Congress. So
          for a perspective on the Navy's role in national
          security, versus the new economy mood on Capitol Hill,
          it's a pleasure to welcome Commodore Dudley Carlson.
                            (INTERVIEW #1)

J.P.:   Nice to see you today, Commodore, thank you very much
          for being with us. I might march right down to my
          friendly recruiting station. Good luck with Congress.
          The Navy's point of view, expressed by Commodore Dudley
          Carlson. We'll talk to a man who also has some
          experience on the seas, but he's having fun---he's
          fishing. Expert fisherman, in just a minute.

```
POS. #4: WXYZ-TV spot (R)                       :30
POS. #5: Callard & Bowser spot (R)              :60
POS. #6: Prince Spaghetti spot (R)              :60
```

ANNCR: This is Focus on WJR. Today's featured sponsor is
          Outdoorama. Enjoy the great outdoors, indoors at the
          Michigan State Fairgrounds Coliseum, Eight Mile and
          Woodward, now through March 3rd.

J.P.:   One look at Buzz Ramsey and you can believe the fish
          story that he's about to tell me; even when he tells you
          that he landed a giant, big, dog-of-a-fish; a 30-pound,
          5-ounce steelhead out of British Columbia's Thompson
          River where he hails from. In fact, I've got a picture
          of it, right here in front of me. The fish is a monster
          who looks like he's 4½ feet long. Buzz has been a
          professional angler for 15 years now, which makes him
          easy to envy---and admire. He conducts fishing seminars
          all over the country and is promotion director for Lure
          Jenson, fishing equipment company. It's a pleasure to
          welcome you to one of the great fishing spots in the
          world---Michigan.

(INTERVIEW #2)

J.P.:   Thanks for being with us. (MUSIC: SNEAK IN THEME) I hope
           some of your skill and luck rubs off on me next time
           out. Buzz Ramsey, world record-holder fisherman, with
           some good ideas for all of us. And a breath of Spring, I
           might add.

(MUSIC: UP AND OUT TO TIME)

(Courtesy of Hal Youngblood, WJR.)

Interview programs intended for regional or national distribution generally
have greater preparation time allotted than can be afforded on the local level.
As a result, their semiscripts may be considerably longer and their individual
segments much shorter to increase aural variety and, therefore, broad listener
appeal. Since they seek a numerically greater (but not necessarily wider) audience, the sense of locality is exchanged for more extensive production values
and carefully preplanned rather than extemporaneous pacing. In this semiscript
for an internationally distributed religious program, the copywriter is charged
with much greater responsibility in total program sculpting than was the case in
the host-governed *Focus* show. Note how brief and how carefully balanced are
the presentation's individual elements.

SACRED HEART PROGRAM

PROGRAM NUMBER: S-461, J-861   SS: Matt 24:43-44
TITLE: The Lady in Room 421   MUSIC: Tonight (ASCAP)
SPEAKER: Father James Poole   Beautiful Day (ASCAP)
                                        The Kingdom of
                                           the Lord (ASCAP)
                                        Miracle of Life (BMI)

(INTERVIEW #1   Sommers, Cervantes)   1:00
ANNCR: There are many myths about growing old.
              We'll discuss some of them today on Lift
              Your Heart.   :06
(MUSIC: THEME UP-INSTRUMENTAL, 1st CHORUS)   :23.5
ANNCR: (MUSIC: THEME UNDER - 1st VERSE - AND OUT)
              The title of today's program is The Lady in
              Room 421. There has been increased
              awareness of the elderly the past several
              years. Yet, there are still many
              misconceptions about aging. These erroneous
              ideas are sometimes accepted not only by
              younger people but by the elderly as well.
              Father Lucius Cervantes is a member of the
              White House Conference on Aging.   :19
(INTERVIEW #2   Cervantes)   :40

ANNCR:	Dr. Lennie Marie Tolliver is the U.S. Commissioner on Aging. We asked her about the latest statistics on the number of senior citizens who live in nursing homes.	:10
(INTERVIEW #3	Tolliver)	1:44
ANNCR:	Perhaps one of the reasons we accept myths about aging is that we have not been exposed to the facts. Abraham Lincoln once said: ''I am a firm believer in the people. If given the truth, they can be depended upon to meet any national crisis. The great point is to bring them the real facts.''	:17
(MUSIC:	'TONIGHT' - UNDER FOR :07, UP FOR 2:13)	2:13
ANNCR:	Another myth about aging concerns the retirement years. It leads us to believe that once we are no longer active in our chosen work, our lives will become lonely and boring.	:11
(INTERVIEW #4	Cervantes)	:28
ANNCR:	Frank is a senior citizen who retired at age sixty-five after working from the time he was fifteen. He is active with senior citizens' organizations and has developed a new interest which he did not have time for while he was working.	:15
(INTERVIEW #5	Frank)	:45
ANNCR:	One of the most common ideas about growing old is that people suffer losses of their mental capacities as they age.	:07
(INTERVIEW #6	Cervantes)	:21
ANNCR:	The Older Womens' League is a private organization which attempts to upgrade the image of the elderly and women in particular. Its president is Tish Sommers.	:09
(INTERVIEW #7	Sommers)	1:13
(MUSIC:	'BEAUTIFUL DAY' - UNDER FOR :13 UP FOR 2:07)	2:07
ANNCR:	At the beginning of today's program, we pointed out a misconception about the attitude of the elderly toward death. Father James Poole tells us about the feelings of the lady in Room 421.	:12
(TALK	Father Poole)	5:00

ANNCR:	Thank you, Father Poole, No matter what your age, you should make preparations for eternal life. In the Gospel of Saint Matthew, Our Lord said to his disciples: ''You may be quite sure that if the householder had known at what time of the night the burglar would come, he would have stayed awake and would not have allowed him to break through the wall of his house. Therefore, you must stand ready because the Son of Man is coming at an hour you do not expect.''	:27
(MUSIC:	'THE KINGDOM OF THE LORD' - UNDER FOR :14, UP FOR 2:00	2:00
ANNCR:	Many retired persons in our country today do enjoy an adequate income from a pension and Social Security. However, this should not encourage us to accept the myth that senior citizens have no money problems.	:13
(INTERVIEW #8	Cervantes, Carter)	:54
ANNCR:	What can we do to help our elderly friends and relatives? The U.S. Commissioner on Aging, Dr. Lennie Marie Tolliver, has some thoughts.	:07
(INTERVIEW #9	Tolliver)	:32
ANNCR:	Old age is a part of life, a gift of God we should appreciate as did The Lady in Room 421.	:05
(MUSIC:	'MIRACLE OF LIFE' - UNDER FOR :04, UP FOR 2:04)	2:04
ANNCR:	We'd like you to have a free copy of today's comments on aging. To receive it, write to the Sacred Heart Program, Saint Louis, Missouri 63108. In Canada, the address is Box 606, Station F, Toronto, Ontario. Ask for the program entitled The Lady in Room 421, number S-461. Music on today's program was by Dave Mattson singing Tonight. Karen Lafferty was featured on Beautiful Day. Tom Netherton sang The Kingdom of the Lord. Miracle of Life was by Ellis and Lynch. Lift Your Heart is a production of the Sacred Heart Program. Your announcer is John McCormick.	

(MUSIC: <u>THEME</u> <u>UP</u> <u>TO</u> <u>END</u>)

(Courtesy of Jerry Irvine, Sacred Heart Program, Inc.)

Semiscripts can be required for noninterview shows, too, but they are still modularly constructed. In this football game opening, the writer has fashioned a unifying frame in which each broadcast's sponsors can be inserted, rearranged, or omitted as conditions warrant:

(MUSIC: <u>RECORD</u> <u>WITH</u> <u>ATTACHED</u> <u>MUSIC</u> <u>BED</u>)

ANNCR: The Detroit Lions are on the air! This game is being
    brought to you on WOOD Radio in Grand Rapids by:

        Budweiser, the King of Beers. Reach for that
        distinctively clean, crisp taste that says Budweiser.
        For all you do, this Bud's for you.

        Ford and your Ford dealer. Have you driven a Ford—
        lately?

        The Farmer's Insurance group of companies. For
        insurance on your car, home, life, or business,
        phone your fast, fair, friendly Farmer's agent.

        Elias Brothers Restaurants. A fresh choice to enjoy
        at every meal. That's the fresh magic of Elias Big
        Boy.

    This game is also brought to you by:

        Sullivan's Riverview Carpet, with more carpet than any
        one store in the world! Sullivan's, Bridge Street at
        the bridge.

        The Bun Basket, the home of the original Tailgater;
        the sandwich designed to be the highlight of any
        tailgating party.

        Also by Roger's Department Store, on 28th Street
        across from Roger's Plaza. You never looked better,
        at Roger's Department Store.

        And by Miera's Family Shoes, at 2 handy locations;
        8-41 West Leonard, and in the Leonard-Fuller Plaza.

    We'll join Frank Beckman with Lion's pro-football, right
    after this.

(Courtesy of James P. White and Paul Boscarino, WOOD Radio.)

Other frequently employed semiscripts are on-air contest promos and associated telephone format sheets. To avoid listener confusion and legal problems, it is imperative that contest particulars and interchange with contestants be carefully written out in advance. The emphasis here must be on clear delineation of game rules, consistency of respondent handling, and still, at the same time, copy that sounds conversationally appealing. The on-air production spot, mini-promo, and telephone format sheet for WCKY's award-winning "Take Stock in Cincinnati" contest are reproduced below as good illustrations of how these types of continuity should be structured.

(PROMOTION SPOT)

ANNCR:　This is (personality name) inviting you to Take Stock in
　　　　　Cincinnati, as WCKY offers shares in a greater
　　　　　Cincinnati area company.
　　　　　The offer (next or this) hour is (number) shares of
　　　　　(corporate name) stock.
　　　　　(Name of stock) closed (yesterday or Friday) at (price).
　　　　　(Number of shares) has a value of $___.
　　　　　Here's how you can Take Stock in Cincinnati and be a WCKY
　　　　　winner. I'll make a phone call at random from the
　　　　　greater Cincinnati area telephone directories. If I call
　　　　　you, just tell me the name of the stock and the number
　　　　　of shares WCKY is offering during the current hour---and
　　　　　you win.
　　　　　Remember, (this or next) hour, the offer is (number)
　　　　　shares of (corporate name) stock. You're always a winner
　　　　　with WCKY when you Take Stock in Cincinnati.

(MINI-PROMO)

ANNCR:　Remember, WCKY's stock offer this hour is (number) shares
　　　　　of (corporate stock). Write it down. We could call you.
　　　　　You're always a winner with WCKY when you Take Stock
　　　　　in Cincinnati.

(TELEPHONE FORMAT SHEET)

ANNCR:　We're playing WCKY's Take Stock in Cincinnati game. Our
　　　　　random phone call has gone out to (name and address).
　　　　　(Mr. or Mrs. or Miss)---if you can tell me the name of
　　　　　the stock and the exact number of shares WCKY is
　　　　　offering this hour---you'll win the stock.
　　　　　　(response/answer/guess from person called)
　　　　　　(wind up conversation---win or lose---with the
　　　　　　　following)
　　　　　You're always a winner with WCKY when you Take Stock in
　　　　　Cincinnati.

(Courtesy of Bruce Still, WCKY.)

PUBLIC SERVICE ANNOUNCEMENTS

Several examples of successful PSAs have been used in previous chapters as illustrations of various copy principles. As they amply demonstrate, public service copy need not be any less creative or appealing than its commercial counterparts. Yet, too many writers approach a PSA assignment with self-imposed blinders. Because the "client" is a church, a charity, or a governmental institution, they construct dignified, straightlaced, and totally boring messages that are too innocuous to enlist anyone's interest or attention.

If anything, PSAs must be even more creative, more vibrant than commercial copy because:

1. the "product" is often an intangible (safety, love, patriotism, etc.), which must be made concrete for the listener;
2. this "product" often asks more of the listener: give, join, call, etc., with a less immediate or less specific benefit to be gained in return;
3. since they receive no money for airing them, stations are free to select for airing whichever PSAs they wish.

The importance of this last point cannot be overstressed. Provided a *commercial* is not libelous, obscene, or in violation of the station's continuity acceptance policies, we know it will be transmitted to listeners because the station is being paid to do just that. Thereafter, it is a matter of whether the advertisement is appealing enough for those listeners to give it heed. In the case of public service announcements, however, we cannot even take airing for granted. Instead, the PSA we write must contend with those prepared by dozens of other copywriters and organizations equally dependent on making a favorable impression on station personnel before they will even have the opportunity to make a favorable impression on that station's listenership. A study of 150 radio stations done by William Toran of the Ohio State School of Journalism found that stations' "chief complaints about PSAs are that they are like newspaper releases (unsuitable for radio) and that they are dull."[1]

In another study, this one of radio stations in the state of Texas, W. Bryant Boutwell also found that

> "as a gatekeeper actively involved in selecting PSAs for a limited amount of broadcast time, the radio public service director is often pressed for time by other station responsibilities and the sheer volume of requests. The burden clearly rests on the communicator's shoulders to deliver a quality, competitive, ready-to-use public service message that succinctly serves the local public interest. . . . There is a distinct advantage in using well-produced tapes with an emphasis on production quality, carefully timed material and a copy style that complements station format."[2]

A stodgy or programmatically incongruous PSA may attract neither the station programmer nor the listener. And because it is the PSA's task to captivate, in sequence, both of these individuals, special care must be taken in its development. All the techniques and appeals previously mentioned in regard to broadcast writing as a whole, or radio writing in general, should also be evaluated when developing the radio PSA. In addition, there are four special considerations that, though they can also be applied to all broadcast copy-writing, seem to have special relevance in radio public service material. For our

1. William Toran, "Guideposts for Radio PSAs," paper distributed at the 1977 Association for Education in Journalism Convention, Madison, Wisconsin, p. 5.
2. W. Bryant Boutwell, "Public Service Utilization by Texas Radio Stations, *Journalism Quarterly,* Winter, 1980, p. 676.

purposes, these considerations will be referred to as THE FOUR PUBLIC SERVICE POSTULATES:

1.   Keep it all together.
2.   Don't re-wage the crusades.
3.   Stodginess stinks.
4.   The station is your public, too.

Keep It All Together

Because the radio PSA has one relatively intangible point to make and must make it via the initially single-sense medium of radio, there is no time to write ourselves off on tangents. Radio does not have an actual visual to articulate the main point while the audio embellishes it. And a public service "product" does not have the "2-liter bottle" concreteness that allows the listener to set it readily in a visual context. The radio public service announcement must therefore be especially focused and pointed. In it:

a.   every phrase should drive the message forward;
b.   one sentence must lead directly to the next;
c.   no part of the message should be susceptible to cutting without breaking the flow-of-ideas progression.

Aristotle, who created some pretty fair copy in his own idiom, called this process *organic unity.* As he discussed in his *Poetics,* organic unity culminates in the whole being greater than the sum of its parts. Each part leads so inevitably to the next part that the conclusion (the central copy point) is itself inevitable. Beethoven's music has this quality of inevitability and so does a good legal brief or debate case. Beginning with an original concept that is appealing or agreeable to the listener, we then add agreement to logical agreement until the message is accepted in its entirety. Since the parts of the message are so fused, the listener cannot carve it up and attack the parts piecemeal. Instead, the whole must either be accepted or rejected and, if a suitably appealing/agreeable concept was selected to begin the message, the chances of acceptance are therefore naturally high.

In this 60-second PSA, the concept of organic unity is well executed. Its opening premise elicits both involvement and a promise from the listener that are hard to retract later:

```
If you had a friend who was dying, how much would you do to save
him? Would you give your blood? Would you give your money? Sure
you would. That's what friends are for. But every year 23,000
people die in car crashes because they have too much to drink,
and then try to drive. And all those people have friends, and all
those friends don't do a thing to save a life. If your friend has
too much to drink, and drives, your friend could die. It would be
so simple to save him. It doesn't take blood. It doesn't take
money.

It just takes caring. Caring enough not to make excuses. Not to
laugh it off as your friend stumbles down the steps. Take his car
```

keys. Call him a cab. Let him sleep it off on your sofa. Drive
him yourself. Maybe you'll have a little trouble convincing him,
but it'll be worth it.

It won't end your friendship. It'll save it.

FRIENDS DON'T LET FRIENDS DRIVE DRUNK.

A public service message on behalf of the U.S. Department of
Transportation.

(Courtesy of U.S. Department of Transportation National Highway Traffic Safety Administration.)

And just to illustrate that a message can possess organic unity and lift-out capabilities too, here is the same approach in 30-second form. Even though running time has been cut in half, the part-to-part linkages remain persuasively intertwined:

If your friend were dying, what would you do to save him? Give
your money? Give your blood? Sure. Well, if your friend drinks
too much and drives, your friend could die. You could save him.
It doesn't take money—or blood.

It just takes caring. Do something. Don't let him drive. Drive
him yourself. It won't end your friendship. It'll save it.
Friends don't let friends drive drunk. A public service message
on behalf of the U.S. Department of Transportation.

(Courtesy of U.S. Department of Transportation National Highway Traffic Safety Administration.)

Don't Re-wage the Crusades

Public service causes are important. And a writer can become much more idealistic about them than about a tube of toothpaste or a liquid breath freshener. This does not, however, provide license to grab the listeners by the lapels and issue shrill orders as to what they should think or believe. In the previously cited Toran study, an exasperated Illinois station manager labelled PSAs he'd received (and presumably their writers) as: "Not entertaining—boring—pontificating style—self-righteous bastards."[3] More elegantly, a London *Times* reviewer once observed that "good causes do not automatically beget good programs." Listeners are pretty rugged individualists and inherently resent being told what to do—especially by some plastic box sitting on the table or in their dashboard. Arguing with the listener only invites that listener to argue back. And in radio, the listener always has the last word and can have it anytime he or she desires. Especially in the public service announcement, where a fundamental but often nebulous attitude is being promoted, confrontation copy will only encourage the audience to talk back. And it is impossible for anyone to talk back and listen at the same time.

3. Toran, p. 19.

Imagine the understandably defensive reactions of young people if a recruitment message snarled like this:

```
Unless you want to be at the bottom of the heap all your life,
you'd better learn a skill. It's a dog-eat-dog world and you just
aren't qualified to make it. So you better come in and join the
Air Force. We know what's best for you and will pay you well
while you're getting it. The Air Force can make you worth
something. Don't just sit there marking time. Get down to your
Air Force recruiter now!
```

Such a pronouncement virtually begs the listener to counter with clever rejoinders like "Who says?," "How do you know?," "Go bag your head!," or several more colorful responses that cannot here be set down. Certainly, the listener would be energized by such a message—but toward all the wrong ends. In the actual PSA that follows, on the other hand, the copywriter covered much the same ground on behalf of the Air Force, but in a far less argumentative, far more positive manner:

```
Did you know that your job competition tomorrow may be wearing
Air Force Blue today? Yes, it's true. Many young people are
taking advantage of Air Force training and employers know the
value of this training. Find out today if you can meet the high
physical and mental standards to enter Air Force technical
training. It's an excellent way to earn a good income while
you're receiving valuable experience. It's an opportunity that's
hard to beat. Contact your local Air Force recruiter. The Air
Force: A Great Way of Life.
```

(Courtesy of the Department of the Air Force.)

Arriving through the extremely personal medium of radio, the public service message is a guest in peoples' homes, or a rider in their cars. It must behave as a guest is expected to behave or the listener has every right to kick it into the street. Don't push your cause with waving banners and blazing eyeballs. Don't try to re-wage the Crusades in your copy or you'll be just as futile as they were.

This Lutheran Laymen's League PSA is effective because, while it makes its point of view convincingly clear, the message does not attempt to jam its offer of help down the listener's Eustachian tube. The benefit is there, engagingly put, but as an *offer*—not a *commandment*.

```
ANNCR:     If your mother was anything like mine, she probably
           taught you not to ask people two questions. The first
           was: 'How much did it cost?'
(SFX:      MECHANICAL CASH REGISTER RINGS ONCE)
ANNCR:     And the second forbidden question was: 'How much do
           you earn?'
(SFX:      MECHANICAL CASH REGISTER RINGS TWICE)
```

ANNCR: But if you're like me, you haven't always listened to
            your mother.

(MUSIC: <u>SYNTHESIZED</u> <u>BASS</u> <u>NOTE</u> <u>THAT</u> <u>BEGINS</u> <u>AS</u> <u>A</u> <u>LOW</u> <u>LEVEL</u> <u>DRONE</u>
            <u>BUT</u> <u>GRADUALLY</u> <u>GETS</u> <u>LOUDER</u> <u>BENEATH</u> <u>NARRATION</u> <u>BELOW</u>)

ANNCR: Money does talk, sometimes so loudly that it taints
            the way we treat ourselves and others. Scrooges and
            J. R. Ewings aren't made overnight. Some of us spend a
            lifetime listening to our money talk without ever
            coming to grips with a warning about the use of money.
            Perhaps your mother quoted it to you from the Bible:
            ''The LOVE of money is the root of all evil.'' <u>(MUSIC</u>
            <u>FADES</u> <u>OUT)</u> Remember? If you would like a free booklet,
            designed to help you keep the use of money in the
            proper perspective, then simply write to this address:

                    MONEY TALKS
                    2185 Hampton Avenue
                    Saint Louis, Missouri Six-Thirty-One-Thirty-Nine

(MUSIC: <u>MULTI-MEDIA</u> <u>CAMPAIGN</u> <u>STINGER</u> <u>UP</u> <u>AND</u> <u>FADE</u>)

ANNCR #2:   This announcement came to you as a public service from
            the International Lutheran Laymen's League.

(MUSIC: <u>UP</u> <u>AND</u> <u>OUT</u>)

(Courtesy of Rev. Kenneth H. Roberts, International Lutheran Laymen's League.)

Stodginess Stinks

Since the subject of many PSAs is initially less stimulating than a new sportscar or alluring perfume, the words we use and their arrangement must take up the slack. Copy traits that are merely moldy in commercials can be downright rancid in public service announcements where we generally *start out* with a subject that's more difficult to handle. Thus, the following lumpish writing tendencies are especially to be avoided:

1. *"five-dollar words"*
    As a class, PSAs have acquired a reputation for a certain ponderous, bureaucratic copy style. Using bigger words than we need will reinforce rather than confound this stereotype.

ANNCR: The voluntary expropriation of your hemoglobin is a matter
            of unquestioned importunateness as Municipal Hospital
            endeavors to replenish its sorely depleted inventory.

Besides the use of some inaccurate terminology, why couldn't the copywriter just say the hospital was badly in need of blood? Overblown prose doesn't make the appeal seem more official—only more unapproachable.

2. *too much alliteration*
    Trying to dress a dull message in a distracting sound costume is just that—distracting. The listener may marvel at the announcer's ability to enunciate the "pervasive

Peruvian poverty that the penniless peasants personify in patient passivity" but will undoubtedly miss the message's central appeal. Thus, the peasants go on being penniless.
3. *redundancy*
The difference between unwanted *redundancy* and desirable *emphasis* is one of location. Both devices use the same word or phrase several times. But redundancy also puts it at the same place in a number of recurring sentences and thereby drains listener interest. Emphasis, conversely, varies the placement so the word or phrase is exposed at novel and unanticipated junctures. In its deft juxtaposition of "wait" and "waiting," the following message illustrates effective emphasis:

```
ANNCR:   Waiting for some things is a part of life. We wait in line
         at stores, gas stations, movies; waiting is simply a fact
         of life. Except when you're hungry. Except when you're
         poor, jobless, under-employed. Then waiting destroys. The
         Campaign for Human Development believes in people working
         together to solve their common problems so that no person
         in America must wait to live a decent life. The Campaign
         for Human Development, United States Catholic Conference.
```

(Courtesy of Francis P. Frost, United States Catholic Conference.)

Redundancy, on the other hand, would negate this cumulative sense of suspense by giving the repeated phrase an all-too-predictable and monotonous position:

```
ANNCR:   Waiting for some things is a part of life. Waiting in line
         at stores. Waiting at gas stations and movies. Waiting is
         simply a fact of life. Waiting is endurable except when,
         (etc.)
```

Another mechanism for repeating a point with emphasis rather than redundancy is to split it up between two voices who, in communicating the concept to each other, are actually doubling our chances of successful communication to the listener:

```
ANNCR:   Here's Joe Campanella and MacLean Stevenson.
JOE:     Why don't I go first, MacLean. After all, I'm a dramatic
         actor and I can set it up right.
MAC:     Oh, actually Joe, I think I ought to go first. I mean,
         with my talk show experience, I can give it a friendly,
         warm feeling.
JOE:     MacLean, I beg your pardon, but I believe it needs a
         straight-forward dramatic delivery---like this:
         On April 15th, the great Coldwater Canyon Chili Cookoff
         will be held at Saint Michael's and All Angels School in
         Studio City on Coldwater Canyon south of Ventura
         Boulevard. Tickets are only one dollar and the net
         proceeds go to the school building fund. MacLean Stevenson
         and I will be there to meet you. Come as early as 12 and
         stay as late as 5. Chili and fun for everyone.
```

```
MAC:     Joe, I don't like to disagree but I would be a lot less
         formal. For instance:

         Hi, guess what? There's going to be a great Coldwater
         Canyon Chili Cookoff and I'm going to be the official
         greeter. How about that. And I'd like you to bring the
         family out to say hello and have some terrific chili. It's
         April 15th. Saint Michael's and All Angels School. Studio
         City, south of Ventura on Coldwater Canyon about a
         friendly mile.

JOE:     Friendly mile?
```

(Courtesy of Bill Lobb, Radio Arts Inc.)

4. *periodic sentences*
   This construction forces the listener to hold several phrases in mind while waiting
   for the main verb to give it all meaning. Pretentious even for print, the following
   periodic sentence is pure torture in radio as the listener must juggle long clauses
   with one ear and strain for the verb with the other:

```
The need for help, for donations of time and money, for the tools
of farming and education, for a care that negates the neglect of
the past and the abject futility of the future, all of these
needs can be met with a Community Chest contribution.
```

Five-dollar words, excessive alliteration, redundancy, and periodic sentences
are obscuring fumes best kept out of your copy. Their pungent and overripe
verbiage simply confirms peoples' worst suspicions about PSAs in general and
radio PSAs in particular. In short, such stodginess stinks.

The Station Is Your Public, Too

As was analyzed earlier, a public service announcement must be written as
much for the station staff as for the listener if it is ever to make that massive
leap out of the mail bag and onto the program log. If it's not submitted in
correct form to begin with, the copy is summarily discarded. Copywriters should
therefore take the following precautions in securing the best possible reception
for their material:

1. Triple-space all copy on standard 8½ × 11 inch paper, leaving ample margins at the
   sides and bottom. Copy should start a third of the way down the page for special
   format reasons that will be discussed in (5) below. Remember, since PSAs are
   "freebies," those that enter a station's copy book in script form will probably be
   read "cold," without rehearsal, by the announcer or disc jockey. Give them every
   typographical chance to pick it up easily.
2. For this same reason, make sure the copy is cleanly typed on reasonably sturdy,
   noncrackly paper. Clean typewriter keys and a well-inked ribbon are musts.
3. If your PSA is not being provided in prerecorded form (and almost all stations
   prefer recordings to scripts they would have to produce themselves), always give
   the station an ample number of script copies to meet its legal and productional
   requirements. The station will want at least one file copy of the script and a copy
   for each of what might be several continuity books that are used in the control
   rooms and announce booths. Anywhere from five to ten copies may be required. If

your PSA is being prepared for tape or disc distribution, provide the recording studio with several scripts so costly time is not wasted when some minor functionary demands his own copy. And even if you are sending the stations recordings, be certain to include at least two copies of the script for their previewing and record-keeping purposes.

4.   Never use a PSA as a Trojan horse for some commercial pitch. At the very least, such a practice will incur the understandable animosity of the station, which you have consciously or inadvertently duped into airing an advertisement for free. Avoid copy like this, and you'll similarly avoid such hassles for all concerned:

```
The Greencrest Brownie troop is having its semi-annual bakesale
at the Selkirk Hardware store, Cherry Street and Main. That's
Selkirk's Hardware where you can also obtain the finest selection
of tools, lumber, and all-round building supplies available
anywhere in the area.
```

Everything occurring after the street address constitutes commercial copy. If Selkirk wanted a pitch, he should have sold a few more nails and *bought* the time himself.

5.   Make certain that the originating source of the PSA is clearly identified. That's primarily what the top third of your first page of copy as mentioned in (1) is supposed to service. What follows is a sample format head for a radio PSA. While some of this information might be rearranged into a variety of patterns, normally it all should be included somewhere within this reserved space. If the PSA source engenders a good deal of broadcast copy, for example, much of this data will exist as preprinted letterhead or logohead.

```
From:                           For release:
Committee for Field Mouse       Wednesday, November 21, 1986
  Preservation                  Message No.: CFP-64R-86
George Doorstop,
  Director, Public
  Relations
1291 Humphrey Street
Alma, Michigan 48080
(517) 339-6085
Time: 30 seconds
Words: 72
```

· ·

```
ANNCR:   As cities annex more farmland, and developers put up new
         subdivisions, a little one's rights (etc.).
```

This format sample clearly provides the station with information as to the source of this material, a code number in order to identify unmistakably this particular message, an indication of how contemporary this announcement is, and a specification of total message length. Particularly when PSAs arrive from small or relatively obscure organizations, the word count/length data lets the station know that this 30-second message will, in fact, fit into thirty seconds. Thus, the station has the assurance that it will not end up giving more free time to the announcement than it will be able to get credit for.

A slightly different data arrangement is used when the subject of the PSA is a limited-duration event. In such a case, it is vital that neither the station nor the copywriter be embarrassed by the airing of event promotion after that event is over. Consequently, the use dates will often begin before the actual start of the observance and will end on, if not slightly before, the event's conclusion.

```
                                    BALTIC CAPTIVE NATIONS WEEK
          From:                         For Use: March 16, 1986
                                                   to
          Lutchek Botski,                      March 24, 1986
            Coordinator
          Baltic Captive Nations
            Council
          3678 Appian Parkway
          Beal City, Idaho, 79114
          (208) 746-0902                 Message No. BCN-21R-86
                    BALTIC CAPTIVE NATIONS WEEK
                      March 19 to March 25, 1986

          Time: 60 seconds
          Words: 143

. . . . . . . . . . . . . . . . . . . . . . . . . . . . . . . . . . .

ANNCR:  Estonia, Latvia, Lithuania. Separate nations with a pride
        and heritage that should not be blurred by the etc.
```

One final note about PSAs. Keep in mind that, unlike advertisers with which the station has a working relationship and a tangible contract to back up that relationship, public service organizations and the people who originate copy on their behalf may be completely unknown to the station staff. In addition, PSA copy arrives totally unsolicited rather than through the orderly and anticipated channels of the commercial time buy. Public service announcements must therefore sell themselves every step of the way in their content, their style, and the ease of use proper format accrues. Like all radio housekeeping copy, the cleverly fashioned PSA *can* have tremendous surprise impact because listeners' expectations of these continuity types have so seldom been inspired to be high.

```
          Production Note: Fred is casual, Miss Jones captivated,
             throughout the spot.
FRED:   Good morning, Miss Jones.
MISS:   Good morning, Mr. Gaston. How are you?
FRED:   Is Mr. Billings in?
MISS:   No, he's out to lunch. It's just me and you.
FRED:   Well then, speaking of lunch—
MISS:   Yes, Mr. Gaston?
FRED:   Fred.
MISS:   Yes, Fred?
```

```
FRED:   How do you like ox?
MISS:   Mr. Billings? Oh, he's all right—
FRED:   No, no. What I'm proposing is---would you like to go to an
        ox roast?
MISS:   Proposing!
FRED:   October 27—that's this Saturday—at the American Legion
        Hall in Hancock. The Legion's raising money so the city
        can restore Wheelwright Park.
MISS:   Frederic; this is so sudden.
MISS:   Not really. Wheelwright Park's been needing new swings,
        slides and a ball diamond for—
MISS:   A diamond!
FRED:   Yeah. Money from the Legion Ox Roast will build one. Kids
        need a place where they can engage in sports.
MISS:   (Dreamily) Engaged!!
FRED:   You can't let kids play in the street. It's our civil
        obligation to—
MISS:   Civil? I'd hoped for a church.
FRED:   Church? This roast is at the Legion Hall. Do you want to—
MISS:   I do! Saturday, October 27th?
FRED:   Right. Four o'clock at the Hancock American Legion Hall.
MISS:   Oh, Fred! We haven't even gotten daddy's approval.
FRED:   To go to an ox roast?
```

Evocative phonetics, fulcrum phrases, a concerted respect for organic unity, a studious avoidance of strident or lumpish copy, and a little ingenuity can justify and satisfy high expectations not only for radio housekeeping copy, but also for every other form of broadcast writing. No, these particular principles and devices are not the exclusive property of audio continuity and PSAs. Rather, such methods have been set down here because these too-often-slighted copy forms are in need of the most help. Functional continuity and public service announcements require the most incisive use of language possible to merit even a chance at the listener's attention.

Chapter Eight

RADIO COMMERCIALS

Most people, when they hear the term *commercial,* tend to think of television. According to veteran broadcast writer and air personality Henry Morgan, this condition applies as much to folks within the advertising industry as it does to those outside it:

> Too often, in recent years, the advertiser's radio budget consists of whatever is left over after the other appropriations have been made. How strange it is that each time radio has had an outstandingly successful campaign, often being the only medium used, there appears a coterie of instant experts to explain it away. "Oh, sure, that's okay for wine." "Oh, sure, it's okay for a magazine." "Oh, sure, it'll sell a movie."
> No kidding.[1]

Charles Martell, executive creative director of J. Walter Thompson/West, confessed to a meeting of the Southern California Broadcasters Association that he was one of those agency types who had given radio short shrift. Martell listed four fears agencies and copywriters must overcome if they are to tap into radio's great communicative potential:

1. The fear of writing.
2. The fear of "flying out on a creative limb with nothing to support us but our imagination and the minds of our listeners."
3. The fear of going to a client without pretty pictures.
4. And the fear that made it impossible to paint pretty pictures in the first place.[2]

Presumably, by this point in your reading, you, like Mr. Martell, have seen beyond these fears to realize that "radio isn't so much written—it's imagined—and if you can imagine it, it writes itself."[3]

This chapter attempts to heighten your feeling of creative partnership with radio, particularly as it pertains to the medium's viability as a vehicle for advertising not only your clients' products, but your own "fearless" talents as well.

NONCOPY DATA

As we have recently discussed the special format requirements of the PSA script, it may be well to set down the counterpart requirements for the commercial script before proceeding to actual copy concerns. Like the PSA script,

1. Henry Morgan, writing in "Monday Memo," *Broadcasting Magazine,* April 28, 1980, p. 14.
2. Charles Martell, speech to the Southern California Broadcasters Association, Hollywood, California, October 18, 1982.
3. *Ibid.*

the radio commercial must be preceded on the page by the key information needed to service it properly. The following radio script heading contains the data usually required in radio copy administration.

```
                      AIMED-WRITE ADVERTISING
                        (radio-TV division)
2/21/86                 client:     B & E Chemicals
3/9/86 rev.
3/13/86 rev. apprvd.    product:    Dynamite Drain Opener
4/2/86 prod.
                        title:      Plunger Parade
                        length:     60 seconds
                        script
                        no.:        BE-167-86R (as recorded)
```

. . . .

Production Note: Announcer is middle-aged female.

ANNCR: I've got five sinks in my house. All different sizes.
        With different size drains. But they had one thing in
        common. They all clogged. So I had five different size
        plungers. Which all worked---sometimes. Then I found out
        about, etc....

Much of this material will, like the information presented at the top of a PSA script, be constituted as preprinted stationery. The specifics that pertain to the particular spot in question are simply typed in on the appropriate lines.

Some of these data require additional explanation. The series of dates in the upper left portion of the copy head pertain, respectively, to when the commerical was originally submitted for review to a supervising officer, when the resulting revision was prepared, the date on which that revision was approved, and, for a message released in recorded rather than script-only form, the date of sound studio production. The complete chronology of the spot is thus available at a glance and any unusual time lag between stages can be noted. If this same lag begins to appear in the development of other commercials, management can conduct an appropriate investigation to ascertain if there is an organizational bottleneck that needs attention.

The spot title is the colloquialism that illuminates the copy's central concept and provides a quick means of identification for those who will be cooperating in its creation and production. Forcing the writer to set down a spot title is also a good quality control device. If the writer has difficulty evolving a title, or if the title does not relate well to the script as a whole, perhaps the central concept is either faulty or missing altogether. In the following adolescent perfume spot, the "good 'ol Karen" designation chosen as a title encapsulates the message's pivotal character as well as its pivotal problem—a problem our product is adroitly positioned to solve.

ANNCR: Good 'ol Karen. She had more male friends than she could
          handle. But she wasn't satisfied. Problem was, they
          treated her like one of the guys. Good 'ol Karen. She
          just couldn't put up with it anymore. She wanted boys to
          treat and respect her like they did the <u>other</u> girls. With
          romance, candle-light and flowers, rather than candy
          bars, hamburgs and study trips to the library. Then good
          'ol Karen discovered Ben Hur perfume. Its sweet, gentle
          fragrance stayed with her longer than the other perfumes
          she tried. And more importantly, it made the boys take
          notice. That's because Ben Hur perfume touches that
          special sense in men. And Ben Hur is only 69 cents for a
          three-quarter ounce bottle. Now good 'ol Karen is asked
          to parties and proms and her boyfriends treat her just
          the way <u>she</u> wants. Ben Hur perfume. Let it bring out the
          <u>new</u> Karen in you.

The title of this spot captured the very essence of its selling storyline. That's
a good indication of a commercial that serves a single, focused, and specific
purpose.

A script number, such as BE–167–86R in our Dynamite Drain Opener format
sample, is a more objective and necessarily bureaucratic means for designating
a given spot. It is used in intra-agency correspondence as well as in correspondence with the stations and networks whose facilities have been contracted
to air the commercial. With a numerical designation, the station does not have
to take the time to audition the entire spot in order to ascertain whether it is
actually the "Plunger Parade" treatment for which time has been purchased.
The number makes such a chancy subjective judgment unnecessary. Further, a
numerical designator serves to identify the commercial as it wends its way
through the various "continuity acceptance" offices at networks and stations.
Everyone concerned will therefore have an accurate record of which spots have
been previewed by the broadcaster and cleared for airing. (Review the section
in chapter 5 on prohibition for a discussion of industry clearance processes.)

Script numbers may be constructed in several different ways but usually with
an eye toward identifying any or several of the following:

a. the originating agency
b. the client or company for whom the spot is written
c. the spot's location in the total sequence of advertisements produced by the agency
    for that client
d. the year in which the spot is produced or in which it is intended for first airing
e. the medium for which the spot is intended
f. the spot length

Our sample "BE–167–86R" indicates that the client is B & E Chemicals (BE), that
the spot is the one-hundred-sixty-seventh treatment for that client which this
particular agency created, and that it is a 1986 *commercial for use on* Radio.
Alternatively, we might use a number like AW–5–167–60r in referring to this

same spot. In this case, the script number first reflects the agency name (AW for Aimed-Write), and then uses a client number (5) rather than a letter abbreviation. Everything Aimed-Write creates for B & E Chemicals would thus be identified via numbers beginning AW-5. The specific spot sequence number then follows (167), as does the designation that this is a 60-second radio spot. As shown in the Chapter 7 PSA sample formats, similar codes can be used in public service announcement identification as well, though more out of convenience than contractual necessity.

GENERIC TYPES OF RADIO COMMERCIALS

Whatever code number system is utilized for a given account, it should be consistent with the numbers being assigned to all other accounts serviced by that same creative agency. Further, the same numerical system should be used regardless of the particular generic category into which a given spot fits. In general, we can divide radio commercials into eight main classifications:

1. straight commercial
2. multivoiced commercial
3. dialogue commercial
4. dramatized commercial
5. device/gag commercial
6. musical commercial
7. integrated commercial
8. pop-in commercial

Straight Commercial

In this category, which is alternatively known as the "univoice" commercial, a single voice delivers the selling message without support from any of the other sound elements available to radio. Most spots sent to stations in script form for live on-air reading by an announcer or disc jockey are therefore, by necessity, straight commercials. Because it cannot depend on music, sound effects, or the vivifying interaction of different voices, this commercial type requires an especially clear and cogent use of the language. On the plus side, a straight commercial is also very inexpensive to produce since only the script need be sent to the stations. It also means that revised versions of the spot can be created very rapidly in order to take advantage of a local condition or seasonal event. An April snowstorm can sell a lot of leftover sleds if appropriate copy can be quickly marshalled.

Of course, the straight commercial also lends itself to prerecorded rendering by a corporate spokesperson who may be prominent in his or her own right. The copywriter must be careful, however that the words themselves do the selling job and don't become dependent on the personality for the announcement's impact. The spot below, for example, could be voiced by a nationally famous or anonymous local announcer without compromising its well-focused pictorial pitch:

ANNCR: Just for a moment, forget the snow and cold outside.
         Picture yourself standing on a lush, sun-drenched

fairway. As you size up your next shot, the distant flag
rustles in a warm ocean breeze. You can have this
daydream come true now---at Green Grommets, Florida's
premier golf resort. Take the Green Grommets Challenge.
Play three of Florida's best golf courses in Green
Grommets' economical 3-day, 3-night package. Every golf
lover should experience Green Grommets and your travel
agent can tell you how. There's no need to let winter get
in the way of your golf game. Get a head start on spring
at Green Grommets.

Multivoiced Commercial

This is a derivative of the straight commercial since, in both types, the voices
talk directly to the listener. In the multivoice, two or more characters who are
not in conversation with each other, are used to deliver the selling message.
The employment of more than one talent is a means of bringing vocal variety to
the spot and/or helps suggest universality. Especially in a commercial that is
required to impart a significant amount of specific information, the multivoiced
approach can keep jogging the listener's attention more than would a straight
spot. Still, don't make the multivoiced technique a crutch on which to hang
weak copy. It may help with a special assignment problem but, like any generic
type of commerical, cannot do the selling job without well-directed copy that is
appropriately styled to the technique selected. In the following multivoiced
application, three mutually supportive testimonials all speak directly to the
listener in a persuasively interlocked fashion:

FRAT LEADER: The fraternity of 'Alpha Pizza PI' welcomes this
                year's pledges to our noble brotherhood of pizza
                pie lovers. The pledges have successfully completed
                the most difficult of initiations. It was tough-
                eating all those inferior pizzas that—

PLEDGE #1:   Yeah, it wasn't too funny when the guys made me eat
                those soggy things from Pizza Pit.

PLEDGE #2:   And me? I hadta choke down all those greasy pizzas
                from Mr. Joey's. I missed a whole day of classes
                trying to recover.

FRAT LEADER: Sure. They've all been there. They know what it's
                like. But it was worth it. Because now the guys can
                really respect the magnificence of Uncle Mario's
                Pizza. Now they're ready to discover what real
                pizza is. I'm going to open this box and—

PLEDGE #1:   Look at all the cheese!

PLEDGE #2:   And Uncle Mario's wholewheat crust. Really
                something to sink your teeth into.

FRAT LEADER: If you're a pizza freak, like the brothers of
                'Alpha Pizza PI,'—

```
PLEDGE #1:    You skip our initiation.
PLEDGE #2:    And initiate yourself to real deep-dish pizza from
              Uncle Mario's.
FRAT LEADER:  That's Uncle Mario's on South Jefferson. Or check
              the yellow pages for Uncle Mario's free delivery
              phone number.
ALL:          All right, Mario!
```

As the Uncle Mario's treatment shows, universality is implied when we have several voices all saying the same thing about the product, service, or condition. Sometimes, these lines accrue from man-on-the-street interviews, which are later edited into an audio montage. Like a semiscript, the copywriter sets down the interviewer's questions and the desired direction in which the responses should be led by that interviewer. Provided a large number of interviews can be taped from which to choose, the results are often more effective than if copywriters try to script out all the lines themselves. In the old days before cassette recorders and audio tape, universality in the multivoiced approach was always prescripted and much more stilted:

```
ANNCR:   For men—
MALE:    I like Smerchies.
ANNCR:   For women—
FEMALE:  I like Smerchies.
ANNCR:   For everybody—
CROWD:   We like Smerchies!
ANNCR:   Yes, smokers everywhere are finding they love the taste
         of Smerchies cigarettes; the cigarette with the
         full-blown flavor from the sun-drenched Virginia
         heartland. Smerchies cigarettes really let you know
         you've been smoking. So for men—
MALE:    It's Smerchies.
ANNCR:   For women—
FEMALE:  Smerchies for me.
ANNCR:   For all America's smokers—
CROWD:   It's Smerchies every time!
ANNCR:   Smerchies cigarettes---the pride of Virginia.
```

If you do fully script out a multivoiced message, make certain it retains believability. If the result comes across as contrived as the old-fashioned Smerchies effort, it is far better to return to a no-nonsense but still conversational univoice approach.

Dialogue Commercial

With this technique, rather than talking to the audience, the multiple voices used *are* in conversation, in *continuous* conversation, with each other. Usually, one of the voices is a salesman surrogate and the other voice or voices represents the consumer by asking the kinds of questions and expressing the kinds of doubts that we would expect the listener to vocalize. Though radio lacks the immediate feedback of the direct selling situation, the dialogue spot allows us to anticipate and simulate that environment. Thus, in convincing our substitute listener, we are talking with and convincing the real listener on the other side of that radio set.

To be effective, the dialogue must seem natural. Foote, Cone & Belding's group copy head Larry Rood pointed out years ago that:

> Many dialogue commercials sound as though the characters are delivering soliloquies while facing away from each other. Often the dialogue sets up the situation through humor and then suddenly one character delivers an advertising message that seems to come from nowhere. The commercial seems to stop while the heavy message is delivered. Try and make that message part of the flow of the dialogue rather than shoe-horned in between some funny lines.[4]

Just listen to the radio for any length of time and you'll discover how few copywriters have learned Rood's enduring lesson. That is why Walter Hampton, N.W. Ayer creative director, felt compelled to observe that "the toughest form of creative is dialogue, and it's tough to find good writers."[5]

To be a "good writer" in this genre, you must insure that none of your dialogue characters ever wheels on his or her heel and makes a pitch directly to the listener. This tactic only destroys the seeming reality of the situation and the vital eavesdropping orientation that listeners, being humanly nosey, enjoy. Dialogue listeners *overhear*, but straight/multivoiced audiences feel themselves to be *addressed directly*. Thus, if you want listeners to be straightforwardly invoked during the body of the spot, stick to a straight or multivoiced technique. Similarly, when a direct-sell line is mandatory at the end of an overheard dialogue, bring in an announcer to do it so the interrelationship and function of the dialogue's characters are not compromised. Dialogue characters should also be thoroughly distinguishable from each other. If taking a line from character A and giving it to B makes no real difference, that line should never have been included in the first place. There is little enough time to establish credible portrayals without wasting it on verbiage that blurs their identities.

The dialogue spot below demonstrates the virtue not only of strong, distinct characters, but also of using an announcer for a compulsory straight-sell tag.

(MUSIC: JAPANESE FLOURISH)

FATHER: Ah, my son, you have troubled countenance.

SON: I know, pappa-san.

FATHER: Today pussy willow in bloom. Sky without cloud. Yet you drag butt. Wassamatta?

---

4. Larry Rood, writing in "Monday Memo," *Broadcasting Magazine*, November 11, 1974, p. 14.
5. Fran Brock, "N. W. Ayer Sharpens Wits for Aggressive Clients," *ADWEEK/Midwest*, January 28, 1985, p. 24B.

SON: Ah, I save and save money to buy colour television, but more I save, more infraction drive colour TV price out of reach.

FATHER: Oh, infraction is a fract of rife.

SON: But I find out Japanese colour TV go to Canada. There, Granada TV <u>rent</u> colour set for small monthly payment in <u>Canadian dollar.</u>

FATHER: Holy mackeral. In Tokyo you can't even blow <u>nose</u> with Canadian dollar.

SON: Granada include all parts, all service, even colour loaner if shop service is needed---no extra charge.

FATHER: No kidding!

SON: So I call Granada long distance, say send me one, and you know what?

FATHER: What?

SON: Granada colour TV available only in Canada.

FATHER: Only in Canada you say? Pi-pi-pir-pirr—Tough ruck!

ANNCR: Granada TV rental. Worry free colour TV. Forever.

(Courtesy of Barry Base, Base Brown Partners Ltd.)

Dramatized Commercial

In this further refinement of the dialogue technique, the characters not only talk about the product-entailing situation but, usually with the help of sound effects, strive to *act out* the scene right before the listener's ears. This is obviously a more complex and more costly endeavor but can be very audience-involving—provided, of course, that the production doesn't get in the way of the selling objective. Here again, character identities must be well established and direct sell lines should be voiced by an announcer rather than by one of the "real people" the production is trying so hard to establish. In addition, dramatic impact must be secured quickly so the spot can get on with the task of product or service promotion. If the entire time is expended in setting the scene, there will be no opportunity to showcase our wares within that scene.

The Weight Watchers spot below illustrates purposeful audio dramatization. Both dialogue and sound effects work in tandem to present a message that proceeds smoothly and compellingly within the proven and previously discussed *Progressive Motivation* structure:

(SFX: DOOR CREAKING, COYOTE HOWLING)

EVIL VOICE: Can I help you?

LADY: Is this—uh—uh—Weight Watchers?

EVIL VOICE: No, but we're a weight loss company too. Come, let me show you-(Evil laugh)

LADY: Oh, but I have an appointment at Weight Watchers.

```
EVIL VOICE:   We have a number of methods. In here, the starvation
              diet—
(SFX:         DOOR OPENS)
EVIL VOICE:   (Laughs)
MAN:          Food---food---a carrot---a crumb.
LADY:         Oh—
(SFX:         DOOR SHUTS)
EVIL VOICE:   Over here, we have the work-out room.
(SFX:         HEAVY PANTING AND RUNNING FEET)
2ND MAN:      Faster. Faster, I say!
(SFX:         WHIP CRACKING)
(SFX:         DOOR SHUTS)
EVIL VOICE:   (Laughs)
LADY:         Oh---Look, I'm going to Weight Watchers.
EVIL VOICE:   Don't go—
ANNCR:        Instead of the horrors of the miracle diets, Weight
              Watchers has a balanced diet and an optimal exercise
              program. We'll even help you change your attitudes
              about food. And it's all done in a friendly, group
              environment. Of all the weight loss programs in the
              world, none have been more successful than the
              Weight Watchers program. We've helped more people
              lose more pounds than any other program.
```

(Courtesy of Doyle Dane Bernbach Inc.)

Device Commercial

The device approach exploits some unusual sound technique as the carrier of the sales message. Odd blends, wails, oscillations, and modulations are combined with either straight copy or dialogue to take advantage of radio's image potential. If the device itself is the build-up and payoff for listening, this category is also known as the *gag commercial*. Hopefully, the message will be such that the audience won't gag when they hear it.

Radio's devices can conjure up a giant, whistling chewing gum bubble, a gelatin with so much jiggle its vibrations crack the plaster, or, as in the classic Stan Freberg message, a ten-ton maraschino cherry in a hot chocolate-filled Lake Michigan. Sound devices can also suggest implausible alternatives to the thoroughly plausible solution we offer on behalf of the client:

```
(SFX:   BIZARRE ELECTRONIC HUMMING. FEATURE AND UNDER)
WIFE:   (Fading on) What in the world have you built down here in
        the basement, dear?
HUBBY:  It's an electronic automobile vacation planner.
WIFE:   Oh? (MACHINE BURPS NOTICEABLY) How does it work?
```

HUBBY: You just feed in the information about where you're going
         here (2 SECONDS OF TINNY TYPING SOUNDS) and this screen
         shows the best route to take. Then these lights
         (ELECTRONIC POPPING AND CRACKING) show the best places to
         stay and eat along the way. And those dials point out
         detour and road conditions.

WIFE: Silly—We can get all of that with a thirty-five dollar
         Acme Auto Club membership, and all of Acme's other travel
         services besides.

HUBBY: You mean I did all this work for nothing?

WIFE: Well, as long as it's finished. Do you think it'll fit in
         the car?

HUBBY: I'll have to knock out the basement wall to get it out of
         here first. (BIZARRE ELECTRONIC HUMMING GROWS LOUDER)

ANNCR: If you want trouble-free travel, join the Acme Auto Club.
         For just thirty-five dollars a year we'll give you all
         the travel assistance you need---without tearing out a
         wall.

(SFX: ELECTRONIC HUMMING AND CLANKING UP FULL; SPUTTERS TO A
         CHOKING EXPIRATION)

Musical Commercial

As pointed out in chapter 6, music can establish itself more rapidly and more
powerfully than any other sound element. Provided the music matches the
product category and blends well with your product's personality and your
campaign style, it can bring an unparalleled sense of dimension to your selling
message. The use of music in commercials can assume four distinct forms:

1. as a heightener of only the main sales point or slogan
2. as a backdrop for the entire commercial
3. as the carrier of a complete and customized vocal lyric
4. as a scene setter/enhancer

In the first category, a musical tag line is linked to what is otherwise a non-
musical production. Lyric tags such as "From the Valley of the Jolly—ho ho
ho—Green Giant," "Ace is the place with the helpful hardware man," "You're
looking smart—J. C. Penney," "You asked for it, you got it. Toy-ooota," "And
like a good neighbor, State Farm is there," all epitomize this limited but nonetheless incisive enlisting of the recall power of music. In this AT & T commercial, singers are used to bumper what is essentially a dialogue pitch.
Through their use, the copywriter can emphasize the client slogan while still
leaving plenty of time for the dialogue scene to be played out before the
listener's ears.

(SONG: REACH OUT, REACH OUT AND TOUCH SOMEONE)
GAILLARD: Hello—
JACK: Hey, Gaillard.

```
GAILLARD:   Jack.
JACK:       How you doin'?
GAILLARD:   Is that you?
JACK:       Yeah.
GAILLARD:   How you doin' buddy?
JACK:       You recognized my voice on the first crack.
GAILLARD:   I sure do, sounds like you're next door.
JACK:       Yeah, well I am next door, pound on the wall. I was
            thinking about coming up and doin' some fishin'.
GAILLARD:   Great!
JACK:       Yeah, are they biting?
GAILLARD:   Are they biting? My grandmother caught a 500-pound
            catfish yesterday and that was out of the well we dug.
JACK:       (Laughs) Yeah, what she use for bait?
GAILLARD:   She used a boa constrictor.
BOTH:       (Laugh)
(SONG:      REACH OUT, REACH OUT AND TOUCH SOMEONE)
JACK:       I'm gonna come up next week then, that's for sure. How
            are Ann and the kids?
GAILLARD:   They're great. Boy are they going to be excited when
            they hear you're coming up.
JACK:       Ah, that's terrific. Think Ann would mind if I stay
            with you guys?
GAILLARD:   Shoot, no Jack, wait a minute, she's right here, let
            me ask her. (Off mike) Hey honey, what do you think
            about Jack coming up and spending some time with the
            family and everything? (PAUSE) (On mike) Jack, let me
            get back to you on that.
(SONG:      REACH OUT, REACH OUT AND TOUCH SOMEONE)
VO ANNCR:   The Bell System.
```

(Courtesy: AT & T Communications.)

Sometimes, the musically heightened slogan has been extracted from a complete spot-length lyric and used as a tie-in to other spots that are primarily straight copy. Such a practice helps keep an entire campaign integrated while, at the same time, avoiding the cost and copy limitations of having to have every commercial fully scored. Though given in Figure 8-1 in its original full-minute score format, the musical statement, "Colt For-Ty-Five is a dynamite taste" is, all by itself, easily and effectively adaptable to a wide variety of otherwise non-musical messages. It is also amenable to a number of musical stylings for smooth integration into diverse station formats.

The second category, music as a backdrop, is exemplified by the Chanel spot below. There is no lyric in whole or part in such an approach. Rather, music

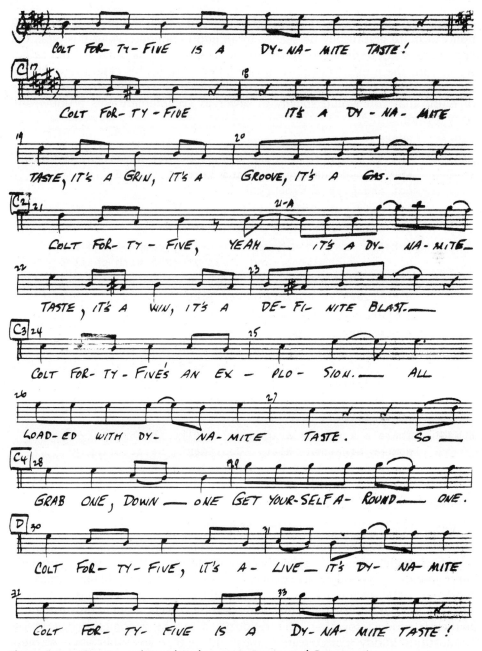

Figure 8–1. *(Courtesy of David Sackey, W.B. Doner and Company.)*

provides the appropriate mood/motif frame into which the product and situation can more graphically be set. As in all good commercials of this type, the copy here is not *dependent on* the music in achieving its objective but rather *works with* the music to acquire an extended and, in this case, more vibrant dimension. As it is omitted on the script, imagine for yourself the precise type of music that you would specify in order to complement this product and copy texture.

(MUSIC: UNDER)

MAN: Why do you give a woman Chanel Number Nineteen? Because she called one evening, and asked if you'd like to go out and grab a hamburger.

          You said sure, why not?

          She said she'd be by in an hour.

          And she was. In a hired limousine, complete to a uniformed chauffeur and a bar stocked with chilled French champagne.

          Hamburgers to go were never like this.

          You drove slowly around the city, looking at the lights. And at her.

          Finally, she closed the window between the front and back seats so the chauffeur couldn't hear the conversation.

          She smiled slightly, and gave you a conversation you'll never forget.

WOMAN: There's a single fragrance to give that woman---Chanel Number Nineteen. Witty. Confident. Devastatingly feminine. Inspire her today, and pick up some Chanel Number Nineteen to go.

(MUSIC: QUICK FEATURE TO TIME)

(Courtesy of Melissa Wohltman, Doyle Dane Bernbach Advertising.)

Music as a carrier of copy that is entirely cast in lyric form, our third category, goes back even to the earliest days of commercial radio. Usually called "jingles," these singing commercials have evolved a great deal from the banal rhymes and melodies of the thirties and forties. Today's jingles or musical images are carefully sculpted to bring a particular demographic/psychographic universe and a particular product together. This rendezvous can be accomplished, says TM Productions' Buddy Scott, because "music, more than any other single element in the advertising arsenal, enables the advertiser to tailor a message to the potential audience's perception of reality, and this is crucial in the decision-making process. Music's unmatched ability to conform with both the real and imagined profiles of an audience has made jingles the choice of more advertisers for commercial effectiveness."[6]

6. Buddy Scott, writing in "Monday Memo," *Broadcasting Magazine*, August 8, 1983, p. 24.

"Contemporary" musical treatments are often selected for lyric spots since most clients want to appear in tune with the times and because a contemporary sound blends well with the formats of the greater number of radio stations. But because few advertisers seek to associate their products with the uncertainty of the *newest* musical trends, the style of the lyric commercial tends to mirror the "Top 40" sound from two or three years previous. Normally, the syntax is kept simple to facilitate meshing with various musical bed permutations:

```
SINGERS:   Time for milk
           Anytime is the right time for milk
           A glass of milk
           On a summer day.
           Backyard barbecue
           Take it on a picnic too.
           If you have a notion
           For cruisin' on the ocean,
           Milk's the perfect ration for your crew.
           In a shake
           Or with a burger
           It's a cool, refreshing breeze to take.
           At the lake
           Don't forget the milk.
           Pour yourself a glass real tall,
           It's time you had a ball
           'Cause any time at all
           Is the time for milk.
```

(Courtesy of California Milk Advisory Board and Cunningham & Walsh, San Francisco.)

Unlike the California Milk Advisory Board lyric, which is a general or "institutional" promotion piece for summer milk consumption regardless of brand, most lyrics in commercials are required to register a *specific product name*. Note the multiple mentions of Stroh's in this vocal treatment:

```
SINGER:    Woah ----
           The time is right
           That feeling's coming through
           Woah and real beer lovers know
           That only one beer will do
           Yeah ----
           Stroh's for the real beer lovers
           Stroh's it tastes like no other
           Stroh's for the real beer lover
           Real beer lovers say
           They go out of their way
           For a Stroh's --- woah ---
           Stroh's for the real beer lover
           Stroh's tastes like no other
```

```
        Stroh's for the real beer lover
        From one beer lover to another --- Stroh's.
```

(Courtesy of Melissa Wohltman, Doyle Dane Bernbach Advertising.)

Though we have given but two examples of lyric commercials here, it should be recognized that, as music producer Frank Gari affirms,

> "music as a marketing tool has never been so widely used and so powerful. 'You Deserve a Break Today' and 'McDonald's and You' have sold a great many of those billions of burgers. It may sometimes be difficult to determine which is remembered the most, the slogan or the music. But would you have remembered 'Coke Is It' without its magnificent lyric and arrangement? Not likely. Good commercial music can be remembered for a very long time."[7]

The final category of musical commercial, in which music is used as a scene setter/enhancer, is epitomized by the Cigna spot that follows. Here, the instrumental bed not only serves as pictorialization agent, but also helps pace and punctuate the entire copy progression. As long as the proper care is devoted to its selection, music can focus your product-in-use scene more quickly and colorfully than can any sound effect or group of words and, if needed, can also be an element off which your talent can play:

```
ANNCR:  At CIGNA, our companies insure thousands of works of
        great art, at hundreds of museums. We'd like to show you
        some of the artwork. But obviously, we can't. Instead,
        we'd like you to listen to some of the artwork we insure.
        Toulouse-Lautrec's 'At the Moulin Rouge.'
            (MUSIC: FRENCH CAN-CAN)
        Degas' 'Dancers Preparing for Ballet.'
            (MUSIC: SELECTION FROM BALLET 'NUTCRACKER SUITE')
        Piet Mondrian's 'Broadway Boogie Woogie.'
            (MUSIC: BOOGIE WOOGIE SAXOPHONE)
        Gilbert Stewart's 'George Washington.'
            (MUSIC: FIFE AND DRUM VERSION OF 'YANKEE DOODLE')
        Hopper's 'Early Sunday Morning.'
            (MUSIC: PEER GYNT SUITE 'MORNING')
        Grant Wood's 'American Gothic.'
            (MUSIC: BLUE GRASS)
        And Philippe De Champaigne's 'Charles the Second, King of
        England.'
        (MUSIC: 'MY COUNTRY 'TIS OF THEE')
        Thank you for listening to just some of the artwork
        insured by CIGNA's companies. You'll enjoy the artwork
        even more if you visit one of the 250 American museums
```

7. Frank Gari, writing in "Monday Memo," *Broadcasting Magazine*, July 2, 1984, p. 24.

for which we provide insurance. CIGNA. We're dedicated to
the fine art of insurance.

(Courtesy of Melissa Wohltman, Doyle Dane Bernbach Advertising.)

One further musical device, though not a category unto itself, must be mentioned. Termed the *doughnut* technique, it is a means of customizing a preproduced national or regional spot to meet local needs and situations. The doughnut normally employs a lyric and an instrumental accompaniment. At a point clearly specified in the accompanying cue-sheet, the lyric stops while the accompaniment continues. This allows the local announcer a "hole" over which can be read information relating to the locations or specials being offered by the client's outlets in that area. In the "closed" doughnut, the preproduced lyric is featured again after the locally filled hole and before the end of the spot. In the "open" doughnut, the hole runs from the point of its introduction to the very end of the message without the lyric ever being reintroduced. Because timing is especially crucial in achieving a smooth "closed" doughnut effect, a safety valve is sometimes added in the form of a brief humming or "la-la" phrase by the singers. If the local announcer runs over the actual hole, the "la-la" lets him know that fact and provides a bit more time to wrap up the live copy without stepping on the lyric. Even if the specific copy in the "hole" does not demand content localization, its reading by the particular station's personality helps to blend the message much more effectively with the program in which it appears.

SINGERS: We're your type for memos and manuscripts
          Love letters for labels and laundry lists
          If words are the way you write
          We're your type.
          (IBM typewriters, IBM typewriters)
          For hunt and pecks, for doctors orders
          For company checks, police headquarters
          For offices big and businesses small
          We're your type.
          (IBM typewriters, IBM typewriters)

ANNCR: As a neighborhood authorized IBM typewriter dealer,
          we're your type---no matter what your need for a
          typewriter. Say you want an IBM Correcting Selectric
          Three.

          Need a typewriter with memory, like the IBM electronic
          65, 85, or 95? We're your type. If you need supplies
          for your IBM typewriters, we're your type. Or if you
          need the service of a repair technician, trained by
          IBM? You guessed it—

SINGERS: IBM typewriters, we're your type.

(Courtesy of Melissa Wohltman, Doyle Dane Bernbach Advertising.)

However you and your client decide to use music, it is well to keep in mind Buddy Scott's observation:

> Success in this area requires incorporating tangible, or even intangible benefits into the development of the jingle, a skillful blending of purpose and psychographics to achieve the goal. This is an area in which music excels, for while the lyrics can extoll the virtues of a product or service, the music itself can project anything from a feeling of confidence, to excitement or exhilaration. You are making two impressions during the same time it normally would take you to make one. In this manner, music also reinforces a product's identity. There's hardly anyone over 20 years old who could not immediately identify the McDonald's jingle, even without the lyrics. The music has become so identified with the product that even without mention of the name, the message is still clear.[8]

Stephen Ford, of Chicago's Godfrey & Ford, has developed a checklist to help insure that *clarity* is indeed the cornerstone of your musical message, in both its lyric and instrumental aspects:

> First, hone in on style. Think of a musical piece which most nearly approximates what you want. A tune on the radio, a popular artist, a classical piece, anything akin to the mood you want to create. We're all pretty much exposed to or bombarded by the same music and four bars truly are worth a thousand words.
>
> Conversely, avoid words like "upbeat" or "contemporary." Such descriptions could refer to anything from Dolly Parton to Rick James. . . .
>
> When dealing with orchestration, communicate in terms of mood. A nice method, particularly for art directors, is to use visual color descriptives. Red could be a trumpet or a screaming electric guitar. Woodwinds are earth tones; clarinets yellow, oboes orange, bass clarinets dark brown, French horns a deep blue, and flutes a light green. This technique works especially well when creating sounds electronically on a synthesizer. . . .
>
> Who is the announcer? Male? Female? The tonal range and attitude of a voice will determine the selection of instruments in orchestrating an underscore. You don't really want John Houseman battling your saxophone.
>
> If you don't have an idea of what sort of musical treatment would be suitable, that's what music houses are for—to offer creative input that could enhance your concept. Maybe put an Addy on your wall.
>
> However, be wary of those producers who talk above you and hide behind a technical bush with words like "echo tweaks," "digital delay" or "square waves." They're probably technicians, not musicians.[9]

In short, when it comes to music, as mentioned in chapter 6—don't be afraid to trust your own instincts and don't be mesmerized by technicalities. Advertising music and its production is a mass communicative tool, not a secret cult.

Integrated Commercial

The ultimate method for blending the commercial with the program content is to weave the selling pitch into the very fabric of the program on which it appears. Though this technique is still popular in the radio systems of some

8. Buddy Scott, "Monday Memo," p. 24.
9. Stephen Ford, "You, Too, Can Be a 'Music Man,'" *ADWEEK/Midwest*, April 16, 1984, p. 18.

countries, the absence of dramas, situation comedies, soap operas, and variety shows on today's radio makes the fully integrated commercial largely a thing of the past. Besides, when announcers like Don Wilson and Harry Von Zell mouthed commercials as cast members rather than as isolated presences, it was often difficult for the listeners to discern the large amount of direct selling to which they had been subjected. From an ethical and public relations stand-point, the virtual demise of the integrated radio commercial was probably more a boon than a bane for the advertising community.

One vestige of this form, the integrated lead-in, does remain popular as a means of making the initial segue between program and commercial a smoother one. Unlike the old fully integrated message, the public realizes a commercial is taking place but, at least, is not initially cued by such tune-out encouraging lines as "and now a word from our sponsor." In a typical integrated lead-in, a sportscaster might say:

```
The way Marino maneuvered in Municipal Stadium yesterday reminded
me of the way a new Mercury from Jonesville Motor Sales
maneuvers. Right, Earl?
```

Announcer Earl would then take over with the actual commercial, and a smooth segue into the advertisement has been accomplished without the danger that the entire sportscast would be perceived as a program-length commercial.

Pop-in Commercial

This is the special term given the 10-second spot that makes one quick memorable thrust and then gets out of the way as its impact still resounds in the listener's consciousness. The pop-in commercial is much rarer today because of time pricing structures that force advertisers to pay a real premium for units of such short length—particularly when not aired as part of a station ID. Neverthe-less, the pop-in spot can have significant potential as a brand recall or image enhancer for clients who are simultaneously advertising via longer spot lengths or nonbroadcast media. Here are examples of radio pop-in approaches:

```
Somebody said that it couldn't be done---but they didn't work for
Vigilante Mutual, your 'can-do' insurance company.
```

```
BOY:   I think lemonade is a kid's drink.
GIRL:  Then you're too immature for the grown-up kick of Lemon
       Whizzer.
```

```
If you're only earning 5% interest, get up off your assets and
see the folks at the Briscoe Savings and Loan. Briscoe pays more,
more often.
```

```
This commercial takes ten seconds. You only need five to unwrap a
luscious Choco-Fruit candy bar. Why waste time? Unwrap a Choco-
Fruit for each hand.
```

```
ANNCR:  At the sound of the rooster, it'll be ten past the hour.
```

```
(SFX:    DUCK QUACKS THREE TIMES)
ANNCR:   Maybe I do need a Minutemaster watch.
```

SPECIAL PROBLEMS: RETAIL, CO-OP, AND DIRECT-RESPONSE ADVERTISING

No matter what generic type of commercial is used, certain kinds of radio advertising present unique difficulties that should be isolated here before we attempt to summarize our radio copywriting section. To an extent, these problem categories overlap, but each will be discussed separately as a means of revealing their special requirements.

Retail Advertising

This category embraces all the copy generated for local outlets that sell a variety of goods directly to the general public. Traditionally wedded to newspaper advertising, these retailers have been one of the last but now one of the most important targets for radio sales departments. Unlike other clients, retailers are looking for *results today*—not just for general image building or brand awareness. They tend to measure these results in terms of (1) the traffic through their stores and (2) the goods moved out of the door. Most successful retailers are good pitchmen—they know their products well and how to describe them in order to consummate sales.

Radio copywriters are therefore well advised to gain a working knowledge of their respective retailing communities. This knowledge-gathering should include conversations with retailers, noting the lines that flow most glibly from their mouths as they talk about their products. The retailer has probably used these lines on customers for years—and used them successfully or they would not be a continuing part of his or her persuasive arsenal. The copywriter who can encapsulate those statements in a spot is thus not only profiting from a consumer-oriented approach that has already proven its worth but is also making the commercial more appealing to the retailer who will have a personal affinity for radio messages that use those favored pitches. In this dramatized commercial for a local lawn-sprinkler dealer, such retailer-proven lines as "how green the grass is on my side of the fence," "saves on the water bill," and "lawn gets watered regularly, like clockwork" are smoothly integrated into an outrageous situation that nonetheless provides the listener with helpful, nonthreatening information.

```
(SFX:      INDIAN DRUMS & CHANT—THEN SCREEN DOOR OPENS)
NEIGHBOR:  Hey out there. It's 2 A.M.!
LEON:      Best time dance for rain. (DRUMS/CHANT UP)
NEIGHBOR:  Leon? Why are you talking like that? Your family's
           Italian.
LEON:      SHHHHHHH! He just pull-em rain-god's leg. (DRUMS/CHANT
           UP)
```

```
NEIGHBOR:   Leon, there's a better way. Didn't you ever notice how
            green the grass is on my side of the fence? That's
            because I had D.N. Ryor Underground Sprinkling install
            an Automatic Toro system. You can't even see the
            pop-up sprinkler heads when not in use. (CHANTING UP
            BRIEFLY) Leon, it's not expensive. D.N. Ryor designs
            to your specifications and budget. My Toro system even
            saves on my water bill. And the best part is the way
            my lawn gets watered, regularly like clockwork.
            Whether I'm here or not. (CHANTING UP) Hey Leon, D.N.
            Ryor's number is 429-3195. 429-3195! Call 'em, Leon!
            I'm through being Mr. Nice Guy.
(SFX:       DOOR SLAMS. CHANTING HALTS)
LEON:       Mr. Nice Guy heap big sorehead.
ANNCR:      See your authorized Toro dealer in the greater
            Michiana area. That's D.N. Ryor Underground Sprinkling
            with offices in Niles and Stevensville.
```

(Courtesy of Joe Borrello and Paul Boscarino, WOOD Broadcasting, Inc.)

In spots for multiple-product retailers such as grocery and department or discount stores, the radio copywriter encounters an additional difficulty. Comfortable with and accustomed to newspapers, these merchants will want you to compress all the product pictures and price balloons from a half or even full-page print ad into one grossly overloaded radio minute. The resulting laundry-list radio commercial makes little or no impact on the listener because not enough time can be devoted to any one item to have it properly situated on the stage of the listener's "mind's eye." The alternative is to find a strong central concept on which the listener can focus and from which individual products can be hung like ornaments on a well-proportioned Christmas tree. The following "what's in a K-mart bag" idea embraces several months' worth of items without fragmenting the selling statement the spot is commissioned to register.

```
KID:        ''What I Learned This Summer'' by T. R. Knight. This
            was my eleventh summer, and I've wised up since my
            tenth summer. Now I can tell what's going on by what my
            Mom brings home from K mart. My Mom is smart. She
            always shops at K mart because K mart always has what
            she wants on sale. In June, she came home with a good
            K mart bag. Tennis shoes, shorts, T-shirts, and a
            softball glove. That's a good K mart bag. Later in the
            summer she brought home another very good K mart bag.
            Swimming suit and more jeans. Summer stuff. Very good
            bag. But, a few weeks ago, I found a bad K mart bag. It
            was full of Back-to-School stuff from the Back-to-
            School Sale---notebooks, lunch bags, school clothes.
```

> This is a bad K mart bag. Keep your eyes on those K mart
> bags. And watch out for one full of bad news Back-to-
> School stuff. It means summer's almost over. It means
> washing your hair a lot and wearing good shirts.

SINGERS: <u>AT K MART.</u>
           <u>WE'VE GOT IT AND WE'VE GOT IT GOOD.</u>

(Courtesy of Sheila I. O'Donnell, Ross Roy Inc., Advertising.)

Sometimes, a multiproduct retail spot may be the most effective when it talks
about all the things the client *doesn't* sell. This approach has the effect of
seeming to narrow the focus of the spot when, in fact, it is allowing a workably
broad and generalized view of the store's entire line—in this case, its line
of clothes.

MAN: Uh, 'scuse me, where would I find the Cheese-o-Matic
         cheese slicers?

WOMAN: Oh, I'm sorry, sir. This is Kempner's.

MAN: Oh, you only carry your own brand of cheese slicers?

WOMAN: No sir, we're a clothing store.

MAN: I see. Well, what brand of cheese slicers do you carry?

WOMAN: We don't carry any cheese slicers. We carry a complete
         line of fashions for men and women.

MAN: Well, could you tell me what part of the store they're in?

WOMAN: What?

MAN: Cheese slicers.

WOMAN: Sir, just think of Kempner's as a clothing store.

MAN: Okay, I'm thinking. Now, where's the slicer?

WOMAN: Sir, no footballs, no pots and pans, and no cheese
         slicers, just clothes.

MAN: You're sure you're not out of them temporarily and are
         embarrassed to tell me?

WOMAN: Uh, sir, folks have always shopped Kempner's for the
         latest apparel and accessories.

MAN: I see.

WOMAN: They think of us for clothing. That's all---clothing.

MAN: Well, where do you suggest I look for a cheese slicer?

WOMAN: I don't know---why don't you try a hardware store?

MAN: Don't be ridiculous, that's where I buy my suits.

WOMAN: What???

MAN: I used to buy them at the gas station, but then the price
         of oil went up so—

ANNCR: Get departments at department stores. Get discounts at
         discount stores. And get good styles, good fit, and good

selection in clothing for men and women at Kempner's
clothing store. If you're a man, or a woman, and you wear
clothes, you'll love Kempner's. 2706 Clover Valley, just
off I-30.

(Courtesy of Fran Sax, FirstCom.)

Co-op Advertising

In a cooperative (co-op) enterprise, the manufacturer shares the cost of advertising its product with the local retailer. Thus, all the pitfalls associated with retail advertising per se can also be encountered in attempting to fashion co-op spots. In addition, the copywriter must wrestle with the problem of two co-equal clients who share a contractual right to co-star status. It is essential that the listener be able to discern which is the brand (manufacturer) name and which the retailer (store) name. If, for example, Gladstone's Shoe Store is featured in a co-op spot with Dexter Shoes, and the listeners are led by the copy to look for the Dexter Shoe Store, they may pass right by Gladstone's, to the long-term detriment of both clients.

As a general rule, it is usually less confusing either to (1) start and end with the brand name, focusing on retailer identity in the center of the spot or (2) devote the first part of the message to the product and the last part to where that product can be obtained. This doughnut commercial for Andersen Windows uses the first method—a practice very common when the manufacturer supplies the doughnut (and pays the bulk of the advertising costs).

SINGER: Come home to quality. Come home to Andersen.
           Come home to quality. Come home to Andersen.

ANNCR: Andersen introduces a double-pane insulating glass more
           energy efficient than triple-pane. It's their new High-
           Performance insulating glass---optional in Andersen
           windows and gliding patio doors from Miller-Zeilstra
           Lumber. It's good news for homeowners here in Western
           Michigan because its special transparent coating keeps
           radiant heat indoors where it belongs in winter---reduces
           heating costs---keeps you comfortable in cold weather,
           even next to windows. For specific details about the new
           Andersen option---High-Performance insulating glass---talk
           to the experts at Miller-Zeilstra. They've been serving
           Grand Rapids area homeowners for over 50 years. Miller-
           Zeilstra is at 8-33 Michigan Northeast, just east of
           Eastern. Open daily 'til 6, and Saturdays 'til 4.

SINGER: Come home to quality. Come home to Andersen.

(Courtesy of James White and Paul Boscarino, WOOD Radio.)

The second method, often known as the dealer tag technique, can also be manufacturer supplied. It initially gives heavy stress to product benefits and then turns major attention to the local retailer. The store may be promoted in the first portion of the spot but generally not by name in order to minimize the danger of listener confusion. The Armstrong spot that follows gives a lot of play to the local dealer's importance—but wisely waits until the actual dealer tag to introduce him by name. The local customizations have been underlined in this example to indicate more clearly their placement in the spot's progression.

(MUSIC:	ESTABLISH <u>AND</u> <u>BRING</u> <u>UNDER</u>)
WOMAN:	Look, I admit that I don't know a lot about buying floors. I mean, I'm sure they've changed a lot since I bought my last one. So when I look for a floor, I want to be sure that I'm getting it at the right store where I can get useful advice.
MAN:	We're your Armstrong floor fashion center store, and we are the right store. Armstrong specially trained our staff so they can give you really helpful professional ideas and advice. We can help you make the right choice with complete product information on each sample, lots of full-color pictures of rooms, and a choice of over 300 different Armstrong floors.
WOMAN:	Go on.
MAN:	What's more, you get a warranty on the installation from us---and a warranty on the floor from Armstrong. And there's even more.
WOMAN:	Even more?
MAN:	Just listen.
DEALER TAG:	Right now, save <u>4</u> dollars on every square yard of beautiful Armstrong Collectors Solarian. That's a <u>20</u> percent savings off our regular price, only at <u>Arklow</u> <u>House</u> <u>of</u> <u>Floors.</u> Visit our store at <u>1518</u> <u>Jennings.</u> This special price for one week only. <u>Arklow</u> <u>House</u> <u>of</u> <u>Floors.</u> Your Armstrong floor fashion center store in <u>Middleburgh.</u>
(MUSIC:	<u>UP</u> <u>TO</u> <u>TIME</u>)

(Courtesy of James P. White and Paul Boscarino, WOOD Radio.)

Whichever technique is used, the co-op copywriter must recognize that the manufacturer plays a determining role in the copy approval process. A recent Radio Advertising Bureau study found that most stations obtain manufacturer approval by reading the copy directly to the manufacturer over the phone.[10] Such precautions are essential. If the manufacturer does not believe his wares and name have been adequately showcased in the commercial, he will not

10. "Co-op Leader," *Broadcasting Magazine,* July 30, 1984, p. 50.

reimburse the local merchant for a portion of the cost of airing it. Since the merchant counts on such reimbursement, the copywriter had better make certain that the script fully justifies its payment—or risk losing a local client.

Direct-Response Advertising

In DR (also known as *per inquiry*) advertising, there is no local merchant. Instead, the commercial itself must consummate the sale by having the listener call or mail in an order. Thus, the direct-response spot must not only create the desire to own but also actually achieve the decision to buy. While it is said that advertising in general is the process of "diverting the consumer past the merchant's door," the DR message must work as the functional substitute for that door and the point-of-purchase salespeople who normally stand behind it. This means, says Ketchum Direct's president, Maryalice Fuller, that "direct response has to be incredibly clear, incredibly precise. Far more so than with all other forms of advertising. And you don't just get that kind of clarity and precision without the highest attention to creativity."[11]

Because of the selling and delivery burdens imposed on it, direct response copy does not have the time to be artsy or allegorical. Every word must be directed not just to the sell, but to the activation of the purchasing decision through dialing or writing in. What is more, with DR, it soon becomes unequivocally apparent whether you have succeeded or failed based on how many units of the product your copy has actually moved. One can't blame poor store location or limited shelf space for a failed direct-response campaign because the commercial *itself* is that store and that shelf as well as the emotional/ rational selling appeal.

For these reasons, David Ogilvy once said: "The best copywriters are direct response copywriters."[12] Their registration of direct-response messages on our consciousness is far greater than many of us comprehend. An example of the salience of DR in our culture is illustrated by the third-grade elementary school class, which, as an art appreciation project, was assigned by their teacher to write advertisements for *The Adoration of the Magi* painting by Fra Filippo Lippi. The students' individual responses to this project showed just how intensely they have assimilated the essence of direct-response broadcast style. No particular type of ad was specified in the assignment and, of course, the concept of direct-response was not even introduced. Nonetheless, here are some of the DR-oriented pieces of copy that resulted:

```
I can sell you this great painting for only $400. Yes, only $400.
For this great religious painting. This painting shows a mother
and father with a baby boy. With great background.
                                                            Blaine
```

11. Richard Szathmary, "Direct Response: Creativity at Its Most Accessible," *ADS Magazine*, November, 1984, p. 27.
12. *Ibid.*, p. 30.

What is your favorite holiday? What? Did you say---Christmas?
Well, do I have a deal for you. I have a painting that would make
a great gift. It has a lot of detail. And it is very, very pretty.

Jenna

Are you an art collector, looking for a priceless painting for
ten dollars? Well, the one you've been wanting is here. The
Adoration of the Magi is waiting for you. The great Fra Filippo
Lippi painted this picture with beauty and grace. It's a round
painting and it's 500 years old.

Dan A.

Hi there. Would you like to buy this famous painting? I am
selling this painting for 100 dollars. This is a good painting
for your church. This painting is not for sale in any store. This
is a good painting for churches. Only $100!

Mike

Have you ever wanted to own your very own painting? Well, here's
your chance! It's by the very, very, very famous painter---Fra
Filippo Lippi. But have you worried about money problems? Well,
this painting only costs $2,109,056.97! What beautiful colors!
Black, orange, pink, purple, green. Magnificent. Wonderful. Are
just some of the words to describe this wonderful painting. It
is---The Adoration of the Magi.

Sarah

(All the above courtesy of Mrs. Alice Stengren's class, Pullen School, Mt. Pleasant, Michigan.)

   The amusing nature of such efforts from eight- and nine-year-old copywriters
should not obscure the fact that these students, subconsciously, have learned
(even *mastered*) several key principles of direct response copy construction:

1. *Make certain that the product cost is clearly and repeatedly stated.* ". . . for only
   $400. Yes, only $400," tells the listeners they have heard correctly and sets down the
   financial commitment in unmistakable terms. Lacking a price sticker on the side of
   the box or can, the DR shopper must have alternative verification of the specific
   cost of the goods.
2. *Get the listener involved early; perhaps by a leading question.* "What is your
   favorite holiday?" and "Have you ever wanted to own your own painting?" are
   queries calculated to garner a positive response from the prospects most likely to
   be interested in what this copy has to offer. "Are you an art collector?," on the
   other hand, may elicit an affirmative reaction from a far smaller universe than our
   client is seeking. Remember, if listeners can answer "no" to your opening question,
   they'll have no further interest in the message that follows it. "No, I'm not an art
   collector," and attention ceases. The listener mentally exits before we've had time
   to unveil that $10 price.
3. *Show how the product can impinge on the listener's life.* Phrases like "would make
   a great gift," and "a good painting for your church" show the prospect the uses to
   which the merchandise can be put. Keep in mind that effective selling involves

solving problems for people. The direct-response product must be a documented problem-solver before the listener is activated to buy.

4. *Take listener objections into account.* You don't want to solve one difficulty by substituting another. "But have you worried about money problems?" is one way to segue into proof that this worry need not be a concern as regards this merchandise. The proof that follows however, must be convincing. (A two million dollar price tag obviously doesn't mitigate monetary concerns!)

5. *Make product exclusivity unmistakable.* "This painting is not for sale in any store" informs the listener that there is no alternative to buying from us. Direct response will never be direct if the audience feels they have the option of shopping around.

6. *Stress the need for immediate action.* Just as we don't want our prospects to assume that there are in-store alternatives to buying from us, we don't want them to postpone their purchase into the indefinite future. DR copy must generate immediate sales and we can't be sure prospects will be within ear's reach of our "radio store" again. "The one you've been wanting is here . . . is waiting for you" and "here's your chance" are phrases that help evoke a sense of urgency and limited availability.

7. *Describe product attributes in positive, tangible terms.* Direct-response radio is no different from other forms of radio copy in that it must place a visualizable depiction in the listener's mind. "Show's a mother and father with a baby boy," and "What beautiful colors! Black, orange, pink, purple, green" are far preferable to "very, very pretty," "good painting," and "wonderful" in helping audience members truly to see the commodity we are holding up to their ears.

8. *Communicate the specific purchase process.* None of our third-graders reached this stage—perhaps because it typically comes last in the DR message and doesn't relate further to their subject painting's definition. In any event, real world direct response copy must set forth the contact method at least twice, whether it's the repetition of a street address or a toll-free telephone number. Creating the desire to own and getting the decision to buy will still be useless functions if we do not provide a well-marked channel to operationalize that desire and decision.

Extrapolating components from the five grammar school scripts we've examined, it is possible to construct a virtually complete DR commercial that might read like this. (Original material—chiefly relating to the purchase process—has been added in brackets.)

ANNCR: Have you ever wanted to own your very own painting? Well, here's your chance. The Adoration of the Magi is waiting for you. The great Fra Filippo Lippi painted this picture with grace and beauty. The Adoration of the Magi. What beautiful colors! Black, orange, pink, purple, green. A good painting for your church or a great gift. And I can sell you The Adoration of the Magi for only $400. Yes, only $400. For this great religious painting. Not for sale in any store, the painting you've been wanting is here. Worried about money problems? [Well, don't be. You can charge The Adoration of the Magi on your Visa or Mastercharge. To reserve your painting, call 1-800-666-7250.] Great background. Beautiful colors. The Adoration of the Magi. [Call 1-800-666-7250 to reserve your painting now.]

After two decades of decline, direct-response involvement on radio is likely to grow, according to advertising agency chief Alvin Eicoff. Radio, he observes, "offers the direct marketer an unbeatable combination: the immediacy of broadcast and the specialized audience of print. The ingredients that make narrowcast cable attractive to direct marketers are also present in radio. . . . In this booming era of direct response advertising, there are enough media dollars for everybody. Direct marketers' searching for imaginative, effective alternatives recognize radio's potential as a direct response vehicle."[13]

PUTTING "PUNCH" IN THE RADIO SPOT

Whatever its generic form, or the special problems its market function entails, *any* radio spot of a half-minute or more can and should accomplish five product-related tasks. While, at first glance, this seems a huge assignment to complete in thirty or sixty seconds, the spot that in some way encompasses all five will possess real marketplace PUNCH. Specifically, this PUNCH consists of:

Product specification(s)
User experience(s)
Notable competitive advantage(s)
Cost/value ratio
Heightened listener benefit

What follows is a classic radio commercial for Carling Breweries' Tuborg Gold beer. Let's see whether it has PUNCH:

A. SCOURBY: In Denmark, beer has been the center of a never-
                ending celebration. Of friendship. And of life. In
                the famed Danish beer gardens, one beer has been
                loved above all. Traditionally light, golden Tuborg.
                (Pause) Today, we join the Danes in their
                celebration---with a beer of noble heritage and
                character. Our Tuborg Gold is now brewed in America,
                with the guidance of Denmark's master brewers.
                By appointment to the Royal Danish Court. So, for
                about what you'd pay for the king of beers, you can
                now enjoy Tuborg Gold. The golden beer of Danish
                kings.

ANNCR: Tuborg Gold. The light beer with the gold label.
                Carling National Breweries, Incorporated, Baltimore,
                Maryland.

(Courtesy of Bruce Dunham, W. B. Doner and Company.)

Product Specifications

Even from this single commercial, the audience is given a considerable amount of information about Tuborg. They know that it is a light, gold beer

13. Alvin Eicoff, writing in "Monday Memo," *Broadcasting Magazine*, February 7, 1983, p. 18.

that originated in Denmark. In fact, all of these data are presented in several different ways for added emphasis.

User Experiences

We do not need to resort to a personality testimonial in order to disclose how other consumers of the product feel about it. The Tuborg spot shows how popular the beer is among the experienced quaffers in the Danish beer gardens and further points out that its quality brought it an appointment to the Royal Danish Court itself. Since Denmark is considered prime beer territory, these experiences carry significant weight. Obviously, citing Tuborg's popularity in France or Italy would be nowhere near as convincing. Nor, if we were advertising wine, would Danish endorsements be very valuable. The product users cited, in other words, should preferably be of a type reputed to have some expertise with the product category under discussion.

Notable Competitive Advantages

As this spot positions it against competing beers, Tuborg has the advantage of a European heritage and supervision ("with the guidance of Denmark's master brewers") while still being brewed domestically. As is often the case, these characteristics are manipulated to tie in closely with the product's:

Cost/Value Ratio

Tuborg, the audience discovers, is a very prestigious beer with a long and "noble heritage and character." Nevertheless, for what they would pay for a domestic premium beer like Budweiser ("for about what you'd pay for the king of beers") the audience can obtain a brand with the same lineage as several more expensive imports. True, Tuborg will be more costly than local beer but seemingly, a much better value than the domestic premium beers with which it competes in price.

Heightened Listener Benefits

In many cases, this is the sum total of the other PUNCH elements. For Tuborg, the audience is shown that, for a relatively low cost, they can enjoy the same light, gold beer that has won the approval of even the Danish royal family and that profits from the attention of Denmark's master brewers.

Here is a commercial with a generically different approach and for a different product category. Let's examine its PUNCH factors:

```
        Production Note: Woman should convey lines like innocent
        girl-next-door. Man emotes with lusty impatience.
SALLY:  Tom, dear, I've got a treat for you when we reach the
        honeymoon cabin.
TOM:    (Devilish) Heh-heh-heh-heh. I know, Sally. I've been
        counting the minutes.
SALLY:  (Hurt by spoiled surprise) Who told you?
TOM:    Told me? Someone had to tell me?
```

SALLY: How else would you know I made your favorite cookies?

TOM: Cookies?

SALLY: Sure. the ones made with Blaine & D'Arcy's new cherry-
           flavored bakers' chips. You said you loved them 'cause
           they taste like fresh-picked cherries.

TOM: (Bewildered) Blaine & D'Arcy's cherry chips <u>do</u> taste
           tartly sweet---like fresh cherries---but honestly, Sally.
           I did have something else in mind for the first night of
           our honeymoon.

SALLY: (Revelation) Of course! I'm sorry, Tom. I'm such a silly.
           We'll stop at the store and get some cherry chips for
           munching. I can get a whole bag of Blaine & D'Arcy's for
           only 59 cents.

TOM: (Defeated) Good grief.

ANNCR: Blaine & D'Arcy's cherry-flavored chips. Their newest
           flavor. Blaine & D'Arcy's. Candy chips for your baking
           that taste like fresh-picked fruit. Good <u>any</u>time.

TOM: Or <u>almost</u> anytime.

Product Specifications

The eavesdropper on this little vignette knows that Blaine & D'Arcy's cherry-flavored chips are a recent addition to their product line (thus evoking the emotional appeal of uniqueness/newness). More importantly, it is clear that they taste "tartly sweet" just like their fresh-picked namesake and are easily obtainable in bags at the grocery.

User Experience

Even though the honeymoon may be off to a rocky start, the spot gives ample evidence of past positive associations the couple has had with the product. She has baked cookies for the trip after success with a previous batch that he enjoyed. They apparently also like eating them right out of the bag since she berates herself for failure to buy the means for replicating that experience.

Notable Competitive Advantages

Unlike Tuborg, this product has no direct competitors other than fresh cherries themselves, which are obviously more expensive and harder to obtain and store. Secondary competition consists of more conventional chocolate and, perhaps, butterscotch and peanut butter chips. Thus, it is important to focus on the novel alternative Blaine & D'Arcy's *cherry* chips now provide.

Cost/Value Ratio

Blaine & D'Arcy's cherry-flavored chips are only 59¢ a bag and seem well worth it since they can do double-duty as a candy-like snack in addition to their testified-to success as a baking ingredient.

Heightened Listener Benefit

Though cherry-flavored chips are not as thrilling as a honeymoon, they seem capable of making even that experience more pleasurable. They are inexpensive, highly portable, easy to obtain and, apparently, offer baking success even for the driftily naïve. They are furthermore, *different* both in product characteristics and in the way these characteristics are introduced to the listener.

For practice, conduct your own PUNCH analysis on the 7-Eleven Slurpee commercial that follows. Then, look for this same PUNCH in the radio spots you write from this point on. That should help you maximize copy utility and marketability in the competitive world of radio commercial creation.

FRANK: Okay, you can start this 7-Eleven Slurpee commercial now.

BOB: Who are you?

FRANK: I'm the Truth-in-Advertising Watch Dog.

BOB: Uh-huh.

FRANK: I'm watching you.

BOB: Right.

FRANK: So watch it.

BOB: Right. Okay, cue the birds. Once upon a time in Slurpee-Land. A million years ago—

FRANK: Don't exaggerate.

BOB: Once upon a time in Slurpee-Land. A hundred years ago—

FRANK: No.

BOB: One day after school—

FRANK: Oh, that's better—

BOB: —there was a beautiful fairy princess named Lorilee—

FRANK: Not believable.

BOB: —there was a girl named Sheila.

FRANK: Okay.

BOB: She just loved slurpin' Slurpees down at participating 7-Elevens.

FRANK: What's a Slurpee?

BOB: It's a cold drink that's made outta ice. And only 7-Elevens have got 'em. She found out that 7-Elevens were selling the 22-ounce cup of freezin' cold treat for only 49 cents!

FRANK: Is that true?

BOB: It's true. It's usually 60 cents. But now it's just 49 cents for a 22-ounce Slurpee. An' so she bought one. And when she slurped it—she grew beautiful long golden locks

FRANK: That's not true.

BOB: She grew short brown locks.
FRANK: Not true.
BOB: A moustache?
FRANK: No.
BOB: Anyway, she went to a 7-Eleven for a 49-cent Slurpee and
          she loved it.
FRANK: True, true and true.
BOB: You're driving me crazy!
FRANK: True.

(Courtesy of Dan McCurdy, The Stanford Agency.)

RADIO RESOLUTIONS

Finally, there are seven copy considerations that inject themselves into every assignment you will encounter as a writer of radio spots. Whatever the generic type of commercial you choose, or whatever type is chosen for you, these radio resolutions can keep you and your copy on the right selling track:

  I.   Avoid pronoun proliferation.
  II. Employ appeals wisely.
  III. Don't write a television soundtrack.
  IV. Stay conversant with contractions.
  V.   Stress sponsor identification.
  VI. Keep humor in bounds.
  VII. Don't underestimate radio.

Avoid Pronoun Proliferation

We have previously established that, unlike newspaper or magazine readers, radio listeners cannot go back to pick up ideas that were missed the first time. By the same token, these listeners cannot regress to find the referent for pronouns like "he," "she," "it," "they," "them," or "that." Since pronouns have such a high potential for listener confusion and diversion, they should be used with great care in broadcast copy. Particularly to be avoided is the use of the relative pronouns "this" and "that" to refer to a complex idea. Listeners will certainly tire of mentally retracing their auditory steps and may well forget the entire point of the spot in the process.

This trainee-written commercial for Sanford's Mucilage illustrates how pronoun proliferation can clog continuous auditory revelation. Even if they bother to remain "tuned in," listeners become so preoccupied with determining the nouns that the pronouns replace, that they have little time to focus on the product use situation.

ANNCR: Many of you may not know what Sanford's Mint-Flavored
          Mucilage is. Some may say it's a new kind of dessert, or
          maybe it's an after-dinner drink. Well, it's not.
          Sanford's Mint-Flavored Mucilage is an adhesive that's
          used like licking a stamp. Just apply it to what you want

bonded. Then lick it and hold its two surfaces together.
It bonds in seconds. And with Christmas getting close,
children can use it to make tree decorations. Yes,
Sanford's Mint-Flavored Mucilage can make it even more fun
for them because it's mint flavored. Its rubber top
regulates the mucilage flow so they get out only what is
needed. The bottle is unbreakable too so you won't have to
worry about their mess. Try Sanford's Mint-Flavored
Mucilage. It's great fun for them because it tastes like
mint.

Count the number of pronouns that have been inflicted on this poor, harmless product and on the poor, harmless listener at whom this spot is aimed. Not only must time be taken to insert mentally the referent for all of these pronouns, but at several points the identity of this referent also may be in considerable doubt. *What* "bonds in seconds?" *Who* will "it" be even more fun for and what is the "it?" *What* has a rubber top and *who* makes that mess? Little wonder if the listener gets bored of the guessing game and turns his or her mind to other things.

Keep pronouns to a minimum in your copy. If a pronoun has been used to avoid the redundant use of the same term, either find an appropriate synonym for that term or try rearranging the sentences so that term does not appear at the same place in succeeding thought units. On radio, most pronouns are confusing and colorless stumbling blocks to listener comprehension. The main exception to this rule, as noted previously, is the pronoun "you," which can often be used to represent each individual listener's name in simulating a sense of one-to-one communion.

Employ Appeals Wisely

If stated in military terms, this resolution would be phrased: *concentrate* your attack. Given all the potential perils of the real-time message that reaches its audience solely by the aural mode, we cannot try to cover everything there is to say about the advertised product or service. A radio spot is *not* a full-page newspaper ad with its variety of typefaces, graphics, and layout patterns. Radio, even 60-second radio, has its greatest chance of success when it selects a single product appeal and paints that appeal vividly. Several years ago, Russell I. Haley of the University of New Hampshire discovered that even for advertising in general, "people only turn their minds on for a very small proportion, perhaps 10 percent to 20 percent of the advertising message to which they are physically exposed. A single-focus ad has a better chance of stimulating a mental reaction than does a multifocus ad. The latter type may slow you down physically, because it has more things to look at—more areas to scan. But an effective ad is one that lets people get its central message quickly and easily."[14] So if you must make more than one major point about the product, resort to separate spots,

14. "Counting Noses, Feeling Pulses Occupies ARF," *Broadcasting Magazine,* October 25, 1976, p. 63.

similarly styled that together will constitute a cohesive *flight* of commercials. In this way, the listener will become acquainted not only with each aspect but also with the fact that all of them relate to the same brand or company.

Varying the product appeal in different spots or flights is often the best mechanism for telling a complete story about the product while avoiding individual message fragmentation. With proper spot rotation (a big concern of agency media planners) and copy coordination, listeners will get an in-depth picture of your client's ware over the days and weeks of the campaign without sacrificing the integrity and utility of the individual spot.

Whether you use the same appeal in different situations, or vary the appeal from spot to spot or flight to flight, make certain that any and every appeal selected is calculated to aim your copy directly at your target audience. Your entire approach, the appeals used as well as the words that convey them, should show the listeners in your universe that you (and by implication, your client) know something about them and their needs. Andrew Purcell of Atlanta's Tucker, Wayne and Company fashioned three criteria to gauge a piece of copy's effectiveness in this regard. These criteria have since become accepted standards.

1. Does the message conform to people's images of themselves?
2. Does it give them meaningful information?
3. Does it help position a product or service in people's minds?[15]

A teen-age-oriented message that uses out-of-date slang, for example, would not conform to the teens' self-vision of being contemporary and may well make the information that slang embellishes seem outmoded and irrelevant.

Sometimes a spot can be entertaining, well-written, and product-centered but *fail* because it relies on a situation having little to do with the interests or experiences of its target audience. In this hypothetical Bubble Joy commercial, the writer has mistakenly used a celebrity popular with the over-fifties in an attempt to reach the product's under-twelve prospects. This mismatch means that only people *uninterested* in buying Bubble Joy will pay attention to the spot.

```
              Production Note: To be done with a recognizable but
              slightly exaggerated Lawrence Welk delivery.
SVELTE:       Hello, friends, this is Clarence Svelte, world famous
              ah-band leader. Many people who watch my show have said
              to me: 'Clarence, your band just wouldn't be the same
              without the bubbles.' So naturally, I depend on those
              bubbles. Only the best bubble liquid goes into my bubble
              machine. That's why I use Bubble Joy. Every bottle of
              Bubble Joy contains enough juice for thousands of ah-
              wunnerful, wunnerful bubbles. Big, ah-round bubbles that
              last ah-long, ah-long time. And with one bottle of
```

15. Andrew Purcell, writing in "Monday Memo," *Broadcasting Magazine*, May 17, 1976, p. 13.

> Bubble Joy, my band can play all night and still have
> bubbles left over for blowing on the bus. Whether you're
> a famous ah-band leader, or blow bubbles just for fun,
> use Bubble Joy. For the biggest, ah-roundest bubbles.
> Just count all those Bubble Joy bubbles: Ah-one, ah-two,
> ah-three, ah-four (Fade to time).

ANNCR: Bubble Joy. Look for the bright red bottle at your
          favorite five and dime. Bubble your pleasure with Bubble
          Joy.

A similar problem occurs when ethnic audiences are clumsily targeted in copy styling. As Caroline Jones of Mingo-Jones Advertising warns, "slanguage has never worked, and probably never will. Especially if it comes from general advertisers. We still call that 'patronizing' advertising, not ethnic."[16] Ethnic markets should be addressed via the same process as any demographic/ psychographic cluster—through careful research into their wants and life-styles rather than by superficial parroting of alleged ethnic verbal patterns.

In short, use appeals wisely. Use one appeal per message. As necessary, vary that appeal or the situations to which that appeal is applied from spot to spot or flight to flight; and project a copy orientation that is on-target with your selected universe's needs and life-styles. No one, for example, can confuse the following footwear retailer with a discount, camping, or athletic shoe outlet. This client is clearly an upscale emporium talking to people willing to pay for fashion.

ANNCR: You dress in designer dresses, designer suits, even
          designer jewelry. Well now, you can dress your feet in
          fashion footwear by major footwear designers. Petoskey's
          newest store underfoot is Signature Shoes with the
          fashions you haven't been able to find. Signature Shoes.
          Across from Country Casuals on Mitchell Street, downtown
          Petoskey. Dress up your feet in fashion footwear from
          Signature Shoes.

(Courtesy of Tim Moore, WKHQ.)

Don't Write a Television Soundtrack

Having been continuously exposed to so many television spots from the virtual moment of birth, it is easy for today's young writers to create radio copy that's really *television*. Specifically, this means scripting *up* to the point at which the product is to be used—and then jumping ahead to discuss the glowing *results* of that use. What's missing? The vital revelation of *product-in-use*. Why does the novice writer miss it? Because in the familiar world of television, the visual can actually view the product doing its thing, thereby leaving the audio free to anticipate and amplify the consequences. But radio is NOT television;

16. Caroline Jones, letter to the editor, *ADWEEK/Midwest*, January 31, 1983, p. 22.

radio cannot illustrate product-in-use *unless* that use is translated into the aural pictorialization of words, music, and sound effects. Note how this commercial introduces Baker's Guild Gold Dragees and then leapfrogs directly to use aftermath. Unfortunately, since the actual manipulation of the product was omitted, listeners are unsure of how the "All Occasion Cake" was achieved; uncertain as to whether they can duplicate this positive result. This makes the commercial much less involving and puts the decision to buy much more in doubt.

```
ANNCR:  I'm the All Occasion Cake. Being in the cake family hasn't
        always been easy for me. Especially with a popular big
        brother like the Birthday Cake. But now I'm special too---
        thanks to Baker's Guild Gold Dragees. Gold Dragees are
        cake decorations that look like tiny gold beads. Before
        trying them, I was a plain, ordinary cake. But now, I'm a
        beautiful All Occasion Cake. For creative cake decorating,
        use Baker's Guild Gold Dragees from your Wise Frog
        grocery store. Baker's Guild: for the sparkling All
        Occasion Cake.
```

You don't necessarily need a lot of time or a battery of sound effects to demonstrate product-in-use aurally. Even thirty seconds of straight copy can do the job if the words are well-chosen and well-arranged, as in this univoice demonstration of the Lintaway. How (with what words) is product-in-use articulation accomplished?

```
ANNCR:  Going out? Got everything you need? Chances are you have
        more than you need. Chances are you have lint. There---on
        your favorite sweater. On your new suit. On that special
        jacket. But now, you can roll lint off with Lintaway.
        Lintaway's specially designed adhesive roller actually
        peels lint off in smooth, easy strokes. Glide the Lintaway
        roller up that sleeve and watch as the lint, hair and
        other unsightly particles vanish. Next time, leave lint at
        home with the handy Lintaway adhesive roller.
```

Stay Conversant with Contractions

We have previously stressed the necessity of a conversational quality in radio writing and, at another juncture, the importance of avoiding time-wasting and colorless helping verbs. If you haven't already noticed, the linkage between these two principles is the contraction. Contractions allow us to simulate conversation, which does use helping verbs, while still precluding the need to set down and articulate those helping verbs, in full. In the following dramatized spot, we have replaced all the original contractions with complete helping verbs which are underlined for easy recognition. Read the spot aloud and note how stilted and unnatural the absence of contractions makes it:

```
DOCTOR:  Nurse, how did this clown swallow a watch?
```

NURSE: Why <u>do</u> <u>you</u> <u>not</u> just remove it, doctor?

DOCTOR: Look, <u>I</u> <u>am</u> chief of surgery. I <u>do</u> <u>not</u> touch anything unless <u>it</u> <u>is</u> a brain transplant. Now, is there a doctor around?

GUY: Did you say doctor?

DOCTOR: Yes, doctor. This man swallowed a watch.

GUY: Oh, wow. Well, look, <u>I</u> <u>am</u> only delivering.

NURSE: Oh, <u>you</u> <u>are</u> a baby doctor.

GUY: No. No my name is—

DOCTOR: Look, why are we arguing? This man's life is ticking away.

GUY: You <u>do</u> <u>not</u> understand.

DOCTOR: Now <u>that</u> <u>is</u> an order.

GUY: All right, man. Scalpel, hemostat, pliers—

DOCTOR: Hey, do you often work in dungarees?

GUY: No, <u>they</u> <u>are</u> not dungarees. <u>They</u> <u>are</u> Cheap Jeans.

NURSE: Oh, I see, I suppose Cheap Jeans help you operate better.

GUY: They <u>do</u> <u>not</u> show blood stains.

DOCTOR: <u>That</u> <u>is</u> wonderful work. You really do know what <u>you</u> <u>are</u> doing.

NURSE: Say, where did you study?

GUY: Automotive high school.

DOCTOR: Automotive? <u>You</u> <u>are</u> no doctor?

GUY: No, my name is Doctor. 'D' like in dog. 'O' as in—

DOCTOR: Oh, no.

GUY: Are you the guy that ordered the B-L-T?

DOCTOR: But <u>you</u> <u>have</u> just performed a perfect operation.

GUY: Wow, stomachs, oil pans—<u>it</u> <u>is</u> all the same trip, baby.

DOCTOR: Do Cheap Jeans come in hospital green? 34 short?

GUY: Red makes more sense.

ANNCR: Pick up your Cheap Jeans at Gimbel's East. <u>They</u> <u>are</u> on the second floor, men's wear department.[17]

As the Cheap Jeans advertisement illustrates, complete helping verbs are sometimes needed—particularly in questions and for emphasis. But as our manipulation of this spot also demonstrates, contractions of these helping verbs are required with much greater frequency.

---

17. Arnold Arlow, writing in "Monday Memo," *Broadcasting Magazine*, November 4, 1974, p. 21.

Stress Sponsor's Identification

The world's most colorful and creative piece of radio writing won't justify itself if the listener fails to discern the brand name being promoted. It used to be that clients and/or agencies would translate this principle into a mathematical formula that decreed how many mentions of the brand name must be included in given length spots. Today, it is recognized that you do not have to necessarily mention the product a dozen times or in every other sentence. The particular *placement* of the mentions within the spot, and the way the spot as a whole hooks the listener are far more important considerations. This Stiller and Meara commercial promotes exceptional brand recognition through their skillful manipulation of a character's name.

```
ANNCR:  United Van Lines presents Stiller and Meara.
ANNE:   Welcome to 'Simpatico Singles.' I'm Rowena Pirhana, and
        you're—
JERRY:  Van. Van Linze.
ANNE:   (Laughing) Oh, like the moving company.
JERRY:  Yeah.
ANNE:   Not married are you, Mr. Linze---or should I say, United?
JERRY:  Er, no.
ANNE:   (Hysterical laughter) United! Get it? If you were married,
        you and your wife would be the 'United Van Linze!'
        (Shrieking with laughter)
JERRY:  Actually, I work for United Van Lines.
ANNE:   How cute!
JERRY:  Van's just a nickname.
ANNE:   Is it true what they say about United, Van? Can you move
        practically anything?
JERRY:  Anything from computers to trampolines.
ANNE:   I thought United only moved household goods.
JERRY:  Not any more. Now United's the total transportation
        company.
ANNE:   You totally transport me, Van.
JERRY:  United moves new products and equipment direct from
        manufacturer to distributor.
ANNE:   Anywhere?
JERRY:  Sure. And United gives the same special handling to
        industrial machinery as they do to your delicate
        Chippendale.
ANNE:   Sounds protective.
JERRY:  We are. That's why individuals and companies trust United
        to move them.
```

```
ANNE:   I find you very moving, Van. Get it?
JERRY:  Got it and I am.
ANNE:   What?
JERRY:  Moving. Right out the door.
ANNE:   Wait, Van.
JERRY:  United Van Lines, Ms. Pirhana. Call 'em.
ANNCR:  For the name of your United Van Lines agent, see the
        Yellow Pages.
```

(Created by Stiller & Meara and Bob Kelly, President of Kelly, Zahrndt & Kelly; and Shirley Browne, Director of Public Information, United Van Lines.)

Especially on radio, a prime component of this audience hook is often the *identity line,* the short but swingy slogan that enhances rapid recognition of the brand or corporate name. It often helps if this identify line has a generic thrust—if it showcases the brand name *and* the product category of which that brand is a member. Brand names in isolation do not exist in the listener's mind for long. So if the identity line also designates the product category (and thereby the product use), the line will enjoy a longer and much more functional life. Here are some past and present identity lines that establish both the brand name and its category/application:

```
When you're out of Schlitz, you're out of beer.

Diet Delight. If it wasn't in cans you'd swear it was fresh
fruit.

Fly the friendly skies of United.

You've got an uncle in the furniture business---Joshua Doore.

When it comes to pizza, who knows? Jenos.

Wheaties---the breakfast of Champions.

Shasta Root Beer---the foam that you feel.

Post Toasties---the best thing that's happened to corn since the
Indians discovered it.

Piccadilly Circles. The English muffin with the meal on top.

You brush with an ordinary toothbrush, but you brrrush with a
Broxodent.

Heinz. The slowest ketchup in the West.
```

Whether or not their spots make use of an identity line, some copywriters like to substitute the pronoun "we" in contexts that would otherwise call for the brand name. This is generally an unwise practice for two reasons. First, each use of "we" is one less use of the client's name in a place where it would be just as easy to be specific. Second, unless the client has one voice under contract on an exclusive basis, the listener is fully aware that this announcer is not, really, the "we" down at Joe's Service Station any more than he was the "we" at the Ajax Appliance Mart whose message he delivered earlier. Phoney "we's" cut down on message credibility and do nothing to facilitate sponsor identification.

Keep Humor in Bounds

Particularly on radio, the trend has been toward more and more humor as a means of advertising an ever-widening range of products and services. The proponents of comedic commercials observe that you can't reason with people if you don't have their attention. Bob Stanford, president of The Stanford Agency in Dallas, reflects that: "I decided years ago that if people are going to give you 30 to 60 seconds of their time, then you ought to give them something in return. Maybe it's a laugh, just a smile or a little feeling of warmth; but it's something."[18] Yet, as Stanford and others realize, the "funny" commercial that has only the joke going for it can be catastrophic.

This volatile situation is especially acute on radio, which lacks the visual element either to augment a truly funny approach or to distract from copy that lays an egg. Humor on radio is always at center stage and will therefore be either very effective or very embarrassing. There is simply no such thing as mediocre radio comedy.

It must be recognized that you can't use comedy to sell everything. As a general rule, the more expensive an advertised product or service is, the less appropriate a humorous appeal becomes. When is the last time you chuckled at a Lincoln or Cadillac spot? Guffawed at an ad for a $40-an-ounce perfume? Giggled at a brokerage firm's or a real estate agent's commercial? Things seem to become less humorous the more money they will siphon from our wallets or bank accounts. If for this or any other more rarefied reason, humor does not seem appropriate to your client and/or your client's product category, don't use it. You can't use humor to sell everything.

You must also beware of the extraneous humor that ad man Robert J. Wanamaker long ago labelled *parasite advertising* because it feeds off, chews away at whatever positive image the product or service heretofore possessed. If listeners remember the joke but not the product that joke was supposed to promote, the quip has sustained itself entirely at the expense of the client with no beneficial return in either brand recall or product knowledge. As Wanamaker described it:

> With parasite advertising, the means become the end. The means of present-ing the selling message (if there is any message) completely overshadow the message itself. And, often the means of presentation are incompatible with the product they are showcasing. How often do you see products presented in irrelevant, incongruous or ridiculous situations in the name of off-beat adver-

18. Bob Stanford, writing in "Monday Memo," *Broadcasting Magazine*, January 14, 1980, p. 24.

tising? Nobody denies that this type of advertising gets talked about. So does the playboy son of the successful father.[19]

Since humor is so prevalent on radio, and since when radio humor fails, it fails so abjectly, copywriters for the aural medium must be especially suspicious and wary of giving birth to anything that might translate itself into parasite advertising. To keep your humor in bounds, and to ferret out parasite advertising before it feeds off *you*, stand your proposed comedic treatment up against these "don'ts and do's" fashioned by Anthony Chevins, president of Cunningham & Walsh:

1. Don't tell a joke. Jokes wear out fast.
2. Never make fun of the product. Have fun with the product, but not at the expense of it.
3. Don't have a surprise ending. Surprise endings are only a surprise one time.
4. Don't make it difficult for the listener/viewer to figure out whether you're laughing at him or with him.
5. Don't ever let the humor get out of hand and get in the way of selling your product. Don't pull the chair from under the listener/viewer.
6. Don't use humor because you can't figure out anything else to do.

Now the do's:

1. Way out front and number one by far is make the humor relevant—relevant to the product—relevant to its benefits—relevant—relevant—relevant.
2. Involve the listener/viewer in the humor in the first 10 seconds of the commercial.
3. Use humor to point out the product's strong selling points.
4. Be charming rather than funny. It is better to get a smile than a belly laugh.
5. Make your humor simple and clear. Make it basic and broad. (Give it a chance to appeal to everybody.)
6. Make sure that the humor is so tightly integrated with the product and its sales message that there would be no way that one could survive without the other. A humorous approach that could be used to sell any number of products by simply picking out one and putting in another is usually worthless—as with all borrowed interest.[20]

The spot below is a typical piece of parasite advertising in which the allegedly humorous theme tramples all over the client. Pay particular attention to how the most potent imagery pertains not to the product (as it is supposed to), but to the "funny" condition that product is supposed to alleviate:

```
WIFE:   (Syrupy) Good morning, dear. How's my little pigeon?

HUBBY:  Awful. My mouth feels like the bottom of a bird cage.

WIFE:   That's terrible. Here. Stick you little beak into this.

HUBBY:  What is it?

WIFE:   It's Apri-Grape. A juice to wake-up crowing about!

HUBBY:  Apri-Grape? With a bunch of starlings molting in my mouth?
```

19. Robert Wanamaker, writing in "Monday Memo," *Broadcasting Magazine*, February 3, 1969, p. 16.
20. Anthony Chevins, writing in "Monday Memo," *Broadcasting Magazine*, May 18, 1981, p. 22.

WIFE: Just try it, ducky. This apricot and grapefruit blend will
           really get you flying.

HUBBY: (Tasting) Hey! This stuff sure plucks up my spirits!

WIFE: (Sexily) Anything for my little rooster.

In contrast, here is an automotive dealership spot. Rather than feeding off the product, this commercial meets each of the Chevins criteria for effective comedy in radio advertising.

(SFX: PHONE RING AND PICK UP)

MAN: Hello. O'Mara Pontiac-Toyota service department.

DICK: Uh, hello, my car is, uh—

MAN: Yes?

DICK: Very ill---don't yell at me.

MAN: Ill?

DICK: It makes a funny noise---like tickity, tickity, don't yell
           at me.

MAN: Tickity, tickity?

DICK: And sometimes it goes chapoogata—chapoogata.

MAN: Would you like to bring it in, sir?

DICK: Yes, I would, don't yell at me.

MAN: Why do you keep saying don't yell at me?

DICK: Because that's what they do at car places. They yell at
           you and they make you break out in hives, and they never
           talk to you after you buy the car.

MAN: Well, not at O'Mara Pontiac-Toyota. We're a friendly place
           with no hype and no yelling from the sales or service
           department.

DICK: You won't say, 'What do you want, punk,' make your eyes
           all buggy?

MAN: No, and if you say your car goes tickity tickity

BOTH: And chapoogata, chapoogata—

MAN: Then you just make a service appointment at O'Mara
           Pontiac-Toyota, and we'll give you fast, efficient
           service.

DICK: I really appreciate this, don't yell at me.

MAN: If you say that one more time, I'm gonna yell at you!

DICK: I knew it, I knew you would yell at me---I knew it—

MAN: No, I didn't mean it---I was kidding—

ANNCR: Let the dealer that delivers, deliver yours today. O'Mara
           Pontiac-Toyota. The relaxed, <u>friendly</u> dealer. 1200 East
           30th, Hutchinson.

(Courtesy of Fran Sax, FirstCom.)

"Don't Yell at Me" was written by Dick Orkin, whose treatments have not only promoted a variety of national and local products, but also the radio industry itself through copy commissioned by the Radio Advertising Bureau. (RAB is an organization devoted to the expansion of radio's sales success and the source of valuable creative assistance for copywriters and sales personnel). Orkin has isolated a major flaw common to many humor commercials—a flaw of which we as copywriters must be cognizant. "Somewhere around 45 seconds in," instructs Orkin, "too many writers get lost and they don't know how to get to a payoff. With comedy, you've promised that if people have listened, you will reward them for listening with something funny."[21] In other words, the comedy spot, like any radio message, must end with strength, with power. We cannot afford to throw away our message conclusion just because we've run out of "funny." A comedy concept that can't sustain itself for a full 60 seconds is comedy that should never have been employed.

While conceding that "Selling is serious business," advertising agency founder W. B. Doner reminded the Adcraft Club of Detroit:

> Humor is one of the most powerful weapons with which to sell. For your client's sales curves, and incidentally perhaps for your own, humor is far more than something to laugh at. . . . McCollum Spielman Research found that humorous commercials penetrate clutter 30 percent better than the norm. Now we are just naive enough to believe that's identical to buying $133,000 worth of media for $100,000. . . . Most significant of all, humor can be, should be, must be *warm*. It can make people like the advertiser. When they like the advertising, the advertiser gets the credit.[22]

Don't Underestimate Radio

Despite its limitations and pitfalls, radio remains the medium in which writers and their words can conjure up the most vivid and self-participatory scenes in the minds of the audience. Hopefully, the last three chapters have provided some of the guidelines and insights necessary to your full realization of radio's potential. Radio is not second-class television. Rather, in Henry Morgan's words, "radio is cheaper, steadier, simpler, purer, cheaper, effective, cheaper, kindlier, less expensive; the results are measurable, the demographics easier to pre-figure, the audience dependable."[23]

Still, especially in the commercial world, there are plenty of institutional barriers to the acceptance of radio as a full partner with television and print. Robert Hodges of Della Femina, Travisano & Partners once graphically portrayed the obstacles that radio must overcome even before it gets out of the conference room:

> Pity the poor agency account executive who has to tell a roomful of client types that they ought to be on radio. He stands there practically naked—no storyboards, no comprehensive layouts, nothing but a typewritten script. He

21. Betsy Sharkey, "Dick Vs. Bert," *ADWEEK/Midwest,* October, 1983, p. H.R.13.
22. Eileen Courter, "Doner: 'Reach the Wallet through the Funnybone,'" *ADWEEK/Midwest,* March 26, 1984, p. 24.
23. Morgan, "Monday Memo," p. 14.

reads the copy (all three dramatic roles) while an assistant account executive does sound effects with his mouth, and hums or whistles the music. And the client sits there thinking, "On this I'm spending a million dollars"[24]

There is no better testing ground of a writer's ability as a wordsmith than the scene Mr. Hodges describes. And that is the central reason radio should not be underestimated by the copywriter. For if you depreciate radio's potential, you are depreciating your own skill as a language marksman, your own ability as a master of the often unadorned word.

Kenneth Roman, president of Ogilvy & Mather, boosts the sound medium as an exciting platform on which to exhibit our talents when he marvels:

> What an opportunity for the writer, constrained on all sides by TV research, to demonstrate creative range. To take risks. To get involved with the listener. To use the unique strengths of a medium that depends on imagery. Radio can— and must—be sold to the copywriter. Not as a place just for humor or music, but one that is ideal for highly creative, noticeable selling ideas. . . . We have learned how to use radio successfully; to move in quickly, as in an airline promotion war; to schedule commercials by time of day; to involve the listener with imagery; to promote a service at the national level for local tie-ins and even for special promotions, and to build brand images as in the soft drinks and beer categories.[25]

With a proper attention to format, selection of the most appropriate generic vehicle, exercise of the proper caution in problem copy types, a commitment to the Radio Resolutions, and a determination to inject PUNCH into every spot you write, radio *will* work because it more directly and more intensely thrusts the audience into the picture-determination process. Ultimately, radio can even allow the listener to construct concrete pictures out of what are, in real life, intangible concepts and relationships:

```
ANNCR:  My music store really had the blues. I didn't know how
        many drums I had in stock. (SFX DRUMS DISORGANIZED).
        And I had 500 more clarinets that I could sell! (SFX
        CLARINETS ORGANIZED) Instead of ordering banjos I ordered
        ukeleles. I don't even sell ukeleles! (SFX UKELELES
        DISORGANIZED) And don't ask me about tubas (SFX TUBA)

        My inventory was a disaster-(SFX DIFFERENT INSTRUMENTS)
        Now I heard that IBM made small computers for small
        businesses like mine. So I bought a small IBM computer for
        my inventory and now I know what to order, when to order
        (THE DISORGANIZED INSTRUMENTS BEGIN PLAYING IN SYNC) and
        how much to order.

        And these days my music store is working in total harmony.
        (THE MUSIC IS EVOLVED INTO A FULL DIXIE BAND) But best of
```

24. Robert Hodges, writing in "Monday Memo," *Broadcasting Magazine*, February 11, 1974, p. 21.
25. Kenneth Roman, writing in "Monday Memo," *Broadcasting Magazine*, August 18, 1980, p. 12.

all, IBM sells so many different kinds of small computers
that I told my brother to buy one for his business—(SFX
COW MOOOOOOOOOO!)

For more information, call IBM toll free at
1-800-631-5582.

(Courtesy of Melissa Wohltman, Doyle Dane Bernbach Advertising.)

In short, radio is not only a worthy competitor of, but also a potent companion to, television. Radio, in the words of (7-Eleven Slurpees') Bob Stanford, "is something special. Its scope isn't limited to a number of inches, measured diagonally or any other way. Radio's color is always brighter, and its depth invariably greater. Radio makes pictures inside your head and there is simply no limit to where you can take that."[26]

26. Stanford, "Monday Memo," p. 24.

PART THREE

TELEVISION COPYWRITING

Key Elements of Television Writing

Television Housekeeping Copy

Television Commercials

Chapter Nine

KEY ELEMENTS
OF TELEVISION WRITING

Though many of the communicative writing principles discussed in the previous chapters on radio also pertain to television, they will not be reintroduced in this section. Instead, the next three chapters concentrate on concepts that apply mainly to the *visual* components of television continuity and commercial creation, or to the particular problems encountered in the interlocking of video and audio. Thus, if you have not already done so, the entire section on radio writing should be read before proceeding into the additional complexities of television.

THE AUDIO/VIDEO COALITION

The most fundamental but, at the same time, the most difficult principle for the new television writer to grasp is that the sound track must enhance, not echo, the visual. Good television audio neither distracts from nor duplicates what the picture is striving to present.

Many writers rebel at this concept either because they don't believe television audio is that important or because they have never learned to write effective audio in the first place. That is why a solid grounding in radio copy creation is so valuable for the television writer. Given a large shooting budget and high-priced production personnel, a lot of visually adept copywriters can come up with a fairly interesting, even relevant piece of pictorial continuity or advertising. But let an assignment come along that for budgetary or conceptual reasons demands a relatively basic and unadorned picture, then many of these same visual artists will fall flat on their eyeballs because their audio is only good enough to stash behind the scenery. Martha Holmes, Needham, Harper & Steers associate creative director maintains that, "There isn't any reason to think that words are less interesting in commercials—as long as the words are not advertisingese, and don't have a list of client strategies in there. People's interest is not necessarily visual . . . what's important is a synergy between what's spoken and the film technique."[1]

Certainly, television is a visual medium. But it is also a frantically competitive one in which every possible advantage must be exploited to break through the

1. Barbara Lippert, "The New Terseness," *ADWEEK/Midwest*, February, 1985, p. C.R. 1.

clutter of the tube into the listener's consciousness. If the audio in your message is only "no worse than anybody else's," you are throwing away an immense opportunity to stand out from the crowd. Think the sound track of a television communication really doesn't matter? Then imagine:

```
shots of various mouth-watering delicacies available at your
local fast food palace—and a soundtrack consisting of a bunch of
pig snorts
```

```
                              or
```

```
action footage of a new pick-up truck bounding across rough
terrain—with an audio that features a tinkling music box
rendition of 'Twinkle, Twinkle, Little Star.'
```

Just now, even with the imperfect conveyance of print, were you able to keep concentrating on the food after the audio barnyard was called up in your mind? Could you keep your focus on the ruggedness of the pick-up truck once its delicate little aural counterpoint impinged on your consciousness? Obviously, most television sound tracks are not this incongruous, but the power of the audio portion of the television message to confuse as well as to complement must always be respected because that power is present in every video assignment you face.

The Michigan Bell script that follows demonstrates how well-selected audio can complement and embellish the visual without making that visual totally dependent on it. This is very important because the basic point of a good television message should be capable of viewer discernment from the visual alone. The audio then serves to amplify that point. A high-interest visual (something every television message should possess) naturally arouses audience attention toward the audio that augments it. It is then up to the audio to fulfill the expectations that the visual and thence the viewer have set up for it. In this Yellow Pages commercial, the picture alone fully conveys the hassles of random, unorganized shopping. Yet, it is the audio that encapsulates the problem into key catch phrases and identifies these with the classified solution:

Video	Audio
MAN IN CAR BACKS OUT OF DRIVEWAY.	(SFX: VW BACKING UP)
	V/O: A simple shopping trip,
CAR BACKS UP TO PLUNGER OF PINBALL MACHINE AND STOPS ABRUPTLY.	(SFX: PINBALL DROPPING IN SLOT)
	V/O: without the Ameritech Michigan Bell Yellow Pages—

Video	Audio
PLUNGER LAUNCHES CAR INTO PINBALL GAME.	(SFX: PLUNGER RELEASE)
	V/O: —could be an unforgettable experience
CAR SPIRALS AROUND PINBALL BUMPER.	(SFX: BOING! BOING!)
	V/O: You could end up in circles—
CAR THROWN RAPIDLY BETWEEN PINBALL GAME BUMPERS.	(SFX: BUZZER)
	V/O: or going no place fast—
PINBALL FLIPPER SENDS CAR INTO ''CLOSED'' SIGN.	(SFX: DING! DING! DING!)
	V/O: and getting there too late.
	(SFX: GENERAL PINBALL MACHINE MAYHEM)
CAR IN FRONT OF ''WRONG AGAIN'' SIGN AT END OF ALLEY.	V/O: Going down one blind alley after another—
CAR COMES TO A HALT IN FRONT OF OWN GARAGE.	—why go through that?
CU OF YELLOW PAGES BOOK ON TABLE NEXT TO PHONE AND DARK LAMP IN FRONT OF WINDOW.	V/O: —when you can go through Michigan's most complete shopping guide, before you leave.
SAME TABLE SHOT SHOWING SHAKING MAN THROUGH WINDOW.	
CU OF MAN'S HAND TURNING ON LAMP OVER BOOK AND PHONE.	The Ameritech Michigan Bell Yellow Pages. Next to the phone, there's nothing better.

(Courtesy of Sheila I. O'Donnell, Ross Roy Inc., Advertising.)

We have just mentioned that the visual alone should be capable of attracting viewer interest in the message as well as giving a basic understanding of what that message is about. In fact, a good test of a piece of television continuity or advertising is to view it, or imagine it, with the sound off. Does the central point of the message still come through? And further, does it make us *want* to turn up that audio so we learn more? The Michigan Bell spot possesses this quality and, although a different approach for a different phone company, so does the Northwest Bell commercial in Figure 9–1. In this storyboard, the visual certainly communicates the announcement's fundamental premise—but in a way that entices the viewer to listen to the sound track for a complete explanation.

Tonight, try turning off the sound on the television commercials and continuity to which you are exposed. How many of these messages attract your interest and attention with the visual alone? And of these, how many tempt you to turn up the audio to get more information? The results of this experiment should give you a general idea of the percentage of messages that really exploit the audio/video coalition to full potential.

GENERAL TELEVISION FORMATS

You have just seen television material presented in script and storyboard formats. Together with the photoboard, these vehicles constitute the main mechanisms by which your television commercial or continuity idea is captured and processed. Let's look at the characteristics of each.

The Script

As the Yellow Pages treatment demonstrated, television scripts are usually fashioned in the conventional two-column format with video directions on the left and the corresponding audio directions on the right. Care is taken in spacing so that the audio indication is always directly opposite the visual it is intended to complement. To do otherwise would make the script very difficult to comprehend and, in shooting stage, would force the television director or film editor to read slantwise in trying to synchronize sound and picture properly. Note that video directions are in ALL CAPS form as, on the audio side, are character names (or VO for "announcer voice-over"). Should they be needed, sound effects and music cues are also in ALL CAPS. Thus, the television audio side follows the same upper case/lower case conventions as the radio script.

For especially complex pieces, either of two more sophisticated script formats may need to be employed. The first of these uses a running column of numbers down the center of the page for precise referencing and production interlock. The following K-Mart "Grand Opening" script illustrates the utility of such a format when dealing with an intricate project (see pp. 240–243).

The second variety of specialized script ignores the left side/right side separation altogether in favor of a detailed "centered" approach in which lower-case video directions run margin to margin and audio proceeds down the center of the page. Such a scripting methodology provides for greatly expanded visual description while, at the same time, allowing the production process more latitude as to the length of subsequences and the precise injection point for

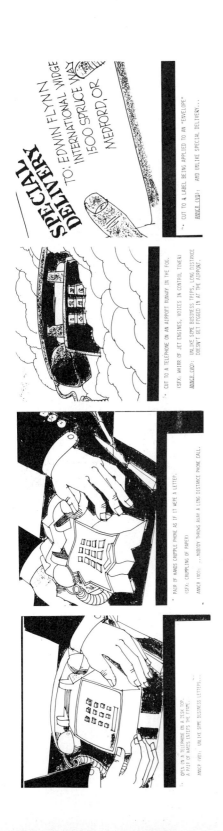

Figure 9–1. *(Courtesy of Lockey Todd-Bennett, Livingston & Company.)*

239

TELEVISION *copy by*

ROSS ROY INC.
2751 EAST JEFFERSON AVENUE
DETROIT, MICHIGAN 48207
TELEPHONE 313-961-6900

CLIENT K MART DISCOUNT STORES

PRODUCT GRAND OPENING

JOB NO.

PROGRAM :60

STATION/NETWORK

SCHEDULE PAGE ONE

PAGE NO. AS PRODUCED

video

OPEN ON PRINCIPAL PLAYER (35-ISH MALE) IN TYPICAL SUBURBAN NEIGHBORHOOD WALKING DOWN SIDEWALK. HE SINGS:

WIDEN AND PULL BACK TO REVEAL SUBURBAN MATRON GARDENING AND SHE JOINS PRINCIPAL PLAYER AND BOTH SING:

CUT TO SMALL TOWN STREET WITH BAKER STANDING IN DOORWAY. THE BAKER JOINS THE GROWING GROUP AND THEY SING:

CUT TO THE FACADE OF A HOTEL AND AS GROUP MARCHES BY A "RICH COUPLE" JOINS THE GROUP AND ALL SING:

CUT AS GROUP NOW PASSES AN OUTDOOR SWIMMING POOL AS MAN IN SCUBA GEAR CLIMBS OUT OF WATER, HEARS THE PASSING GROUP, FALLS BACKWARDS INTO THE WATER AND THEN JOINS GROUP SINGING:

CUT AS GROUP PASSES SCHOOL HOUSE AND PICKS UP TWO STUDENTS AND ONE "OLD" LADY WHO DOES CARTWHEEL AND THEY ALL SING:

CUT TO PARK LIKE SETTING WITH GAZEBO. A TENNIS PLAYER AND NANNY PUSHING "PRAM" NOW JOIN IN AND THEY SING:

CUT TO HIGH ANGLE SHOT OF RURAL DIRT ROAD AS PLAYERS MARCH IN SINGLE FILE DOWN THE ROAD. WIDEN SHOT TO REVEAL TELEPHONE LINESMAN AT TOP OF TELEPHONE POLE. LINESMAN TURNS TO CAMERA AND SINGS WITH THE GROUP:

audio

1.
2. I know a place....
3.
4.
5.
6.
7. I know a place....
8.
9. Where life is good.....
10.
11. Where life is good....
12.
13. A brand new place.....
14.
15. A brand new place.....
16.
17. In your neighborhood....
18.
19. Your neighborhood.....
20.
21.
22.
23. Come to my place....
24.
25. Where dreams come true......
26.
27.
28. They come true....
29.
30.
31.
32. My saving place......
33.
34. Can save alot of dollars for you.
35.
36.
37.
38.
39.
40.
41.
42.
43.

TELEVISION *copy by*

ROSS ROY INC.
2751 EAST JEFFERSON AVENUE
DETROIT, MICHIGAN 48207
TELEPHONE 313-961-6900

CLIENT K MART DISCOUNT STORES

PRODUCT GRAND OPENING

JOB NO.

PROGRAM :60

STATION/NETWORK

SCHEDULE PAGE TWO

PAGE NO. AS PRODUCED

video

CUT TO LOW ANGLE SHOT OF URBAN TOWNHOUSES AND SNAP ZOOM IN ON "HOUSEWIFE" AS SHE OPENS FRECH DOORS AND STEPS OUT ONTO SECOND LEVEL PORCH IN BATHROBE AND HAIR CURLERS. THE GROUP SINGS:

CUT TO LOW ANGLE SHOT OF K MART STORE FRONT AS THE GROUP LED BY THE PRINCIPAL PLAYER WALK OVER CAMERA TOWARDS STORE. THE GROUP SINGS:

CUT TO STRAIGHT ON SHOT OF INSIDE STORE LOOKING OUT TO THE PARKING LOT AS GROUP FILES IN DOORS AND PAST CAMERA. ZOOM ON TO PRINCIPAL PLAYER. THEY SING:

CUT TO DOWN THE MAIN AISLE SHOT AS GROUP FANS OUT OVER STORE LOOKING AT MERCHANDISE AND SINGING:

CUT TO THREE SHOT OF PRINCIPAL PLAYER AND TWO FEMALE FULL TORSO MANNEQUINS IN THE LADIES WEAR SECTION. THE PRINCIPAL PLAYER DUCKS AND WE ZOOM PAST HIM TO LONG RACKS OF CLOTHES AS THE REST OF THE GROUP HOLDS UP THE MERCHANDISE AND THEY SING:

CUT TO ECU OF AUTOMOBILE TIRE WITH THE LINESMAN'S HEAD STICKING THRU AND THEY SING:

audio

1.
2.
3.
4.
5. My saving place......
6.
7.
8. K mart....
9.
10. K mart....
11.
12. Is your saving place.
13.
14. Yes, it is.
15.
16. You'll meet value....
17.
18. Face to face (everyday)
19.
20.
21.
22. K mart.
23.
24.
25.
26. Sells great
27.
28.
29.
30.
31.
32.
33. Merchandise.
34.
35.
36.
37.
38.
39.
40.
41.
42.
43.

Left Panel (Page Three)

TELEVISION *copy by*

ROSS ROY INC.

2751 EAST JEFFERSON AVENUE
DETROIT, MICHIGAN 48207
TELEPHONE 313-961-6900

CLIENT K MART DISCOUNT STORES

PRODUCT GRAND OPENING

JOB NO.

PROGRAM :60

STATION/NETWORK

SCHEDULE PAGE THREE

PAGE NO. AS PRODUCED

video

CUT TO COSMETICS DEPARTMENT AS THE LADIES IN THE GROUP DANCE DOWN AISLE "PRIMPING" AND "FUSSING". THEY SING:

CUT TO DOWN THE AISLE SHOT OF PLAYERS IN THE SHOE DEPARTMENT. SOME ARE MILLING AROUND AND THE OTHERS ARE SEATED AND "CROSSING" AND "UNCROSSING" THEIR LEGS IN TIME TO THE MUSIC. ZOOM INTO PRINCIPAL PLAYER. THEY SING:

CUT TO MENSWEAR DEPARTMENT AS THE GROUP "SHOPS" AND THE PRINCIPAL PLAYER IS SITTING ON TOP OF THE CHANGING BOOTH: THEY SING:

CUT TO SPORTING GOODS DEPARTMENT AS FEMALE PLAYER (STUDENT) WITH FOOTBALL HELMET ON PASSES A BALL TO OTHER STUDENT. THE GROUP SINGS:

CUT TO DOWN THE AISLE SHOT AS PLAYERS POP OUT FROM BEHIND THE COUNTERS AND SING:

CUT BACK TO THE SHOE DEPARTMENT ON TIGHT SHOT OF PRINCIPAL PLAYER AS HE SING:

CUT TO DOWN THE AISLE SHOT OF REFRIGERATORS AND FREEZERS. AS CAMERA PULLS BACK THE PLAYERS REACH IN AND OPEN THE DOORS OF THE APPLIANCES SEQUENTIALLY. THEY SING:

audio

1.
2.
3. You're gonna get value...
4.
5.
6.
7. At a low, low price.
8.
9.
10.
11.
12.
13.
14.
15. Here at my place.
16.
17.
18.
19.
20.
21. You know you're going to get more....
22.
23.
24.
25.
26. You get more.
27.
28.
29.
30. My saving place.
31.
32.
33. Has got a lot of........
34.
35.
36.
37.
38.
39.
40.
41.
42.
43.

Form No. 2-1061   6-72

Right Panel (Page Four)

TELEVISION *copy by*

ROSS ROY INC.

2751 EAST JEFFERSON AVENUE
DETROIT, MICHIGAN 48207
TELEPHONE 313-961-6900

CLIENT K MART DISCOUNT STORES

PRODUCT GRAND OPENING

JOB NO.

PROGRAM :60

STATION/NETWORK

SCHEDULE PAGE FOUR

PAGE NO. AS PRODUCED

video

CUT TO DOWN THE AISLE LONG SHOT OF CHECKOUT COUNTERS AS GROUP COMES THRU. PRINCIPAL PLAYER IS ON TOP OF COUNTER. THEY SING:

CUT TO OUTDOOR ECU SHOT OF "K" ON SIGN AND PULL BACK TO LONG SHOT AS "PRINCIPAL PLAYER" COMES UP FROM BEHIND "K" AND THE GROUP ON THE ROOFTOP FILE BY SINGING:

LEAVE ROOM IN BLUE SKY ABOVE STORE FRONT FOR SUPER INFORMATION

FADE TO BLACK.

audio

1. Value in store.....
2.
3. Your saving place.
4.
5.
6.
7.
8. K mart.
9. K mart is your saving place.
10.
11. Sing it for me children.....
12.
13. You'll meet value face to face....
14.
15. It's ok at K mart.
16.
17. Your saving place.
18.
19.
20. Good day at K mart.
21.
22. Your saving place.
23.
24.
25.
26.
27.
28.
29.
30.
31.
32.
33. (Courtesy of Paul J. Stano,
34. Ross Roy Inc. Advertising)
35.
36.
37.
38.
39.
40.
41.
42.
43.

Form No. 2-1061   6-72

individual copy segments. The compelling Citation demonstration below indicates how such scripting works.

```
Commercial opens on a Chevy Citation (in mortise). Hatchback is
open. We see the interior of the car. Pop in pieces of a
disassembled garage. SUPER:  CHEVY CITATION.
     ANNCR: (VO)          Chevrolet demonstrates the room in the
                          Chevy Citation.
Cut to spokesman standing by Citation and a garage.
     ANNCR: (OC)          You're probably not surprised that this
                          compact car fits into this compact garage.
                          But what would you think—
CU of spokesman
     ANNCR:               —if the garage fits into the compact car?
Through stop-motion photography garage disassembles, and becomes
a pile of material and then each piece goes into Citation cargo
space—then hatch closes.
     MUSIC & SINGERS:  IT'S THE FIRST CHEVY OF THE EIGHTIES
                       THE FIRST CHEVY OF ITS KIND
                       THIS COULD BE THE CAR YOU'VE HAD IN MIND
Cut to Citation in neutral setting. Spokesman is standing near
car.
     ANNCR:               Take a Citation demonstration drive---at
                          your Chevy dealer's today.
SUPER:  THE FIRST CHEVY OF THE '80s.
     MUSIC & SINGERS:  CHEVY CITATION
BOWTIE/LOGO:  CHEVY CITATION
```

(Courtesy of Chevrolet Division and Campbell-Ewald Company.)

   Whether the standard arrangement or one of the two specialized formats is used, the professionally structured television script provides the writer with the opportunity to probe visual concepts without having to draw the illustrations. Since many copywriters are somewhat the other side of cave paintings in their artistic abilities, the video script is a blessing for all concerned. It is used as one of the bases of consultation when the copywriter periodically gets together with an art director for the actual sketching of the proposed visual segments. In between these conferences, the script allows the writer to work alone in refining the treatment so that valuable artistic time is not wasted before the message concept has really jelled in the writer's mind.

   The evolution of a television script is graphically shown in the following four treatments supplied through the courtesy of Bruce S. Dunham, Jr., of W. B. Doner and Company. Though several more "fine-tuning" stages occurred between the creation of these four scripts, the major copy development, which spread over eleven months, is well represented here. Clearly, television script maturation is neither a quick nor approximate business. Every word and every pictorial aspect must be scrupulously examined and evaluated in deriving the most cohesive and incisive treatment possible.

Read over these four scripts carefully. Note the progressive modifications made in both audio and video and try to discover for yourself what made these changes necessary and what they helped to accomplish in message clarification. As a television copywriter, you will soon have to make these same determinations in regard to your own commercial and continuity material.

Version #1

Video	Audio
SPOT OPENS ON A PACKAGE OF AMERICAN TUBORG.	ANNCR V/O: This is Tuborg, the world famous beer of Denmark.
CAMERA GOES IN CLOSE TO LABEL TO SHOW THAT IT IS BREWED IN THE U.S.A.	As you can see, Tuborg is now brewed in America.
DISSOLVE TO WIDER SHOT AS HAND COMES INTO FRAME AND EXECUTES A LONG SLOW POUR. THERE IS AN UNUSUAL SIGNET RING ON ONE OF THE FINGERS. THE DESIGN IS A COAT-OF-ARMS.	Imported Tuborg used to be a very expensive beer. But now that Tuborg is also brewed in America---it is affordable by anyone who loves the flavor of good light Danish beer.
	(PAUSE)
GLASS COMES BACK INTO FRAME.	
CAMERA PANS TO COPY ON LABEL THAT READS ''BY APPOINTMENT OF THE ROYAL DANISH COURT.''	It is the only beer in America brewed by special appointment for the personal enjoyment of the kings of Denmark and Sweden.
CUT TO REGAL-LOOKING SPOKESMAN AS HE SMILES, REPOURS AND TOASTS THE VIEWER WITH A TONGUE-IN-CHEEK SMILE.	Now, if Tuborg is good enough to be a beer for Kings, shouldn't it be good enough for your next Saturday night beer bash?
SUPER POPS ON TUBORG.	

Video	Audio
MANDATORY: Tuborg of Copenhagen, Ltd., Natick, Mass.	

Version #2

Video	Audio
OPEN ON MEDIUM SHOT OF BOTTLE OF TUBORG BESIDE RICHLY DESIGNED GOBLET.	ANNCR V/O: This is Tuborg, the famous beer of Denmark.
START ZOOM TO CLOSE-UP OF LABEL THAT IDENTIFIES THE BEER AS BEING BREWED IN THE U.S.A.	now brewed in America
DIZ TO PART OF LABEL THAT IDENTIFIES APPOINTMENT TO DANISH COURT.	by special appointment to The Royal Courts of Denmark
BOTTLE ROTATES TO ALLOW VIEWER TO READ LABEL COPY THAT IDENTIFIES APPOINTMENT TO SWEDISH COURT.	and Sweden.
DIZ TO WIDER SHOT OF PACKAGE AND GOBLET.	Now you may think a beer brewed for Kings would be expensive.
HAND ENTERS FRAME AND GRASPS BOTTLE FOR POUR.	It was.
AS BEER IS POURED INTO THE GOBLET, ONE CAN SEE THAT ON THE MIDDLE FINGER THERE IS A RICHLY CARVED RING BEARING THE ROYAL COAT OF ARMS OR THE SEAL OF STATE OF DENMARK.	But now Tuborg is affordable by anyone who loves the authentic taste of good light Danish beer.
THE FILLED GOBLET IS HOISTED OUT OF FRAME AND CAMERA STARTS SLOW ZOOM INTO THE PACKAGE.	And for about the same money you've been paying for the king of beers—

Video	Audio
THE DRAINED GOBLET IS THUNKED DOWN BESIDE PACKAGE AND CONTINUES TO ZOOM TO THE CROWN ON THE LABEL. TUBORG LOGO AND MANDATORY POP ON.	now you can get Tuborg, the beer of kings.

Version #3

Video	Audio
OPEN ON CLOSE UP OF BOTTLE NECK, READING ''Tuborg Gold.''	ANNCR V/O: This is Tuborg Gold—
CAMERA TILTS DOWN BOTTLE, PICKS UP CROWN ON MAIN LABEL,	the golden beer of Danish kings—
AND PANS ACROSS TO READ:	
''By appointment to the Royal Danish Court/the Royal Swedish Court.''	by appointment to the Royal Courts of Denmark and Sweden.
DISSOLVE TO CU OF LABEL ON BOTTLE BEING TILTED BY HAND FOR A POUR, AND READ, ''Product of USA.''	Tuborg Gold is now brewed in America—
DISSOLVE TO BEER BEING POURED INTO DANISH GLASS WITH RAISED IMPRIMATUR OF CROWN ON ITS FRONT.	and affordable to anyone
DISSOLVE TO HAND WEARING REGAL RING LIFTING GLASS UP AND OUT OF FRAME.	who loves the authentic taste of light, golden Danish beer.
DISSOLVE TO BEAUTY ''STILL LIFE'' OF BOTTLE AND FOOD ON A TABLE BEFORE BEAUTIFUL STAINED GLASS WINDOW, MOVING IN AS THE DRAINED GLASS IS SET DOWN BY	So, for about what you'd pay for the king of beers---now you can have Tuborg Gold, the beer of kings.

Video	Audio
HAND INTO THE FRAME, ENDING ON CU OF LABEL, FINALLY READING LARGE, ''TUBORG GOLD.'' SUPER MANDATORY: Tuborg of Copenhagen, Ltd., Baltimore, Md.	

Version #4

Video	Audio
OPEN ON CLOSE UP OF BOTTLE NECK, READING ''Tuborg Gold.''	ANNCR V/O: This is our Tuborg Gold—
CAMERA TILTS DOWN BOTTLE, PICKS UP CROWN ON MAIN LABEL,	the golden beer of Danish kings—
AND PANS ACROSS TO READ:	
''By appointment to the Royal Danish Court/the Royal Swedish Court.''	now affordable to anyone who loves the true taste of light, golden Danish beer.
DISSOLVE TO BEER BEING POURED INTO DANISH GLASS WITH RAISED IMPRIMATUR OF CROWN ON ITS FRONT.	For Tuborg Gold is now brewed in America.
DISSOLVE TO HAND WEARING REGAL RING LIFTING GLASS UP AND OUT OF FRAME.	By appointment to the Royal Danish Court.
DISSOLVE TO BEAUTY ''STILL LIFE'' OF BOTTLE AND FOOD ON A TABLE BEFORE BEAUTIFUL STAINED GLASS WINDOW, MOVING IN AS THE DRAINED GLASS IS SET DOWN BY HAND INTO THE FRAME, ENDING ON CU OF LABEL, FINALLY READING LARGE, ''TUBORG GOLD.'' SUPER MANDATORY: Carling National Breweries, Inc., Baltimore, Md.	So, for about what you'd pay for the king of beers---you can now have Tuborg Gold, the golden beer of Danish Kings.

The Storyboard

This sequence of selected sketched stills of the proposed television treatment helps to keep concept creation and evaluation visually oriented. In some situations, even the first attempt at an assignment is done in storyboard form by a copywriter/art director team. At other times, it is the copywriter who comes up with an initial script draft and perhaps even refines it before bringing the draft to the artist for visual workup. For reasons of economy and efficiency in conserving valuable artist time, several script rewrites may occur between each storyboard.

With a visual block on top and an audio box on the bottom, each storyboard frame or panel strives to illustrate the sequence of visual action, the camera settings, angles, and optical effects desired, and the dialogue, music, and sound effects being considered for use.

As it is being prepared, the storyboard provides the opportunity for good interplay between copy and art people. This interplay can be most effective when the two people involved are not afraid to make suggestions about the other's area and to accept suggestions about their own. Art directors *have* been known occasionally to come up with a better word or phrase than the copywriter had originally captured. And copywriters, in their own scattered moments of pictorial brilliance, do stumble on more compelling visual ideas than the artist at first had in mind. Since the professional well-being of both depends on their *collective* ability to derive a successful audio/visual communication, the copywriter and the art director each have something to gain from pooling rather than departmentalizing their knowledge and insight.

Only partly in jest, copywriter Peter Kellogg warns: "If you walk into an art director's office with an idea and say, 'Here it is!' you're just asking to get your head chewed off. Art directors, you see, like to think that they have some part in the creative process, and you've got to convince them they do . . . Besides, sniffing spray mount and magic markers all day seems to affect their brains. So it's always wise to proceed with caution."[2] TV poses special problems for the relationship anyway, according to creative director Bob Kuperman of BBDO/West, because, "the job of the art director and copywriter is not as clearly defined in television as in print, where one does the layout and the other writes the body copy. Television is more of a team effort."[3]

The result of effective copywriter/art director partnership, the two storyboards that follow (Figures 9–2 and 9–3) illustrate intermediate stages in the maturation of the same Tuborg television production to which the four scripts pertain. From the 'boards, it is relatively easy to see how the script modifications determined and, were themselves determined by, refinements in the storyboard. With its self-contained audio/visual segments, the storyboard format also facilitates easy and quick rearrangement of frames in the pursuit of more effective idea flow.

2. Peter Kellogg, "Artful Deception Fills a Copywriter's Day, *ADWEEK/Midwest*, April 16, 1984, p. 38.
3. Arnold Schmidt, "'New Wave' Ads Summon New Creative Roles," *ADWEEK/Midwest*, September 27, 1982, p. 76.

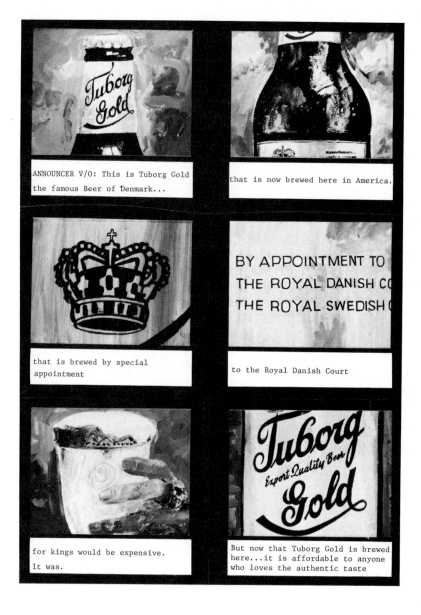

ANNOUNCER V/O: This is Tuborg Gold the famous Beer of Denmark...

that is now brewed here in America.

that is brewed by special appointment

to the Royal Danish Court

for kings would be expensive. It was.

But now that Tuborg Gold is brewed here...it is affordable to anyone who loves the authentic taste

Figure 9–2. *(Courtesy of W. B. Doner and Company.)*

OPEN ON CLOSE UP OF BOTTLE NECK, READING "Tuborg Gold."

- -

ANNCR V/O: This is Tuborg Gold --

CAMERA TILTS DOWN BOTTLE,

- -

the golden beer

"By appointment to the Royal Danish Court/ the Royal Swedish Court."

- -

of Denmark and Sweden.

DISSOLVE TO CU OF LABEL ON BOTTLE BEING TILTED BY HAND FOR A POUR,

- -

Tuborg Gold

DISSOLVE TO HAND WEARING REGAL RING LIFTING GLASS UP AND OUT OF FRAME,

- -

who loves the authentic taste of light, golden Danish beer.

DISSOLVE TO BEAUTY "STILL LIFE" OF BOTTLE AND FOOD ON A TABLE BEFORE BEAUTIFUL STAINED GLASS WINDOW,

- -

So, for about what you'd pay for the king of beers...

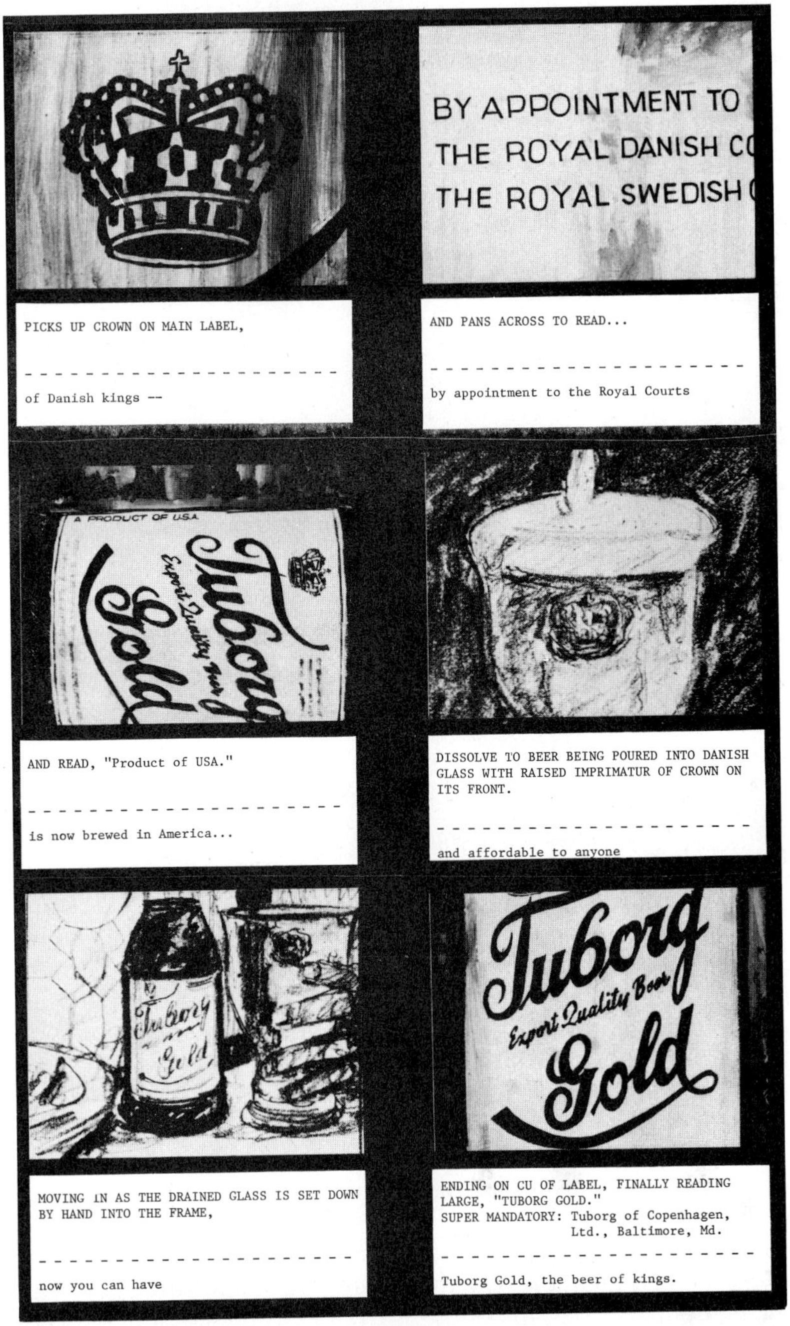

Figure 9–3. *(Courtesy of W. B. Doner and Company.)*

ANNCR V/O: This is our Tuborg Gold . . .

the golden beer of Danish kings . . .

now affordable to anyone who loves the true taste of light, golden Danish beer.

For Tuborg Gold is now brewed in America.

By appointment to the Royal Danish Court.

So, for about what you'd pay for the king of beer . . .

you can now have Tuborg Gold, the the golden beer of Danish kings . . .

Carling National Breweries, Inc. Baltimore, Md.

Figure 9–4. *(Courtesy of W. B. Doner and Company.)*

Technically, the first quick sketches, suitable only for showing to co-creators, constitute what is called a *rough* or *loose* storyboard. Later versions (like Figures 9–2 and 9–3), which are polished enough to exhibit to the client and more precisely delineate each frame, are called *refined, tight,* or *comprehensive* 'boards. In short-deadline or low-budget projects, however, it is not uncommon to proceed directly from a *rough* into actual production—provided that the rough is definitive enough to motivate executive approval.

The Photoboard

After the last stage storyboards are prepared and approved, but before dubbing or distribution is authorized, a photoboard is often made up to give those who have the final power of decision the clearest possible idea of the actual creative and production values present in the finished commercial, PSA, or piece of continuity. In many cases, the photoboard is constructed from selected stills lifted out of the tape or film footage from the completed message itself. In other situations, where reviewers want to see the photographic/telegenic effect earlier in the message's evolution, photoboards replace the later (refined) storyboards. In such instances, the still photographs themselves are shot and pasted up as 'board panels for scrutiny before videotape or film production is authorized.

The photoboard in Figure 9–4 represents the culmination of the Tuborg "Label" commercial. You can see that it matches the copy called for in script version #4 but that the visuals have been further refined. This photoboard is also, in total affect, a good deal more polished than either of the stages represented in the two storyboards. In addition, since the visual component has already been shot as production *rushes* (total exposed tape/film footage from which the final version will be edited), a photoboard does not require the storyboard's verbal description of the pictures.

After final approval, the photoboard can also be used to provide stations and networks with a hard-copy record of the spot's submission to them for initial continuity acceptance and subsequent airing. Photoboards can also be sent to distributors of the product as a means of documenting the marketing efforts that the manufacturer is exerting on this commodity's behalf.

Additional Media for Television Message Creation

Over the years, the desire for closer quality control earlier in the message construction process together with advances in visual technology have brought about a variety of storyboard/photoboard hybridizations. Crudest of these is the *PDT* or *Panoramic Design Technique,* which uses a scaled, magnetized blackboard and a Polaroid or other self-processing still camera. Instead of drawing and redrawing the same backgrounds, implements, and talent in frame after frame, the artist can sketch a scene on the blackboard with chalk, and then position and reposition people and props in front of it. If the product or subject of the message is small enough, a magnet can be attached to it for easy mounting and remounting directly on the board. Staff members from the office or shop can be recruited to stand in front of the board and thereby simulate the way in which on-camera talent will be used in the treatment's final version. Once everything is properly sketched and positioned, individual snapshots are then taken of the board and the people and props in front of it. These are then affixed to the visual block of a standard layout for discussion and presentation.

The PDT approach generally brings a much more dimensional and real-life quality to the proposed treatment than can be accomplished by a storyboard's approximate sketches. At the same time, it is a much quicker and much less expensive method for message capture than the refined storyboard whose individual frames eat up so much more of a well-paid artist's work day. Still, the *Panoramic Design Technique* does not lend itself to every situation. Messages that promote large objects or that demand expansive or detailed settings obviously present reproduction problems that exceed the capability of this very basic device. When used in reasonably small-scale assignments, however, the PDT can mean big savings.

A more sophisticated mechanism is the *animatic,* which is a storyboard whose sketched panels are transferred onto film or videotape. If a more "true to finished product" effect is desired, it is possible to commission limited animation to obtain some actual movement. To go one step farther, the *photomatic* can be employed. This technique is identical to that used in animatics except that photographs are utilized instead of an artist's illustrations. Animatics and photomatics are not inexpensive but, particularly with commercials that need careful pretesting before large-scale distribution, they provide much more realism than a static board or script and are considerably less costly than the complete production of a message whose test results may cause it never to be broadcast.

Alternatively, the prototype television idea can be produced and presented as a 35 mm slide show. In this methodology, a still camera shoots drawings, graphic titles and, perhaps, even the actual exterior scenes called for in the proposed commercial. For supervisor and client review, the resulting slides are then projected on a screen to the accompaniment of a live "voice over" read by the copywriter or a "rough cut" audio tape on which suggested music, sound effects, and talent voice elements have been recorded.

These mechanisms for television message creation, refinement, and evolution are not cheap. A 1984 *ADWEEK* survey indicated that, among the 62 responding top national brand advertising directors, "the average costs for production included $2,500 per storyboard; $10,000 for an animatic; $12,000 for a photomatic; and $100,000 for a finished commercial. Prebroadcast testing of a finished commercial added another $11,000 to the overall bill."[4] Obviously, *local* spots would cost much less in real dollars but would often be just as significant an expenditure in proportion to the local advertiser's available budget. With such sums involved, television copywriting demands the best ideas you can bring to an assignment and cultivation of a highly productive (if not necessarily sublime) relationship with your art director co-creator.

TELEVISION PRODUCTIONAL TERMINOLOGY

As in the case of radio, the professional television copywriter must know and use the proper "lingo" of the electronic medium if words and sketches are to be translated into desired moving and talking images. Directions for television audio are fundamentally the same as for radio so need not be reintroduced here. They can be found in their entirety back in chapter 6. What does require cataloging at this point is the *visual* terminology writers must employ in communicating their concepts to production crews. One cautionary note: Some copywriters, once they acquire a working knowledge of video jargon, tend to *overuse* it; to overspecify every visual detail so that the production personnel are entirely locked into what might not be the best visual treatment of the sequence in question. Give as many directions as needed to convey the main intent of your shot progressions but don't become so detailed that the hands of your video or film production experts are totally tied. Allow them some leeway to take advantage of opportunities that might present themselves on set or on location.

In this Oldsmobile spot, the copywriter has clearly described the overall effect and visual progression required while leaving subsidiary details to the

---

4. Debbie Seaman, "Millions Spent on Commercials You Never See," *ADWEEK/Midwest*, July 30, 1984, p. 29.

best professional judgment of the director and others responsible for creating the footage.

Video	Audio	
1 SALESMAN AND PROSPECT PULL UP IN FRONT OF DEALERSHIP, UNDER BANNER WHICH READS: ''TEST-DRIVE OLDS. GO DRIVEHAPPY TODAY.''	SALESMAN:	Well, what'd you think of your Olds test drive, Mr. Johnson?
	MR. JOHNSON:	(HOLD BACK HIS EXCITEMENT) Not bad. Not bad. See ya.
2 JOHNSON DUCKS ALONGSIDE DEALERSHIP AND DONS GROUCHO MARX GLASSES, NOSE AND MUSTACHE.	V/O ANNCR:	Some people will do almost anything to keep going drivehappy in a new Oldsmobile.
3 JOHNSON WALKS INTO DEALERSHIP AND FINDS OTHER PROSPECTS ALSO WEARING MARX GET-UP.		But it's not necessary.
4 QUICK CUTS OF VARIOUS MARX PROSPECTS HAPPILY DRIVING DIFFERENT OLDSMOBILES. SUPER WORDS: ''GO DRIVEHAPPY IN A CUTLASS CIERA, OLDS FIRENZA.'' PROSPECTS GIVE OKAY SIGN.	SINGERS:	DRIVEHAPPY. <u>OLDS CAN MAKE YOU A LITTLE DRIVEHAPPY. DRIVE ONE TODAY.</u>
5 MR. JOHNSON'S DISGUISE FALLS OFF.	SALESMAN:	Mr. Johnson! Again!
6 MATTE DOWN SHOT AND SUPER TAG:	V/O ANNCR:	Test-drive Olds— and you could go drivehappy too.

(Courtesy of Roger Bodo, Leo Burnett Company of Michigan, Inc.)

We now turn to the specific pieces of visual terminology with which the television copywriter should be familiar. These designations can most easily be divided into four categories: (1) camera movements, (2) shot lengths and angles, (3) control room transitions and devices, and (4) other writer-used technical terms. As in the case of our radio terminology discussion, it is not the intent here to cover the entire vocabulary of television and film production. Instead, attention will be limited to words the copywriter is most likely to need in preparing the actual script.

Camera Movements

This category consists of directions that call for maneuvering of the camera and its base or some manipulation of the camera "head" alone while the base on which it is mounted remains stationary.

Dolly In/Dolly Out.   When this movement is specified, the entire camera is pushed toward or away from the subject of the shot, who or which usually stays immobile.

Truck Left/Truck Right.   This term specifies a lateral movement of the entire camera parallel to the scene being shot. Alternatively, trucking left or trucking right may be referred to as tracking.

Crane/Arc/Boom.   These designations, which have become more or less interchangeable, require that the television or film camera be mounted on a long manual, hydraulic, or electric arm which allows for shots that demand smooth, flowing changes in height and/or semicircular sweeps toward and away from the scene. A much more restricted derivation of this type of movement is the *ped up/ped down,* where the camera is raised or lowered on its base without changing its angular relationship to or distance from the scene.

Pan Left/Pan Right.   This is a more limited version of the truck since only the camera head turns to follow the action as that action modulates to one side of the set or the other. Since the camera's base does not move, the panning procedure also more graphically changes the shot's angle on the scene than does the *truck,* which keeps a constant parallel relationship with the scene and its elements. In the case of character movement, for example, a trucking shot would give the feeling of *walking with* an actor whereas the pan would have the effect of following his approach to or departure from the viewer's psychological location at scene center.

Tilt Up/Tilt Down.   If you stand in place and change the subject of your visual attention by the simple raising or lowering of your head, you will achieve the same effect created by the *tilt* as the camera head tips up or down on its base. The tilt allows television to change the altitude of the viewer's gaze without changing the perceived distances from the perimeter of the scene.

Shot Lengths and Angles

These designations refer to how close or how far the subject of the shot will seem to be in terms of the viewer's perspective as well as to the angular relationship between viewer and subject. The effects of shot lengths and angles are achieved by manipulation of available lens components and/or by the actual movement of the camera in any of the ways just discussed. The basic shot length continuum extends from the full shot (FS) to the extreme close-up (ECU).

Full Shot (FS) or Cover Shot (CS).   The entire scene is encompassed by this shot, which may thus include the whole set or even an outdoor epic's entire horizon. Because it often occurs at the opening of the message in order to acquaint the viewer with the total visual environment, the full shot/cover shot is also known as an *establishing shot.*

Long Shot (LS) or Wide Shot (WS).   Long shots may or may not reveal the entire scene; if they do, they can be interchangeably referred to as full shots. In any event, long shots do encompass a comparatively wide angle of vision and would, in the case of the talent, show a character from head to toe. The term *wide shot* is also used to denote this same orientation.

Medium Shot (MS).   This is a very broad category that includes all visual fields too close or "narrow" to be called long shots and, on the other hand, perspectives too wide to be referred to as close-ups. Though medium shots can thus vary widely depending on the scope of the scene in question, we generally think of them as framing only the upper two-thirds of a standing character and with minimal additional revelation of the set behind him. When two or three characters are featured, a *medium two-shot (M2S) or medium three-shot (M3S)* can be requested. (Any more than three persons would require so wide an angle as to be called a long shot.) For more definitive designation, the terms *medium long shot (MLS)* and *medium close-up (MCU) can also be employed to refer to each end of the medium-shot spectrum.*

Close-Up (CU).   In the close-up, the specific character or prop fills most of the viewing screen. For example, only the head and shoulders of a person would be seen, and thus the CU may also be referred to as a "tight" shot. The *extreme close-up (ECU or XCU)* is the ultimate extension of this principle so that a pianist's hands or a single leaf on a tree can consume most of the picture area and draw the viewer's total focus.

Zoom In/Zoom Out.   Though it is technically a lens function to be treated under this section, the zoom in or out is functionally a technological replacement for the physical and comparatively awkward *dollying* of the entire camera. Through either manual or electronic changes in the lens' optics, a good zoom lens can smoothly bring viewer orientation from a full shot to an ECU and, if desired, back again without the need to move the camera base at all. In the case of outdoor productions, a zoom could traverse hundreds of feet—a far greater distance than the camera itself would be capable of moving within the TV spot's time confines.

To summarize shot lengths, and to review your knowledge of the relevant abbreviations, the following continuum is presented for quick reference. Working from left to right, it proceeds from the "widest" shots, in which individual elements seem the most distant, to the "tightest" shots, in which even a very

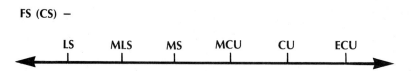

small part of a human or set element can be made to dominate the entire screen.

In our discussion of shot lengths, we have tended to use the word *angle* to refer to the width of the resulting picture. This is because the closer we focus on a single object, the narrower our peripheral vision becomes. Thus, as has been already implied, "long" shots are also "wide" shots and "close-ups" are also "tight." Writers of television commercial and continuity copy tend to use either or both of these descriptive sets, depending on what seems to convey the clearest depiction of the visual effect they have in mind. Camera angles can also be designated in another way in order to describe more graphically the spatial and psychological relationship between shot subject and viewer. A *point-of-view (POV)* shot, for example, looks at the scene through the eyes of a character or implement within it. In Figure 9–5, which is a frame from a promo for the Ontario Ministry of Industry & Tourism, the POV might be referred to as that of the gridiron's turf or (if you wanted to inject tragedy), POV DOWNED QUARTERBACK.

A similar effect is obtained when the writer calls for a SUBJECTIVE CAMERA, in which the lens is addressed by on-camera talent as though it were a specific being. The first three frames of the Scotts commercial in Figure 9–6 use this technique (SUBJECTIVE CAMERA: DANDELIONS) to heighten viewer involvement by having the audience addressed directly as though they were the weeds.

Over the shoulder shots are another derivation in which one character is viewed by looking over the shoulder of the other. A *reverse angle* shot can then be called on to give the viewer the scene from 180° away—looking "over the shoulder" of that second character back at the first. Either separately or in conjunction with any of these other techniques, *high angle* and *low angle* shots can draw special relationships or promote unique vantage points in order to illustrate more powerfully the message's main tenet. Notice how a variety of carefully linked shot lengths and angles helps convey the central concept and psychological involvement exploited for Paul Masson Champagne in Figure 9–7. In this photoboard, numbered Frame 7 is an OS PLAYER (over-the-shoulder shot, with the shoulder being that of the football player). The following numbered Frame 8 is then a reverse angle to complete the exchange. (Technically, Frame 8 is a ¾ REV ANGLE since we see the player from Gielgud's *side* rather than from directly behind his head. This is done here to enhance viewer participation by using the audience's rather than the product spokesman's frame of reference.) Notice too how a high angle shot such as Frame 7's seems to diminish the subject's (Gielgud's) size in relationship to the athlete and how Frame 8's low angle shot makes that athlete seem even more giant-like.

Figure 9-5. *(Courtesy of Carole McGill, Camp Associates Advertising Limited.)*

As a general rule, tighter (closer) shots tend to have more utility in television than a preponderance of wider (longer) framings. According to Neil Kesler, president of Airfax Productions, this is because

> generally, television is viewed on a 19-inch color television set in a room that can have any number of distractions. The set itself is probably not a new one, and the colors often are not exactly right—the set might not be functioning properly, or it might not be tuned properly. The sound, too, is frequently no better than what emanates from the cheapest radio. . . . One certain way to reach that viewer—to make him sit up and pay attention—is with close, tight shots that cannot be ignored. . . . All this is not to say that all commercials should be continuously filled with close-ups (or that there is no place in advertising for big budget, elaborate commercials). The monotony would be disasterous. Instead, the close-up should be considered a major weapon in the creative arsenal, used selectively to focus the viewer's attention. Television is such an intimate medium that it's often a mistake to reject that intimacy.[5]

Control Room Transitions and Devices

In television, the *video switcher* is the vehicle that controls not only which visual source is in fact being taped or aired, but also the way in which one visual source is replaced by or juxtaposed with another. Television's switcher allows for the immediate assemblage of selected shots; which film normally accomplishes in post-shoot editing. Videotape can be edited too, of course, but with sometimes prohibitive technical costs and requirements. Particularly for the low-budget, locally produced spot, it is usually most efficient and economically desirable to use the switcher as your editor and put your message together as the cameras are capturing it.

Fade In/Fade Out. Virtually all television messages "fade in" from "black" at the beginning and fade out or "fade to black" at their conclusion. Due to the

5. Neal Kesler, writing in "Monday Memo," *Broadcasting Magazine*, August 20, 1984, p. 12.

PRODUCT: TURFBUILDER PLUS 2
TITLE: "WHAT DANDELIONS"

LENGTH: 30 SECONDS
COMM'L NO.: ITOM 2330

(MUSIC UNDER)
MAN: Gentlemen, it's curtains.

I told you dandelions not to come back again.

But you didn't listen, did you?

No more Mr. Nice Guy.

ANNCR. (VO) Turfbuilder Plus 2 Weed and Feed from Scotts

gets rid of dandelions, root and all, and 40 other weeds.

while it helps thicken your lawn with Turfbuilder fertilizer.

MAN: See. I told you I meant business.

WIFE: (VO) Ralph, are you out there

talking to those dandelions again?

MAN: What dandelions? You see any dandelions?

ANNCR. (VO) Say goodbye to dandelions.

Figure 9–6.   *(Courtesy of Melissa Wohltman, Doyle Dane Bernbach Advertising.)*

abbreviated nature of television commercials and continuity, these fades are very rapid and may not even be specified in the script. For longer messages such as dramatic programs, varying the length of a fade can help to raise or lower more definitively television's version of the theatrical curtain.

   Cut.   This is the quickest and simplest method for changing from one shot to another. Today's visually literate audiences are so accustomed to this instantaneous transition that it often does not even impinge on their consciousness. Properly punctuated cuts can do a great deal to aid in the pacing of even very brief visual mesages, and *intercutting* (rapid switching back and forth between two or more shots) has proven to be of significant utility when the creative

Figure 9–7.   *(Courtesy of Melissa Wohltman, Doyle Dane Bernbach Advertising.)*

concept requires a rapid, pulsating delivery. *Cutaways* are a further variation on the term and are especially prominent in certain types of commercials in which we briefly replace the main scene with some laboratory or animated demonstration of a specific property that the product possesses. (The Scott's spot in Figure 9–6 used a cutaway to show, via accelerated animation, how Turfbuilder Plus 2 worked to kill dandelions and thicken grass.) Since cuts are by far the most commonly used transition, a cut or "take" is assumed whenever any other transition between two segments is not specified in the script.

Dissolve.   In this transition, one picture source seems gradually to "bleed through" and then finally replace another. Dissolves may be slow or fast and, in either case, provide a more fluid and gentle transition than the comparative punchiness of the cut. When the progress of the dissolve is stopped so that both picture sources remain discernible to the viewer, the result is called a *superimposition,* or SUPER for short. *Matched dissolves* are hybrids in which we obtain a cumulative effect by dissolving from one similar or like thing to another. The old clock-face matched dissolves utilized to show passing time, or the series of dissolves that make the pile of dirty dishes get smaller and the stack of clean ones get taller are both common (even trite) applications of this technique.

Contemporary solid-state electronics also makes possible a virtually infinite number of customized transitions that are programmed by the *special effects bank,* which works in conjunction with the video switcher. Many of these effects are made possible by a *chroma-key*—the generic name for an apparatus that allows the removal of a given color from the original scene so a visual element from another source can be inserted in its place. Special effects terms such as "split screen," "sunburst dissolve," and "checkerboard transition" are quite descriptive of the function each provides.

A standard cluster of special effects devices are known as *wipes.* Instead of one picture "bleeding through" the other, as in the dissolve/superimposition, a *wipe* allows one picture visually to push the other off the screen. Common direction-denoting varieties are *vertical, horizontal, diagonal, corner* and *iris* (circular) wipes. A *split-screen* is simply the midpoint of a vertical, horizontal, or diagonal wipe. *Squeeze-zoom,* meanwhile, is a manufacturer-derived term referring to the namesake device's ability to compress, expand, and manipulate individual elements within a frame.

Squeeze-zoom and other proliferating electronic special effects phenomena use auxiliary terminology that is much more obscure because many of these state-of-the-art effects owe their existence to a computer. This marriage of television switching apparatus and computer hardware/software systems begets an almost bewildering array of tools from which to choose and an equally bewildering jargon all its own. For the copywriter, however, it is best to stick to a commonly understood phrase when attempting to specify some rarefied piece of special effects wizardry. The production and graphics people can put it in their own parlance later, but they will at least start out with an accurate conception of what you want.

The NBC Style ID shown in Figure 9–8, for example, results from a new computer program "utilizing a metal reflecting technique which produced reflections and metallic shadow effects. The effect was produced by Cranston/Csuri software developer Shaun Ho. 'The metallic surface of an object rotates and the surrounding environment is reflected through the color bands appearing on the surface,' Ho explained. 'Various effects can be achieved when the animator designs different-colored environments to be reflected on the metallic surface.'"[6] This technical description obviously is not something with which most copywriters can or should contend. So instead, for practice, translate the

6. Cheryl McClenahan, "Computer Graphics—NBC Style," *ADWEEK/Midwest,* August 27, 1984, p. 18.

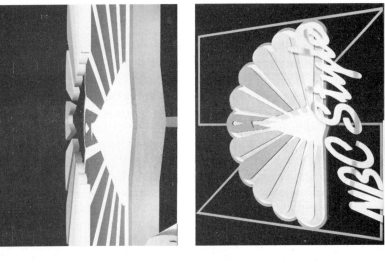

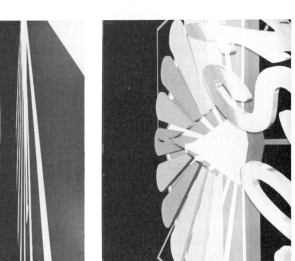

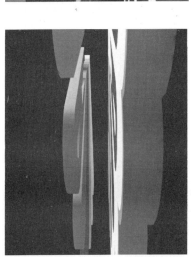

Figure 9–8. (Technical Director/Animator: John Berton; Data Generation: Maria Palazzi; Technical Director/Software Developer: Shaun Ho; Art Director: Ron Tsang; Hardware: Marc Howard. For NBC Sports: John Schipp, Mgr. of On-Air Promotion and Advertising. Courtesy of NBC Sports and Cranston/Csuri Productions, Columbus, Ohio.)

Figure 9–7 Paul Masson concept into script form by deciding what *words* you would use to incisively describe the visual effects it delivers.

One overriding admonition must be heeded about special effects. Keep in mind that you are not selling, promoting, or identifying the transition or effect itself. Any technique that calls attention to itself at the expense of your subject is to be studiously avoided. If you should find yourself concentrating on what jazzy electronic explosion you can shoehorn into your next television spot or promo, it's time to stop and reexamine your priorities. "Special *defect* is my term," says Grey Advertising's executive vice president Richard Kiernan, "for a totally inappropriate use of special effects. Things like using a laser beam to create an apple pie when the strategy calls for old-fashioned-like-Grandma-used-to-bake. That kind of special effect not only doesn't reinforce the strategy; it undermines it. Or the bank that uses computer graphics in the attempt to dramatize warm, friendly, personalized service. Another special defect. . . . The magic, I maintain, is in how organic the solution is to the selling proposition. If you lose sight of the objective, then special effects can become special defects."[7] Any truly appropriate visual device will evolve naturally out of whatever it is you are trying to say in your message. The message's selling concept, not the effect, must come first. Leave the extraneous kaleidoscopes to the entertainment programs, which have thirty or sixty *minutes* to play with and can afford to be irrelevant.

Other Writer-used Technical Terms

Here are a variety of additional visual production designations that are common to television and are often used on a script or storyboard to communicate the writer's intent to those who will pick up the project from there:

Abstract Set: a plain and neutral background that uses only a few scattered implements to suggest the message environment. A single gas pump might represent a complete service station or a few framing tree branches simulate an entire forest. Though the abstract set is certainly not realistic, there is also less visual clutter in which the viewer might lose the product or central point of your message.

Animation: drawing/cartooning that is sketched and photographed in a sequence that gives motion to a series of still pictures. May be computer-generated.

Aspect Ratio: the constant three units high by four units wide dimensions of the television screen. The copywriter should keep this in mind when planning the television message since aspect ratio will circumscribe every visual idea funneled through the television medium.

Background Projection or Rear Projection (RP): throwing a still slide or motion picture from behind a translucent screen so performers can use the result as scenery and stand in front of it without blocking the projector's illumination beam.

Backlight: illumination from behind a subject in order to distinguish it more clearly from the background area.

7. Richard Kiernan, writing in "Monday Memo," *Broadcasting Magazine*, August 15, 1983, p. 24.

Beauty Shot: still picture of the product set in an environment that heightens its appeal, prestige, or appearance.

BG: commonly used abbreviation for the *background* of a scene.

Black: the condition of a video screen when it is processing no video information.

Bumper: a graphic, slide, or brief animation used before or after a program or commercial segment.

Bust Shot or Chest Shot: a more specific designation for the Medium Close-Up (MCU) calling for a picture of a talent from the chest to just above the head.

Cameo: lighting a foreground subject against a completely black background.

Crawl: a device used to reveal printed words (usually credits) or associated artwork in a gradual horizontal or vertical progression on the screen. Crawls were formerly accomplished via a manually or electrically powered "drum"; the all-electronic *character-generator* is now usually used. It is activated by a typewriter-like keyboard, which produces coded electronic impulses.

Cyc (Cyclorama): a U-shaped, stretched curtain that provides a neutral background for a television studio set.

Depth of Field: that swath of territory in front of the camera lens in which all objects and subjects are in focus.

Downstage: the area nearest the camera lens; seemingly closest to the viewing audience.

Drop: a piece of scenic background, normally painted on canvas.

Edge Wipe: wipe in which the edges are manipulated to give the key subject more prominence.

FG: commonly used abbreviation for the *foreground* of a scene.

Film Chain: equipment linked together to permit the showing of 35mm slides and motion picture film on television and normally consisting of the slide and film projectors plus a multiplexer and a specially adapted television camera.

Film VO: script indication that a piece of film includes the copy set forth on that script.

Fisheye Lens: lens that delivers an extremely wide angle picture to provide a field of view of up to 180°.

Flashback: quick return to an earlier time/scene to show how the current scene evolved and/or graphically to contrast conditions portrayed in each.

Flip Cards: pieces of cardboard, cut into proper aspect ratio, that contain credits or other simple visual information. Flip cards are also known as *super cards* (from "superimposition") or *camera/studio/easel* cards and come in *lower one-third* (for names and subtitles) and *full-frame* varieties.

Follow Shot: use of a single, stationary camera to follow the action of a moving subject or object.

Follow Spot: high intensity, narrow-beam light used to illuminate subjects in motion.

Freeze Frame: stopping the motion of a film or tape so a single frame can be viewed as a still picture. May result in a *beauty shot* (see above).

Graphic Tablet: device on which the artist draws with an electronic pen (light-pen) to produce an image on the associated video screen.

Hard Light: a strong directional beam from a spotlight that produces sharply defined shadows.

Headroom: area between the top of a subject's head and the upper edge of the TV screen.

High Key: relatively even illumination with few discernible shadows.

In Mortise: literally, "in a box"; placing the subject within a graphically rendered frame—often to set it off from "supered" titles that appear on the border this frame creates.

Jump Cut: a disturbing or unnaturally abrupt transition between two pictures.

Kinescope (Kine):   a comparatively poor quality film recording of a live television program or segment made by making a motion picture from the image on a television monitor.

Limbo: a perfectly neutral and empty background.

Matte Shot: a portion of the picture is blanked out and replaced by a separate picture or pictures of any of a variety of sizes; often accomplished via chroma-keying.

Montage: composite picture created from many separate images or a series of rapidly intercut visuals designed to create a certain association of ideas.

MOS: abbreviation for "Mit Out Sound," thus signifying a silent piece of film or tape footage.

Multiplexer: special optical sampling device that allows one television camera to service several slide drums and/or movie projectors (see *Film chain*).

Negative Image (Reverse Polarity):   electronic manipulation that makes the "white" parts of a television appear "black" and vice-versa.

NI: old, but occasionally still used abbreviation for "network identification."

OC: abbreviation for "on-camera"; person speaking is shown in the shot. Generally used to cancel a previous "voice-over" direction (see *VO*).

Pixillation: frame-by-frame animation technique using live actors or actual props rather than cartoon characters. When projected up to standard speed, pixillation makes talent/subject movements comedically jerky and abrupt.

Reaction Shot: any picture designed to reveal the emotional response of a character to some previously shown, or about to be shown, event.

Shared ID: in television, commercial material that is placed on a flip card, slide, or film together with some graphic representation of the station identification.

S.I.:   a sponsor identification line.

SOF: abbreviation for "sound on film"; a motion picture with its own synchronized sound track.

Soft Focus: a slight defocusing of the picture resulting in a hazy effect indicative of dreams or semiconsciousness.

SOT: same as SOF when the medium is videotape rather than film.

Specific Illumination: lighting of highly localized and discrete areas.

Stock Shot/Stock Footage: still or motion pictures of subjects than can be used in many different messages. An urban street scene, picture of a jet-liner taking off, or view of a charming old farmhouse can all constitute stock footage.

Swishpan: an extremely rapid camera pan that is perceived on the screen as a blur.

Tease: very brief promo for an upcoming program segment or the opening "grabber" in a long-form commercial.

Telecine: equipment for projecting film and slides on television (see *Film chain*).

Undercut: changing the background of a scene without modifying fore-ground subjects—usually accomplished via matte or keying.

Upstage: the area farthest from the camera lens; seemingly the most distant from the viewing audience.

Vector: process of creating pictures on a video screen through use of a light-pen (see *Graphic tablet*).

VO: abbreviation for "voice-over"; words spoken by someone not shown in the shot.

VTR: abbreviation for "videotape recorder" or for the recording it makes.

X/S: abbreviation sometimes used to designate an over-the-shoulder shot.

PRODUCTION METHODS FOR THE TELEVISION MESSAGE

All these shot lengths, camera movements, transitional devices, and special terminology have no relevance until they are grouped and amalgamated in creating a single unified message. And, despite the great variety in the terms and baggage of television, there are but five basic processes from which the television spot, PSA, or piece of continuity is begotten.

Live

This is the quickest, cheapest, and also the most risky technique for producing anything for televison. The annals of video are filled with sagas of refrigerator doors that refused to open, fry pans that wouldn't scour clean, and puppies who not only refused to eat the sponsor's dog food but also directed a socially unacceptable comment at the dish that contained it. Still, if kept simple, the live message provides the most rapid turnaround time for copy changes and the greatest adaptability to specific events and conditions. Many program promos and other forms of similar continuity are thus viable as live copy—especially when read on-camera by a personality who is already well established on the individual show or station.

Slides and Flip Cards

This is the next least expensive method to on-camera, live presentation and employs video obtained either from 35 mm slides in the film chain or flip cards placed on easels in front of a studio camera. This series of still "pics" is then complemented by an audio message that can either be rendered live or recorded on an audio cartridge, perhaps with a complementary music bed. Station IDs, spots for small local clients, and local PSAs mesh well with this inexpensive but still visually flexible production method. The Designated Driver slide reproduced in Figure 9–9 is an example of this kind of device. It was provided by the National Safety Council to stations that could then voice-over this slide specific information about their locality's drunk driving prevention efforts.

For convenience, many stations produce the slide or flip card message on videotape so it can be cued up and run by the duty engineer without the need for additional announcer, studio, or film chain involvement. A program promo

Figure 9–9. *(Reprinted with permission from the National Safety Council.)*

for a Philadelphia station's "Bright Futures" high school senior salute was produced this way via a cogent graphic flip card (see Figure 9–10) and a brief
announcer voice-over that were both then committed to videotape for easy
storage and retrieval.

Videotape

Since its industry entry in the latter fifties, videotape has replaced much of
television's live fare and, with recent breakthroughs in economical electronic
editing, is even now coming to challenge film as the most-used medium for
program material as well as for commercials and continuity. Tape provides live
picture quality but with a safety net—you can reshoot that demonstration (studio
time permitting) until it comes out right, and yet its visual quality will make it
seem as spontaneous to the viewer as though it were done live. As noted
above, with advances in solid-state technology and video cassette machines,
even material originating as a slide/card presentation can be easily taped for
later retrieval to free the studio cameras and personnel for other things.

If not provided as a service by a station on which you are placing commercials,
video studio time can be expensive. Still, if your spokesperson does not talk on
camera, even this cost can be mitigated by preproducing the audio track at a
much lower cost-per-hour sound studio. Then you can use your rented video
facilities for only as long as you need to "lay down" a good visual with which
the previously finished audio can easily be linked.

Film Voice-over

This same basic technique can be applied to film as well. If no one talks on
camera, film can be quickly shot anywhere, stock footage can be rented as
needed, and a nicely fashioned audio can be married to the result at the
editing/assembly stage. Because many producers still prefer the softer "look,
tone, and mood" of film, it will remain a viable if not a preferred medium for
many PSA and commercial assignments for the foreseeable future. Another
advantage of the film voice-over for spots slated for airing on multiple stations

Figure 9–10. *(Courtesy of Jim Denney, WPVI-TV.)*

is that the dubbing/distribution costs for film are significantly lower than for videotape. (If the campaign is of long duration, or will be re-used in the future, however, tape becomes the more cost-effective duplication medium given film stock's deterioration problems.) Particularly if the voice-over technique can be used, even very small organizations and accounts can afford the flexibility of film production should they wish it. In such low-budget endeavors, the shooting can even be done in 16mm rather than in the more expensive 35mm motion picture stock preferred by large agencies and studios.

Film Lip-sync

Especially if outdoor location shooting is involved, this can be the most time-consuming and therefore expensive approach to message creation for television. Since the characters in the presentation talk on camera, great care must be taken to record their dialogue properly and synchronize it with the visual being captured at the same time. This process can become especially complex as the scene is consecutively reshot from several angles—each with its own sound bed—that must later be edited into a matching whole without visual or audio "glitches." Sometimes, later sound stage dubbing, in which the characters repeat their lines to match the previously filmed lip movements, must be scheduled in order to achieve acceptable audio quality and synchronization. Because indoor shooting normally allows for greater control of the sound environment than when filming outdoors, subsequent sound stage work can usually be avoided with interior scenes, at least as far as the dialogue is concerned. Other sound sources like music may also have to be layered in, however, and unlike video-tape production, this can seldom be done when the film cameras are rolling.

It is possible, of course, to mix and match elements from several of these five productional methods in order to achieve your television objectives within the available budget. Just keep in mind that, whatever techniques(s) is (are) employed, they should not call attention to themselves but rather, should help to articulate the central point of your spot, PSA, or continuity segment. And don't, whatever you do, try to use a production method that the budget really can't afford by cutting productional and picture-value corners. The result will look shoddy and so, by implication, will whatever it is that your message is striving to promote. Far better to employ a less expensive productional methodology and do it *right*.

A BLURB ABOUT ANIMATION

The above point acquires special relevance when dealing with the *animated* or cartoon presentation. Certainly, through its ability to vivify concepts and happenings impossible in real life, the animated commercial provides the maximum in creative freedom and flexibility. In addition, the specially customized cartoon "spokesthing" can be an almost priceless asset to brand recall and a ready-made tie-in between the television message and such nonbroadcast media as print layouts, billboards, display cards, and direct mail pieces. Smokey the Bear and the Hawaiian Punch man demonstrate that this phenomenon can work for both PSAs and commercials.

Alternatively, if a creative tie-in with the product can be uncovered, and if the rights can be obtained, an *already popular* animated character may be recruited to promote your client. Such a character combines the elements of the celebrity testimonial with the inherent charm of cartoon characters who, unlike real people, are difficult for viewers to dislike. Animated characters also are able to demonstrate the product in ways real people can't, as in this Uniroyal spot (Figure 9–11) that enlists a prominent inhabitant of the comic strip "B.C." The spot's effectiveness is further heightened by the appropriateness of using a caveman to demonstrate the fundamental necessity of the Uniroyal steel-belted radial, a tire seemingly second in importance only to the invention of the wheel itself.

Unfortunately, even if you can avoid "lease fees" for a popular animated character by creating your own, animation is still very expensive. And if cartooning action must be matted (overlaid) onto footage of real-life scenes and characters, as in the well-paced Cookie Crisp spot in Figure 9–12, the cost can go through the roof. So if your account is on a small budget but an animated scene or spokesthing is considered essential, don't hire some art school dropout to animate the whole sequence simply because the price is right. Better to hire a top-notch artist to draw a few, well-rendered, single pics between which you can intercut and that lend themselves to use in several different messages or contexts.

In the spot for Ocean Spray Cranberry Sauce (Figure 9–13), a simple but concept-encompassing piece of cartooning is used to attract attention and set up the "cut-away" to the actual demonstration. All of animation's advantages are accrued without the necessity for cartoon/real life matting and without expensive end-to-end animation.

If you just have to have wall-to-wall animation, you can, as an intermediate step, contract for *limited animation* in which the artist is required to produce only four or five drawings per second of running time as compared to the fifteen or sixteen drawings per second needed for *full animation*. The realistic

UNIROYAL

UNIROYAL TIRES
:30 Second T. V.
"Invention"

ORSON WELLES: "When man invented the wheel, it was probably ...

... a lucky accident.

But it was to avoid unlucky accidents ...

... that man deliberately invented the Uniroyal Steel Belted Radial Tire.

Twin Belts of steel gave man the road-holding grip ...

... the puncture resistance ...

... the extra mileage he'd always wanted.

Today, Uniroyal Steel Radials are original equipment on some of the world's best-selling wheels.

Uniroyal.

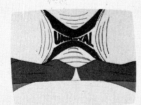

From the first man ...

... the last word ...

... in Steel Radials.

Figure 9–11. (Courtesy of Barry R. Base, Base Brown Partners Ltd.; Copyright Field Syndicate Inc.)

Figure 9–12. *(Reprinted with permission of Ralston Purina Company.)*

appearance of character movement is compromised in this trade-off, but, since most of today's television cartoons also use limited animation, your spot will look no more jerky by comparison than they do.

A variety of computer-assisted or -controlled animation techniques are also coming on the market. (Review the NBC Sports Style graphic in Figure 9–8 for an example of what these can accomplish.) As a whole, these new methods can simplify attaining previously available animation effects and make possible a whole range of additional ones. The highly sophisticated Motion Control System (MCS), for example, uses a computer-controlled tracking camera with pan and tilt head, an all-motorized boom arm, and a forty-foot track to combine stop

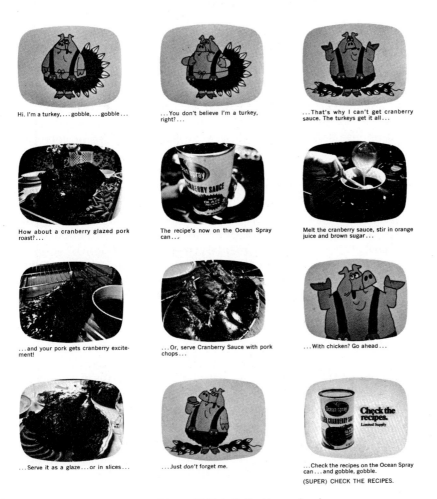

Hi. I'm a turkey,...gobble,...gobble...

...You don't believe I'm a turkey, right?...

...That's why I can't get cranberry sauce. The turkeys get it all...

How about a cranberry glazed pork roast?...

The recipe's now on the Ocean Spray can...

Melt the cranberry sauce, stir in orange juice and brown sugar...

...and your pork gets cranberry excitement!

...Or, serve Cranberry Sauce with pork chops...

...With chicken? Go ahead...

...Serve it as a glaze...or in slices...

...Just don't forget me.

...Check the recipes on the Ocean Spray can...and gobble, gobble.
(SUPER) CHECK THE RECIPES.

Figure 9–13. *(Courtesy of Irene Taffel, Kelly-Nason Inc.)*

motion and live action in one take, repeat and modify shots, and accomplish double and triple exposures—all right in the camera.[8] Because of their complexity, however, these new devices have not appreciably reduced costs. Even in the new tech era, presentable animation remains something your client must be willing to pay for. If that willingness is not present, stick to brief cutaway sequences, stills, or creative concepts that can avoid animation entirely.

For the extensively animated sequence that uses music (and most long segments of cartooning seem virtually to cry for it), the copywriter needs to be aware of the most efficient sequence of creative events and plan the work accordingly. From a synchronization standpoint, it is much easier for the artist to fit the action to a prerecorded music bed than for a musician to compose

8. Cheryl McClenahan, "Motion Control Makes Streaks, Flips and Scans Happen," *ADWEEK/ Midwest*, April 25, 1983, p. 4.

music that exactly matches a finished piece of animation. Thus, the writer and the art director must first develop and get approval for a storyboard that sets down the essential progression of the proposed message and the specific characteristics of the animated spokesthing(s) it will feature. Once copywriter, artist, and approval board have a clear idea (and the *same* clear idea) about the tone and purpose of the message and its cartoon talent, the composer can be brought in for storyboard orientation. The creative team can then provide the composer with a precise and noncontradictory explanation of the project out of which a tailored score can be fashioned. Once the score is set down, it is a comparatively easy job for the animator to draw and polish the finalized cartoon movements to match the meter and accents of that score.

Animation, like all of television's gestating formats, methodologies, and terminologies, is a tool to be used in pursuing the most potent audio/video coalition possible. For it is through this coalition that television communication becomes a cohesive rather than a fragmentary message experience. Scripts, storyboards, camera movements, shot lengths, flip cards, videotape, and the other devices introduced in this chapter are all complementary or alternate means to the same end. Use them as needed to produce the most effective copy concepts possible. Don't let them use you lest you become a purveyor of *hardware* instead of *ideas.*

No matter how state-of-the-art or costly the technique, it is irrelevant if not motivated by the strong, central selling concept that you, the copywriter, must engineer. As Needham, Harper & Steers chairman Keith Reinhard cautions, "Many of the new, super-expensive commercials are more sophisticated in a certain way and yet they're also simpler in a certain way. They can deceive you, because they too often operate on the premise that because you can do certain things with a computer, you can often do without an idea."[9]

Fortunately, of course, we can't do without that idea. Because if we could, that would mean the television copywriter is expendable, too.

9. "Creative Upsurge," *ADS Magazine,* December, 1984, p. 16.

Chapter Ten

TELEVISION

HOUSEKEEPING COPY

Like its radio counterpart, television housekeeping copy can basically be divided into two categories: continuity (again, in the narrow sense of the term) and public service announcements. Also as in radio, continuity for television requires a special adeptness on the part of the writer to make a quick, "clean" impression and then gracefully get out of the way for the next program segment.

There is a lot of television continuity to be written; a lot of other continuity with which each ID or station promo, for example, must compete. The growth of new television services and delivery systems via cable, microwave, satellite, and home video has propelled both mature and fledgling television enterprises to unprecedented efforts to establish an identity with the viewing public. This identity is comprised of two parts: (1) the image of the transmitting entity (station, network, or cable service) itself and (2) the sum total of the programmatic appeals encompassed in that entity's offerings. In short, today's viewers need to be constantly reminded of who you are, what you did for them yesterday (*proof of performance* promotion), and what you will do for them today and tomorrow.

On most stations, cable systems, and networks, the biggest client nowadays is the station, network, or system itself. As early as 1980, a Denver television station "used more than $2.5 million worth of its time to advertise itself and its programs."[1] On the network level, by 1984, NBC's in-house promotion group was producing "some 8,000 promotions for NBC corporate, primetime, daytime and Saturday morning and a separate East Coast unit produced another 2,500 for news and sports."[2] The creative services directors and promotion managers in charge of such efforts have never been busier, better compensated, or more in need of skillful copy constructed by skilled copywriters. In fact, a 1983 study by Hayes Anderson of San Diego State University found virtually all responding promotions executives listing copywriting as a "very important" skill for people in their jobs and units.[3] Thus, it should not be surprising that the first order of business in this chapter is:

1. Robert Rimes, writing in "Monday Memo," *Broadcasting Magazine*, April 6, 1981, p. 14.
2. Betsy Sharkey, "Bringing a Network Back from the Dead," *ADWEEK/Midwest*, March, 1985, p. 16.
3. Hayes Anderson, presentation to Broadcast Education Association Convention, Las Vegas, Nevada, April 9, 1983.

IDs AND STATION PROMOS

Just as in radio, these two varieties of continuity writing can occur separately or as one and the same thing. A station identification may simply give the governmentally mandated information in audio and video form and then apply the remaining eight seconds to a commercial pitch (see the "Shared ID" definition in the "other technical terms" section of the previous chapter). In this case, the audio copy is not much different from that found on a radio billboard spot with the slide/flipcard graphic or succeeding graphics accentuating the station call letters, channel number logo, and perhaps the name or corporate symbol of the client being promoted.

But as the competition for viewers and the dollars they bring has everywhere intensified, more and more stations are preferring to reserve this ID time for their own self-promotional purposes. Many television outlets now boast their own "signature slogans" that come complete with moving graphic and music bed over which the local announcer can read customized and timely promotion copy. Often, these ID enhancement devices are prepared by some outside production or consulting firm that makes them available to clients on a market exclusivity basis.

The music beds that back up these graphics have many of the same style and copy characteristics used to showcase IDs on radio. But, because television stations do not have a single well-delineated music format to which they must adhere, most TV identification music and lyrics tend to reflect a "safe" though up-tempo, middle-of-the-road orientation. The average television station's viewing audience is comprised of a much more heterogeneous mass than the usually segmented groups to which most radio stations strive to appeal. Thus, though the ID stylings may vary somewhat from one part of the television station's viewing day to another, the music and the copy are seldom allowed to wander too far from mainstream acceptability. This is something to keep in mind whether you write for a national specialty firm or, what is more probable, have to come to grips with station promotional copy as a staffer at the local outlet level.

Sometimes, in-station and specialty house creative forces combine to produce a station promotional campaign that blends local referents with a slick, pretested approach developed for use in markets around the country. In such a cooperative effort, local writers/promotions people must evolve insert copy pertaining to their station and/or secure visuals that seem to capture best the spirit of the market that station serves. The specialty house then uses this material in customizing their predeveloped station image package to specific local conditions.

The following instruction sheet prepared by TM Productions for prospective station clients is one example of how this cooperative process evolves. In this "YOU" Campaign, as in any specialty house production designed for local tailoring, the result is only as good as the input provided by each station's writer/promotions people. Though, as in this case, the local writer may not be called on to create a single line of copy, it is that writer's responsibility to *deliver the most appropriate visual ideas possible.* And such responsibility, as you should have figured out by now, is just as much a part of "television writing" as is the selection of words for announcer voice-overs.

CUSTOMIZED TELEVISION SPOT

The ''YOU'' Campaign includes an optional 30-second television commercial fully customized for your station. Or, an alternate plan provides both a 20-second and a 10-second customized television spot. The visuals will reflect the personality of your audience, your city, and your station, backed by the 30-second (or other) version of the central ''YOU'' Campaign Jingle. The spot will culminate with the display of your present call-letter logotype along with the sung musical logo.

What You Need to Furnish:
1. At least 12 photos of your city.
Please provide more than the minimum to allow us to select those photos that work best in the context of the commercial. The photos should be ''atmosphere'' shots that reflect your city's personality, and at least five of them should depict local landmarks that will be instantly recognizable to your audience. All photos should be high-quality color <u>prints</u> for which you have obtained appropriate releases. Slides or transparencies should be converted to prints. Minimum print size: 3" × 4", maximum: 11" × 14". All photos will be returned to you.
2. At least 12 photos of people.
The generic ''YOU'' Campaign commercial has been targeted to an 18-to-25-year-old demographic group. The ''people'' photos you supply should be close-up shots of happy, attractive people either alone or in groups. Several shots should show people engaged in some activity. Should you wish to target your spot to a more specific audience, please supply a minimum of 10 photos of people who represent that audience. The same quantities, types, and dimensions specified under ''city'' photos apply here. Releases should be obtained from the persons whose photographs you use.
3. A printed copy of your station's call letters.
These should be <u>in the lettering style</u> in which they should appear in the commercial. The lettering should be black on a white background, and each letter should be at least 3/4" high.

Where to Send It:
Operations Department   Please include the name and
TM PRODUCTIONS, INC.   phone number of the person at your
1349 Regal Row   station who can be contacted regarding any
Dallas, Texas 75247   question about your customization.
(214) 634-8511

Figure 10-1.

DELIVERY SCHEDULE
TM will acknowledge receipt of your materials and will ship your
finished commercial to you in two to three weeks. You will
receive one (1) two-inch high-band videotape for broadcast, and
one (1) 3/4"-inch video-cassette for your library.

Courtesy of TM Productions, Inc.

Most often in the form of lyrics, the copy for station promotional IDs is not
markedly different from that used in the counterpart continuity on radio. (Turn
back to chapter 7 to review radio samples.) The main difference between television and radio promos may well be that, since we now have a visual to occupy
center stage along with the support of words and music, even less copy is
usually required. For not only must some "breathing room" for the music be
allowed, but the viewer must also be given the opportunity to concentrate on
the visual without the potential clutter of overloaded dialogue or voice-overs.
Though the following piece of lyric copy was pulled from a *60-second* station
promo, note that the number of words is much smaller than would normally
be employed in a radio message of the same length and type. Note too that,
when used as a complement to the visual, an ID/promo slogan line tends to be
much more repetitive so as to assist its registering with an audience that is
simultaneously being exposed to a vast array of visual stimulation.

<u>Where</u> <u>You</u> <u>Belong</u> <u>Basic</u> <u>I</u>   :60
This is where you belong, let us share our world with you—
Where you belong, with friends who are nice to have around,
now you've found—
Where you belong, Channel 11, where you belong—
(MUSIC PAD)

This is where you belong, Baltimore 11, where you belong,
Channel 11, where you belong—

(Courtesy of TM Productions, Inc.)

In television, as in radio, station ID/promo copy is constructed in such a way that shorter versions are created by taking lift-outs from longer ones. This is not only a money-saving practice but also makes for consistency in the promotional style and concept throughout the programming day. And just like its audio cousin, the television self-promo, whether locally or specialty-house produced, must be a mirror image of how the station's sales, promotion, and programming departments view their facility. Any continuity, no matter how brilliant, that does not mesh with the station's overall programming image and sales orientation is only worth its weight in ulcers.

Network IDs and promos, of course, exhibit most of the same characteristics as their station/specialty service counterparts but with the additional advantages of bigger budgets and large in-house staffs to accomplish the job more quickly and continuously. As in TM's "YOU" package, the NBC network's "Let's All Be There," like any effective television image creation, features a high-definition logotype (Figure 10–2), image-riveting ID enhancements of that logo (Figure 10–3), and well-written tie-in instructions and support materials (Figure 10–4). Notice especially that the ID graphics shown in Figure 10–3 can be customized. They bring the local station's identity and the network's image into one interlocked theme/styling rather than creating two disparate and conflicting statements.

Lyric copy also is a major part of network promotion, with the same concern for theme-establishing repetition and network/local station cross-promotion. Figure 10–5 sets forth the music and lyrics for the "pure" NBC network song.

Without melodic modification, the same musical bed can be used in either a *basic* or *complete* custom version for local station enhancement. In basic customization, many of the original network lyrics remain, with station call letters (or channel number) inserted at key junctures. These drop-ins have been underlined on p. 283 for your information.

Figure 10–2. *(Excerpt of LET'S ALL BE THERE courtesy of The National Broadcasting Co. Inc. © 1984. The National Broadcasting Company, Inc. All Rights Reserved.)*

1A Your station logo in center on plane above BE THERE. It begins moving toward us.

1B Your station logo starts large frame left. It moves back away from us to the right side of frame.

1C Your station logo starts large frame left. It moves back away from us to the right side of frame.

2A Your station logo accelerates upward through the frame revealing the BE THERE.

2B The words LET'S ALL are written on as your station logo continues its move back.

2C The words LET'S ALL are written on as your station logo continues its move back.

3A The BE THERE is now accelerating toward us. As it travels, the words LET'S ALL are written on. The LET'S ALL BE THERE continues toward us to a cut point.

3B In this frame we see the final position of the slogan and station logo.

3C In this frame we see the final position of the slogan and station logo.

It is difficult to perceive the full impac
Please refer to the closed ci

MULTI-PURPOSE LOGO TREATMENT	ACTION WINDOW OPTION	TAIL GRAPHIC WINDOW OPTION

1D Your station logo starts large frame left and moves back.	1E As the window and your station logo animate into position, BE THERE shoots through the window.	1F From action we travel through an opening in a letter form. We see the window in the background.

2D It continues its move back to the right.	2E LET'S ALL writes on. The window is swinging forward LET'S ALL BE THERE moves up and out of the frame.	2F The night of the week moves back as your station logo animates in and swings forward.

3D It settles on the right side, allowing your station to use it for shared ID as well as legal ID.	3E The window completes its swing. As your station logo animates into its final position.	3F The night of the week and your station logo lock in place as the window is straight on. *Station logo replaces peacock in the customized tail graphic option.*

animation through these early slides.
ed. (Scheduled for May 11).

Figure 10–3. *(Excerpt of LET'S ALL BE THERE courtesy of The National Broadcasting Company Inc.* © *1984. The National Broadcasting Company, Inc. All Rights Reserved.)*

LET'S ALL BE THERE for the most compelling, memorable campaign in television history. NBC's got it all this year. Theme continuity by unanimous affiliate request. State-of-the-art 3D raster graphics animated on the same equipment that produced the Network Graphics. Music that adds new meaning to the words upbeat, exciting and joyous, and all at 1983 prices.

Custom Promo Network, the exclusive NBC licensee, has incorporated many suggestions made by the Affiliate Promotion Committee into this year's package. CPN can also provide you with additional custom services and any special needs you may have.

The first 21 orders received by May 18th will be delivered by June 8th, one month earlier than in previous years. All following orders will be produced, 21 per week, in the order that completed forms are received. Confirm early and get on the air first in your market.

For maximum station promotion impact, LET'S ALL BE THERE this year.

=== BASIC CUSTOM PACKAGE ===

ANIMATION

Your station logo, channel # and/or call letters in campaign donut.

Your station logo, channel # and/or call letters in flexible basic ID format (Multi-purpose logo treatment).

Animated logo on black (Keyable).

Three slides: station logo on black, on background and in format.

Animation will be delivered on 1'' videotape unless otherwise specified.

MUSIC

Affiliate custom arrangement of the network theme.

:60's, :30's, :20's, :10's and :03,5/:04's.

Vocals and instrumentals, instrumentals to tags and donuts :30's and :60's.

The Basic affiliate lyrics will include channel # mentions which can be substituted with your station call letters and one reference to your market area.

Music will be delivered on both 7½ and 15 ips quarter inch monaural tape.

=== MINI PACKAGE ===

ANIMATION

Available only to stations in markets 101 + ADI.

Promo donut with your station logo* animated in place, in the tail.

Animated logo on black can be used to build shared or legal ID.

* *Station logo, channel # and/or call letters will be set in station's choice of our standard typefaces and according to station layout.*

MUSIC

Same as basic package.

=== OPTIONS ===

ANIMATION

Available at additional cost:

Twelve Tail graphics with station logo, with or without window.

Seven days of the week plus, TONIGHT, TODAY, WEEKDAYS, WEEKNIGHTS AND TOMORROW.

Additional logo sizes and positions (quadrants, etc.)

Live ID format with animated station logo and window in aspect ratio.

Additional first generation transfers in 2'' or 1'' C format.

Station logo animated in alternate color.

Call letters added in only part of package.

Legal ID with call letters and city of origin added in standard typefaces, in 3D move or in place.

Channel # with station call letters in non-standard typefaces animated in format.

Local show title or slogan Custom Tail Graphics.

Additional custom options available upon request.

=== MUSIC ===

COMPLETE CUSTOMIZATION
(includes additional 60-second *stereo presentation mix*)
provides you with the opportunity to promote local programs in place of the basic affiliate lyrics.

ADDITIONAL BROADCAST STEREO MIX. ALL EDITS
(all cuts, available with complete customization only.)

NEWS/DOCUMENTARY VERSION
60-second instrumental only includes opens, closes, bumpers, pads and ID's.

SOFT/IMAGE VERSION
:30 second lyric with customized donuts, tags and instrumentals :10's & .035's

=== COSTS ===

The 1984 package prices have been frozen at 1983 levels. The cost depends on your market size. Custom Promo Network will provide you with a quotation.

For your convenience, Custom Promo Network will have a suite at the BPA to answer questions and accept orders; however, earlier orders are encouraged.

Contact: Carol Bauer
Custom Promo Network
7800-A River Road
N. Bergen, N.J. 07047
(201) 662-1400 Office
(201) 662-1992 Home

LET'S ALL BE THERE with NBC for the 1984-85 campaign.

Figure 10–4. *(Excerpt of LET'S ALL BE THERE courtesy of The National Broadcasting Company Inc. ©1984. The National Broadcasting Company, Inc. All Rights Reserved.)*

```
WESH-TV let's all be there
Those special moments that can bring
   us all together, make us smile,
   make us laugh or cry or cheer.
NBC let's all be there
You and me let's all be there
People come together in the moments that they share
On WESH-TV let's all be there
   (be there/be there) WESH-TV let's all be there
WESH-TV let's all be there
People come together in the moments that they share
WESH-TV let's all be there
Central Florida's together in the moments that we share
Share on WESH-TV let's all be there.
```

(Excerpt of LET'S ALL BE THERE courtesy of The National Broadcasting Company Inc. ©1984. The National Broadcasting Company, Inc. All Rights Reserved.)

In complete customization, virtually every line of the original lyric is transformed to in some way heighten the identity of the individual station or its locality:

```
Channel 8 let's all be there
Those special programs when
   the stars are shining brighter
It's the fun and it's the pride of Tampa Bay
Channel 8 let's all be there
WXFL let's all be there
People come together in the moments that they share
On Channel 8 let's all be there
   (be there/be there) Channel 8 let's all be there
Tampa Bay let's all be there
All the shows you love and all the moments that we share
On Channel 8 let's all be there
Tampa comes together in the moments that we share
Share on Channel 8 let's all be there.
```

(Excerpt of LET'S ALL BE THERE courtesy of The National Broadcasting Company Inc. ©1984. The National Broadcasting Company, Inc. All Rights Reserved.)

Despite the fact that the lyrics are prepackaged, they nonetheless strike the viewer as being highly relevant to stills and sequences representing a variety of shows with which they can be paired. Many different visual montages can be constructed featuring different groupings of programs. But all programs, network or local, profit equally from musical references that seem to be constructed just for them.

"LET'S ALL BE THERE" MUSIC

"LET'S ALL BE THERE"
Words by David Buskin and Steve Sohmer
Music comp. by David Buskin, arr. by Rob Mounsey

Figure 10–5. *(Excerpt of LET'S ALL BE THERE courtesy of The National Broadcasting Company Inc. © 1984. The National Broadcasting Company, Inc. All Rights Reserved.)*

Figure 10–5. *(cont.)*

One caution must be expressed to the promo writer working in-station at a network affiliate. A high definition local campaign like TM's "YOU" and a masterfully intrusive network-derived approach like "Let's All Be There" can, if intermixed, create a hopelessly schizophrenic station personality. Care must be taken in planning, writing and scheduling your own promotional efforts so these blend in with, or at least stay out of the way of, the network barrage. Whether your station promotion is entirely self-produced or customized from a specialty house theme, it must not be crumpled by collisions with the network's own image builders. Adopting a local customization of the network concept may be the safest approach in assuring on-air image consistency.

If you must use a separate and distinct local campaign, then as a general rule, use network-derived image builders around network shows and your own image package at times that are locally programmed. If a logical link just can't be found between the network thematic package and your own, then keep them mutually isolated to avoid confusing your own viewers on your own air. At the least, you should be able to design or acquire some ID graphics that bridge the gap between the two themes at times in the program day when network and local features abut.

PROGRAM PROMOS

Network *program* promos cannot generally be separated from network promos *per se.* This results from the networks' belief that people tend to watch programs in terms of days of the week (for prime time) or within broad time frames (afternoon, late night, weekend sports). Thus, *block promos* in which two or more temporally adjacent shows are featured, have come to the fore. Since the individual programs are thus subordinated to the block, the integrating factor is that each of these offerings is available *on the same network* in audience-flow-seeking tandems.

For local station program promos, the outlet's own image package is similarly engaged, though specific shows tend to be more individually highlighted than at the network level. (Promos illuminating an entire program series, incidentally, are known as *generics* and those pushing a particular episode are called *topicals.*) In-station, a single music theme and slogan are often modified to meet each of the more specialized requirements of promoting the station's news, movie, and other locally originated features. This Action News promo, for example, is musically and thematically linked with the more general "Where You Belong" station promo previously presented:

```
Action News Promo I    :60
Look for us, we'll be there, Action News is everywhere—
And if what you're looking for is all the news in
   Baltimore and everywhere, then we'll be there—
Look for us, we'll be there, Action News is everywhere—
```

```
From the Allegheny mountains, to the eastern shore
  and everywhere, then we'll be there—
Action news is everywhere.
```

Courtesy of TM Productions, Inc.

As evidenced in the earlier "Where You Belong Basic" lyric, the television sound track can also be constructed in "doughnut" form to permit the smooth integrating of local voices and contemporary happenings into the communication. For a news promo like "Action News," this live insert copy could banner a top story to be covered in an upcoming newscast.

In formulating packaged productions to meet every conceivable local continuity need, some specialty houses now go even further and provide a variety of musical stylings of their main music theme to match the type of movie (comedy, melodrama, mystery, etc.) being shown and plugged that day. The station's continuity writer can then simply use this bed over which to prepare a suitable piece of voice-over copy. This customized adaptability is even being extended to news themes. For its "Action News" package, TM provides what it describes in the package's promotional literature as:

> three different, though thematic, newsthemes, ranging in style and tempo from fast, ultra-dynamic, to easy laid-back smoothness. You now have a range to choose from and, because they *are* thematic, can select your closing theme to match the mood of your final news story. Obviously when a major tragedy occurs, a different musical mood is required. Now you have that versatility with the Where You Belong Newsthemes I, II, and III.

Such preproduced, yet flexible image devices certainly help the local station writer retain a consistent, high-profile personality in all the continuity—IDs, station promos, program promos—required in day-to-day programming. The writer must then take special care that his or her own copy has a polish and coherence to match that of the prepackaged music/lyric bed. For, though such packages are of tremendous help to the station writer, they can also backfire badly in making mediocre local copy look even worse by comparison. Don't, in short, think that the sudden availability of these specialty house services makes the job of the in-station writer any easier. In most cases, they make it more demanding by enforcing a uniform rigor in all your continuity assignments.

Whether, as a television station copywriter, you have an image-enhancer package with which to contend or whether your promos are self-produced "from top to bottom," the copy and visuals must be blended in such a way that they *make* their point clearly and then *make way* for the commercial or program segment that follows. Sometimes, this process can be aided by combining a standard four-second station ID with a ten-second program promo, as in the following generic message for WKRC-TV's news block. Via this method, two distinct continuity tasks can be simultaneously accomplished with a consequent reduction of potential message clutter. Note, too, how the station's network affiliation has been slickly dovetailed in the promo's visual:

Video	Audio
OPEN ON NICK AT THE ANCHOR DESK IN KEY POSITION. BEHIND HIM IS THE <u>FIRST TEN SECONDS</u> OF THE ABC ANCHOR PROMO. NO AUDIO FROM FILM.	MUSIC: <u>NEWS VAMP UNDER ENTIRE</u> <u>SPOT</u> <u>NICK</u>: Eyewitness 12 will be in New York City to report to you LIVE from the Democratic National Convention all next week. We'll feature special close-up reports on the delegations from Ohio,
ON CUE ''SO'' DISSOLVE TO LEGAL ID SLIDE WITH LOGO IN KEY POSITION NORMALLY USED FOR NEWS ID's.	Kentucky, and Indiana. So, for <u>complete</u> election coverage, watch Eyewitness 12 at 5:30 and 11.
DO NOT GO TO LOGO IN BLACK. FADE TO BLACK.	

(Courtesy of Taft Broadcasting Company.)

Of course, television program promos can also be a good deal longer to mesh with the traffic department's still-standard units of thirty and sixty seconds. The following half-minute spot featuring WXYZ-TV's evening anchor lets the viewer conclude how much work (and consequent viewer benefit) is involved in the Channel 7 newscast by acting out a behind-the-scenes vignette. The need for talent self-praise is thereby avoided, but the promo still positions the newscast, personality, and station in a very positive light. Says promotion consultant Henry Price,

> We know from both research and practical experience, that viewers can be impressed with a television station and yet choose not to watch a newscast on the same station. Why? Usually because another newscast is offering the viewer direct benefits in return for watching. Those benefits vary from market to market, but they all have one thing in common: a viewer orientation. Every general manager, news director and promotion manager should take a few moments from time to time to ask himself or herself: 'What message is my promotion giving viewers?' If that message is 'brag and boast' or just a nice jingle with pretty pictures, the station may have problems.[4]

The Bonds promo below does *not* have problems because it shuns boasting in favor of spotlighting, through the viewer's own eyes, the labors that go into making a comprehensive newscast look effortless.

4. Henry Price, writing in "Monday Memo," *Broadcasting Magazine*, January 24, 1983, p. 30.

Video	Audio
M2S BONDS SEATED AT DESK, SECRETARY STANDING NEXT TO HIM	<u>BONDS:</u> What's the week look like, Mary?
MS MARY	<u>MARY:</u> Well, I cancelled the theatre tickets so you can cover the UAW bargaining. Thursday's dinner is off---the assignment in Flint is on. I got you out of that golf outing tomorrow so you can spend the day here writing your commentary for tomorrow night. And your seats for Friday's game—
CU BONDS	<u>BONDS:</u> Yeah?
M2S BONDS AND MARY	<u>MARY:</u> My brother-in-law says thanks.
DIS. MLS TWO GUYS ON BAR STOOLS WATCHING TV IN BG	<u>BONDS:</u> (voice from set) Good evening, this is Bill Bonds...(fade)
PAN LEFT TO FEATURE GUYS	<u>GUY 1:</u> Now that's a job for you.
	<u>GUY 2:</u> Yeahhhhhh—
	<u>GUY 1:</u> An hour a day
	<u>GUY 2:</u> One hour.
SUPER 7 LOGO	<u>VO:</u> Channel 7 Action News. It isn't easy being first.

(Copyright © 1983 American Broadcasting Company.)

    As the Bonds spot illustrates, especially in the case of promotion copy for locally produced shows, the program is often best showcased by focusing on the personality who is featured on it. There is no functional need to distinguish between "program" and "personality" promos since both aspects are so mutually interdependent. Because a "person" is more tangible and involving than a "program," some of the most successful show advertisements accrue from careful exposure of that show's talent. Just make certain the talent is ultimately and clearly tied to a "home base"—to the show or shows on which the viewer can find him or her, as in this 30-second treatment.

Video	Audio
BOYS COME UP OVER CREST OF HILL CARRYING KITE	MUSIC: LIGHT WOODWIND AND STRINGS UNDER VO: Even when Eric Nefstead was a kid, his head was in the clouds.
TWO SHOT, FRONT, BOYS LOOKING UP	BOY ERIC: You know what kind of clouds those are, Tommy? TOMMY: (Sarcastically) White ones!
CU BOY ERIC POINTING AT THE SKY	BOY ERIC: They're fairweather cumulus clouds. That means it's great kite flying weather.
TWO SHOT FROM BEHIND BOYS, SEEING KITE IN TREE	TOMMY: If we ever get it out of the tree.
CU KITE IN TREE	MUSIC: STINGER; THEN SNEAK IN EYEWITNESS NEWS DITTY UNDER
DIS. TO KITE: ZOOM OUT TO SEE IT IS UNDER WEATHER DESK WITH MAN ERIC SITTING AT DESK. HE TURNS TO CAMERA AND SMILES.	VO: Meteorologist Eric Nefstead, down-to-earth weather reporting from a forecaster who knows what he's talking about.
SHOT FREEZES AND EYE-NEWS LOGO IS SUPERED.	Weeknights at 5:30 and ten on 19 Eyewitness News.

(Courtesy of Charles E. Sherman, WHOI-TV.)

A strong personality appeal backed by well-honed copy can carry a full-minute message, too—especially when it clearly targets local interests and feelings while, as in the Bonds and Nefstead promos, revealing talent qualifications:

<u>Production</u> <u>Note</u>: Lavalier mike and wireless so we don't see a cord on cover shots.

Video	Audio
OPEN ON A VERY WIDE COVER SHOT OF THE INSIDE OF THE ROTUNDA OF UNION TERMINAL. BEGIN SLOW ZOOM BEFORE WE COME UP.	(WE HEAR ECHOING FOOTSTEPS BEFORE WE SEE NICK ENTER FRAME)
NICK ENTERS FRAME, LOOKING AROUND HIM AT THE BUILDING.	(DELIVERY IS CASUAL, REMINISCENT BUT LIGHT AND SPIRITED FOR BOTH NICK AND ANNOUNCER)
CONTINUE ZOOM TO MS AS NICK CONTINUES WALKING. WHEN CAMERA REACHES MS, WE BEGIN TO FOLLOW NICK AS HE CONTINUES HIS STROLL.	NICK: I remember coming home from basic training on a train. We came here---to Union Terminal. That was more than twenty years ago. (Pause, looks around) It was pretty busy then. But I remember coming here just a few years ago to wave good-bye to a friend who was taking the last regular passenger train to leave from the terminal. Times change quickly sometimes. (Sentence should not stop; effect should be as if Nick has taken a breath and continued the same sentence)
DISSOLVE TO NICK WALKING IN FRONT OF TERMINAL (Begin dissolve on ''Times change quickly...'') SHOT IS WIDE COVER SO WE CAN SEE THE DOME (low angle?)	
	NICK: Some say it stands in the way of progress. Others claim it's a piece of their past, that it's the most significant art deco structure

Video	Audio
	in the world. Either way you look at it, right now---it's empty.
NICK CONTINUES WALKING AND LOOKING AROUND AS CAMERA PULLS AWAY TO WIDEST COVER POSSIBLE. DISSOLVE TO SWIRLING LOGO. JUST AS LOGO LOCKS IN PLACE, ADD SUPER (LOWER THIRD) READING ''with Nick Clooney''	<u>ANNOUNCER (VO):</u> a neighbor of yours is on the news tonight. He tries to understand BOTH sides of local problems, like what to do with Union Terminal. Not because he HAS to, but because he WANTS to. NICK CLOONEY, anchoring Eyewitness 12, 5:30 and 11. (or) <u>WEEKEND AUDIO/VO ANNCR:</u> A neighbor of yours is on the news weeknights on TV-12. He tries to understand BOTH sides of local problems, like what to do with Union Terminal. Not because he HAS to, but because he WANTS to. NICK CLOONEY anchoring Eyewitness 12, 5:30 and 11.

(Courtesy of Taft Broadcasting Company.)

Note that the above piece of continuity also provides an alternate audio outro for weekend use. By writing a variety of outro voice-overs and having each recorded on a separate audio cart, the copywriter can adapt a message to a variety of days or day parts without the necessity to reshoot the piece. The appropriate cart can simply be inserted over the visual as it is being aired without the need to store several different videotape or film clip versions. Putting such an adaptable audio insert at the *end* rather than at the beginning or middle of the message also makes it much easier for selection and cueing.

Syndicated programs, sold to stations for local airing on a market exclusivity basis, are usually accompanied by prewritten promos that the syndicating source has provided. But a given episode may lend itself to special exploitation by the local station. A home-grown star might be featured, for example, or the specific episode may have a seasonal theme that helps bolster the station's holiday program schedule. Perhaps, as in the following illustration, that particular script was even shot in the station's own city. Whatever the case, the alert continuity writer can create special appeal for the show and the station if, in conjunction with the promotions and traffic departments, a tailored topical plug can be constructed and scheduled:

Video	Audio
OPEN WITH DOUGHNUT	<u>MUSIC:</u> <u>'Let us be the one...'</u>
ADD PARTRIDGE FAMILY SUPER	<u>LINDA (VO):</u> Monday evening, TV-12 brings you an extra special episode of the
DISSOLVE TO SINGING FOOTAGE	Partridge Family, the one that was filmed at Cincinnati's own King's Island Amusement Park. Join David Cassidy, Shirley Jones,
DISSOLVE TO STILL FRAME OF BENCH	Johnny Bench---as a waiter--- and
DISSOLVE TO FOOTAGE OF COVER SHOT	the famous King's Island Characters, along with a few of your neighbors in 'I Left My Heart in Cincinnati,' a
BACK TO DOUGHNUT AND FADE TO BLACK	special Partridge Family adventure, Monday at 6:30 here on TV-12.

(Courtesy of Taft Broadcasting Company.)

Network offerings also provide solid opportunities for promo exploitation on behalf of local station shows. For, as a means of pushing their own stars and series, networks often make talent from their shows available for "cross-pitch" messages to be aired by their affiliate stations. Sample copy for such messages may be supplied by the network itself or, if conditions permit, the station is given the opportunity to contribute its own copy for the star to perform, as in this 30-second piece written for Ted Koppel by WXEX-TV. Although not the case here, the networks sometimes provide a "doughnut" script in which their talent need record the open and close only once and then, simply read a short piece of specialized "hole" copy for each separate station. This can then be edited between the standard open and close on behalf of each affiliate without forcing the talent to undertake an entire 30- or 60-second script for every station. Were this procedure to have been followed with the Koppel piece, the copy within the brackets would constitute such a customized hole.

Clearly, local copywriters who know the various options open to them and who can carry out the advance planning required for proper coordination with the network or syndicator promotions people, have a treasure trove of extra resources to make their station look prestigious and keep their total continuity package more slickly integrated.

Video	Audio
MLS TED ON NEWS SET	TED: I'm Ted Koppel, ABC News <u>Nightline,</u> helping you keep up with our rapidly changing world by bringing you up to date on today's major events.
SLOW ZOOM IN TO MCU TED	The newsmakers of the day will be here at night. Innovative, live television reporting---a trademark of ABC News.
	<u>Eyewitness News</u> shares that commitment, bringing you up to the minute central Virginia news with Pat Robertson, Jim Ramsey and Ralph Hipp. Watch TV 8's <u>Eyewitness News</u> followed at 11:30,
	by ABC News <u>Nightline</u>—the last word in television news.

(Courtesy of WXEX-TV.)

In summarizing the requirements for any effective television promotion campaign, Tuesday Productions' Bo Donovan sets down six realities that must be respected:

1. Your competition is not just the other stations in town but also the long and growing list of alternative well-advertised viewing activities. Keep all your competitors in mind when you plan an advertising campaign.
2. Advertising is selling. If you're not thinking of comparative ads, testimonial ads, endorsement ads and dozens of other kinds before positioning your station, you're not giving your campaign the thought it requires.
3. If your approach is too "safe," you'll get the poor response you deserve. If you're pushing vanilla when your competitors are selling tutti frutti, you won't motivate viewers to watch your station.
4. If your campaign doesn't reflect the ideas or enthusiasm of your staff, it will probably fail. When a new campaign is launched, you deserve their input and full cooperation. They deserve respect for the jobs you hired them to do.
5. Once a workable plan has been devised, understand from the outset it will go through minor revisions. Don't give up on a good campaign idea until it's been given a real chance to succeed in terms of time, money and effort.

6. You will find that surveying the competition, reviewing the alternatives, being bold, involving your staff and sticking with a good idea will pay dividends. Use all the resources at your disposal and you'll be amazed that you can survive, even in the jungle we call broadcasting.[5]

   Though just a single spot, this message for Cable Network News' *Moneyline* encapsulates Donovan's central principles. The competition (magazines and newspapers in this case) is kept in mind, comparative selling is accomplished through bold, enthusiastic statements and visual pacing, the character of *Moneyline* and its hard-driving CNN parent comes through clearly, and the idea of trusting your business fortune to this program is pulled all the way through the promo.

Video	Audio
ZOOM IN TO FORTUNETELLER WITH CRYSTAL BALL	<u>VO:</u> What medium do you use to summon up financial news?
MS <u>MONEYLINE</u> TALENT ON SET GENERIC FINANCIAL SCENES	For business news with substance, make nightly contact with <u>Moneyline</u> on CNN. <u>Moneyline</u> is there every weeknight at 7 eastern.
DIS. CU MAILBOX W/MAGAZINES	No waiting for the weekly magazines with the news you missed.
DIS. MONEY BEING PRINTED	Profit from <u>Moneyline</u>'s
FINANCIAL REPORTER	clear practical reporting
DIS. CU NEWSPAPER AND READING GLASSES	instead of pages of newspaper fine print.
DIS. FORTUNETELLER PLACING COINS ON STOCKS	Don't leave your fortune
CU FORTUNETELLER	to just any old medium.
CU COINS; REVEAL CHYRON INFORMATION AND LOGO	Trust it to <u>Moneyline,</u> weeknights at 7 eastern on CNN.

(Courtesy of Karen Boldra and Diana Krouse, Cable News Network.)

5. Bo Donovan, writing in "Monday Memo," *Broadcasting Magazine*, March 21, 1983, p. 50.

TRAILER PROMOS

Particularly if you find yourself writing for a program producer or syndicator, you may also be required to take film or tape footage that has its own sound track and add additional voice-over narration to it. This footage normally consists of a brief clip or clips from the program being plugged, which your voice-over copy then transforms into promo material. Since you are dealing with two separate audio tracks, a more complicated and distinctive script format is required, as evidenced in the following trailer for a Walt Disney feature. The term *trailer* comes from the original movie house practice of having the promo for next week's serial episode follow or "trail" the current week's installment. Thus, trailers tend to mirror their snappy, direct-sell heritage and, especially on television, use short, attention-grabbing quick cuts to overcome home distractions swiftly and lock in the thematic essence of the offered motion picture. The trailer below is, in fact, an aired *commercial* for a Disney theatrical movie, but the same format and technique are used to pitch upcoming *televised* motion pictures and dramatic or action/adventure series. Notice that the typical trailer format reverses normal television practice by placing visual directions in lower case and narration in upper case. This is done because it is the narration that is being added to what is already mixed (finished) picture and dialogue.

Picture Dialogue	Narration Title
Day. Ext. MS, Low Angle, Herbie's wheels spin, then car speeds o.s. left. LS Herbie turns street corner, travels to f.g. Title POPS ON and Camera PANS R. with car.	(In The Clear) NARR. & TITLE: DISNEY GOES SOUTH OF THE BORDER AS HERBIE GOES BANANAS.
CU POV inside Herbie's trunk with boy's back to camera; Prindle and Shepard visible far b.g. PRINDLE: ''There he is...	
MS Prindle and Shepard run to f.g. PRINDLE: ''in the car.''	
LS Prindle and Shepard with backs to camera standing in middle of street watch Herbie	

Picture Dialogue	Narration Title
far b.g. rear up and travel toward them.	
MS fast truck in to Prindle and Shepard leap o.s.	(In the Clear)
MLS Prindle and Shepard with backs to camera jump out of Herbie's way. Car races to f.g.	
MLS Herbie being hoisted on to ship.	THE LOVE BUG TAKES A TRIP ON THE LOVE BOAT.
Day. Int. Ship. Banquet Room, MLS guests look at Herbie crash through doors in b.g. Waiter holding a cake rides on Herbie's hood.	(In The Clear)
MCU Blythe drops piece of cake, looks wide-eyed at o.s. Herbie.	
MS Camera PANS L. with car as it bumps into table; waiter flies off car, slides left on table.	
CU Blythe with mouth open wide.	
MS stunned Blythe and group in b.g. watch waiter slide across table.	
CU Blythe. Partially visible waiter throws cake into Blythe's face.	
Day. Ext. Ship. MCU Paco peers out VW side window. PACO: ''Sorry.''	

Picture Dialogue	Narration Title

MCU Blythe.
  BLYTHE: ''By the powers
  vested in me as Captain of
  this ship,...	

MLS Herbie upside down on ship
platform.
  BLYTHE: (o.s.) ''I deem
  this vehicle a menace...	

LS Herbie dumped overboard.
Camera PANS DOWN with car
splashing into water.
  BLYTHE: (o.s.) ''I herewith
  commit it to the sea...
  a fate well deserved.	

Day. Ext. Bullring. MLS Herbie races to f.g. and o.s. left.	BUT HANG ON TO YOUR CHIQUITAS AS HERBIE
MS Herbie traveling to f.g.	BOUNCES BACK ON TO A DIFFERENT KIND OF
MCU Herbie bumps into back of car.	TRACK.
MS black car crashes through arena gate.	(In The Clear)
MS Matador facing b.g. holding cape in front of bull. Black car and Herbie in far b.g.	
MLS crowd cheers.	
MLS bull charges to left.	
MCU, side angle, Herbie with cape draped over hood, rear up.	

Picture Dialogue	Narration Title
MCU, side angle, bull runs under raised Herbie.	
MLS crowd stands and cheers.	THE FANS GO BANANAS...
Day. Ext. MLS dilapidated bus comes to a stop on deserted road; its engine blows up.	YOU'LL GO BANANAS.
Int. Bus. MCU Aunt Louise, Melissa and D.J. react frightened.	(In The Clear)
Ext. Bus. MLS, Low Angle, parts fly off vehicle.	(In The Clear)

Night. Ext. LS Herbie travels to f.g. toward Shepard, Prindle and Quinn who jump out of way. Title DURING ABOVE pops off.	NARR. Walt Disney
	  & Productions'
	TITLE: HERBIE GOES BANANAS
	  © Copyright MCMLXXX
	      Technicolor®
	  Walt Disney Productions
	    All Rights Reserved
	
	IT'S ALL-NEW LAUGHTER BY THE BUNCH!

INTERVIEWS AND SEMISCRIPTS

Interview programs, particularly at the local level, are becoming almost as prominent a part of television public service schedules as they are on radio and for the same community relations-related reasons. (See section on "Interviews" in chapter 7.) From a structural standpoint, the television interview's intro and outro each must accomplish the same three purposes as their radio cousins but with some added dimensions that must be taken into consideration.

Arousing listener interest about the television interview, for example, may prove more difficult given the comparatively undynamic but nevertheless prominent visual of two or more people sitting and looking at each other. Film clips, tape segments, or selected still pics that relate to the guest's subject can help overcome the initial "talking head" doldrums. If this is not possible, the opening of the program itself should be visually scripted and produced in such a way that viewers' attention is grabbed long enough for a compelling statement of the topic to sink in and, hopefully, keep them watching.

Making the guest feel at home, the third function of any broadcast interview intro, is even more difficult on television, where bright lights and moving cameras can cause nonmedia visitors to feel especially isolated and uncomfortable. Thus, the continuity writer's well-chosen words of welcome are probably even more crucial in this environment than they were on radio, where the guest had only to contend with a blind and stationary microphone.

Other aspects of the television interview in particular, and of television semi-scripts in general, tend to follow much the same procedures and possess much the same requirements that these forms entail on radio. The one unblinking overlay, however, is the presence of the visual dimension that the continuity writer may need to embellish subtly via suggested props or pics. The following continuity bed for the opening portion of a *Good Afternoon Detroit* program from WXYZ-TV is indicative of the semi-scripts used by many successful interview and magazine shows. In this script, the term *homebase* refers to the standard in-studio conversation set.

ITEM 1. STUDIO TEASE
HOMEBASE

> JOHN: Greenfield Village is a place for family fun and we'll be finding out what's going on this Fall—
>
> MARILYN: And Perry King, will be telling us about the latest twists in his career---next!

ITEM 2. END BREAK.
VTR SOT. FLASH CAM.

ITEM 3. STUDIO COLD OPEN.
HOME BASE.
SUPE: John Kelly

> JOHN: Good afternoon, Detroit. Handsome actor Perry King was one of the stars of the TV adventure series—The Quest. Today, Perry is joining us to talk about what it's like to be an actor who's more interested in acting than being a star.

ITEM 4. HOMEBASE
SUPE: Marilyn Turner

> MARILYN: Sylvia Glover is on a shopping trip to learn how to get away from it all---anytime she wants.

JOHN: We'll have a look at elegant back-to-school fashions for the mature student—

MARI: And we'll find out that the folks at Greenfield Village are gearing up for a great Fall season—

JOHN: Good afternoon, Detroit!

ITEM 5. ANIMATED OPEN

ITEM 6. HOMEBASE.

JOHN: Good afternoon, Detroit. It's Friday, we're heading into the weekend.

    (AD LIB—GAIL PARKER— LETTING GO KIDS)

MARI: So today on our People Poll, we want to know: Is it easier to raise boys or girls?

JOHN: Figure with boys, you don't have nearly the worry about clothes---or keeping 'em clean. Just hose those guys down every couple of days and they're fine--- almost maintenance free. Is it easier to raise boys or girls?

MARI: To let us know what you think, call 298-6070--- and say ''A'' for boys or ''B'' for girls. We'll let you know how the calls are coming in during the show and have

the totals at the end of
the hour.

ITEM 7. HOMEBASE.   JOHN: In the last week or so
we've been looking at
back-to-school clothes
for teenagers, college
kids, and kids who are
too young to even go to
school. Well, what about
the moms? They deserve
to be looking good this
Fall too. Here's Dayna
Eubanks with a peek at
the latest for the
mature woman. Dayna?

ITEM 8. 3:00 VTR SOT

ITEM 9. HOMEBASE.   MARI: Many of us think anti-
freeze is something our
cars only need in cold
weather. But it also
acts as a coolant---so
it's really a year-round
prescription and here's
survivor Jim Ochs to
tell us more.

ITEM 10. RE-RUN VTR
SOT FEATURE.

ITEM 11. STUDIO BILLBOARD   JOHN: (VO) Linda Hirsch is
TEASE.   standing by with the
latest on the soaps—

MARI: (VO) And shopper Sylvia
Glover is up in the air
over her latest spree.

JOHN: (VO) Don't go way.

ITEM 12. VID TEASE.
SUPE: Just ahead—
Perry King!!!

ITEM 13. COMMERCIAL #1	COMMERCIAL #1

ITEM 14. VID TEASE   <u>BOOTH VO:</u> There'll be music in
SUPE: Next week—   the air next week
                                          when we'll be joined
                                          by Motown's own—
           Smokey Robinson   Smokey Robinson—
                                          And we'll be looking
                                          at the career of
           Tom Jones   heart-throb Tom
                                          Jones.

ITEM 15. COMMERCIAL #1a.	COMMERCIAL #1a

ITEM 16. VID BUMPER
SUPE: Coming up—
      Greenfield Village!!!

ITEM 17. HOMEBASE   <u>MARI:</u> Once again, Linda Hirsch
                                    is dipping into the
                                    mailbag to answer some
                                    of the questions you've
                                    sent in. Linda?

ITEM 18. VTR SOT
SUPE: Linda Hirsch

ITEM 19. HOMEBASE   <u>JOHN:</u> Nobody can accuse actor
                                    Perry King of not being
                                    versatile. He's played
                                    everything from
                                    Shakespeare to the role
                                    of the dashing Errol
                                    Flynn-like character in
                                    ABC's <u>The Quest.</u> Now
                                    he's changing again---
                                    this time in the role
                                    Ronald Reagan once
                                    played in a remake of
                                    <u>The Hasty Heart.</u> So what
                                    else is new? That's what
                                    we're going to find out.
                                    Marilyn?

```
ITEM 20. INTERVIEW
VTR SOT
SUPE: Perry King
  (upper left) Courtesy of
        Showtime Pay-TV


ITEM 21. VIDEO TEASE
SUPE: Come fly with Sylvia!!
```

```
ITEM 22. Commercial #2          COMMERCIAL #2
```

```
ITEM 23. PEOPLE POLL BOARD      BOOTH VO: Remember today's
                                          People's Poll
                                          question---is it
                                          easier to raise:
                                          ''A'' boys?
                                          ''B'' girls?
                                          Call 298-6070 and
                                          say ''A'' or ''B.''
```

```
ITEM 24. Commercial #2a         COMMERCIAL #2a
```

```
ITEM 25. VID BUMPER
SUPE: Kay's Coming!
```

Networks and other regional or national distributors use semi-scripts in energizing their shows, too. Here is the continuity for a typical CBS *60 Minutes* program. Note particularly how the opening story intros (which are done *in mortise* and then bumpered by the famous ticking stopwatch) succinctly package the story tension in each of the features to follow. Like the opening mini-segments in *Good Afternoon Detroit*, this lubricates viewer anticipation for the show as a whole while still providing definitive information about its several parts. Each interview intro in the opening composite is then built on when that story is actually handled—but in a way that doesn't require that the viewer be tuned in at the program's beginning.

In addition, the conclusion of *60 Minutes* illustrates two further semi-script/promotion techniques. The closing credits are rolled over a segment from one of the earlier-covered stories as a punctuating reprise of a key program-delivered insight. Then a bumper announcement is fashioned in the *60 Minutes* style to cross-promote the network's regular evening newscast. In this way, successful shows can be exploited as vehicles to direct viewers to like programs offered by that same broadcaster.

DIANE SAWYER: If you set out to find an all-American,
                             true-blue soldier, you would probably
                             come back with someone just like Captain
                             Edward Pearson. How, then, did it happen
                             that Edward Pearson's Air Force career is
                             in ruins; that, not long ago, he found
                             himself facing an Air Force court-
                             martial? Well, the Pentagon says Captain
                             Pearson was a marijuana smoker.
                             Is it true? Do you smoke pot?

CAPTAIN EDWARD PEARSON: No.

SAWYER: Have you ever?

CAPTAIN PEARSON: No.

SAWYER: Never tried it?

CAPTAIN PEARSON: No.

                             (STOPWATCH BUMPER)

MORLEY SAFER: If you were a businessman, like these
                             men, what would you think would be the
                             most unlikely of all businesses you'd be
                             in? How about the jail business, like
                             this jail, the first adult jail to be
                             operated for profit? A private company
                             runs it. They not only house and feed the
                             inmates, but they're also responsible for
                             their education, rehabilitation and drug
                             and alcohol treatment. They hire, pay and
                             train the guards, who are not government
                             employees but employees of—

WOMAN (answering ringing telephone):   Good morning. Corrections
                             Corporation of America.

                             (STOPWATCH BUMPER)

VERNON WALTERS (Ambassador-at-Large, trouble shooter):   Castro
                             once said to someone I knew very well,
                             ''If you've come here to threaten me, you
                             should know I've been threatened by every
                             President of the United States since John
                             Fitzgerald Kennedy. You should also know
                             that I know how your government works,
                             and I know that your congress will not
                             allow any of your Presidents to do to me
                             what they'd like to do to me.'' Unquote.

MIKE WALLACE: Insiders say the person to whom Castro
                             said that was Ambassador Walters himself,

when he went to see Castro for Ronald
Reagan on a secret mission in 1982.
(STOPWATCH BUMPER)

WALLACE:	I'm Mike Wallace.
SAFER:	I'm Morley Safer.
HARRY REASONER:	I'm Harry Reasoner.
ED BRADLEY:	I'm Ed Bradley.
SAWYER:	I'm Diane Sawyer. Those stories and more, tonight on 60 MINUTES.

(Announcements)

DIANE SAWYER:

If you set out to find an all-American,
true-blue military man, you'd probably
come back with someone just like Captain
Edward Pearson, a 27-year-old Air Force
Academy graduate, a top-rated flyer, who
wanted nothing more than an Air Force
career the rest of his life. How, then
did it happen that Edward Pearson's Air
Force career is in ruins: that the
Pentagon charged him with smoking
marijuana?
The Air Force says you're a pot smoker.
(STORY BODY)

(Announcements)

MORLEY SAFER:

''The business of America is business,''
said Calvin Coolidge, and this story more
than confirms that wisdom. ''Crime Pays''
is not how to get away with it; it's how
to cash in on it. The care and feeding of
criminals in this country costs about
$10-billion a year. A number of bright
entrepreneurs decided, with that kind of
cash available and the heat that the
government's taking about overcrowding
and rehabilitation, that maybe they could
do a better job of running corrections
than the government; that, if confinement
were treated as a business, maybe someday
there'd be a profit. That ''someday'' is

	now. It's happened in Tennessee, here in the Hamilton County Jail, Chattanooga, the first adult jail to be operated for profit. A private company runs it. They not only house and feed the inmates, but they're also responsible for their education, rehabilitation and drug and alcohol treatment. They hire, pay and train the guards who are not government employees, but employees of—
WOMAN (answering ringing phone):	Good morning. Corrections Corporation of America.
SAFER:	Corrections Corporation of America was formed solely to manage and operate detention centers, jails and prisons. These are the men who are the corporate wardens of that jail in Chattanooga. They also run a detention center for illegal aliens for the Immigration Service in Houston and a center for juvenile offenders in Memphis. Tom Beasley, president; Travis Snelling, vice president.
	(STORY BODY)

(Announcements)

ANNOUNCER:	60 MINUTES, a CBS News weekly magazine, will continue.

(Announcement)

ANNOUNCER:	This is CBS.

(Announcements)

MIKE WALLACE:	The ''Trouble Shooter'' is Vernon Walters, Ambassador-at-Large for Ronald Reagan. He has traveled more than a million miles since February, 1981, when he took the job; he speaks eight languages, has traveled to a hundred countries. Formerly an Army general, formerly Deputy Director of the CIA, this 67-year-old roving ambassador was with Harry Truman in 1950 when he met with

Douglas MacArthur at Wake Island. He was
with Richard Nixon when, as Vice
President, Nixon's car was stoned by
Venezuelan mobs. Walters spirited Henry
Kissinger in and out of Paris at the
beginning of the secret peace talks with
the North Vietnamese. Back in 1959, he
was escort officer for Fidel Castro, when
the bearded revolutionary made his first
UN appearance in New York as Cuba's new
leader. Walters is no policy-maker, but
his views, expressed with characteristic
bluntness, represent a major line of
thought inside the Reagan Administration.
Last month, we asked him just what it is
that he does.
(STORY BODY)

(Announcements)

HARRY REASONER:
Last week, during our story about the
famine in Ethiopia, Monsignor Robert
Coll, who heads Catholic relief in that
country, said—
(BODY OF STORY UPDATE)
    SECTION
I'm Harry Reasoner. We'll be back next
week with another edition of 60 MINUTES.

(Announcements)

(Production credits during replay of
excerpt from ''Crime Pays'' segment)
TRAVIS SNELLING (Corrections Corporation of America):   ...versus
bringing people to the classic large
dining facility, which has always been a
corrections problem. And, so, we're
operating probably 20---15-to-20% under
what the national norm is per day, per
inmate, and I'll guarantee you our food
quality and nutritional levels are equal
to or better than anywhere in the
country.

CORRECTIONAL GUARD:
Enjoy your lunch, guys. (Speaking
Spanish)

ANNOUNCER:
This is CBS.

	(Announcements)
ANNOUNCER:	Armed robber Bonnie Fawcett got a parole, held two jobs and became a model citizen. Now she's back in a Texas jail.
BONNIE FAWCETT:	It just seemed like that no matter how hard you try, it doesn't matter. (Crying) I'm sorry.
ANNOUNCER:	So, then, why are Bonnie and 53 others being locked up all over again? Their story, tomorrow, on the CBS EVENING NEWS WITH DAN RATHER.
ANNOUNCER:	This is CBS.

(Courtesy of Robert Chandler, CBS News.)

Sometimes the semi-script may take the form of a *routine sheet;* a blocked-out schedule of events that contains the names and lengths of the individual segments that together comprise the program. Routine sheets normally include little or no voiced continuity, though the continuity writer must often aid in their preparation and/or use them as a guide to the spoken material they mandate. Should you find yourself working in broadcast journalism, a similar type document that lists the stories in a newscast is called a *run-down sheet.* It likewise is simply a nonscript guide to the order and running times allotted to the voiced and pictured subjects slated for the broadcast. Typically abbreviated routine sheet style is exemplified in this standard outline for NBC's enduring *Meet the Press:*

ITEM	AT	LENGTH	VIDEO	AUDIO
(1)	12:30:00	(:10)	Globe/VT-Open	VT
(2)	12:30:10	(:05)	Hello-MK/RM	Live-MK/RM
(3)	12:30:15	(1:00) appx.	Intro-Kalb	Live-MK
(4)		(1:15) appx.	Intro - Mudd	Live-RM
(5)		(4:00) appx.	Q & A-Mudd/Kalb & Guest -Chyron Supers	Live-Mudd/Kalb & Guest

ITEM	AT	LENGTH	VIDEO	AUDIO
(6)		(:05)	Cml. Cue-Mudd or Kalb	Live-Mudd or Kalb
(7)		(:10)	Wide Shot of set	Anncr: (Meet the Press, the world's longest-running television program, is a presentation of NBC News.''
(8)		(:10)*	Cml. Billboard-Open VT or ESS	Anncr.
(9)		(1:00)	1st Commercial Position/VT	VT
(10)		(:02)	MTP-ESS	VT
(11)		(7:00) appx.	Q & A-Mudd/Kalb & Guest -Chyron Supers	Live-Mudd/Kalb & Guest
(12)		(:05)	Cml. Cue-Kalb or Mudd	Live-MK or RM
(13)		(1:00)	2nd Commercial Position/VT	VT
(14)		(:02)	MTP-ESS	
(15)		(7:00) appx.	Q & A-Mudd/Kalb & Guest -Chyron Supers	Live-Mudd/Kalb & Guest
(16)		(:05)	Cml. Cue-Mudd or Kalb	Live-RM or MK
(17)		(2:00)	3rd Commercial Position	VT

ITEM	AT	LENGTH	VIDEO	AUDIO
(18)		(:02)	MTP-ESS	
(19)		(2:15) appx.	Discussion-Kalb & Mudd	Live-Kalb & Mudd
(20)	12:57:20	(:10)	Kelly Transcripts -ESS	Anncr.: ''For a printed transcript of Meet the Press, please send one dollar....and a stamped, self-addressed envelope to.... Kelly Press, Box 8648, Washington, D.C. 20011.''
(21)	12:57:30	(:10)*	Cml. Billboard- Close VT or ESS	Anncr.
(22)	12:57:40	(:30)	Credits-Chyron Stills-ESS	Anncr./cross plug
(23)	12:58:10	(:15)	News Logo/VT	VT

*Some weeks there are two major sponsors and commercial billboards run 15 seconds instead of 10 seconds.

(Courtesy of William Placek, National Broadcasting Company, Inc.)

Though only for nonair or closed-circuit utilization, the *presentation* ("dog and pony show") treatment is a fleshed-out cousin of what we have called the semi-script. In the presentation script, you are chiefly concerned with coordinating still pics/slides with a live speech. It may also include written "wrap-arounds" to relevant pieces of film or tape footage. These wrap-arounds also will be delivered by the live presenter. Since the presentation script thus encompasses the same materials as other forms of radio/television continuity, and since it is a vital aspect of the broadcasting and advertising industries' internal decision-making processes, the presentation script's construction is accomplished by someone who, regardless of title, is in fact fulfilling the functions of a broadcast copywriter.

As in any radio and television writing, the aim here must be to keep the copy conversational so the presenter seems to be talking *with* rather than lecturing *to* the audience. Clean, clear interlock between script segments and their illustrative visuals is also of pre-eminent concern. Nothing short-circuits a dog and pony show faster than when the dogs and ponies get out of sync: when the pics are scripted in such a way that they come too fast or too slow for the meaning and style of the presenter's aural delivery and perceivers' comprehension. A well-formatted outline combined with language that clearly relates to the pic on the screen are necessities. As an example of an effectively fashioned presentation, here is the start of a closed-circuit script in which Steve Sohmer (then CBS Promotions vice president and subsequently, NBC Entertainment executive vice president) unveiled CBS' "Looking Good Together" theme campaign to his network's affiliates.

```
OPEN ON CBS METALICIZED
''EYE'' WITH ''PROMO
BRIEFING'' TITLE
```

MCU SOHMER IN CHAIR	Hello, I'm Steve Sohmer---and this is promo briefing. We've begun work on the most closely coordinated, carefully planned and detailed promotion campaign ever mounted by a network and its affiliates.
''LOOKING GOOD TOGETHER'' LOGO	Our theme is: <u>Looking Good Together.</u> And our mark---our logo---grows out of the very spirit of what we are.
''STAR'' SLIDE	The star for entertainment--- and for excellence.
ADD ''CIRCLE'' OVERLAY	The circle: our symbol of continuity---and the unbroken ring of the family.
ADD ''BUNTING'' OVERLAY	The bunting for America---and Americans, the beautiful.
ADD ''LOOKING GOOD'' TITLE	<u>Looking Good</u>---boldly stated, filled with optimism and light.

ADD ''TOGETHER'' TITLE TO COMPLETE LOGO	And Together---a very special word, with many, many facets— many meanings as you will see.
CALENDAR CHART #1 (THEME)	Early in June, we are taking Looking Good Together to the people of America; once again seizing the initiative, and taking advantage of the air time opportunities June and July provide for establishing our theme.
CALENDAR CHART #2 (ADD ''SINGALONG'')	Then, starting at the beginning of July, a unique phase we call ''Singalong''. Both of these will be a major network effort---and provide an extraordinary local tie-in opportunity for affiliates.
CALENDAR CHART #3 (ADD ''PREMIERE'')	Then, in August, we'll start running premiere spots for our new shows.
CALENDAR CHART #4 (ADD ''TOPICAL'')	And our topical promos will go on-the-air late in that month.
''LOOKING GOOD TOGETHER'' LOGO	But first, let's talk about how we're going to put our theme across together.
MCU SOHMER IN CHAIR	In our theme promos, your viewers will see themselves portrayed with warmth, humor, love. While we dramatize how television provides a gathering place for the family---companionship to the lonely---a break for the work-weary---diversion---delight--- a vehicle to transport people. And throughout these promos we'll return again to the intimacy shared between our

```
                                      viewers and the CBS stars they
                                      adore. Rub your eyes---because
                                      you've never seen promos like
                                      this:

''SINGLE MAN'' CLIP                   (ROLL TAPE: SINGLE MAN: 75)
```

(Courtesy of CBS.)

PUBLIC SERVICE ANNOUNCEMENTS

Research indicates that less than one percent of total television time is devoted to public service announcements. It is further estimated that a given PSA campaign must compete for airtime with at least 100 other PSA campaigns at any given moment. There is no better indicator of the competitive nature of the television PSA field than these statistics. Everything that was said in chapter 7 about the requisites and rigors of radio public service writing can be repeated with double emphasis when it comes to television. In addition, a number of visual concerns also impinge themselves on the PSA creation process and must therefore be addressed in this section.

March to the Beat of the Station's Drummer

The engineering and productional functions required in creating and transmitting television content are considerably more complex than those demanded by radio. Consequently, the personnel and equipment at the television station can seldom accommodate material that does not come ready for airing. At the optimum, this means that PSAs should arrive at the station in finished 16mm sound-on-film or broadcast format videotape. A survey of 419 stations conducted by Planned Communications Services Inc. indicated that the most preferred format was 16mm SOF, with slide/script being the least favored.[6] If 16mm sound film or broadcast quality video tape is totally beyond the resources of the agency for whom you are preparing the announcement, a silent 16mm film with a preproduced audio tape sound track would be the next best, but far less desirable alternative. Only in the case of a local organization, whose message really helps address a fundamental community need, should 35mm slide or flip card formats even be considered.

But let's assume that your copy is communicating a local message the station is interested in addressing and that still pics, if properly prepared, will be accepted. In that case, the following procedures should be followed to avoid the station's having to go any farther out of its way to serve the needs of the community and your client organization:

1. Take the visuals that have been selected for the PSA and have them all made into 35mm slides. Flip cards are much more trouble to handle than slides since they

6. "PSA Performance and Preferences," *Broadcasting Magazine,* May 26, 1980, p. 58.

require actual studio production. Slides, on the other hand, can be taped or aired directly from the control room's film chain. The minimal expense which slide creation entails is an investment that any media user should be prepared to absorb in order to make everyone's life easier.

2. Provide one slide for every ten seconds of running time (three slides for a "thirty," six slides for a "sixty"). This is, if not a "happy" medium, at least a livable one that provides for some visual interest on the one hand, but does not demand pre-rehearsed and split-second intercutting on the other. No station has the time to produce a technical extravaganza that comes disguised as a 30-second "freebie" kit.

3. Keep the copy "spacious"—don't pack the message so tightly that the technicians have trouble catching each slide's cue line or don't have time to check the monitor for proper word/picture matching. This also means, of course, that multiple copies of your PSA script must be provided along with the preproduced audio tape. If they like your message, the station will probably transfer it to videotape and then simply replay the tape whenever the PSA is scheduled. Thus, it is especially important that your copy and script allow for a "clean" and trouble-free taping the first time so as not to antagonize any of the technicians who may be involved in its replay.

4. Make certain that the visuals selected are intrinsically related to the central point of your PSA and are necessary to the realization of that point. Too many low-budget public service announcements try to use pictures because they are conveniently lying around rather than because they are appropriate to the message itself. If highly relevant and meaningful illustrations are not available, and if resources don't permit their procurement, then fashion the communication for radio, where it can have positive rather than negative impact.

One Concept to a Customer, Please

In the earlier chapters on radio, it was stipulated that messages with a duration of a minute or less should not attempt to deal with more than one main idea. Yet, when they "graduate" to television, some writers seem to feel that the availability of a visual makes possible the inclusion of two, three, or even more copy points. Such an attitude can spell disaster. True, television does have both audio and visual vehicles for the conveyance of data, but this also more than doubles the stimuli load audience members are asked to ingest. Adding multiple copy points to the mixture only guarantees that, no matter how much information is originally taken in, little if any will possess the needed salience for viewer retention and later recall.

This principle is especially important to the television public service announcement in which a usually intangible "product" requires disciplined and definitive explication. For the video PSA to succeed, every picture and supporting sound must contribute to the reaching of the one, key conclusion for which the message was written in the first place. The initial vagueness of most public service subjects makes it especially critical that the sequence of selected pictures leads inevitably to viewer comprehension, if not actual acceptance, of the announcement's central tenet. The organic unity that, on radio, flows from the careful progression of heard words and sounds is, on television, dependent on the frame-to-frame linkage of compelling and interrelated visuals (as featured in Figure 10–6).

Figure 10–6. *(Courtesy of The Advertising Council, Inc.)*

Concept-focusing visuals need not always be outdoor epics. Sometimes, as illustrated in the following script, a much more circumscribed, single-scene approach is what is needed for concept concentration. The number of mutually distinctive visual settings the spot uses is, by itself, no index of whether the television public service announcement will be a success. Rather, as both the treatments in Figure 10–6 and on page 318 demonstrate, the quantity and character of your pictorial scenes should be determined solely on the basis of that one, main point you are trying to make.

Video	Audio
	(APPROPRIATE SFX THROUGHOUT)

```
LS MAN FORCED INTO CAR
LS BACK SEAT—MEN SIT DOWN
MS MAN IN MIDDLE
CU BUCKLES SEAT BELT
CU GANGSTER ON RIGHT
CU MAN IN MIDDLE
CU GANGSTER ON LEFT
LS THREE MEN
CU GANGSTER ON RIGHT
CU MAN IN MIDDLE


LS THREE MEN—CAR STOPS,
GANGSTERS FLY FORWARD


MS MAN IN MIDDLE                     ANNCR (VO): Next time someone
                                     takes you for a ride,


CU SEAT BELT


CU MAN IN MIDDLE                     buckle up.


SUPER LOGO:


''A Public Service from Motor
Vehicle Manufacturers
Association''
```

(Courtesy of Jim O'Donnell, National Television News.)

Believability Is Not an Option

Another way of analyzing the appropriateness of PSA visuals is to try to ascertain their *believability* within the confines of the single statement their message is striving to register. Like an involving novel or, for that matter, an appealing product display, the believable PSA entices viewers to put themselves "in the picture"—to participate mentally and emotionally in the little vignette being spun out before their eyes. And for the public service announcement, which often promotes a state of mind rather than a less personally entangling decision to buy, the credibility of the communication may itself constitute the element you are trying to sell. The audience has to conclude, for example, that the National Guard is a valuable national resource; has to agree that buckling up is important even if you aren't being abducted. In short, the message has to appeal to what persuasion theory calls *enlightened self-interest:* we are willing to believe in and subscribe to bannered principles and advocated practices because of "what's in it for us." Thus, we are not asked to support the National Guard because that is the "patriotic" thing to do. Rather, we are shown that such support makes possible the protection of our own futures. Likewise, we see that buckling up isn't just a safety procedure "they" command, but a way to keep from having our brains bashed out.

Believability in the PSA is thus anything but an option. It is an indispensable quality that comes from (a) sincere-sounding copy, (b) natural casting, and (c) comfortable but not dull photographic values.

a. *sincere-sounding copy*

This is credibility's cornerstone and the element over which the writer has the greatest direct control. Good copy can make unknown talent seem as familiar as (and perhaps more believable than) the famous faces that are often beyond the resources of a public service budget. Review what was said about the Proletariat Promenade back in chapter 5. For sincere-sounding copy is, above all, copy that *makes sense* and makes it in a way that strikes the audience as neither pompous nor patronizing. Both lyric and straight material can possess sincerity, as this Traffic Safety Administration production demonstrates.

Video	Audio
FADE UP ON MLS OF WIFE, HUSBAND & CHILD IN LARGE HAMMOCK. MOVE IN TO MCU OF MOTHER AND CHILD.	JANIE SONG: I want to watch the sun come up another fifty years.
DISSOLVE TO LEFT SIDE MCU SHOT OF ALL THREE.	
	I want to write a novel that will bring the world to tears
DISSOLVE TO MCU OF FRONT SHOT OF MOTHER AND CHILD.	And I want to see Venice
DISSOLVE TO CU OF CHILD.	I want to see my kids have kids
DISSOLVE TO CU LEFT SIDE SHOT OF MOTHER AND CHILD.	I want to see them free
DISSOLVE TO MLS OF ALL THREE— MOVE IN TO MS.	I want to live my only life I want the most of me

Video	Audio	
DISSOLVE TO LEFT SIDE MS OF MOTHER AND CHILD		I want to dance
DISSOLVE TO MS OF RIGHT SIDE OF MOTHER AND CHILD.		I want to love
DISSOLVE TO CU LEFT SIDE OF MOTHER AND CHILD.		I want to breathe
FREEZE FRAME AND DISSOLVE TO B & W.	ANNCR VO:	Janie died On an endless road in America
PULL BACK FROM B & W PHOTO IN A PICTURE FRAME AND DOLLY PAST EMPTY BED		Because a lonely man was driving drunk out of his mind. Problem drinkers who drive are responsible for more than 40 deaths every day. Get the problem drinker off the road.
	JANIE SONG:	I want to know what's out there beyond the furthest star
		I even want to go there if we ever get that far
TITLE: ''GET THE PROBLEM DRINKER OFF THE ROAD''		And I want to see Venice.
FADE TO BLACK.		
FADE UP TO TITLE: ''WRITE: DRUNK DRIVER	TAG VO:	Help. Do something about

Video	Audio
BOX 1969, WASHINGTON, D.C. U.S. DEPARTMENT OF TRANSPORTATION NATIONAL HIGHWAY TRAFFIC SAFETY ADMINISTRATION.''	the problem drinker. For his sake. And yours.

(Courtesy of U.S. Department of Transportation National Highway Traffic Safety Administration.)

b. *natural casting*
Because television announcements that show people tend to be more interesting *to* people, casting is an important consideration most of the time. Even though the copywriter may not make the actual casting decisions, it is his or her scripted specifications that, when translated via the art director's sketches, form the blueprint from which the producers will make their talent decisions. This selection process deserves as much of your input as possible because, if the audience does not like the people who appear in your message, they will apply this distaste to the message itself. Take some time to write a vivid and compelling production note that really delineates the type of person you had in your mind during script creation. Then, read over that description to make certain it describes the sort of individual who would most likely be found in the environment in which your vignette transpires. If an implication of universality is desired, well-selected, differentiated casting as shown in the photoboard for Independent Sector (Figure 10–7), can fill the bill for television in the same way the multivoiced technique performs for radio.

c. *comfortable (but not dull) photographic values*
A believable PSA does not exude an institutional formality in the direction and placing of its shots. Nor, on the other hand, are its production techniques so *avant garde* that only spaced-out video freaks understand them. Yet, the tendency of some PSA writers is to swing from one extreme to the other in their video planning. They try either to respect some assumed "propriety mandate" from the sponsoring agency or, on discovering that to be an imaginary constraint, go wild in an attempt to "out-hip" the most bizarre commercial copy around. It is as though a public service announcement must be either more straitlaced or radical than anything else on the tube in order to get viewer attention. This, of course, is anything but the case. Provided the central concept has been well honed, a PSA can compete with any other commercial or continuity fare on television—and compete in the productional mainstream rather than on the "up tight" or "far out" fringes. In the Figure 10–8 message for The Atlanta Ballet, the central concept is given full reign through an appropriately innovative, but by no means bizarre, pictorial progression.

Good copy, on both the audio and video sides of the page, can just as effectively serve a nonprofit institution as it can a profit-centered mouthwash manufacturer. As long as the videography/cinematography flows directly out of the subject (as chapter 11's Demo-Deriving Quintet discussion will explore), a PSA's pictorial values should require neither apology nor hype. The Center for Voluntary Action "Mannequin" treatment (Figure 10–9) demonstrates the audience-embracing elements that accrue from nurturing a PSA visual to an appropriate and self-confident maturity.

Figure 10-7. *(Courtesy of The Advertising Council, Inc.)*

Beware the CEBUS Factor

If, for whatever the reason, the viewing audience is unable to believe in your message or its leading elements, the CEBUS factor will rise up and smite any recollection of your announcement. Standing for Confirmed Exposure But UnconScious, CEBUS is a motivational research term that describes the phenomenon whereby a person's sensory system was exposed to a stimulus but without any conscious registering. In CEBUS tests, David Ogilvy and Joel Raphaelson reveal, "75 percent of viewers cannot recall the average television commercial the day after they have seen it."[7] If CEBUS is a problem of such

---

7. David Ogilvy and Joel Raphaelson, "Agency Boredom with Analysis Cripples Execution," *ADWEEK/Midwest*, September 27, 1982, p. 72.

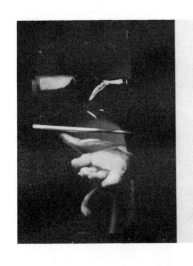

They brought great stories to life. And dazzled audiences each night.

We'll give you a thrill -- right down to your toes.

But then, some new shoes stepped into the picture. And boy, could they dance. And romance.

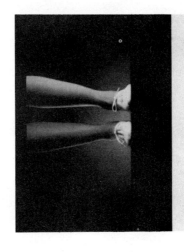

If you're up for one surprise after another, call 892-3303 and get your season tickets to The Atlanta Ballet.

Once upon a time, people thought that ballet was all pliets and pirouettes.

Figure 10–8. *(Courtesy of Julie Burmeister, writer and producer, Ogilvy & Mather Advertising.)*

323

Volunteer/:60 "People who need people."

Public Service Announcements available in color in :60 and :30 lengths on 16mm film

MUSIC: NANCY WILSON SINGING
"PEOPLE WHO NEED PEOPLE"

MUSIC: ORCHESTRA ONLY AFTER
INTRO

MS. NANCY WILSON (V.O.): Some
people feel that we're becoming a
nation of mannequins.

Nothing but heartless clothes racks

no longer caring about, or for, each
other's needs.

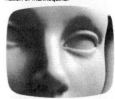

They say we've become blind to the
suffering of the sick and the old . . .

deaf to the pleas of the disadvantaged.

If it's true, pity us . . . because it's not
those of us who need help who are
the handicapped

. . . it's those of us who won't give it.

I'm Nancy Wilson asking you to have a
heart, and write Volunteer, Washington
D.C. 20013.

It'll make you a better human being.

MUSIC UP AND OUT.
"PEOPLE WHO NEED PEOPLE"

Volunteer

**A Public Service Campaign of the Advertising Council
for The National Center For Voluntary Action
and its Local Voluntary Action Centers**

Volunteer Advertising Agency: Bozell & Jacobs, Inc.

Figure 10–9.   *(Courtesy of The Advertising Council, Inc.)*

magnitude as regards tangible products, it is easy to see its import for the
initially intangible subjects pitched in public service announcements.

CEBUS is easily triggered by a message that lacks credibility because people
seldom pay extended attention to things they don't believe; especially when, as

on television, there are so many announcements competing with each other for initial notice and later recognition. Always recheck your copy, proposed visuals, and suggested casting to make certain each element contributes the maximum to believability and the minimum to the CEBUS factor.

For practice, analyze the components of the "Hospital" photoboard in Figure 10–10. Do they create an initial interest? Sustain that CEBUS-defeating interest through cumulative believability? Are there any aspects that strain credibility? If so, how would you change them?

Don't play games with the CEBUS factor. That is what a few individuals tried to do in the late fifties with so-called *subliminal* advertising. The theory was that

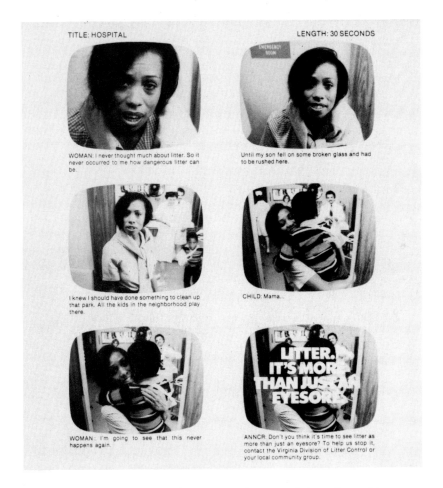

TITLE: HOSPITAL LENGTH: 30 SECONDS

WOMAN: I never thought much about litter. So it never occurred to me how dangerous litter can be.

Until my son fell on some broken glass and had to be rushed here.

I knew I should have done something to clean up that park. All the kids in the neighborhood play there.

CHILD: Mama...

WOMAN: I'm going to see that this never happens again.

ANNCR: Don't you think it's time to see litter as more than just an eyesore? To help us stop it, contact the Virginia Division of Litter Control or your local community group.

Figure 10–10. *(Courtesy of The Virginia Division of Litter Control.)*

stimuli that came to the viewer at a level above the limits of sensory detect-
ability but below the threshold of consciousness (below the *limen* level), would
have an involuntarily persuasive impact on that viewer. Subliminal (sub-*limen*)
messages, in essence, attempted to disguise the negative CEBUS factor as
a positive, motivating attribute. Not only was it never definitively shown to
work, but the storm of quite understandable protest about such underhanded,
thought-controlled practices has made subliminal advertising both a functional
and regulatory outcast. A January 23, 1974, policy statement by the Federal
Communications Commission has warned for years that:

> Use of subliminal perception is inconsistent with the obligations of a licensee,
> and therefore we take this occasion to make clear that broadcasts employing
> such techniques are contrary to the public interest. Whether effective or not,
> such broadcasts are clearly intended to be deceptive.

The U.S. Bureau of Alcohol, Tobacco and Firearms also has acted in this
area through a 1984 rule that prohibits subliminal advertising techniques in
alcohol beverage promotion.[8] If you can't entice viewers to perceive your
message, you have failed as a copywriter. And any *premeditated* use of subconscious stimuli is, particularly for PSAs, impossible to reconcile with the high-
minded causes public service announcements, by their very definition, are
supposed to advocate.

Don't Smother Your Visual

When discussing ID construction earlier in this chapter, the point was made
that the copy must be used sparingly to allow "breathing room" for the music
and visual. This same principle applies equally to public service announcements. Unfortunately, some PSA writers are like once-a-month preachers trying
to jam four sermons into each single appearance.

Granted, the subject of your piece is laudable, humane, and vital. And it may
be aired quite infrequently. But packing it with so much copy that the viewer
must become primarily a *listener* throws away the unique advantage of television. The perceptive PSA writer knows that the silent speech of gestures, facial
expressions, and camera revelations can have far more television impact than a
continuous stream of dialogue or voice-over copy. True, the subject of a public
service announcement may be more difficult to delineate than a soft drink or a
"living girdle," but talking your script to death is no way to exploit the potential
of video. In all your television writing, and particularly in PSAs where the
tendency to "pontificate" is so strong, write copy as sparingly as a compelling
visual will allow. In this way, the words you *do* utilize will have special force and
significance.

In this 60-second treatment, any more words would simply intrude on the
visual and blunt the resounding quality of the copy that *was* employed:

8. "Alcohol Ban: the View from BATF," *Broadcasting Magazine*, February 25, 1985, p. 75.

Video	Audio
STRING HANGS TOP CENTER. A HAND REACHES UP TO PULL IT DOWN.	MUSIC: ELECTRONIC THEME THROUGHOUT
HANDS REACH UP, EACH PULLING DOWN A COLORED CORD.	
CAMERA PANS UP CORDS AS THEY WEAVE AND SPIN LIKE A MAYPOLE AND FORM A STURDY, MULTI—COLORED KNOT.	ANNCR (VO): When our single efforts join together—then there is hope.
CU OF INTERTWINED STRANDS	
THE ROPE APPEARS TO BE PULLED DOWN RHYTHMICALLY. AS IT'S PULLED A PANEL SLOWLY LIFTS TO REVEAL A BRILLIANT SUNRISE.	SOUND OF A PULLEY IN OPERATION.
ZOOM IN.	
SUPER:	ANNCR (VO): Campaign for Human Development, United States Catholic Conference, Washington, D.C.

(Courtesy of Creative Services, U.S. Catholic Conference.)

Tag for Success

In order to be accepted for airing, all public service announcements should feature, aurally and/or visually, the name of the sponsoring organization. Usually, this identification occurs at the message's conclusion as a "tag" or "signer." This tag need be neither extensive nor detailed but should include the name and logo of the originating agency. A brief mention of the organization's home city ("United States Catholic Conference, Washington, D.C.") is also appropriate, and sometimes required.

If your intention is to have viewers write or call in, then ample time must be allowed to permit registering and repetition of the mailing address or phone number. In such instances, it is often necessary to devote the last 6 seconds of a 30 second spot to a full-screen tag that provides the essential contact information. Nationally or regionally distributed spots that require local tagging follow the same practice: the copywriter creates a 24-second piece, followed by 6 seconds of black (or freeze frame) that will be custom tagged by the local organization in each city. The audio also may be left "open" or continue the PSA's music or sound effects bed right through the tagging procedure.

Whether a short or long tag is used, there is no need to waste valuable time and viewer attention with the words: "This is a message from. . . ." Today's television audiences understand that the organization identified on the screen is the source of the spot and require no functionless reminder. As in the American Heart Association PSA below, effective public service announcements establish their agency's name but spend the bulk of their time unveiling what that agency can do for the viewer.

Video	Audio
HIGH ANGLE WS BERNIE PLAYING PIANO - BOOM DOWN AND DOLLY INTO MS	MUSIC: BERNIE PLAYING & SINGING ''MISS AMERICA'' SONG.
	BERNIE: Hi. I'm Bernie Wayne. When I wrote this in 1954, coronary bypass surgery was only a dream. A dream that has come true, largely because of research supported by the American Heart Association.
MCU BERNIE PLAYS ANOTHER TUNE.	Thousands of people have been helped by this research, including me. I can now continue writing music.
DIS AHA LOGO	The American Heart Association. We're fighting for your life.

(Courtesy of Virginia Tannebring, American Heart Association.)

Chapter Eleven

TELEVISION COMMERCIALS

Despite all the rules, strictures, and warnings of the last two chapters, you must not lose sight of the fact that television writing can be a very rewarding professional endeavor. And particularly in the area of television commercials, these significant rewards can be both monetary and creative.

In proportion to the number of words included, television commercial writers probably get more money per word than do those for any other medium—even when the vital but unspoken words expended on the script's video side are included in the computation. More importantly, from a psychological standpoint, copywriters in television advertising experience the fun of dealing with a communications vehicle that is more flexible than any other channel human beings have contrived—a vehicle that is becoming *more* flexible all the time. The danger, of course, is that we become so captivated by television's possibilities that the ads we create become too diffuse. We mistakenly try to show everything to everyone in a single spot.

Keeping our message persuasively on-target is always a copywriter concern and a concern that is magnified given the multitude of television tools but the paucity of time that any video spot has in which to use them. In television commercial creation, therefore, it is essential that a focused objective be arrived at and, once agreed on, used as a yardstick against which every piece of dialogue and visual technique is measured.

OBJECTIVE DEFINITION

In previous sections on television as well as in our radio discussion, we have talked about the need for clear articulation of what our message is trying to do. If for no reason other than cost, this specific goal-setting is given greatest emphasis in the television commercial. For in comparison with radio, television tends to be far more expensive to produce and very costly to air with station and network rate card prices continuing to soar. So much money will usually be invested in the preparation, testing, and broadcast placement of the television commercial that there can be no question as to what the spot is supposed to accomplish. This is why the actual objective often finds its way onto working copies of the script as a constant reminder of the project's reason for being; an unblinking quality control mechanism for the copy and picture ideas that must both typographically and conceptually follow it.

In this example of a standard noncopy data bloc for a television spot, the objective is not "to sell gum." That any spot is supposed to "sell" its product goes without saying. Rather, this commercial's written objective specifies a universe (subteens), a product characteristic (taste), and a viewer benefit flowing from that characteristic (the brightening of one's disposition/mood).

```
                    AIMED-WRITE ADVERTISING
                    radio-TV broadcast copy

SIMMONS GUM COMPANY                    SIGC-3862[1]
6-8-86                                 'TOOTH-TREAT TROLL'
6-21-86 rev                            TOOTH-TREAT GUM
7-8-86 rev adv. apprvd.
```

Objective: To demonstrate to subteens that the taste of Simmons Tooth-Treat Gum is so enlivening that it brightens the disposition of almost anyone.

Production Note: The locale is a picturesque though sinister-looking bridge spanning a forest ravine. A sharp-featured, scowling dwarf appears from under the bridge. Young (7-10 year old) boy and girl who encounter him are of contrasting types---one a dark brunette, the other a light blond.

Video	Audio
1. OPEN ON ESTABLISHING SHOT OF RAVINE.	MUSIC: LONELY, EERIE 'STORY-BOOK TYPE' THEME
	TROLL: I hate people etc.

Even if you are not required to set down the commercial's objective as part of the scripts you submit, fashion one for yourself at the earliest exploratory stage of the project and then fine-tune it as your thinking and/or directions from the client proceed. There is no better way to enforce communication precision than the construction of and adherence to such a goal-focusing statement.

Don't, however, lock yourself in too soon; don't set the objective in concrete before your deliberations and the product data have a chance to jell. True, time usually is of the essence, but take some of it to derive a direction that you've completely explored and with which you can effectively deal. Hours expended in the construction of ten meandering and therefore unusable approaches

---

1. For ease of tracking, many television commercials are now identified by a uniform eight-character code from the ISCI (Industry Standard Commercial Identification) system. The code designator is comprised of four letters assigned to a specific advertiser followed by four numbers to signify a particular spot. You will find these ISCI codings printed on several of the photoboards reproduced in this book, including this chapter's Figures 11–2, 11–4, 11–6, 11–7, and 11–11.

would have been far better devoted to the gestation of one, solid objective and a single spot that, like the ERA Real Estate creation in Figure 11–1, straightforwardly addresses it. What is this ERA photoboard's objective? Its clarity makes this question very easy to answer.

OBJECTIVE PORTRAYAL

Once you've refined, honed, twisted, and shifted that idea to the point that it constitutes an *incisive conclusion about a specific product benefit,* you can, with television, dig for the pictorial progression that will lead the viewer inevitably to that conclusion.

Figure 11–1. *(Courtesy of David R. Sackey, W. B. Doner and Company Advertising.)*

Here are three objectives, each containing its own product benefit and definitive verdict about same. What visual ideas would *you* put into play to articulate these objectives in commercials of your own creation?

```
The Bic Banana is the modern means to express yourself
distinctly.
```

```
Even for expert gamesplayers, the Othello game is the miraculous
compromise between challenge and simplicity.
```

```
Your gravel road won't stay road without Allied Calcium Chloride.
```

Do you have your pictorial progressions in mind? Now, fashion each progression into a single visual-specifying sentence, jot it down, and compare your three approaches to those adopted by the trio of advertising agencies that serviced these accounts. To reacquaint you with the three main creative vehicles in which television spots are conceived, the Bic Banana commercial is presented in Figure 11–2 in photoboard form, the Othello treatment in script form, and the Allied announcement (Figure 11–3) in storyboard form.

Video	Audio
GAMESMAKER APPEARS IN YOGA POSITION	(both VOICE & ANNC. Offcamera) ANNC.: The great gamesmaker. His search for the perfect game brought us
GAMESMAKER CAUSES CHECKER GAME TO APPEAR THRU CLOUD OF SMOKE	A simple game (SFX: THUNDER) checkers— VOICE:
GM REACTS TO VOICE	Dull. D.U.L.L. Dull! ANNC.:
GM CAUSES CHESS GAME TO APPEAR THRU CLOUD OF SMOKE.	A challenging game–(SFX: THUNDER) Chess— VOICE:
GM REACTS TO VOICE	Too complicated! ANNC.:

Wells, Rich, Greene, Inc./767 Fifth Avenue/New York, N.Y. 10022/Plaza 8-4300

CLIENT: Bic Pen Co.   CODE NO.: WBBM 3327
PRODUCT: Bic Banana   TITLE: "Shakespeare"
                                         LENGTH: :30

V.O.: For years, Shakespeare struggled to express himself.

And today, there are still people trying to figure out what he was talking about.

"To be or not to be."

What does it mean?

If he had a Bic Banana, he would've written: "I am. Take it or leave it."

(SFX: Pleased sounds from people in coffee house) Because you can express yourself with a Bic Banana.

You could write, sign, draw, mark, and mainly go crazy! You don't find that kind of expressiveness in a ballpoint.

In a ballpoint you find: "Wherefore art thou, Romeo"

In a Bic Banana you're gonna get,

"Romeo, you keep yourself nice. Let's get married."

Get a Bic Banana.

It comes in ten expressive colors!

Figure 11–2. *(Courtesy of Kenneth Olshan, Wells, Rich, Greene, Inc.)*

Video	Audio
GM CAUSES BACKGAMMON GAME TO APPEAR THRU CLOUD OF SMOKE.	An exciting game! (SFX: THUNDER) Backgammon—
	VOICE:
GM REACTS TO VOICE	Luck, just luck.
	ANNC.:

Figure 11-3. (Courtesy of Barry Base, Base Brown & Partners, Limited.)

Video	Audio
GM CAUSE OTHELLO TO APPEAR THRU LIGHTNING AND SMOKE	And finally—(SFX: THUNDER) Othello
GM NODS AFFIRMATIVE	VOICE:
	Othello?
	ANNC.:
GM DEMONSTRATES GAME	Othello, the new game of games that combines the simplicity of checkers with the challenge of chess and the excitement of backgammon.
	VOICE:
GM REACTS TO VOICE	Sure took you long enough.
	ANNC.:
PRODUCT SHOT OF OTHELLO IN A CLOUD OF SMOKE	Othello, the game of games—
PRODUCT LOGO GABRIEL LOGO	—by Gabriel

(Courtesy of Charles Einach, Nadler & Larimer.)

COMPULSORY DEMONSTRABILITY: THE D.D.Q.

As all three of the above objectives and their subsequent portrayals appreciate, television is the medium of *demonstration*. With its simultaneously moving audio and video lines, television is the real "show and tell" vehicle. Your viewers have come to expect a demonstration from the products they see on the tube and your client is paying big money to put it there. So as a copywriter, it is incumbent on you to use this costly capability to the fullest. The television commercial that does not demonstrate does not belong on television.

Can all products or services be demonstrated? Yes. Provided you are willing REALLY TO ANALYZE the assignment subject before you. And the best way to structure this analysis is via the following five-step question/answer process that we label *The Demo-Deriving Quintet:*

1. What is the subject's key attribute?
2. What benefit flows from that attribute?
3. What implement(s) make(s) the benefit most tangible?
4. What scene best showcases the implement(s)?
5. What happens in that scene? (What's the pictorial progression?)

1. What Is the Subject's Key Attribute?

You may recall our previous focus on "key attributes" in conjunction with the chapter 6 discussion of *Poetic Packaging*. There, the emphasis was on isolating this prime component of our product so the proper radio sounds could be enlisted to describe it. Here, we are seeking to cull out that same key attribute as the first step in determining which pictures will best delineate it. Most often this key attribute is, by itself, intangible, as in the "unobtrusiveness" core of the IBM copier commercial in Figure 11–4.

2. What Benefit Flows from That Attribute?

The important word in this second-level question is, of course, *benefit;* benefit in relation to the viewers at whom the commercial is directed. It is one thing,

Figure 11–4. *(Courtesy of Melissa Wohltman, Doyle Dane Bernbach Advertising.)*

for example, to use slow motion and freeze frame to show tennis players that your client's ball stays on the racket longer. But unless this attribute is unequivocally translated into the greater *control* that is thereby brought to your game, the viewer will be unimpressed. Similarly, we can expend 60 seconds or more in illuminating the coarse texture of our breakfast cereal. This will be wasted effort, however, if our geriatric universe isn't able to comprehend the digestive advantages this texture provides. In the IBM 'board, the isolated benefit is copier reliability—still, by itself, an intangible concept but one that brings the product's "unobtrusiveness" essence closer to home for its target executive audience.

It is this second step of our D.D.Q. analysis that most closely parallels and, under ideal circumstances, really determines the assignment *objective.* For, from a logical standpoint, we should ascertain the key attribute of our subject's product or service *before* latching onto an objective. Once we have identified the subject's prime element, once we have completed Step 1, we can then much more clearly translate this element into a consumer-related benefit—and fashion an objective that most efficiently proclaims that benefit. Recall that the Bic Pen objective centered on an "express yourself" benefit, the Othello game objective on the achievement of a simple yet challenging pastime, and the Allied Calcium Chloride objective on the preservation of nonjarring roadways. All three objectives thus brought their corporate essences into a consumer-relevant context to complete the Demo-Deriving Quintet's Step 2.

3. What Implement(s) Make(s) the Benefit Most Tangible?

Now, with the frustratingly nonvisual, initial two steps decided, and with the indispensable framework they provide in place, we can proceed to deal with concepts at which a camera can point. We can choose a pictorial referent for that product-derived and consumer-related benefit. In the IBM spot, the selected referent for reliable copiers is a paradoxically invisible machine. In the Bic commercial, Shakespeare symbolizes the ability to express oneself well. And in the Kendall Oil script and resulting photoboard (Figure 11–5) an unmarred ring of gold epitomizes the product's impressive maintenance abilities.

Video	Audio
KENDALL CAN AND GOLD RINGS IN FOREGROUND	ANNCR. (VO): Kendall Motor Oil protects engines from friction.
HAND PICKS UP RING.	To prove how well,
ECU OF ANNCR. AND RINGS.	ANNCR. (OC): we plated ordinary piston rings with pure gold,

TITLE: "GOLD RING" :30

ANNCR. (VO): Kendall Motor Oil protects engines from friction.

To prove how well,

ANNCR. (OC): we plated ordinary piston rings with pure gold

and ran them inside this engine for 5,000 miles.

Kendall friction fighters are better than car makers demand...

But can Kendall protect even soft gold?

Look......... No visible wear! That's protection!

Friction Fighting Kendall Motor Oil... for protection worth its weight in gold.

Produced by Al Paul Lefton Company Inc.

Figure 11–5.   *(Courtesy of Ken Merritt, Al Paul Lefton Company Inc.)*

Video	Audio
CUT TO: MED. SHOT ANNCR. AND ENGINE	and ran them inside this engine for 5,000 miles.
HOLD UP CAN.	Kendall friction fighters are better than car makers demand—

Video	Audio
CUT TO HAND RIM RINGS	but can Kendall protect even soft gold?
ECU ANNCR. AND RINGS.	Look---No visible wear! That's protection!
BEAUTY SHOT OF CAN AND RINGS. <u>TITLE</u>: 'Protection worth its weight in gold'.	Friction Fighting Kendall Motor Oil---for protection worth its weight in gold.

(Courtesy of Ken Merritt, Al Paul Lefton Company, Inc.)

It should be clear by now that the range of pictorial implements from which you, as a copywriter, can select is as broad as the ever-widening technology of film and tape can provide. Today, small, local accounts can obtain productional services that, until recently, were available only to the costly, national distributed commercials of the largest companies in the land. But this does not mean you select a visual implement simply because it's now within budgetary reach or because a lot of other commercials are using it. That is nothing more than "me-too" advertising; a dangerous practice because it only invites more imitation with consequent loss of identity. And "in those cases where 'me-too' advertising has led to 'me-three' look-alikes," reports commercial testing expert Dave Vadehra, "anything short of innovative will surely be as boring to the viewer as it is confining to the advertiser."[2] If, on the other hand, your chosen benefit implement is a natural and inevitable outgrowth of the conclusions reached in the Demo-Deriving Quintet's first two levels, that implement's intrinsic relationship to your product will make copying by others counterproductive.

4. What Scene Best Showcases the Implement(s)?

In some assignments, this aspect is decided almost simultaneously with the third step above. To endanger a gold piston ring, for instance, it immediately follows that we need an engine in a service garage. To picture an "invisible" office machine, we require an office interior. That the IBM copier itself did not even appear in its commercial is entirely appropriate since we primarily seek visual referents for the *product benefit* rather than being content only with static, inexpensive shots of the product itself.

2. Richard Morgan, "The Decline of Me-Too Advertising," *ADWEEK/Midwest*, February, 1984, p. C.R. 8.

In other assignments, such as in the Bic approach, the selected benefit implement may mandate placement in more than one environment. To make Shakespeare a convincing *modern* "expresser," therefore, he and the benefit he represents jump from the Elizabethan court to a contemporary coffee house. This environmental interplay thus sets up a clear contrast between the benefit-symbolizing referent and the scene in which it reacts, and consequently provides a real motivating force for the message as a whole. Similarly, in the Figure 11–6 Weight Watchers commercial, the equation of the product line with diverse favorite restaurants is engendered first in restaurant settings. Then this point is

Figure 11–6. *(Courtesy of Melissa Wohltman, Doyle Dane Bernbach Advertising.)*

driven home by transporting the favorite food *to the home* while leaving the calories behind.

Under still other circumstances, the implement and its environment both work together to heighten a developing *comparison* rather than a contrast. The Ocean Spray spot in Figure 11-7 is a focused example of this demonstration strategy. The concept of the product as a refreshing liquid treat is exemplified in a street vendor and his cart. This benefit is then amplified by putting him in a natural street environment into which a desired comparison with the more conventional lemonade can be worked easily and smoothly.

KELLY , NASON INCORPORATED *Advertising*	Client: OCEAN SPRAY Product: GRAN-GRAPE/CRAN WAGON	Title: LEMONADE STAND Comm'l. No.: OGSG-6013 Length: 30 SECONDS

FRANK: Cranberries!!!
KIDS: Hi Frank!

FRANK: How's business?
KID: Too much competition.

FRANK: Sell Ocean Spray Cran-Grape... sweet juicy grapes and tangy cranberries- all natural flavor.

Try it with ginger ale...

and even ice cream.

KIDS: Wow!!

FRANK: There are lots of ways to use Ocean Spray...Cran-Grape, Cranberry Juice Cocktail, and Ocean Spray Cranapple.

KIDS: Cran-Grape! Ocean Spray Cran-Grape!

FRANK: Cranberries!!!

Figure 11-7. *(Courtesy of Irene Taffel, Kelly, Nason Inc.)*

5. What Happens in That Scene?
(What's the Pictorial Progression?)

Finally, after carefully thinking through the first four levels of D.D.Q. analysis, we are in a position to determine the scenario, the actual storyline of our commercial. It is important that the tale we are spinning unfold in a manner that continues to hold viewer attention while, at the same time, keeping the product benefit at center stage. The story that is so dominant that the mission it serves gets lost is a story that should never have been told. Fortunately, if the first four levels of *Demo-Deriving* have been scrupulously and honestly dealt with, the resulting scenario should be so product/benefit actuated that it is impossible to separate the story from the goods in whose support it evolved. Such is certainly the case with the Figure 11–8 Champion commercial, in which two interrelated stories are separated by a locally customizable solution segment in Frame 4.

This Champion spot also doubly conforms to what John O'Toole, the board chairman of Foote, Cone & Belding, years ago isolated as the need for *commercial tension:*

> It seems to me that something has to happen very quickly in a commercial, much as in a print ad, to engage and hold the prospect. I suspect it must occur in the first five seconds.
>
> It also seems to me (and again, this is not dissimilar to the print experience) that the commercial must establish a tension, a sort of magnetic field compelling enough to overcome the viewer's natural tendency to discuss the preceding program material, to listen to someone else do so, to go to the bathroom or to simply disengage his mind.
>
> In addition, it seems to me that the tension must center on, or lead quickly to, some question the viewer might want answered, some need or want or problem he suddenly recognizes or acknowledges, some insight into the reality of his life. Whichever, it must relate logically to the product or service that is being advertised.[3]

All spots need not be as dramatically life-threatening as the Champion commercial to achieve a storyline that both demonstrates a benefit and possesses the O'Toole-advocated tension. For other clients and objectives, a much simpler scenario may be called for. As evidence, page 344 features a truly classic demonstration for the Broxodent Automatic Toothbrush (Figure 11–9)—a demonstration that additional props and characters would only clutter.

Despite the obvious differences among the clients and treatments that have been presented in the preceding pages, they all share and exhibit a persuasive demonstrability that flows unstoppably from the central attribute of each product being advertised. Notice that nowhere in the *Demo-Deriving Quintet* have we mentioned camera angles, special effects banks, or fancy superimpositions. Instead, the process allows the subject itself to determine what should be done and the visual components that most naturally should be called on to do it. There is plenty of time to worry about specific production techniques once each of *Demo-Deriving's* five questions has been successfully met and, in order,

3. John O'Toole, writing in "Monday Memo," *Broadcasting Magazine*, April 17, 1978, p. 14.

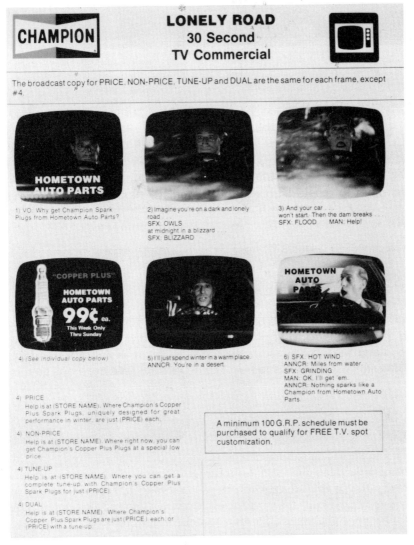

The broadcast copy for PRICE, NON-PRICE, TUNE-UP and DUAL are the same for each frame, except #4.

1) VO: Why get Champion Spark Plugs from Hometown Auto Parts?

2) Imagine you're on a dark and lonely road . . .
SFX: OWLS
at midnight in a blizzard . . .
SFX: BLIZZARD

3) And your car won't start. Then the dam breaks . . .
SFX: FLOOD   MAN: Help!

4) (See individual copy below)

5) I'll just spend winter in a warm place.
ANNCR: You're in a desert.

6) SFX: HOT WIND
ANNCR: Miles from water.
SFX: GRINDING
MAN: OK, I'll get 'em.
ANNCR: Nothing sparks like a Champion from Hometown Auto Parts.

4) PRICE
Help is at (STORE NAME). Where Champion's Copper Plus Spark Plugs, uniquely designed for great performance in winter, are just (PRICE) each.

4) NON-PRICE
Help is at (STORE NAME). Where right now, you can get Champion's Copper Plus Plugs at a special low price.

4) TUNE-UP
Help is at (STORE NAME). Where you can get a complete tune-up with Champion's Copper Plus Spark Plugs for just (PRICE).

4) DUAL
Help is at (STORE NAME). Where Champion's Copper Plus Spark Plugs are just (PRICE) each, or (PRICE) with a tune-up.

A minimum 100 G.R.P. schedule must be purchased to qualify for FREE T.V. spot customization.

Figure 11-8. *(Courtesy of Dan Nelson, W. B. Doner and Company.)*

answered. To "think production" any earlier is to sell a video technique rather than a client's wares.

The reason that people with no experience in broadcast production often make better television copywriters than those who come out of the television industry is that the former lack the background to concentrate on anything but the *message concept.* The broadcast or film veteran, on the other hand, has spent so much time with the machinery of the medium that questions of execution keep getting in the way of the much more central questions of content. If you have, or are acquiring, a television or film production background—fine. That knowledge will help you polish your finished scripts and 'boards so that

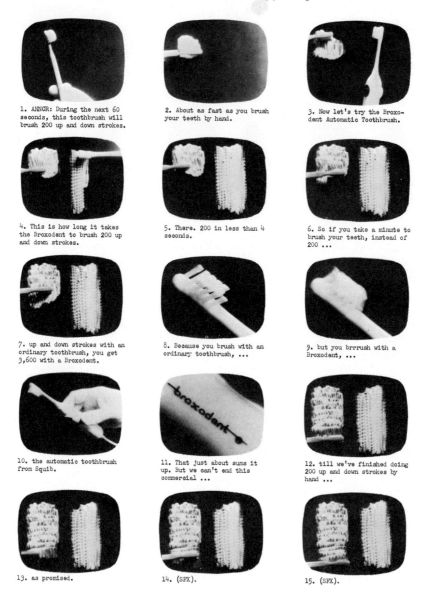

1. ANNCR: During the next 60 seconds, this toothbrush will brush 200 up and down strokes.

2. About as fast as you brush your teeth by hand.

3. Now let's try the Broxodent Automatic Toothbrush.

4. This is how long it takes the Broxodent to brush 200 up and down strokes.

5. There. 200 in less than 4 seconds.

6. So if you take a minute to brush your teeth, instead of 200 ...

7. up and down strokes with an ordinary toothbrush, you get 3,600 with a Broxodent.

8. Because you brush with an ordinary toothbrush, ...

9. but you brrrush with a Broxodent, ...

10. the automatic toothbrush from Squib.

11. That just about sums it up. But we can't end this commercial ...

12. till we've finished doing 200 up and down strokes by hand ...

13. as promised.

14. (SFX).

15. (SFX).

Figure 11–9.   *(Courtesy of Robert Levenson, Doyle Dane Bernbach Advertising.)*

they will more easily jump the gap between the creation and production phases of a commercial's development. Just don't let your technical expertise clutter up your mind and your advertisement any earlier in the process. Don't, whatever you do, let the production run away with the message in the conceptual stage or it will invariably run away with the message once it gets "on the tube."

Keep structuring your commercial development process via the *Demo-Deriving Quintet.* It will not only help keep your television creations "on track" but will also make you a more focused and disciplined visual writer. And just to review the Quintet's five steps, and the progressive interaction of each of those steps on the others, let's follow the labors of one trainee group as it tried to evolve a spot for a hypothetical Terry Cuff Ring campaign.

The Terry Cuff Ring (an actual though largely unadvertised product) is an oval-shaped and open-ended, flexible metal band, imported from England. Cyclists clamp it above their ankle to keep pant cuffs from snagging in the bicycle chain.

What is the Terry Cuff Ring's key attribute? After unproductive forays into aspects of "protection" and "safety"—forays that broke down in later steps—the trainees (in some unjustified panic) clutched at the idea of *convenience*.

What benefit flows from convenience? Most obviously, quickness of use. The Terry Cuff Ring can be slipped onto one's leg in far less time than it takes to position and tie a lace or small piece of rope.

What implement(s) make(s) the benefit most tangible? This too is very obvious in this case and, with a little fine-tuning, the trainees decided upon a trouser leg that sported a substantial cuff.

What scene best showcases the implement? To determine this took some time and seemed to present several possible ways to go until one of the trainees perceptively pointed out that: (1) the product was English-made; (2) English-made goods have a positive (if not wholly deserved) reputation for quality; and (3) there were American-made versions of the Terry Cuff Ring from which it must be distinguished. An English motif seemed to be the natural response to these factors, and what is more English than a bobby (English policeman)? Whose trouser leg more appropriate than his?

What happens in that scene? Whatever the event, it was crucial that it set up an episode in which the previously selected "quickness of use" benefit could prominently be showcased and that it be the bobby who derived this benefit. After more trainee discussion the scenario took shape:

A typical British crook (complete with little tweed cap, black eye mask, and turtle neck sweater) bursts out of a village thatched-roof bank carrying a bag of money. He runs toward his cycle but, enroute, sees and is seen by our stalwart bobby who is standing down the street near his own bicycle that sports a ''Constable'' sign on the handlebars. The nervous robber, after some obvious disconcertion, jumps on his bike but his heavy trouser leg is already enmeshed in the chain. Frantically, he pulls the tie string off the bag of money and attempts to lace it around his cuff. A view of the bobby then displays his exquisite poise and confidence as he pulls a Terry Cuff Ring out of his pocket and effortlessly places it on his trouser leg. The robber is still tying his lace with money falling out of the now-open bag as the bobby rides up and arrests him. The Terry Cuff Ring triumphs again.

Visual technology, and, in fact, the determination of the entire sound track, could come later. What the trainee group had succeeded in doing was to shape a compelling demonstration that possessed flow, held interest, and clearly defined both the specific product and the benefit that the viewer would accrue from using it. If you want to write television copy that *is* truly television, go ye and do likewise. Provide your television treatments with demonstrations that are so intrinsic, so relevant, that you never need to call on some overexposed announcer to scream the CEBUS-activating words: "Here's proof."

THE PRODUCT NAME HELPS, TOO

As you concentrate on your treatment's objective, the portrayal of that objective, and the means by which you mesh a visual demonstration with both of the above, don't forget that the product name must come through it all loud and clear. The viewer has to be made aware, and be able to recall, that the *Terry Cuff Ring* helped the bobby, the *Broxodent* beat the ordinary toothbrush by 56 seconds, and that it's *Champion Spark Plugs* to thank for dependable starts. Brand recall is as important in television as it is on radio and should be promoted as part and parcel of the benefit-displaying demonstration.

The same *identity line* formulation principles that were presented in the chapter on radio commercials can also be applied to television but with the additional requirements that the ID line have conspicuous *visual* relevance to the demonstrations being featured. Thus, to make it on television as well as radio, the commercials in which these ID lines are featured must let the viewer *see* that Allied's Calcium Chloride does indeed "keep the road out of the ditch"; *see* that Kendall Motor Oil's protection is "worth its weight in gold"; *see* that you brush with an ordinary toothbrush but you "brrrush with a Broxodent." And, as in radio, the televison ID line that is *also generic*—that also signifies its product-use category—usually has a longer and more functional life expectancy. Here are some video identity lines each of whose collective components meet all these criteria:

```
Joy cleans down to the shine; and that's a nice reflection on
you.

Krylon Paint; no runs, no drips, no errors.

Head and Shoulders hates your dandruff but loves your hair.

Arm & Hammer---a nice little secret for your refrigerator.

Our L'eggs fit your legs.

Skoal; the tobacco you don't have to smoke to enjoy.

The Michigan Bell Yellow Pages; next to the phone there's nothing
better.

Miracle Whip; the Bread spread from Kraft.

Nothing sparks like a Champion.
```

Whether or not an ID line is part of your brand recall strategy, this recall needs to be stimulated by both audio and video cues that are well integrated into the fabric of your spot as a whole. Probably the ultimate in sight and sound brand IDing was the bizarre, but nonetheless carefully calculated, Bic Banana promotion featured in Figure 11–10.

Fortunately for the sanity of copywriters and viewers alike, most products and most spot objectives do not lend themselves to such a brand recall binge. As the "Banana Schoolhouse" treatment illustrates, however, opportunities that do exist and can be exploited by well-directed creativity deserve every rave that they get. Not because they're "weird," but because they work; because they shoehorn the product name into every nook and cranny of the message while still accomplishing a visual objective and the demonstration that makes it manifest.

A more recent and more mainstream example of audio/visual brand recall enhancement is the Cold Factor 12 approach in Figure 11–11. Here, the product is either visually or aurally identified in every frame from #2 to the end. Further, the "12-hour staying power" application itself is emphasized in the spot's successive moon and sun backdrops.

THE STORYBOARD PRESENTATION

In checking for sound track and pictorial brand recall as in evaluating the commercial's overall concept progression, the storyboard is most often the

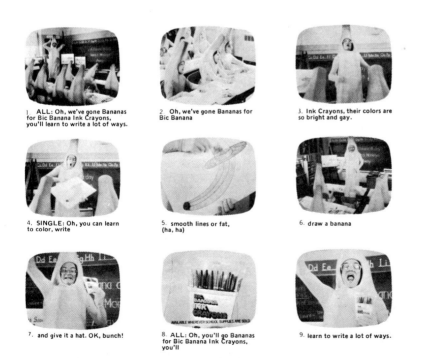

1. ALL: Oh, we've gone Bananas for Bic Banana Ink Crayons, you'll learn to write a lot of ways.

2. Oh, we've gone Bananas for Bic Banana

3. Ink Crayons, their colors are so bright and gay.

4. SINGLE: Oh, you can learn to color, write

5. smooth lines or fat, (ha, ha)

6. draw a banana

7. and give it a hat. OK, bunch!

8. ALL: Oh, you'll go Bananas for Bic Banana Ink Crayons, you'll

9. learn to write a lot of ways.

Figure 11–10. *(Courtesy of Kenneth Olshan, Wells, Rich, Greene.)*

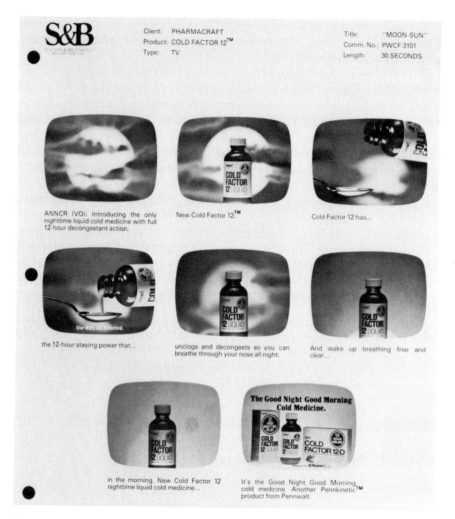

Figure 11–11. *(Courtesy of Mimi Rydre, Sullivan & Brugnatelli Advertising Inc.)*

central focus of attention and main creative battleground. Since both writer and art director sink or swim by what is on that 'board as well as by how well they *present* what is on it, you must know how to handle yourself and your multi-frame progeny in the review sessions, where their fate is ruthlessly determined.

First of all, it must be made unequivocally clear that a good presentation won't save a bad 'board but a bad presentation can certainly kill a good one. If you are as glib of tongue as you are of pen the fates have shone kindly on you. But don't come to rely on your "gift of gab" as a substitute for disciplined and well-ordered preparation of your assignments. Water-cooler mythology notwithstanding, client representatives, creative directors, and account supervisors do not hold their seats in those storyboard review sessions because they are easily duped.

By the same token, the best 'board still needs some well-fashioned promotion to transform it from a static piece of cardboard into a dynamic, breathing story. Even walking in with an approach in which you are supremely confident, you must be aware that the storyboard review session requires you to perform three simultaneous selling jobs on its behalf:

1. You are selling yourself as an articulate, knowledgeable product-wise copywriter. Your art director is normally there to help you with the presentation but your creative judges expect the most precise treatment defense to come out of your mouth. You, after all, are supposed to be the duo's wordsmith.
2. You are selling your 'board as an appropriate, even heaven-sent answer to the client's marketing needs. Once you've shown yourself to be a competent professional, you must then prove that you've fully applied this competence to the 'board at hand.
3. You are selling the product or service being featured in that 'board. This, of course, is the ultimate task of all advertising, but your approach will never get a chance to accomplish it if you have not surmounted the previous two selling barriers.

Assuming that, as a backdrop, you understand the tri-leveled, persuasive role you are expected to play, let's proceed with the five-step unveiling that constitutes the review session's usual liturgy:

1. State the specific purpose, the defined objective, that the spot is intended to achieve. Depending on the situation, this may also involve an explanation of *why television* is required to meet the objective, why (if television commercials for the product are already being run) this additional treatment is needed, and how it will fit in with the style and orientation of all other advertising the client is currently running or planning to run on behalf of this product. This may include a discussion of print as well as broadcast campaign material and strategies.

   Don't slight this first step just because it appears more a marketing than a creative concern. Copywriters today are as involved in writing copy platforms and strategies as they are in penning commercials with modern competitive forces no longer permitting writers to be oblivious to the dynamics of the marketplace. The evolution of VALS and other psychographic targeting systems discussed in chapter 4 indicates just how extensively copy styling and market delineation must now intermesh. Only after you have justified your proposed orientation in terms of business realities can your storyboard presentation proceed to the subsequent explication of creative values.
2. Unveil your treatment's video properties slowly. Do this via a frame-by-frame progression that serves to put the picture in your reviewers' minds. Explain any technical terms and effects quickly and simply. You don't want your presentation to become a telefilm production seminar any more than you want your finished commercial to submerge the message in the medium.

   Even in an informal review session, a pointer is helpful in directing attention to the proper frame without blocking anyone's view. A collapsible antenna from an obsolete transistor radio makes it easy always to have a pointer in your pocket and is another indication that you're in well-prepared command of the situation.

3. Next, with pointer at the ready, go through the entire commercial again, now articulating the audio as you direct attention to each succeeding picture. Read dialogue in a style as similar as possible to the way in which you expect the talent to read it. If the music background is important, you may also want your art director to hum along or, especially if your partner is tone deaf, a cassette recorder can be called on to suggest the general musical effect you have in mind. Above all, keep your portrayal of the audio clear so everyone knows exactly what the sound track is saying.

4. Now present the entire storyboard again, combining both audio and video descriptions. This is your chance to make that whole greater than the sum of its parts—and your audience's opportunity to put the complete communication into interlocked perspective. If the reviewers (who are handsomely paid to pay close attention to your proposed spot) don't understand the concept by this time, the bored and listless consumers on the other side of the tube will never get it. Step 4 should pull everything together with all the assurance of a steel trap springing shut.

5. Finally, close with a solid and meticulously prepared summary statement that reemphasizes the storyboard's objective, the mechanism by which it meets that objective, and the indispensable way in which the television medium is enlisted to serve the project's needs. At this juncture, the meeting is normally opened for questions and follow-up discussion. You answer these questions in a resolute and nondefensive manner that spotlights the 'board rather than your proprietary interest in it.

For practice, take the following Buick "Bad to the Bone" storyboard (Figure 11–12 and stage your own five-step exposition of it to your favorite full-length mirror. This should familiarize you with the presentation process without the additional confounding variable that comes from ego-involvement with a 'board you yourself have created. This exercise will also force you to dig out and articulate the spot's central objective and the manner in which it's portrayed. Once you're satisfied with your handling of "Bad to the Bone," you should be ready to attempt a storyboard demonstration of one of your own creative concepts.

Before leaving the judgment arena, here are the seven deadly sins that copy trainees are especially tempted to commit in the zealous fostering of their 'boards. Mending your ways now will prevent your concepts' damnation later:

1. The objective is clearly stated—but is never really linked to the treatment being proposed. Reviewers are thereby left to wonder whether they misunderstood the objective or whether the advocated approach is at all compatible with it.

2. The consumer benefit is stated in negative terms ("this spot for the Futzmobile is intended to keep people from buying an imported car"). Audiences seldom remember what they *shouldn't* do—especially if you haven't really bannered what they are *supposed* to do.

3. The overall presentation lacks flow. Instead of each step smoothly seguing into the next, reviewers are assailed with such stop/start lines as: "That completes step two. Now let's move on to the audio." Your oral transitions, in short, should be as fluid and graceful as your written and pictorial ones.

4. The presentation is projected into the storyboard rather than out to the reviewers. This gives the impression that you are self-conscious about the approach being proposed—and sets up a reviewer suspicion that you may have a right to be. Use

the aforementioned pointer and a few inconspicuous notecards so you can talk to the people rather than the props. This avoids blocking the line of sight and doesn't force you into the awkward contortions required to read audio blocks off the storyboard itself.

5. Production costs are totally ignored. Saying, "I don't care what this costs because it's a zowie approach" will never stretch a ten thousand dollar budget to thirty thousand—or a fifty thousand limit to seventy. Do some prior research to obtain at least an approximation of your 'board's shooting price tag. And, if no one bothered to tell you, find out the budgetary range that the particular account has devoted to video production in the past.

6. "Brand recall" is advanced as the commercial's objective. Yet, as you should be aware by now, brand recall is useful and feasible only when it is tied to a specific, consumer-related benefit. It is the articulation of this benefit that constitutes the core of your spot's objective and through which brand recall can be implemented. People don't remember names that mean nothing to them.

7. Inadvertently, or out of an acute sense of frustration, the client or assignment is belittled in an attempt to make the treatment look more praiseworthy: "This is a terrible account to try to do anything with on television but—." To paraphrase a famous theatrical truism, there are no terrible accounts, only unimaginative copywriters.

Most important of all, you must be careful not to assume your 'board is yourself. Put some distance between you and it—not physical distance, or professional distance, but *psychological* distance. All advertising review sessions, and storyboard presentations in particular, can generate a lot of sometimes heated discussion and often pointed criticism. If you see your 'board as a total projection of your psyche—if you can't separate attacks on it from attacks on you—real psychological damage can result. Serena Deutsch of Riverside Psychotherapy Associates, who treats a number of patients from the advertising community, warns that a creative person's strong identification with his or her work can be dangerous. "If they so identify with their work and the work is attacked, then they feel attacked," Deutsch observes. "Sometimes they have trouble seeing the difference."[4]

AVOIDING THE STORYBOARD

Now that you've absorbed all the whys and wherefores of storyboard presentation, let it be said that there are those in the industry who would circumvent their use altogether—not the use of presentation sessions but the employment of storyboards in them. Such a situation makes the review arena all the more rigorous for the copywriter since there is now nothing to capture that judgment panel's attention except your words on paper and in the air. It is as though you are back pushing a radio concept but, due to the cost factor, with stakes that are much, much higher.

4. Debbie Seaman, "Creatives Take Their Problems to Creative Therapy," *ADWEEK/Midwest,* September 24, 1984, p. 50.

Figure 11–12. *(Courtesy of H. E. Savage, Buick Motor Division, General Motors, and James Ramsey, McCann-Erickson Inc.)*

Two decades ago, advertising veteran Alfred L. Goldman made one of the strongest cases on record for *not* using storyboards, a case that revolves around these key points and that is still used as anti-'board ammunition today:

> We discovered that beyond the selling words, pictures, and ideas, there was a "fourth" dimension: a kind of total impression that not only underscored the words, pictures and ideas, but which turned out to be an experience in itself; a kind of "cathedral effect" (thank you Mr. McLuhan) that spread its wings over the entire commercial and helped win friends and influence sales.
>
> Second only to the basic selling idea, and far more vital than isolated words and pictures, this total impression is something that no storyboard can deliver.
>
> In fact, the storyboard tends to kill it. We are looking at a print interpretation of a motion picture idea. And we are looking at it in a logical series of pictures with captions on a frame-by-frame basis. What's more, we are forced to accept what a talented artist can do with a drawing pencil in the suffocating confines of a little box measuring a few inches wide by a few inches deep.
>
> Neither the artist nor the still camera can capture the essence of the idea as it will emerge on a fluid piece of film. There is a distortion of values, too,

because we illustrate "pretty girl goes here" and "pretty package goes there" and it has nothing to do with the true dimensions of time and space as they will occur in the finishing commercial. . . .

So how can you beat the storyboard booby trap? . . .

Go to the client with a script. Let your creative people play it out by creating a movie in the client's mind. They can explain, describe, act out, flash pictures, use sound effects and do whatever they must to set the stage and position the players just as if they were describing a feature film they had seen. Then, read the script against this background and the whole reel will unwind in the client's mind and he'll get the full "cathedral effect" of your commercial. When he "buys" the idea, he is buying a *tour de force* rather than meaningless isolated pictures and words as they appear in a storyboard.[5]

Much more recently, Bob Abel, the president of his own commercial production company, contributed additional arguments to the "ban the 'board" cause. Abel maintains that if agencies

concentrate on the concept, on the idea and on the strategy, a storyboard is unnecessary. In fact, the agency will be better off without one. This might sound like sacrilege, but most agency storyboards only indicate those things the agency already knows how to do and those techniques with which the agency is already familiar. When you want to make a breakthrough commercial, you must be able to use techniques you've never tried before and don't yet know how to do. This is the only way you can push the production company to creative and technical levels that go beyond anything it has achieved previously.[6]

Toward the possibility that you someday find yourself in a "no storyboard" ballpark, prepare now to erect the "cathedral effect" of which Goldman spoke. And even if you never have to face a television review session without your trusty 'board, the communication dexterity that comes from successfully presenting pictures without pictures will stand you in good stead in describing radio treatments, too. Words are words whether scrawled on paper or gliding through your dentures. Particularly in the advertising business, you must learn to string them effectively together in both contexts.

As an exercise to hone your oral abilities, take the following Fireman's Fund script and "play it out" for a friend. Then evaluate your effectiveness by having that friend tell it back to you. Did the commercial's objective survive the translation? If so, you're on your way. If not, if the point of the spot got lost between A and B, you really didn't comprehend the objective yourself or you lost sight of it in your efforts to convey pictorial brilliance and snippets of sound track. Strive to make your oral presentation as much a cohesive, *demonstrative* totality as is the commercial creation on which that presentation is based.

5. Alfred Goldman, writing in "Monday Memo," *Broadcasting Magazine*, May 1, 1967, p. 20.
6. Robert Abel, "How to Create a Breakthrough Commercial," *ADS Magazine*, September–October, 1983, p. 72.

Video	Audio
1. OPEN ON MIKE IN CU.	<u>MIKE:</u> You know, choosing business insurance can be a slippery business.
2. WIDEN SHOT AS HE TAPS HAT.	So Fireman's Fund suggests: play it safe with this sign:
3. CUT TO RED SPOTLIGHT.	(<u>MUSIC: STAB.</u>)
4. CUT TO BLUE SPOTLIGHT.	(<u>STAB.</u>)
5. CUT TO TWO SKATERS' FEET AS THEY MEET AMIDST SPRAY OF ICE.	(<u>STAB.</u>)
6. DISSOLVE TO SKATERS CIRCLING RED CIRCLE IN ICE.	(<u>RELEASES INTO WALTZ. ESTABLISH AND DUCK UNDER.</u>)
7. DISSOLVE TO GIRL SKATING ACROSS SIGN.	<u>MIKE:</u> (V/O) It belongs to someone—
8. DISSOLVE TO BOY LIFTING GIRL HIGH IN AIR.	—who sells our insurance.
9. DISSOLVE TO BOY SKATING ACROSS SIGN.	Who's free to choose from several companies—
10. DISSOLVE TO SPINNING FEET.	—to get you—
11. DISSOLVE TO BOY LEAPING ACROSS EAGLE IN SIGN.	—the best policy and price.
12. DISSOLVE TO BOY'S SPINNING FACE.	

Video	Audio
13. DISSOLVE TO PULLBACK AS SKATERS SKATE ACROSS FULL FLYING I SIGN.	MIKE: In short, your independent insurance agent. Who serves <u>you</u> first. So for great insurance—
14. CUT BACK TO MIKE IN CU. SKATERS AND RINK BEHIND HIM.	—call one today, and break the ice!
15. DISSOLVE TO END TITLE:	(V/O) In the Yellow Pages: Fireman's Fund Insurance Companies.

Fireman's Fund Insurance
Companies

Subsidiaries of American
Express

(Courtesy of Fireman's Fund Insurance Companies and Cunningham & Walsh, San Francisco.)

You may wish to ask yourself whether the trial presentation of the Fireman's Fund script was easier or more laborious than your practice unveiling of the Buick 'board. The answer to this question will help reveal for you the unique differences between script and storyboard "selling" as well as your own presentational strengths and weaknesses.

If you found both exercises difficult, remember that this difficulty will be ego-compounded when it's your *own* creations that have to be pitched. Nevertheless, whether boosting a 'board or selling a script, you must strive to make your approach stand out—and stand out in a credible, relevant way. For, if it can't attract favorable attention in a session called specifically to debut it, you can't expect your message to survive in the wilderness of television air schedules.

Attracting consumer attention to the television commercial is becoming a greater challenge all the time. QC Productions' Tony Quin and Bob Cambridge remind copywriters that "your commercial will be viewed in the context of many other images and commercials, all competing for the viewer's attention. Only the best, in terms of creativity, execution and impact, will break through the blur and drone and become embedded in the viewer's consciousness. The viewer is a tough nut to crack, but it can be done."[7] One key reason it can be

7. Tony Quin and Bob Cambridge, writing in "Monday Memo," *Broadcasting Magazine*, April 11, 1983, p. 22.

done is that "your audience," observes Barry Day of McCann-Erickson World-wide, "carries around in its dustbin of a mind just about every reference you're capable of dredging up. TV sees to it that nothing gets thrown away and every-thing is in a constant present tense. All that matters is that you treat the refer-ences with reverence, style and wit."[8]

A RUMINATION ON 'DR,' INFOMERCIALS, AND RETAILING

We cannot close this chapter without a brief consideration of copy creation for the direct market and local merchant trenches. Direct response advertising for radio was discussed in chapter 8; all the tenets introduced there also apply here to television DR messages. That is, the TV direct response ad should (1) state the product cost clearly and repeatedly; (2) get the viewer involved early; (3) show how the product can impinge on the viewer's life; (4) take viewer objections into account; (5) make product exclusivity unmistakable; (6) stress the need for immediate action; (7) describe product attributes in positive, tangible terms, and (8) communicate the specific purchase process.

Since television has both sound and picture available to accomplish these objectives, the copywriter enjoys greater flexibility in message design. Phone numbers can be supered on the screen, for example, thus freeing the sound-track for other information. Remember, in most television DR messages, you are, in direct marketer Freeman Gosden's words,

> selling the offer, not your product. This is especially true in lead generation programs where you are trying to get people to identify themselves as someone who might be interested. Once you have enticed them with the offer, you can sell them in person, by phone or by mail much more easily. . . . State your offer prominently. If you bury your offer, you might as well not even use one. People are used to seeing offers prominently displayed. They also want to learn all they can about the offer—because that is what they are responding to. . . . State your offer's benefit clearly. People are not buying your product and they are not really buying your offer. They are buying the benefits of your offer. Offers are not perceived to be good unless you tell the audience they are good. Benefits, benefits, benefits."[9]

The following direct-response commercial epitomizes this selling of the offer (free information on cut-rate travel fares) and its fundamental benefit ("getting the world on sale"). The ultimate product, on which the writer wisely chose not to concentrate, is DTI Membership. This spot also illustrates the accomplish-ment of each of our earlier-mentioned DR objectives—even though it is only 60-seconds in length. True, the specific membership cost (the actual product) is not mentioned, but the price-tag for the offer (club information) is communi-cated: it is *free* and so is the call to order it.

8. Barry Day, " '84's 10 Best," *ADS Magazine*, December, 1984, p. 32.
9. Freeman Gosden, "Marketing and Making an Offer," *ADWEEK/Midwest*, April 30, 1984, p. 68.

Video	Audio
2 EMPTY AIRPLANE SEATS KEYED OVER FILM FOOTAGE OF PLANE IN SKY.	<u>ANNCR. (VO):</u> The unsold airplane seat. Until now, nobody flew in it!
EMPTY CABIN KEYED OVER FILM FOOTAGE OF OCEAN LINER.	The unsold cruise cabin. Until now, nobody sailed in it!

MEMBERSHIP CARD KEYED OVER SKY WITH DIS ACTION.
<u>SUPER:</u> (lower third)
    Unsold trips at discount
    prices
	But now---with this card---as a member of DTI, you can buy unsold travel space. And save up to 60% off the regular price.

DIS MEMBERSHIP CARD TO REVEAL 2 EMPTY SEATS. EMPTY SEATS DISSOLVE TO SEATS OCCUPIED BY TWO MODELS. <u>SUPER:</u> 1-800-000-0000	If you can travel on 6 weeks' notice or less, you should call now for free information about this unusual travel club.

DIS PHOTOS OF PARIS, ROME, SPHINX, ETC.
<u>SUPER:</u> (lower third)
    Full-fare service at
    15%-60% discount
	While everyone else is paying <u>full-fare</u> <u>rates</u> for exciting trips to all parts of the world,
	
	DTI members pay only a <u>fraction</u> of the regular rate for the <u>same</u> <u>trip</u>---and the same <u>guaranteed</u> reservations.

MEMBERSHIP CARD KEYED OVER SKY, DIS TO FULL SCREEN
<u>SUPER:</u> (lower third)
    Call now for free brochure
    with DTI trips and prices
	You are invited to <u>join</u> <u>the</u> <u>club</u>---so call now for free information about DTI—

SPINNING WORLD GLOBE IS DISSOLVED IN BEHIND CARD. <u>SUPER</u> REMAINS.	—<u>where</u> <u>the</u> <u>world</u> <u>is</u> <u>on</u> <u>sale</u> every day of the year. Here's the number:

Video	Audio

KILL LOWER THIRD SUPER AND REPLACE WITH:
SUPER:
   Call FREE
   1-800-000-0000
	For free information in the mail about DTI membership, call 800-000-0000. The call is free. 800-000-0000.

Written and produced by Barney Kramer, President and Creative Director, Direct Response Broadcasting Network, Phila. PA.

    Infomercials, a commercial category introduced in chapter 3, can also constitute a form of DR advertising. Expending anywhere from 90 seconds to 8 minutes, these descendents of the old newsreels and "PR" films provide a great deal more time to register the subject of your message. As its name implies, however, the *infomercial* decrees that more than just offer/benefit sell take place. The viewer must also be given specific and tangible *information* that can be of interest and value *in its own right.* In this 90-second spot, for example, the audience learns about the importance of a will.

Video	Audio

SILHOUETTE OF DOCUMENT
SUPER: (CRAWL UP OVER SIL.)
   This may be . . .
   (same as audio)
	ANNCR. (VO):
	
	This may be one of the most important documents of your life. It represents everything you own—and protects everyone you love.

CONTINUE CRAWL:
   Your will
   Now only $25
	Your will. You can have yours now for only $25.

DIS SLIDE LEFT (OF PREVIOUS VIDEO) REVEALS SPOKESMAN STANDING IN LAW LIBRARY	GENE CRANE: Do you know who will inherit your property if you do <u>not</u> leave a will?
SLOW ZOOM IN ON SPOKESMAN AS HE WALKS TOWARD DESK	Your house, your car, your savings—everything you've

Video	Audio
SUPER: Your property will be distributed by the State	worked for all of your life will be distributed by law--- and you will have <u>nothing</u> to say about it.
CU SPOKESMAN BEHIND DESK SUPER: Consumer Legal Services Trust	That's why every adult in America who owns <u>anything</u> should have a will. Now, thanks to Consumer Legal Services Trust,
HE PICKS UP QUESTIONNAIRE FROM DESK SUPER: Your will drawn up by a lawyer only $25	anyone who <u>wants</u> a will, can <u>have</u> a will, prepared by an attorney, for only $25---if you call for it now.
ZOOM IN ON QUESTIONNAIRE SUPER: (lower third) 1-800-000-0000	If you do call, you will receive this Will Questionnaire in the mail. It's simple and easy to complete and return from the comfort of your own home.
HE PUTS QUESTIONNAIRE ON DESK SUPER: (DIS EFFECTS) No lawyer to visit No time lost No costly legal fees	There is no need to visit a lawyer. No need to take time from work. And no need to pay hundreds of dollars in legal fees.
CU SPOKESMAN SUPER: (lower third) Your legal, simple will Prepared by a lawyer	Your Will will be prepared according to your wishes by an attorney in your state, and will be sent to you---in the mail---ready to sign.
SUPER: (lower third) Call now to order Your will for $25	So, if you want to protect the people you love, this is your opportunity to call and order your will now for only $25. Here's the number:
FULL SCREEN CHYRON	ANNCR. (VO):

Video	Audio
Call Free 1-800-000-0000	To order your legal will in the mail for $25, call 800-000-0000. The call is free. 800-000-0000.
Visa and Mastercard accepted	
A prepaid legal services program administered by Don Caldwell Corp. Sacramento, CA 95820	

(Written and produced by Barney Kramer, President and Creative Director, Direct Response Broadcasting Network, Phila. PA.)

Clearly, DR infomercials are not elegant, but they communicate their points in a manner most calculated to facilitate audience understanding. The five minute infomercial below for Grocerama provides enlightenment on nutrition as well as on the economics of food distribution. It also has time to dramatize much more extensively how Grocerama can impinge on the viewer's life. Spots of this length owe much of their increasing popularity and exposure to cable television networks, which have the schedule flexibility, available time, and more specific "narrowcast" audience to accommodate the infomercial's needs and the market requirements of its sponsors.

Production <u>Note</u>: Talent is mid-thirties woman. She's attractive but not gorgeous and dressed in skirt and blouse equally appropriate to secretary, teacher or homemaker.

Video	Audio
FADE UP ESTAB. SHOT OF LARGE SUPERMARKET AND PARKING LOT, FRAMED SO STORE NAME NOT VISIBLE.	<u>VO:</u> The great American supermarket. How many times has it ruined <u>your</u> day?
PAN RIGHT TO CENTER ON TALENT'S RED SEDAN ENTERING LOT	First it's finding a place to park.
MLS TALENT CAR BEATEN TO LAST PARKING SPACE BY PICK-UP TRUCK	SFX: LIVE ACTION, TIRES SQUEALING, HONKING
MCU TALENT FRAMED BY CAR WINDOW LOOKING EXASPERATED	And parking's the easy part.

Video	Audio
DIS TALENT ENTERING MAMMOTH MARKET (SHOT WITH FISHEYE LENS TO LOOK EXTRA WIDE)	Then you have to find the groceries. And without a road map.
DIS M2S TALENT W/SHOPPING CART AND STOCKBOY	TALENT: Excuse me, where do keep your olives?
	BOY: Huh?
	TALENT: Your olives.
	BOY: I don't work on that side of the store, lady.
DIS MLS TALENT AT END OF LONG CASHIER LINE; SHOPPING CART NOW FULL	VO: Check-out is fun too.
DIS INCREASINGLY TIGHTER SHOTS OF TALENT FROM CASHIER POV. TALENT LOOKING AT WATCH, EDGING CLOSER TO REGISTER.	SFX: LIVE ACTION, BANGING OF GROCERY CARTS, CASHIERS YELLING OUT PRICES, CHILDREN CRYING, ETC.
DIS M2S TALENT AND CASHIER; CASHIER HOLDING 4-PACK OF BATHROOM TISSUE	CASHIER: There's no price on this.
	TALENT: It's a dollar thirty-nine.
	CASHIER: Who says so?
	TALENT: The sign on the display.
	CASHIER: (yelling into mike) Toilet paper price check on 11, Al!
DIS WIDER SHOT TO SHOW IMPATIENT CUSTOMERS IN LINE BEHIND TALENT	VO: And when it comes time to pay—

Video	Audio
	INTERCOM VOICE: That toilet paper's a buck thirty-nine.
FEATURE TALENT AND CASHIER	CASHIER: (ringing up price) OK, that'll be ninety eight dollars and twelve cents.
	TALENT: (repeating while writing) Ninety eight dol—
	CASHIER: We don't take checks like that.
WIDEN TO SHOW CUSTOMERS GETTING MORE IMPATIENT	TALENT: What?
	CASHIER: We don't take those checks.
	TALENT: Why not?
	CASHIER: Because they're pink.
	TALENT: What??!!
DIS MS TALENT AWKWARDLY LOADING GROCERIES IN CAR	VO: At least, it's a pleasure when the shopping's done.
EMPTY SHOPPING CART ENTERS FRAME AND BANGS INTO TALENT'S CAR DOOR	TALENT: (To camera) Sure---a pleasure.
WIPE TO MS SPOKESMAN STANDING IN FRONT OF FREEZER.	SPOKES: You don't have to put up with supermarket battles any longer. Not with Grocerama in your corner.
SPOKESMAN STEPS ASIDE TO REVEAL GROCERAMA LOGO ON FREEZER DOOR	Grocerama is the new shop-at-home food plan that lets you

Video	Audio
	order all your grocery needs by phone.
TALENT PULLS FREEZER DOOR OPEN TO REVEAL NEAT, WELL-STOCKED FREEZER	Yes, steaks, chops, vegetables, frozen fruit, ice cream, and all kinds of canned goods for the cupboard.
ZOOM IN, PAN ACROSS FOOD	You name it. Grocerama gets it for you and brings it to you every week.
DIS MCU TALENT IN HER KITCHEN	TALENT: (To camera) But I like to choose my own food.
MCU SPOKESMAN	SPOKES: Of course you do. That's why Grocerama gives you as wide a choice as most supermarkets.
DIS M2S TALENT AND WHITE-JACKETED GROCERAMA SERVICE REP IN TALENT'S LIVING ROOM, SHOWING HER ITEMS IN GROCERAMA CATALOG	SPOKES (VO): Our professional Grocerama sales representative helps you plan for your every grocery need. He does a complete analysis of your current buying habits before making suggestions about Grocerama options.
DIS MS SPOKESMAN AT DESK, HOLDING UP CHECKLIST	SPOKES (OC): This exclusive Grocerama food analysis system was prepared by nutrition experts to ensure

Video	Audio
	that what you buy is not only what you want, but what you need for healthy living.
DIS ''BASIC 4'' CHART	SPOKES (VO): We've all heard of the Basic 4 food groups: dairy products; meat, fish and eggs; vegetables and fruits; and bread and cereals. But do you always remember them when you shop?
DIS ''CALORIES SOURCES'' CHART	And how about the sources of calories? Fats, carbohydrates and protein. Do you know how each of these contribute to health?
DIS ''VITAMINS/MINERALS'' CHART	What about minerals and vitamins— magnesium, zinc; vitamins A, B-one and D?
DIS BACK TO SPOKESMAN	SPOKES (OC): Well, Grocerama's patented nutritional analysis takes all of these dietary needs into consideration in helping you create the tastiest, healthiest meal plan imaginable.
MCU TALENT IN KITCHEN	TALENT: But I can't afford all of this.

Video	Audio
MCU SPOKESMAN	SPOKES: Not only can you afford it, but you'll probably save money over what you're spending at the supermarket now.
SPOKESMAN HOLDS UP DISTRIBUTION CHART, ''X's'' OUT SUPERMARKET	That's because Grocerama buys in bulk from distributors and delivers the groceries direct to you. Grocerama eliminates the middleman's profits to put more money in your pocket.
MCU TALENT	TALENT: But I'll still have to go to the supermarket for some things.
MCU SPOKESMAN	SPOKES: Only if you want to. Because Grocerama's modular shopping plan also lets you obtain laundry products, health and beauty aids, even bathroom tissue---and at lower prices than you're
WIDEN AS SPOKESMAN RISES, GOES BACK TO FREEZER	probably used to paying at the supermarket. Grocerama will even supply the freezer if you need one.
MCU TALENT	TALENT: Can I check this out?
MS STANDING SPOKESMAN	SPOKES: You certainly can. Just dial this number

Video	Audio
SQUEEZEZOOM SPOKESMAN IN MORTISE, SUPER LOCAL OR 800 NUMBER HERE	for a free, no obligation booklet on Grocerama services. Check out how Grocerama can free you from the supermarket battleground. Discover just how easy it is to eat healthier for less.
MLS GROCERAMA TRUCK PULLING INTO RESIDENTIAL DRIVEWAY RE-SUPE PHONE NUMBER	<u>VO:</u> Grocerama does your shopping for you, and delivers it right to your door. To find out more, just dial this number. There is absolutely no obligation to buy anything.
MLS TALENT OPENING DOOR TO WHITE-UNIFORMED GROCERAMA DELIVERY MAN; ZOOM IN	<u>TALENT:</u> (Turns to camera) What a pleasure. Good-bye supermarket. Hello Grocerama!
GROCERAMA LOGO ON BLUE BACKGROUND RE-SUPE NUMBER	<u>VO:</u> Why waste any more time or money shopping the old way? Call this number now and learn how Grocerama can start working for you. Grocerama. Better food. Better health. Better prices.

Both the above infomercials represent DR thrusts, but direct response is only one of four main kinds of infomercials that you may be called on to write. The other three forms consist of (1) in-house training modules, (2) in-store demonstrations, and (3) long-form PSAs. Training modules may be on such topics as employee safety, retirement options, how to use new data processing systems, or improved methods for selling the company's wares to face-to-face clients. These modules are normally created or purchased by the corporate relations or internal communication arm of a company to improve productivity, morale, or general interaction.

In-store or in-mall demonstrations are designed to attract and hold the attention of passersby through a video minidocumentary that in some way relates to a new product or brand line. Often written by the manufacturer or an independent producer under contract to the manufacturer's or chain's marketing wing, these in-store efforts have the advantage of continuous replayings without "interruption" from entertainment programming.

Long-form PSAs are often prepared by the charity or public service organization itself for showing at seminars, church meetings, and service club gatherings. Whatever the type, infomercial copy, like that for any television commercial, should respect the need for compulsory demonstrability and clear audio/video interlock. More time does *not* mean you can afford to waste your audience's valuable and fleeting attention through irrelevant or unnecessary images.

Retail advertising spots on television are not as lengthy as infomercials. Nor must they consummate the sale as in DR messages. Like these two forms, however, retail copy must be especially hardworking since it is promoting both a business and at least some of its multitude of wares. (You may wish at this point to review our discussion of retail radio advertising in chapter 8 to reacquaint yourself with some dynamics of this genre.)

Especially since the mid-seventies, the commercial television industry, led by its sales promotion arm the Television Bureau of Advertising (TVB), has attempted to show local and regional retailers that television is an effective and affordable advertising vehicle for them. TVB's annual Retail TV Commercials Workshops and its various sales clinics all strive to provide industry writers and sales personnel with the same extensive assistance in this and other commercial areas as does the Radio Advertising Bureau (RAB) for its counterpart industry. But, though local retailers have long been accustomed to the fact that radio is at least an option as one of their marketing tools, the concept of television is still frightening; it remains obscured in the ominous fog of the "super production mystique."

Co-op efforts have, in part, helped dissipate some of this fog since the manufacturer handles the burden of production. The Champion spot back in Figure 11–8 is an example of such a co-op enterprise as is the Figure 11–13 Culligan commercial (a variant of which was presented in chapter 5). Here, the last two frames provide a sparkling water background on which dealer customization can be supered and enhanced by a local voiceover tag. Nevertheless, in the majority of cases, retailers must still depend on their own—or their copywriter's—devices to prepare the video message.

As a copywriter, you will probably not be directly involved in the television salesperson's task of persuading that department store, beauty parlor, or lumberyard to use video. You may, however, be called on at least to assist in the pitch by designing a sample commercial that showcases the perspective client in an effective, yet frugally produced manner. And, should the retailer make an initial commitment to try television, you, as an in-station or agency

Figure 11–13. *(Courtesy of Kathy Mullins, Marsteller Inc.)*

wordsmith, must be the prime person to satisfy that local business's expectations for a penetrating and cost-efficient production—expectations that the station or agency sales folks may have uplifted to a disturbingly high level.

Fortunately, one of the inherently persuasive charms of local television advertising accrues when it *looks* local. As Louisville Productions' President Richard Gordon once told a convention of the National Retail Merchant's Association:

> Whether you are Bloomingdale's or Bacon's, May Company or Belk, you are still local and should appear that way. Your spots should stand out from the impersonal national spots. This does not mean a sacrifice of image or quality, but they should be different. . . . The spot should say that here's a local store

with the fashion and items the customers want. Don't try to be national when being local is an advantage.[10]

Subsequently, some *national* retailers such as the giant J.C. Penney chain have initiated use of television "doughnut" approaches. Through this mechanism, a nationally produced open and close is sent to the individual outlet's manager together with a variety of slides emphasizing different copy points. The local executive may then select whichever slides are most appropriate to "custom-complete" the body of his or her local spot while retaining an overall similarity of style with Penney stores in other markets.

Many times, however, the local retailer must rely on the in-station or same-city agency writer for top-to-bottom television treatment creation. This is especially true of the small regional chain or one-outlet independents who may be finding their way to television with greater and greater frequency through the TVB's efforts as well as the increasing availability of comparatively low-cost advertising exposure via broadcast-competing cable systems.

Under such circumstances, you have only to plunge in by remembering that the small retailer, unlike many national advertisers, is primarily concerned with stimulating "next day" traffic at the store. Long-term image building is fine, but not at the expense of tomorrow's customer volume—or that of this afternoon. As Stuart Sleppin, head of New York's Ad Counseling Productions points out:

> Most often agencies convince the client that his needs would be best suited if he were to be treated like a product. I'm sure most of us have sat at a meeting in which the client is told: "What you really need is an image." If the client were realistic, he'd come right back: "What I really need is customers." . . .
>
> I believe that one reason for our success is that we approach every retail account as if we were a customer—not an art director or copywriter. In our creative meetings, the bottom-line question is never: "Would the commercial bring me into the store?" We realize that our creative people are not necessarily our retailer's customers. Rather, our bottom-line question is: "Would that commercial bring in the customer who would shop at the store?"[11]

In this spot for a local grocery, customer values are well articulated by both the audio and video. Just as important, the commercial has been constructed to have a long life and yet, still be seasonally, even weekly, adaptable. Try to discern how this adaptation could most simply be accomplished.

Objective: To demonstrate that Townsend's produce is so fresh that mothers can let their children shop for it and still be certain of good quality.

Production Note: Johnny is 6-8 years old. Mother's voice featured exclusively throughout.

10. "From Down Louisville Way: Some Shrewd Advice on Selling While Keeping the Local Image," *Broadcasting Magazine*, January 16, 1978, p. 55.
11. Stuart Sleppin, writing in "Monday Memo," *Broadcasting Magazine*, December 10, 1979, p. 12.

Video	Audio
1. M2S IN KITCHEN. MOTHER GIVES SMALL CHANGE PURSE TO SON JOHNNY AND SENDS HIM OFF.	<u>MOTHER:</u> Run down to Townsend's and get two pounds, please.
2. WHEN JOHNNY EXITS FRAME, SHE FACES CAMERA.	I send Johnny to Townsend's Market because—
3. MLS OF TOWNSEND'S EXTERIOR. FEATURE ''TOWNSEND'S MARKET'' SIGN ON STOREFRONT.	<u>(V.O.):</u> at Townsend's, I'm sure of getting the best produce for my money.
4. MCU SLIDE OF LARGE SHINY RED APPLE DISPLAY IN FG, WITH JOHNNY'S FACE OVERLOOKING IT.	Townsend's apples, like all their fruit and vegetables, are the freshest apples in town.
5. MCU OF JOHNNY AT CHECK-OUT COUNTER. CASHIER'S HANDS GIVE HIM GROCERY BAG OF UNDISCLOSED CONTENTS; DROP CHANGE BACK IN HIS COIN PURSE.	And this week, they're at especially low prices.
6. LS OF TOWNSEND'S EXTERIOR TO INCLUDE ENTIRE STREET CORNER. DIS. TO—	Townsend's Market on Hillcrest and Dale is nice and close, too.
7. M2S AS JOHNNY ENTERS KITCHEN AND IS GREETED BY MOTHER	(<u>END</u> V.O.) My, that was quick.
8. MOTHER LOOKS DOWN INTO BAG AND SMILES	Townsend's Market—mmmmmm.

If you weren't able to ascertain the modular nature of this script, re-examine segment 4. Currently, Townsend's wants to generate "next day" (or even *same day*) traffic by promoting its apples. But by merely substituting a slide of a different display, and changing the fruit/vegetable-specifying segment 4 audio, the treatment can become a promotion for Townsend's oranges, tomatoes, bananas, or any other produce item sold by the pound. The spot thus has the capability of an almost unlimited number of modifications—and at virtually no additional cost beyond that required to produce the initial commercial "bed." Expenditures can be further reduced by using slides rather than film/tape footage for segments 3, 5, and 6. And, if Townsend's is in a four-season climate zone, these slides could even be shot to reflect the different times of the year. Because we never see Johnny outdoors, the footage of him and his mother at home (segments 1, 2, 7, and 8) could be used year-round as long as telltale costuming like a snowsuit or bathing togs was not used in the kitchen scene.

In summary, television messages for retailers, like those for any client, should demonstrate their subject's benefit in a cogent, believable, honest, and cost-efficient manner. Creative Director Ed Butler puts television copywriting in the most stark relief when he concludes that, "the point is, you can say all the right things, but unless you stop the viewer cold, you're talking to yourself."[12] As your scripts start talking through television, let us hope you have plenty of hearers.

12. Ed Butler, "Formula Advertising Just Died a Well-Deserved Death," *ADWEEK/Midwest*, April, 1985, p. F.C. 7.

PART FOUR

CAMPAIGN COPYWRITING

Broadcast Campaigns

Political, Controversy, and Crisis Campaigns

Cross-Media Campaigns

Chapter Twelve

BROADCAST CAMPAIGNS

Up to this point, our concern has focused on the prewriting analysis, script creation, and postdraft evaluation of individual pieces of radio and television copy. Now it is time to view the process in compound form; to examine how an entire broadcast campaign is constructed and the individual messages within it coordinated into a mutually reinforcing whole. Even though the discussion in this chapter centers primarily around *commercial* strategies, keep in mind that the same basic steps and procedures can, and usually should, be followed in forging well-aimed station promotion, program promotion, and PSA packages as well. It should be noted, too, that cross-media campaigns in which both print and broadcasting are employed, campaigns on which we'll focus in chapter 14, would also comply with the same basic mode of operation. The essential and common ingredient to all of these situations is *Concept Engineering:* determining and executing the most viable plan of action possible given the resources and time available.

CONCEPT ENGINEERING VERSION 1—MAKING LISTS

A good way to begin to draw a bead on that proposed campaign or client whose business you're courting is to construct a paper-and-pencil inventory of the currently existing marketing situation. Not only will this help acclimate you to the problems and potentials of the project but, as a writer, will also make you feel more comfortable about the assignment once you've put some of your own words down on paper—in no matter how prosaic a register. Making lists starts you grappling with the task and, just as important, gives you concrete reassurance that you are making progress in coming to grips with it.

Of course, before you can construct any list, you have to find out as much as possible about your subject. There are many ways to do this. After his agency acquired the Texaco account in 1934, Jack Cunningham, one of the founders of Cunningham & Walsh, "spent two weeks wearing the Texaco star, pumping gas, greasing axles and changing oil. From his time at the point of sale, Cunningham learned that customers cared more about the cleanliness of a service station's restrooms than they cared about the gasoline sold there. For several years to follow, it was clean restrooms that sold Texaco's petrol."[1]

---

1. Chuck Reece, "Admen Remember Jack Cunningham," *ADWEEK/Midwest*, March 4, 1985, p. 2.

You may not feel the need (or have the time) to go to such extremes. But Cunningham's dedication certainly illustrates how central is acquired product/ market knowledge to the campaign tailoring process. Once you have gained an understanding of product and market specifics, by whatever means, the list-making process can proceed in the assurance that it is based on fact.

1. List the Positive Attributes

The first and most obvious portion of your inventory should encompass all the reasons that someone (or different groups of someones) would want to utilize/patronize the product or service. Set down each of these in a consumer-benefit form and include at least one for each of the SIMPLE rational appeals discussed in chapter 4. Keep an entirely open mind at this point, for you can never predict which benefit may, once the total analysis is completed, exhibit the greatest success potential. Write down every conceivable product merit, no matter how bizarre, and allow the process to isolate the *most* meritorious later.

2. List the Weaknesses

The perfect product or service never existed in this imperfect world and don't assume yours will break the pattern. The honest and ultimately triumphant campaign always takes its own drawbacks into consideration and proceeds accordingly. As you may recall from chapter 1, the in-house agency sometimes lacks the capability or willingness to view its corporate output in this light. Such self-imposed blinders too often ignore marketplace realities and substitute management's hallucinations for public attitudes. A weakness glossed over in campaign planning is almost certain to surface like a bloated whale in campaign execution. Get all the product or service drawbacks out on paper, where you can see and deal with them *in advance.*

3. Retrieve the Exploitable Weaknesses

Once you've made a candid appraisal of product limitations, see if you can't transform them into positive attributes by casting them in a new light. This can harvest the most persuasive advertising because it shows consumers that what they thought was a negative factor is really, on closer examination, a laudable characteristic. Thus, for a certain candy mint, "you pay a few cents more, but for a breath deodorant it's worth it." Similarly, an insurance company's inability to contact personally every household is explained away by the popularity of the policies that are keeping its agents so busy. And, as revealed in the classic spot in Figure 12-1, blatant product cheapness still does not preclude quality and durability.

In fact, retrieving an exploitable weakness might even save the business itself. The story is told of the small salmon packing plant which was losing more and more share of market because its steam-based canning processes turned the naturally pink salmon meat to *white.* Though the process was just as hygienic as the methods employed at bigger plants, and though the steaming did not adversely affect taste, consumers were simply suspicious of white salmon. The

MAN: Some idiot probably spent a lifetime making this lighter feel good in your hand. Big deal. But for $1.49 and thousands of lights it's a pretty good lighter.

Bic Butane.

LADY: This lighter comes in a lot of colors like blue, yellow, orange, white and green, but it isn't avocado green. Anyway, for $1.49 and thousands of lights it's a pretty good lighter.

Bic Butane.

LADY: Personally I don't smoke. But for $1.49 and thousands of lights, it's a pretty good lighter.

Bic Butane.

Figure 12–1. *(Courtesy of Kenneth Olshan, Wells, Rich, Greene Inc.)*

plant did not have the money to install another process and all seemed lost until an astute copywriter unearthed the perfect exploitable weakness theme:

(Company name) Salmon---the only salmon guaranteed not to turn pink in the can.

In one stroke, the conventional became the unacceptable and the regional market for *white* salmon rebounded to an all-time sales high.

4. Amalgamate the Benefits and Excuses

Next, take all the positive attributes from list #1 and all the feasible excuses from list #3. Merge them into one composite slate and condense this to the fewest possible essentials. You want to have a comprehensive catalog of benefits related to your product or service without a confusing and potentially replicative overlap. At this juncture, you should now have before you the total range of differentiated options, each of which may conceivably be selected as a main campaign theme, depending on the demographic/psychographic profile of your client's target audience. This comprehensively sets the stage for the winnowing process that follows.

5. List the Approaches Taken by the Client in the Past

Since we began with the assumption that you are planning a new campaign, it must also be assumed that the current approach is not working or has simply run its course, as did the other approaches that might have preceded it. Generally, it is deemed undesirable to reharvest a previously abandoned campaign theme from which all the usable fruit has already been picked and consumed. Thus, list #5 serves to eliminate items from #4 that have been stressed in the past. Should you *want* to resurrect an earlier theme, however, cross-checking it with list #4 should ascertain whether there is a solid and readily identifiable current benefit from which that theme can issue. It may be discovered that the particular approach failed to work before because it really didn't relate to a meaningful product advantage or mismatched an advantage with an inappropriate target audience, such as pitching a tire's durability to high-income types who only buy tires with a new car attached.

6. List What the Competition Is Stressing

This particular catalog may be long or short depending on how many major competitors there are and how many different campaigns each may be running. In our own campaign, we usually attempt to emphasize some aspect that the "other guys" are not talking about in order to differentiate more effectively our product from theirs. Nevertheless, if your product is unequivocally and demonstrably superior to a competitor in terms of the element that competitor is currently stressing, you may want to "take him on" at his own game. In either event, list #6 has given you an inventory of what tunes the others are singing. It can therefore serve to eliminate their approaches from your composite list of options or it can alert you to the fact that encroaching on any of these "occupied" themes may set up doubtful brand recall and/or perilous comparative advertising considerations.

7. Weigh the Options That Remain

After crossing off those benefit approaches from list #4 that are (1) undesirably replicative of past campaigns or (2) dominated by the competition, you are left with a final and residual slate of possibilities. From this slate, and in conjunction with client representatives and their target audience specifications, the benefit-expressed campaign theme must be selected. For maximum effectiveness, all subsequent advertising for the product, service, program, or station should be expressed in terms of this theme. Otherwise, you run the risk of advertising against yourself—of seeming to promote two separate and competing accounts rather than a single, consistently packaged one.

8. Pick a Product Personality

Based on your theme and the benefit it conveys, a product personality, expressed in a consistent and meticulously tailored writing style, should be allowed to emerge. Product personality will come through in your spots whether you want it to or not, so take the initiative to fashion one that is most appropriate to the campaign, the client, and the target audience that client is attempting to reach. Too many campaigns are afflicted with vapid or even schizoid image traits because, though the benefit theme has been carefully determined, the verve and style of the words conveying that theme have not been scrupulously monitored from spot to spot. In such cases, the product or client may, for instance, sometimes come across as somber, at other times appear simply businesslike, and on still other occasions appear downright dictatorial.

Product personality is the single most perplexing concept for a novice writer to grasp because, though certain personalities seem generally associated with particular benefit themes or product categories, there are now lighthearted insurance companies as well as deadly serious breakfast cereals. Like an old friend whose actions have a comfortable and reassuring predictability, a product personality's familiarity flows from a distinctive yet elusive way of saying and doing things.

Copywriters strive mightily to understand and re-create this same attribute in the material they write for a particular product; to endow it with a cohesive "attitude familiarity" that is carried through that account's every spot. The sustaining of this attitude usually becomes so second-nature to a copy group, in fact, that major product personality modification can in most cases be accomplished only when the account changes agencies. "Good advertising people believe," observes SSC&B's former president Malcolm MacDougall, "that each product is born with a special purpose, endowed with a unique personality and blessed with a soul. They believe that their advertising is a part of that soul."[2]

If you still don't understand the dynamics of product personality, take a look at the photoboards in Figures 12–2 and 12–3. Both were created by the same agency for two different fruit drink clients. Take your time and study each carefully.

Though each photoboard is targeted to an adult market, do these two spots exhibit the same product personality? If you think so, go back and look at them again. Then try to conceive of each written in the tenor of the other. Could a treatment stressing the quality of its utilized grapefruit do so with an unblushing evocation of the allurement appeal? Would a premium-priced fruit drink from France want to stress the wholesomeness of its ingredients and ignore its status as a French import with all that heritage implies? Obviously not. Instead, the visual exploitation of the "good for you, America" grapefruit works best when the focus is indeed on the grapefruit. The swingy sparkle and bounce of Orelia, on the other hand, requires an approach that spotlights the kind of people who exhibit these qualities. The Ocean Spray Grapefruit drink, in short, benefits from a mantle of nutritiousness while the Orelia profits from a continental aura of sex. Thus, by epitomizing key product attributes and their most closely associated consumer rewards, product personality becomes an irreplaceable mechanism for campaign cohesion and memorability.

2. Malcolm MacDougall, "How to Sell Parity Products," *ADWEEK/Midwest,* February 13, 1984, p. 30.

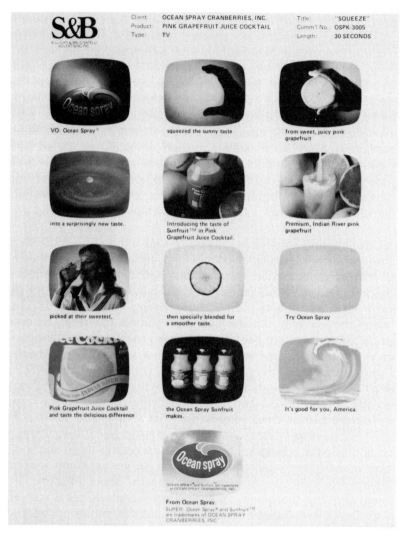

Figure 12–2. *(Courtesy of Mimi Rydre, Sullivan & Brugnatelli Advertising Inc.)*

Grey Advertising's executive vice president, Richard Kiernan, takes the concept of personality even one step further by giving it equal weight with the product and positioning components of a campaign in determining what he calls *Brand Character.* As Kiernan testifies, it is:

> that extra dimension—*who* the brand is—combined with the positioning and the product that Grey calls Brand Character.
>
> Product + Positioning + Personality = Brand Character.

A totality that expresses how a brand looks and feels to the consumer. What its unique character is that distinguishes it from its competition. That lifts it above the crowd.

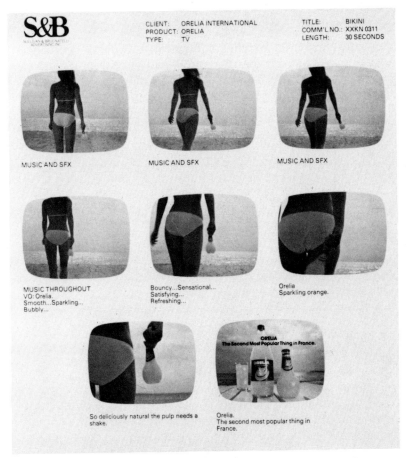

Figure 12–3. *(Courtesy of Mimi Rydre, Sullivan & Brugnatelli Advertising Inc.)*

A television campaign that helps create that strong character has a look, a sound, a feeling as personal—as identifiable—as those characteristics which distinguish one person from another.

And, like the character of a person, it endures. The brand with a strong character is recognizable from commercial to commercial, from campaign to campaign over the years. Just as a person is recognizable over the years no matter how much weight they have put on (or taken off), what clothes they are wearing or how they've changed hair styles.[3]

We've already examined the product and personality ingredients of Kiernan's Brand Character equation. Positioning and its roots are explored in the following section.

3. Richard Kiernan, writing in "Monday Memo," *Broadcasting Magazine*, August 25, 1980, p. 24.

CONCEPT ENGINEERING VERSION 2—CONSTRUCTING
THE CAMPAIGN PROPOSAL

Frequently, a ranking copywriter is called on not only to compose a broadcast treatment but also to take a hand in the vital preliminary preparation that leads to the development of a *campaign proposal* (for a new client or campaign) or *copy platform* (for a particular spot or flight). Unlike Version One's previously discussed lists, which remain the copywriter's private working sketches, campaign proposals and copy platforms are themselves submitted to a variety of other people within the agency and client organizations. The quality of these submissions must be high because the script may never be produced, the account never won, if the platform or proposal respectively, lacks clarity, precision, and persuasiveness. Writing solid proposals is especially crucial since they are the prerequisite to attracting entire accounts; entire accounts that may bring in the means to pay your entire salary. Proposal realization is normally the sum of five component steps:

1. Client analysis
2. Competition analysis
3. Advertising Objective (AO) development
4. Creative Selling Idea (CSI) construction
5. Sample message creation

Let's take a careful look at each phase of the process.

1. Client Analysis

The more you know about the firm whose products you're seeking the opportunity to sell, and the more you know about each of those products, the larger will be the range of options that open themselves to you. The comprehensive client analysis shows the firm you are courting that you have taken the trouble to learn a lot about its operation and have compiled all the relevant information needed to marshal a proper campaign response. For your own formulation purposes, of course, the client analysis serves to garner the raw material out of which those Version One lists of positive attributes and weaknesses can easily and accurately be assembled.

Even though clients themselves can usually be counted on to supply a great deal of data about themselves, smart campaign creators have learned not to rely exclusively on such materials. This is because client-originated information may be flawed or incomplete for either of two reasons:

1. Clients are so close to their business that they fail to take note of elements that, though mundane to them, may be of unusual appeal to lay consumers. One brewer, around his firm's copper tanks all his life, was surprised that a touring creative team took such interest in them. When exploited in a "gleaming copper kettles" approach, however, this client-dismissed aspect became a successful and tangible referent for the firm's fire-brewing benefit. As writers, we are (fortunately) as initially ignorant of the operations of most of the businesses for whom we write as are the consumers at whom we aim our messages. We, sometimes better than the client, can therefore isolate those methods and modes of operation that are of greatest potential interest to current or prospective customers. We can spotlight an

implement or process that, while mundane to the client, can be of great benefit-illustrating significance to us and the broadcast audiences to whom we are writing.

2. Client-originated information may also be deficient because top management, or those who work for them, are afraid to lay bare product/corporate weaknesses. Management (or more often, management's nervous hireling) tries to "gild the lily" and treat the copywriter or agency as just one more consumer of its public relations plaudits. Then they wonder why the subsequent advertising blows up in their faces because the public wasn't told about the mandatory eight-week delivery delay or that the additive didn't help pre-1982 engines. Experienced copywriters and market-wise clients have discovered that the firm's public relations department is usually *not* the best liaison with its advertising agency. To do its job, the agency needs the ugly truth rather than the rosy glow that emanates from the PR office.

Take the data that the client or prospective client provides and thoroughly evaluate it as filtered through your own appraisal of client/product strengths and weaknesses. If you can, visit the firm's office, store, or plant. Take note of everything, for you can never tell when a seemingly insignificant on-site discovery can later be the key to a blockbuster campaign.

2. Competition Analysis

Once you have briefed yourself and *been* briefed on all available account data, you are in a position to define and scrutinize the competition's scope and character. Putting it another way, you are ready to complete a broadened framework for Version One's list #6.

The first requisite of a functional competition analysis is the *competition yardstick;* a definitional framework that separates the real from the imagined rivals. Since the client analysis has already provided you with a clear portrait of your own account, it is relatively easy to isolate its main wares and use these as discriminatory criteria. If your client's restaurant caters to the cocktail crowd, you probably should not worry too much about threats posed by family eateries and diners, for example. In short, your client's key activities become the central qualities that any other firm must possess in order to constitute real competition. Here are some sample yardsticks, each of which would usually be preceded by the phrase "Competition for (client/product name) would include. . . ."

any gas station within eight miles that also features complete engine repair service;
any store that sells shoes for the whole family;
every all-seasons sporting goods establishment whether self-contained or part of a department store;
every presweetened cereal intended primarily for consumption by children;
any plumbing and heating contractor that handles both installation and maintenance.

Once yardsticks such as these ferret out the *primary* rivals, a work-up statement on each rival can be prepared. Such statements are not required to have the depth of the original client analysis but instead need concentrate only on describing each competitor's condition *relative to the strengths and weaknesses of your own account.* Hopefully, a pattern will at this point begin to emerge and you will discover that your client or product is consistently superior (or at least, *different from*) all competitors in regard to certain specific qualities or ways of doing business.

It might be that your firm has longer hours, a more convenient location, or more years of experience than any of its rivals. Or, your product may be less expensive, faster to use, or easier to store than those manufactured by other companies. Whatever the case, such distinctive advantages have now been identified as potential prime agents for the total campaign strategy.

As the last part of our competition analysis, it is necessary to uncover which advertising vehicles the competition is using and what approaches they are taking via these vehicles. Your broadcast material may qualitatively and stylistically vary a great deal depending on whether your opponents are exploiting radio and television in a significant and high-profile manner. You can't, for instance, outspend a much larger rival so you may want to consider capitalizing on that very size discrepancy through copy that orchestrates your benefit to the tune of an underdog motif (we're the little company that does more for you because we need your business more).

3. Advertising Objective (AO) Development

With the completion of steps 1 and 2, all the results are in and it is time to make the unequivocal choice of the central theme that all advertising for this particular product will be designed to promote. Bolstered by an incisive and, we trust, unblushing measurement of marketplace realities, we are now in a position to adopt an approach calculated to achieve the most positive recognition possible for the client whose aims we are serving.

From a workability standpoint, the AO must be narrow enough to delineate your client clearly from the competition yet broad enough to encompass several related subthemes that may later evolve in campaign fine-tuning. We want to provide "growing room" for our overall approach without making the AO so vague that we lose the sense of client uniqueness. If, for example, that same Advertising Objective could be put to use by a rival, it should never have been selected in the first place. As in the following classic examples, the AO will usually include a specification of target audience (universe) and delineation of our key client benefit or benefit-complex:

Communicate to above-average-income families with children that Pizza Hut restaurants employ dedicated people whose primary responsibility is to serve customers.[4]
Let air travelers know that only Western Airlines gives every passenger first-class legspace on every flight.[5]
Show kids that Milk Duds is America's long-lasting alternative to the candy bar.[6]
Assure women forty-five and over that Second Debut moisturizing lotion is an effective cosmetic ally for all the good and productive years that lie ahead.[7]
Persuade the soft-drink-user spectrum that Dr Pepper is neither a root beer nor a cola but a popular beverage for every occasion.[8]

4. Sam Moyers, writing in "Monday Memo," *Broadcasting Magazine*, July 21, 1975, p. 10.
5. Louis Brown, writing in "Monday Memo," *Broadcasting Magazine*, June 9, 1975, p. 8.
6. Al Ries, writing in "Monday Memo," *Broadcasting Magazine*, August 26, 1974, p. 11.
7. Mel Rubin, writing in "Monday Memo," *Broadcasting Magazine*, July 9, 1979, p. 10.
8. Frank DeVito, writing in "Monday Memo," *Broadcasting Magazine*, February 16, 1981, p. 24.

Convince blue-collar males that Miller Beer possesses the traditional American attributes of "value, worth and quality."[9]
Introduce women twenty-five to fifty-four to Snuggle's *low-priced* fabric softening and
static-cling reducing capabilities.[10]

The selected advertising objective is then recast into a *positioning statement*
that allows the essence of the AO to be articulated in the spot. You would
never want to use the above Pizza Hut objective as copy, for example, but the
positioning statement "our people make our pizza better" expresses its central
tenet in a more abbreviated and conversational form that easily lends itself to
script inclusion. Likewise, "when a candy bar is only a memory, you'll still be
eating your Milk Duds" is a swingy, copy-ripe translation of the necessarily
clinical AO whose cause it promotes. And "snuggly softness that's really less
expensive" deftly works in the Snuggle product name as a benefit adjective
while still mirroring its AO motivator.

From a marketing standpoint, positioning is, in the words of positioning
theory's founding father Al Ries, "looking for a hole that doesn't belong to
someone else."[11] Positioning, therefore, is what all of our earlier-mentioned
lists and proposal steps have been geared to facilitate. We are trying to find
what might be called the "high ground of advantage"—the orientation toward
our product or service that clearly and auspiciously sets it apart from the
competition. According to Mr. Ries's long-accepted tenets:

> The first rule of positioning is this: You can't compete head-on against a
> company that has a strong, established position. You can go around, under or
> over, but never head-to-head. The leader owns the high ground.
> The classic example of No. 2 strategy is Avis's. But many marketing people
> misread the Avis story. They assume the company was successful because it
> tried harder. Not at all. Avis was successful because it related itself to the
> position of Hertz. Avis pre-empted the No. 2 position. If trying harder were
> the secret of success, Harold Stassen would be President. . . .
> Too many companies embark on marketing and advertising programs as if
> the competitor's position did not exist. They advertise their products in a
> vacuum and are disappointed when their messages fail to get through.[12]

From a somewhat different though associated perspective, repositioning means
accommodating a prime product characteristic to a *new* consumer-use benefit.
With so few people baking from scratch anymore, the Arm & Hammer people
may have foreseen ever-deepening retail problems for their baking soda. But
through repositioning, the anachronistic baking ingredient became the modern
"nice little secret for your refrigerator." To heighten further its benefit as a
deodorant for closed spaces, the advertising that flowed from this repositioning

9. William Meyers, "The Campaign to Save a Flagging Brand," *ADWEEK/Midwest*, April, 1985,
   p. F.C. 22.
10. Merri Rosenberg, "Snuggle: A Hard Sell in a Cuddly Package," *ADWEEK/Midwest*, April, 1985,
   p. F.C. 36.
11. Ries, *Broadcasting Magazine*, August 26, 1974, p. 11.
12. "Do's and Don'ts of Broadcast Promotion Star at BPA Seminar," *Broadcasting Magazine*,
   November 26, 1973, p. 30.

also was set up to demonstrate how, once its refrigerator days were over, the stuff could be used to freshen a drain or kitty's "drop-box."

Similarly, Sara Lee has offset a big decline in frozen dessert sales by moving from an image of plebian pound cake convenience to that of purveyor of "Elegant Evenings" cheesecakes and croissants, hawked by a Parisian-sounding actress who queries, "Zis Sara Lee, she is French, no?" For its part, the hair-dyeing Miss Clairol was also saved by the studied repositioning repetition of the "Does She or Doesn't She?" question. "Previously," recalls marketing consultant Faith Popcorn, "the only women who dyed their hair had been blue-haired or of questionable reputation. Clairol's repositioning of hair coloring made it a legitimate option for self-respecting proper American women of any age."[13]

Positioning statements, and the Advertising Objectives that mandate them, are obviously of extreme importance for both old and new products and use-benefits. They are also the prime indication that today's copywriter must be part creator and part market strategist, a professional at home in both worlds. In fact, David Ogilvy has observed that campaign results depend less on "how we write your advertising than on how your product is positioned. It follows that. . . . [a positioning strategy] should be decided before advertising is created."[14]

4. Creative Selling Idea (CSI) Construction

From the AO, and the positioning statement that mirrors it, are spun a number of related, more detailed and more focused applications. Each application can, in turn, form the skeletal idea for a spot or flight of spots. Definitionally, a CSI is:

a consumer-related *benefit*
(+)
a *technique* for presenting it
(as applied)
specifically to this product or service.

CSIs must be very carefully constructed if they are to contain all of the above ingredients as well as relate unmistakably to their parent Advertising Objective.

Frequently, a novice writer will construct CSIs that are long on technique but in which the benefit is buried if not missing altogether; or the benefit may be there but its execution is vague or unworkable within the creative and budgetary confines of the campaign. Worst of all, the benefit and technique may show real labor and promise but fail to showcase the product properly or be totally outside the parameters set by the coordinating AO. This last malady, of course, would result in the sort of campaign fragmentation that all the previous stages of proposal development have worked so diligently to preclude.

Advertising executive Paul Goldsmith warns,

> When a creative person sits down to conceive an advertisement, he will often find it tempting to wander away from the agreed-upon strategy. Clearly, a

13. Faith Popcorn, "Repositioning with Real Sell," *ADWEEK/Midwest*, December 12, 1983, p. 42.
14. Craig Tanner, "Taking a Leaf from Ogilvy's Book," *ADWEEK/Midwest*, March 7, 1983, p. 32.

desired quality is the discipline to keep the work within the confines of the product positioning. A scintillating piece of copy for a new car that highlights the fact that you need never carry a spare tire, when the strategy talks about better mileage, is a flop no matter how clever or brilliantly executed. 'That's brilliant!' 'That's funny!' 'Beautifully done!' All are wasted words when the client says, 'This is not the strategy we agreed upon.'[15]

On the other hand, here is an Advertising Objective for Marlene's Dress Shop and three *disciplined* CSIs that flow from it. Notice how each includes all three components of a good Creative Selling Idea and how each relates back to the umbrella AO. Note too that each CSI could constitute the basis for a single spot as well as a whole series of clearly related spots that would thereby comprise an *integrated flight:*

Advertising Objective:
Attract over-35 women to Marlene's by stressing the shop's concern for sensible fashions.

Creative Selling Ideas:
1. Straight spots featuring female school teacher(s) who find(s) Marlene's blouses are comfortable to teach in and still look smart.
2. Husband uni-voice testimonials to the economical altering service Marlene's provides to ''tailor-make'' their clothes—even after the sale.
3. Marlene talks to the ladies about her fashionable yet adaptable headwear.

As another example, here is how an eatery might be positioned through AO/CSI framing:

Advertising Objective:
Establish for area lower-income families and singles that Taco Heaven is the place to go for inexpensive and appealing Mexican food.

Creative Selling Ideas:
1. Multivoiced spots of teens enjoying an after-school snack at Taco Heaven---affordable munchies even on an allowance budget.
2. Testimonials by blue-collar and clerical workers that eating at Taco Heaven converts lunchtime into a mini Mexican vacation.
3. Dialogue spots in which one homemaker tells another how Taco Heaven's menu entices her children to eat fresh vegetables, and for a lower-than-grocery-store cost.

15. Paul Goldsmith, writing in "Monday Memo," *Broadcasting Magazine,* September 22, 1980, p. 12.

5. Sample Message Creation

As the final step in your proposal development, you are ready to engage in what most copywriters (vocationally, at least) like best. You can now create a sample series of announcements that reflects all the market data and decision making with which the first four stages of the proposal are preoccupied. The messages constructed and presented at this, the final, stage of the proposal, may either all relate to a single CSI—and thereby constitute an integrated flight—or they may derive from several different CSIs in order to demonstrate the range of campaign possibilities which exist within the framework of the advocated AO.

Lest we forget that successful public service campaigns must be forged on fundamentally the same proposal anvil as a commercial strategy, here is the objective for the United States Catholic Conference's Campaign for Human Development together with a sample spot to illustrate how each of its subgoals are to be realized. Because of the intangibility of their products and, consequently, of their AOs, public service organizations often use subgoals rather than CSIs to manifest the various components of the belief or action that they advocate. By defining the parts, the subgoals therefore help collectively to characterize the whole.

Objective: To heighten public awareness of the problems of poverty as well as to illuminate some of the solutions such as [subgoals] community organizing, caring, and working together.

Subgoal #1—Community Organization

30-second TV spot

Video	Audio
CONVENTION SCENE CAMERA MOVES DOWN CENTER AISLE	VOICE OF MEETING CHAIRMAN: The Third Annual Convention of the Northeast Community Organization is hereby called to order.
CU, SIGNS: Trinity United Methodist NE Mothers for Peace Our Lady of Lourdes	ANNCR. (VO): A convention--- but a different kind.
WOMEN WORKING AT TABLE	The elderly, the poor, little people getting together

Video	Audio
MAN STANDING AT MICROPHONE SIGN: Strength in Action	to stand up against big wrongs in their neighborhood. Wrongs like industrial pollution,
CU: INDIVIDUALS SPEAKING INTO MICROPHONES	Landlord abuse—wrongs they didn't think they could change until they got together. (SOUND OF APPLAUSE)
CU: PEOPLE APPLAUDING	
CUT TO FULL SCREEN: Campaign for Human Development U.S. Catholic Conference Washington, D.C. 20005	Campaign for Human Development

Subgoal #2—Caring

60-second TV spot

Video	Audio
TWO INDIAN WOMEN WITH AN INFANT WALKING IN A BARREN FIELD	<u>MALE</u> <u>VOCALIST</u> <u>WITH</u> <u>GUITAR</u> (VO): It's the same old earth It'll always be.
OLD INDIAN MAN	With a newfound worth, and dignity;
QUICK CUTS OF PEOPLE, INCLUDING:	Livin' with the joy of bein' free—
TRUCK DRIVER TRAINING MEN STUDYING ENGINE	
	<u>CHORUS:</u>
CHICANO RADIO ANNOUNCER PARKING ATTENDANT	bein' free—
	<u>SOLOIST:</u>
TWO WOMEN OUTSIDE STORE	you and me.
FAMILY EATING HOTDOGS	
GIRL SELLING FLOWERS IN STREET	<u>CHORUS</u> <u>JOINS</u> <u>HIM</u> <u>IN</u> <u>REFRAIN:</u>
CAB DRIVER	The joy of people workin'
OFFICE WORKERS (MEN & WOMEN)	together
TRAFFIC COP	People determined to win,
STONE MASON	Building for tomorrow,
GIRL ON BIKE	Startin' to dream again.

Video	Audio
CHILD IN DENTIST CHAIR WOMAN LOOKING AT PAPERS GIRL AT WORK SITE TELEPHONE CABLE MAN	<u>ANNCR. (VO)</u>: The Campaign for Human Development is all of us—together with hope---learning to care.
	<u>CHORUS</u>:
FREEZE FRAME: MAN WAVING	Learnin' how to care, Learnin' how to live and hope,
<u>LOWER THIRD SUPER</u>:	And learnin' how to share
	<u>ANNCR. (VO)</u>:
Campaign for Human Development U.S. Catholic Conference Washington, D.C. 20005	Campaign for Human Development United States Catholic Conference

Subgoal #3—Working Together

30-second radio spot

HARRY: (VO RATTLING OF DICE) All right, let's see if you can get past me on this turn, Joe.

JOE: All right, let's see, Harr, let's see. (DICE ROLL AND STOP) Oh, no, no, look at that!

HARRY: Looks like you didn't make it, Joe, and is it going to cost you!

JOE: Oh, I guess, but Harry, that's it. I'm wiped out.

HARRY: Oh, too bad, old buddy, but that's life.

ANNOUNCER: For too many people, that <u>is</u> life. But we believe it shouldn't be. <u>The Campaign for Human Development.</u> <u>People Together—With Hope.</u> The United States Catholic Conference.

(All of the above courtesy of Francis P. Frost, Creative Services, U.S. Catholic Conference.)

   Even though less expensive than television to produce and air, all-radio campaigns should also flow from careful Concept Engineering in order to impact the marketplace maximally. The coordinating objective for the following First National/Wichita flight is *to show lower-to-middle-income people that*

First National bankers aren't stodgy businesspeople but folks with a sense of humor who provide significant help on a one-to-one basis. In executing this concept, CSI #1 stresses commitment to customer services, CSI #2 showcases customer courtesy, and CSI #3 illuminates the bank's attention to one's important needs rather than giveaway gimmicks.

<u>CSI #1—Commitment to Service</u>

(SFX: CHAMPAGNE BOTTLE POPS OPEN)

MAN: Happy Anniversary, Doris.

WOMAN: Thank you, dear.

MAN: Ten wonderful years together.

WOMAN: (Sigh) And every anniversary spent here inside First National Bank of Wichita.

MAN: Don't you like the way I fixed up the vault? I got candles and flowers—

WOMAN: Look, Larry, I know you're a dedicated banker.

MAN: Right! Because people don't—

WOMAN: —want to talk to banks, they want to talk to bankers!

MAN: So I've got to be here.

WOMAN: But that's why the First National Bank of Wichita has the 24-hour money card service.

MAN: Yes, I know. They're really convenient and our customers love them.

WOMAN: Can't we go dancing?

MAN: Well, Hon, I've got to be ready tomorrow in case Mrs. Boardman has a question about savings plans or interest rates.

WOMAN: What about me?

MAN: Do you have a question about interest rates, too?

WOMAN: Larry, I do not want to spend my entire anniversary dinner inside the First National Bank of Wichita.

MAN: (Laughs) Doris, I had more than this planned.

WOMAN: You mean it?

MAN: Sure, we can step outside.

WOMAN: Yeah, and I can watch you make a withdrawal at the 24-hour Money Card Center.

MAN: Right.

WOMAN: Oh, be still, my beating heart!

MAN: I know, I get all goose bumpy too.

WOMAN: Uh huh.

ANNCR: The First National Bank of Wichita. Come talk to a banker who wants to talk to you.

CSI #2—Courtesy to Customers

WOMAN: So, Mr. Bagley, you're applying for a job as one of the
         First National Bank of Wichita's friendly tellers?

MAN: That's right, Missy!

WOMAN: Uh huh. Well, let's suppose I'm one of the First National
         Bank of Wichita's loyal customers. I walk up to your
         window and you say—

MAN: Next window.

WOMAN: Uh, no.

MAN: Get in line.

WOMAN: No, no.

MAN: I'm out to lunch.

WOMAN: No.

MAN: Supper?

WOMAN: No.

MAN: Late night snack?

WOMAN: No, Mr. Bagley, the First National Bank of Wichita is
         known as a friendly neighborhood bank. So we say—

MAN: Turn down that stereo.

WOMAN: No.

MAN: Get your dog off my lawn!

WOMAN: No!

MAN: Who swiped my newspaper?

WOMAN: Look, we provide service with a smile, recognize our
         customers and say things like—

MAN: Hi, Baldy. Wanna cash a check?

WOMAN: Mr. Bagley, you're just not right for the First National
         Bank of Wichita. I'm sorry.

MAN: You're sorry. Boy, I'll never get my old job back.

WOMAN: What was that?

MAN: Librarian.

WOMAN: Librarian?

MAN: (Loudly) I don't know why they fired me.

WOMAN: Could you keep your voice down?

MAN: One day, I'm workin' in the library. The next—

ANNCR: The First National Bank of Wichita. Come talk to a banker
         who wants to talk to you about our 24-hour Money Card
         service. The First National Bank of Wichita.

CSI #3—Attention to Important Needs

MAN: And look, if we open an account at this bank, they'll give us Scratch N' Sniff checks in three scents---pine, barbeque, and rocky road.

WOMAN: Hal, that's a flashy gimmick. We want a bank that offers solid service.

MAN: Yeah, but—

WOMAN: And the First National Bank of Wichita has always done business the right way.

MAN: Yeah, but look what this other bank will give us: a hot tub in the vault and free haircuts while you wait in line.

WOMAN: Hal, please, let's go to the First National Bank of Wichita. They've got everything we'll need from special savings accounts to Keogh retirement plans!

MAN: What about—swizzle sticks?

WOMAN: Huh?

MAN: Here's one that gives you a swizzle stick with the teller of the month on it.

WOMAN: Why would we want that?

MAN: Who cares, it's free!

WOMAN: First National Bank of Wichita is the place for us. Whether it's financial advice or friendly help with all kinds of money services, they have it all.

MAN: Gee, and I so looked forward to owning my own whoopee cushion.

WOMAN: What?

MAN: That's what they give you at this place, look—

WOMAN: Hal—

MAN: And here's one that repairs screen doors—

ANNCR: Flashy gimmicks like free china or silverware? Or solid money management so you can look forward to a comfortable retirement? Ask about a Keogh Plan of your own, at the First National Bank of Wichita.

(All of the above courtesy of Fran Sax, FirstCom.)

Looking at our five-stage proposal process in retrospect, it can be seen to resemble schematically the Figure 12-4 hour glass. We start off as broadly as possible, gathering and analyzing client data from every conceivable source and perspective. This leads to developing a discriminatory competition yardstick and a consequent narrowing of focus to encompass only those other firms and products that meet that yardstick's specified criteria. From this we taper the

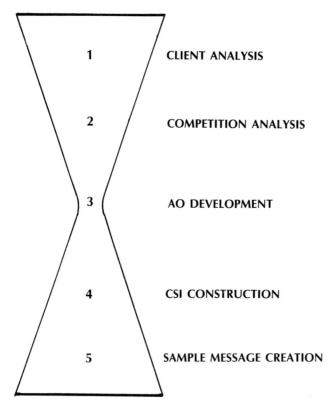

1   CLIENT ANALYSIS

2   COMPETITION ANALYSIS

3   AO DEVELOPMENT

4   CSI CONSTRUCTION

5   SAMPLE MESSAGE CREATION

Figure 12-4.   Proposal Hour Glass.

process even more in the construction of an Advertising Objective and associated positioning statement. Together, these set the boundaries within which
our product can be discussed and revealed to its greatest advantage. Several
applied Creative Selling Ideas or subgoals branch out from this coordinating
AO, and these CSIs and subgoals, in turn, can each give birth to several closely
associated spots and series of spots.

Through it all, the AO functions as key controlling agent. The first two stages
of proposal development are devoted to its careful sculpting and the last two
stages to its preservation and attainment. The Advertising Objective, in short,
constitutes the *synergism* (look that up in your Noah Webster) between broad-
based market research and multifaceted creativity.

PROPOSAL-RELATED ACTIVITIES AND IMPLEMENTS

Particularly as an in-station copywriter, you may never be called on to construct a full-scale proposal of the type just described. Your local accounts may
have long since been presold or attracted by a special price structure or ratings
report that the station salespeople are pushing. Under such circumstances, your
main responsibilities will be to write the copy for these local paying customers
in the manner to which they and/or your sales staff are accustomed. If client

merchants simply like to see/hear themselves on the air, you accept the fact that they are spending money to sell themselves rather than their businesses and showcase these people as best you can.

There comes a time, however, when even the most prosperous station needs to solicit some new accounts or, due to changing market or client management conditions, revamp existing copy approaches. Perhaps a new competitor has emerged for your client or that client has moved into a new line or area of endeavor that presents a whole new slate of competitors. Under such conditions, the *prospects file* becomes a crucial resource—and one for which you, the copywriter, may be responsible.

Simply put, the prospects file is made up of profiles of those area businesses that are either potential clients or potential or actual competitors of current clients. Each profile usually consists of a somewhat abbreviated version of proposal stage #1 (client analysis) plus a semistandardized stage #2 (competition analysis).

Since you don't have the time, nor the immediate need, for truly comprehensive client analyses in this prospects file resource bank, each sketch will normally just set down the main characteristics of each business and any advantages or weaknesses for which it is particularly noted. The limited depth of these profiles, in turn, makes it impossible to draw up *detailed* and customized competition analyses from them. As the prospects file is an initial familiarizer rather than a finalized end product, however, *individualized* competition analyses for a bunch of businesses that may never become your clients would only be a waste of effort.

Instead, certain categorized competition surveys can be written in such subject areas as restaurants, financial institutions, auto repair shops, etc. Copies of these can be placed with each prospective client profile belonging to that category. If the classification is an especially large one given the market situation, you can also break down these categories into subunits. Restaurants, for example, can be divided into fast food places, pizza parlors, and formal dining establishments, with separate competitive summaries written for each division.

For purposes of illustration, let's say that one of your station's sales personnel is trying to woo business from a furniture emporium that has not previously advertised on your outlet. This salesperson should be able to obtain from the prospects file a prewritten, generic competition analysis covering local furniture stores as a whole. This can be supplemented with the individual sketches on each of the stores, including, of course, the profile on the store being courted. As that store becomes more interested and requests more detailed advertising suggestions, its abbreviated profile can be expanded and updated on the basis of the information to which it now gives you or your sales staff access. The generic competition analysis can also be customized to take into account the particular strengths and activities of this store and, if necessary, the other three stages of a full-dress proposal can now be prepared.

If the furniture store joins your list of time-buyers, the preresearch will have immediately paid off. But even if the store decides to forgo spot buys with your station or through your agency at this time, all the effort has not been wasted.

For, in the courting process, you have acquired a good deal more information about that store and, therefore, about the furniture business in your market; information that can help you serve that firm more quickly in the future. And even if the store *never* signs a contract with you, your prospects file has still been enriched by much more specific and comprehensive material about it— material that can be very useful in constructing pitches or formal proposals to that store's competition.

A closely allied procedure in which you as a copywriter may be involved is called *spec writing.* In spec writing, you prepare sample spots for businesses that are not yet your clients. Technically, the last stage of formal proposal development can be labelled spec writing but, more commonly, the term relates to the creation of a catalog of generic spots for each of the prime business categories from which your station or firm would expect to draw clientele.

In this latter use of the term, spec writing can be an extremely frustrating experience for the copywriter since, in many ways, you are writing in a vacuum. If you have access to a prospects file, you at least have a general idea about the competitive arena in which your sample spots must function and a broad out-line of the advertising approaches being used in it. Nonetheless, you are still forced to create prototype advertising for an as yet unnamed product or business; advertising that your station's sales or agency's account force might use to entice several different firms in that same classification.

Worse yet, you may find yourself in a regional or national spec writing situation in which you have only the broadest of market data to guide you. And, in a few cases, you may even be ordered to prepare a *general spec spot inventory*—a series of treatments that could be auditioned by prospects in a wide variety of business categories to show them the advantages of radio or television or the type of creative styling your firm can employ to showcase them.

Under such circumstances, you can only, like Charles M. Schulz's poor old Charlie Brown, bull your neck and grit your teeth and swing. Use whatever product classification parameters and data that are available to you in orienting your hypothetical approach to the very real marketplace consumers at which this approach is supposedly aimed. Even if you have been given only the broadest description of the types of business or services to which your spec spots are expected to appeal, you can, at the minimum, make sure each announcement you write includes a rational appeal, an emotional appeal, a consumer-involving benefit, and the other main qualities that have been dis-cussed over the last eleven chapters. Since even the most vaguely assigned piece of spec writing still has to have some sort of product or service in it in order to *be* a spot, you can at least formulate a workable benefit approach from the general product classifications to which your spec spot can be applied.

The following spec spot has been adroitly created by master copywriter Dick Orkin to promote virtually any economy furniture store anywhere in the country. The underlined sections can be removed and replaced with another emporium's name without in any way compromising the integrity of the concept. That is spec writing at its finest and most difficult.

WIFE: Charles, it's not necessary for you to build all our furniture yourself!

MAN: But where could you find a couch like this?

WIFE: This is not a couch!

MAN: What is it then?

WIFE: This is a lot of bleach bottles stapled together and covered with an old shower curtain.

MAN: But think of all the money we're saving!

WIFE: There's a better way to furnish our home! Brandon Furniture! They're inexpensive, but they have a wide selection of quality furniture.

MAN: Like our coffee table.

WIFE: This is just an old tire.

MAN: So?

WIFE: So where do you put stuff on it?

MAN: I didn't say it was perfect.

WIFE: Take me to Brandon Furniture so we can get rid of this junk!

MAN: This dining room table you call junk?

WIFE: Because it's our old worn out screen door balancing on two garbage cans—

MAN: But think of the money we're saving!

WIFE: It's nothing compared to what we'd save at Brandon Furniture.
For example, this lamp you're making out of tuna fish cans. What's it costing you?

MAN: Um—well, let's see. 500 cans of tuna fish, at $800, plus two kitty cats to eat the tuna—

WIFE: Charles—

ANNCR: Think how much farther your money will go during Brandon Brothers Fall Clearance. Everything on the floor is up to one-half off now through the end of the month. Save now during Fall Clearance prices at Brandon Brothers Furniture. Jupiter Road at Kingsley.

(Courtesy of Fran Sax, FirstCom.)

Unless anchored by a particularly strong category concept (like the Orkin spot above) spec-written spots usually are not designed to get any actual airplay. From everything we have said in this and previous chapters, it should be clear that the most successful broadcast advertising arises from careful scrutiny of a *particular* product with *particular* benefits for a *particular* target audience, and *particular* advantages over a *particular* list of competitors. The speculative spot, conversely, is intended to evince creative selling technique. Except when constructed by an outstanding copywriter with a multimarket use plan firmly in mind, the spec spot's sole priority is to sell *itself* and the station or agency that is using it to attract new clients.

CASE STUDIES

A discussion of broadcast campaign construction and its motivating creative strategies would not be complete without the presentation of some classic illustrative examples of campaign development in action. The cases that follow will not articulate every step in proposal evolution. To do so would require an entire book in and of itself. Instead, they collectively serve to exemplify the interaction of market analyses and conditions with creative design and development.

Case #1: Ronzoni Macaroni[16]

The Ronzoni company was the "little guy" in a "big guy" dominated field. As an initially single-market company competing in that market against the nationally active subsidiaries of giant conglomerates, how does a family-owned business survive?

It survives through an advertising approach that makes the most of this family-run characteristic; in other words, an approach that, in classic positioning theory, finds what's different and then sells it. When the Murray Firestone & Associates agency first acquired the Ronzoni account, its staffers conducted on-site research and found that no single phase of the business was run without the personal supervision of a member of the Ronzoni family. They also found that, in the old Italian sections of Greenwich Village and the East Bronx, when you asked for a "package of pasta" in a grocery store, you were handed a box of Ronzoni.

With a consequent Advertising Objective *to let people know that Ronzoni quality was a family as well as a brand name hallmark* and a positioning statement that "there's always a Ronzoni watching the pot," these market observations were put into creative action. The camera crew went right to the factory and showed Richard Ronzoni and his cousin Ron in their normal day's work: checking the ingredients, the preparation, and the taste of Ronzoni spaghetti sauce. In another spot, the action was placed in an East Bronx Italian neighborhood where, as the visual cuts from one Italian delicacy to another, the voice-over concludes:

```
Next time you're in an Italian neighborhood, go into a store and
ask for spaghetti. No special brand---just spaghetti. And see
what you get.
```

16. Extracted from Murray Firestone, writing in "Monday Memo," *Broadcasting Magazine,* March 31, 1975, p. 14.

The final shot then focused on the box of Ronzoni being laid right on the counter.

This campaign's slice-of-life response to market realities brought Ronzoni's share of its home-base New York pasta market up 33 percent during an eight-year period and helped propel the client from single-city status as a pasta manufacturer to multicity success as a purveyor of a complete line of pasta, sauce, frozen-food, and egg-noodle products.

Case #2: Pizza Hut[17]

A franchiser that had been in operation since 1958, Pizza Hut, Inc. later encountered more and more competition in the national marketplace. Its agency, Noble-Dury & Associates, therefore set out to find a campaign approach that would continue to make Pizza Hut stand apart from its newcomer rivals for the "above-average-income families with children" trade. Unlike Ronzoni's, the Pizza Hut organization is a publicly held corporation that needs brand identity and brand image to tie together its scores of unrelated (from a family standpoint) franchisees.

From extensive research efforts that included attitude-awareness and usage studies, group interviews, and other survey techniques, three primary benefits seemed to surface constantly in regard to this client: (1) the consistent popularity of its food product; (2) the courteous service provided by its employees; and (3) the unrushed, comfortable atmosphere of its uniformly designed places of business. As all three of these characteristics flowed directly from the Pizza Hut people, the key consumer benefit-complex (as expressed in the client analysis summation) seemed to be that:

```
The people who run the restaurants are enthusiastic and
dedicated. Great care is taken in food preparation and all
products are made by hand. Courteous service is provided by
trained waitresses. The atmosphere is pleasant and conducive to
relaxation and total enjoyment of a meal. The manager and his
people are determined to please each customer.
```

From this portrait of the client as filtered through a comparison with the attributes of key competitors, emerged the AO:

```
Communicate to above-average-income families with children that
Pizza Hut restaurants employ dedicated people whose primary
responsibility is to serve customers.
```

This AO, in turn, fostered the original positioning statement, "Our people make our pizza better," and, when the franchise's menu was expanded the following year, the broadened application, "Our people make it better."

To bring life to the claim, Pizza Hut spots, like those for Ronzoni's, used real-life employees and locations whenever possible in both the video and the sound track. From waitresses washing the windows to managers accepting fresh

17. Extracted from Moyers, *Broadcasting Magazine*, July 21, 1975, p. 10.

vegetable deliveries, copy execution of the research-mandated strategy led to increased Pizza Hut sales and, just as importantly for the future, increased brand awareness throughout the country.

Case #3: Benihana[18]

Though there is hardly a citizen who cannot accurately define what a pizza is, there is a far less widespread understanding of the true character of Japanese food. As Kracauer & Marvin Advertising found in planning a campaign for the Benihana of Tokyo restaurant chain, most Americans perceived Japanese cooking as leaning heavily to rice and uncooked seafood. Thus, the agency's advertising strategy could take far less for granted than could that for Pizza Hut or, for that matter, Ronzoni's. As a demonstration vehicle, television was figured to have the capability to dispel the culinary clichés about Japanese cuisine at the same time it was showing the enjoyment that eating at a Benihana restaurant could provide. In addition, television was selected as a preemptive strike medium against the competitors who had been riding in on Benihana's pioneering coattails in market after market. All three of these goals reduced themselves to one fundamental objective:

`To introduce the restaurant-goer to Benihana's special mystique.`

Via the Creative Selling Ideas that spun off this objective, several unique but complementary creative treatments were employed. One spot featured the testimony of Benihana's founder, Rocky Aoki, who pointed out:

`When I came to this country nine years ago, most Americans`
`thought Japanese cooking meant only sukiyaki. Or raw fish. But I`
`had a dream. I'd introduce hibachi cooking to America.`

As Rocky talked, the trademark theatricality of the Benihana chef who cooks your meal at your table was being visually demonstrated as was the tempting (and definitely non-raw-fish) character of hibachi steak.

In an associated commercial, a man rattled off a list of anxieties about what Japanese food would do to him. Suddenly, the Benihana chef appears, performs his cooking extravaganza, and leaves the man chastened but happily digging into his steak. Thus, the spot not only broke the Japanese food stereotype but also illuminated the unique performance aspect at Benihana that differentiated it from rival Japanese eateries. Another treatment in the same vein filtered the whole scene through the Benihana chef's perspective and featured a rookie about to make his in-restaurant debut. An old-pro chef provides the nervous youngster with a pep talk and sends him out to give what ends up being a masterful performance, thus simultaneously demonstrating the consumer-related benefits accruing from the Benihana dining experience while creating interest-heightening empathy for the Benihana chef.

---

18. Extracted from Hans Kracauer, writing in "Monday Memo," *Broadcasting Magazine*, March 4, 1974, p. 15.

After only six weeks on the air, this three-pronged but carefully focused campaign increased volume at several Benihana locations by as much as 35 percent.

Case #4: Calavo Avocado Guacamole[19]

A carefully directed radio campaign can have just as much impact in its own way as can a television plan—even in cases where, like Benihana, the product itself is in basic need of defining. Such a definitional problem was met head-on and solved by the old Anderson-McConnell agency in an historic campaign on behalf of its client, the Calavo Growers of California.

The product to be marketed was Calavo's guacamole—a frozen avocado dip which, though one-of-a-kind as to its ingredients, had to compete with the much better known dip flavors manufactured and promoted by much larger corporations. It was, in short, a Ronzoni-size problem and Benihana definitional task all rolled into one.

With a small budget that made radio the only feasible broadcast delivery system, the Anderson-McConnell creative group went about their analytical work. Given the uniqueness of the product and its name, an extensive client and competition analysis was unnecessary. The Advertising Objective, after all, was virtually automatic:

To identify and introduce to party-givers what guacamole is and who makes it.

Because avocados were still a fairly exotic item in most parts of the country, it was doubtful that consumers would make that key original purchase simply for their own snacking as they would, say, a new brand of peanut butter. Rather, special foods are purchased for special occasions—for parties, in other words, so those people whose social and economic status enabled them to give parties became the campaign's target audience. And since parties are supposed to be fun, a light, humorous approach seemed not only natural, but almost mandatory—as long as the humor did not decrease the attention given to product definition. Here are two of the spots that executed this concept.

Spot #1 (30 secs.)

(MUSIC:	COCKTAIL DANCE-BEAT BEGINS)
(SFX:	INTERMINGLE PARTY SOUNDS)
WOMAN:	Would you like to try the avocado dip?
MAN:	Sure, is it anything like the tango?
(MUSIC:	UP AND STOPS FOR:)
MAN:	Do you realize that Calavo is the only one in history to successfully freeze a ready-to-serve avocado dip?

19. Extracted from Clinton Rogers, writing in "Monday Memo," *Broadcasting Magazine*, June 10, 1968, p. 18.

2ND MAN:	Holy guacamole!
(MUSIC:	<u>STARTS</u> <u>AND</u> <u>STOPS</u> <u>FOR</u>:)
WOMAN:	Listen---if <u>she's</u> serving this jazzy avocado dip, it <u>must</u> be easy to serve. Why, it takes her two hours to make instant coffee.
(MUSIC:	<u>STARTS</u> <u>WITH</u> <u>FOLLOWING</u> <u>VOICES</u> <u>OVER</u> <u>IT</u>)
MAN:	GWA-ka-mole, eh?
WOMAN:	<u>WA</u>-ka-mole. Calavo Avocado Guacamole.
MAN:	(In rhythm) Calavo Avocado Guacamole (BEAT) Dip.
ALL:	(In rhythm) Calavo Avocado Guacamole (BEAT) Dip. (Fading off) Calavo Avocado Guacamole (BEAT) Dip. (Repeat to fade out at time.)

. . . .

<u>Spot #2</u>   (60 secs.)

(MUSIC:	<u>COCKTAIL</u> <u>DANCE-BEAT</u> <u>BEGINS</u>)
(SFX:	INTERMINGLE PARTY SOUNDS)
(MUSIC:	<u>STOPS</u> <u>FOR</u>:)
MAN:	(Pompous) It's a scientific breakthrough, do you hear? Frozen avocado dip, fully prepared and ready to release its provocative flavor at the touch of a can opener. What do you say to that, eh?
2ND MAN:	What <u>can</u> I say? Holy guacamole!
(MUSIC:	<u>STARTS</u> <u>AND</u> <u>STOPS</u> <u>FOR</u>:)
WOMAN:	Calavo Avocado Guacamole, Roger?
3RD MAN:	You're talking my language, Elaine.
(MUSIC:	<u>STARTS</u> <u>AND</u> <u>STOPS</u> <u>FOR</u>:)
MAN:	Honey, did you know that this avocado dip is frozen at 300 degrees below zero?
2ND WOMAN:	Speaking of that, dear, did you notice I'm the only woman at this party without a mink coat?
(MUSIC:	<u>STARTS</u>:)
2ND MAN:	GWA-ka-mole, eh?
3RD WOMAN:	<u>WA</u>-ka-mole. Calavo Avocado Guacamole.
3RD MAN:	(In rhythm) Calavo Avocado Guacamole (BEAT) Dip.
ALL:	(In rhythm) Calavo Avocado Guacamole (BEAT) Dip. (Repeat to fade out at time.)

Definition, boisterous brand memorability, and continuing universe-oriented interest make this Calavo campaign a classic low-budget success story. As it unmistakably proves, careful campaign planning can bring significant dividends to small as well as large account applications.

Case #5: Riceland Rice[20]

To succeed, the Calavo and Benihana campaigns had to define and promote a product among consumers who were highly unfamiliar with it. The Riceland Rice account, handled by Noble-Dury & Associates, had exactly the opposite task. It had to demonstrate to heavy users of rice—to people who are already virtual rice experts—that Riceland was the brand for them. As the largest selling brand of regularly milled rice in America, the Arkansas-based farmer-marketing organization that *is* Riceland knew that reaching heavy users of rice was essential to sales growth since only 36 percent of all households use rice once a week or more. But this market is further complicated by the fact that it is divided into two segments: those who use precooked rice (like Minute and Uncle Ben's), and those willing to take the extra ten or twelve minutes to use a regular milled variety such as Riceland. Thus, Noble-Dury had to devise an advertising position that had merit for both precooked and regular-milled users in the half of the country in which its client's product was distributed.

Through further client analysis, the agency found that Riceland was already the leading regular-milled brand and that it was served in the most popular restaurants in the heaviest rice-using states (Arkansas, Louisiana, South Carolina). From these marketing data, a two-pronged Advertising Objective was derived:

To show users of precooked rice that Riceland offers <u>better flavor</u> for the extra few minutes of cooking time needed.

(and)

To illustrate for users of regular rice that Riceland offers <u>constantly</u> good flavor.

Out of this dual AO came the single positioning statement:

Riceland Rice---for people that know about rice.

Neither an elegant nor a particularly glossy line, it nonetheless succeeded because it was on-target with the style and preferences of the heavy-user universe at which it was aimed. The commercial executions struck this same responsive chord. Shot in key restaurants located in heavy rice-consuming areas, each spot used music indigenous to the pictured locale to bolster further the credibility of the visual testimonials and make the positioning statement come alive for rice lovers. Photoboards of these spots are featured in Figures 12–5 to 12–8.

Case #6: Tri-State Buick/Opel Dealer Association[21]

The Riceland flight clearly visualizes its product for the audience. But can a television campaign succeed that never once shows the wares it is promoting?

20. Extracted from Don Wirth, writing in "Monday Memo," *Broadcasting Magazine,* July 4, 1977, p. 8.
21. Extracted from Don Fergusson, writing in "Monday Memo," *Broadcasting Magazine,* May 28, 1973, p. 14.

RICELAND RICE

30-second Television Commercial
"Mannie Crusto"

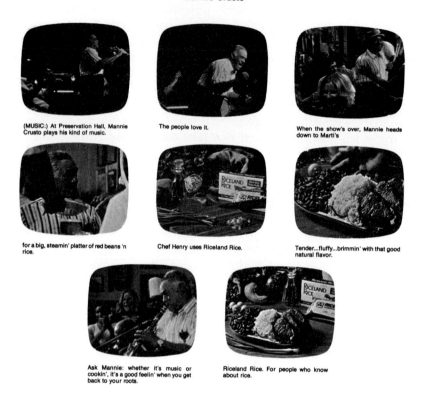

(MUSIC:) At Preservation Hall, Mannie
Crusto plays his kind of music.

The people love it.

When the show's over, Mannie heads
down to Marti's

for a big, steamin' platter of red beans 'n
rice.

Chef Henry uses Riceland Rice.

Tender...fluffy...brimmin' with that good
natural flavor.

Ask Mannie: whether it's music or
cookin', it's a good feelin' when you get
back to your roots.

Riceland Rice. For people who know
about rice.

Figure 12–5.

The people at Shiffman/Fergusson Advertising thought so and proved it in the planning and execution of a campaign for the collective Buick dealer associations in New York, New Jersey, and Connecticut.

Budget limitations constituted an immediate and unyielding parameter. None of the individual state associations could themselves afford television, and even their pooled funds did not provide what most would consider a very significant resource. So stretching production dollars across more than one model year was a necessity.

From a market research standpoint, too, the Buick dealers had a problem. For even though they now featured models in every price range, the public perception persisted that Buick was a high-priced vehicle appealing mainly to older people. In addition, client analysis turned up the unhappy truth that factory communications concentrated on selling the styling and quality of Buick automobiles, but not their affordability. Little wonder that Shiffman/Fergusson's Advertising Objective had to focus on:

RICELAND RICE
30-second Television Commercial "Pierre Part"

MUSIC	MUSIC	ANNCR: Here in Pierre Part, Louisiana,
people come to the Rainbow Inn	for a good Cajun band	and Jimmie Cavalier's shrimp creole.
Jimmie knows the freshest shrimp and the tastiest peppers	deserve the tenderest, fluffiest rice. Riceland Rice.	If you want the best shrimp creole on the bayou . . .
or in your own home . . .	use the best rice!	Riceland Rice. For people who know about rice.

Figure 12–6.

Convincing young car buyers and middle-aged and older blue-collar workers in the tri-state market that Buick is an affordable as well as a desirable car.

Out of this AO came the positioning statement, "If you price a Buick, you'll buy a Buick," as well as Creative Selling Ideas aimed at each target audience: the young car buyers on the one hand and the older working class prospects on the other.

The youth-directed flight used humorous situations to get its message across. One commercial in this set focused on an Italian race car driver and his interpreter. The interpreter pointed out that the race car driver had been behind

RICELAND RICE
30-second Television Commercial "Heber Springs"

MUSIC
ANNCR: Maybe it's crazy to drive hundreds of miles

for chicken 'n rice.

But not when it's Mrs. Beardsley's chicken 'n rice.

MUSIC

She runs the Stockholm Restaurant

in Heber Springs, Arkansas. And the things

Mrs. Beardsley does with her Riceland Rice

you've just gotta taste to believe. It always cooks up tender

and tastes terrific.

Do like Mrs. Beardsley:

Get Riceland Rice for some good eatin'.

Riceland Rice. For people who know about rice.

Figure 12–7.

the wheel of many prestigious cars but preferred the American Buick. In fact, he liked it better than spaghetti—because it didn't cost much more than spaghetti. The spot ended with the signature, "If you price a Buick, you'll buy a Buick."

The flight aimed at the more mature buyers featured older, real-life working men such as a hot-dog vendor, tollgate operator, and hansom-cab driver and showed each in his work setting, testifying to enjoying a Buick even though he had thought he couldn't afford one. Viewed driving his hack back to the horse barn at New York's Central park, the hansom-cab driver says:

RICELAND RICE

30-Second Television Commercial
"Perdita's"

MUSIC: (VO) Charleston, South Carolina.

Where you can ride back through the Centuries.

And here at Perdita's Restaurant,

you'll be tempted with entrees like Crab Remick....

prepared with fresh seafood...

and Riceland Rice.

Nothing compares to Riceland's texture and natural flavor.

If you can't spend a day in Charleston and Perdita's, spend 14 minutes preparing the world's finest rice.

Riceland Rice. For people who know about rice.

Figure 12-8. *(Credit: These four photoboards courtesy of Nobel-Dury & Associates, Nashville, Tennessee*
CLIENT: Riceland Foods, Stuttgart, Arkansas
PRODUCT: Riceland Rice
CREATIVE DIRECTOR: Bill Mostad
COPYWRITER: Don Wirth
PRODUCER: Mannie Crusto: *Bill Mostad*
Pierre Part, Heber Springs, Perdita's: Don Wirth
PRODUCTION COMPANY: Morrison Productions, New Orleans
DIRECTOR: Hobby Morrison)

Bet you thought all a guy like me could afford was a Ford or Chevy or watcha call your half-pint Pontiac. Well, I got myself a Buick for no more money---and it couldn't have happened to a more deserving fellow.

After the driver puts his cab away, the viewer sees a close-up of him through the window of his automobile (what we assume to be his Buick) as he says, "I really enjoy my weekends in this buggy." Again, the illustration of the positioning statement, "If you price a Buick, you'll buy a Buick."

All right, this was a well-coordinated, well-executed campaign for Buick. But notice something else about it—*no Buick was actually ever shown!* At most, all that was featured was part of a window frame during the hansom-cab driver's testimonial. What was shown was, as the agency put it, "the sizzle, not the steak," and thus every commercial was timeless. Each spot could be used for years without the need for reshooting every time the manufacturer changed its chrome strips or hub caps. Production funds could easily be stretched across the otherwise constraining boundaries of model years, and new spots could be added (as affordable) to the pool of existing ones, thereby creating ever greater rotational flexibility through an ever-expanding spot inventory. As long as the market-derived AO and positioning statement provided the common denominator, any year's commercial could be used far into the future without danger of campaign fragmentation.

Case #7: WRQX[22]

Chapters 7 and 10 notwithstanding, we tend to forget that stations are products, too, and that their promotion (on their own air) and advertising (via other media vehicles) require the same careful campaign/creative strategy development as do the promotion and advertising for a box of rice or macaroni. In deriving a television approach for Washington D.C.'s WRQX (known as Q107), Needham, Harper & Steers had to find ways to transform a radio station's sound into a visual commodity. Q107's Contemporary Rock format, in short, had to be packaged into a highly focused video embodiment.

Since the station's own format-justifying research was already available, it was obvious from it that the target audience was composed of men and women, ages 18 to 34, with secondary emphasis on teens, ages 12 through 17. Just as obvious, since WRQX had only recently changed to its Contemporary Rock format, the Advertising Objective for television had to be:

> To get target audience listeners to tune-in for a first-trial sampling of Q107 by exemplifying what kind of music the station plays and where it's located on the radio (FM) dial.

The positioning statement therefore told the selected universe that:

```
Q107 plays the hits you want to hear.
```

To achieve the proposition, the television treatments depicted the same kinds of people as comprised the aimed-for demographics—and showed them having fun in contemporary, up-beat situations that blended well with "Top 40s" music and lifestyle. Because the target viewers could easily relate to the "real people" in the spots, Q107 was established as the station their friends (actual and hoped-for) listened to for enjoyment, relaxation, and right-now popularity. Humorous copy, up-tempo lyrics, and animated graphics all stressed the identity line, "Hits

---

22. Extracted from materials courtesy of Gerald Downey, WRQX.

happening right on Q," and thereby focused on the station's playlist and on its location at the extreme right of the FM dial. Everything the viewer saw or heard was always sliding, turning, moving, or mentioning "right"; getting them away from the heavy concentration of stations to the left and center of the dial and "right" over to Q107.

Video	Audio
OPEN ON MS CHRISTINE WEARING ''Hits Happening Right on Q'' T-SHIRT. SHE'S SEATED AT CONTEMPORARY BREAKFAST NOOK; LOTS OF PLANTS IN BG.	CHRISTINE: I have a way of getting up
CAMERA TRUCKS RIGHT.	in the morning that's really remarkable. I like to wake up with the Dude.
ECU TABLE RADIO AS SHE DIALS IT RIGHT TO Q. PAN RIGHT, FRAME MCU CHRISTINE	And, aah, on Q107. DUDE WALKER (VO): 6:20 on Q107 with your Dude awakening. Time to wake-up. (SFX: Q-Fex) And now the Eagles, on Q. . . (MUSIC: IN AND UNDER
BEGIN DOLLY BACK TO MLS	CHRISTINE: Not only are they warm and lots of fun, but everyone knows they play more music. So next time your alarm goes off, wake up on the right side, right on Q107. A remarkable way to wake up.
SHE REACHES TO FINE TUNE RADIO, SMILES AT CAMERA	(MUSIC: FEATURE TO TIME)

(Courtesy of Gerald Downey, WRQX Radio.)

In this and the other Q-commercials, the emotional appeals of laughter, people interest, uniqueness, and allurement were intermixed with a constant rational appeal of performance in showing WRQX's universe why they'd like the station and what they had to do to get there. This well integrated creative strategy certainly worked, for, within one year of its execution in television and associated media, WRQX became the number 1 rated station in Washington, D.C.

Case #8: Pretty Feet (and Hands)[23]

Taking a product much older than the format of WRQX, Revlon's John Muhlfeld achieved equal success through determined *re*positioning. His firm's Pretty Feet had been introduced some twenty years before as a lotion for rubbing away rough skin and calluses on women's feet. Unfortunately, Pretty Feet had initially been positioned too narrowly. As a podiatry aid, the product performed very well but, given such a limited use, one bottle would last a woman for years.

After acquiring Pretty Feet from a series of previous corporate owners, Revlon and its agency, Cadwell Davis Savage, conducted a thorough product and market analysis, finding that (1) women's hobbies and vocations had become much more physical in the two decades that had elapsed since product unveiling; (2) Pretty Feet worked equally well to remove rough skin, calluses, and stains from the hands, elbows, and other exposed parts of the body.

With this information, the agency adopted an Advertising Objective aimed at repositioning Pretty Feet by showing physically active women that the product was indispensable as an all-around skin care/repair application. This new strategy was enhanced by modifying the name of the product to Pretty Feet & Hands and by television commercials that, in two stages, accomplished the name change and broadened use pattern right in front of the viewers' eyes and ears. In the first commercial, a dancer was seen in performance and then back in her dressing room where she reveals:

```
I dance through a pair of shoes a week. If it weren't for Pretty
Feet, I'd have ugly feet. Pretty Feet rolls away the rough, dry
skin I don't want---leaves the skin I do want. Then I discovered
it does the same for my hands---rolls away chapped, dry skin.
Maybe they should call it Pretty Feet & Hands.
```

An announcer voice-over then muses:

```
Maybe we should call it Pretty Feet & Hands.
```

A few months later, with rechristening accomplished, the second stage commercial took to the air featuring a dancing couple followed by the young woman's revelation that:

```
I dance through a pair of shoes a week---think of my feet. Thank
goodness for Pretty Feet & Hands. It rolls the rough stuff off my
feet and peels the dry skin off my hands.
```

Through this carefully sequenced campaign, the product was liberated from retail outlets' summer-oriented foot care sections and relocated on the year-

23. Extracted from John Muhlfeld, writing in "Monday Memo," *Broadcasting Magazine*, August 21, 1978, p. 16.

round hand and moisturizer shelves, thereby increasing point-of-purchase visibility and uninterrupted product exposure. Repositioning had been successfully accomplished because the television campaign had issued directly out of marketplace realities and marketing needs.

Case #9: Second Debut[24]

Another skin care product requiring renovation through Concept Engineering was Second Debut, a moisturing lotion manufactured by Beecham, Inc. Under the guidance of Shaller Rubin Associates, a small New York advertising agency, a detailed re-analysis of the product was undertaken—a re-analysis that ran right into the unvarnished truth that in name and use, the product is not for the young woman. Unlike Pretty Feet & Hands, it was not the item's appellation that needed changing but rather, the faulty creative strategy that refused to accept the fundamental implications of the item's name. As Mel Rubin, the agency's chairman, put it, "You don't have to be a genius to know that before a woman will admit she's making her second debut, she's probably already making her third. So, we start with the first simple step: How do women forty-five and over like this product?"

Since the resulting client analysis found that existing users in this age group liked the product just fine, the agency settled on an Advertising Objective that would assure over-forty-five females that Second Debut was an effective cosmetic ally for all the good and productive years that lay ahead. The spin-off positioning statement, "I'm making my Second Debut now; I've got what it takes to see it through now," was cast in cheerful lyric form to keep the product use experience positive and to facilitate tight integration between television spot soundtracks and the supporting radio commercials. Leading with, "Look out world, here I come again; I'm more of a woman than I've ever been," and concluding with the positioning statement, the lyric copy was universe-directed without being threatening or accusatory.

To provide a central and relevant product spokesperson for Second Debut, actress/singer Rhonda Fleming was selected. After more than two decades, Miss Fleming was not only making her own "second debut" as a singer, but also possessed an enviable physical appearance. Furthermore, she actually used and liked the product—no need for testimonial disclaimers here. As a trained singer, Miss Fleming could perform the lyric herself for yet another integrating element in the total broadcast campaign; a campaign that brought Second Debut back to the marketplace forefront through a hardnosed creative strategy, sensitively implemented.

Case #10: Snuggle[25]

It is one thing to reestablish market position and quite another to accomplish market penetration in the first place. Lever Brothers' Snuggle brand fabric softener, through the help of a cuddly teddy bear, was able to carve out a

---

24. Extracted from Rubin, *Broadcasting Magazine,* July 9, 1979, p. 10.
25. Extracted from Rosenberg, *ADWEEK/Midwest,* April, 1985, p. F.C. 36.

hefty national market share even before it became a national brand. In fact, in markets where it competed head-to-head with Procter & Gamble's long-entrenched Downy, Snuggle garnered 28 percent of fabric softener purchases in just a little more than two years.

In order to meet the objective of proving to women age twenty-five to fifty-four that Snuggle was the effective *and lower priced* fabric softener/static cling reducer, Lever's agency, SSC&B, launched a television campaign in which Snuggle, a teddy bear, became the actual personification of the product. "He's the very essence of softness," noted agency Executive Vice President Carolyn Hirschklau, "who also happens to demonstrate the end benefit of the product. The bear sells very hard, but he sells by example." (See Figures 12–9 and 12–10.)

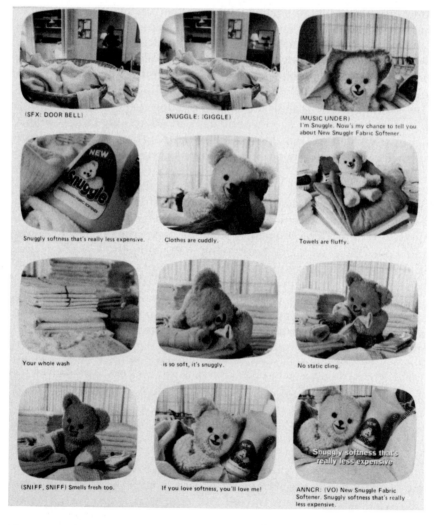

(SFX: DOOR BELL)

SNUGGLE: (GIGGLE)

(MUSIC UNDER)
I'm Snuggle. Now's my chance to tell you about New Snuggle Fabric Softener.

Snuggly softness that's really less expensive.

Clothes are cuddly.

Towels are fluffy.

Your whole wash

is so soft, it's snuggly.

No static cling.

(SNIFF, SNIFF) Smells fresh too.

If you love softness, you'll love me!

ANNCR: (VO) New Snuggle Fabric Softener. Snuggly softness that's really less expensive.

Figure 12–9. *(Courtesy of John Speirs, Lever Brothers, and Carolyn T. Hirschklau, SSC&B Inc.)*

Figure 12–10. *(Courtesy of John Speirs, Lever Brothers, and Carolyn T. Hirschklau, SSC&B Inc.)*

Ending with the tagline/positioning statement, "snuggly softness that's really less expensive," the spots mystically revealed a talking teddy who appears only when everyone else is gone. This established an aura of magic—not only for the bear but also for how the namesake product assumedly worked. Combined with the gentle theme music that underscored all six commercials in the flight, the Snuggle teddy lulled the viewer into a warm feeling of acceptance toward the product—a styling that was worlds apart from the prosaic slice-of-life approach being used by market giant Downy. Snuggle's benefit-epitomizing cuddliness also hooked viewers into readily suspending their disbelief while brand recall was driven home. Through its success, the comparatively low-budget Snuggle campaign demonstrated that sometimes concept and execution can be so intertwined as to be indistinguishable from each other.

A CAMPAIGN CONCLUSION

Having studied two versions of Concept Engineering, and after your exposure to ten separate case studies, you should have developed a working acquaintanceship with the components of broadcast campaign construction. As a culminating exercise, analyze the Subaru campaign reflected in the Figure 12–11, 12–12, and 12–13 photoboards.

What does this campaign's Advertising Objective appear to be? Is this reduced to a cogent Positioning Statement? What CSI is reflected in each of the three commercials? Is there one CSI or do the individual spots emanate from separate

Figure 12–11. *(Courtesy of copywriter Lee Garfinkel; Levine, Huntley, Schmidt & Beaver, Inc.)*

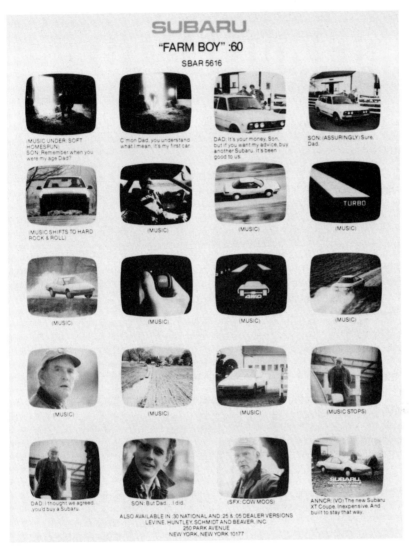

Figure 12–12. *(Courtesy of copywriter Lee Garfinkel; Levine, Huntley, Schmidt & Beaver, Inc.)*

ones? Does the creative execution seem to flow directly from the AO and at what universe(s) does it appear to be aimed? Answering these questions should help you consolidate your knowledge of campaign construction—perhaps to the point at which you can one day create a case-study success of your own.

It should be clear from all of our case studies that successful broadcast campaigns are neither generated by, nor aired in, a vacuum. Rather, they are the outgrowth of a great deal of laborious research and step-by-step intellectual

Figure 12–13. *(Courtesy of copywriter Lee Garfinkel; Levine, Huntley, Schmidt & Beaver, Inc.)*

analysis. As Paul Harper, chairman of Needham, Harper & Steers once remarked at the agency's Professional Conference:

> It is the right combination of shoe leather and scholarship that eventually leads you to a key fact about the market that everyone else has overlooked. It is only by separating truths from half-truths, straw from chaff, that you eventually find the shining needle—a competitive weakness, a proprietary strength—that nobody perceived before in quite the same way.
> That is the beginning of advertising victory.[26]

26. Paul Harper, *Victory in Advertising* (New York: Needham, Harper & Steers, 1980), p. 4.

Chapter 13

POLITICAL, CONTROVERSY, AND CRISIS CAMPAIGNS

As we have discussed in the first eleven chapters, the seemingly simple act of penning a few dozen words for a radio or television message is, in reality, a very complex and hazard-prone enterprise. And, as chapter 12 points out, the inter-weaving of multiple messages into a cogent and coherent campaign creates further responsibilities and considerations with which the copywriter must contend. In this chapter, we'll add another series of copywriter concerns—concerns that arise when the subject of your message is inherently contentious, frequently emotion-laden, and often intangible. We are, of course, talking about broadcast commercials and campaigns designed to elect a political candidate, advance one side of a controversial issue, or mitigate a crisis of confidence in which an otherwise conventional advertiser suddenly finds itself embroiled. The principles of spot and campaign construction previously discussed also apply here but are complicated by the abrasive nature of the subject matter with which your messages must deal.

POLITICAL ADVERTISING

Commercials designed to promote the candidacy of a particular individual for a public office are today known as *polispots.* Beginning with the 6,000 "Minute Men" who delivered identical Republican-promoting pitches over local radio stations in 1928, American polispots have grown in prominence, sophistication, and perceived importance ever since. No longer limited to national or even state-wide contests, candidate commercials are now a significant part of many local elections as well, with thousands and even millions of dollars being spent to influence voters in a single city or county.

Although they constitute only one of four primary avenues for reaching the electorate, most political advisers view polispots as the *preferred* thoroughfare, due primarily to the limitations seen to constrict the other three:

1. *Print advertising* is felt to be undynamic and uninvolving. It is further believed to be poorly read—and then only by the people already interested in the candidate or party. Thus, print is not widely perceived as the way to make inroads into the vital noncommitted constituencies. (You might review what was said about the "So What" audience in chapter 4.) For these reasons, James Severin, president of the

Severin/Aviles political consulting firm, observes: "I don't think there are any consultants left who are respected or eating that do anything in print anymore."[1]

2. *Personal appearances* may be romanticized as a noble throwback to grassroots politics but, as football raconteur Don Meredith once commented, "Things aren't like they used to be and never were." William McKinley never left his Ohio front porch in his successful 1896 presidential campaign, and Harry Truman's 31,000 mile whistle-stop saga of 1948 is seen as a desperation-fueled exception to the rule. More to the point, when it comes to contacting the general electorate rather than party functionaries, personal appearances are grossly inefficient. They reach only a few people at a tremendous expenditure of time. Worse, such sojourns fatigue a candidate—a very dangerous condition in an era when microphones and cameras are always present to record every slip. A tired candidate is at his or her unnatural worst and might even be perceived as punchy by viewers of the nightly news.

3. *Free media* is the term that encompasses that nightly news show, interview programs, and other unpaid exposure the candidate enjoys—particularly on radio and television. But even though free media do not cost the candidate anything in dollars, appearances on this forum are also outside of the candidate's control. In free media, it is the reporters, correspondents, and interviewers who call the shots and who, quite naturally and rightfully, have interests other than those of the candidate at heart.

Little wonder, then, that political candidates and their advisers have turned to the electronic paid media with ever-increasing frequency—and that broadcast copywriters are facing greater and greater opportunities and challenges in this arena. Candidate-controlled paid broadcasting can reach millions of people— and the right people—simultaneously. And while longer form paid broadcasts successfully play to party activists who seek them out, only polispots have the proven capacity to grab that fleeting attention of the uncommitted throngs. It is to the emerging guidelines concerning the construction of these polispots, therefore, that we now turn.

What Polispots Are Not

Before going any further, it must be made clear that effective polispots need not be superficial. In his content analysis of the 1980 United States presidential campaign, Leonard Shyles scrutinized a large number of primary election spots. His findings concluded that "televised political spot advertisements are not merely frivolous diversions. Such commercials can accurately define the issues of a political campaign. . . . These data suggest that political commercials attend to contemporary issues and reflect the political concerns of the times, regardless of how entertaining and emotionally engaging such messages might also be."[2] In short, like any well-fashioned commercial, a professional polispot is based on a rational appeal while recognizing that emotional packaging is vital for any message transported by an entertainment medium.

Nevertheless, a political commercial *is* a much different animal than an agency pitch for soap or dog food, and this difference extends to the way it is

1. "Political Advertising Tab in Fall Expected to Hit $250 Million," *Broadcasting Magazine*, September 3, 1984, p. 36.
2. Leonard Shyles, "Defining the Issues of a Presidential Election," *Journal of Broadcasting*, Fall, 1983, pp. 342–343.

conceived and produced as well as to its eventual content. As a polispot copy-writer, you must first recognize that the dynamics of an election campaign provide little lead time for spot development. Thus, polispot writing's abbreviated time line is more like that faced by the in-station copywriter than by an agency counterpart. Unexpected events and maneuverings by the other side can force literally overnight creations and execution changes.

Second, in so far as they feature the candidate, polispots are not usually dealing with professional talent but with media amateurs (the success of the Reagan exception thereby proving the rule). Demanding too much from the office-seeker's on-mike or on-camera performance can only result in an obviously staged portrayal that makes even the competent seem incompetent at best, or shifty at worst. In fact, given the time frame and talent limitations of the genre, political commercial creation is in some ways like producing local retail advertising in which the store owner insists he be a part of the message. Unlike the store owner, however, the candidate really *is* the product.

A third general difference between polispots and conventional commercials is that political messages, particularly for television, are often written *after,* not before they are shot. Footage of the candidate, supporters, and related events is gathered; the writer/producer's job then is to screen, select, and organize this material into a focused and meaningful message or series of messages. One cannot go back and reconstitute a rally, and a candidate's campaign schedule does not permit two or three days of pre-scripted shooting per commercial. Consequently, the political copywriter may spend a lot more time in an editing room than at a typewriter.

Fourth, a campaign committee is not like a regular client where designated marketing vice presidents and account executives do designated things in a clear chain of command. Instead, a political "coordinating" committee may be twenty people in a room telling you forty different things with no clear delineation of responsibilities or of who holds ultimate decision-making power. This is one reason traditional advertising agencies avoid political accounts, leaving them to freelance specialists or to agency executives on temporary leave from their normal duties.

A fifth distinction between candidate and commercial commodity advertising is that most packaged goods and services constitute minor purchases. If the consumer makes an unhappy choice, it can be rectified on the next trip to the store. Whom to vote for, on the other hand, is an immutable decision that lasts for years and may impact all areas of the consumer's life. Most citizens sense this important attribute and are therefore much more wary of polispot claims.

Finally, and most fundamentally, the personal stakes in a political campaign are much higher. "Clients are different from candidates," cautions advertising veteran Ed Buxton. "If their new campaign or new product bombs out, they can write it off and start over. The candidate—poor bastard—is not so lucky. He is out on his lonesome, in the cold, and usually in debt."[3] We will not speculate here on the implications of this turn of events for that candidate's polispot

3. Ed Buxton, "Adman, Pass By," *ADWEEK/Midwest,* May 7, 1984, p. 26.

copywriter. Suffice it to say that a diversified account list is not an unwise precaution.

Six Polispot Objectives

Given the gloomy alternative to victory, the overriding objective of political advertising is, of course, to get the candidate elected. But this ultimate goal can only be attained via the accomplishment of several subsidiary objectives along the way—subsidiary objectives in whose service your copy is recruited.

1. Make Like the Greeks. To a significant extent, candidate advertising is like classic drama. You strive to position your client as the "good guy" by deifying whatever virtue you can find. Along the way, you may recruit a Greek chorus of current officeholders, other famous personalities, and people-on-the-street to highlight and validate this portrayal of virtue. In this television spot for Senator Carl Levin, his record on Social Security legislation and his own monologue combine in a center-stage display of his sense of fairness.

Video	Audio
	ANNCR. (VO):
STILL PHOTO—BLACK AND WHITE	Tens of thousands of people had their
OTHER STILLS OF ELDERLY PEOPLE FILL QUAD	Social Security disability payments cut off between 1981 and 1983. Abruptly and unfairly.
STILL FRAME OF LEVIN COMES THROUGH QUAD AND MOVES TO UPPER OR RIGHT CORNER. BILLS COME FORWARD, ONE AT A TIME.	Carl Levin took action. His emergency legislation to restore Social Security payments and his bill to reform the disability system have meant that those who deserve help get it.
DIS. TO LEVIN ON CAMERA	LEVIN:
	We want people removed from the rolls who don't belong there. On the other hand, we want people to be given that protection if they're

Video	Audio
	entitled to it. And we should want that with equal passion.

DISCLAIMER/SLOGAN TITLE

(Courtesy of Stephen Serkaian, Office of Senator Carl Levin.)

Meanwhile, Levin's radio spots merge endorsements from several real and identified constituents in order to establish a chorus of acclaim for his stewardship:

ANNCR:	People from the Upper Peninsula know what kind of Senator Carl Levin has been for Michigan. People like Bruce Lange from Calumet.
LANGE VOICE:	He represents the people in the U.P. as well, if not better than the people downstate. I'm working with displaced workers and I see these people that are down there and Carl has feelings for those people.
ANNCR:	Gene Cofflin of Iron Mountain.
COFFLIN VOICE:	We've been very pleased because he has been so responsive. We call his office---they respond; both the local office in Escanaba and in Washington.
ANNCR:	Tom Selly of Ishpeming.
SELLY VOICE:	Senator Levin was of great help in my dealings with the Veterans Administration. An individual citizen could not get there from here without someone like Senator Levin to help.
ANNCR:	What kind of Senator has Carl Levin been for the Upper Peninsula? A Senator who's proven he cares about us.
	(Disclaimer Tag)

(Courtesy of Stephen Serkaian, Office of Senator Carl Levin.)

Recognize, however, that from both ethical and workability standpoints, Levin could not have dramatized these virtues if they were not *documentable*. When you attempt virtue fabrication, your candidate's opponents and the news media will be only too happy to expose the fiction. In his 1968 presidential victory, Richard Nixon was positioned as *competent*—not as particularly likeable or straightforward. It would have been easier to attack his claim on the latter two virtues than it was to assault him on the former.

2. You Pick the Battlefield. Like Nixon's preemption of the competency "high ground of advantage," it is important that your spots strive to set the

Campaign Copywriting

agenda early—strive to stake out issues in which your candidate has the discernible edge. In this way, your officeseeker, rather than your opponent, becomes the standard of comparison. During the 1980 Democratic presidential primary race, for example, it is generally accepted that

> President Carter's forces hoped to make the candidate's character a primary issue. Carter was widely thought of as a decent and honest family man whereas [Senator Edward] Kennedy's car accident at Chappaquiddick—in which a young woman drowned—and his attempts to explain the accident had raised questions about his morality and judgment in a crisis. . . . These issues, according to this analysis, became top items on the media's agenda and so, too, on the public agenda. Carter's performance and the economy were far lower on the list.[4]

By staking out the advantageous battleground early and convincingly, the Carter forces were successfully able to deflect attention from the country's economic ills—at least for the time being.

Yet, unfortunately for Carter, the character issue that played so well against Kennedy was not extendable to the general election struggle against Ronald Reagan, whose judgment and morality were not in question. As a polispot copywriter, therefore, it is wise to pick a theme (an Advertising Objective, if you will) that can be used for the duration of *both* the primary and general election campaigns. Notice how this Gary Hart television spot preempts the "New Leadership" position against both his Democratic primary rival (Walter Mondale) and the opponent either would have to face in the general election (Ronald Reagan).

Video	Audio
ALL VIDEO IS MCU 'LIVE ACTION' CLIPS FROM HART APPEARANCES	HART: How many of you voted for Reagan in (fade)...
	ANNCR (VO): Senator Gary Hart.
	HART: Ronald Reagan represents the past. I think the last administration and Mr. Mondale represent the past.
	ANNCR (VO): New leadership for our economy.
	HART: It means an education system. It means a trained

4. Melvin DeFleur and Everette Dennis, *Understanding Mass Communication* (Boston: Houghton Mifflin Company, 1981), p. 330.

Video	Audio
	work force. It means investment in private plants. It means managers who are going to put their profits back into their plants. It means training for workers and I strongly believe that workers ought to be able to own stock in a company because (fading) that gives them a chance...
DISCLAIMER/SLOGAN GRAPHIC	<u>ANNCR</u> <u>(VO)</u>: New leadership. We can't afford to go back.

(Courtesy of Raymond Strother, Raymond D. Strother, Ltd.)

For consistency, the same battlefield also should be chosen when the candidate's surrogates are speaking. As with the commercial campaigns discussed in chapter 12, you don't want to change your theme (your AO) with every change in spot technique. In other words, the CSIs should all service the same AO. Hart's "New Leadership" motif, for example, easily transcends technique shifts:

Video	Audio
MCU OF WORKER IN NATURAL ENVIRONMENT	<u>WORKER</u>: A good many of us in this valley gave Reagan a chance because we were so disillusioned with Carter and Mondale. Reagan's failed us. We're still disillusioned with Mondale. He's still the same Fritz Mondale. We <u>do</u> need somebody new. We like Gary Hart. I do, and I'm going to vote for him. We've had Mondale. We don't need him again.

Video	Audio
DISCLAIMER/SLOGAN GRAPHIC	ANNCR (VO):
	New leadership.
	We can't afford to go back.

(Courtesy of Raymond Strother, Raymond D. Strother, Ltd.)

3. Fashion Slogans, Not Boomerangs.   There was little chance that either a former vice president or a sitting president could use "New Leadership—We Can't Afford to Go Back" against Gary Hart. But such is not always the case. In their efforts to develop memorable and high-profile slogans, some copywriters play into the hands of the opposing camp by giving them a thematic (positioning) statement that is all too easy to juxtapose or distort. Barry Goldwater's 1964 "In Your Heart You Know He's Right" was transformed by the Democratic opposition to "In Your Heart You Know *He Might*"—an unsubtle reference to Goldwater's alleged enthusiasm for unleashing a nuclear war. George Wallace's "Send Them a Message" theme of 1972 was used against him by Jimmy Carter in the Democratic primaries four years later. The futility of a 1976 vote for Wallace in the mutual struggle to defeat a Republican incumbent was summed up in the deft expropriation: "This Time, Don't Send Them a Message; Send Them a President."

Even though a copywriter usually can't worry about what might happen four years hence, you should at least make certain that your positioning articulation is not going to fly back in your face during the current election. Congressman Phil Gramm's advisers at Ailes Communications took a pivotal event direct from his political past to fashion a line that used sense to make sense. The "Common Sense—Uncommon Courage" slogan was made so integral a part of Gramm's public record that it became virtually unassailable.

Video	Audio
BLUE FIELD/WHITE LETTERING FILLS SCREEN SAFE AREA: When was the last time you witnessed an act of political courage?	ANNCR (VO THROUGHOUT): When was the last time you witnessed an act of political courage?
PG ARRIVING AT AIRPORT	(SYNC SOUND MIXED) Congressman Phil Gramm became a Republican when liberal
FREEZE FRAME TIP O'NEILL LEAVING WHITE HOUSE	Democratic leaders removed him from the budget committee—

Video	Audio
<u>PG</u> ENTERING NEWS CONFERENCE	—for leading the fight to pass President Reagan's tax and spending cuts.
<u>PG</u> AT NEWS CONFERENCE PODIUM <u>SUPE:</u> Congressman Phil Gramm <u>SUPE:</u> date	<u>PG (SYNC):</u> ''...that I should be punished for representing the people who sent me to Washington is unfair. That they should be disenfranchised in an effort to silence my voice on the number one issue in America—the budget---is intolerable.''
REPORTERS/PHOTOGRAPHERS/CREWS	ANNCR: Phil Gramm had the courage to let the people choose.
<u>PG</u> AT NEWS CONFERENCE PODIUM	<u>PG (SYNC):</u> ''...the only honorable course of action is to resign my seat in Congress and to seek re-election as a Republican.''
<u>PG</u> PLANE ARRIVES	(<u>MUSIC: GRAND & HEROIC IN/UNDER</u>)
<u>PG</u> AT CAMPAIGN RALLY	ANNCR: Gramm took his message to the people.
<u>PG</u> WITH PEOPLE ON STREET	<u>PG (SYNC):</u> ''...I had to choose between y'all and Tip O'Neill and I decided to represent y'all...''

Video	Audio
<u>PG</u> ENTERING VICTORY RALLY <u>SUPE</u>: date	ANNCR: And the people overwhelmingly re-elected him. (SFX: APPLAUSE IN/MIXED WITH <u>MUSIC</u>)
<u>PG</u> AT PODIUM HOLDING PHONE	ANNCR: President Reagan called Phil Gramm a man...
DIS. REAGAN ON PHONE FREEZE IN BOX NEXT TO <u>PG</u>	RR <u>(SYNC)</u>: ''...that has courage, that has principle, and God bless you...''
DIS. TO: ANIMATED GRAPHIC/DISCLAIMER	(SFX/<u>MUSIC</u>: APPLAUSE AND <u>MUSIC</u> UP TO CLOSE) ANNCR: Phil Gramm for United States Senate. Common Sense—Uncommon Courage.

(Courtesy of Robert Bradsell, Ailes Communications Inc.)

4. Rally the Troops. Since the landmark Lazarsfeld, Berelson, and Gaudet study of the 1940's,[5] research has consistently shown that few people actually *change* candidate preferences as a result of mass media blandishments. At the same time, however, the Lazarsfeld and many subsequent studies do indicate that media messages are quite important in *reinforcing* and *activating* those people already favorable to the subject candidate's cause. Important objectives for polispots, therefore, are to encourage supporters and lure the uncommitted. Complacency is the frontrunner's greatest enemy, so his or her spots will do well to rally the troops to the importance of the battle at hand. Thus, this

5. Paul Lazarsfeld, Bernard Berelson, and Hazel Gaudet, *The People's Choice* (New York: Columbia University Press, 1948).

Mondale primary spot drives home the earnestness of the struggle with stark copy and unrelieved crisis imagery.

Video	Audio
OPEN ON ECU OF RED TELEPHONE IN LIMBO AND SEEN FROM THE BACK. PHONE SLOWLY REVOLVES TO REVEAL FLASHING RED LIGHT INSTEAD OF A DIAL.	ANNCR: (VO THROUGHOUT) The most awesome, powerful responsibility in the world lies in the hand that picks up this phone. The idea of an unsure, unsteady, untested hand is something to really think about. This is truly the issue of our times. On March 13 vote as if the future of the world is at stake.
MONDALE PIC IN MORTISE WITH DISCLAIMER BELOW	Mondale. This President will know what he's doing. And that's the difference between Gary Hart and Walter Mondale.

(Courtesy of Roy Spence, Jr., GSD&M.)

Radio can encourage supporters, too. Jim Martin's successful bid for the governorship of North Carolina relied heavily on copy unabashedly designed to activate fellow conservatives.

ANNCR: It's really not a tough decision. Jim Martin is a conservative who supports Ronald Reagan and will cut state taxes.

Rufus Edmisten is a liberal who supports Walter Mondale and thinks taxes are fine the way they are.

Jim Martin is opposed to state funding of abortion on demand.

Rufus Edmisten is for state funding of abortion on demand.

Shouldn't we have a governor who believes in the things we believe in? Jim Martin for governor.
(Disclaimer)

(Courtesy of Donald Ringe, Ringe Media, Inc.)

No matter what the race or issues involved, the polispot that does not cater to the candidate's supporters is not performing political advertising's most essential function. It is not always necessary to speak so directly to your partisan constituency as does the Martin spot, but every commercial should demonstrate, at least implicitly, that your candidate has those supporters' interests in mind.

5. Use Paid Media to Entice Free Media.   One of the most important advantages an athletic team or a candidate can possess is *momentum*—the intangible feeling telling fans and supporters that things are going "our" way. Even with a lead on the scoreboard or in the polls, failure to make further gains can result in both dangerous complacency on which opponents can capitalize and lack of interest on the part of sportscaster and journalist alike. Since free media exposure is vital to continued visibility, polispots are sometimes used mainly to attract increased media attention and get the polls moving again.

A standard method for drawing media notice is to issue a proposal or challenge that ignites public comment or opponent reaction. This is exactly the tack taken by the Lehrman campaign in this pointed television announcement:

Video	Audio
FULL SCREEN GRAPHIC: 　　Lew Lehrman 　　Crime Proposal #2	<u>VO</u> <u>ANNCR</u> (Compressed with slight echo): 　　Lew Lehrman—Crime Proposal 　　Number Two.
VERTICAL WIPE TO REVEAL <u>LL</u> MWS <u>LL</u> ON STOOL/INFINITY BACKGROUND <u>SUPER</u> <u>LOWER</u> <u>3RD</u>: 　　A violent crime occurs every 3 minutes in New York State.	LEHRMAN: Criminals commit thousands of violent crimes while out on bail.
LOSE SUPER BEGIN SLOW ZOOM TO MS COMPLETE SLOW ZOOM TO MS	When one of these savages commits another crime, you'd think he'd get a double sentence! But under present law, he gets no extra time. The second crime is free! Except for the innocent victim. For years, DA's

Video	Audio
	have begged for a consecutive sentence law.
BEGIN ZOOM TO MCU/ COMPLETE ZOOM TO MCU <u>SUPER LOWER 3RD:</u> Lew Lehrman	As governor, I'll keep the legislature in session until hell freezes over. And we'll get the law changed.
DOUBLE VERTICAL WIPE TO LOGO	(SFX: DRUM ROLL CLOSE TAG)
GRAPHIC/DISCLAIMER	<u>VO</u> ANNCR:
	Lew Lehrman for Governor. A leader to make New York safe again.

(Courtesy of Robert Bradsell, Ailes Communications Inc.)

6. Mesh with What's Hot, Not What's Not.   As a final polispot premise, it must be recognized that political commercials are placed on a fundamentally entertainment-driven medium and viewed or heard within an entertainment matrix. So to be effective, it naturally follows that they reflect themes, subjects, and attitudes that are in the popular mind at the moment. Since political campaigns have such a brief run as compared to commercial ones, there is also the associated need to exploit every possible device for getting quickly into a listener/viewer consciousness that is all too easily distracted. Riding an in-vogue subject or slogan is a proven way to blend well with the broadcast scene and yet, at the same time, still enjoy an independent identity.

There is no better example of successful hitchhiking on popular idioms than Walter Mondale's borrowing of the battle cry from the celebrated Wendy's commercial featured in Figure 13-1. His "Where's the Beef?" query to opponent Gary Hart crystalized the theretofore poorly articulated charge that Hart's platform lacked substance. Wendy's, actually, had already done much of Mondale's conceptual work for him, but his campaign staff was astute (or *creative*) enough to forge a meaningful relationship with this burger-born bonanza.

In capitalizing on what's hot, you might (under the right circumstances) even pattern your polispot after not just an entertaining commercial, but an entertainment *program*. On behalf of client Mitch McConnell, Ailes Communications used the continuing popularity of TV "chase" scenarios as a weapon against incumbent Senator Dee Huddleston. The result was entertaining, hard-hitting, and ultimately effective because it graphically dramatized a documentable charge.

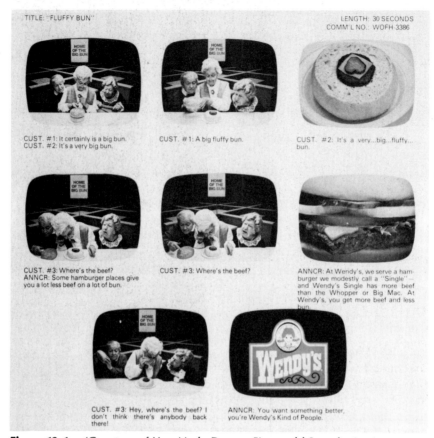

TITLE: "FLUFFY BUN"

LENGTH: 30 SECONDS
COMM'L NO.: WOFH-3386

CUST. #1: It certainly is a big bun.
CUST. #2: It's a very big bun.

CUST. #1: A big fluffy bun.

CUST. #2: It's a very...big...fluffy... bun.

CUST. #3: Where's the beef?
ANNCR: Some hamburger places give you a lot less beef on a lot of bun.

CUST. #3: Where's the beef?

ANNCR: At Wendy's, we serve a hamburger we modestly call a "Single"— and Wendy's Single has more beef than the Whopper or Big Mac. At Wendy's, you get more beef and less bun.

CUST. #3: Hey, where's the beef? I don't think there's anybody back there!

ANNCR: You want something better, you're Wendy's Kind of People.

Figure 13–1. *(Courtesy of Linn Nash, Dancer Fitzgerald Sample, Inc.)*

Video	Audio
HUNTER WITH 5 BLOODHOUNDS, DOGS SNIFFING ''DH'' T-SHIRT	(SFX: BLOODHOUNDS BARKING IN MELEE)
CU, BLOODHOUND POV	<u>HUNTER (VO)</u>:
	My job was to find Dee Huddleston
MCU DOGS SNIFFING <u>DH</u> PHOTO	and get him back to work.
MWS HUNTER BEING LED BY DOGS ACROSS CAPITOL LAWN (LOW ANGLE)	(<u>MUSIC: CHASE MUSIC</u> UNDER VOICE AND SFX)

Video	Audio
	Huddleston was missing big votes on Social Security---the budget---defense. Even agriculture.
MWS HUNTER BEING LED BY DOGS THRU FIELD (LOW ANGLE)	
MWS HUNTER LED BY DOGS THRU CROWD ON BUSY SIDEWALK, HUNTER WAVING T-SHIRT FOR DOGS TO SNIFF (HEAD ON)	Huddleston was skipping votes— but making an extra 50 thousand dollars giving speeches.
MWS HUNTER PAUSES WITH DOGS BETWEEN 2 ARROW SIGNS POINTING IN OPPOSITE DIRECTIONS. HE LOOKS ONE WAY, THEN THE OTHER.	I just missed him when Dee skipped votes for his thousand-dollar Los Angeles speech.
HUNTER LED BY DOGS TO SWIMMING POOL. SUNBATHER WITH SUNGLASSES AND NEWSPAPER POINTS TO RIGHT.	(SYNC) ''Let's go boys, we got him now.''
HUNTER LED BY DOGS SPLASHES THRU SURF	I was close at Dee's 2 thousand-dollar speech in Puerto Rico—
WS LED BY DOGS ALONG BEACH, OVER SUNBATHER'S SHOULDER. TALKS TO SUNBATHER WHO POINTS TO RIGHT.	(SYNC) ''Seen Dee Huddleston? Thank you very much...''
MS EYELEVEL: HUNTER SEATED ON GROUND WITH DOGS LAPPING AT HIS FACE	(SYNC) (To dogs, out of breath) ''...We can't find Dee...Maybe we oughta...let him make speeches...
DIS PANEL TURN TO ANIMATED GRAPHICS/DISCLAIMER	and switch to Mitch for Senator.''
	(MUSIC: UP TO CLOSE) (SFX: SINGLE DOG BARKS)

(Courtesy of Robert Bradsell, Ailes Communications, Inc.)

Polispot Types

Candidate commercials are usually grouped into three broad typologies: image spots, issue spots, and negative spots. Even though there is some overlap among this trio, the techniques they use tend to be quite distinct and their intended impacts much different.

1. Image Spots. These commercials focus on the personal characteristics of the candidate they are promoting. According to political scientist Richard Joslyn, "These characteristics most often tend to be personality traits. . . . Qualities that seem to be valued in the arena of political advertising are leadership, honesty, concern, responsiveness, strength, determination, perseverance, vigor and purpose."[6] Leonard Shyles adds that "'image' is similar in meaning to a loose modern construction of Aristotle's 'ethos' concept, or the 'source credibility' of the candidate."[7]

For front runners, an image approach is generally preferred since it maintains contact with the voters without raising issues or launching attacks that could prove offensive to parts of the constituency. Image campaigns strive to strike a harmonious chord in which candidate and listener/viewer feelings coincide. People like someone who appears to share their life's view, and that life's view can be presented in very general terms since it is itself a generality. Ultimately, then, the image approach is designed to make the voters feel good about themselves and, by extension, feel good about the candidate. This 1980 Reagan spot illustrates this phenomenon at its most basic.

```
ANNCR:    Some of our leaders say our country has to stop growing;
          that our children may have to accept a lower standard of
          living than we've had. Ronald Reagan doesn't buy that.
REAGAN:   This is the greatest country in the world. We have the
          ability to solve our economic problems---our energy
          problems---even our social problems. We have the talent.
          We have the drive. We have the imagination. Now all we
          need is the leadership. (Disclaimer/tag)
```

(Courtesy of Danny Eizen, Elliott Curson Advertising, Ltd.)

Image appeals can work at the state and local level, too, when they continue to build and praise the commonality of interests that unite candidate and constituent:

```
MARTIN:   Everybody wants your vote, including me. I'm Jim Martin
          and I've said all along that I'm running for governor
          because I know how to get things done---whether cutting
          taxes or improving education.
```

6. Richard Joslyn, "The Content of Political Spot Ads," *Journalism Quarterly*, Spring, 1980, p. 94.
7. Leonard Shyles, "The Relationships of Images, Issues and Presentational Methods in Televised Spot Advertisements for 1980's Presidential Primaries," *Journal of Broadcasting*, Fall, 1984, p. 406.

```
            While I ask you for your vote, I also want to thank you,
            all of you who took the time to share with me your
            vision for the future of our state.

            It can be a great future, and I hope enough of us have
            come to know each other well enough that we can make
            that future great together.
ANNCR:      (Disclaimer/tag)
```

(Courtesy of Donald Ringe, Ringe Media, Inc.)

Image messages can also serve the purpose of *polishing* a candidate's aura but, because of their subtlety, are seldom able to change it radically. During her tenure in office, Chicago Mayor Jane Byrne's combative image was so pronounced that a radio station even made it part of a concise promotion pun (see Figure 13-2). The image spots in Byrne's re-election effort tried to project a controlled, if not mellow, leader, but the change was so drastic that the image itself became an *issue,* and a damaging one. By its very nature, an image polispot should be low key and nonargumentative. If it becomes a flashpoint of contention, it cannot hope to accomplish its bridge-building goals.

2. Issue Spots. A *candidate-related* issue message (we'll discuss noncandidate *controversy* issue ads later) "involves either the mention of a current *political* issue or a discussion of the candidate's stand on the issue."[8] The issue may be major or minor, but it should be one on which your candidate clearly

Figure 13–2. *(Courtesy of AnnMarie Stepovy, WBBM.)*

8. Ronald Faber and M. Claire Storey, "Recall of Information from Political Advertising," *Journal of Advertising,* Vol. 13, No. 3, 1984, p. 39.

holds the advantage (review our earlier discussion of "You Pick the Battle-field"). The most decisive issues are not always the most important but rather, those with which the audience can most readily identify. Thus, the constituency must be carefully assessed before any issue is targeted for exposition.

Intrinsically, issue polispots are more risky than image messages because of their potential for voter alienation. Issue ads also expose the candidate to opponent attacks on his or her position. For these reasons, front runners tend to avoid issue orientations whereas pursuing candidates tend to embrace them. Still, a leading candidate may want to mount at least one issue flight if it is an issue that can be dominated. In this way, favorites deflect criticism for "not taking stands" while publicizing a safe position on which they know they are not vulnerable.

Some strategists tend to divide issue polispots into "soft" and "hard" categories. A "soft issue" is one on which almost everyone can agree. By raising it, the officeseeker can bolster his or her general image while reaping the additional benefits that come from an evidenced willingness publicly to take a stand. Virtually no one but drug dealers, for example, could disagree with the posture that is struck in this message:

Video	Audio
PAN AND CUT ON VARIOUS DRUGS AND PARAPHERNALIA ON DISPLAY BOARD	MARTIN (VO): They call it dope for a reason. And it comes into North Carolina by the plane, boat and truckload every day. In fact, North Carolina has the second highest drug trafficking in the nation.
WIDEN OUT TO REVEAL JIM BESIDE BOARD TALKING TO CAMERA	I'm Jim Martin. As Governor, I'll mobilize our police and National Guard to slam the jail house doors on drug pushers. And I'll bring state-wide drug education programs to our schools.
JIM POINTS OFF CAMERA, PULL OUT TO REVEAL HE IS IN JUNIOR HIGH CLASSROOM	We've got to stop the dope out there before it finds its way in here.
DISCLAIMER/TAG GRAPHIC	

(Courtesy of Donald Ringe, Ringe Media, Inc.)

Even soft issue ads must still accurately reflect the candidate's attitude and willingness to act. Were Mr. Martin not totally committed to drug enforcement, his TV spot would constitute a broken promise certain to be used against him by future opponents.

"Hard issue" commercials, in contrast, take a position on a subject about which there is more widespread disagreement. In scripting a hard issue approach, the copywriter at least must be certain that (1) the candidate's supporters are completely in tune with this stand, and (2) the candidate's position can be clearly and concisely articulated without any danger of public misperception. The Phil Gramm spot presented earlier satisfied both of these conditions and, in truth, Gramm had no choice but to take a "hard" tax/spending stand to explain the party switching that this stand apparently precipitated. The first Jim Martin spot in our discussion also exemplified a hard issue orientation on both tax cutting and abortion—issues on which he knew his opponent to be much more locally vulnerable than he.

The Mondale spot below seems to take an unusually risky hard issue stand— especially for a frontrunner. It must be noted, however, that it was prepared for airing in a state (New Jersey) that had already passed handgun control legislation and, therefore, where Mondale's position was comparatively advantageous (especially given the somewhat selective use of a Gary Hart quote).

Video	Audio
ECU OF ''SIX SHOOTER'' BARRELED HANDGUN LYING ON LIMBO TABLE, GUN SLOWLY REVOLVES	<u>ANNCR (VO)</u>: Handgun control. A tough issue to tackle. Yet, New Jersey already has. That's why it's important to ask the presidential candidates where they stand. Dan Rather did.
SUPER: Gary Hart: ''I have <u>opposed</u> federal gun control laws.''	Gary Hart said: 'I have opposed federal gun control laws.'
LOSE SUPER	Walter Mondale
SUPER: Walter Mondale: ''I <u>favor</u> control of Saturday-night Specials and Snub-nosed handguns.''	favors handgun control. It's one thing to talk about the future.

Video	Audio
LOSE SUPER	It's another to support laws to protect our families. So they <u>have</u> a future.
MONDALE SHIRTSLEEVE PIC AND DISCLAIMER TITLE	Mondale for President.

(Courtesy of Roy Spence, Jr., GSD&M.)

That the tightening of the Democratic primary race forced a faltering front runner to move to a hard issue strategy only reemphasizes the caution with which hard issue advertising must be approached. Use it when necessary but again, only on your own battlefield.

3. Negative Spots.   The Mondale gun control script might be assumed to be a negative commercial. Technically however, since it compares and articulates the positions of both candidate and opponent, it constitutes a piece of *comparative issue advertising.* Negative spots, on the other hand, are unrelenting attacks on an opponent. Because of their stridency in only *attacking* rather than *comparing,* negative polispots are seldom employed by front runners who do not wish to be perceived as bullies. A long-shot candidate, conversely, can exploit negative advertising with much greater safety since he or she can play the role of the underdog who is only trying to get a fair hearing.

No matter who uses them, negative attacks should almost never be made by the candidate; instead, they are assigned to others while the candidate profits from, but stays above, the fray. The unrestricted growth of PACs (political action committees) in the United States has signaled a resurgence in negative advertising since PAC money is usually devoted to defeating an incumbent rather than specifically supporting a challenger. Even without the independent advertising presence of special interest groups, negative advertising would remain part of the broadcast landscape since the burden any challenger assumes is to demonstrate that the incumbent opponent has done something *wrong.*

The McConnell "Bloodhounds" script presented earlier is a prime example of reputable negative advertising carried out on behalf of a candidate by others. As in that verifiable approach, any negative pitch must be based on facts or it will be perceived as mudslinging and end up damaging your own candidate's image.

Legitimate negative strategies also avoid patently irrelevant attacks because these are seen as both unfair and absurd by a significant portion of any electorate. In 1952, overzealous Adlai Stevenson supporters aired an unauthorized anti-Eisenhower pitch in which a "private citizen" says:

I don't like generals for president. Twenty years ago the Germans had a general for president whose name was Von Hindenburg and then Hitler moved in and took over the country. No thank you, general---I'll stick with a man with experience in government. I'll stick with Adlai Stevenson.[9]

Stevenson's chances were slim to begin with and fortunately, the above slur received limited and localized airplay before it was pulled. Still, the damage that could have been done far outweighed anything constructive that such an outlandish smear might have accomplished.

Thirty years later, some misguided writers still think gratuitous villification is a feasible copy strategy. In the 1982 Tennessee senatorial race, incumbent Jim Sasser's opponent broadcast this television spot:

Video	Audio
MCU OF HANDS HOLDING A CROWBAR TO PRY OPEN A CRATE LABELLED ''U.S. AID.''	ANNCR (VO): When it comes to spending taxpayers' money, Senator James Sasser is a master. Take foreign aid. While important programs are being cut back here at home, Sasser has voted to allow foreign aid to be
HANDS GRAB FOR THE STACKS OF DOLLARS THE CRATE DISGORGES	sent to committed enemies of our country---Vietnam, Laos, Cambodia, Marxist Angola and even Communist Cuba. You can bet James Sasser is making a lot more friends abroad than he is here in Tennessee.
MCU CASTRO LOOK-ALIKE LIGHTING CIGAR WITH A DOLLAR BILL	CASTRO: Muchissimas gracias, Señor Sasser.[10]
DISCLAIMER GRAPHIC	

Sasser won—probably because of, rather than in spite of, this outlandish bit of character assassination.

9. Paul Porter, "Did You Know Ronald Reagan Shot Lincoln?" *The Washington Post Outlook,* January 23, 1972.
10. "The Dirtiest Three from Campaign '82," *ADWEEK/Midwest,* January 1983, p. B.R. 9.

The above aberrations notwithstanding, negative advertising that is responsible, accurate, and relevant does make a contribution by informing the public of inconsistencies, failures, or abuses of which they should be aware. That this information is provided as part of an effort to elect an opponent does not, by itself, make the practice wrong, unprincipled, or misguided. As long as the criticism is valid and verifiable, the copywriter should feel free to consider its use if campaign strategy thereby will be furthered. In the following above-board negative spot, the copywriter has stuck to the facts and exposed opponent vulnerability without resorting to personal vituperation.

Video	Audio
McDANIEL PHOTO #1 (B/W) IN MORTISE. SUPER: Roger McDaniel LOSE SUPER	<u>ANNCR VO</u> (soft/grandfatherly): This is Roger McDaniel. He's a young lawyer who thinks he should be a senator.
SOFT CUT TO CU, SAME PHOTO IN MORTISE	But what has he done?
SOFT CUT WITHIN MORTISE TO McDANIEL PHOTO #2	Well, he was in the state legislature,

SUPER:
   Sponsored no legislation
  —missed 50 votes
 	
LOSE SUPER
	where in 1980, he sponsored <u>no</u> legislation---and missed 50 votes. Three times more than any other senator.
	McDaniel didn't like the job much. He didn't show up for work.

PUSH BOX TO LEFT AND SMALLER, REVEAL 2ND BOX TO RIGHT WITH <u>TK</u>, THEN SOFT CUT WITHIN BOX TO PHOTO #3	The same year, he was Teddy Kennedy's Wyoming campaign chairman.
SOFT CUT WITHIN, TO #3, REVERSED	McDaniel now claims to be a conservative.
SOFT CUT WITHIN, TO <u>TK</u>, REVERSED	Do you think he just fooled Teddy Kennedy?

Video	Audio
PUSH LEFT BOX CENTER AND LARGER, COVER 2ND BOX	Or is he trying to fool us?
DIS MW FREEZE, SMALL BOX LOWER 3RD	Actions speak louder than words.
SUPER DISCLAIMER FOR WALLOP	We want our senator to work for us.

(Courtesy of Robert Bradsell, Ailes Communications Inc.)

As stated earlier, candidates themselves try to remain statesmanlike by letting their surrogates articulate the negative attacks. In the spot above, for example, opponent Wallop is not even identified in the soundtrack. In certain circumstances, however, a candidate can make points with the voters by showing he or she has the conviction to make the charge personally. If the polispot is well fashioned, the candidate can still appear statesmanlike—and candid as well:

Video	Audio
MWS <u>DD</u> SITTING ON EDGE OF DESK IN OFFICE SUPER: Senator Dave Durenberger	DURENBERGER: People ask me what I think of Mark Dayton. I don't know him well, but he seems sincere
LOSE SUPER	about his beliefs.
BEGIN SLOW ZOOM TO MCU	He put together a series of programs called ''The Minnesota Agenda,'' which---on the surface---appears to have something for everybody. But what Mark doesn't say---or maybe doesn't know---is that those programs
COMPLETE ZOOM TO MCU	will double the federal deficit. As I said, Mark's probably very sincere. But that's the kind of mistake

Video	Audio
	that comes from inexperience. Or perhaps from growing up never having to ask the price of anything.
DIS TO LOGO/GRAPHIC DISCLAIMER	ANNCR (VO):
	Re-elect Senator Dave Durenberger. A leader we know---and trust.

(Courtesy of Robert Bradsell, Ailes Communications Inc.)

Whether the attack is launched by the officeseeker or, more often, by a surrogate, it should stress the reasonable and avoid the strident. Hatchet jobs are intensely resented by listeners and viewers—even if they are conceded to be partly true. Worse, unbridled smears strongly suggest that the campaign has dissolved into panic—that your candidate is a "loser" who will try anything to stay in the race.

Other Polispot Techniques

In our treatment of polispot objectives and types, we have explored several well-proven techniques. Here are nine other devices on which the copywriter also can call if the campaign strategy requires it and if the candidate's personal qualities mesh with it.

1. Homespun Honesty. What worked for Lincoln can work for others as long as the folksiness is genuine (and aired in a locale where folksiness is prized). If it is phoney, the newshawks in the free media will pick up on the stylistic discrepancy and paint the candidate to be devious, rather than guileless. As with any image, homespun honesty cannot be manufactured but must be a quality the officeseeker naturally exhibits in public life as well as on camera. For the following message to succeed, it was imperative that Mike Strang not be previously thought of as a "politician," and that he really talked and believed as the spot revealed.

Video	Audio
MCU MIKE TALKING DIRECT TO VIEWER.	MIKE:
	I'm Mike Strang, and I'm running for Congress. I hope that doesn't make me a

Video	Audio
	politician, because, frankly, politicians bother me. Especially the ones who just can't wait to go and raise your taxes. Just look at Mr. Mondale. I don't believe in that. Never have. In the legislature, I helped keep taxes down. Because I agree with President Reagan— letting the people keep their money is good for the economy. The <u>Democrats</u> in Congress may go with Mr. Mondale and vote to raise your taxes. But here's one man who <u>won't</u>.
DISCLAIMER GRAPHIC	

(Courtesy of Anita Warren, National Republican Congressional Committee.)

2. We All Make Mistakes. After decades of ever-increasing polispot implementation, candidates have learned that admitting a mistake not only may not hurt them, but can actually make them more likeable, appealing, and human. The degree of the mistake must, or course, be taken into consideration. Lyndon Johnson could no more have characterized Vietnam escalation as a well-meaning "goof" than Richard Nixon was able to make light of what he clandestinely did in the Oval Office with his "cheap Sony equipment." In less onerous instances, however, owning up to a mistake—especially a relatively minor one—can pay disproportionate dividends and defuse the issue before the opponent has a chance to exploit it:

ROUNDBOTTOM: I'm Governor Irv Roundbottom and I believe the only way we learn from our mistakes is to admit to them. So I'm admitting to you that my move to cut state expenses by reducing my staff was a boner. We did save you, the taxpayer, sixty-five thousand dollars over a 9-month period. But in the process, we lessened our ability to quickly address the questions and problems citizens bring to the governor's office. I think two weeks is too long to wait for a response from your governor. So I'm bringing the staff back up to strength. My opponent

```
                    may call me a spendthrift. But what good is a
                    penny-pinching governor you can't contact?
ANNCR:              (Disclaimer/tag)
```

3. *Cinema Verité.* "Real life" sound and sight footage can impart a powerful sense of authenticity to the polispot. It also narrows the audience's perceptual distinction between free and paid media messages and therefore heightens the credibility of the political commercial. As mentioned in our opening discussion, the use of a cinema verité type approach also puts special demands on the copywriter by requiring you to accomplish after-the-fact scripting in which footage already shot must be molded into a well-structured copy event. Viewers, of course, must not be made aware of the sequence of message production but should only notice the polispot's central thematic statement. The television voice-over that follows was fashioned around visuals of Congressman Bateman that, documentary style, showed him performing the tiring and tireless duties of which the copy speaks.

Video	Audio
LIVE ACTION SEQUENCES AS EDITED	ANNCR (VO):
	The road from our nation's capital to the First District of Virginia is one this man knows well. He's our Congressman, Herb Bateman. The First District---is his district. Its people---his people. And its needs and concerns are his, as well. And though Congressman Bateman works hard in Washington, there are the times that mean the most---back here, with the people he serves. He has half a million constituents from the Penninsula, to Northern Neck and the Eastern Shore. Small businessmen who need help getting federal contracts. People with questions on everything from the federal budget to cleaning up the Bay.

Video	Audio
	And people who sometimes feel forgotten; Congressman Bateman is there to show them they're not.
	His days back home are long ones. But when, once more, he's on the road, back to the business of our nation's capital, Congressman Bateman takes back with him our voices---<u>our</u> concerns.
DISCLAIMER GRAPHIC	Re-elect Congressman Herb Bateman.
	He's been good for Virginia.

(Courtesy of Anita Warren, National Republican Congressional Committee.)

4. Catch the Opposition in the Act. The cinema verité technique reveals the *candidate* in real-life situations. Catching the *opposition* in the act takes the device one step further by negatively turning the microphones and cameras on the competition. Since the tools of electronic journalism are now so ubiquitous, most public figures find themselves the subject of a multitude of footage. Sometimes, due to a mental error, misassessment of an issue, or a basic "slip," such footage becomes grist for a comparative or negative polispot. But to be perceived as effective and fair, this audio-visual recording of your opponent must pertain to a subject of substance and significance to the constituency. Such significance was certainly present when Michigan Senator Carl Levin's opponent once made the mistake of seeming to endorse foreign automobiles:

Video	Audio

HEADLINE CHARACTER GENERATED:
  ''Auto Jobs Disappear
     Despite Recovery''
  Detroit News
  August 7, 1983
	<u>ANNCR (VO):</u>
	
	In October 1983, 133,000 auto workers were unemployed.

CARL IN COMMITTEE	Senator Carl Levin was in Washington fighting to strengthen the American auto industry.

Video	Audio
LOUSMA IN TOYOTA HALL	Jack Lousma was in Japan giving a public speech in Toyota Hall.
	LOUSMA (SYNC):
	I feel, as a matter of fact, that I have a small investment in this hall because you see, back home in the United States, I do have a Toyota automobile.
LEVIN STANDING UP, TALKING (MOS)	ANNCR (VO):
	We deserve a Senator who understands our problems and has proven he will fight for Michigan.
FREEZE, SQUEEZE AND TITLE	We have one in Carl Levin.

(Courtesy of Stephen Serkaian, Office of Senator Carl Levin.)

5. Heroic Stills. The use of still photographs accrues the same basic attributes as cinema verité's moving footage plus providing three additional advantages:

a. Still photographs are normally much more available than motion picture or video-tape footage. As a copywriter, you thus have many more pictorial options from which to select.
b. The use of stills can compensate for a candidate with awkward verbal or physical mannerisms. Film and video cameras are very unkind to clumsy individuals who nonetheless may be bastions of competence and integrity. By cutting or dissolving between *still* pictures, instead of exhibiting live action footage, a polispot can make even gawky persons look quick, graceful, and adroit.
c. Perhaps because of their documentary mystique or sense of print authenticity, still pictures have a distinct ability to make their subject candidate appear more heroic.

By manipulating stills of your side and their side, a polispot can also constitute what amounts to a pictorial chess game in which your candidate visually check-mates the opposition and dominates the picture tube board:

Video	Audio
MONTAGE: MULTIPLE DIS FACES IN BOXES MOVING THRU FRAME— BH, RR, JC, WM	ANNCR (VO): In the race for Congress this year, keep your eye on the teams.
BH and RR BOXES PAIR OFF AND MOVE TO UPPER 3RD, CENTER	Bill Hendon and President Reagan want to:
SUPER: Hold the line on taxes	Hold the line on taxes;
LOSE SUPER SUPER: Balance the budget by controlling spending	Balance the budget by controlling what the government spends;
LOSE SUPER SUPER: Continue economic recovery and create new jobs	And continue the economic recovery that has already created more than 6 million new jobs.
LOSE SUPER JC & WM BOXES PAIR OFF AND MOVE TO UPPER 3RD, CENTER	James McClure Clarke and Walter Mondale want to:
SUPER: Raise our taxes by at least $157 a month	Raise our taxes by at least 157 dollars a month per family;
LOSE SUPER SUPER: Jeopardize economic recovery with policies that failed	And jeopardize the economic recovery with Carter-Mondale policies that failed.
LOSE SUPER JC & WM BOXES MOVE FORWARD AND CENTER	The choice is clear. Clarke and Mondale—

Video	Audio
CUBE TURN TO <u>BH</u> & <u>RR</u> BOXES, CENTER, <u>BH</u> BOX MOVES FORWARD ALONE	Or Hendon and Reagan.
<u>SUPER:</u> GRAPHICS DISCLAIMER	

(Courtesy of Robert Bradsell, Ailes Communications Inc.)

6. Supering for Power.   Because of how viewers have been indoctrinated in their media perceptions, printed words (as long as there are not too many of them) are more credible than spoken ones. And printed words on TV (such as the supered graphics above) are more powerful and salient than those in printed handouts. Thus, supering a fact gives it more perceptual prominence than having the candidate *say* it. This technique was further demonstrated in the Mondale handgun commercial presented earlier; it is also shown in the following McConnell for Senate message, in which supered graphics are deployed over a still of incumbent Huddleston opponent to indict his stands on key issues.

Video	Audio
BLACK/PALE BLUE FINE-LINE GRID COVERS ENTIRE SCREEN; TILT TO FORCE 3RD DIMENSION	(SFX: SYNTHESIZED MINOR-CHORD TONE STARTS AT ZERO, BEGINS CRESCENDO WITH FIRST VIDEO. CRESCENDO BUILDS STEADILY THROUGHOUT SPOT)
FROM TOP 3RD CENTER, B/W PHOTO OF <u>DH</u> IN BLACK-BORDERED BOX; STARTS AS DOT, EXPANDS WITH TONE CRESCENDO	
<u>SUPERS:</u> (LOWER ½, NUMBERS KEYED RED, KEY WORDS UNDERSCORED RED	
<u>SUPER:</u> Missed 25% of Social Security votes	<u>ANNCR (VO):</u> Missed twenty-five percent of the Social Security votes—
<u>SUPER:</u> Made $50,000 giving speeches	—but made an extra 50-thousand dollars giving speeches.

Video	Audio

SUPER: <u>FOR</u>
  Grain embargo
  Panama Canal giveaway
	Votes <u>for</u> the grain embargo
	and the Panama Canal giveaway—

SUPER: <u>AGAINST</u> School prayer	—but voted <u>against</u> school prayer.

SUPER:
  Opposed President Reagan
    more than Ted Kennedy
	Opposed President Reagan's
	policies more than Ted
	Kennedy.

SUPER:
  One of the BIGGEST SPENDERS
    in Congress
	Rated one of the biggest
	spenders in Congress by the
	non-partisan National
	Taxpayers Union.

SUPER:
  Voted to raise your taxes
    44 times
	Voted to raise your taxes
	forty-four times!

<u>DH</u> PHOTO BOX STOPS EXPANDING, FILLS TOP 3RD SAFE AREA	(SFX: TONE REACHES MAX. CRESCENDO, TAGGED WITH MINOR- CHORD CHANGE, THEN SILENCE)
PANEL TURN TO ANIMATED GRAPHICS/DISCLAIMER	(<u>MUSIC</u><u>:</u> <u>DRUM</u> <u>ROLL</u> <u>END</u> <u>TAG</u>) For a Senator Kentucky can really depend on, switch to Mitch.

(Courtesy of Robert Bradsell, Ailes Communications Inc.)

7. Metaphor Magic. Like the subjects of many of the public service announcements presented in chapters 7 and 10, polispots fundamentally focus on intangibles. A vote or a public issue is not a concrete entity, and the issue clusters of which a campaign consists only add to the amorphousness. So it is often a good idea to try to derive a palpable metaphor to embrace and characterize the struggle from your candidate's perspective. Metaphors drawn from sports or war have special utility in this regard because they epitomize the associated ideas of conflict, victory, causes, and defeat. In a 1981 spot for the National Republican Congressional Committee, for example:

> A group of runners appears out of the mist. And as a close-up of the runners' faces reveals—in the words of the production script—the "dedication and pain it takes to be a winner"—the voice-over talks of the Republican effort "to cut

a bloated economy and make America tough again," and adds, "It's not an easy job. . . . Sure, we've still got a long way to go. But you can feel something good happening out there." Then the picture freezes on the runners a step away from the finish line, as the voice-over says, "We're beginning to feel like winners again."[11]

Metaphors can also be used negatively to indict an opponent's record or motives in a highly intense manner but without the need to involve your candidate personally in the attack. The Sullivan for Senate campaign fashioned one such device in this satiric Western tableau where the humor cushions the blow's sting, but not its substance.

Video	Audio
LOW ANGLE SKY SHOT WITH CLOUDS OF DUST, BLOWING LEAVES	(MUSIC: WESTERN THEME) (SFX: THUNDERING HOOVES, WHINNIES)
	ANNCR (VO): (COMPRESSED WITH MED. ECHO):
	America loves heroes!
SLOW ZOOM OUT, PAN TO RIGHT...PM LOOK-ALIKE, DRESSED AND MADE UP AS COWBOY, MOVES INTO FRAME—MCU, LOW-ANGLE HEAD & SHOULDERS BOUNCING, AS IF RIDING GALLOPING HORSE. SUPER: Title	Out of Washington come the thundering hooves of the mighty horse---Waffle! And the Great Straddler— Pat Moynihan!
MWS/SLIGHT ELEVATION, REVEALING COWBOY, ON SADDLE, RIDING SPLIT-RAIL FENCE	No matter what the issue, Pat Moynihan's on both sides!
FWS HIGH ANGLE, HEAD ON SUPER (LEFT FOOT): For it SUPER (RIGHT FOOT): Against it	The death penalty— He's for it, and against it.
SUPER (LEFT FOOT): For it	Nuclear disarmament— He's for it,

11. "Republican Plan to Control House Under Way with TV Ad Campaign," *Broadcasting Magazine*, October 5, 1981, p. 25.

Video	Audio
SUPER: (RIGHT FOOT): Against it	and against it.

SUPER (LEFT FOOT):
    For it
 SUPER: (RIGHT FOOT):
    Against it
	The President's tax cut—
	 He's for it,
	
	 and against it.

MWS SEMI-PROFILE	For straddling issues, no one beats—
SUPER: Title	The Great Straddler— Pat Moynihan.
PUSH TO SMALL BOX, LOWER 3RD FS FREEZE FRAME SUPER: Disclaimer	(MUSIC/SFX: UP AND OUT) Elect Florence Sullivan. She'll take a stand.

(Courtesy of Robert Bradsell, Ailes Communications Inc.)

8. The Radio Rifle.   Though new delivery systems are slowly changing the pattern, commercial television remains a broad-reach or "shotgun" medium that attracts a wide and heterogeneous spectrum of viewers during the course of a programming day. Commercial radio, on the other hand, has evolved to the point at which individual stations deliver a much narrower and specific audience segment. The radio medium is thus seen as a rifle that can target individual groups through the careful selection of stations on which a given spot will run. Radio spots are also much cheaper to produce and to air. All of this means that the aural medium gives the polispot copywriter the opportunity to create a comparatively large number of commercials and to have them say more specific things to more specific constituencies than is possible on the wide-swath medium of television. A rural radio station, for instance, might be sent a spot lauding the candidate's stand on agricultural price supports. At the same time, an urban facility airs commercials that stress the candidate's commitment to rapid transit. Especially when used as a supplement to broad stroke television exposure, such radio rifling can pay major dividends in matching candidate stands with the attitudinal or geographic interests of listeners.

Though they follow the same formula, the following two Carl Levin radio messages employ specifics that are tailor-made to appeal to distinct counties in the Senator's home state:

VOICE #1:   Ottawa County is Republican. Muskegon is a
 Democratic County. But it really hasn't made any <br> difference to Senator Levin whether we were

	Republicans or Democrats. He was still willing to do whatever he could to help us. Through Senator Levin's efforts, we were able to get the money released and go on with our sewer project.
ANNCR:	Whether it's a community problem affecting thousands of people or a problem that affects just a few, Carl Levin is there when we need him.
VOICE #2:	When our flag which we fly at the Hume Home began to deteriorate, we were a little ashamed to fly it. One of our residents contacted Senator Levin. And in just very short order, we had a beautiful flag which we use now at the Hume Home with pride.
ANNCR:	What kind of Senator has Carl Levin been for Muskegon? A Senator who's proven he cares about us. (Disclaimer)

. . . .

ANNCR:	What kind of Senator has Carl Levin been? People like Garnette Trip, Jack Mathias and George Fragelo know what kind of Senator Carl Levin has been for Alpena County.
TRIP VOICE:	It's hard to believe he's not from Alpena County from the way he represents this area because he's able to speak with the people here and he recognizes their needs.
MATHIAS VOICE:	I am a Republican but I do endorse Senator Levin and I plan to vote for him based on his performance with regard to our community. We've created something like 130 jobs and Senator Levin's assistance helped make that possible.
FRAGELO VOICE:	My feelings about Carl Levin as a United States Senator are about the same feelings that they had when they made the picture of Bo Derek. He's a ten.
ANNCR:	What kind of Senator has Carl Levin been for Alpena County? A Senator who proves he cares about us. (Disclaimer)

(Courtesy of Stephen Serkaian, Office of Senator Carl Levin.)

As you probably noticed, these two spots also demonstrate that in radio, too, the copywriter's job is often that of orchestrating previously gathered pieces of tape rather than penning an end-to-end commercial.

Under certain circumstances, you may even wish to use the more personal medium of *radio* to attack the other side's use of "big buck" *television*. This tactic is especially effective in countering a slick television blitz your antagonist has mounted. For far fewer dollars, well-fashioned radio messages have the potential to undermine if not torpedo opponent TV efforts:

```
ANNCR:          (With sincerity)
                Television has changed the world. It can make you
                think you know a person you really don't—
                Like Mark Dayton.
                TV's Mark Dayton tells you his Minnesota Agenda
                will solve all your problems.
                The real Mark Dayton must know that all those
                programs would double the federal deficit.
                TV's Mark Dayton tells you we must restrict foreign
                imports.
                The real Mark Dayton, while he was a state
                employee, drove an expensive foreign car.
                TV's Mark Dayton tells you he was a legislative
                aide to Senator Mondale for Small Business and
                Education.
                The real Mark Dayton was a part-time employee of a
                Public Welfare subcommittee.
                TV's Mark Dayton tells you he believes in Social
                Security.
                The real Mark Dayton, when he ran his own
                organization, didn't contribute to Social Security
                for himself or his employees, but chose a
                tax-sheltered annuity instead.
                Television's Mark Dayton—
                The real Mark Dayton—
                Quite a difference
                Yes, television has changed the world.
                But even on radio, people can see the truth.
DURENBERGER:    Paid for by Durenberger for U.S. Senate.
```

(Courtesy of Robert Bradsell, Ailes Communications Inc.)

9. Positive Reminders. In the race to gain ground and "keep the polls moving," a political copywriter should not forget to pen *maintenance promos*— spots that recollect for the faithful what the candidate has done for them or how that candidate's stands mirror their own. If all your efforts are spent in pursuit of the uncommitted, some of your supporters may feel neglected—and they might just neglect to vote! This brief 1980 Reagan polispot certainly did not reveal any new information about him. It did, however, reassure Reagan voters as to the propriety of his (and their) beliefs.

ANNCR: Ronald Reagan spoke out on the danger of the Soviet arms
          buildup long before it was fashionable. He's always
          advocated a strong national defense and a position of
          leadership for America. He has a comprehensive program
          to rebuild our military power.

REAGAN: We've learned by now that it isn't weakness that keeps
          the peace. It's strength. Our foreign policy has been
          based on the fear of not being liked. Well, it's nice to
          be liked. But it's more important to be respected.

ANNCR: (Disclaimer)

(Courtesy of Danny Eizen, Elliott Curson Advertising, Ltd.)

Polispot Cautions

In accomplishing polispot objectives through use of the message types and techniques just discussed, several warnings, unique to this form of writing, must be observed. Some of the warnings have already been covered in the sections above, but other cautions transcend individual type or technique considerations.

1. Don't Forget the Disclaimer. An entire battery of laws and station regulations mandate that the source of the commercial be revealed, either aurally or visually. Many stations and networks further demand that this identification, or *disclaimer* (so titled since the station *disclaims* any responsibility for or endorsement of the message) be presented either at the beginning or end of the message. In this way, the listener or viewer is less likely to mistake the station as the announcement source. For commercials emanating directly out of the candidate's office, a typical disclaimer reads:

Paid for by Citizens for Roundbottom

or

Paid for by the Roundbottom for Governor Committee

If the message is sponsored by an independent group, such as a political action committee (a PAC) and is not endorsed by any candidate, the disclaimer must say something like:

The preceding (or following) announcement paid for by Lawyers for
a Liberal South Dakota. Not authorized by any candidate.

For radio, of course, the statement must be transmitted as spoken copy. For television, a visual graphic (such as those used in many of our previous examples) is sufficient. This then allows the option of having the audio devoted to a more dynamic selling tag. In any case, if the disclaimer is not there, the originating station is forced to require you to add it. On radio, this means removing other important copy from your message in order to conform to the spot's time limits. On television, it may result in a very cluttered visual conclusion with supered words muddling the impact of a final frame not originally laid out to accommodate them.

2. Maintain a Sufficient Spot Inventory. Unlike commercial advertising endeavors, broadcast campaigns on behalf of a candidate usually last only a few weeks and purchase more, rather than less, airtime at campaign conclusion. Under such conditions, if you produce only one or two spots, listeners/viewers will tire of the messages quickly since they are exposed to each so often within a comparatively brief time span. Therefore, you must create a sufficient number of announcements so people are not continuously going to meet the same message at the same time of day. And no matter how many polispots are produced, each nonetheless must relate to your overall campaign theme—to what, in chapter 12, we called the AO.

3. Stay Away from Super-Slickness. Today's voters may be politically naïve, but they are sophisticated radio listeners and television viewers. And enough citizens are at least aware of the charge that polispots "people package" to make the super-slick image message a dangerous gamble. Particularly in state and local races, a slightly "homemade" look to the spot may actually raise a candidate's credibility—especially when it is patently obvious from the opposition's extravaganzas that those are being assembled by some "big time out-of-staters." This Jim Martin commercial demonstrates how avoiding glossy production values helps put the focus back on the actual copy and what it is saying.

Video	Audio
MARTIN OC IN BLACK LIMBO	MARTIN: I'm Jim Martin and I'm as tired of slick political commercials as you are. I'm running for governor.
SLOW ZOOM IN	I started out teaching at Davidson and I've been a North Carolina Congressman for the past 12 years. I know about education and I understand the responsibilities of leadership. I'm Jim Martin and I'm running for governor because, like you, my greatest concern is

Video	Audio
	for the future of our children and our state.
ANIMATED LOGO	ANNCR (VO):
	Jim Martin for Governor

(Courtesy of Donald Ringe, Ringe Media, Inc.)

3. Forsake The Ottinger Effect.   As we've mentioned, free media and paid media exist side-by-side. Since the broadcast audience is surely going to be exposed to both, you must make certain that both are projecting, if not the same image, at least not contradictory ones. Putting it more bluntly—*you can't package qualities that don't exist.* In 1970, Congressman Richard Ottinger ran for a United States Senate seat and was positioned in his campaign spots as a decisive, dynamic, even charismatic leader. But his performance in a live debate showed his *personality* to be just the opposite. Actual *competence* was not really showcased in either forum, but the fabricated personality of the polispots killed Ottinger's campaign when it shattered in the free media's glare. As political campaign analyst Edwin Diamond summarizes it:

> There are big chunks of uncontrolled time on television—the so-called free media of local and national newscasts as well as the live debates sponsored by the League of Women Voters. What happens in these venues influences reactions to the controlled messages of paid media. The ad people can't make the case that their candidate is presidential or has the right stuff in the paid media if the free media are telling another story. The cognitive dissonance between the two images is usually resolved in the voter/consumer mind in favor of the "real"—and, more often than not, the free media are perceived as more real than paid media.[12]

In short, it is better to copy-cast your candidate in his or her own personality than to select a personality costume that looks and sounds rented as soon as it is out of the protective box of the polispot studio. Reversing both the sequence and net outcome of the Ottinger episode, Canadian Prime-Minister-to-be Brian Mulroney's writers successfully used a man-on-the-street testimonial to argue that Mulroney's performance in the free media (specifically, a just-concluded debate) mirrored the cool-headed qualities inherent in their man. In this way, the paid media message became a reverberated reinforcement for, rather than a lame repudiation of, what the free media were said to be saying.

SINGERS: Across this great big country
               People feel it, people know,
               Mulroney is the leader,
               Who could make this country go.

12. Edwin Diamond, "Fritz' 'Beef' vs. Gary's Appeal," *ADWEEK/Midwest*, March 19, 1984, p. 36.

STREETER:	I think people want to see a leader who is effective on his feet and can get an idea over clearly and can defend his position clearly and do it with tact. And I think he proved that in the debate. He didn't slander the opponents, he merely said how things were.
SINGERS:	We're voting PC Now We're voting PC
STREETER #2:	Mulroney is winning the hearts of Quebec and with both the West and in Ontario and Eastern Canada. There's no question that he's the only truly national leader at this time.
SINGERS:	'cause we're voting PC Now We're voting PC Now We're voting PC We're voting PC Now We're voting PC
ANNCR:	This has been a paid announcement by the PC Party of Canada.

(Courtesy of Peter MacKenzie, Progressive Conservative Party of Canada.)

4. Know the Territory.   To avoid The Ottinger Effect, you need to know your candidate. It is just as important to understand the candidate's *constituency*— both its people and its places. A polispot must not only ring true in what it says about its subject officeseeker, but must also be perceived as accurate in terms of what it says about the state or district in which it airs. If this local under-standing is not clearly present, the credibility of the candidate will suffer.

Recently, a young prairie-state man ran for the United States Senate. Hand-some and personable, he was also the son of the state's most famous and successful football coach. No Ottinger Effect here—he was who he said he was and projected the same appealing charm in public as on tape. The key polispot of his campaign showed him confidently walking with his wife through a pas-toral field, eyes raised toward the future, to the accompaniment of a stirring musical underscore. But the spot failed. And so did the campaign. Because his rural constituents knew what the copywriter did not. No one ever walks through a cow pasture with upraised eyes!

Below is another prairie region spot. But unlike the previous example, this one evinced candidate cognizance of the real priorities of the region—not pasture panoramas but more responsive energy and rail service policies. Thus, even though not a resident of the territory, Mulroney shows himself to be in tune with the prairie provinces' most pressing needs.

SINGERS:	Across this great big country People feel it, people know, Mulroney is the leader,

```
                    Who can make this country go.
                    We're voting PC Now.
MULRONEY:           You and I know that we can achieve more when we work
                    together, yet for many years conflict has marked
                    relations between our federal and provincial
                    governments. The lack of progress experienced in
                    energy, freight rates and passenger rail services
                    isn't going to change unless there's a new climate of
                    co-operation between Ottawa and the Prairie provinces.
                    You help me and we'll do it together.
SINGERS:            We're going to do it all together
                    'cause we're voting PC Now
                    We're voting PC Now
                    We're voting PC
                    We're voting PC Now
                    We're voting PC
ANNCR:              This has been a paid announcement by the P.C. Party of
                    Canada.
```

(Courtesy of Peter MacKenzie, Progressive Conservative Party of Canada.)

5. Keep Governmental Symbols Positive.   Whatever they may think of the individual candidates, the people most likely to vote are also those who have the greatest respect for the process and hallmarks of goverment. Incumbents are thus wise to link themselves with the edifices and tools of their office as a means of capitalizing on feelings of local, regional, and national pride. While overdoing this association by wrapping oneself in the flag is not credible, using symbols of the realm as a backdrop creates a very positive impression without any need for the incumbent to brag about them.

Not holding title to the office being sought, challengers must be more creative in finding authority-confering symbols. If they already hold a lesser political office, they can, of course, appropriate the emblems of that post to enhance credibility. A mayor running for Congress might be seen hard at work at City Hall, or a governor seeking the Presidency might use scenes from the State House. (Using old footage, even ex-governors successfully can enlist this device, as Jimmy Carter and Ronald Reagan both proved.) Alternatively, a contender might be seen at his or her place of business or working in some other professional capacity while the copy draws parallels between that experience and what is needed in political office.

What a challenger must not do, however, is to seem to confuse the incumbent opponent with the office by treating government symbols in a negative way. Showing a picture of the White House while talking of the shortcomings of its current occupant, for instance, attacks the institution more than the officeholder and will be misperceived, if not resented, by a significant portion of the electorate. The copywriter must ensure that an office archetype is always shown as something to be respected and striven for—otherwise, why is your candidate seeking to assume it?

CONTROVERSY ADVERTISING

The International Advertising Association has defined controversy advertising as:

> Any kind of paid public communication or message, from an identified source and in a conventional medium of public advertising, which presents information or a point of view bearing on a publicly recognized controversial issue.[13]

Partisan Spot

The bridge between controversy and political advertising is the partisan or political action spot, in which the disputation involves voting for or against the policies of a political party in general rather than any one candidate in particular. Most of the polispot's previously discussed objectives and techniques apply to the blanket partisan commercial with the additional problem that the intangible of "party" is now added to the intangibility of an issue or belief. The copywriter must make doubly certain, therefore, that concrete implements are called on to define and register the controversy's essence and the correctness of your side's stand on it. In this National Republican Congressional Committee treatment, the point is made by alternating positive historical symbols of government with indicting contemporary representations of who is allegedly abusing that institution.

PORTRAIT OF THOMAS JEFFERSON	ANNCR (VO): When the Democratic Party was born, its founders had a vision.
DISS TO U.S. CAPITOL	Of fairness. And free and open debate in the House of Representatives.
HEADLINE ANNOUNCING DEMOCRAT TAKEOVER OF HOUSE OF REPS.	The Democrats have controlled the House for 29 years.
TIP O'NEILL	And look at the result.
GAVEL STRIKES: SUPER: Democrats Falsify Congressional Records	They've falsified Congressional records.
SUPER: Speaker Breaks Own Rule	The Speaker broke his own rule about TV cameras in the House.
DISS BACK TO JEFFERSON PORTRAIT: IT WEEPS	Is this the proud record he foresaw? The House is out of order.

13. International Advertising Association, *Controversy Advertising* (New York: Hastings House Publishers, 1977), p. 18.

<u>SUPER:</u> Vote Republican　　　　　Bring back the pride. Vote
　　　　　　　　　　　　　　　　　　Republican.

(Courtesy of Anita Warren, National Republican Congressional Committee.)

Other Controversy Categories

In addition to blanket partisan messages, broadcast controversy spots can be divided into three other categories: corporate image, corporate advocacy, and product legitimacy.

Why do we buy this space?

For more than 12 years now, we've been addressing Americans with weekly messages in principal print media. We've argued, cajoled, thundered, pleaded, reasoned and poked fun. In return, we've been reviled, revered, held up as a model and put down as a sorry example.

Why does Mobil choose to expose itself to these weekly judgments in the court of public opinion? Why do we keep it up now that the energy crisis and the urgent need to address energy issues have eased, at least for the present?

Our answer is that business needs voices in the media, the same way labor unions, consumers, and other groups in our society do. Our nation functions best when economic and other concerns of the people are subjected to rigorous debate. When our messages add to the spectrum of facts and opinion available to the public, even if the decisions are contrary to our preferences, then the effort and cost are worthwhile.

Think back to some of the issues in which we have contributed to the debate.

● Excessive government regulation—it's now widely recognized that Washington meddling, however well intentioned, carries a price tag that the consumer pays.

● The folly of price controls—so clear now that prices of gasoline and other fuels are coming down, now that the marketplace has been relieved of most of its artificial restraints.

● The need for balance between maintaining jobs and production and maintaining a pristine environment—a non-issue, we argued, if there's common sense and compromise on both sides, a view that's now increasingly recognized in Washington.

Over the years, we've won some and lost some, and battled to a draw on other issues we've championed, such as building more nuclear power plants and improving public transportation. We've supported presidents we thought were right in their policies and questioned Democrats and Republicans alike when we thought their policies were counterproductive.

In the process we've had excitement, been congratulated and castigated, made mistakes, and won and lost some battles. But we've enjoyed it. While a large company may seem terribly impersonal to the average person, it's made up of people with feelings, people who care like everybody else. So even when we plug a quality TV program we sponsor on public television, we feel right about spending the company's money to build audience for the show, just as we feel good as citizens to throw the support of our messages to causes we believe in, like the Mobil Grand Prix, in which young athletes prepare for this year's Olympics. Or recognition for the positive role retired people continue to play in our society.

We still continue to speak on a wide array of topics, even though there's no immediate energy crisis to kick around anymore. Because we don't want to be like the mother-in-law who comes to visit only when she has problems and matters to complain about. We think a continuous presence in this space makes sense for us. And we hope, on your part, you find us informative occasionally, or entertaining, or at least infuriating. But never boring. After all, you did read this far, didn't you?

Mobil®

Figure 13–3. *(This ad appeared in* The New York Times, *February 9, 1984. © 1984 Mobil Corporation. Reprinted with permission of Mobil Corporation.)*

1. Corporate Image. Like image polispots, *corporate* image messages strive to invest the sponsoring entity with a positive halo. It may be that, though this specific sponsor has not been singled out for attack, it is part of a generic category that is the subject of public debate or mistrust. Or perhaps the sponsor *is* well known and that distrust is highly focused on it. Either way, it is the job of the corporate image message to defuse hostility without actually tackling the underlying issues that might be involved. At the same time, the corporate image controversy pitch strives to secure its client's legitimacy as a source of valid opinion. The Mobil Corporation print layout in Figure 13–3 is a good example of general image building and legitimacy establishment. For practice, decide how you might condense this approach into a well-honed 60-second radio treatment.

2. Corporate Advocacy. Since, by its nature, advocacy is perceived as argumentative, most sponsors prefer the safer image course. Once a major public controversy that directly or indirectly involves that sponsor has been touched off, however, there is little choice but to meet the issue head on. Such a volatile situation presents an immediate need to encourage listeners or viewers to take a side—your client's side—before the public opinion battle is lost. The following Minnesota Business Partnership spot adopts an almost cruel visual metaphor to characterize the threatened legislative actions of the opposition. In this way, it powerfully advocates its position without becoming a visible combatant itself.

Video	Audio
1-2 YEAR OLD BABY SITTING WITH CANDY IN HAND	MUSIC: [MUSIC BOX 'BRAHMS' LULLABY] VO: Raising taxes in Minnesota used to be like taking candy from a baby.
BABY IS DISTRACTED BY SOMETHING ON THE LEFT—ADULT HAND ENTERS FROM RIGHT AND PLUCKS SOME CANDY	VO: But lately, some of our state lawmakers have had to resort to tricks.
BABY IS DISTRACTED TO RIGHT—HAND COMES FROM LEFT	VO: Right now, hidden in a bigger tax bill are provisions that spell permanent income tax hikes for most Minnesota taxpayers.

```
CANDY CONTINUES TO BE TAKEN          VO:  They think we won't
                                          notice a little increase
                                          of twenty to thirty
                                          percent.


BABY IS VISIBLY UPSET                VO:  Who do they think we are—
                                          children? Call or write
                                          your legislator and tell
                                          him to hold the line.
                                          Let's hang on to what
                                          we've got left.


SUPER: NO MORE TAX INCREASES
```

Figure 13-4. *(Courtesy of Deb Tarum, Fallon McElligott Rice.)*

3. Product Legitimacy. Sometimes the issue is the product itself—whether and/or how its sale should be promoted. In nudging a controversial commodity into the marketplace, the usual strategy is to try to champion the audience's right to choose; their right to know their options and make their decisions accordingly. Choice is not just the strategy but the central theme of the Today commercial in Figure 13-5. As a means of accentuating the difference between "The Sixties" and "Today," the first two-thirds of the spot was shot in black-and-white. The visual transformed to contemporary color with the words "Until Today." Being in tune with the times is thereby added as a reinforcing sub-theme without directly raising potentially argumentative statements of values.

Six Controversy Campaign Objectives

As with polispots, at least half a dozen goals can be set in activating a contro-versy campaign. Certainly, no campaign need realize all of these objectives, but

Figure 13–5. *(Courtesy of Patti Halpert, keye/donna/pearlstein.)*

a familiarity with each will make a copywriter more aware of, and prepared for, the major task or tasks that must be faced.

1. Restore Balance to Public Discussion. In democratic countries, at least, most of the citizenry believe in people's right to be heard. Even though this belief is not automatically extended to corporations or organizations, appealing to the audience's sense of fairness will usually beget a willingness to listen—provided, of course, your message is presented in an interesting and involving manner. Babies and taxes are again interrelated in the W. R. Grace & Company approach in Figure 13–6. As the spot makes clear, the company is not "looking

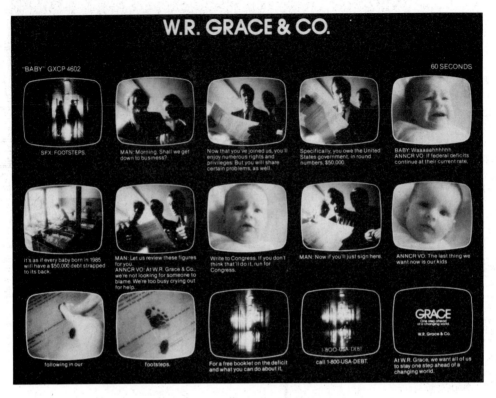

Figure 13-6.   *(Courtesy of Stephen B. Elliott, W. R. Grace & Co.)*

for someone to blame" (which would only precipitate an argument) but simply seeks help and is willing to share its own thoughts on the deficit in a free booklet. This Direct Response type of strategy thus defers any aggressive issue confrontation until viewers have been coaxed into obtaining more explicit and complete print material.

2. Establish Your Right to Be Party to Issue Resolution.   A portion of any controversy—sometimes a major portion—swirls around "who can play"; who has the credentials to participate in determining the outcome and how we shall reach it. A "special interest group," for instance, must prove itself to be a "*public* interest group" (or at least, a group with the public's interest in mind) before its advocacy will be accepted. The firearm manufacturer's position on gun control legislation probably faces an insurmountable task in showing it speaks with anything but pocketbook motivation. The manufacturer could, however, provide the ammunition (no pun intended) that sympathetic but less vested interest spokessources could articulate in support of its stand.

Though it admittedly has had far greater success placing print than broadcast advertisements, much of Mobil Corporation's public effort (such as the Figure 13-3 layout) has persuasively taken the position that "while a large company may seem terribly impersonal to the average person, it's made up of people with feelings, people who care like everybody else." It is on behalf of these people, then, rather than corporate self-interest, that Mobil asserts the right to address energy and other business issues in which it (or its "people") can demonstrate expertise.

3. Strive to Influence the Public Agenda. This objective is akin to the polispot's goal of "picking the battlefield." But since there is no candidate context to provide a natural framework for issue articulation, the controversy spot often must try to bring an issue to the fore in its own right and for its own sake. In the script that follows, The American Security Council (a nongovernmental action group) uses an arm wrestling metaphor in an attempt to sway public attitudes to (1) focus on the issue of world peace, and (2) consider it within an attitudinal orientation of "peace through strength." Clearly, agenda influencing is often a process that involves not only publicizing a problem, but also simultaneously advocating an attendant solution to it.

Video	Audio
FADE UP FROM BLACK	(SFX: AMBIENT BACKGROUND SOUND MIXED WITH SLOW, SOFT HEARTBEAT)
TIGHT SHOT ACROSS TOP OF PROFESSIONAL ARM WRESTLING TABLE; NON-DESCRIPT BG.	
LARGE, MUSCULAR ARM ENTERS SCREEN RIGHT, ELBOW FIRST, IN WRESTLING POSITION, BANGING DOWN INTO PLACE AND FILLING SCREEN. WRISTBAND INDICATES THE SOVIET SICKLE-AND-HAMMER EMBLEM ABOVE THE LETTERS ''USSR''	
SECOND ARM ENTERS SCREEN LEFT, FIRMLY GRASPS OPPOSING HAND	
CAMERA POV CUTS ACROSS TABLE, NOW SHOWING ARM AND GLOVE WITH POLISH FLAG AND WORD ''POLAND''	
ARM WRESTLING ACTION BEGINS, POV CHANGES TO REVEAL T-SHIRTS WORN BY CONTESTANTS ALSO INDICATE NATION BUT FACES ARE NEVER SEEN	(SFX: HEARTBEAT MIXES WITH AMBIENT SOUND OF GRUNTS, STRUGGLE AND HEAVY BREATHING)

Video	Audio
	<u>ANNCR (VO):</u>
POLISH ARM STRUGGLES, IS SLOWLY AND FIRMLY PUSHED DOWN UNTIL PINNED	It's a fight no one can afford to lose. That's the way it is, like it or not.
POV SHOOTING DOWN ON TABLE SHOWING VICTORIOUS SOVIET ARM PINNING OPPONENT	
REPEAT SHOT FROM OPEN. NEW ARM CHALLENGING SOVIET IS ''AFGHAN''	(SFX: SAME AMBIENT BACKGROUND; HEARTBEAT SLIGHTLY FASTER, SLIGHTLY LOUDER)
ACTION RESUMES, SAME POV SHOT	The Soviets know their own strength---and now, so do many others. It may not be the best of worlds, but it's the only one we've got. We have to live
AFGHAN LOSES	in it, and so do they---and so do our kids.
	(SFX: HEARTBEAT INCREASES; SAME AMBIENT BACKGROUND)
REPEAT SHOT FROM OPEN. NEW ARM CHALLENGING SOVIET IS ''USA''	If you believe that peace comes through having the strength to <u>keep</u> the peace— join us. We're the Coalition For Peace Through Strength. We believe that if you really want to talk to the Russians,
USA & USSR ARMS START OUT EQUAL	they have to have a reason to listen to you first.
SOVIET ARM SLOWLY STARTS TO GAIN ADVANTAGE	We're the Coalition For Peace Through Strength.
SOVIET ARM PUSHES USA ARM DOWN CLOSE TO PINNING POSITION. USA ARM STARTS SLOW STRUGGLE BACK UP, FIGHTS SOVIET ARM TO A POSITION STILL AT SLIGHT DISADVANTAGE	And we believe that the future of freedom depends on an America that's willing to depend upon itself.

Video	Audio
ACTION FREEZES	(SFX: VERY LOUD HEARTBEAT, GRUNTS, GROANS, ETC.)
	(SFX: OUT SUDDENLY)

DIS TO TITLE:
  Peace Through Strength
  Boston, Virginia 22713
  (Tel.) 1-800-PEACE-84
	Peace Through Strength
	Join us.
	Call: 1-800-PEACE-84.

(Courtesy of Donald Ringe, Ringe Media, Inc.)

4. Defend/Extend a Point of View. Unlike the previous one, this objective need not concern itself with agenda influencing. Here, the issue is already squarely in the public eye, and the message can proceed directly to the task of championing the client's position on it. Many people, in fact, see this goal as being synonymous with controversy advertising *per se*. Though our discussion has identified additional goals with which controversy advertising might be involved, there is no question that stark point-of-view advocacy is the most salient task of most controversy campaigns.

The concept of open housing, for example, is no longer a *legal* dispute in the United States. Nonetheless, it remains an *attitudinal* controversy as far as significant numbers of people are concerned. So the following award-winning treatment defends open housing by extending it into a serene and nonthreatening struggle (a checker game) that plays down race and plays up humanity.

> Production Note: Relaxed, warm conversational tones. Periodic sounds of checkers on game board and soft street activity. BM is elderly black man; WM is elderly white man.

BM: Beautiful day. Just playin' checkers on the porch with my buddy.

WM: Your neighbor, since open housing.

BM: Been better 'n ten years.

WM: Since you won a game? Jumped your king.

BM: Since open housing. No race; no handicap; and no national background standing between someone and a place to live.

WM: And no more going crosstown just to teach you the checkers game.

BM: Well, we sure covered a lot of ground to get open housing.

WM: Wonder if we'll be neighbors in the great beyond?

BM: Why not? Behind the pearly gates, open housing's always
         been the game plan. Your move.
BOTH: (Chuckle)

(Courtesy of Susan Montgomery.)

5. Rebut Charges.   This is an objective a copywriter hates to face because it
becomes a goal only when the other side has already put your client on the
defensive. Under such circumstances, it is too late to strive to influence the
public agenda and not enough just to extend a general point-of-view. Instead,
your client has already been indicted in the public media, and you have little
choice but to respond directly to the thrust or thrusts of that indictment. As
mentioned in our analysis of the "Heck, No" audience in chapter 4, you cannot
ignore or sidestep the main charge being leveled. That will only confirm in
people's minds that the allegation is true—and that you are "shifty" besides.
Like the Tincanada spot below, your best strategy is to isolate the accusation
and neutralize it by describing clearly extenuating circumstances (not excuses)
while seeking to establish a common bond with your audience.

ANNCR: The recent rate hike in local telephone service has
         worried a lot of people. And it's making some of them
         angry. Angry at Tincanada Telephone. Like you, we're
         worried and angry too. Not just because we're area
         residents. But because we <u>are</u> Tincanada. That's right.
         We're the folks being blamed for that added charge on
         your local phone bill.

VOICE: So what gives us the right to be angry or worried? Just
         the fact that the rate increase is beyond our control
         too. But we're taking the rap.

ANNCR: You see, recent government tariff regulations on long
         distance access charges have forced us to pay a lot more—
         a lot more to those long distance companies to get your
         calls in and out of our community. So to stay in
         business, we're forced to raise this revenue from local
         service customers. People like you. Who Tincanada has
         valued as friends for 50 years.

VOICE: That's what worries and angers us the most. The fact that
         Tincanada's in danger of losing your friendship over new
         regulations created in Washington. Let's get mad
         together---but not at each other.

6. Urgent Correction of Facts.   When it raises its rates, a phone company
should anticipate a negative consumer reaction. Occasionally, however, an
entirely unforeseen event will strike a company and threaten its existence. This
is the hardest condition of all for a controversy copywriter to cope with, and
the reason we discuss such "crisis advertising" separately in the last section of
this chapter.

Further Controversy Copywriting Techniques

Though they are encompassed in some of the copy solutions presented earlier, five controversy-combatting devices are so common and can serve to realize so many different objectives as to merit special showcasing here.

1. Offer Alternatives. The Today contraceptive commercial in Figure 13–5 helps epitomize this approach in its "time you had another choice" tagline. Such an offering of other options helps get the audience beyond an argumentative stance and into a posture of examining new choices. Most people would feel better dealing with a concern in an affirmative manner than keep it continually churning. Alternatives, when skillfully presented, provide just such a resolution. The following television message for the Minnesota Business Partnership graphically portrays a burgeoning budget surplus that the state's personal income tax allegedly caused. This irritating condition is made more graphic by a bloated suit device; but the spot does not leave the matter there. Instead, it progresses toward the "explosively" framed alternative: "Write your legislator now."

Video	Audio
MS OF MAN IN A CONSERVATIVE BUSINESS SUIT SYMBOLIZING THE STATE OF MINNESOTA. SUIT GRADUALLY EXPANDS AS MORE AND MORE CURRENCY ''GROWS'' INSIDE IT.	ANNCR (VO): Two years ago, the State of Minnesota started collecting a personal income surtax to help balance the budget. It worked.
MAN'S SUIT AND SHIRT NOW QUITE ROTUND BUT HIS EXPRESSION REMAINS IMPLACABLE	In fact, it continues to work. So well, that this biennium, the state will collect 400 million dollars more than is needed to balance the budget.
SUIT/SHIRT NOW ALMOST GLOBAL	In a state where you already pay

Video	Audio
	almost twice the national average in state income tax the last thing you really need—
SUIT/SHIRT EXPLODES SPEWING MONEY EVERYWHERE	(SFX: LARGE EXPLOSION)
	—is a surtax.
DISCLAIMER TAG	Write your legislator now.

(Courtesy of Deb Tarum, Fallon McElligott Rice.)

2. *Justify Your Action.* Particularly when you urge your audience to take a concrete and negative action, it must be made clear that the action is both warranted and sensible. The Minnesota Business Partnership's Figure 13-4 call to resist further taxes was portrayed as the only "adult" thing to do. The boycotting of Malone & Hyde food stores as advocated in the following television commercial is endorsed as a righteous response to the firm's alleged harshness toward individual workers and the public's competitive options.

Video	Audio
PLATE SHOT WITH ADO OUT	ANNCR (VO):
LONG CRANE SHOT FROM ABOVE: TWO WOMEN STANDING IN POOLS OF LIGHT	Meet Sandra Beacham and Neola Donnerson. Between them, 37 years of service to Memphis shoppers as employees at Montesi Food Stores. Malone & Hyde bought the Montesi stores and closed them down
SLOW ZOOM IN AND DOWN	the day after Christmas, 1983, eliminating over 800 jobs and about 20% of the competition— in one stroke---with no warning—without even a thank you.
TIGHT CU OF FACE	MS. BEACHAM:
	How could they do this to us?

Video	Audio
RACK FOCUS, TIGHT CU OF FACE	**MS. DONNERSON:** How could they do this to the people of Memphis?
PLATE SHOT WITH ADO WINDOW: Please don't shop Malone & Hyde. Paid for by Local 1529 UFCW, AFL-CIO	**ANNCR (VO):** Has Malone & Hyde earned your family's food dollars?

(Courtesy of Stephanie Adler, The Kamber Group.)

3. Associate with Others. Picturing your sponsor as a "lone ranger" fighting singlehandedly against injustice may have a certain dramatic appeal, but it is not calculated to involve the passive broadcast audience, which is content to let that sponsor continue to carry this courageous burden unaided. People have so many personal and continuing responsibilities that they are understandably reluctant to assume any more. Consequently, it is important that the call to action is seen as part of a group effort that has wide acceptance and won't require much individual sacrifice. The following parody on the movie *Ghostbusters'* musical theme puts the request for help in a nonthreatening and deceptively humorous package. The message makes clear that the listener will be joining "thousands of Americans nationwide" through the simple and painless act of buying a different brand.

SINGERS: Listen up you all
It's a personal call
For you to become
Turkeybusters
And if you know what's fair
And if you know what's right
Then you will become
Turkeybusters

(MUSIC: INSTRUMENTAL BED UNDERSCORE)

ANNCR: Join the thousands of Americans nationwide who know that unfair and unreasonable treatment of workers isn't in the American spirit of Thanksgiving (later, Christmas). Boycott Marval Turkeys and Marval Turkey products. Become one of the Turkeybusters.

SINGERS: I ain't buyin' Marval.
So this holiday
Listen to what we say
And be a Marval

```
                   Turkeybuster
                   Turkeybuster
                   Turkeybuster
ANNCR:        Sponsored by Local 400, United Food and Commercial
              Workers.
```

(Courtesy of Stephanie Adler, The Kamber Group.)

4. Become the Victim. The opposite of being the solitary crusader is adopting the role of the abused. When carefully handled, this tactic can arouse sympathy for your cause, trigger underdog sentiment on your behalf, and cast the opposition as the villain. Few people would accept the Colorado Independent Banks as a helpless victim, but by using a child to represent their stand visually, a human rather than corporate harm is projected.

Video	Audio
MS CONTINUOUS MOTION DOLLY, WITH CUTS, TRACKING 11-YEAR-OLD BOY THRU A DOOR—UP A FLIGHT OF STAIRS—DOWN A HALL—INTO HIS ROOM. ROOM IS MIDDLE-CLASS KID'S ROOM FILLED WITH CONTEMPORARY KID'S STUFF. BOY IS CARRYING A LETTER. (SCENE SHOT WITH SLIGHT FOG FILTER)	<u>(MUSIC: SAD, NOSTALGIC UNDER</u>) <u>ANNCR (VO)</u>: We're gonna give it to you straight. If branch banking is passed, it's gonna cost you money.
MS MODERATE ANGLE, BOY SITS ON BED, BEGINS TO OPEN ENVELOPE APPREHENSIVELY	When you try to borrow, interest rates will be higher. When you try to save,
MCU EYE-LEVEL. BOY PULLS OUT LETTER AND BEGINS TO READ IT, LOOKS PUZZLED	interest rates will be lower. Either way, it costs you.
MCU SEMI-PROFILE. BOY LAYS LETTER ON BED.	And branch banking will hurt in other ways.
ECU LETTER (NOTE FROM BIG BANK SAYING HIS SAVINGS ACCNT. HAS BEEN CLOSED BECAUSE BANK NO LONGER HANDLES ACCOUNTS UNDER $100)	Small savings accounts will be discouraged---and then phased out. After all, big banks need big money.
MCU EYE-LEVEL, BOY PICKS UP LETTER	They don't have to be concerned

Video	Audio
CU EYE-LEVEL, BOY LOOKS PUZZLED	with the little people.
PULL BACK TO MS, BOY NEATLY FOLDS LETTER, PUTS IT BACK IN ENVELOPE, HOLDS ENVELOPE IN LAP, STARES STRAIGHT AHEAD LOOKING CRUSHED. FREEZE.	It shouldn't happen here in Colorado. That's why we're giving it to you straight. Branch banking will hit you where you live—
<u>SUPER</u>: Vote <u>NO</u> to Branch Banking (Disclaimer)	in more ways than one.

(Courtesy of Robert Bradsell, Ailes Communications Inc.)

5. Alert the Constituency. Paul Revere's storied midnight ride was a plea for support ("To Arms, To Arms") as well as an alarum ("The British Are Coming"). Advocacy statements can often be enmeshed in a warning so objective assessment (the arrival of the redcoats) and subjective espousal (armed opposition) become mutually indistinguishable. Thus, while updating a news event (the Las Vegas strike continues), the radio commercial that follows also unequivocally registers its own recommendation (stay away).

ANNCR: Your get-away to Las Vegas could turn into a vacation
         nightmare. The strike there continues. And acts of
         violence have become as commonplace as a silver dollar.
         Combine that danger with the inconvenience of cancelled
         shows, closed restaurants and inadequate service, and then
         ask yourself:
         What are the odds of a good time in Las Vegas?
         Lousy. So don't get away---stay away. From Las Vegas. It's
         no place for you or your family.
         Paid for by the Hotel and Restaurant Employees Union.

(Courtesy of Stephanie Adler, The Kamber Group.)

CRISIS ADVERTISING

The journalistic Paul Reveres of today have an infinitely greater and more sustained influence than he did. An alarum raised by one of their stories can spread almost instantaneously across the country and impact the actions of millions of people. As a result, when your client's product or service is the subject of this scare, a copywriter has little time to act before permanent damage is done. Since the aforementioned "urgent correction of facts" is such a crucial operation in today's world of precipitate communication, we close this chapter with a separate examination of crisis advertising techniques.

As *ADWEEK*'s Christy Marshall points out, when a public crisis hits a company, there are basically only five possible courses of action:

Stop advertising.
Kill the product or dump the celebrity (if the crisis involved your spokesperson).
Pull the product, reformulate it, repackage it, replace it on the shelves.
Break a campaign to set the record straight.
Ignore it and pray it will go away soon.[14]

Four of these five options are company actions that will not employ the copywriter. Therefore, we need not concern ourselves with them here. The remaining choice, "breaking a campaign to set the record straight," is, on the other hand, a copywriter-centered task that demands all the skill a wordsmith can muster. To delineate possible scripting responses, we'll examine two of recent history's most successful crisis campaigns: those for Johnson & Johnson's Tylenol and the Hygrade Corporation's Ball Park Franks.

The Tylenol Crisis

In October, 1982, a number of people in the Chicago area died after taking poison-tainted Extra-Strength Tylenol capsules. Though it was soon determined unequivocally that the poison had been introduced by someone after the capsules had been distributed, this fact had to be communicated promptly and in a way calculated to *preserve* the brand's good name. The term *preserve* is important. Because it is more feasible to bolster a subject still perceived somewhat positively than to wait and have the uphill battle of restoring credibility to a term that, in the public's mind, has already been thoroughly polluted.

Working closely with the client, executives from Compton Advertising decided to take their case to the airwaves with a straightforward report designed to set the record straight. For credibility's sake, use of any outside talent was ruled out. Instead, the agency screentested a number of top executives from Johnson & Johnson's McNeil Consumer Products subsidiary (the actual manufacturer of Tylenol) and selected Dr. Thomas Gates, McNeil's medical director, as the on-camera spokesman. The resulting Gates commercial (Figure 13–7) ran more than a dozen times in network primetime.

As the grainy Tylenol photoboard evidences, what had to be communicated—and communicated quickly—was a sense of urgent concern rather than premeditated slickness. Production values were necessarily underplayed as a consequence. After explaining the facts of the situation, Dr. Gates's message incorporated several of the controversy copywriting techniques we've just studied. The copy offered the twin alternatives of (1) switching from Tylenol capsules to the much-harder-to-tamper-with tablets via (2) the company's offer to "replace your capsules with tablets." The precautionary action of withdrawing all capsules from the stores was justified as necessary to maintain consumer trust and characterized as a temporary measure until "capsules in tamper-resistant containers" could be developed. The spot also associated the

14. Christy Marshall, "Crisis Advertising: What's an Agency to Do?" *ADWEEK/Midwest*, August 13, 1984, p. 25.

Figure 13–7. *(Courtesy of F. Robert Kniffin, Johnson & Johnson.)*

company with the consumer by observing that "this act damages all of us" and made it clear that the company, like the people poisoned, was an innocent victim of a criminal act by an outsider.

This no-nonsense trust strategy was extended some two months later when the now triple-sealed capsule packages had reached store shelves. The reintroduction was heralded in a 45/15 commercial. The 45-second portion was devoted to a testimonial by San Diego housewife Paige Nagle, who affirmed that "Tylenol is worthy of my trust" and that the product's "more than just a pain reliever, it's something we can count on." As a trust/confidence builder, the testimonial avoided any mention of capsules, poisoning, or packaging. The

15-second announcer voice-over then explained the three safety seals as they were shown and warned against the purchase of open packages. Rather than reawaken memories of the disaster, the announcer's copy concentrated on the fact that Tylenol capsules were being "reintroduced" and thus fulfilled the promise that Dr. Gates had made in the previous spot.

Six months after the tragedy, Tylenol had recaptured 80 percent of its previous market share,[15] a tribute both to product quality and a level-headed copy reaction to what might have been a panic-inducing situation.

The Hygrade Crisis

About the same time as the Tylenol episode, the Hygrade Corporation was rocked by a charge that a consumer had found a metal object in one of the Hygrade-manufactured Ball Park Franks. Three other complaints about hot-dog-encased nails and razor blades soon followed. The company immediately halted shipments, issued a voluntary product recall, and quickly obtained metal detectors to examine one million hot dogs. As in the Tylenol case, Hygrade's agency, W. B. Doner & Company, marshalled its forces and prepared to launch creative work as soon as (but not before) all the facts were available. Looking back, agency executive vice president Skip Roberts emphasized:

> All the God and motherhood advertising appeals in the world would not give us one edge up forward if our customers were not convinced that the premium product, although they had enjoyed it for years, was still fit for human consumption.[16]

Only a few days later, polygraph tests on two of the complainants failed to support their "metallic" charges and a third failed to appear for the test. With examinations of both the meat and its accusers thus completed, the crisis advertising strategy was launched. "We recommended," recalled Roberts, "that our advertising be based on simple truths—we had a problem; the problem had been solved; and we were ready to go back on the market."[17] Within a day, the Figure 13–8 print ad was created, as was a TV spot based on it. As account executive Debbie Cragin explained, "We simply ran it as a crawl with an audio read of the copy."[18]

To avoid prolonging the sense of crisis, the print ad ran only once in sixteen newspapers in Detroit, outstate Michigan, Ohio, Chicago and Pittsburgh.[19] The 30-second television version ran on the three major Detroit television stations for only one day. Despite such brief exposure, the credibility of the print-on-TV device (recall the "Supering for Power" polispot technique analyzed earlier)

15. Maria Fisher, "Tylenol Makes Extra-Strong Comeback," *ADWEEK/Midwest*, March 21, 1983, p. 20.
16. Eileen Courter, "Reputation, PR Helped Hygrade Survive Hot Dog Hoax," *ADWEEK/Midwest*, April 4, 1983, p. 43.
17. *Ibid.*
18. Debbie Cragin, letter to Peter Orlik, January 30, 1985.
19. Emmett Curme, "Hygrade Counters Ball Park Rhubarb with Safety, 'Thank-You' Campaign," *ADWEEK/Midwest*, November 15, 1982, p. 57.

TO OUR BALL PARK CUSTOMERS:

Thank you for bearing with us.

We at Hygrade Food Products Corporation, along with the United States Department of Agriculture, have just completed an exhaustive investigation and inspection of Hygrade's Livonia, Michigan plant, and over 600,000 pounds of our product. The results: All facilities are operating according to the highest standards, and all product leaving our plant has been verified 100% safe . . . just as it's always been.

Our withdrawal of Ball Park Franks from the marketplace was entirely voluntary. U.S.D.A. inspectors have agreed that such action is no longer necessary, and normal distribution is now being resumed in all areas.

There is no evidence that any individual was ever in any danger. Nonetheless, we have taken the precaution of installing permanent ultra-sensitive metal detection systems in our plant. We want to maintain your trust in us and provide every possible measure of protection and safety.

We wish to thank our many employees who so willingly volunteered their own time to assist in this inspection. And we thank you, our customers, for your support and understanding.

Hygrade Food Products Corporation

Figure 13–8. *(Courtesy of Debbie Cragin, W. B. Doner & Company Advertising.)*

plus what Cragin labelled "the timeliness and directness of the message"[20] combined to bring the potentially disasterous episode to a positive conclusion for Hygrade. And like the Tylenol response, the creative work in this case also exploited an amalgam of controversy copywriting techniques. The company justified its action in product removal as well as its subsequent quick return to "normal distribution" by citing the safety verification that was sought and obtained through "an exhaustive investigation and inspection."

The company's cooperation with the U.S.D.A. and that governmental agency's positive findings invested the commercial with additional legitimacy. Finally, though it did not make it a major issue, the fact that Hygrade examined "over 600,000 pounds of our product" and that this was accomplished through "employees who so willingly volunteered their own time," demonstrated that the company and its people were the episode's only real victims and

20. Cragin, letter of January 30, 1985.

should not be victimized further by unwarranted consumer avoidance of the Hygrade product.

Unlike the more predictable pitfalls encountered in political and institutional-ized controversy advertising (and the availability of campaign planning that can anticipate many of these pitfalls), the demand for crisis advertising comes sud-denly and with no advance warning. Gary Hart knew he was going to challenge Walter Mondale, and the United Food and Commercial Workers knew they were going to mount an action against Marval Turkeys. On the other side, Mondale could foresee the Hart threat and Marval was aware of its labor difficulties. For Tylenol and Hygrade, however, no helpful foreshadowing was available. When such crises occur, the copywriters involved can only count on their own quick cognizance of the available techniques and their abilities as communicators to execute these techniques to their fullest, most persuasive potential.

What advertising chieftain Paul Harper of Needham, Harper & Steers recently said about advertising in general pertains in special measure to political, contro-versy, and crisis campaigns in particular:

> It takes persistence to win in advertising. . . . Only tough, resilient, and well-armed advertising people, convinced that they are right, can sell great ideas and keep them sold.[21]

21. Paul Harper, *Victory in Advertising* (New York: Needham, Harper & Steers, 1980), p. 10.

Chapter Fourteen

CROSS-MEDIA CAMPAIGNS

Up to now, the thrust of this book has been exclusively toward creating copy and campaigns for radio and television. More and more, however, broadcast copywriters, particularly at in-station or other "lone wordsmith" shops, face the task of generating print media tie-ins to their broadcast output. An advertising agency writer can usually rely from the start on the design sense and layout expertise of an art director; but copy professionals in more solitary straits must often depend on their own devices for at least the initial stages of the cross-media campaign's development. Accordingly, then, this chapter focuses on the key problems of creating for *type* in addition to *tubes*.

CROSS-MEDIA SHOULDN'T MEAN CROSS-PURPOSES

The most common failure in any cross-media campaign is the failure to project a consistent image from medium to medium. As a consequence, we end up promoting what seems to the consumer to be two or three *different* entities rather than an ever-deepening familiarity with the same one.

Take the following hypothetical campaign, for example. The small Dimflicker Light and Power Company uses billboard, newspaper, and radio advertising to communicate with its customers and to project its corporate image. Yet, as the following three sample treatments show, Dimflicker is a much different company on billboards than it is in newspapers, with its radio presence projecting still a third countenance.

In its "piggybank" billboard approach (Figure 14–1), Dimflicker evinces a light-hearted, almost juvenile attitude to the subject of its chief stock in trade—energy. The company appears to have avoided the heavy-handed institutional orientation common to many utilities, and its visual, if somewhat "cutesy," does tie in with the *single* copy point to which any billboard layout is restricted. The mood of the display is unquestionably happy, with no indication that there is anything to fear either from Dimflicker or about the service it provides. Though the piggybank motif may be somewhat trite, it does make the twin concepts of saving and economy immediately tangible, and, when combined with the light bulb, visually relevant to Dimflicker's main reason for being.

But if the Dimflicker of billboards is jovial and optimistic, the newspaper Dimflicker (Figure 14–2) is surly and cynical. Here, the firm has taken an almost 180° turn and adopted a self-righteous attitude packaged in a stark, institutional framework. Even the headline's play on words seems more threatening than

Figure 14–1. *(Illustration by Ann Rittenhouse.)*

humorous, and the subhead reinforces an overall feeling of antagonism. Other than the lightbulb in the corporate-symbolizing "logo" (a logo that didn't even appear on the billboard), there is nothing to identify this power company with the friendly folks who brought you the smiling piggybank. Even the basic thematic orientation has changed from one of "economical energy" to that of spiraling costs. Consumers exposed to both the billboard and newspaper messages have every reason to wonder just what kind of an organization Dimflicker really is and what in the world it's trying to tell them. Unfortunately, the company's radio spots do not clarify its intent:

<u>Production</u> <u>Note</u>: Smooth, sultry, female voice.

DEBBIE: I'm Debbie. Want to know what turns me on? My new
          sunlamp that tans me from all the way up here (pause) to
          down around there (pause) to the tips of those ten,
          tantalizing toes. And like all my appliances, I couldn't
          turn my sunlamp on to turn <u>me</u> on if it weren't for
          Dimflicker Light and Power. Dimflicker's the energy
          company that pulls my chain and flips my switch every
          time. Let's both turn on to Dimflicker. Together.

The institutional heavy-handedness of the newspaper advertisement is certainly gone here. And there's not a piggybank anywhere in sight. There is also not the slightest vestige of a coherent relationship between the above radio treatment and either its billboard or newspaper counterparts. Dimflicker seems to progress from pal to propagandist to procurer and back again (depending on

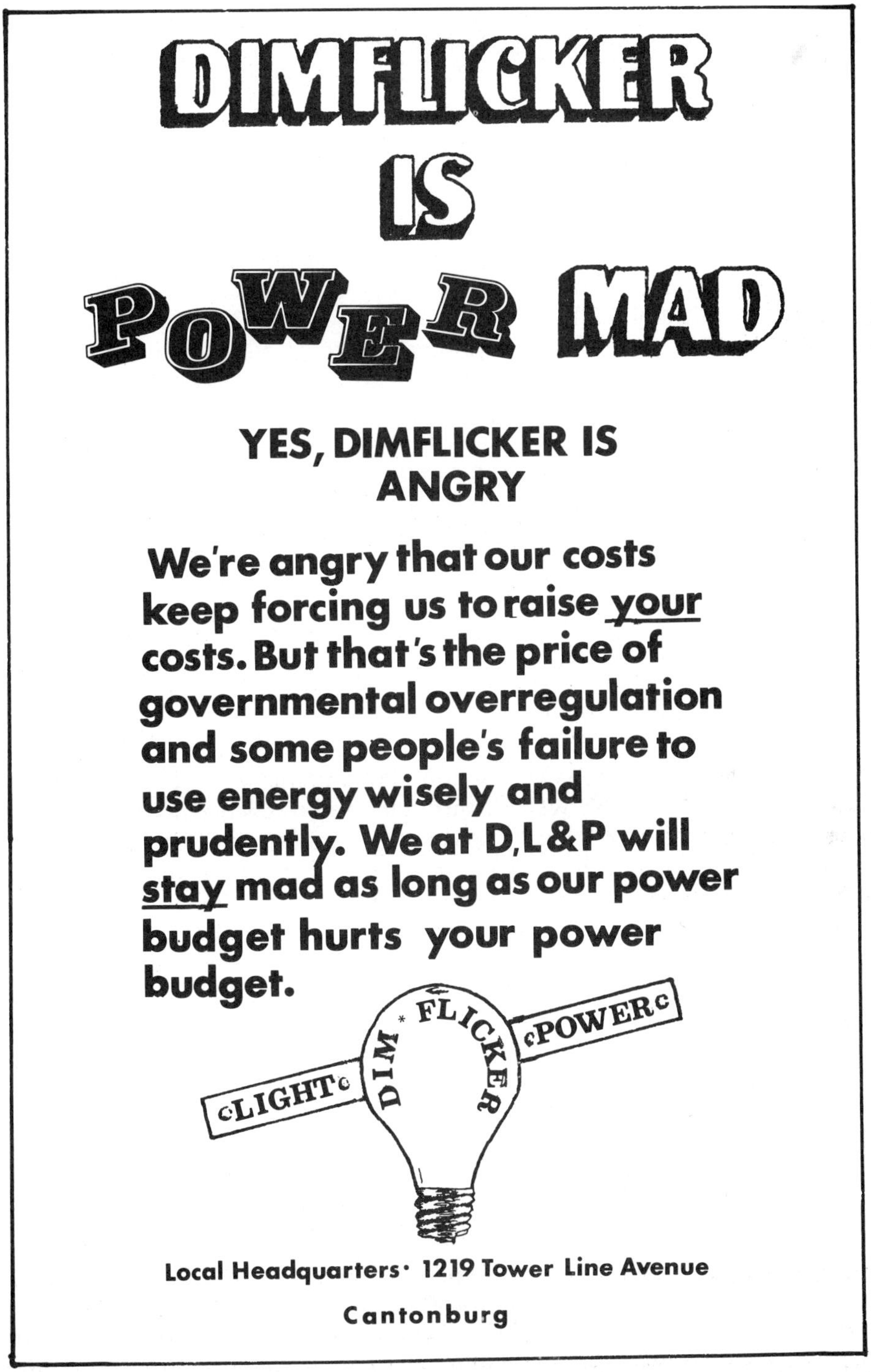

Figure 14–2. *(Illustration by Ann Rittenhouse.)*

the order in which the individual consumer perceives the three media ads). With Debbie, we even lose the lightbulb symbol that provided the sole unifying feature between the two visual layouts. What she contributes has very little to do with electricity except in a colloquial sense.

It is fortunate for Dimflicker Light and Power that there can be only one electric purveyor in town. For, though the company projects three entirely different images, there are no competitors with which any of these images can be confused. On the other hand, there *are* hundreds of firms in *highly competitive* fields whose individual cross-media campaigns also seem to speak in just as many tongues. This lack of consistency at best casts blurred shadows on consumer identification of the company or service and at worst fails to establish the firm or its product in the consumer's mind *at all*. Instead, the various unrelated strands of the campaign may even be perceived as pitches for several *different* competitors.

Via Concept Engineering Versions 1 and 2, chapter 12 provided several techniques for keeping the broadcast campaign on a single, coherent, and market-defined track. Many of these same techniques can be applied with equal utility to the cross-media effort. Still, it must be recognized that the inherent and previously discussed differences between print and broadcast communication make the possibilities of campaign fragmentation far greater when media of both types are used to promote the same entity. The constant cognizance of these differences by the copywriter is a prime preventative of what we might call the Dimflicker Phenomenon.

In contrast to the scattered communications of our hypothetical utility firm, let's examine the cohesion of the following "Someplace Special" package developed for client stations by TM Productions. Proving that unified campaigns can be initiated accidentally as well as through careful calculation, "Someplace Special" began as an announcer's spontaneous ad-lib on Pittsburgh's KDKA. One day, the morning man remarked on-the-air that he was fed up with the negative remarks outsiders were directing toward Pittsburgh. To conclude his rebuttal to their sneers, he used the phrase, "Pittsburgh, Someplace Special." The favorable response to this expression, and the phrase that encapsulated it, was so immediate and dramatic that the station latched on to "Someplace Special" as a theme. On-air copy and complementary print media materials were created and used to achieve a focused, high-recall triumph in the packaging and communication of station identity.

TM Productions later bought the rights to this campaign and made its elements adaptable to client stations in a number of cities, of course, on a one-to-a-market basis. The creative work set forth below illustrates how "Someplace Special" was adapted to the needs of WTIC, Hartford, Connecticut; a station that, with its 50,000 watts, likes to identify itself with all of New England.

Since the product *is* a radio station, it is natural that special attention be devoted to the on-air promotional material the station itself carries. The principles related to construction of this type of copy have been amplified earlier, especially in chapter 7. Thus, the purpose here is to show how such radio scripting dovetails with the other elements of the cross-media campaign.

As an outlet featuring MOR (middle-of-the-road) tunes, WTIC naturally uses a lyric package that lends itself to that musical style while it still conveys the essence of the "Someplace Special" motif. Here is a typical "sixty" from that package:

```
Some things are special to ya,
some things just always seem to give.
Some things are special to ya,
just make you want to get up and live.
New England, you're someplace special,
New England, you're someplace special,
New England, and WTIC,
we're just right for each other.
Some places are special,
some places always make you smile.
Some places are special,
some places make it all worthwhile.
New England, someplace special,
New England, someplace special,
New England, and WTIC,
we're just right for each other,
we're just right for each other.
```

(Courtesy of TM Productions, Inc.)

Notice that the modular construction of this lyric allows the last nine lines to serve as the "lift-out" for a self-standing 30-second promo and that the final three lines can serve as a separate 10-second piece. Similarly, the second half of the alternate "sixty" that follows can also function alone for greater flexibility in promotion airings:

```
There's a special place for very
   special people.
And special people like you need a
   special place to hide away.
It's a special place for someone special;
   WTIC and you.
It's a special place for very special
   people.
Oh, New England, New England, you've got
   special people,
And for those special people
there's a special place for someone special;
WTIC and New England (echo fade).
```

(Courtesy of TM Productions, Inc.)

What is aimed for here is a single, warm, and cogent image with a simplicity that makes it easily identifiable and the station's call sign, therefore, assuredly *memorable.*

The clarity of the slogan is carried over into the graphic designs used in the print media tie-ins. The associated *velox* (a screened, sharp-definition photographic print that can be used in page paste-ups as though it were a drawing containing dots and lines) features the same basic theme together with a graphic reproduction of recognizable landmarks indicative of the station's coverage area. This Figure 14–3 design is readily adaptable to a variety of print

Figure 14–3. *(Courtesy of TM Productions, Inc.)*

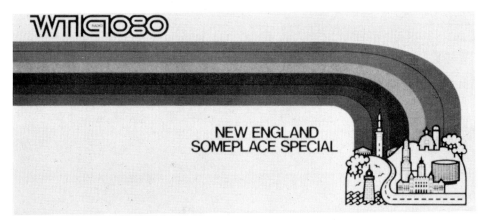

Figure 14–4.   *(Courtesy of TM Productions, Inc.)*

media, including billboards, and can be used alone or, in the case of newspaper or magazine layouts, combined with additional copy to promote specific programs or events. For further enhancement of the same image in *full-color* media, a rainbow is added, thus making the graphic representation of the station's aural image serviceable for color billboards or the often neglected but beneficial support media of stationery and business cards. Here, again, the material is designed to meet the particular technical requirements of each medium without compromising or cluttering the central theme statement and desired image (see Figures 14–4, 14–5, 14–6).

Figure 14–5.   *(Courtesy of TM Productions, Inc.)*

Figure 14–6.   *(Courtesy of TM Productions, Inc.)*

PERSONALITY IS A TRANSLATABLE ASSET

What "Someplace Special" epitomizes, and the Dimflicker campaign so sadly lacks, is *client personality;* the same quality discussed in reference to broadcast campaigns. Client (or product) personality is just as attainable in the cross-media plan if the copywriter takes the time to devise and hone the key concept and has the sense to call on an artist to provide the core visuals.

At the start, let this artist know the uses to which the graphics will be put since the range of applications required will do much to dictate ultimate design. Once the artist has prepared several rough pencil sketches of your thematic concept, pick one—and only one—to avoid any danger of the Dim-flicker Phenomenon rearing its multiple heads. Make certain your selected treatment is easily adaptable to all projected print uses as well as to the slides and studio cards that can help to tie in potential television treatments. If your graphic design is a clear statement of a high-impact personality, then even such brief uses of television as video billboards and shared ID's can contribute a great deal to image penetration at a comparatively low cost.

"The Spirit of Texas" image package for Dallas's WFAA–TV, for example, begins with the bold Figure 14–7 depiction in which the vibrant term *spirit*

Figure 14–7.   *(The Spirit of Texas is copyrighted by WFAA-TV, Belo Broadcasting Corporation. Syndication rights granted to TM Communications.)*

seems to soar right off the screen. In its lucidity, the artwork is equally at home as an ID slide or outdoor billboard. The concept can then be inlaid on complementary artwork (Figure 14–8) for print media extension and exploitation. Like "Someplace Special," "Spirit of Texas" calls on an associated lyric for broadcast image deepening and even adapts this lyric to slice-of-life pictorial vignettes that, as TV promos, envelop WFAA in a warm human-interest glow:

```
         #1  IMAGE SONG  :60
The Spirit of Texas—
It's alive and in our eyes,
One look and you'll see it.
We share your dreams and share your pride,
Hey Texas, you've got it!
The Spirit of Texas, it's alive on Channel 8,
Come help us celebrate the Spirit of Texas on 8.
—The Spirit of Texas—
It's in every song we sing,
One look and you'll know it.
The excitement that we bring,
Hey Texas, you've got it.
The Spirit of Texas, it's alive on Channel 8,
Come help us celebrate the Spirit of Texas on 8.
```

Figure 14–8. *(The Spirit of Texas is copyrighted by WFAA-TV, Belo Broadcasting Corporation. Syndication rights granted to TM Communications.)*

The general lyric's "celebration" subtheme is then musically and visually illustrated in shorter "event" promos:

#2 <u>GRADUATION</u> :30

```
It's the dream you've had for years,
It's happened, you've earned it.
Through the laughter and the tears,
Hey Texas, you've got it!
The Spirit of Texas, it's alive on Channel 8,
Come help us celebrate the Spirit of Texas on 8.
```

#3 <u>WEDDING</u> :30

```
Counting hours, making plans,
A new life so special.
Now that moment's close at hand,
Hey Texas, you've got it!
The Spirit of Texas, it's alive on Channel 8,
Come help us celebrate the Spirit of Texas on 8.
```

*(Music composed by Jim Kirk, TM Communications. Lyrics written by Lee Armstrong,
Bill Barlow and Wally Wawro, WFAA-TV. The Spirit of Texas is copyrighted by Belo
Broadcasting Corporation. Syndication rights granted to TM Communications.)*

Getting back to graphic preparation, once the visual concept has been solidi-
fied, the artist will then prepare what is called a *color comprehensive* (a
"comp") of your selected sketch. The comp will precisely represent how the
final design will look before *repro* (reproduction) in the various visual media.
Once you and your client (which may be your own station) approve the comp,
the artist will then supply *mechanicals*. Mechanicals are pieces of camera-ready
art that can be plugged into print/photographic processes with a minimum of
further preproduction work. If the client's personality was well thought-out in
the beginning, and if you have selected a distinct graphic design that positively
radiates this personality, the result should be intrusive marketplace penetration
and consistent community recognition for the subject of your campaign.

In developing the cross-media personality, you might, as George Gribbin
once proposed to a meeting of the American Association of Advertising Agencies,
try thinking of the campaign's subject as an actual person. Then ask yourself
whether you would pick for a friend a person who acts the way the campaign
does. It is doubtful, for example, that you would care to cozy up to an individual
who comes on like the Dimflicker newspaper ad shown earlier. A bold, even
argumentative, headline isn't necessarily bad—as long as it seems to promise
companionable assistance. But like any self-centered acquaintance, the Dimflicker layout projects a personality that focuses inward, rather than outward; a
personality that arrogantly takes your concerns into consideration only when
they further its own. Contrast Dimflicker's "bad press" with the similarly out-
spoken, but still friendly newspaper/magazine overtures by and for Minne-
apolis/St. Paul's KSJN as shown in Figures 14–9 and 14–10.

Like many people toward whom we feel an affinity, the effective cross-media
personality need not necessarily be a "buddy" image but might, instead, con-

Figure 14–9.   *(Courtesy of Deb Tarum, Fallon McElligott Rice.)*

vey an aura of competence, elegance, integrity, graciousness, kindliness, or beguilement. We respect people who possess these and similar attributes and, though often not able to conceive of them as "pals," still wish to consider them as *friends*—perhaps very close friends. That is why a wide variety of campaign personalities can appeal positively to us—as long as that wide variety is not evidenced by the same client! As stated in chapter 12, product personality must, like a good friend, have a comfortable and reassuring predictability.

In the cross-media campaign, of course, this predictability must not only carry from spot to spot, but also from spot to print medium and, perhaps, back

Figure 14–10.   *(Courtesy of Deb Tarum, Fallon McElligott Rice.)*

again. In the Scoundrel treatments in Figures 14–11 and 14–12, an involving and consistent personality is unmistakably manifested in both the product's magazine and television exposures. Using Gribbin's device of thinking of products as friends, we can see that Scoundrel is definitely not of the "chum" variety—but this friend's personality is still highly compelling, nonetheless. The Scoundrel ads also illustrate the utility of design consonance when crossing from one medium to another. Scoundrel exhibits a photographic/casting coherence whereas "Someplace Special" and "Spirit of Texas" achieve their unified styles through an artist's sketches. Yet, from our perspective, this distinction is unimportant. Scoundrel's photos and the station-characterizing drawings do equally

Figure 14–11.   *(Courtesy of Robert Zimmern, Grey Advertising Inc.)*

Figure 14–12. *(Courtesy of Robert Zimmern, Grey Advertising Inc.)*

effective jobs of instigating retentive personalities that are easily translatable to both print and electronic environments.

It *is* important to realize that, as in any effective cross-media effort, the Scoundrel campaign did not require that the consumer see the magazine layout *before* the television spot (or vice-versa) in order to comprehend it. Even though we often speak of messages in one medium supplementing or enhancing more extensive presentation via another, each communication must *still* be able to stand on its own. The product's central statement as well as its personality must unequivocally shine through with the same brightness in the supplementary medium as it does in the prime one. Remember, consumers are not exposed to media *budgets,* they're exposed to media *messages.* Looking at the Scoundrel television and magazine treatments, one cannot tell which is the prime medium and which the supplemental one. But what *is* readily discernible is the character and constancy of the product's personality that clearly enhances *one* perfume rather than *two.*

In fact, a truly successful cross-media venture should not depend on perceivers of the message via one medium *ever* seeing its counterpart treatments on another. Certainly, campaign strategists seek to increase the frequency by which a given consumer is reached through the careful coordination of complementary delivery vehicles. But the astute copywriter will never allow campaign coordination concerns to obscure the need for each message, print or broadcast, to communicate *in its own right* though still with the same focus, and the same personality as all the other campaign facets to which audience members might be exposed.

For further practice with the concept of cross-media personality, examine Figure 14–13, a magazine layout for Jostens class rings. How would you promote this product in a radio spot? On television? At whom (what universe) would your message be aimed and why? What is your positioning statement? In other words, isolate the print piece's key stylistic elements and then derive the closest possible translation of these elements for audio and video environments. Take some time and answer the questions we've just posed before reading on.

THINK

TIME

HERE

Now that you've developed a Jostens cross-media effort in your mind, let's see how Carmichael-Lynch, the company's advertising agency, handled this assignment.

Figure 14–13. *(Courtesy of Cathy Madison, Carmichael-Lynch, Inc.)*

Music, as we've previously discussed, is an effective campaign integrater that can come to the fore in radio as well as add depth to a television spot. Carmichael-Lynch developed a nostalgic song to transmit "Keep the Good Times Round"—its ring-replicating positioning statement. This song, as noted in Figure 14–14, became a centerpiece communication on radio and provided the key component of the television soundtrack.

The TV commercial (Figure 14–15) then used the radio melody as the motive force to propel the viewer toward the print ad's pictorial conclusion. The spot features a 1950s couple making the drive-in scene in a 1954 red Chevy convertible. The date climaxes with the couple sitting in the car under a starlit sky.

Figure 14–14.   *(Courtesy of Cathy Madison, Carmichael-Lynch, Inc.)*

Then, in the event freeze-framed by the magazine ad, the stars materialize into Jostens class rings as a comet streaks across the horizon graphically to accentuate "keep(ing) the good times round." Television thus amalgamated the radio and print contributions and enhanced the audience's awareness of subsequent exposures to these other media messages.

Now, let's take a central concept as encapsulated in the graphic in Figure 14–16. What is the personality of KRQX that this logo suggests to you? What might be the format (the product) of this station, and how would your copy, in on-air promos and newspaper ads, *express* this sound? A campaign, of course, does not normally start with a logo and work backward, but this little exercise should help you better comprehend the fundamental interrelationship that must exist between (1) client/product; (2) copy style; and (3) visual design/execution. If you can avoid mixing apples, oranges, and (especially) lemons, the total of these three elements will be a definitive and highly marketable cross-media *personality*.

LAYING OUT THE PRINT PIECE

Because typography and design involve the specialized sorcery of a variety of people and machines, and because this is still a book on *broadcast* copywriting, little time or space will be spent here on the complexities of the print layout process. Certainly, an artist should always be engaged whenever graphic design requires anything above the level of paleolithic stick figures. Broadcast writers who find themselves involved in a cross-media effort should, however, understand the basic avenues for communicating with printers or compositors.

Figure 14–15. *(Courtesy of Cathy Madison, Carmichael-Lynch, Inc.)*

Figure 14–16. *(Courtesy of Wally Wawro, WFAA–TV.)*

Most layouts with which you will be involved contain the primary ingredients of headline, illustration, and copy block. Additional components might include subheads, coupons, picture captions, and logos (which were originally known in the print media as *logotypes*). Another essential item, which accrues from what is left after the above units are added, is called *white space.* Sufficient and well-arranged white space helps attract attention to the layout and enhances its readability. Too little white space in a newspaper or magazine spread has the same effect as an overloaded television soundtrack or a radio spot with too many words: perceiver frustration and tune-out. The KSJN–FM advertisements in Figures 14–17 and 14–18 demonstrate how effectively exploited white space makes even unillustrated layouts *seem* pictorial. These ads also prove that a well-integrated series of print layouts can have the same cumulative effect as a unified broadcast flight and can clearly define product (in this case, a classical music format) without having to resort to scores of words.

White space is an element that can have several variations. In come cases, as in the WBBM skyline treatment in Figure 14–19, it may be appropriate to reverse the tonalities so white space becomes "black space." The principle is exactly the same (in fact, the black space is still technically referred to as white space), but the design may acquire greater salience than surrounding layouts using black and white in the more conventional way.

Much like the storyboard/photoboard evolution in television message creation, the print layout also goes through several stages. Most often, these stages are referred to as the *thumbnail sketch, rough layout,* and *semi-comprehensive layout* (semi-comp), with each getting closer to what will become the finished comprehensive. As a copywriter, your personal design concern will normally be

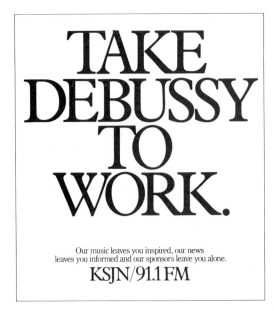

Figure 14–17.   *(Courtesy of Deb Tarum, Fallon McElligott Rice.)*

HANDEL WITH CARE.

Our music leaves you inspired, our news
leaves you informed and our sponsors leave you alone.

KSJN/91.1 FM

Figure 14–18. *(Courtesy of Deb Tarum, Fallon McElligott Rice.)*

limited to the first two stages, and even here, you may already be collaborating extensively with a layout specialist.

The thumbnail sketch is simply a preliminary miniature of a full-size ad. As its name implies, it can be done very quickly, usually in several versions, to see how all the basic elements in the display can be most appealingly aligned. Few, if any, words appear on a thumbnail sketch since the objective is to get the overall visual feel of the ad rather than to fine tune its copy content.

The rough layout is the chosen version of your thumbnail sketch brought up to full size. Even here, a copywriter's (as opposed to an art director's) layout is expected and allowed to be very rough indeed with stick figures and shaded boxes entirely sufficient. As long as the piece is neat and contains properly proportioned elements, you can then proceed to "key" the layout to your script. "Keying" involves assigning identical letters to identical elements on both your script and rough layout. In this way, anyone involved in the print production process can clearly understand what words constitute what part of the total advertisement.

An example of an unartistic copywriter's rough sketch as keyed to the companion script is reproduced in Figures 14–20 and 14–21 on pp. 498–499. Notice that, in addition to keying, the writer has also used left-margin labels as a further cross-referencing of script parts with layout sections and has given special prominence to the large headline by typing its three words on separate lines.

In the same way that a radio message must fit a finite and unexpandable unit of time, a print media ad must fit an unenlargeable unit of space. And, just as you allow the powerful television visual to predominate by avoiding "wall-to-wall" copy in the soundtrack, so, too, do you enable print media white space to

Figure 14–19. *(Courtesy of WBBM.)*

work its enticements by not obliterating it with verbiage. In calculating copy "fit," therefore, it must be realized that any chart or table presents the maximum number of words that can physically be accommodated within a given boundary using a certain size and style of type. The need for white space and the other elements of layout design as architecturally arranged in the WBBM ad in Figure 14–22, for example, decrees a far sparser use of copy than any chart allows. Remember, professional copywriters, even those primarily engaged in broadcasting, want the print media ads on which they labor to look *and be* more sophisticated than something that belongs in the classifieds.

Often, you and a layout expert will set up the structure of the print piece even before you have written, or at least, before you have *finalized*, the body copy. In these cases, your layout collaborator will be able to give you a fairly precise estimate of the number of words the selected type size will permit within the space reserved for the verbal body of your message. Since people in layout have access to such exotic-sounding calculators as Haberule Copy-Casters and Lee Streamlined Visual Control Copyfitters in figuring the number of allowable characters, there is little purpose in your attempting to memorize typesize-to-square-or-line-inch tables. In working with print experts, you will gradually come to know that all type is measured on a point system in which 72 points equals one typographer's inch.

Standard Pica type, in which this line is set, is 12 point.

The smaller the point number of your selected type, the more characters that can be accommodated within a given space. Type size derives from the *heights* (not the widths) of its capital letters, with standard heights varying from 5½ to 72 points.

This line is set in Agate type, which is 5½ point.

Until recently, newspapers sold space in agate lines, fourteen agate lines to one column inch.

Now, however, in a long-overdue move to standardize buying and filling newspaper space, agate and column measurements are out and inches are in, courtesy of the Standard Advertising Unit (SAU) system. For major United States newspapers, the new scheme officially came on nationwide line on July 1, 1984, and brought uniformity to what had been chaos in ad space dimensioning. Under SAU, the standard broadsheet page is "13 inches wide and 21 inches deep with six 2 and 1/16 columns and 1/8 inch between columns."[1] The page can be divided into combinations of 57 standard ad sizes where formerly, up to 439 different column sizes were being used. (Similar and related standardization also was accomplished for the smaller *tabloid*, as compared to broadsheet-type, newspapers.)

According to the Newspaper Advertising Bureau's Charles Kinsolving, an industry committee in 1981 asked agencies: "'Would you rather do one

1. Blake Hallanan, "Drumroll Please: The SAU Finally Is Arriving," *ADWEEK/Midwest*, April, 1984, pp. 40–41.

13,000 Sympathetic Towtrucks }Ⓐ

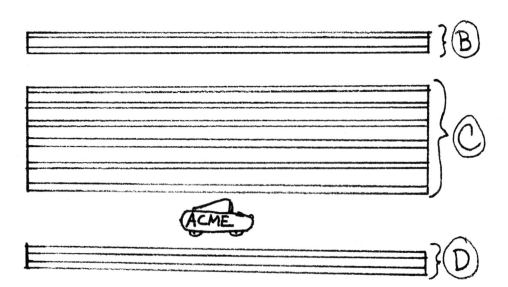

Figure 14–20.

Head:

Subhead:

Copy:

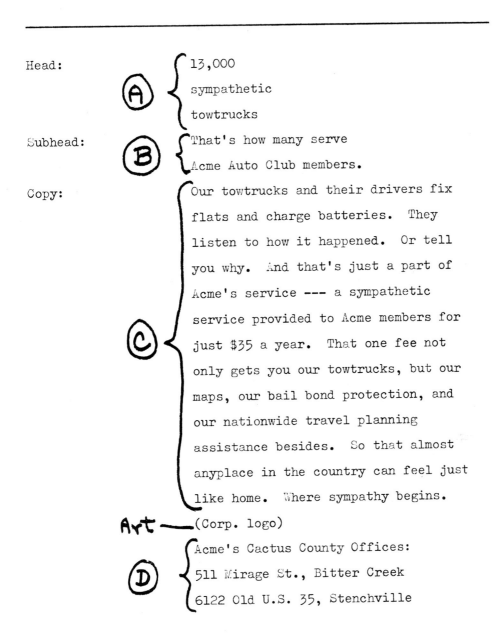

(A) 13,000
     sympathetic
     towtrucks

(B) That's how many serve
     Acme Auto Club members.

(C) Our towtrucks and their drivers fix
     flats and charge batteries. They
     listen to how it happened. Or tell
     you why. And that's just a part of
     Acme's service --- a sympathetic
     service provided to Acme members for
     just $35 a year. That one fee not
     only gets you our towtrucks, but our
     maps, our bail bond protection, and
     our nationwide travel planning
     assistance besides. So that almost
     anyplace in the country can feel just
     like home. Where sympathy begins.

Art ---(Corp. logo)

(D) Acme's Cactus County Offices:
     511 Mirage St., Bitter Creek
     6122 Old U.S. 35, Stenchville

Figure 14–21.

Newsradio 78 Means Business in Chicago.

Throughout the day WBBM's Financial Editor Len Walter broadcasts the latest market readings and financial news direct from the Midwest Stock Exchange. And our Chicago Tribune Business Reports tap the expertise of that newspaper's huge business staff.

From the CBS Network we bring you: Today in Business, summarizing the day's trading on the NYSE; Business Update, monitoring the world markets; and two programs for the financial non-genius: Inside Business with William S. Rukeyser, and Your Dollars with Money Magazine's Marshall Loeb.

Turn to WBBM. You'll find our business reports are quite a commodity.

**Turn to us first.
WBBM
Newsradio 78.**

Figure 14–22. *(Courtesy of Barbara DiGuido, WBBM, CBS Radio.)*

mechanical and pay for extra space it doesn't fit, or continue to make different size mechanicals for each space?' The response was to pay for the extra space and keep the mechanical intact instead of constantly changing it."[2] Consequently, not only does SAU simplify the artist's work by requiring but a single mechanical, but it also tends to improve ad reproduction quality since mechanicals don't have to be resized to fit a whole spectrum of nonstandard formats. For the copywriter, the hoped-for result is a less hassled artist/layout person who might even be easier to work with.

Beyond these basic print apportionment facts with which you should generally be familiar, it is more prudent to depend on layout experts for copy calculation. In planning and typing your final script, you may find it helpful to ascertain from your print associate how many characters each line of the ad's copy block can carry, given the type size and typeface (style) selected. You will already know the number of lines allowed by the layout. Then, simply set your typewriter margins for the same number of spaces as accommodated characters per line and type up your copy accordingly to see if the words will fit within the line allocation.

2. Ibid., p. 41.

In addition, you should be aware of a terminology distinction. Though this chapter has tended to use the terms *layout* and *design* interchangeably, the latter is officially reserved for the initial conception of the ad. Thus, if you are a copywriter developing a print piece without the initial services of an art director, you would, in fact, be the ad's *designer. Layout* people then work within the twin constraints of this design and printing technology to bring the communication to fruition.

Finally, since most of this discussion has dealt with magazine and newspaper advertisements, a brief word should be said about designing messages for outdoor billboards. A billboard communication is really the most time-limited of all mass media messages because, on average, a motorist has only 3.5 seconds to ingest it. Thus, from a design standpoint, a billboard must restrict itself to short headlines (six to nine words are generally felt to be the maximum) and/or to a single arresting graphic. As to content, the billboard must set forth an immediate *promise*—one that clearly states what the billboard's occupant *does for* its reader.

Cuteness on a billboard, if not self-explanatory, does not communicate. One radio station, for instance, tried to describe its location on the dial between two competing outlets with the billboard slogan:

K---:   BETWEEN A ROCK AND A SOFT PLACE

Though a clever line for radio programmers who are familiar with format slang, few billboard *readers* were able to decipher the station's message and ascertain that it could be found between an album-oriented-rock facility and an "easy listening" purveyor.

The Figure 14–23 WXYZ–TV billboard, conversely, makes no such mistake. It explicitly lets its readers know that the displayer is a "good" evening newscast provider located on Channel 7. The two headlines are short and well-separated for readability. The graphic is arresting and the promise/product clearly delineated.

ANCILLARY NONBROADCAST VEHICLES

In addition to newspaper and magazine advertisements, billboard layouts, and the point-of-purchase (in-store) displays that can derive from any of these, your labors in the print field may lead to the creation of copy for a variety of specialized communication devices. Though the purposes, format, and content of these devices may differ from *mass* media writing, the same requirements for clarity, consistency, and calculated personality apply.

Many of these ancillary vehicles are "take-aways" (items given out at stores, station promotion events, county fairs) or "leave behinds" (materials dropped off at the prospective customer's place of business or home). They are natural and often mandatory by-products of a main campaign thrust and, since they are particularly useful in station promotion, a common chore for the in-station copywriter. Though balloons, bumper stickers, buttons, and ball-point pens carry very little copy (and thus don't add much to your workload), other materials—

Figure 14–23.   *(Copyright © 1983 American Broadcasting Company.)*

particularly those aimed at time-buyers and prospective advertisers—may be much more verbal and demand greater toil.

A "sales kit" (referred to as an "information packet" if done for a public service entity) will contain several of these copy-heavy elements. For a station, these elements usually include the omnipresent rate card, a coverage map, sketches and biographies of key personnel, format/program descriptions, and recent press releases (or their resulting clippings) that reflect positively on the operation and its drawing power. All of these items, together with the firm's stationery and business cards, should project a consistent image and a clear personality. If, as in the case of the "Someplace Special" package presented earlier, the key image and generic items have been produced by an outside firm, the local copywriter must be very careful that the additional day-to-day material he or she generates blends in well with the prepackaged elements. To be successful, any campaign must be localized, and that is where the on-the-scene copywriter can be the making or breaking factor.

Exposure in other media organs is facilitated through well-written and easily digestible "news releases" that use strong copy to project a message clearly worth retelling. Like a compelling bit of gossip or a snappy joke, a well-written news release will be "retold" because it is enjoyable and advantageous for the reteller to do so. Media agencies are no different from individuals in this regard, and the effective copywriter-initiated news release will keep the interests of those potential retellers uppermost in mind. This requirement applies to corporate and institutional endeavors as well as to creations promoting stations such as Q107's "Ground Hog" release (Figure 14–24).

News releases are designed to reach your target audience via the mass media; other ancillary print pieces are intended for first-hand delivery to specific individuals. When produced in quantity and sent via the postal service, these pieces constitute what has long been known to the advertising industry as *direct mail.* If carefully fashioned, these same items can also constitute part of a

Q107 News Release Q107 News Release Q107 News Release **Q107 News Release**

FOR IMMEDIATE RELEASE   CONTACT: Gerald Downey

January 22, 1980   (202) 686-3112

"PARDON ME, BOY...IS THAT THE PUNXSUTAWNEY GROUND HOG?"

(WASHINGTON, D.C.) - In a continuing effort to keep their listeners among the best-informed in the Washington area, WRQX (Q-107) Musicradio, the ABC-Owned FM Station in Washington, D.C., will send a correspondent to Punxsutawney, Pennsylvania, for a first-hand account of the annual ritual known as Ground Hog Day.

The twist is: the "stringer" will be a Q-107 listener!

Q-107 News Director Doug Limerick has arranged to send one lucky (?) listener, and a guest, to the home of "Punxsutawney Pete", the legendary shadow-spotting ground hog, to report on whether or not the little nipper sees his shadow, February 2nd. Ostensibly, if Pete sees his shadow, the Nation is in for six more weeks of Winter; if not, Spring can't be far behind!

The morning of Friday, February 1st, Q-107's lucky prize-winner will be whisked away in luxury, on a Continental Trailways coach to Pittsburgh, where he will transfer to a bus to Punxsutawney. There, the correspondent, and guest, will spend two unforgettable nights at the magnificent Country Villa Motel (free TV!).

Just before dawn, February 2nd, a friendly member of the Punxsutawney Chamber of Commerce will escort the Q-107 "stringers" to the Shadow Casting Ceremony, followed by a "family style breakfast buffet", at the famous DeFelices Restaurant! That evening, the sumptuous cuisine of the Ground Hog Day Banquet is theirs to behold, compliments of Q-107!   (more)

WRQX Radio • 4400 Jenifer St., N.W. • Washington, D.C. • 20015 • (202) 686-3078
Represented nationally by Blair Radio

Figure 14-24. *(Courtesy of Gerald Downey, WRQX.)*

<u>1st Ad - Q-107/Punxsutawney</u>
_____

       The winner of Q-107's "Trip to See the Ground Hog" will be
determined by impartial drawing, from among listeners who qualify by
phoning the Dude Walker Show (6 - 10 AM) throughout the week of
January 28 - 31. Each hour, the "nth" caller will be awarded a nice
qualifying prize, plus a chance to win the Grand Prize.

       The qualifying prize is a tube of Ground, "Whole Hog" Sausage!

       Said Walker, "At first, we were going to ask listeners to
<u>spell</u> Punxsutawney, in order to qualify. Then we realized that serious
injury could result from attempting to spell Punxsutawney before 10 AM!"

       Asked if he thought the offer would meet with good public
response, Limerick commented, "Any radio station whose listeners would
send in more than 600 requests for 'Anti Slush Turtle Kits', like ours
did a few weeks ago, is <u>bound</u> to realize terrific response to something
as big as a 'Trip to See the Ground Hog'!"

       Messrs. Walker and Limerick are resting comfortably, and
are expected to continue their daily show, without interruption.

*** Q-107 ***

Figure 14–24. *(cont.)*

sales kit or information packet that a company or institutional representative passes across the desk in a prospective client or contributor's office. As in the case of the news release, the "mail-out" or hand-out must be written to anticipate the *recipient's* wants and needs and should seem to cater to these as much or more than to the interests of the piece's disseminator. Thus, the (W)KHQ flier in Figure 14–25 is *not* just a print rehash of an on-air promo but a carefully tailored reminder to *advertisers* that the young station has met its audience delivery expectations and *their* audience attainment requirements.

    An even more meaningful and long-life ancillary device is one that provides the prospect with something *besides* data; one that gives the mailbox or across-the-desk recipients something that can be put to use in their day-to-day activities. For Q107, such a vehicle is a full-size appointment book, two pages of which are reproduced in Figure 14–26. The book's layout continuously identifies the station through placement of its logo in the lower right-hand corner of the righthand page, which is the culmination point of the normal eye scan. Meanwhile, the utility of the piece to the user is enhanced through a copy approach featuring media terminology and thereby expressing the common language, the business bond, between the station and the book's accepter. Use of this

Figure 14–25. *(Courtesy of Tim Moore, WKHQ.)*

leave-behind is encouraged because the copy creates a pleasing interface with the professional endeavors of the person to whom it is given. *Usability* and *relevance* are essential attributes of any leave-behind and are prominent features of this Q107 gift.

The Q107 press release and appointment book project the same fun-loving, upbeat personality as is striven for in the station's on-air sound and its mass media advertising (review Case Study #7 in chapter 12). Notice that all the writing and graphic design elements emphasize a single identification: Q107. Expecting people to remember call letters, station slogan, and location on the

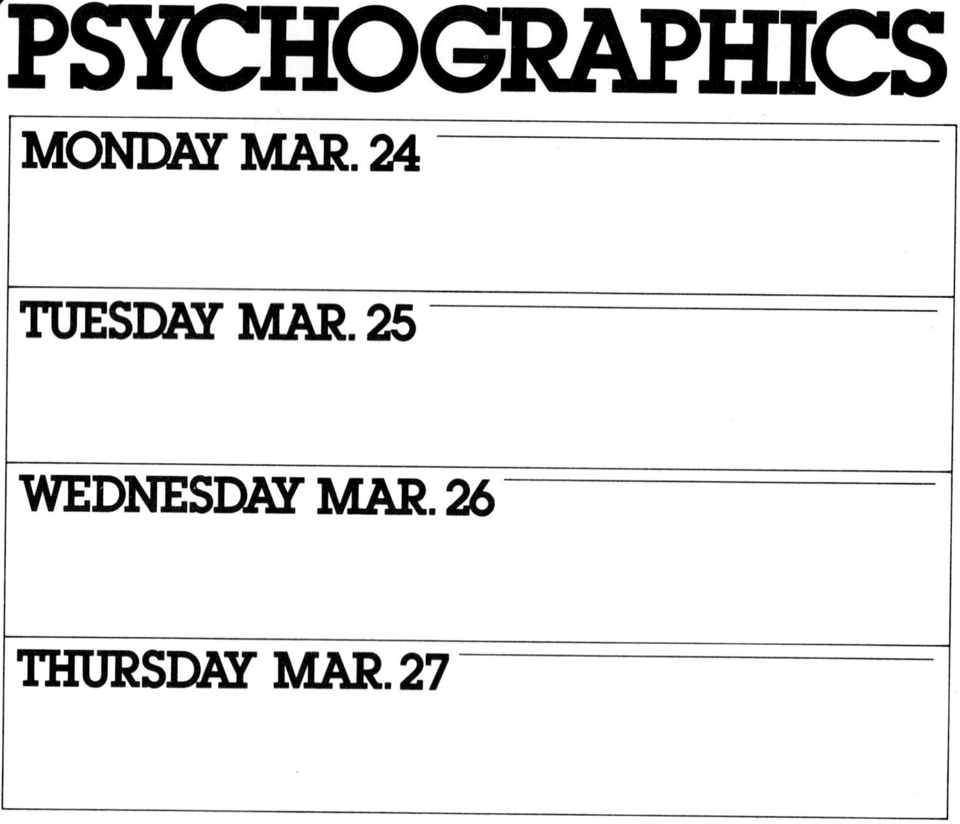

PSYCHOGRAPHICS

MONDAY MAR. 24	
TUESDAY MAR. 25	
WEDNESDAY MAR. 26	
THURSDAY MAR. 27	

Figure 14–26. *(Courtesy of WRQX.)*

dial would only dilute and obscure perceiver recognition. So *one* ID—Q107—is selected and adhered to throughout every copy element generated by and for the station.

Whether promoting a broadcast outlet, a purveyor of products, or a non-profit institution, any well-tooled cross-media campaign presents a consistent, positive, and highly recognizable face to the world. Artwork and layout play a significant part in accomplishing this task, but so, too, does carefully planned and skillfully executed copy. Copy makes specific what design can only suggest.

Whether in primary or in ancillary vehicles, competent broadcast writers will not shrink from opportunities to showcase their subject and talents *in print*. Though some of the techniques and much of the technology are different, the main requisite, in print and in broadcasting, is for purposeful, well-engineered word bridges linking people for their mutual advantage.

A FINAL WORD FROM THE SODA BAR

By this juncture, you've been acclimated to the tools and principles of broadcast copywriting, have suffered the rigors of writing for radio, and been ex-

A company run by crazed art directors.
or
The study of personality traits found in a particular group
of individuals or a target audience.

FRIDAY MAR. 28

SATURDAY MAR. 29

SUNDAY MAR. 30

February							March							April					
M	T	W	T	F	S	S	M T W T F S S							M T W T F S S					
				1	2	3						1	2		1	2	3	4	5 6
4	5	6	7	8	9	10	3 4 5 6 7 8 9							7 8 9 10 11 12 13					
11	12	13	14	15	16	17	10 11 12 13 14 15 16							14 15 16 17 18 19 20					
18	19	20	21	22	23	24	17 18 19 20 21 22 23							21 22 23 24 25 26 27					
25	26	27	28	29			24 25 26 27 28 29 30							28 29 30					
							31												

HITS HAPPENING RIGHT ON Q

Q107 FM MUSICRADIO

Figure 14–26. *(cont.)*

posed to the discipline of creating for video. Finally, you have endured at least a small measure of the grappling between market conditions and creative inclinations, grappling that is the necessary prologue to a well-fashioned broadcast or cross-media campaign—whether in the service of product, public cause, or politician. As agency president Malcolm MacDougall observes: "The words that appear in advertising today are the most expensive words ever written. Each and every one should be agonized over, crunched into a ball and tossed into the wastebasket, until just the right word is found—the word that perfectly fits the selling message, the word that has that special power to arrest, to penetrate, to persuade, to create customers."[3]

If you are utterly frustrated by all of this—great. Most creative people are. But since all art is ultimately a delicate balance between the discipline of form

---

3. Malcolm MacDougall, "The Advertising Cliché Code," *ADWEEK/Midwest,* April 22, 1985, p. 52.

and the discipline of content, promising copywriters also find a stimulating encounter in the whole rule-clogged mess. Just don't become so intense in winning the encounter that you burn yourself out, like the kid who used up all his July 4th sparklers before it got dark enough to see them.

Instead, try to follow the long-trusted advice of veteran copywriter and creative director Don Cowlbeck and—

> Listen very carefully for the sound of your *own* soda-straw starting to suck bottom. When you hear it, go fishing.
>
> We are in a pressurized profession. "I need that next Tuesday." "We have to do something about our marketing situation in Phoenix." "I don't know what—that's what I pay you people for." "It's no big problem; how's about we discuss it tomorrow at a breakfast meeting. Say, 4 A.M.?"
>
> What fun! What a challenge! How much better than the hum-drum, ho-hum, another-day-another-dollar existence of others less fortunate than we.
>
> But there comes a time when each of us, under pressure, becomes cranky, finds his energies dissipated, himself unproductive and unhappy. My final secret—and perhaps most valuable one—is when your personal straw starts to suck bottom—go fishing.[4]

As your author and guide through the world of broadcast copywriting, let me wish you every success as a wordsmith and leave you with one final and (after fourteen arduous chapters) heartfelt word—

```
S-S-S-SSLURP!
(I hope the bass are biting.)
```

4. Don Cowlbeck, writing in "Monday Memo," *Broadcasting Magazine*, March 20, 1972, p. 19.

APPENDICES

Appendix A

ADDITIONAL
SUGGESTED EXERCISES

In a chapter-by-chapter listing, here are several proposed assignments designed to solidify your knowledge of and practice in principles introduced throughout *Broadcast Copywriting*. These exercises are intended to augment those proposed within the chapters themselves and can be used "as is" or amplified with additional instructor-supplied elements. Don't forget to include your best resulting efforts in your developing writer's portfolio.

CHAPTER ONE—THE BROADCAST COPYWRITER'S WORLD

1. List the principal advantages and drawbacks found in each broadcast copywriting environment. Given your own current status, experience, and goals, which environment seems to offer the greatest potential for *you?*
2. Survey and list the name and location of every firm, institution, and/or individual within fifteen miles that generates broadcast copy. To which writer environment category does each most closely relate?
3. Draw a doughnut on a piece of paper. In the "hole," write in all the types of material encompassed by the *narrow* definition of "continuity." In the "ring," write in all the *additional* copy types that the broader definition of continuity also embraces. Save this "doughnut" for future reference and as a possible aid in portfolio organization.
4. Listen to a half hour of programming on each of two differently formatted radio stations. Make a descriptive list of the segue devices used to bridge the gaps between the separate items of broadcast material. Do these devices differ in number or type from one station to the other? If so, in what way(s)?
5. Using this book's *Table of Contents* as a starting point, develop an organizational plan for your professional portfolio. Prepare the cover page/table of contents and secure a three-ring binder and tabbed divider sheets. Label each tab to correspond to the categories of writing into which you plan to segment your copy samples, both broadcast and nonbroadcast. Then use this binder as the repository for your best and most representative past, present, and future writing efforts.

CHAPTER TWO—THE COMPONENTS OF COMMUNICATION

1. Jot down the basic message content you derive from each of the next ten people with whom you come in spatial contact. In how many of these situations was it intended that you be a receiver? In how many was this not intended? How can you tell? (Or, *can* you tell?) Through which specific media (communication/communications/mass communications) were these messages transmitted?
2. Make a list of as many communications vehicles as you can think of, omitting those that belong to the mass communications subgroup. What are the means by which

each of these vehicles attracts your attention? Which of these same attention-getting methods are usable on radio? Which are usable on television?

3. Make a list of the next dozen TV commercials to which you are exposed, dividing it into two categories: (1) messages that seem to address you as an individual and (2) messages that seem to address you as part of a mass audience. Which verbal and/or pictorial elements contributed most to each of your categorization decisions? Which category, in your opinion, had a higher percentage of successful commercials?

4. Repeat Exercise #3 using as your subject matter the next dozen *radio* commercials to which you are exposed.

5. Examine the photoboard in Figure AP-1. What, if any, are the physiological barriers to your full comprehension of it? What, if any, are the experiential barriers? Show the 'board to a friend of the opposite sex, asking the same questions. Were your barriers (or lack of them) the same?

6. Diagram in detail the components and subcomponents of the Broadcast Communication Process as they exist in a media agency for which you have worked or with which you are familiar. How does your model compare with our theoretical model? Which portions of your model have proven to be more susceptible to breakdown or overload? How would you, as a *writer* working in that situation, have to compensate for this in your mode of operation?

Figure AP-1. *(Courtesy of Melissa Wohltman, Doyle Dane Bernbach Advertising.)*

CHAPTER THREE—THE BROADCAST COPYWRITER'S TOOLS

1. Take a piece of print advertising and, without changing the words or their arrangement, try to repunctuate it for broadcasting. Read it aloud in its "before" and "after" versions to discover how, even by itself, proper broadcast punctuation can improve oral flow.
2. Punctuate the following radio commercial (from which all original punctuation has been removed) to achieve maximum clarity for the announcer and the listener. Have a colleague read it aloud as punctuated to gauge your success.

```
ANNCR:   Brummels Sales and Service invites you to stop in and
         visit the microwave oven center a separate department
         befitting the stature of this miraculous modern
         convenience where you'll find the entire line of Sharp
         microwave ovens on display but please don't bring Grandma
         that sweet little lady has spent a lifetime simmering and
         slow baking and it just wouldn't do for her to see how
         fast and easy it is to cook with microwave efficiency does
         that dear woman really want to know about Sharp's
         capabilities for every kind of cooking all in the same
         oven it would break her heart to realize that thanks to
         Sharp fussing over company meals is now a thing of the
         past she won't have to be aware that Sharp's new fangled
         gadgetry cooks by time or temperature rotates food for
         even cooking and even turns itself off keeping the food
         warm until it's served up so do yourself a favor when you
         go to Brummel's leave Grandma at home you never know she
         might want a Sharp microwave oven for Christmas see the
         complete Sharp line in the microwave oven department at
         Brummel's Sales and Service your complete home furnishing
         store at 44th and Clyde Park Avenue.
```

(Courtesy of Joe Borrello and Paul Boscarino, WOOD Broadcasting, Inc.)

3. Visit the local library and assemble a short, annotated list of the word-finder and style aid books that are available. Make a priority determination of which of these you would eventually like to add to your own working library and in what order.
4. If you are not sufficiently proficient at the typewriter to manage forty-five words a minute, take a typing course. Seriously.
5. Spend an hour or two at a local computer store to research the price and basic operation of selected home word processors. Derive a list of personal advantages and disadvantages in switching to a word processor as compared to continued reliance on a typewriter. (If you already use a word processor, you may wish to pursue this exercise from the opposite angle—reasons for/against switching *to* a conventional typewriter.)
6. For practice in message condensation, try to rewrite the following 60-second radio spot as a 15-second message that is built around the same main copy point.

```
ANNCR:   Smile. (SFX: CAMERA SHUTTER) This one's for you. The
         crisp, true-to-life picture you get, instantly, with the
         new Polaroid SLR 680---the camera that combines
         flexibility and control with the ease and immediacy of
```

instant photography. And you can get it now, at Sterling Jewelry and Distributing Company. The SLR 680 features Autostrobe, the built-in electronic flash that recharges automatically, and a unique folding design for easy carrying. Just press the button, the 680's sophisticated electronic circuitry takes over---managing focus, flash and exposure setting automatically. Delivering in seconds a developing picture that lets you share the moment as it happens. Pass it around and share the smiles. And right now, purchase an SLR 680 for only $159.90 from Sterlings, and get a ten dollar smile-back rebate from Polaroid, and free smile insurance too. Take a picture you don't like, and Polaroid will replace the film free. Ask for complete details at any one of the three Sterling Jewelry and Distributing Company locations. Share the moment, share the smiles, with Polaroid's new SLR 680, the state of the art in instant photography.

(Courtesy of Wally Wawro, WFAA.)

7. Monitor one hour of a commercial television station's programming and one hour of that transmitted by a Top 40 or MOR (Middle-of-the-road) commercial radio station. Log the length of each commercial, PSA, ID, and station or program promo. What is the difference between the television and the radio station in number and length of these announcements? Into what length clusters does each station group these messages? What is the average number of messages per cluster?
8. Repeat Exercise #7 with a different radio and a different television station. Is there any discernible difference in your findings? Taking the four stations together, list individual message lengths from most to least frequent. What does this result mean to you as a broadcast continuity and commercial writer?

CHAPTER FOUR—RATIONAL AND EMOTIONAL APPEALS AND STRUCTURES

1. Select any item from those sitting on your dresser or kitchen counter. Try to write six 30-second radio spots for this item, each of which is centered on a different Rational Appeal.
2. Take the same item as in Exercise #1 and try to attract attention to eight messages for it by using a different PLEASURE Emotional Appeal in each. Strive to focus each Emotional Appeal within no more than the first two or three sentences of the copy.
3. Keeping the Rational Appeals constant, rewrite the Stiller & Meara "I Love New York" PSA so it is propelled by an allurement rather than a laughter Emotional Appeal. Are the SIMPLE and PLEASURE appeals still mutually supportive? Repeat the experiment, and ask the same question using the rivalry appeal.
4. Find eight print media advertisements—each of which uses a different PLEASURE as its prime Emotional Appeal. Analyze each of these advertisements by answering the following questions about it:
   a. Does another PLEASURE supplement the main one?
   b. What demographic group is aimed for?
   c. What demographic group(s), in your opinion, is/are actually attracted?
   d. Could this treatment be applied cross-media? (Radio? Television? Billboards?) If so, how?

5. Find six print media advertisements—each of which uses a different SIMPLE as its prime Rational Appeal. Analyze each advertisement by answering the following questions about it:
   a. Do other SIMPLE appeals supplement the main one?
   b. What is the prime PLEASURE appeal being used?
   c. What demographic group is aimed for?
   d. Could this same SIMPLE appeal be used with other PLEASURE appeals in promoting this same product?

6. Compose a 30-second single-voice radio spot for Firmstrand Round Toothpicks aimed at "heck noers" who think toothpicks, in their namesake use, are only for barbarians.

7. Convert the Mortein flyspray TV treatment into a 60-second radio commercial. Try to preserve as much as possible of the original's pictorial imagery and do not change the utilized rational and emotional appeals.

8. Using the Brontomobile four-door sedan as the product, write four 30-second radio treatments, each of which promotes it among a different attitudinal type of audience, specifically:
   a. those who love its styling but just can't make up their minds to buy
   b. those who think it a gas guzzler and ecological disaster
   c. those who are initially attracted to its appearance but are skeptical of its large size and cost
   d. those who really hadn't thought about buying any car this year.

9. Taking the spot written for Exercise #8 d, analyze it to see if it follows the five-step Progressive Motivation. Rewrite it as necessary to conform to this "Double-E, Double-D, A" structure.

10. Writing three separate spots, redirect the concept shown in Figure AP-2 (p. 516) to target clearly: (a) Sustainers, (b) Achievers, and (c) the Societally Conscious.

11. Rewrite the following Rudy's radio spot into two versions that respectively target (a) Emulators and (b) Experientials.

> <u>Production</u> <u>Note:</u> Talent is late-thirties male with hint of a drawl.

ANNCR: Sometimes I'm driving down the road early in the mornin', watchin' the world wake up. The sun's peekin' over the trees. And the dew's all over the grass. Early in the mornin'—that's when I have to go to work. And that's when I'm really hungry. Lunch is a long way off. So I pull in to Rudy's for a man-on-a-budget breakfast that tastes like home. I can sit down to a hot breakfast and relax for a little while. Sometimes, I read the free newspaper, but usually I find a good buddy to talk to. When I pull out of Rudy's, I've got a friendly feelin' that'll last the whole day. And still some money in my jeans. Rudy's. On County Line Road in Seney. Rudy's---for a meal to please your stomach and your wallet.

CHAPTER FIVE—THE CDVP PROCESS

1. Find five more examples of creativity in currently running radio and television spots. Write each down in the "equals/proves" format. Keep track of how long it took to accomplish this search. What does this say about the prevalence of true creativity?

Figure AP-2. *(Courtesy of Barry Base, Base Brown & Partners Limited.)*

2. Scan general circulation print media ads until you find four examples from each of the five categories of words requiring definition. What percentage of these terms were adequately defined within the copy in which you found them? By what devices were the successful definitions accomplished? Could the same definitional approaches be easily used on radio? On television?

3. Write five 30-second radio definitional treatments for the Expo Giraffe (a telescoping duster for reaching out-of-the-way nooks and crannies), each of which uses a different one of the five definitional mechanisms (negation, location, etc.). Which method seemed to work best for this product on the radio medium? Why?

4. Apply the five tests of definitional effectiveness to your treatments written for Exercise #3. Which treatment(s) pass(es) all five tests? Did your application of the method you previously cited as "best" pass them?

5. Try the Fuller Brush Odyssey on the following piece of copy. Rewrite as necessary so it feels comfortably conversational coming out of your own mouth:

```
ANNCR:  For many years, most individuals believed the only way to
        thoroughly cleanse pots and pans was to use the ever-
        popular steelwool or metal scouring pad. However, times
        have changed and in this day and age, when almost
        everything is coated with Teflon, steelwool just isn't
        very practical. The Whiz-Away Cleanee pad is. The Whiz-
```

Away is a heavy-duty, simulated sponge covered with a tough nylon net that scours away dirt and grease without harming the Teflon. This not only makes the Whiz-Away pad practical, but economical too. So, if you believe that a cleaning product should possess the attributes of practicality and economy, then you should be utilizing the Whiz-Away Cleanee pad for your entire range of cleaning tasks.

6. Apply the three Validation tests to the next television commercial or PSA you see. Did it pass all three? What devices were used for those it passed? What devices would *you* have used to meet those it failed? Repeat this same experiment on the next radio commercial or PSA you hear.
7. Find four print media ads, each of which violates a different Prohibition. Rewrite them for radio and in a way that corrects these violations.
8. Remodel the Gramma Hubbard's Hominey Bread commercial so it becomes believable to twenty-nine to forty-nine-year-old housewives.

CHAPTER SIX—KEY ELEMENTS OF RADIO WRITING

1. Write two different dealer tags for the insert at the end of the Porsche spot. One of these should tie-in to the "cold" concept on behalf of a Minnesota dealer, the other to the "hot" aspect for an Arizona dealer.
2. Set up three 10-second "backdrop painting" promotion pieces for each of two competing radio stations in your locality. Try to make the copy divergent enough in style that the two stations project unmistakably distinct personalities.
3. Plot the beat patterns for the sentences in any two pieces of broadcast copy you have written previously. Are sentence lengths and rhythms sufficiently varied to promote pleasing flow? If not, rewrite, and check your beat patterns again.
4. Rewrite the copy in a 80 to 100 word newspaper ad into a 30-second radio spot. Did you have to leave details out? Rearrange idea units? Restate or add materials?
5. Read the following Mulchburg Chamber of Commerce PSA aloud. Mark the passages that cause you to stumble, then smooth them out through incisive rewriting.

ANNCR: The week of October 13th to October 20th as you know is Stamp Out Litter Week. Litter is a problem to everyone so the Mulchburg Chamber of Commerce is sponsoring the clean up activities during the week. Litter is everyone's concern so everyone must work together to help our problem. The Chamber of Commerce wants you to join them cleaning up the Filmore Park area and make our park free from litter. The community event begins at 2 P.M. so bring your rakes, shovels and garden gloves to help the clean up process. Hot cider and doughnuts will be provided after clean up so you can meet with your friends. Remember October 13th and Stamp Out Litter Week is for you and only you can help the litter problem.

6. Take a poem of 24 or more lines and try to convey its essence via a 30-second radio spot. Ask yourself the same questions as in Exercise #4.

7. Try to write a 60-second radio spot for *lavender* Fuller Paint that is as successful at aurally conveying that color as Robert Pritikin's commercial was in capturing yellow.
8. Here are four more items for Poetic Packaging practice. Pull out the key element in each and derive a poetic package to showcase it:
    a bicycle tire
    a can of lima beans
    a two-wheeled, fold-down, camper-trailer
    a box of moth balls
9. For practice in radio script formatting, write your own counterpart of the Owen's Elixir spot: a commercial whose script contains an example of each of the nine main productional direction situations. Write it for the Burly Moving and Storage Company.
10. Relying on sound effects, create a 30-second spot for the Zapper Microwave Oven. Strive to use as few words as possible.
11. In the following script, music cues are indicated but the actual descriptions have been omitted. Fill in these blanks as clearly and concisely as possible.

(MUSIC: _____)

ANNCR: Today, on <u>Shoes of Our Lives,</u> Katy arrives home from work and quickly gets dressed for an early-evening date with Bart. Minutes later, Katy is anxiously standing at the door, awaiting Bart's toot of the horn. All of a sudden, she looks down—and is terrified.

(MUSIC: _____)

ANNCR: Her shoes! They're dull and scuffed. Without hesitation, Katy grabs the Ajax Shoe Polish Kit.

(MUSIC: _____)

ANNCR: But won't Katy end up with black polish under her fingernails? A sure turn-off for Bart.

(MUSIC: _____)

ANNCR: Not with the Ajax convenient polish applicator. It keeps the polish on the shoes---not on her fingertips. Will Katy keep Bart waiting? Not with Ajax. Ajax Shoe Polish dries instantly to build a scuff-resistant barrier around Katy's shoes.

(MUSIC: _____)

ANNCR: Listen in next time to <u>Shoes of Our Lives</u> when we hear Bart say: 'Why Katy! The softness! The feel! I've never felt this way about any woman's shoes before.'

(MUSIC: _____)

ANNCR: The Ajax Shoe Polish Kit. Don't shoe up without it.

(MUSIC: _____)

CHAPTER SEVEN—RADIO HOUSEKEEPING COPY

1. Write a 30-second station promo that features a strong, central theme. Construct it in such a way that you can take a 10-second and a 20-second lift-out from it. (All or part of the 10-second version may, of course, be part of the 20-second approach.)

2. Compose a lyric to the public domain tune of "Oh, Susannah" on behalf of KYPE, a country-and-western formatted outlet in Lost Souls, Nevada, 98.5 on the FM dial.
3. Create a 10-second and a 30-second promo for the following show:

```
Show Title:   The Pet Gourmet (pronounced GOR-MÈT)

Hostess:      Alice Ennis

Subject:      Preparing nutritious and varied meals for many kinds
              of pets.

Station:      KNNL, AM 760

Time:         9:15 to 9:30 A.M., Saturdays
```

4. Construct five fulcrum phrases to promo WYUK, a "beautiful music" station in Beaverville, Kentucky, at 1100 on the AM dial.
5. Write an intro and outro for a hypothetical interview program on which the mayor of your city is the featured guest. Make sure that both pieces of copy fulfill their stipulated three objectives and that each is no more than thirty seconds in length.
6. Develop two 30-second spots for the *Sacred Heart Program*: one that promotes the series as a whole (a *generic* promo) and another that publicizes "The Lady in Room 421" episode (a *topical* promo).
7. Construct a 60-second radio PSA to promote your community's yearly GIVE A COIN FOR MOSQUITO CONTROL WEEK. Use as many relevant, tangible images as possible.
8. Go back over the PSA written for #7 and check it for organic unity by removing each sentence in turn, and ascertaining if it is missed. Omit those that aren't missed as you rewrite the announcement.
9. Complete the 30-second PSA for the Committee for Field Mouse Preservation. Avoid statements that may intensify controversial ecological issues.
10. Complete that 60-second PSA for the Baltic Captive Nations Council. Strive to activate the listener to attend one or more of the events hypothetically scheduled for Baltic Captive Nations Week.

CHAPTER EIGHT—RADIO COMMERCIALS

1. Finish the 60-second uni-voice, "Plunger Parade" spot for B & E Chemicals. Make certain that "plungers" remain the central element in your treatment.
2. Construct the noncopy data block that most likely would have preceded the Green Grommets spot. Assume that the initiating agency bears your name, that the spot was first submitted three weeks ago, revised ten days ago, and approved today.
3. Write a 60-second *multi-voiced* spot for the Vigilante Mutual Insurance Company's new, high-risk auto insurance policy. Don't let the message lapse into a dialogue approach.
4. Compose a 30-second *dialogue* spot for Bossie's Pride Homogenized Milk. Write two versions: one with a straight-sell announcer tag and one without it:
5. Now, compose a 60-second *dramatized* spot for Green Grommets that does *not* require an announcer tag.
6. Create a 30-second *device* commercial for Granada TV rental. Retain the Japanese motif used by the dialogue spot in the chapter.
7. Write out three clear, concise descriptions for different types of music backdrops that could be used in the chapter's "Good 'ol Karen" spot. What would be the resulting differences in impact, appeal, or target audience?

8. Convert your original "Plunger Parade" spot completed for Exercise #1 into a musical commercial by specifying a suitable, effective backdrop for it. If you do not believe any musical treatment is appropriate for this particular piece of copy, isolate your rationale for this belief.

9. Write a lyric for a 30-second musical commercial for Cruncherooni Potato Chips. Make this lyric the total copy in one spot, then take a lift-out from it to use as a scene/setter, enhancer for an otherwise uni-voice approach in a second commercial.

10. What generic type of commercial does the following epitomize? Now, write two pop-in versions in the same style.

BOB: It's time for our 7-Eleven Ham and Cheese lucky phone
          call. The Ham and Cheese sandwich has the great flavor of
          juicy ham and American cheese on a big, big bun—

(SFX: TELEPHONE DIALING UNDER)

BOB: And it's the sandwich of the month at all participating
          7-Elevens. This hour's lucky phone call is for Mr. Y. Y.
          Wickie—

(SFX: TELEPONE RING UNDER)

BOB: If Mr. Wickie answers by saying---7-Eleven Ham and Cheese
          sandwich---and he is doing a hula while ringing
          sleighbells and holding a duck over his head, he'll be
          this hour's big winner.

(SFX: TELEPHONE BEING ANSWERED; SLEIGH BELLS JINGLING UNDER;
          UKULELE MUSIC UNDER; DUCK QUACKING UNDER)

FRANK: 7-Eleven Ham and Cheese Sandwich.

BOB: Is this Y. Y. Wickie?

FRANK: No, you must have the wrong number.

(Courtesy of Dan McCurdy, The Stanford Agency.)

11. Study the following TV script. Then convert this concept into an effective 60-second radio retail spot.

Video	Audio
LS OF GIRL TRYING ON WEDDING DRESS, SHOWING IT TO HER MOTHER. EXCITEDLY JUMPS ON BED, BREAKING GLASSES	ANNCR: With glasses from Denton Optical this won't happen—
DOLLY IN TO MS FOR GIRL PICKING UP THE GLASSES SHE SAT ON	GIRL: Oh no!
CUT TO MLS OF SAME GIRL AND A GUY AT THE ALTAR	ANNCR: Or this—

Video	Audio
MS OF COUPLE KISSING	<u>PREACHER:</u> I now pronounce you man and wife. You may kiss the bride.
CU OF GIRL'S FACE. HER GLASSES HAVE SLID DOWN TO THE TIP OF HER NOSE	<u>GIRL:</u> Why me?
FADE TO MLS OF SAME COUPLE STANDING ON TOP OF EMPIRE STATE BUILDING. CUT TO MS OF COUPLE AS GIRL LEANS OVER AND GLASSES FALL OFF	<u>ANNCR:</u> Or even this.
PAN SHOT OF GLASSES DOWN SIDE OF BUILDING TILL THEY HIT THE GROUND	
CU OF SHATTERED GLASSES ON GROUND. FREEZE FRAME <u>GRAPHIC:</u> ''DENTON OPTICAL COMPANY, 523 BRYAN''	<u>ANNCR:</u> For breakproof, slip-proof glasses and frames, come to Denton Optical Company. With over 40 years experience to serve you

(Courtesy of Wally Wawro, WFAA–TV.)

12. Gladstone's Shoe Store, 5712 Broadway, is featuring the new Dexter "Bush-Buster" high-top sport oxford on sale for $34.95. Encompass this information in a uni-voice 30-second co-op spot. Then, produce a 60-second dialogue co-op on the same subject.
13. Sell Granada TV rental as a direct response item in a 60-second spot. Don't forget to communicate the specific purchase process (a toll-free number).
14. Analyze one of your previously written 30-second spots to see if it has PUNCH. If not, rewrite until PUNCH (as we have used the term) is achieved. Repeat the experiment on one of your previously written sixties.
15. Create a 60-second Bubble Joy spot that, unlike the one in the chapter, *does* attract and appeal to children age twelve years and under.
16. Rewrite the Baker's Guild spot to include/demonstrate vivid product-in-use.
17. If you have not already done so in completing previous exercises, construct *generic* ID lines for each of the following:
    Dynamite Drain Opener
    Vigilante Mutual Insurance
    Bossie's Pride Homogenized Milk
    Cruncherooni Potato Chips

18. Evaluate the Cheap Jeans "Surgeon" spot via Anthony Chevins's "do's and don't's" for radio comedy. Does the spot measure up or not? Specifically, why or why not?

CHAPTER NINE—KEY ELEMENTS OF TELEVISION WRITING

1. Fashion a *script* version of the Northwest Bell "Phone Alternatives" storyboard. Take care that both your format and content meet the specific requirements of television and of this particular commercial.
2. Repeat Exercise #1 using the Scotts "What Dandelions" photoboard as your subject.
3. For practice in format composition, recast the Chevy Citation "Garage" spot into a conventional "left side video/right side audio" style.
4. Convert the chapter's Michigan Bell "Pinball" script into *storyboard* form. Your pictures need not be works of polished art, but subjects sketched within them should be in proper size relationship to shots called for in the script.
5. Write a 10-second voice-over to accompany the WPVI–TV "Bright Futures" graphic.
6. Using the proper productional terminology, write the verbal descriptions of each shot in the Ocean Spray "Pigasus" photoboard.
7. Monitor at least six 30-second television spots and jot down the number and length/angles of the spots used. Repeat the exercise at another time of day with another six commercials. Find the average number of shots used per announcement. What particular shot length/angles were most often used?
8. How many of those twelve spots analyzed in Exercise #7 seem to be created in each of the five productional methodologies (live, tape, etc.)? Which was the most commonly employed methodology, which the least common?
9. Write a script that converts the Oh Henry! spot (Figure AP–3) into a *non*animated treatment.

CHAPTER TEN—TELEVISION HOUSEKEEPING COPY

1. Write up clear, concise descriptions of the 24 photos you would send to TM Productions in order to customize the "You" campaign for a station in your city. Each picture idea should satisfy the criteria set down in the TM instruction sheet.
2. Assuming "wall-to-wall" vocalizing, try to harvest the following lift-outs from the long CBS lyric given below:
   > two "30's"
   > one "20"
   > two "10's"

   Then, using a storyboard format, take one of each length spot and suggest visuals to accompany these lyric segments—visuals that would promote the CBS affiliate in your locality.

```
Looking good together, looking good, looking good.
Looking good together, looking good, looking good.
Good things to share, good friends are there.
Looking good together---you and CBS, you're looking good.
The fun you love's on CBS,
The laughter and the sighs.
There's comedy and drama,
And stars get in your eyes.
Day or night all lives are right
When CBS is there.
There's just no better looking,
And it's all right to stare.
```

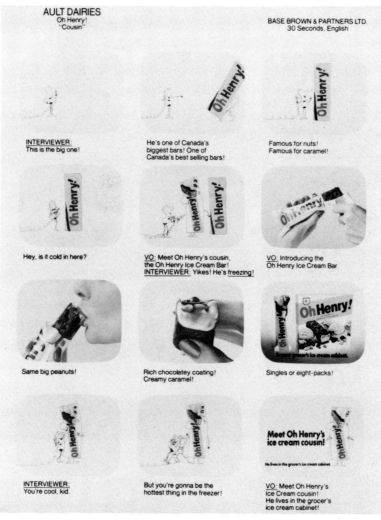

Figure AP-3. *(Courtesy of Barry Base, Base Brown & Partners Limited.)*

```
Looking good together, looking good, looking good.
Looking good together, looking good, looking good.
Gather 'round—there's going to be
New people to meet.
And good friends, from good years, gone by.
Funny people, scary people,
The bitter and the sweet.
For the best in sports and news reports
Sit up---and say ''eye''.
Mystery,
Comedy,
Singing,
```

And dancing.
Movies,
And specials;
The thrill of romancing.
Looking good together, looking good, looking good.
Looking good together, looking good, looking good.
Good things to share, good friends are there.
Looking good together---you and CBS, you're looking good.
And best of all, what's best this fall,
Is at the same address.
Where good friends get together:
You and C-B-S—yes, yes.
Looking good together, looking good, looking good.
Looking good together, looking good, looking good.
When you're watching C-B-S;
You're looking good.

(Courtesy of CBS.)

3. Script a "location" promo for one of your area's local television personalities as per the Nick Clooney "Union Station" piece. Remember to tie in the station's identity clearly.
4. Prepare a script for a 60-second program promo that plugs your station's weekly half-hour interview show, *Civic Spotlight,* featuring Community Affairs Director Jane Banton.
5. Take a lift-out from the script created for Exercise #4 in order to harvest a 20-second promo for the same show.
6. Using the *Good Afternoon, Detroit* format as the pattern, semi-script a *Good Afternoon, (Your Campus/Company)* program up to the second commercial break. Include people and subjects actually available and of interest to viewers on your campus/in your company.
7. Create the first two minutes of a 10-minute slide/live delivery presentation script in which you will unveil your station's new promotion package, to be customized by you, using "Let's All Be There" tools. Your audience consists of station executives and key stockholders.
8. Write the script for a 30-second, 35mm slide PSA promoting your community orchestra's upcoming season. Follow closely the stipulated guidelines for this particular productional methodology.
9. Transform The Atlanta Ballet photoscript into an *all-script* format. Take special care with the selection and specification of music for the spot.
10. Compose a *script* version of the Virginia Division of Litter Control's "Hospital" photoboard. Your production note should clearly set forth the casting requirements.
11. Construct a 30-second storyboard for your state health department's campaign against venereal disease. Work to make it both believable and in good taste, and do not overwork your copy at the expense of the visual.

CHAPTER ELEVEN—TELEVISION COMMERCIALS

1. Complete the "Tooth-Treat Troll" 30-second script, keeping it true to its central and stated objective.

2. Discern and write down the objective of the Mobil photoboard, Figure AP–4. Then, try to create another pictorial progression that meets this same objective.
3. Analyze the Partager Wine "Fisherman" photoboard (Figure AP–5, page 526) by reconstructing, on paper, the answer to each of the Demo-Deriving Quintet's questions as they might have led to this treatment.
4. Repeat Exercise #3 using the chapter's Broxodent photoboard as your subject.
5. Prepare a full-fledged script based on the trainee group's scenario for the Terry Cuff Ring spot.
6. Your product is Glub-Glub Fish Food, which comes in a three-ounce can and is appropriate for both goldfish and more exotic tropical varieties. Apply the Demo-Deriving Quintet to arrive ultimately at a solid scenario, written in the manner of the trainee group's Terry Cuff Ring summation. Then, translate this scenario into 30-second storyboard form.
7. If not already accomplished in conjunction with your labors on the other exercises, fashion *generic, visual* ID lines for each of the following:
   Glub-Glub Fish Food
   Terry Cuff Ring
   Tooth-Treat Gum

Figure AP–4. *(Courtesy of Melissa Wohltman, Doyle Dane Bernbach Advertising.)*

Figure AP–5. *(Courtesy of Melissa Wohltman, Doyle Dane Bernbach Advertising.)*

as well as:
Sinfully Satin Shampoo (a bright pink, perfumed dandruff inhibitor)
Large Leonard (an industrial strength porcelain cleanser)

8. Develop a 30-second storyboard for Sinfully Satin Shampoo that:
   a. is conceived via the Demo-Deriving Quintet
   b. uses the generic, visual ID developed for this product in Exercise #7.
9. Prepare, rehearse, and present (to whatever captive audience you can find) your 'board created for Exercise #8. Use the five-step storyboard presentation procedure. Be careful that your exposition does not commit any of the "seven deadly sins."
10. Transform the 'board created in Exercise #8 into a *script,* and construct and give a presentation of this script. Was this process easier or more difficult than the storyboard exposition in Exercise #9? Which seemed to you to provide a more accurate and meaningful forum for your treatment?

11. Repeat Exercises #8, 9, and 10 with Large Leonard as your product. Did you reach the same conclusions this time in regard to the questions posed in Exercise #10? Why or why not?

12. Assume that the Cold Factor 12 product featured in Figure AP–6 is available only on a direct-response basis. Rewrite the Figure AP–6 spot into a 60-second "DR" script that adheres to all eight of the direct-response tenets.

13. Write a 4-minute infomercial based on the ERA Real Estate print ad in Figure AP–7 (p. 528). Retain Harry Morgan as the talent.

14. Write the dealer-specifying audio copy for the last 10 seconds of the chapter's Culligan co-op photoboard.

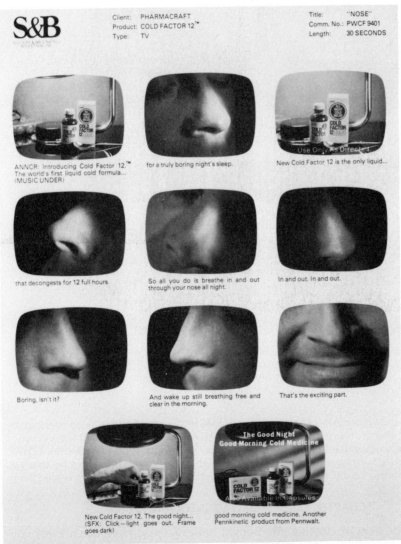

Figure AP–6. *(Courtesy of Mimi Rydre, Sullivan & Brugnatelli Advertising Inc.)*

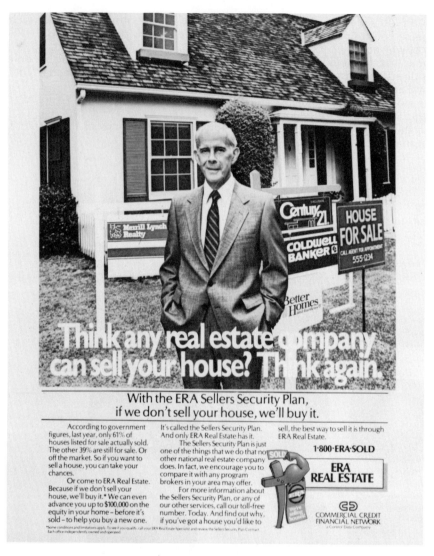

Think any real estate company can sell your house? Think again.

With the ERA Sellers Security Plan,
if we don't sell your house, we'll buy it.

According to government figures, last year, only 61% of houses listed for sale actually sold. The other 39% are still for sale. Or off the market. So if you want to sell a house, you can take your chances.

Or come to ERA Real Estate. Because if we don't sell your house, we'll buy it.* We can even advance you up to $100,000 on the equity in your home – before it's sold – to help you buy a new one.

It's called the Sellers Security Plan. And only ERA Real Estate has it.

The Sellers Security Plan is just one of the things that we do that no other national real estate company does. In fact, we encourage you to compare it with any program brokers in your area may offer.

For more information about the Sellers Security Plan, or any of our other services, call our toll-free number. Today. And find out why, if you've got a house you'd like to

sell, the best way to sell it is through ERA Real Estate.

1·800·ERA·SOLD

ERA
REAL ESTATE

COMMERCIAL CREDIT
FINANCIAL NETWORK
a Control Data Company

*Some conditions and limitations apply. To see if you qualify, call your ERA Real Estate Specialist and review the Sellers Security Plan Contract. Each office independently owned and operated.

Figure AP–7. *(Courtesy of David Sackey, W. B. Doner and Company Advertising.)*

15. Convert the Figure AP–2 Sealtest spot (p. 516) into a script-form co-op message by having it also promote Blue Jay Supermarkets. Keep spot length at 30 seconds.
16. Construct a modular television script for a 30-second spot that pushes Clyde's Rent-It Shack. Write the script in such a way that only one frame need be changed to key on the rental of trailers, cement mixers, and lawn thatchers respectively.

CHAPTER TWELVE—BROADCAST CAMPAIGNS

1. Taking the item of clothing you bought most recently, write down every conceivable positive attribute it possesses. Which one most influenced your purchase? Which attribute is most important to you now? Is the latter the same aspect in

which you believe most potential purchasers of this piece of apparel would be primarily interested?

2. Set down six positive attributes possessed by the subject of the following spot— each of which is rooted in a different SIMPLE appeal. Which of these would have the broadest application? Which would be the most unique in comparison to the way competing storage services are positioned? In which appeal is the following spot itself based? Is the appeal successfully realized?

MAN: Last week I tried working out in my apartment. But (SFX: LOUD CRASH) when the neighbors started complaining about the noise, I figured I better find a new place. This week, I'm working out at Bouma Self-Storage. Yup, (grunt) I rented out my own storage space and that's where I'm lifting weights. I get to work out in peace (SFX: LOUD CRASH) and nobody complains. (Painful cry) Wonder if Bouma can do anything about hernias?

ANNCR: Bouma Self-Storage. Call 'em today at 364-8777 or toll-free 800-442-2608.

(Courtesy of Joe Borrello and Paul Boscarino, WOOD Broadcasting, Inc.)

3. Write down all the drawbacks to living in your current place of residence. How many of these can be converted into advantages? Formulate an AO and three CSIs to flow from one of these "retrieved weaknesses." Don't forget to specify a target audience in that AO.
4. Select a dry-cleaning establishment in your town and work up an analysis of it and its broadcast advertising needs based on the eight procedures called for by Concept Engineering Version 1. Remember that on-site research is one of the most potent means of information gathering.
5. Reposition the BIC butane lighter as the "he-man's pal." How would the BIC photoboard set forth in the chapter have to be changed to reflect this positioning?
6. Derive four additional CSIs for Marlene's that all flow from the AO stipulated in the chapter. Do not replicate the CSI's already specified.
7. Repeat Exercise #6 with Taco Heaven as your subject.
8. Construct three CSIs for the stipulated Miller Beer AO, three for the Milk Duds AO, and three for the Western Airlines AO.
9. Write positioning statements for the chapter-specified Western Airlines, Marlene's, and Taco Heaven AO's.
10. Create an additional radio spot for First National/Wichita that flows from its CSI #1—Commitment to Service.
11. Derive a 30-second TV spot for First National/Wichita that flows from CSI #4. (You must first determine what CSI #4 is to be. Make certain it is encompassed by the First National AO given in the chapter.)
12. Select a nonfranchise restaurant in your locale and construct a complete Broadcast Advertising Proposal for it as specified in Concept Engineering Version 2. Specifically, your proposal should include:
    a. title/cover page
    b. client analysis
       1) the business itself
       2) current advertising vehicles and approaches
    c. competition analysis
       1) one-sentence competition yardstick
       2) description of all competitors who qualify under the terms of this yardstick
       3) analysis of these competitors' current advertising vehicles and approaches

    d. Advertising Objective
      1) the one-sentence AO
      2) formulation of the positioning statement that flows from it
    e. Creative Selling Ideas
      1) presentation of ten CSIs which fit within the AO parameters
      2) indication of which CSI will be used as the basis for a sample integrated flight
    f. integrated dual-media flight of sample spots all based on the same CSI:
      1) two 60-second radio spots
      2) one 30-second radio spot
      3) two 30-second television scripts
      4) a 10-second television lift-out from one of the above thirties

13. Put together a prospects file on all the furniture stores within a five-mile radius of your town's center. Draw up the individual profiles first before constructing your composite competition summary.
14. Compile a catalog of spec-writing exhibits for the gas station/service station category. Include in your collection:
    a. a 30-second television script
    b. a 20-second television script
    c. a 60-second radio script
    d. three generically different types of 30-second radio treatments (a uni-voice, a dialogue, a device commercial, etc.)
    e. an 8-second shared radio ID.
15. Research and write up a case study on a local advertiser's successful radio campaign. How did it outflank the competition and what, if anything, has been the competition's broadcast advertising response?

CHAPTER THIRTEEN—POLITICAL, CONTROVERSY, AND CRISIS CAMPAIGNS

1. Write a 60-second radio spot for the mayor of your city that uses two brief testimonials from prominent citizens to achieve the "Make Like the Greeks" objective.
2. Repeat Exercise #1, but now create a 30-second TV spot in which a single announcer voice-over is used to laud the mayor.
3. Assuming your father or mother were running for state legislator, how would you position either? What would be the selected attribute "battlefield"? What personal characteristics might you want to avoid focusing on?
4. Write a sample 30-second radio commercial that flows from your decisions in Exercise #3.
5. Create six slogans that could be used to position your professor or boss as a political candidate. Make certain these are positive and non-preemptible.
6. As a Gary Hart copywriter, try to design a 30-second TV message that counters the Mondale "red telephone" commercial reproduced in the chapter.
7. Repeat Exercise #6, attempting this time to discredit Mondale's adopting of the "Where's the Beef?" line.
8. Design a 60-second radio image spot for Senator Dee Huddleston that is intended to deflect the criticism of him raised in the chapter's Ailes Communications commercials.
9. Selecting from his or her current stands, write a 30-second "hard" issue and a 30-second "soft" issue TV spot on behalf of the chief executive of your state or province.
10. Convert the anti-Sasser "Castro" spot into a legitimate negative treatment that concentrates on his foreign-aid voting record but omits the "Commie-lover" slurs.

11. Assume you are the copywriter for Governor Roundbottom's opponent. Fashion a 30-second negative TV spot that rebuts Roundbottom's "We All Make Mistakes" staff reduction explanation.

12. Specify the video descriptions for the Herb Bateman spot with the aim of creating the most noble and "true-to-life" impression possible.

13. Try to create a spot for former astronaut Jack Lousma that counters the damage done by Levin's "Toyota quote" commercial. You might wish to explore the "We All Make Mistakes" or "Heroic Stills" techniques in this regard.

14. Look through your personal photo albums and design a 30-second image-building TV spot for yourself built from readily available pictures. Write accompanying soundtrack copy to promote your hypothetical campaign for mayor.

15. Create a spot for Senator Patrick Moynihan that uses the Western motif in a *positive* sense on his behalf. You may need to research Moynihan's background to find relevant specifics on which your metaphor can build.

16. Write a 60-second radio image spot for the United States Used Car Dealers Association designed to improve the credibility of its members.

17. Convert the Today contraceptive commercial into a 60-second radio dialogue spot that establishes the legitimacy of the product category in general and the primacy of Today in particular.

18. Carbon-Slick, a strip-mining coal company, has indicated a willingness to begin operations in your economically depressed town. But its proposed activities will destroy the sanctuary for a rare species of crow. Create a 30-second TV treatment that establishes the right of your client, The Audubon Society, to try to preserve the birds by narrowing Carbon-Slick's range of operations.

19. Repeat Exercise #18, except you are now a copywriter for Carbon-Slick seeking to defend the company's right to mine fully all available acreage.

20. As a copywriter for Malone & Hyde, use the "Become the Victim" technique in combating Local 1529's efforts to have customers boycott your stores. The format is a 60-second radio spot.

21. One of The Midasville State Bank's loan officers has embezzled $49,000 from the institution. Word of this act started a run on the bank that forced its closing for two days. It is now Saturday and the bank will re-open for the first time on Monday. Write a 30-second TV spot and a 60-second radio commercial that will convince depositors to keep their money in Midasville State.

CHAPTER FOURTEEN—CROSS-MEDIA CAMPAIGNS

1. Using the Dimflicker billboard as the central campaign concept, write a sample newspaper ad and a sample radio spot that conforms to and amplifies this theme.

2. Isolate a cross-media campaign in your area that falls prey to the "Dimflicker Phenomenon." What contradictory images do the various aspects of this campaign project? Pick the one image that seems to have the greatest potential and extend its use to all other relevant media through creation of sample ads.

3. Write 30-second radio counterparts to both the "Mind Over Chatter" and "Radio Activity" KSJN print ads. Keep the style and personality consistent.

4. Create a 60-second radio uni-voice spot for Scoundrel that mirrors its print and television treatments. Then, write clear and concise descriptions of three music beds over which this uni-voice copy might be read.

5. Redesign the Eldorado magazine ad in Figure AP–8 (p. 532) into an unillustrated same-size newspaper layout that projects an identical image. Now, create a 60-second radio spot that conforms to the style of both print pieces. What is the target audience for the magazine ad? Remember to address the *same* audience in your newspaper and radio approaches.

Figure AP–8. *(Courtesy of Lori Wackerman, D'Arcy MacManus Masius.)*

6. Recreate a rough sketch and "keyed" script for the WBBM print layout reproduced in Figure AP–9.
7. Convert the essence of the WOOD print ad (Figure AP–10, p. 534) into a sketch for a billboard display that meets the chapter-presented criteria for outdoor 'boards.
8. Below is a concept for an October promotion. Assuming that a station in your locality will use it, flesh out this concept into:
    a. a news release like that bannering WRQX's "Ground Hog" stunt
    b. sample 10- and 30-second radio announcements to be aired by the station during the promotion
    c. a rough sketch and "keyed" script for a nonillustrated newspaper ad $4\frac{1}{4}''$ wide by $6\frac{15}{16}''$ deep. (Note that this is a small layout; don't forget white space requirements.)

OCTOBER PROMOTION
THE GREAT HALLOWEEN CATERED CAPER

The object of this contest is to win a catered Halloween party.

The promotion works in this manner: Listeners send in postcards with their name, address and telephone number, and these cards are drawn randomly throughout the day. (Duration and number of winners is to be determined by the station.) Each entrant whose card is drawn wins a pumpkin, and their card goes into a hopper to be included in the drawing for the grand prize which is a catered Halloween party at the winner's home. (Station is to determine number of guests at party.) Runner-up prizes might include such Halloween items as: costumes, masks, candy, apples, brooms, more pumpkins, cider, etc.

The party might be further embellished by doing a remote broadcast from the home—or by having one of your own scary air personalities or someone else on your staff in attendance.

Newsradio 78 Tastes Good, Too!

From Monday, April 16 through Friday, April 20, Sherman Kaplan's <u>In the Kitchen</u> will feature recipes for Asparagus Parmigiano, Fish Etoufeé, Sally Lunn Bread, Dixie Peanut Brittle (yum!) and Easy Skillet Gumbo.

Listen every weekday at 10:38 am as culinary experts join Sherman on Newsradio 78 to share their cooking secrets and recipes.

Know what's cooking.

**Turn to us first.
WBBM
Newsradio 78.**

Figure AP–9. *(Courtesy of Barbara Di Guido, WBBM–AM.)*

Entry blanks might be made up and placed with participating sponsors. Certificates to redeem the pumpkins might be worked in a trade deal with a local market who might also provide other prizes. The drawing for the grand prize could even be done at the market or at other sponsor's locations—perhaps even at the catering company.

The more prizes, the better. It encourages a better response from your audience. After all, we don't want someone to say they don't 'have a ghost of a chance' in this Halloween contest.

(Courtesy of Bill Lobb, Radio Arts, Inc.)

APPENDIX C—INDUSTRY CODES AND POLICIES

1. In the presented codes, find as many statements as you can that pertain to commercial copy aimed at children or within/near children's programs. Write a 60-second radio spot and a 30-second television treatment for *Polly Panda* (a $13.95 battery-operated, one-foot-high stuffed animal that actually chews on leaves and burps.) Both your spots should conform to all these children's advertising strictures.
2. Repeat Exercise #1 in terms of firearms advertising and the Militiaman 22-caliber rifle, sold by the Midstates Hardware Store chain. Which of the reprinted codes

SET YOUR ADVERTISING SIGHTS ON THE #1 RADIO COMBINATION IN WESTERN MICHIGAN

NEWS WOOD 1300

WEATHER WOOD 1300

BEAUTIFUL WOOD FM 105.7 MUSIC

WOOD 1300 PERSONALITY

WOOD 1300 SPORTS

CALL WOOD AM & FM TODAY!

WOOD WORKS

WOOD AM/FM
180 NORTH DIVISION AVENUE
GRAND RAPIDS, MICHIGAN 49503 (616) 459-1919

Figure AP–10. *(Courtesy of Joe Borrello and Paul Boscarino, WOOD Broadcasting, Inc.)*

completely prohibit the advertising of products in this category? Since you cannot place your spots on their facilities, make certain your copy conforms to all the requirements of outlets that do accept firearms commercials.

3. Examine the NBC policies as regards weight control/reduction products. Create a 30-second television spot for Flab-o-Weigh, a liquid weight-control dietary supplement. Your spot should be acceptable to the network.

4. In what ways does NBC address the subject of *comparative* advertising? How would the following piece of copy have to be changed to conform to *all* these standards?

ANNCR: Going cross-country? Green Mountain Transit advises you to ride with us rather than risk delay on a Blue Star bus. Unlike our competitor, Green Mountain inspects the drive train of every bus before every trip. That means less chance of breakdown; less likelihood you'll be stranded. Though Blue Star thinks cheaper rates are preferable to good maintenance, we at Green Mountain Transit know your safety's worth a few cents more. So forget the Blue 'bomb'. Ride the Great Green---Green Mountain Transit.

5. Write a 60-second radio spot for Tinker's Tavern in LaGrange, North Dakota. Your copy should not violate any of the NBC, Westinghouse, or WLUC guidelines as to alcoholic beverage advertising.

6. Find two funeral service/associated product advertisements in local print media. Which of these, if transformed into broadcast copy, could meet the WTVJ acceptance requirements?

7. Find and analyze all references to direct-response advertising contained in the Appendix C policies. Apply these "DR" guidelines to the two short "DR" spots presented in chapter 11 (DTI travel memberships and Consumer Legal Services Trust). What changes, if any, would need to be made in these two commercials to secure their acceptance on the various guideline-issuing outlets?

8. Examine five radio spots you've recently written to ascertain whether they would meet Bonneville Broadcasting's Guidelines for "easy listening" formatted stations. Rewrite where necessary to make all five messages as Bonneville-compatible as possible.

9. Isolate all references to political and controversy advertising found in the Appendix C guidelines. Select any four political and any three controversy spots from chapter 13 and determine whether each complies with the various broadcaster-stipulated regulations. Where needed, rewrite the copy to make the commercials acceptable to as many of the guideline-issuing broadcasters as possible.

COPY CORRECTION

PRACTICE

One of the best ways to become sensitized to your own writing weaknesses is to analyze the mistakes of other writers. In the following pages, several trainee-created commercials have been reproduced exactly as originally submitted. Study them carefully. Find as many flaws as you can and mark these in pencil, using the common proofreading symbols listed below and any other notations needed. Then, refer to the precorrected versions of these same spots, which are included at the end of this Appendix. Did you uncover all the errors? Or, did you overlook the same problem(s) in the trainee scripts that you often miss in your own writing?

COMMON PROOFREADING SYMBOLS

add punc: missing punctuation; add as indicated.

amb (or, *vag*):   ambiguous; vague; word or phrase has no clear meaning or can be understood in several different ways.

AWK: awkward; sound and/or sense are hobbled here.

FS (or, *ROS*):   fused or run-on sentence; two independent thoughts have been jammed together.

HK: hackneyed; trite; find a more unique way of stating this.

LT: lacks transition; one thought does not lead smoothly into the next.

Punc: wrong punctuation.

RA: rearrange; words or phrases are not in clearest or most effective order.

Red: redundant; same things are being repeated in the same way.

Ref: referent for this word is unclear.

Sf: sentence fragment; the thought unit lacks the vital information to make it meaningful.

Sp: spelling error.

TL: thought unit too long for audience comprehension.

VSag: verb/subject agreement lacking; singular verb with plural noun or vice versa.

WP: wrong phrase; choose another for this context.

WW: wrong word; choose another for this context.

30 seconds

It's that time of year again. The christmas season. You
can see, hear, taste and feel it. Can't always smell
christmas though. In this day of artificial trees, large
get-togethers, and lots of seasonal cooking that pure
christmasie scent just can't compete. This year bring
that seasonal scent into your home with Bayberry sachet
and air freshner. The aerosol spray that makes christmas/
christmas. It's Bayberry for the fragrance of the holiday
season.

30 seconds

You can tell winters coming. Frost in on the ground in
the morning. The wind is becoming a out more nippy. When
you notice these signs, you know its time to winterize your
car. And the best place to winterize in the central Iowa
area is Jack's Shell Station in Pemberton. Jacks been
through thirty of these severe Iowa winters and he knows
how to prepare your car for the coming season. Let Jack's
automotive experience work for your car this winter. Bring
your car in to Jacks Shell at seventeen eighteen Mission
in Pemberton.

                                           60 seconds

Fensterwald Fidelity Bank -- where you come first! We have

been around long enough to know you and your needs, but we

haven't been around so long we take you and your business

for granted. We have good, friendly, efficient service.

We understand that when you come in you don't want to

spend time in long lines, especially if you do your banking

during your lunch hour. Besides our checking, drive-in

and quick loan services, Fensterwald Fidelity Bank also

helps you make money on your savings. We compound five

and a quater per cent interest on your money daily ---

and pay it quarterly. And it's a secure feeling you'll

have when you see those quarterly payments added to your

account. We're easy to find, too. Fensterwald Fidelity

Bank is located on the corner of Gennett and Green in

Webster, close to stores and businesses. Come in and see

us soon.

                                        30 seconds

Need cake decorations for that special occassion coming
up at your house? Visit your nearby Red Owl Grocery
Stores for complete decorating supplies. This week Red
Owl Grocery Store is featuring Gold Crest gold dragees.
The small golder balls are useful for trimming cakes,
spelling out names and messages or making your cake look
extra special. Remember, Gold Crest gold dragees, those
small gold balls make your work look better.

60 seconds

Attention all offices and business across the country. For
the next 60 seconds, the makers of Sanford's Mint Flavored
Mucilage would like to explain to you what mucilage actually
is and the benefits it can have for your business. Mucilage
is not a trick or a gimmick --- it is an adhesive used to
help lick the problems of lose evelopes and folders. Just
apply the mucilage to the surface you want to seal and lick
when you're ready. Sanford's mint flavored Mucilage will
keep your seals together stronger and longer. You'll be
amazed how Sanford's mint flavored mucilage really works.
Sanford's mucilage comes in an unbreakable bottle for the
super low price of only 29¢ - so the next time you hear the
word mucilage - think of the good sealer by Sanford's.
At Sanfords we're making it our business to seal up the
problems of business in America.

                                    30 seconds

Cleaning dirt is a demanding job requiring a specialized tool

designed for tough problems of rubbing and scrubbing. The

Whiz Away Cleaner is more than just a scouring pad. It's

tough heavy duty nylon, for long lasting scrubbing power that

can handle any mess you need to Whiz Away. Also great for out

of doors wash up and bathroom messes. Don't bother with sponges,

dishclothes or scouring pads. Get them away with the Whiz Away

Cleaner.

<pre>
                              60 seconds

Altoids, the delicious spearmint candy imported from England.

The refreshing flavor of a mountain stream as it dribbles into

a crystal clear pool. Distinguished as the London atmosphere:

the Winchester Cathedral, the Big Ben and the Queen's mansion

preserved in every box. The most popular selling candy in all

of Europe and thereabouts. Adopted by the Royal Court, Altoids,

made with the highest quality standards in mind. Ask the Bobby

with the cool spearmint candy tucked in his mouth as he walks

his beat or the university professor not to mention a future

rock star. The anser is all the same, Altoids in the blue box

for only $.98 refreshes, soothes and adds that little extra

pride in everything you due. Altoids locks you into the

English tradition without the time and cost of having to cross

the stormy Atlantic to get some.
</pre>

30 seconds

Strongheart Dog Food believes that we owe it o you

to not advertise with any singing dogs, or dancing

dogs, or talking dogs either. We're just gonna give

it to you straight. Strongheart Dog Food is one hundred

per cent nutritionally complete and has a delicious bef

flavor. That means that not only will your dog be

healthy, but he'll be happy too. We think that's

important. Plus Strongheart Dog Food is economically

priced because let's face it, we don't have to hire any

singing, dancing, or talking dogs to do our commercials.

30 seconds

Why are there frozen vegetables all over the counter?

The bag the vegetables were in wouldn't tear open easily,

so you pulled harder to open it. The bag then bursted

open, spilling tonight's dinner all over the sink. The

Kitchen King Bag Slitter can help you avoid this scene.

The Kitchen King Bag Slitter slices the bag open with one

hand, while the other hand holds the package. The Kitchen

King Bag Slitter allows you to keep control of the

package thereby keeping dinner off the counter and on the

table.

Spot begins here!

30 seconds

do these ideas go together?

Cap

It's that time of year again. The (christmas) season. You

can see, hear, taste and feel it. Can't always smell

Cap

(christmas though. In this day of artificial trees, large

Too Long

get-togethers, and lots of seasonal cooking, that pure

Cap   Red

(christmasie (scent) (just can't compete.) This year, bring

which? — (that) (seasonal (scent) into your home with Bayberry sachet

Indicate pronunc

and air freshner. The (aerosol) spray that makes (christmas/

Cap

(christmas.) It's Bayberry for the fragrance of the holiday

Cap

season.

WW — has acquired negative connotations

Vag

Wp

how? cop-out line

Bayberry what?

Spot never makes that seasonal smell clear, specific, tangible.

What IS Bayberry??

don't need
this line

30 seconds   *bookish*

apos   *Sp*

You can tell winter's coming. Frost (in) on the ground/ in

the morning. The wind is (becoming a bit more nippy.) When
                                    apos

you notice these signs, you know it's time to (winterize) your
                                                                              term
car. And the best place to (winterize) in the central Iowa   *never*
                                                                              defined
                                                      apos
area is Jack's Shell Station in Pemberton. Jacks been

through thirty of these severe Iowa winters and he knows

                      Vag
(how to prepare) your car for the coming season. Let Jack's
                                  Vag
automotive experience (work for) your car this winter. Bring
                              apos
your car in to Jacks Shell at seventeen eighteen Mission

in Pemberton.

                                              Sp

to do what? Spot lacks tag.

Specific benefit must be made
                    clear; tangible
What does winterizing involve?

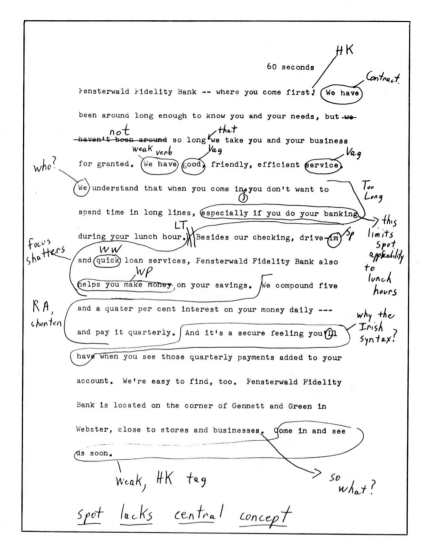

Additional Practice: find the misspelled word the "corrector" missed.

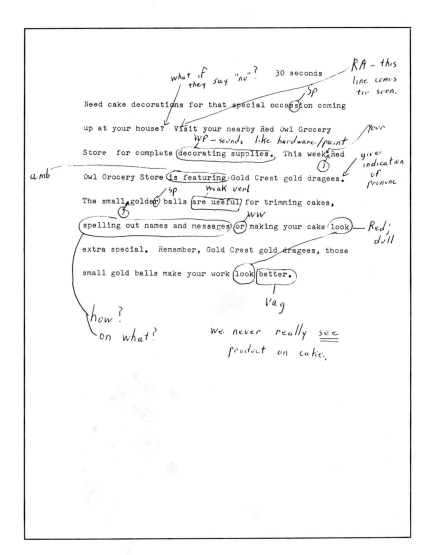

what if they say "no"?   30 seconds

RA – this line comes too soon.

SP

Need cake decorations for that special occassion coming

up at your house? Visit your nearby Red Owl Grocery

your

WP – sounds like hardware/paint

Store for complete decorating supplies. This week Red

?

give indication of province

a mb

Owl Grocery Store is featuring Gold Crest gold dragees.

sp

weak verb

The small golden balls are useful for trimming cakes,

?

ww

spelling out names and messages or making your cake look — Red; dull

extra special. Remember, Gold Crest gold dragees, those

small gold balls make your work look better.

Vag

how?

on what?

we never really see product on cake.

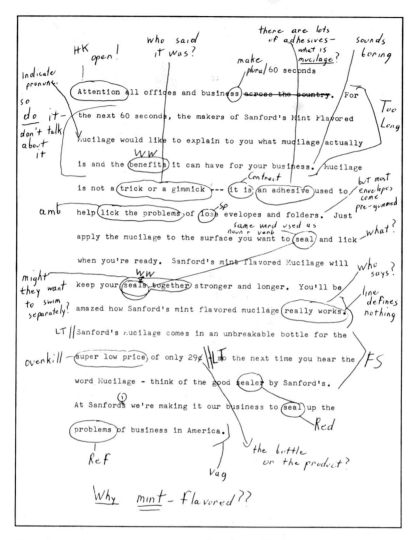

There is another uncorrected misspelling here. Find it.

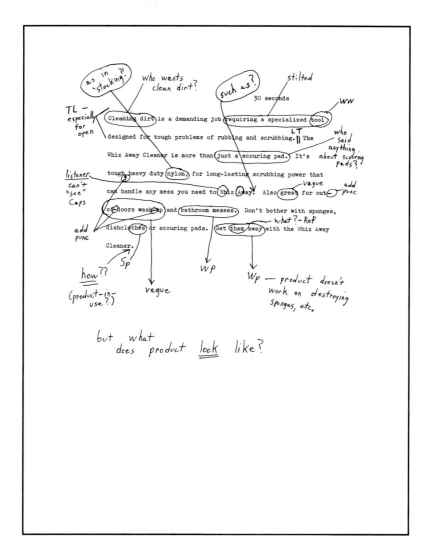

as in ?!
'stocking'

who wants
clean dirt?

such as ?

stilted

30 seconds

WW

TL —
especially
for
open

Cleaning dirt is a demanding job requiring a specialized tool

LT

who
said
anything
about scouring
pads?

designed for tough problems of rubbing and scrubbing. ‖ The

Whiz Away Cleaner is more than just a scouring pad. It's

listener
can't
"see"
Caps

tough heavy duty nylon, for long-lasting scrubbing power that

vague

add
punc

can handle any mess you need to Whiz Away. Also great for out

add
punc

of-doors wash up and bathroom messes. Don't bother with sponges,

dishclothes or scouring pads. Get them away with the Whiz Away

what? - Ref

Cleaner.

Sp

how ??

(product-in-
use?)

vague

WP

WP — product doesn't
work on destroying
sponges, etc.

but what
does product look like?

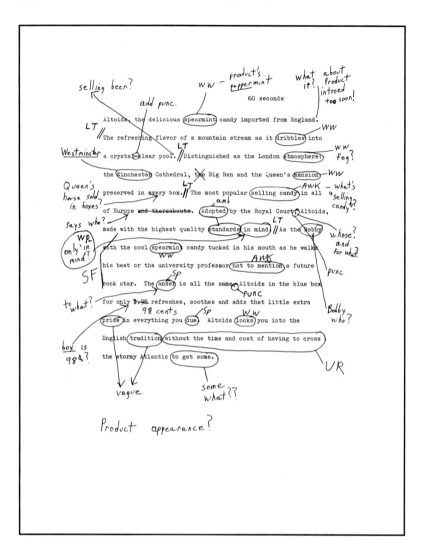

selling been?

ww — product's peppermint

60 seconds

what about it? Product introed too soon!

add punc.

Altoids, the delicious (spearmint) candy imported from England.

LT

//The refreshing flavor of a mountain stream as it (dribbles) into

ww

Westminster a crystal clear pool. // Distinguished as the London (atmosphere?)

LT

ww fog?

the (Winchester) Cathedral, the Big Ben and the Queen's (mansion) ww

Queen's house sold in boxes?

preserved in every box. // The most popular (selling candy) in all

LT

AWK — what's "selling candy"?

says who?

of Europe and thereabouts. (Adopted) by the Royal Court, Altoids,

amb

made with the highest quality (standards) (in mind). // As the Bobby

WP only in mind??

LT

whose? and for who?

with the cool (spearmint) candy tucked in his mouth as he walks

SF

ww

AWK

his beat or the university professor (not to mention) a future

punc

SP

rock star. The (anser) is all the same. Altoids in the blue box

PUNC

to what?

for only $1.98 refreshes, soothes and adds that little extra

Bobby who?

98 cents

SP

ww

(pride) in everything you (due). Altoids (locks) you into the

box is 98¢?

English (tradition) (without the time and cost of having to cross

the stormy Atlantic (to get some.)

UR

vague

some what??

Product appearance?

30 seconds   ~~Sp~~

Strongheart Dog Food ~~believes that we owe it to you~~   *Sp*

doesn't   use
~~to not advertise with any~~ singing dogs, ~~or~~ dancing
                    to advertise. Strongheart just   *weak*
                                                          verb
dogs, or talking dogs ~~either~~. ~~We're just gonna~~ *gives*

it to you straight. Strongheart Dog Food is one hundred

per cent nutritionally complete and (has) a delicious (bef) — *Sp*
                                                      So
flavor. ~~That means that~~ (not only) will (your dog) be

~~healthy, but he'll be happy too. ~~We think that's~~   *This*
                                                           says
                    And   *nothing!*
~~important~~. ~~Plus~~ Strongheart Dog Food is economically
        B   *Pay*
priced, ~~because~~ ~~let's face it~~, we don't have to ~~hire~~ any

singing, dancing, or talking dogs to do our commercials.

Strongheart speaks for itself.

30 seconds

~~Why are there~~ Frozen vegetables ~~a~~ll over the counter~~X~~.

The bag the vegetables were in wouldn't tear open, ~~easily,~~

~~S~~o you pulled harder, ~~to open it.~~ The bag (then) burst~~ed~~

~~open,~~ spilling tonight's dinner all over the ~~sink.~~ ~~The~~
counter. Let

Kitchen King Bag Slitter ~~can~~ help you avoid this scene.

The Kitchen King Bag Slitter slices the bag open (with one

hand,) while (the other hand) holds the package. ~~The Kitchen~~

~~King Bag Slitter allows you to~~ Keep control of the
fixings from spilling.
package. ~~thereby~~ Keeping dinner ~~off the counter and on the~~

~~table.~~

Need tag line!

AWK; RA — product
doesn't <u>have</u>
hands!

INDUSTRY CODES
AND POLICIES

The pages that follow present a cross-section of the self-regulatory standards through which the broadcasting industry strives to police commercial and continuity material submitted for airing. Even though such regulations are in a constant state of evolution, these relatively recent versions are included to give the copywriter some concept of the considerations and standards used to measure message suitability. And, since self-regulation is often a multitiered affair, relevant sections of representative network, group, and individual station guidelines have been reproduced along with those pertaining to children's advertising from the National Advertising Division of the Council of Better Business Bureaus.

In relation to the commercial networks, NBC's Advertising Standards and Advertising Guidelines that immediately follow are made available courtesy of Ralph Daniels, Vice President, Broadcast Standards, the National Broadcasting Company, Inc.

From the Children's Advertising Review Unit, National Advertising Division of the Council of Better Business Bureaus, Inc., the *Self-Regulatory Guidelines for Children's Advertising* are reprinted courtesy of Rita Weisskoff, the Children's Advertising Review Unit Director.

As an example of copy standards that are format-based, the Bonneville Broadcasting System's Commercial Standards for "easy listening" music stations have been supplied courtesy of Ronald Jamison, Bonneville's Director of Sales & Marketing.

The strictures on copy aired by Group W stations (Westinghouse Broadcasting and Cable, Inc.) are set forth in pages provided by Randolph Brooksbank, Group W's Director, Commercial Standards and Practices.

Finally, as specimens of local station standards, guidelines from WBAY–TV (Green Bay, Wisconsin), WLUC–TV (Marquette, Michigan) and WTVJ (Miami, Florida) conclude Appendix C. WBAY–TV's material was made available by Evelyn Keseg, Director of Administration, Nationwide Communications, Inc. The Code of Operations from WLUC–TV comes courtesy of Robert Ganzer, the station's General Sales Manager. Douglas Barker, Station Manager of WTVJ, provided that outlet's written policy memos.

The last section of Appendix A, Additional Suggested Exercises, furnishes some recommendations for projects that will help you become familiar with these codes and with the scope of industry guidelines in general. For broadcast copy, self-regulation is a fact of life that the copywriter can view as either an irritant or an aid. Since broadcasting is such a "fish bowl" environment, however, most prudent professionals would rather know in advance what they cannot do than be reprimanded (or worse) after the fact—after an ill-conceived message has already aired and the public damage already done.

NBC BROADCAST STANDARDS FOR TELEVISION

NBC BROADCAST STANDARDS FOR TELEVISION

INTRODUCTION

NBC is mindful that television is a home medium designed to appeal to audiences of diverse tastes and interests. Consequently, the Company recognizes its obligation to maintain the highest standards of taste and integrity in all its programming. In general, programs should reflect a wide range of roles for all people and should endeavor to depict men, women and children in a positive manner, keeping in mind always the importance of dignity to every human being.

In 1934, NBC became the first broadcasting organization to adopt a Code of Broadcast Standards. This Code has been revised periodically to meet the changing interests and expectations of a nationwide audience and to express NBC's own concern that its program service acknowledge the needs of the millions of homes we enter every day of the year.

The standards set forth in this Code must, of necessity, be expressed as general principles to be applied with sensitivity and intelligence on a case-by-case basis. The responsibility of interpreting and implementing those principles and proposing new or modified standards, rests with NBC's Broadcast Standards Department.

The general provisions of this Code apply in principle to the NBC Radio Division although the Radio Networks and the owned Radio Stations administer them independently.

Each NBC owned television station has its individual Broadcast Standards unit, which applies these standards to locally originated broadcasts in terms of community needs and interests.

News and information programs produced by NBC News are supervised by that Division which has its own set of policies and procedures.

(Courtesy of National Broadcasting Company, Inc.)

ADVERTISING STANDARDS

Clearance Procedures

While the ultimate responsibility for advertising rests with the advertiser, advertising agencies preparing commercial messages intended for broadcast on NBC facilities should consult the Broadcast Standards Department in advance of production. Such advance discussion enables the Broadcast Standards Department to provide initial guidance on questions that might arise under NBC standards.

For each commercial, advertising agencies are asked to submit shooting script or storyboard, a new product sample and label/package insert, substantiation for all material claims and authentication of all demonstrations and testimonial statements.

When the pre-production discussions have concluded, the agency produces the commercial and must submit the finished version for screening and final clearance.

NBC accepts advertising only after securing satisfactory evidence of the integrity of the advertiser, the availability of the product or service, the existence of support for the claims and the authentication of demonstrations, compliance with applicable laws and the acceptable taste of the presentation. Advertisers should deal affirmatively with the results expected from the use of the product or service, not dwell excessively on the results of failure to use the product or service.

Billboards

Billboards may be used as stipulated by NBC, provided they include no more than the identity of the program and the sponsor's name, product or service and a brief factual description of the general nature thereof. Only products, services or companies being advertised in the program may be billboarded. Any claims allowed must be supported. Billboards may not mention contests, offers, promotional teasers or cross-references to other programs.

Charitable Appeals

An advertiser may surrender commercial time to
schedule an approved public service announcement or theme.
Appeals within a commercial announcement will be considered on
a case-by-case basis and will require submission of complete
details of how the contributions will be handled. Clear
sponsorship identification is required in these instances.

Comparative Advertising Guidelines

NBC will accept comparative advertising which
identifies, directly or by implication, a competing product or
service. As with all other advertising, each substantive
claim, direct or implied, must be substantiated to NBC's
satisfaction and the commercial must satisfy the following
guidelines and standards for comparative advertising
established by NBC:

1. Competitors shall be fairly and properly identified.

2. Advertisers shall refrain from disparaging or unfairly
attacking competitors, competing products, services or other
industries through the use of representations or claims,
direct or implied, that are false, deceptive, misleading or
have the tendency to mislead.

3. The identification must be for comparison purposes and
not simply to upgrade by association.

4. The advertising should compare related or similar
properties or ingredients of the product, dimension to
dimension, feature to feature, or wherever possible by a
side-by-side demonstration.

5. The property being compared must be significant in
terms of value or usefulness of the product or service to the
consumer.

6. The difference in the properties being compared must
be measurable and significant.

7. Pricing comparisons may raise special problems that
could mislead, rather than enlighten, viewers. For certain
classifications of products, retail prices may be extremely
volatile, may be fixed by the retailer rather than the product
advertiser, and may not only differ from outlet to outlet but

from week to week within the same outlet. Where these circumstances might apply, NBC will accept commercials containing price comparisons only on a clear showing that the comparative claims accurately, fairly and substantially reflect the actual price differentials at retail outlets throughout the broadcast area, and that these price differentials are not likely to change during the period the commercial is broadcast.

8. When a commercial claim involves market relationships, other than price, which are also subject to fluctuation (such as but not limited to sales position or exclusivity), the substantiation for the claim will be considered valid only as long as the market conditions on which the claim is based continue to prevail.

9. As with all other advertising, whenever necessary, NBC may require substantiation to be updated from time to time, and may re-examine substantiation, where the need to do so is indicated as the result of a challenge or other developments.

Challenge Procedure

Where appropriate, NBC will implement the following procedures in the event a commercial is challenged by another advertiser.

1. If an advertiser elects to challenge the advertising of another advertiser, he shall present his challenge and supporting data to NBC in a form available for transmittal to the challenged advertiser.

2. The challenged advertiser will then have an opportunity to respond directly to the challenger. NBC will maintain the confidentiality of the advertiser's original supporting data which was submitted for substantiation of the claims made in the commercial. However, NBC will ask the challenged advertiser to provide it with a copy of its response to the challenger and, where the response is submitted directly to NBC, the challenged advertiser will be requested to forward a copy of its response to the challenger.

3. Where NBC personnel do not have the expertise to make a judgment on technical issues raised by a challenge, NBC will take appropriate measures in its discretion to assist the advertiser and challenger to resolve their differences, including encouraging them to obtain a determination from an acceptable third party.

4. NBC will not withdraw a challenged advertisement from the broadcast schedule unless:

  a. it is directed to do so by the incumbent advertiser;

  b. the incumbent advertiser refuses to submit the controversy for review by some appropriate agency when deemed necessary by NBC;

  c. a decision is rendered by NBC against the incumbent advertiser;

  d. the challenged advertiser, when requested, refuses to cooperate in some other substantive area; or

  e. NBC, prior to final disposition of the challenge, determines that the substantiation for the advertising has been so seriously brought into question that the advertising can no longer be considered substantiated to NBC's satisfaction.

5. NBC may take additional measures in its discretion to resolve questions raised by advertising claims.

Dramatizations and Reenactments

Dramatized or reenacted events must be clearly disclosed as such and may be utilized only when based on an actual occurrence.

Government Action Regarding a Product or Service Being Advertised

In the event government action is proposed with respect to a product or service or claims being made for it (as for example, the issuance of a complaint or proposed rules by the FTC or the FDA), Broadcast Standards will determine whether the subject questioned is part of a current schedule on NBC's facilities. If so, the substantiation and the authentication originally furnished by the advertising agency in support of the commercial message will be reevaluated in light of the matter being questioned by such proposed government action. The schedule will be maintained, if NBC is satisfied that either the advertising is acceptable under existing standards or that it presents a matter about which it would be inappropriate for NBC to make a judgment. This is done so that NBC action will not have the effect of adjudicating the question being considered by the governmental agency. A similar evaluation will be made of any proposed commercial message which involves subjects questioned by government action initiated prior to acceptance of the commercial for broadcast by NBC. If the governmental agency finally resolves the issue against the advertiser, NBC will withdraw its schedule.

Cross References in Advertising

References by advertisers within their commercial time to another program they are sponsoring are permitted provided that the references do not identify a competing facility, the day, or hour of the program. Statements urging the viewer to check television listings for such information are permissible.

Advertisers may not refer to other programs scheduled at a later hour on the same day on a competing facility.

Guarantee and Warranty Offers

Whenever the terms "guarantee," "warranty" or similar words that constitute a promise or representation in the nature of a guarantee or warranty appear in a television advertisement, certain additional information concerning material terms and conditions of such a guarantee or warranty offer must be clearly and unambiguously disclosed to the viewer.

In general, any commercial announcement in which a guarantee/warranty is mentioned should also disclose:

a. the nature and extent of the guarantee;

b. the identity of the guarantor;

c. the manner in which the guarantor intends to perform;

d. information concerning what a purchaser wishing to claim under the guarantee need do before the guarantor will perform pursuant to its obligations under the guarantee; and

e. where applicable, whether a warranty is full or limited.

This disclosure must be made so it will not be misunderstood by the typical viewer. Simultaneous disclosure in both the audio and video often proves to be the best and most certain method of achieving full, clear and effective disclosure. However, a commercial announcment using only audio may constitute clear and conspicuous disclosure because of the clarity and completeness of the representation and the non-distracting manner of presentation. Video disclosure alone may not necessarily satisfy the above criteria.

Placement and Scheduling

NBC reserves the right to determine the scheduling, format and length of commercial breaks during and adjacent to programs carried over its facilities and the acceptability, number and placement of commercials, promotions and other announcements within such breaks, including those involving cast or celebrities.

In-program advertisements must be placed within the framework of the sponsored program. The program must be announced and clearly identified before the first commercial placement and terminated after the last commercial placement.

Research or Surveys

Reference may be made to the results of bona fide surveys or research relating to the product advertised, provided the results do not create an impression the research does not support.

Sound Level

The sound level of commercials should not appear to exceed that of the surrounding program.

Sponsor Identification

Identification of sponsorship shall be made in all commercials and programs in accordance with the requirements of the Communications Act, the rules and policies of the Federal Communications Commission and with the NBC Compliance and Practices Manual.

Time Standards for Advertising

In order to maintain the quality, audience appeal and integrity of programs presented on the NBC Television Network, NBC shall apply the following Standards to the amount, format and scheduling of non-program material.

1. Definition of Non-Program Material

Non-program material includes commercials; station breaks; promotional announcements; sponsor billboards; announcements that must be logged as commercial matter pursuant to FCC regulations and the NBC Compliance and Practices Manual; and show credits which exceed the allocations specified on pages 8 - 10 of the General Entertainment Program Standards.

The following shall not be considered non-program material:

   a. public service announcements

   b. paid political announcements not in excess of four minutes per hour during a limited number of broadcast hours

   c. credits for theatrical films, opening program titles, episode titles, starring and co-starring credits

   d. audio or "voice over" promotional announcements which are presented simultaneously over show credits and do not exceed 30 seconds in length

   e. announcements regarding the scheduling of special news programs

   f. scheduling information contained in programs of indeterminate length regarding an immediately upcoming program whose regular broadcast time has been affected

   g. certain prize-related announcements broadcast as part of a game, contest or award program or program element

   i. station call letter and network identification

2. Time Limitations for Non-Program Material

    a. Prime Time

        For purposes of these Non-Program Material Time
        Limitation standards, Prime Time is defined as a
        consecutive three hour period designated by NBC
        between the hours of 6:00 PM and 11:00 PM.

        Non-program material in Prime Time entertainment
        programs will not exceed 10 minutes per hour.

        Non-program material in Prime Time sports programs
        shall not exceed 16 minutes per hour.

    b. All Other Time Periods

        Non-program material in programs not scheduled
        during Prime Time shall not exceed 16 minutes per
        hour.

    c. Special Promotional Material

        NBC may, in its discretion, from time to time vary
        the Prime Time and Other Time Periods Standards to
        accommodate promotional material for special
        programming.

    d. Children's Programs

        For purposes of these Standards, children's
        programming is defined as those programs initially
        designed primarily for children 12 years of age
        and under.

        Notwithstanding the Non-Program Material Time
        Limitations set forth in a and b above, in no
        event shall the "commercial matter" (any
        advertising message or announcement for which a
        charge is made or consideration received) in
        children's programs exceed:

        (1) 9 1/2 minutes per hour during weekend and
            Prime Time children's programs and

        (2) 12 minutes per hour during weekday,
            non-Prime Time children's programs.

Fractional periods of less than one hour will be pro-rated on the basis of one hour.

3. Unit of Sale

    The NBC Television Network makes sponsorship opportunities available in units of not less than 30 seconds in length for the advertising of a sponsor's product or service (except for advertisements placed in "news capsules").

4. Multiple Product Advertisements

    The NBC Television Network will not accept a single commercial which advertises more than one product or service unless:

    a. the participation purchased is at least 60 seconds in length and contains no more than two announcements;

    b. the commercial presents the products or services of a single advertiser which have a related or common purpose and use, and such products or services are portrayed in a unified and integrated manner and setting; or

    c. the commercial is less than 60 seconds in length, but presents the products or services of a primary and secondary advertiser. The time devoted to the product or service of the secondary advertiser may not exceed one-sixth of the total time of the commercial.

Visual Supers

When superimposed copy is essential to qualify claims, it must be presented so it can be read easily against a plain, contrasting background, held sufficiently long and be large enough to meet NBC technical specifications (available on request).

Unacceptable Commercial Presentations, Approaches and Techniques

NBC does not accept in advertising:

1. Claims or representations, direct or implied, which are false or have the tendency to deceive, mislead or misrepresent.

2. Unqualified references to the safety of a product, if package, label or insert contains a caution or the normal use of the product presents a possible hazard.

3. Appeals to help fictitious characters in supposed distress by purchasing a product or service or sending for a premium.

4. "Bait and switch" tactics which feature goods or services not intended for sale but designed to lure the public into purchasing higher priced substitutes.

5. The use of "subliminal perception" or other techniques attempting to convey information to viewer by transmitting messages below the threshold of normal awareness.

6. Unacceptable products or services promoted through advertising devoted to an acceptable product.

7. The misuse of distress signals.

8. Disrespectful use of the flag, national emblems, anthems and monuments.

9. Direct or implied use of the office of the President of the United States or any governmental body without official approval.

10. Newsroom settings and techniques.

11. Sensational headline announcements in advertising of publications prior to the identification of sponsor.

12. Scare approaches and presentations with the capacity to induce fear.

13. Interpersonal acts of violence and antisocial behavior or other dramatic devices inconsistent with prevailing standards of taste and propriety.

14.   Damaging stereotyping.

15.   Unsupported or exaggerated promises of employment or earnings.

16.   Presentations for professional services which do not comply with applicable law or ethical codes.

Unacceptable Commercial Classifications

1.   Cigarettes.

2.   Hard liquor.

3.   Firearms, fireworks, ammunition and other weapons.

4.   Presentations promoting a belief in the efficacy of fortune telling, astrology, phrenology, palm reading, numerology, mind reading, character reading or other occult pursuits.

5.   Tip sheets and race track publications seeking to advertise for the purpose of giving odds or promoting betting. See Lotteries, page 27.

6.   The sale of franchises.

7.   Matrimonial, escort or dating services.

8.   Contraceptives.

9.   "Adult" or Sex Magazines.

10.   X-rated Movies.

11.   Abortion Services.

12.   Ethical Drugs.

13.   Anti-Law Enforcement Devices.

Advertising Contests

Any advertiser supplied contest furnished to NBC for proposed broadcast must be initially reviewed to insure that it is not a lottery, that the material terms are clearly stated, and that it is being conducted fairly, honestly and according to its rules.

1. Contest information is further reviewed to make certain that:

    a. The security arrangements are adequate to prevent "rigging".

    b. The terms, conditions and requirements under which contestants compete for prizes are clearly stated in the "Rules" so that there is no reasonable opportunity for any misunderstanding.

    c. The value, nature and extent of the prizes is clear.

    d. The public interest will not be adversely affected.

    e. The contest meets with Federal, state and local laws.

2. Complete details and continuity must be submitted to the Broadcast Standards Department at least ten business days prior to the first public announcement of the contest.

3. All broadcast copy regarding contests must contain clear and complete information regarding:

    a. Complete contest rules or when and how they may be obtained by the public.

    b. The availability of entry forms and how to enter, including alternate means of entry where appropriate.

    c. The termination date of the contest.

    d. Any restrictions or eligibility requirements.

    e. The Prize suppliers, when applicable.

    f. For chance contests, the necessary language:

        No Purchase Necessary

        Void Where Prohibited

    g. For skill contests, judging criteria must be stated.

4. A complete copy of the rules, the entry blank, a completed NBC Compliance and Practices Questionnaire, promotional material and/or any published information (e.g., newspaper advertisements) about the contest should be included with the broadcast copy.

5. All contest rules must be complete and contain:

   a. Eligibility requirements.

   b. Restrictions as to the number of entries made by an individual.

   c. The nature, extent and value of the prizes.

   d. Where, when and how entries are submitted.

   e. The basis on which prizes will be awarded.

   f. The termination date of the contest.

   g. When and how winners will be selected, including tie breaking procedures, when necessary.

   h. How winners will be notified.

   i. Time limits to claim or use prizes, if any.

   j. Restrictions as to the number of times an individual can win.

   k. Reference to "participating dealers" if not all outlets are involved.

Beer and Wine

Advertising of beer and wine is acceptable subject to federal, state and local laws and the requirements of the NBC Alcohol Products Advertising Guidelines.

Children

1. Commercial messages placed within children's programs or in station breaks between consecutive programs designed specifically for children, advertising of products designed primarily for children and advertising or other messages designed primarily for children are subject to all applicable provisions of NBC's Children's Advertising Guidelines.

2. Within programs designed primarily for children 12 years of age or under, appropriate separator devices shall be used to clearly delineate the program material from commercial material.

3. Advertising concerning health and related matters which are more appropriately the responsibility of physicians and other adults shall not be primarily directed to children.

4. Commercial messages shall not be presented by a children's program personality, host or character, whether live or animated, within or adjacent to the programs in which such personality, host or character regularly appears.

5. Taking into account the age of the actors appearing within a commercial as well as the composition of the audience it is likely to reach, advertising approaches and techniques shall not disregard accepted safety precautions.

Door-to-Door Sales Representatives and In-Home Selling

All such advertising must be in accordance with applicable federal, state and local laws and shall be reviewed with special care. The reputation and reliability of the sponsor and the supervision exercised by the advertiser over its sales representatives, are important considerations. Each proposed commercial is evaluated on a case-by-case basis to insure its acceptability.

In general, advertising recruiting door-to-door representatives primarily for the sale of medical products and services having direct health considerations is not acceptable.

Employment Agencies

Reputable concerns are considered on a case-by-case basis and subject to exercise of care in order to avoid over-promising results.

Funeral Homes

The advertising of funeral services and mortuaries requires restrained presentation.

Health Related Product Advertising

All advertisements for health related products shall comply with the NBC Health Care Products Advertising Guidelines.

1. Ethical Drugs

NBC does not accept advertising for ethical drugs. Institutional advertising for pharmaceutical manufacturers, industry associations, and other responsible sponsors is considered on a case-by-case basis.

2. Proprietary Products (Over-the-Counter Medications)

The advertising of proprietary products presents important considerations to the health of consumers. The following principles and procedures govern the acceptability of such advertising on NBC facilities:

   a. The advertiser must give assurance that the advertising for the proprietary product complies with all applicable governmental rules and regulations;

   b. Advertising for proprietary products is accepted only after relevant data, including adequate substantiation regarding both product efficacy and any particular claims asserted, have been submitted to Broadcast Standards for examination and appraisal;

   c. NBC does not accept advertising for products used in the treatment of conditions known to be chronic or irremediable or for conditions in which self-diagnosis or self-medication might present an element of danger unless:

      1. They can be self-administered without the order and supervision of a physician;

      2. They carry on their labels the cautions required by the Federal Food, Drug and Cosmetic Act of 1939; and

      3. Appropriate cautionary references are included in the advertising proposed for broadcast;

d. No claims must be made or implied that the product
   is a panacea or alone will effect a cure;

e. Words such as "safe," "without risk," "harmless,"
   or terms of similar meaning may not be used in an
   unqualified manner;

f. Advertising appeals may not be made to children
   for such products.

3. Statements from the Medical Profession

Physicians, dentists or nurses, or actors
representing them, may not be employed directly or by
implication in any commercial for proprietary products or
other products involving health considerations.
Advertisements of an institutional nature which are not
intended to sell specific products or services to the
consumer, public service announcements by non-profit
organizations, as well as presentations for professional
services, may be presented by physicians, dentists or nurses,
subject to prior approval by Broadcast Standards.

Investments

Advertising of the services of financial institutions
must be consistent with all applicable federal, state and
local laws and regulations. The mention of specific
securities in commercials requires the prior approval of the
Law as well as Broadcast Standards Department.

Legalized Lotteries and Gambling

The lawful advertising of government organizations
that conduct legalized lotteries is acceptable provided such
advertising does not unduly exhort the public to bet.

The advertising of private or governmental
organizations that conduct legalized betting on sporting
contests is acceptable provided it is not instructional in
nature and is limited to institutional type announcements that
do not unduly exhort the audience to bet.

Acceptable advertisements for legalized lotteries or
betting shall comply with the NBC Guidelines on Gambling,
Betting, Lotteries and Games of Chance.

"Personal" Products

Advertising for "personal" products, when accepted, must be presented in a restrained and tasteful manner and comply with the NBC Personal Products Advertising Guidelines.

Premiums and Offers

1. Full details and continuity including "build-up copy," and a sample of the premium or offer, must be submitted to Broadcast Standards well in advance of commitment.

2. The termination date of any offer should be announced as far in advance as possible. Such announcement will include the statement that responses postmarked not later than midnight of the business day following withdrawal of the offer shall be honored.

3. All audience responses to premiums, offers or contests made by advertisers must be sent to a stated Post Office box or to an outside address arranged for by the advertiser.

4. As to the Premium Merchandise offered:

   a. A premium or offer may not be harmful to person or property.

   b. The lesser of one half the total time or 20 seconds in a self-contained portion of any commercial message may deal with the premium scheduled in a Children's program. Such premiums and offers will be subject to all other applicable Premium and Toy advertising requirements of the NBC Children's Advertising Guidelines.

   c. Descriptions or visual representations of premiums or offers may not enlarge their value or otherwise be misleading.

   d. The advertiser must provide NBC with written assurance that it will honor any request for return of money based on dissatisfaction with premiums or offers and that a sufficient supply of the premium or offer is readily available so as to avoid audience ill-will caused by delivery delay or impossibility of delivery.

5. The advertiser will hold NBC and its affiliated stations harmless from any liability which may arise in connection with any premium or offer.

6. The premium or offer may not appeal to superstition on the basis of "luck-bearing" powers or otherwise.

7. Mail order offers should indicate any additional postage/handling charges, as well as expected delivery time.

Testimonial Policy

The following seven point provision constitutes NBC policy relating to testimonials included in advertising of products, services or organizations.

1. Testimonials used, in whole or in part, must honestly reflect in spirit and content the sentiments of the individuals represented.

2. All claims and statements in a testimonial, including subjective evaluations of testifiers, must be supportable by facts and free of misleading implication. They shall contain no statement that cannot be supported if presented in the advertiser's own words.

3. Advertisers are required to disclose any connection between the advertiser and the endorser that might materially affect the weight or credibility of the endorsement.

4. In the event a consumer endorsement does not fairly reflect what a substantial proportion of other consumers are likely to experience, the advertising must clearly disclose this fact.

5. Expert endorsements are permitted only as long as the endorser continues to hold those views.

6. The laws of certain states require written consent of individuals for the use of their names. The advertiser must submit to NBC, in writing, confirmation of such consent or a blanket release assuming full responsibility for obtaining such consent for each testimonial covering its period of use on NBC facilities.

7. NBC staff employees may not give personal testimonials.

Public Service Announcements

The following guidelines are designed to assure that public service announcement time on NBC is used as effectively as possible.

1. All public service announcements proposed for network use apply to a nationwide audience.

2. The sponsoring organization must be national and devoted to public service or charitable activities. Announcements must pertain solely to public service or charitable causes and may not promote directly or indirectly the sale of commercial products or services or deal with sectarian, politically partisan or controversial subjects or issues, nor be designed to influence legislation or other government action.

3. Public service time for fund or membership solicitation is given only to demonstrably responsible organizations. In assessing the qualifications of sponsoring organizations, NBC may consult the Advertising Council, the National Information Bureau or comparable agencies for their evaluations and recommendations.

4. Public service announcements must deal affirmatively with the causes they advocate. Announcements that attack or demean other persons, organizations or causes are not acceptable.

5. The final judgment concerning acceptability and scheduling of public service messages rests solely with NBC.

6. All appeals and solicitations for charities and other non-profit organizations on NBC television facilities must have prior approval of the Broadcast Standards Department.

NBC Broadcast Standards for Television

Advertising Guidelines

NBC BROADCAST STANDARDS FOR TELEVISION

NBC CHILDREN'S ADVERTISING GUIDELINES

I. Introduction and Application

Inasmuch as children are this nation's greatest natural resource and in view of their still developing cognitive and perceptive abilities, NBC recognizes a special responsibility to protect them from unfair exploitation. Accordingly, the following special guidelines have been promulgated to assist advertisers and their agencies in the preparation of commercials:

a) for products primarily used by children; or,

b) which are broadcast in or adjacent to children's programs; or,

c) which are designed for or have the effect of primarily appealing to children.

II. Guidelines - General

Although not specifically reiterated herein, all NBC policies governing truthfulness and accuracy of claims and representations, and documentation therefor, apply to children's advertising. Our general children's advertising guidelines include the following:

1. Commercials may not overglamorize, distort or exaggerate the characteristics or functions of a product or service.

2. As a general matter, exhortative language is not acceptable. Children shall not be directed to purchase or ask a parent or other person to purchase a product or service.

3. Approaches which have the tendency to irritate, confuse or overglamorize, are unacceptable.

4. Commercials which portray attitude and behavior inconsistent with generally accepted social values and customs are unacceptable.

5. Advertising approaches which promote a product or service on the basis of peer pressure are unacceptable.

6.   Commercials which are frightening or provoke anxiety, or which contain realistic war settings or depictions of violent, dangerous or anti-social behavior, are unacceptable.

7.   Commercials generally, as well as specific depictions therein, shall conform to recognized safety standards.

8.   Personal testimonials or endorsements by real-life authority or celebrity figures, are not acceptable.

9.   Non-prescription medications and supplemental vitamin products may not be advertised in or adjacent to children's programs.

10.   Potentially misleading simplifications such as the use of "only" or "just" with regard to price, are unacceptable.

11.   When additional items such as batteries, computer programs and the like must be purchased for proper operation of the advertised product, this fact must be clearly disclosed in the audio portion of the commercial.

12.   Since competitive or superiority claims or techniques can create dissatisfaction in a youngster's mind, such claims are generally unacceptable. Notwithstanding this prohibition, NBC will, on a case-by-case basis, consider acceptance of such claims when they relate to health, safety or other pro-social characteristics of a product or service.

13.   Where applicable, a product's method of operation and source of power must be clearly disclosed.

14.   Where applicable, advertising must disclose aurally when a product requires partial or full assembly.

15.   Where disclosures are required under these guidelines, simplified language, understandable by the audience to which the advertising is primarily addressed, is strongly encouraged (e.g., "You have to put it together"). When audio disclosures are required hereunder, the advertiser is encouraged to include an accompanying video disclosure as well.

III.   Toys

    The following additional guidelines apply specifically to advertising for toys or advertising designed for children which emphasizes a product's play value.

1.   Any view, demonstration, or play environment depicted must be limited to that which a child is reasonably capable of reproducing.

2.   The use of stock film footage, real-life counterparts of toys, fantasy and animation are acceptable only if: (a) they are confined to the first one-third of the commercial, and (b) no child appears within them.

3.   The primary advertised product must be clearly disclosed in the body of the commercial. There shall not be any implication that optional extras, additional units or items that are not available with the toy, accompany the toy's original purchase.

In the closing four to five seconds of the commercial the original purchase must be disclosed by video with audio disclosure where necessary for clarification.

4.   Advertising shall not employ costumes and props which are not available with the toy as sold or are not reasonably accessible to the child without additional cost.

5.   As a general matter, the number of items shown in a play situation should not exceed two per child or a maximum of six per commercial. Notwithstanding the foregoing the depiction of a greater number of items will be considered by NBC if such can be reasonably supported by the advertiser, taking into consideration the nature of the items, their cost, and the overall execution of the commercial.

IV.   Children's Premiums and Offers

The following additional guidelines shall apply to children's premiums and offers:

1.   The amount of time devoted to a premium or offer shall be a continuous segment and shall not exceed one-half of the commercial. The segment may not contain stock footage, real-life counterparts, fantasy or animation.

If the lead-in to the premium or offer segment contains no sell copy for the premium, the product spokesperson may deliver the lead-in, and the voice-over as well.

2.   The premium/offer shall be clearly depicted in a still visual presentation.

3.   Comparative, exclusivity or superiority claims are not permitted.

4.   Except when directed toward a pro-social or public service objective, exhortative language is not acceptable.

5.   Disclosure of essential information such as price, separate purchase nature, offer dates, etc., should be made in the audio portion of the announcement and if deemed appropriate, simultaneous disclosure in the video will be required.

6.   Conditions attached to "Free" premiums or offers must be clearly disclosed simultaneously in the audio and video. In the video, the word "Free" must not be larger than any other conditions disclosed.

7.   A reasonable number of items may be shown per child.

8.   Prior to production of the commercial, a sample of the premium or offer, with instructions, should be submitted for review. The sample should be accompanied by details of the promotion, including air dates, promotion dates, number of participating outlets, and any conditions attached to obtaining the premium or offer.

V.   Food

        The following additional guidelines shall apply to food advertising directed to children:

1.   Advertisements for foods shall be in accord with the commonly accepted principles of good eating and seek to establish the proper role of the product within the framework of a balanced regimen. Any representation of the relationship between a food and energy must be documented and accurately depicted.

2.   Each commercial for breakfast-type products shall include at least one audio and one video depiction of a balanced meal.

3.   Special, enriched foods designed to serve as a substitute for a meal may be advertised as such provided their purpose and nutritional value are featured in the advertising and supported by adequate documentation.

4.   When ingredients are referenced they shall be accurately represented.

5.   Commercials for foods shall not, directly or by implication, suggest or recommend indiscriminate or immoderate use or consumption.

VI.   Feature Film "Trailers"

As a general matter only "G"-rated feature films or films otherwise suited for a general family audience may be advertised in or adjacent to children's programs.

VII.   Sweepstakes

1.   All prizes must be appropriate for the audience to which the advertising is primarily addressed.

2.   All NBC guidelines relative to the advertising of contests are applicable.

VIII.   Adult Oriented Commercials

1.   Advertising of products or services covered by NBC's Children's Advertising Guidelines will be exempted on a case-by-case basis from the application of the Guidelines provided:

> a)   The commercial, on the overall, is clearly designed to appeal to adults; and,
>
> b)   The commercial is not scheduled in or adjacent to children's programs.

2.   The advertising of any product designed primarily for use by adults shall be reviewed on a case-by-case basis to determine acceptability for telecast in or adjacent to programs designed primarily for children, taking into account safety and similar considerations.

NBC HEALTH CARE PRODUCTS ADVERTISING GUIDELINES

Inasmuch as self-medication is a normal facet of everyday living, the following guidelines are promulgated to assist advertisers in the preparation of responsible health care product advertising which is factually accurate and useful to the consumer.

1. Advertising of products which require a physician's prescription is unacceptable.

2. Non-prescription medications and supplemental vitamin products are not acceptable for advertising in or adjacent to children's programs.

3.   a) Commercials for health care products shall not directly or by implication include health professionals such as physicians, dentists, nurses, pharmacists, therapists, their aides or assistants or actors representing such professionals.

        b) Laboratory settings may be utilized to dramatize research which has been conducted for a product or service provided that any laboratory technician so depicted is properly identified as such.

        c) Institutional and public service announcements as well as advertising on behalf of health professionals may include appearances or portrayals of such professionals provided the advertising is not inconsistent with applicable state law and/or NBC policy.

4. All claims of product effectiveness must be supported to NBC's satisfaction by clinical testing, properly represented consumer testing, responsible medical opinion, or other scientific evidence.

5. All commercials must clearly advise consumers to follow label directions.

6. The use of the word "safe" without appropriate qualification is unacceptable.

7. All claims and demonstrations must be consistent with a product's normal capabilities including the limitations and directions for product use indicated on labeling.

8.　Except with respect to incidental background appearances, children may not be utilized in advertisements for adult medications.　Children may be utilized in advertisments for children's medications.　In such announcements use of medication by a child may be depicted only under strict adult supervision.

9.　Commercials for over-the-counter medications shall only promote their occasional use and treatment of minor to moderate conditions.

10.　Commercials which portray directly or by implication dependence upon medication or alteration of mood as a result of medication, are unacceptable.

11.　Portrayal of immediate relief and before/after situations shall be confined to those circumstances which are supported by clinical documentation.

12.　Commercial approaches or techniques associated with illegal drugs or the abuse of legal medications are unacceptable.　Use of the terms "non-habit forming" or "nonaddictive," are unacceptable.

13.　Authority figures may not offer personal testimonial opinion.

14.　Ingestion of medications shall not be visually depicted.

15.　Direct or indirect references to or comparisons with prescription medications which have the effect of equating strength or effectiveness of the advertised product with a prescription medication are unacceptable.　Notwithstanding the foregoing, for a period of six (6) months after a prescription medication becomes available for sale over-the-counter, advertising may reference such fact.

16.　Demonstrations and other portrayals of conditions requiring medication shall be handled tastefully.

NBC PERSONAL PRODUCTS ADVERTISING GUIDELINES

I.   General

A.   Application: These guidelines apply to products and
services of a personal nature such as but not limited
to: catamenial devices, panty shields, douche products,
genital deodorants and irritation medications, deodorants, mouth washes, bathroom tissues and related products, personal nonprescription medications, enema products, menses-related medications, incontinence products,
laxatives, hemorrhoid products, pregnancy test kits and
undergarments.

B.   Scheduling: As a general matter personal products
may be scheduled only on weekdays from 9 AM to 4 PM and
after 10 PM local time, and on weekends after 10 PM local
time (except in the central time zone where applicable
hours are weekdays from 8 AM to 3 PM and after 9 PM, and
on weekends after 9 PM). Products presently subject to
the foregoing time restrictions are: catamenial devices,
panty shields, cosmetic douches, medicated douches, feminine itch products, genital deodorants, menses-related
medications, enema products, incontinence products and
pregnancy test kits. NBC may exempt certain adult-
oriented programs from the foregoing scheduling restrictions.

C.   Standard of Review: Personal Product advertising
will be reviewed in accordance with stringent standards
of taste taking into account the composition of the audience. Use of children will be considered only on a
case-by-case basis.

II.   Product Categories

A.   Catamenial devices, panty shields, cosmetic douche
      products

1.   Graphic audio and video depictions of absorbency,
cleanliness, anatomy, insertion, application, or duration
of efficacy, are not acceptable.

2.   Straight-forward statements of grooming, freshness,
and femininity, as well as descriptions of product features such as packaging, disposability, pre-mixing, etc.,
are acceptable.

3.   Use of mixed social situations are limited to incidental appearances.

4.   Advertisements for cosmetic douche products will include "use only as directed" or "follow label directions." These products may not be promoted for health reasons.

B.   Personal Care and Grooming Products

1.   Genital Deodorants

a)   Representations of product fragrance are not acceptable.

b)   Generalized statements of product efficacy ("lasts," "helps you feel fresh for hours") are acceptable.

c)   Claims equating the product with maintaining cleanliness, health or hygiene are not acceptable.

2.   General Body Odor, Mouth Odor, Underarm Deodorant Products

Representations of odor problems and application demonstrations will be presented in a restrained and inoffensive manner. Axilla demonstrations of product use are not acceptable. Representations of odor problems or wetness are not acceptable.

3.   Bathroom Tissue and Related Products

Direct or indirect references to product use and function or mention of specific areas of the anatomy are not acceptable.

C   Personal Non-Prescription Medications

1.   General

a)   NBC's Health Products Advertising Guidelines are applicable to internally administered products.

b)   Sound health practices such as urging the audience to seek a physician's diagnosis are encouraged.

2.   Menses-Related Medications

   Representations equating edema or general swelling
   to other than menses-related causes are not acceptable.

3.   Laxatives/Binders/Hemorrhoid Products

   a)   Graphic representations of symptoms, relief or
         product mechanics are not acceptable.

   b)   Advertising may only represent products for
         "occasional use" and must include advice to
         "use only as directed."

4.   Male Groin Irritation Products

   a)   Use of graphic language such as the term "jock
         itch," will be minimized.

   b)   Advertisements containing the term "jock itch"
         are limited to scheduling after 11 PM (Eastern
         Standard Time) or in sports programs.

5.   Medicated Douches/Feminine Itch Products

   a)   Advertising may promote health-related claims.

   b)   Advertisements will include the caution "if
         symptoms persist, see your doctor."

   c)   Any product designed for external feminine
         itch must so state by audio or video.

   d)   The terms "itch and irritation" will be mini-
         mized.

D.   <u>Male and Female Undergarments-Adult and Children</u>
      <u>(Baby Products Excluded)</u>

1.   The use of live models wearing only undergarments is
not acceptable except incidentally on packaging that does
not exceed one-third of the screen.

2.   The use of mannequins should not create an impression that a live unclad model is being depicted.

3.   In advertisements for children's undergarments, live
models wearing only undergarments may be utilized provided the child model appears to be pre-pubescent.

4.   The NBC Weight Reduction and Control Guidelines are applicable to those products which promote weight control.

E.   Incontinence Products

1.   The display of incontinence products is allowed if tastefully presented. Live models are not acceptable.

2.   Demonstrations of the absorption capabilities may not involve the pouring of actual fluids.

3.   Advertisements will include the caution "if symptoms persist, see your doctor."

4.   Inasmuch as incontinence is a condition which affects persons of both sexes and all ages, advertising may not state or imply that the condition is peculiar to a particular segment of the population.

F.   Pregnancy Test Kits

Advertisements shall include an audio and video disclaimer reminding viewers (a) to use the products exactly as directed and (b) to follow recommendations for seeing their doctors.

NBC ALCOHOL PRODUCTS ADVERTISING GUIDELINES

1.   The advertising of distilled spirits and products made with or derived from distilled spirits is not acceptable.

2.   The advertising of beer, malt and wine products (up to 24% alcohol content) is acceptable only when portrayed in good taste, consistent with applicable Federal and local laws and in conformance with the NBC Alcohol Products Advertising Guidelines.

3.   Advertising hereunder is acceptable only when portrayed in a manner which does not encourage or sanction product abuse or misuse.

4.   The use of alcoholic beverages or products shall not be portrayed as being necessary to maintain social status, obtain personal achievements, relieve stress or as a solution to personal problems.

5.   Advertising shall not be addressed to, portray, or encourage use of alcoholic products by persons who are, or appear to be, below the legal drinking age.

6.   Alcoholic products shall not be advertised as similar to or equated with non-alcoholic products, e.g., soda, fruit drinks, etc., which have particular appeal to adolescents or persons below the legal drinking age.

7.   The use of alcoholic beverages or products shall not be promoted as a "mark of adulthood" or "rite of passage".

8.   Advertising will conform to recognized safety standards. Use of alcoholic beverages or products will not be represented before or during any activity requiring alertness, dexterity and/or sober judgment. Advertising which states, suggests or implies that autos, motorcycles or other vehicles can be safely operated in conjunction with alcoholic beverages is unacceptable.

9.   On-camera consumption may not be represented or implied. Depiction or implication of excessive consumption is not acceptable.

10. Statements, references or representations of alcoholic products as "extra strength", are unacceptable.

Rev. 8/84

11. Products shall not be promoted for the intoxicating effect which may be achieved by their alcohol content.

12. Advertising hereunder shall not portray excessive drinking or pronounced loss of inhibitions.

13. Advertising shall not suggest or imply that intoxication, excessive drinking, or loss of control or inhibitions, is a proper subject of humor.

14. Advertising shall not depict the use of alcohol as the sole purpose of any activity.

15. Advertisers are required to comply with all applicable federal, state and municipal laws and regulations concerning the advertising of alcoholic beverages. Disclosure of the name and address of the beverage producer will be mandatory in all cases. The corporate name of a distiller/distributor may only be used when required by law for purposes of identification or when it is part of the brand name of an acceptable product. It shall be the responsibility of the advertiser to ensure compliance with all legal requirements.

16. Advertising by retail liquor outlets for beer and/or wine products is acceptable provided there is no aural or visual reference to products otherwise unacceptable under these guidelines.

17. Advertising for establishments and other businesses which primarily offer non-alcoholic products and services, e.g., restaurants and airlines, may make limited and incidental references to the availability of "cocktails."

18. Advertising of drinks mixed with distilled spirits or references to them are not acceptable.

19. Products which may be used with distilled spirits are acceptable providing there is no direct or implied reference to distilled spirits or the names of drinks associated with them. For example, references to "Bloody Mary," "Martini," "Screwdriver," etc., are not acceptable.

20. Glassware and other props normally associated with distilled spirits or specific hard liquor drinks are not acceptable except in connection with the limited and incidental references permitted under Guideline 17 above.

21. Advertisements that present messages which alert the public to the dangers of alcohol abuse will be reviewed on a case-by-case basis.

NBC GUIDELINES FOR ADVERTISING RELATED TO THE CONTROL OF SERUM CHOLESTEROL

Serum cholesterol levels are affected by various physiological, genetic, environmental and dietary factors. Specific dietary factors which influence reduction of serum cholesterol levels are decreased consumption of total fat, saturated fat, and cholesterol; and increased polyunsaturated fat intake.

Given the variability of these factors and the complexity of the relationship between serum cholesterol and coronary heart disease, the following guidelines have been promulgated to insure that commercials which make direct or indirect reference to fats or cholesterol do not mislead, place undue emphasis on one or more of the wide variety of factors enumerated above, or oversimplify a complex health problem:

1.   Straight-forward, non-health related references to fat or cholesterol as product attributes may be included in advertising subject to appropriate claims documentation.

2.   Cholesterol references must be unambiguous so that there is no confusion between serum cholesterol (that which is in the blood) and dietary cholesterol (that which is present in foods).

3.   References to dietary cholesterol or fats which distort their importance are unacceptable.

4.   References to the amount of cholesterol or fats present in or absent from foods, and references to the effect of these substances on serum cholesterol levels shall neither exaggerate nor distort their importance.

5.   References to valid clinical studies shall accurately state the purpose and scope of the study and the results thereof.

6.   Claims that consumption or avoidance of an individual food or component will reduce serum cholesterol, or that an individual food is important or more important than other components in a diet, are unacceptable.

7.   Claims that a fat or cholesterol restricted diet can provide a health benefit beyond helping to reduce serum cholesterol, are unacceptable.

8.   Specific health benefit claims such as longevity, avoidance of coronary heart disease, etc., are unacceptable.

9.   References to coronary heart disease can be made only when related to the three major risk factors: cigarette smoking, high blood pressure and elevated serum cholesterol.

10.   Advertising may not create the impression that only one segment of the population need be aware of cholesterol restricted diets and related issues.

11.   Advertising approaches which tend to play upon anxieties and potential fears of consumers are unacceptable.

NBC WEIGHT REDUCTION AND CONTROL GUIDELINES

1.   Advertising relating to weight reduction for the obese and those excessively overweight is unacceptable since such conditions commonly derive from a variety of causes that may require medical treatment.

2.   As a general matter, effective weight loss for persons who are moderately overweight will result from regular exercise and reduced caloric intake. Advertising for weight reduction products and services should thus avoid implications that:

    a)   a product in itself can cause weight loss without cutting caloric intake; or

    b)   one's appetite will be completely satisfied.

3.   Since weight is a highly individual problem subject to many variables which affect a person's ability to lose weight, advertising should avoid:

    a)   representations of losing a specific number of pounds;

    b)   representations of "before" and "after";

    c)   representations of reducing specific areas of the anatomy independent of a general weight loss unless substantiated by competent medical authority and/or appropriate clinical data; or

    d)   references that dieting is easy or that weight loss can be quickly achieved.

4.   Commercial copy should make no claims directly, or by implication, that weight loss is permanent.

5.   Weight loss may not be attributed to low calorie foods except as a part of a calorie restricted diet plan.

6.   Advertisers should avoid representations that ridicule overweight persons or depict them as social outcasts.

7.   Products or services making claims for weight reduction for pre-adolescent children are unacceptable.

8.   Claims that vitamins, minerals or laxatives will aid in bringing about weight loss are unacceptable.

9.   The comparison of an over-the-counter product with the efficacy of a prescription product may not be made.

10. Testimonials are acceptable provided they meet NBC's Testimonial Guidelines and do not make claims otherwise disallowed hereunder for weight reduction products.

11. All guarantees must conform to NBC policy and applicable law. Claims of guaranteed weight loss may not be made.

12. The preceding guidelines also apply to commercials for health spas, salons and trimming devices as well as commercials for weight gain products and services. In such commercials, excessive weight loss may not be attributed to exercise and use of machines alone without referencing the need for a low calorie diet plan.

NBC GUIDELINES ON GAMBLING, BETTING, LOTTERIES AND GAMES OF CHANCE

The following guidelines apply to lawfully licensed betting, gambling, lottery and other games of chance activities advertised over NBC facilities:

1.   Commercials for any publication, "tip sheet," electronic, or mechanical device whose primary purpose is the giving of odds or promotion of betting, are unacceptable for use on NBC broadcast facilities.

2.   The lawful advertising of governmental organizations that conduct legalized lotteries is acceptable provided such advertising does not unduly exhort the public to bet. The advertising of private or governmental organizations that conduct legalized betting on sporting contests is acceptable provided it is not instructional in nature and is limited to announcements that do not unduly exhort the audience to bet.

3.   Advertising permitted under these guidelines:

   a)   shall not mislead nor exaggerate one's likelihood of winning money or other prizes;

   b)   shall not present fictitious winners or winnings nor misrepresent actual winners or winnings;

   c)   shall not state nor imply praise for those who participate in the advertised activity or denigrate those who abstain.

4.   Advertising for hotels and resorts which have casino facilities is acceptable provided that the advertising complies with applicable laws. Notwithstanding the foregoing, no such advertising may depict or promote gambling activities nor may the word "casino" be included in the advertising except as part of the legal name of the hotel or resort, e.g., "Acme Resort Hotel and Casino."

5.   Products, games of chance, contests and advertising approaches not specifically referred to in the foregoing shall be reviewed on a case-by-case basis pursuant to the policies set forth in both NBC's Compliance and Practices and Broadcast Standards for Television manuals.

SELF-REGULATORY GUIDELINES
FOR CHILDREN'S ADVERTISING
Third Edition, 1983
Children's Advertising Review Unit
National Advertising Division
Council of Better Business Bureaus, Inc.

The Children's Advertising Guidelines have been in existence since 1972 when they were published by the Association of National Advertisers to encourage truthful and accurate advertising sensitive to the special nature of children. Subsequently, the advertising community established the Children's Advertising Review Unit to serve as an independent manager of the industry's self-regulatory programs. The Unit edited and republished the Children's Advertising Guidelines in 1975 and revised them in 1977.

This third edition has been edited by the Children's Advertising Review Unit to be sure the Guidelines are responsive to current conditions. The assistance of children's advertisers and their agencies has been invaluable, resulting in a clarification of individual Guidelines and an improved format.

Interpretation of the Guidelines

Because children's knowledge of the physical and social world is in the process of development, they are more limited than adults in the experience and skills required to evaluate advertising and to make purchase decisions. For these reasons, certain presentations and techniques which may be appropriate for adult-directed advertising may mislead children if used in child-directed advertising.

The function of the Guidelines is to delineate those areas that need particular attention to help avoid deceptive advertising messages to children. The intent is to help advertisers deal sensitively and honestly with children and is not meant to deprive them, or children, of the benefits of innovative advertising approaches.

The Guidelines have been kept general in the belief that responsible advertising comes in many forms and that diversity should be encouraged. The goal in all cases should be to fulfill the spirit as well as the letter of the Guidelines and the Principles on which they are based.

Scope of the Guidelines

The Guidelines apply to all advertising addressed to children under twelve years of age, including print, broadcast and cable television advertising. One section applies to adult-directed advertising only when a potential child-safety concern exists (see page 598, *Safety*).

Principles

Five basic Principles underlie these Guidelines for advertising directed to children:

1. Advertisers should always take into account the level of knowledge, sophistication and maturity of the audience to which their message is primarily directed. Younger children have a limited capability for evaluating the credibility of what they watch. Advertisers, therefore, have a special responsibility to protect children from their own susceptibilities.
2. Realizing that children are imaginative and that make-believe play constitutes an important part of the growing up process, advertisers should exercise care not to

(*Source*: Self-Regulatory Guidelines for Children's Advertising, *Third Edition, 1983. Children's Advertising Review Unit, National Advertising Division, Council of Better Business Bureaus, Inc.*)

exploit that imaginative quality of children. Unreasonable expectations of product quality or performance should not be stimulated either directly or indirectly by advertising.

3. Recognizing that advertising may play an important part in educating the child, information should be communicated in a truthful and accurate manner with full recognition by the advertiser that the child may learn practices from advertising which can affect his or her health and well-being.

4. Advertisers are urged to capitalize on the potential of advertising to influence social behavior by developing advertising that, wherever possible, addresses itself to social standards generally regarded as positive and beneficial, such as friendship, kindness, honesty, justice, generosity and respect for others.

5. Although many influences affect a child's personal and social development, it remains the prime responsibility of the parents to provide guidance for children. Advertisers should contribute to this parent-child relationship in a constructive manner.

Product Presentations and Claims. Children look at, listen to and remember many different elements in advertising. Therefore, advertisers need to examine the total advertising message to be certain that the net communication will not mislead or misinform children.

1. *Copy, sound and visual presentations should not mislead children about product or performance characteristics.* Such characteristics may include, but are not limited to, size, speed, method of operation, color, sound, durability and nutritional benefits.

2. *The advertising presentation should not mislead children about perceived benefits from use of the product.* Such benefits may include, but are not limited to, the acquisition of strength, status, popularity, growth, proficiency and intelligence. Social stereotyping and appeals to prejudice should be avoided.

3. *Care should be taken not to exploit a child's imagination.* Fantasy, including animation, is appropriate for younger as well as older children. However, it should not create unattainable performance expectations nor exploit the younger child's difficulty in distinguishing between the real and the fanciful.

4. *The performance and use of a product should be demonstrated in a way that can be duplicated by the child for whom the product is intended.*

5. *Products should be shown used in safe environments and situations.*

6. *What is included and excluded in the initial purchase should be clearly established.*

7. *The amount of product featured should be within reasonable levels for the situation depicted.*

8. *Representation of food products should be made so as to encourage sound usage of the product with a view toward healthy development of the child and development of good nutritional practices.* Advertisements representing mealtime in the home should clearly and adequately depict the role of the product within the framework of a balanced diet.

9. *Portrayals of violence and presentations that could unduly frighten or provoke anxiety in children should be avoided.*

10. *Objective claims about product or performance characteristics should be supported by appropriate and adequate substantiation.*

Sales Pressure. Children are not as prepared as adults to make judicious, independent purchase decisions. Therefore, advertisers should avoid using extreme sales pressure in advertising presentations to children.

1. *Children should not be urged to ask parents or others to buy products.* Advertisements should not suggest that a parent or adult who purchases a product or service for a child is better, more intelligent or more generous than one who does not.

2. *Advertisements should not convey the impression that possession of a product will result in more acceptance of a child by his or her peers.* Conversely, lacking a product should not convey the impression that the child will be less accepted by his or her peers. Advertisements should not imply that purchase and use of a product will confer upon the user the prestige, skills or other special qualities of characters appearing in advertising. Benefits attributed to the product or service should be inherent in its use.
3. *All price representations should be clearly and concisely set forth.* Price minimizations such as "only" or "just" should not be used.

Disclosures and Disclaimers.   Children have a more limited vocabulary and less developed language skills than adolescents and adults. They read less well, if at all, and rely more on information presented pictorially than verbally. Studies have shown that simplified wording, such as "You have to put it together" instead of "Assembly required," significantly increases comprehension.

1. *All information which requires disclosure for legal or other reasons should be in language understandable by the child audience.* Disclaimers and disclosures should be clearly worded, legible and prominent. In television advertising, both audio and video disclosures are encouraged.
2. *Advertising for unassembled products should clearly indicate that they need to be put together to be used properly.*
3. *If any item essential to use of the product is not included, such as batteries, this fact must be disclosed clearly.*
4. *Information about products purchased separately, such as accessories or individual items in a collection, should be disclosed clearly to the child audience.*

Comparative Claims.   Advertising which compares the advertised product to another product may be difficult for young children to understand and evaluate. Comparative claims should be based on real product advantages that are understandable to the child audience.

1. *Comparative advertising should provide factual information.* Comparisons should not falsely represent other products or previous versions of the same product.
2. *Comparative claims should be presented in ways that children understand clearly.*
3. *Comparative claims should be supported by appropriate and adequate substantiation.*

Endorsements and Promotion by Program or Editorial Characters.   Studies have shown that the mere appearance of a character with a product can significantly alter a child's perception of the product depending on the child's opinion of the presenter. Advertising presentations by program/editorial characters may hamper a young child's ability to distinguish between program/editorial content and advertising.

1. *All personal endorsements should reflect the actual experiences and beliefs of the endorser.*
2. *An endorser represented, either directly or indirectly, as an expert must possess qualifications appropriate to the particular expertise depicted in the endorsement.*
3. *Program personalities, live or animated, should not promote products, premiums or services in or adjacent to programs primarily directed to children in which the same personality or character appears.*
4. *In print media primarily designed for children, a character or personality associated with the editorial content of a publication should not be used to promote products, premiums or services in the same publication.*

Premiums.   The use of premiums in advertising has the potential to enhance the appeal of a product to a child. Therefore, special attention should be paid to the advertising of premiums to guard against exploiting children's immaturity.

1.   *If product advertising contains a premium message, care should be taken that the child's attention is focused primarily on the product.* The premium message should be clearly secondary.
2.   *Conditions of a premium offer should be stated simply and clearly.* "Mandatory" statements and disclosures should be stated in terms that can be understood by the child audience.

Safety.   Imitation, exploration and experimentation are important activities to children. They are attracted to commercials in general and may imitate product demonstrations and other actions without regard to risk. Many childhood accidents and injuries occur in the home, often involving abuse or misuse of common household products.

1.   *Products inappropriate for use by children should not be advertised directly to children.* This is especially true for products labeled, "Keep out of the reach of children." Additionally, such products should not be promoted directly to children by premiums or other means. Medications, drugs and supplemental vitamins should not be advertised to children.
2.   *Advertisements for children's products should show them being used by children in the appropriate age range.* For instance, young children should not be shown playing with toys safe only for older children.
3.   *Adults should be shown supervising children when products or activities could involve an obvious safety risk.* For example, using an electrical appliance or playing in or near a swimming pool.
4.   *Advertisements should not portray adults or children in unsafe acts, situations or conditions or in acts harmful to others.* When athletic activities (such as skateboarding) are shown, proper safety equipment should be depicted.
5.   *Advertisements should avoid demonstrations that encourage dangerous or inappropriate use or misuse of the product.* This is particularly important when the demonstration can be easily reproduced by children and features products accessible to them.

The Children's Advertising Review Unit

The Children's Advertising Review Unit of the National Advertising Division of the Council of Better Business Bureaus was established in 1974 by the advertising industry to promote responsible children's advertising and to respond to public concerns.

The basic activity of CARU is the review and evaluation of child-directed advertising in all media. When children's advertising is found to be misleading, inaccurate or inconsistent with the Guidelines CARU seeks changes through the voluntary cooperation of advertisers.

CARU provides a general advisory service for advertisers and agencies and also is a source of informational material for children, parents and educators. In addition, CARU maintains a clearinghouse for research on children's advertising and has published an annotated bibliography.

CARU's Academic Advisory Panel helps evaluate advertising and information provided by advertisers in support of their advertising claims. The Panel also advises on general issues concerning children's advertising and assists in revisions of the Guidelines.

BONNEVILLE BROADCASTING SYSTEM

COMMERCIAL STANDARDS
(For "Easy Listening" Formatted Stations)

In addition to serving the needs of your market, your goal is to sell commercial time. To do this, you need good ratings. Good ratings can only be obtained and maintained by close adherence to the rules of the format. Following strong standards of commercial acceptance and scheduling is a very important part of these rules.

We play so much music in this format, that by the time a commercial break arrives, listeners are not only ready for it, they actually need the pause. Since they are, in effect, "tuned in" for some messages, there is no need to hit them over the head to get their attention with a loud or otherwise intrusive spot. To the contrary, that approach will more likely "turn them off."

The very best spot for this format is a friendly, conversational delivery by one announcer.

The following types of commercials should be *avoided* because of *presentation* or *sound:*

1. Hard sell or fast pace.
2. Loud or hard music.
3. Loud or otherwise offensive jingles or jingles amateurishly performed.
4. Sound effects (especially the loud ones such as phones ringing, cars crashing, sirens, etc.).
5. Voice or music designed to get attention through annoyance.
6. Voice of the sponsor or members of his family or his employees.
7. Humorous spots, especially those done by local people, which seldom are humorous. However, even well-done spots become a turn-off factor after a little repetition.
8. "Schtick Voices" such as Jonathan Winter's Maudie Frickert or stereotypes such as a Mad German Scientist or the Jewish Mother (which often tend to insult ethnic groups no matter how good the material).

The following should be *avoided* because of *content:*

1. Anything to do with death, funeral parlors, cemetery plots, even funeral flowers.
2. Personal products or those dealing with hygiene. Even though they may be presented well, they are very distasteful and will turn our listeners away.
3. X-rated movies or movies of a higher rating but with suggestive titles.
4. Business or services of dubious reputation. If a listener is taken by one of these outfits, he will tend to blame you for "recommending" it.
5. Advertisers that ask listeners to mention your call letters or mention the announcement, or send entries to your station. If your audience doesn't respond, for whatever reason, you'll be accused of having no selling power . . . of being a background music station.

There are certain *techniques* which must also be *avoided:*

1. *Two voice spots:* There's nothing much you can do about it when it comes in from an agency already recorded (assuming the voices themselves are acceptable). But don't do two voicers at the station if the spot can be effectively delivered by one person.

(Courtesy of Bonneville Broadcasting System.)

2. *Music behind spots:* Number one, since we play so much music we need spots with nothing more than the announcer's voice as relief. Number two, the music selected usually differs in tempo from our programmed music. Also, the announcer usually has to match his reading pace on the spot with the tempo of the music, often forcing him to either talk fast or do the pseudo-sexy announcer of the 1930's approach, both of which are bad. If there's no logical reason to hear music on the spot, why use it?
3. *Piggyback spots:* they sound like a double spot. *Donut-spots* (with a beginning by one voice, a middle by another voice and a close with either a third voice or the original opening voice) sound like three spots. Donut jingles are acceptable.
4. *Tagging spots so they run longer than the length contracted for.* Not only does the tag add another voice, it adds to the length and makes the break seem even longer than it actually was. Spots without a tag but which run longer than the length contracted, are equally bad.
5. *Increasing the pace of your announcer to "shorten" long copy.* If your announcer can't maintain his friendly, conversational pace and still complete the spot in the proper length, edit the copy.
6. *Female voices that are shrill or "sexy" and children's voices* can also be intrusive and should be avoided.

Sales and programming must work closely on this problem of commercial acceptance. While it is difficult for a salesman who has worked hard landing an account to have his spots turned down (especially when he hears them running on every other station in town), the person who makes the final decision must always remember what the wrong kind of spots can do to the station's sound, and therefore its ratings and demos.

Every effort should be made to save the account by coming up with new copy, editing the objectional part out of the original spot, or equalizing the sound when this is sufficient. The salesman, on the other hand, can help his cause by finding out as far in advance as possible what the spots will be like, so that programming can start working on it if there is any doubt about the acceptability.

WESTINGHOUSE BROADCASTING AND CABLE, INC.
GROUP W SPECIAL CATEGORIES

I. Advertising for the categories listed below are UNACCEPTABLE for Group W stations regardless of copy submitted:

Abortion services
Contraceptive products
Gambling
Hair transplants or any hair treatment involving surgery
Hard liquor
Mace or tear gas sprays
Magazines such as Playboy, Penthouse, Playgirl, Oui, etc.
Paid announcements for religion or religious groups
Products or services involving hypnosis
Sale of guns other than antique
Sun tanning salons
X-Rated movies

II. Advertising for the categories listed below MAY BE ACCEPTABLE BUT ARE SUBJECT TO APPROVAL BY HEADQUARTERS COMMERCIAL STANDARDS & PRACTICES ONLY:

(Courtesy of Westinghouse Broadcasting and Cable, Inc.)

Any commercial longer than sixty seconds
Any copy mentioning "cocktail lounge" and then must be minimal reference in connection with a restaurant, hotel or airline.
Casinos
Cocktail mixes
Commodity accounts for any product or service
Dating and singles service
Franchise accounts
Hemorrhoid products
Home pregnancy test kits
Insulin syringes
Legal, medical or dental services
Off-track betting
Personal hygiene products
Products or services involving astrology
Race track copy
Self-protection products
State lotteries
Stop smoking products or services
Transcendental meditation or other groups of this type
Weight reduction products or services

III. Time restriction for scheduling personal hygiene, hemorrhoid and laxative commercials:

Group W TV Stations

Personal hygiene copy may be scheduled, after approval, Monday through Friday, 9 AM to 4 PM and after 10 PM. Saturday and Sunday only after 10 PM.

Laxative and hemorrhoid product copy may be scheduled, after approval, but *not in children's programming areas.* No more than one hemorrhoid product commercial or one laxative product commercial may be scheduled in any half hour between 7–9 AM, 11:30 AM to 2 PM, or 5 to 8 PM.

Group W Radio Stations

Personal Hygiene copy may be scheduled, after approval, only between 9 AM and 4 PM and after 8 PM.

Laxative copy may be scheduled, after approval, but will not be aired between 7 and 9 AM, 11:30 AM and 2 PM, or 5 to 8 PM.

Hemorrhoid products may be scheduled, after approval, but not more than one spot scheduled in the restricted time periods between 7 and 9 AM, 11:30 AM and 2 PM, or 5 to 8 PM.

PERSONAL HYGIENE AND HEMORRHOID COMMERCIALS MUST STILL BE APPROVED BY THE NEW YORK COMMERCIAL STANDARDS & PRACTICES OFFICE BEFORE THEY MAY BE SCHEDULED.

WBAY–TV GREEN BAY—COMMERCIAL POLICY

Time Standards

It is the WBAY-TV policy to carry no more than 16 minutes of commercial matter in any 60-minute segment of a typical broadcast week. This 16 minute normal limitation may be exceeded in the following special and limited circumstances:

(Courtesy Nationwide Communications Inc.)

a. To provide additional commercial matter during periods of unusual consumer information and advertiser demand, such as the Christmas and Easter seasons, or periods of local community promotions;

b. To provide consumer information at times when the normal channels of mass communications in the community have been significantly disrupted by strike or natural causes;

c. To permit the scheduling of "make goods" because of the occurrence of a natural catastrophe, equipment failure, or other emergency situation; or of the broadcast of a Presidential address and news conference; or lengthy programming such as plays, operas and commencement exercises which are not conducive to interruption by commercial messages;

d. To carry an occasional demonstration, trade show exhibition, or fashion presentation, which because of the materials exhibited, might be construed by the viewing audience as more commercial than normal in its content; and

e. In the event that within the last 14 days before an election a political party or candidate requires time for equality of opportunity when all other times are sold out.

Under these circumstances, WBAY-TV Channel 2 may carry up to 18 minutes of commercial matter per hour, not to exceed more than 10% of the hours of any broadcast week.

Continuity Acceptance

WBAY-TV demonstrates our high regard for our audience and for our station image by advertising only those goods and services that are acceptable to the station by whatever measure we deem appropriate. It is for this reason that contracts for the sale of time are not considered binding until they have been approved for credit and accepted by the appropriate station executive.

The station requires full disclosure of the identity of the sponsor/advertiser as well as proof of the legitimacy of the subject matter. When there is any reason to question or the need to secure pertinent additional information regarding any advertising, the station will carefully and fully investigate prior to accepting a contract for advertising.

The station will satisfy itself that the products or services are acceptable to the State of Wisconsin agencies charged with the supervision and enforcement of laws that pertain to advertising and sales. In unusual cases the station will further verify the advertising claims and the values purported as well as the business reputation of the advertiser.

Ideally, we would like to be able to endorse the products, services, and business firms that are advertised on WBAY-TV. From actual experience over the years serving our community we believe many of our audience infer this endorsement. We do not sell our time on this premise, but it is the philosophy behind our acceptance of advertising.

WLUC-TV MARQUETTE, MICHIGAN
CODE OF OPERATIONS

WLUC-TV is aware of the professional responsibility stations have for carrying out programming and advertising in the public interest, convenience and necessity.

An overall Policy of Operations follows, which shall be used as a guide by station management. However, any deviation from this Policy requires prior approval by the Corporate office of WLUC-TV. All stations must operate in accordance with requirements of the Communications Act of 1934, as amended, and the Rules and Regulations of the Federal Communications Commission.

(Courtesy WLUC-TV.)

Program Standards:

1. Station programming should reflect the communities we serve, and also offer challenging concepts and other subject matter to stimulate and explore social change. Programs should be selected with care to make sure their purpose is not for the purpose of shock or sensationalism.
2. If programming is deemed inappropriate for a general family viewing audience it should not be scheduled prior to the second hour of prime time. Advisories should be used when any program contains material that might be disturbing to significant segments of the audience.
3. Programs designed primarily for children require special consideration. These programs may be entertainment, instructional or cultural, but should include positive sets of values to help them become responsible adults.
4. Public service time should be provided as a station response to the specific needs of its community. The station should review requests carefully with respect to the reputation of the group involved, the public interest, and the manner of presenting the announcement or program.
5. Certain program content merits special attention:
   a. *Violence.* The use of violence for its own sake and the detailed dwelling upon brutality or physical agony, by sight or sound, are not permissible.
   b. *Chemical Dependency.* Alcoholism and narcotic addiction should not be presented except as a destructive habit.
   c. *Alcohol and Tobacco Use.* The use of liquor and the depiction of smoking should be consistent with plot and character development.
   d. *Minorities & Human Relationships.* Material relating to sex, race, color, age, creed or religion should be used with special sensitivity.
   e. *Obscenity/Profanity.* Stations shall not broadcast any material which management determines to be obscene, profane or indecent.
   f. *Hypnosis/Superstition.* The creation of a state of hypnosis on camera is prohibited. Program material pertaining to fortune-telling and the like, is unacceptable if it encourages people to regard it seriously.
   g. *Game Programs/Contests.* Such programs must be genuine contests and must be presented with no control over results. In compliance with the Federal Lottery Law, State laws, and FCC Rules, contests may not constitute a lottery.
   h. *Misrepresentation.* Fictional events or non-news material shall not be presented as authentic news telecasts, or give a false impression that dramatized material constitute news. File footage must be labeled as such or identified by date.
6. Professionalism in broadcast journalism is encouraged. News reporting must be factual, fair and without bias. Advertising in news programs should be clearly distinguishable from the news content. News should be telecast in such a manner as to avoid panic and unnecessary alarm. Commentary should be clearly identified as such. Management should exercise due care in the supervision of content, format, and presentation of newscasts originated by the station, and in the selection of newscasters and commentators.
7. Stations are encouraged to present programs which respond to controversial public issues. Fair representation should be given to opposing sides of issues which materially affect a substantial segment of the local market. These programs should be identified as such and should not mislead viewers to believe the program is of the nature of entertainment or news. If stations or reporters express their own opinions about issues of general public interest, those opinions must be identified as editorials or commentaries.
8. Political telecasts must be clearly identified as such.

Advertising Standards:

1. The principles of acceptability and good taste included in Program Standards apply also to advertising where appropriate.

2. Stations should refuse their facilities to an advertiser where they doubt the integrity of the advertiser, the truth of the representations made, or the compliance of the advertiser with applicable legal requirements.

3. Representations which disregard normal safety precautions shall be avoided.

4. Commercials placed in or near programs designed for children require special consideration, both as to content and presentation. They should not mislead as to the product's performance and usefulness. Commercials within programs initially designed for children under 12 years of age must be clearly separated from program material by an appropriate device. No children's program personality or cartoon character may deliver commercial messages within or adjacent to the programs in which he appears.

5. The advertising of alcoholic beverages is acceptable if done in good taste; subject to federal, state and local laws. Federal law prohibits any reference to alcohol content.
   a. Beer and wine advertising must be scheduled when audience composition is suitable for the product being advertised.
   b. Hard liquor (distilled spirits) advertising may be accepted. However, special consideration must be given to acceptance by the market being served, and whether the advertising is in the public interest. Copy should in no way encourage over-indulgence, and advertising must be scheduled after 10:30 P.M. local time.

6. The advertising of firearms/ammunition is acceptable provided it promotes the product only as sporting equipment and conforms to recognized standards of safety and all applicable laws and regulations. Mail order advertising of these products is not acceptable. Advertising of fireworks is acceptable, where state law permits.

7. Advertising of fortune-telling, astrology and the like is unacceptable.

8. Personal endorsements shall be genuine and reflect personal experience. They shall contain no statement that cannot be supported if presented in the advertiser's own words.

9. Station management must exercise great care to prevent the presentation of false, misleading or deceptive advertising. If necessary, advertisers must make available documentation to support the validity and truthfulness of statements made in their commercial messages.

10. The advertising of medical products and professional services is of intimate and far-reaching importance to consumers. Care should be taken that claims made are not misleading or exaggerated. (Professional services to include chiropractic, hospital and legal services.)

11. The acceptance of personal product advertising should be determined with strong emphasis on ethics and good taste. If such advertising is accepted, the presentation must be restrained and of an inoffensive nature. It must be scheduled when audience composition is suitable for the product being advertised. All advertising claims must be substantiated.

12. Contests should be conducted with fairness to all entrants, and shall comply with all laws and regulations. Care should be taken to avoid any situation where all of the three elements which constitute a lottery—prize, chance and consideration— are involved. The only exception to this lottery advertising restriction would be for legalized governmental lotteries. All contest details should be clearly stated or easily available. Winners names should be released and the prizes awarded as soon as possible after the close of the contest. Stations should be particularly alert to avoid contests and promotions that may create a public nuisance.

13. Premiums, offers and direct response advertising require careful examination by the station before the first announcement is made to the public. Before accepting offers involving a monetary consideration, station management should be satisfied as to the integrity of the advertiser and the advertiser's willingness to honor com-

plaints, by returning the monetary consideration if necessary. There should be no misleading descriptions or visual representations which would distort their value in the minds of the viewers. Assurance should be obtained from the advertiser that products offered are safe to use.

14. Fraudulent billing is absolutely prohibited at WLUC–TV. This practice often is called "double billing."

Any bill, invoice, letter or other document purporting to show the amount of advertising purchased by a customer must be accurate and complete. It must show the actual amount charged for the advertising; if a rate is shown, it must be the actual rate charged. Any information regarding dates and times the advertising was broadcast also must be accurate.

Also prohibited is providing false information regarding the broadcast of any advertising or other material. An example of this practice would be providing an affidavit to a customer (or a broadcast network) that a certain program had been broadcast, or an advertisement telecast, when in fact it had not.

Any violation of the above prohibitions will result in immediate dismissal of the employee involved. Furthermore if anyone, of whatever rank, instructs or requests the employee to violate these prohibitions, it must be reported immediately to an officer or director of WLUC–TV. Failure to do so will be grounds for discharge.

COMMERCIAL ACCEPTANCE POLICY MEMOS, WTVJ TELEVISION, MIAMI

Overall Statement: WTVJ primary policy requires that we review all commercial advertising for truth, taste, and legal requirements.

Airlines Advertising in Event of Accident, Hi-jack or Strike

1. *Major accident/crash* resulting in multiple serious injuries and/or casualties . . . incurred by:
   a.   Commercial airline of USA origin anywhere in the world
   b.   USA military aircraft within continent of USA
   c.   Commercial airline of foreign origin within continent of USA
   d.   Private, non-sked or corporate aircraft within continent of USA

Policy: All airline advertising will be postponed for 48 hours . . . or . . . for as long as the story is prominently featured in the news.

2. *Accident with no casualties or multiple major injuries*

Policy: The advertising of the *airline involved* scheduled within or adjacent to news programs will be postponed for 24 hours . . . or . . . for as long as the story is prominently featured in the news.

3. *Hi-jacking.*

Policy: The advertising of the *airline involved* scheduled within or adjacent to news programs will be postponed for 24 hours . . . or . . . for as long as the story is prominently featured in the news.

4. *Immobilizing strike*

Policy: The advertising of the airline involved will be postponed until the strike is resolved. This hiatus should not result in loss of revenue to WTVJ.

(Courtesy WTVJ Television.)

Requests by individual airlines for additional hiatus in advertising because of accident or hi-jacking will be considered on a case by case basis. Our agreement to an additional hiatus is contingent upon no loss of revenue to WTVJ.

Direct Response Advertising Policy

WTVJ will selectively accept "direct response" advertising based on the merits of each individual request.

By "direct response" we mean that type of spot advertising that requires the viewer to phone, write, or send money. The following criteria must be met before station can accept order:

1. Commercial must pass all normal copy acceptance standards of the station. In particular, such commercial must not be strident and must conform to station standards of good taste.
2. Commercial must clearly disclose the company name and actual address of the advertiser. The name of the offer and a P.O. Box or phone number is insufficient.
3. Write-in, phone-in instructions must not include any reference to station in audio or video form.
4. Station will not handle, in any way, mail, phones or money.
5. Advertisers who do not ship merchandise within 30 days must disclose within the commercial the number of weeks to allow for delivery.
6. Advertiser's credit and in particular his ability to deliver product promised, if any, must be researched and documented.
7. Mention of a guarantee within the commercial requires that the nature and extent of the guarantee also be disclosed.
8. Extra charges . . . C.O.D., postage and handling, delivery, etc. . . . must be disclosed in immediate conjunction with the price quoted for the merchandise advertised.
9. In cases when advertiser requests money for product, in advance, from viewer, then an adequate bulk supply of product must be sent to station to cover situations where any viewer complaint of failure to deliver can be covered. This supply must arrive no later than 14 days following the first telecast. If not in house by then, schedule will be pulled.

Note that the above are minimal requirements and the meeting, thereof, does not, even so, imply or guarantee final acceptance by station.

Acceptance of Advertising for Funeral Services & Associated Products

This revision summarizes WTVJ policy and consolidates policy changes made since the memo of 1/3/78.

1. *Primary Policy.* Because of viewer sensitivity to the subject, WTVJ restricts acceptance of this category of commercial to institutional funeral home advertising and advertising of the availability of cemetery facilities.

All commercials are subject to individual review by WTVJ for the following:

1. Commercials must be executed in good taste and with restraint. Exhortative language or approaches may not be used. Strong emotional appeals are disallowed whether thru copy, musical background or video representation.
2. Graphic depictions, descriptions and specifics of products and services may not be included.
3. Use of prayers or the reading of scriptures can not be utilized in any way that would imply commercial exploitation of religion.

2. *ACCEPTABLE TIME PERIODS—WITH EXCLUSIONS.*
   Monday thru Friday: Sign-On thru 5:00 P.M.
                         10 P.M. thru Sign-Off
   Saturday and Sunday: Sign-On thru 6 P.M.
                         10 P.M. thru Sign-Off
   EXCLUSIONS: NEWS, PUBLIC AFFAIRS and CHILDREN'S SHOWS are excluded from the acceptable time periods. Station break adjacencies to Children's shows are also excluded.

Acceptance of Advertising for Legal Services

All commercials are subject to individual review by WTVJ for the following:

1. Commercials must be executed in good taste and with restraint. Exhortative language or approaches may not be used. Strong emotional appeals are disallowed.
2. Copy approach may not be exploitive of the emotions, fears, insecurities, or lack of knowledge of potential clients.
3. Any and all Florida State regulations for attorney advertising must be complied with.

It is the feeling of WTVJ that legal advertising should be presented in a professional manner to reflect the special responsibilities of this profession to the public.

Advertising of Mature Magazines

Commercials for mature magazines and publications are subject to individual review by WTVJ.

Mature magazines and publications are those generally considered "For Adults Only" due to content and/or depiction of nudity, sexuality, and/or excessive violence.

A storyboard or the produced commercial must be submitted to WTVJ prior to placement of schedule. A representative issue of the publication is also requested for review.

Any publication evaluated as the counterpart to an X-Rated movie is not acceptable for advertising on WTVJ no matter how innocuous the commercial presentation.

Acceptable commercials may air after 10 P.M. thru to sign-off nightly with the exclusion of the 11 o'Clock Newscast.

WTVJ Legal Guide and Policy for Paid Political Advertising

1. All paid political announcements and programs must be in compliance with the regulations of the Federal Communications Commission, Federal Elections Commission and the State of Florida Elections Laws.
   A. *FCC Regulations. Political announcements and programs must include a statement that the broadcast is paid for and disclose clearly who paid for it . . . and in whose behalf.*

This statement must use the words "paid for by" or "sponsored by" and correctly identify the person or persons or corporation, committee, association or other unincorporated group or entity by whom the consideration was paid.

This statement may be made audio or video . . . or both. Visual identification must be legible and in view long enough to be read . . . e.g. 3 seconds. Audio identification must be intelligible.

Statement of sponsorship identification must be made at the beginning or at the end of a spot announcement. Programs longer than five minutes must show sponsorship identification both at the beginning and at the end of the program.

All required disclosures must correspond to the information supplied to WTVJ on the Political Broadcast Agreement Form Application and on the subsequent confirmed Contract.

    B.   *Florida Election Laws.* Section 106.143 requires that all political advertisements state: "Paid Political Advertisement" or the abbreviation "Pd Pol Adv".

Political advertising for state, county, area, and municipal candidates and issues must state "Pd Pol Adv" in addition to the FCC required Paid For By statement.
Under Florida Law all candidates must establish a campaign depository or fund from which all political campaign expenditures are paid.
Hence the paid for by statement for a candidate subject to Florida Law should state:
Pd.Pol.Adv. Paid for by _____ Campaign Fund.
                    (name of candidate)
The Pd. Pol. Adv. identification need not be in juxtaposition to the paid for by information . . . but must be at the beginning or at the end of the announcement.
The only exception to the *Candidate's Campaign Fund* sponsorship identification would be a political announcement paid for by a state or county executive committee of a political party on behalf of the candidate.
In a General Election the candidate's political party must be disclosed.
Political advertisements endorsing a candidate(s) must state whether the permission of the candidate had been obtained.

    C.   *Federal Election Commission Requirements.* FEC requires that a political announcement paid for by a third party (other than by the federal candidate or his/her authorized election committee) must state whether or not it was authorized by the candidate or the candidate's committee.

2.   *WTVJ POLICY*
    A.   No political announcement may air within or adjacent to any local or network news program or newsbreak nor within or adjacent to news-type programs. News-type programs include Newswatch, Tiempos, Montage and Face the Nation. In addition, political announcements may not air within or adjacent to any programs of political debate or news-type programs about candidates.
       Note: Effective 9/24/84 political announcements are totally excluded from 10 PM to 11 PM Monday thru Sunday.
    B.   No regular members of the WTVJ staff may take part in a political announcement or program . . . either on or off camera.
       Slide or silent film or videotape political announcements requiring a voice-over must be accompanied by a provided audio tape. WTVJ staff announcers may not be used to "sell a candidate or issue." Staff announcers may be used only to read sponsorship identification or political party affiliation.
    C.   Political announcements and programs must be received by WTVJ at least two working days prior to first air date to allow for screening for compliance with legal requirements and technical standards.
       Politicals found legally non-compliant will not be aired on WTVJ. The schedule will be placed in hiatus until compliant replacements are received. When it is possible . . . and so requested and approved by the purchaser of broadcast time, WTVJ will make the necessary changes and additions at WTVJ's standard production rates.
    D.   Chyron and videotape production must be paid immediately on completion by campaign check or voucher as outlined on Sales Information Bulletin #2489.
       Note: WTVJ no longer produces slides of any kind. Chyron (electronic type) is available at standard rates.

Exclusion of Commercials from News and Public Affairs Programs

1. WTVJ excludes from news and public affairs: Funeral and Cemetary advertising, Personal Products, Politicals, Ballot Issues, Paid Promos for Religious Programs.
2. Certain other commercials are also subject to exclusion:
    A. Commercials that may be perceived by viewers as an endorsement by WTVJ.
    B. Commercials that, within a news environment . . . may mislead the audience to assume that it is about to hear or is hearing an actual news report.
    C. Image advertising by organizations often concerned with public issues that are subject to immediate news coverage.

    Advertisers that may fall into this classification include:

    Business and Trade Associations, Professional Associations, Labor Unions and Associations, Citizens Groups, Consumer Associations and Utility Companies and Corporations.

    Advertisers in this classification are required to submit proposed advertising to WTVJ prior to placement of schedule.

    Commercials for associations, groups, unions and associations must clearly and fully indicate sponsorship identification using the words "paid for by" or "sponsored by."

WTVJ reserves the right to add to or delete from the news exclusion list at any time.

INDEX

9108   4-8-88

P.330   Video (Non-Copy Data)